The Development of Memory in Infancy and Childhood

Studies in Developmental Psychology
Published Titles

Series Editor
Charles Hulme, University of York, UK

The Development of Memory in Infancy and Childhood

Edited by Mary L. Courage and
Nelson Cowan

Psychology Press
Taylor & Francis Group
HOVE AND NEW YORK

First published 2009
by Psychology Press
27 Church Road, Hove, East Sussex BN3 2FA

Simultaneously published in the USA and Canada
by Psychology Press
270 Madison Avenue, New York, NY 10016

*Psychology Press is an imprint of the Taylor & Francis Group,
an Informa business*

Typeset in Times by RefineCatch Limited, Bungay, Suffolk
Printed and bound in Great Britain by
TJ International Ltd, Padstow, Cornwall
Cover design by Bob Rowinski Code 5 Design

British Library Cataloguing in Publication Data
A catalogue record for this book is available from the British Library

Library of Congress Cataloging-in-Publication Data
The development of memory in infancy and childhood / edited by Mary
L. Courage and Nelson Cowan. – 2nd ed.
    p. cm.
    Rev. ed. of : The development of memory in childhood. c1997.
    Includes bibliographical references and index.
    ISBN 978-1-84169-642-3
    1. Memory in children.   I. Courage, Mary.   II. Cowan, Nelson.
    III. Title:
Development of memory in childhood.
    BF723.M4D485 2009
    155 4′1312 – dc22

                                  2007048595

ISBN: 978-1-84169-642-3

Contents

Contributors

Deborah Alley, Department of Psychology, University of California, 1 Shields Avenue, Davis, CA 956161, USA

Tracy Alloway, Child Development Research Unit, Durham University, Queen's Campus, University Boulevard, Thornaby, Stockton on Tees, Durham TS17 6BH, UK. Email: t.a.alloway@durham.ac.uk

Patricia J. Bauer, Department of Psychological and Brain Sciences, Duke University, 9 Flowers Drive, Box 90086, Durham, NC 27708-0086, USA. Email: patricia.bauer@duke.edu

David F. Bjorklund, Department of Psychology, Florida Atlantic University, Boca Raton, FL 33431, USA. Email: dbjorklu@fau.edu

Rhonda Douglas Brown, Department of Psychology, Teachers College 603b, P.O. Box 210002, Cincinnati, OH 45221-0002, USA. Email: rhonda.brown@uc.edu

Paola Castelli, Department of Psychology, University of California, 1 Shields Avenue, Davis, CA 956161, USA. Email: pcastelli@ucdavis.edu

Mary L. Courage, Department of Psychology, Memorial University, St. John's, NL A1B 3X9, Canada. Email: mcourage@mun.ca

Nelson Cowan, Department of Psychological Sciences, University of Missouri, 207 McAlester Hall, Columbia, MO 65211, USA. Email: cowanN@missouri.edu

Kimberly Cuevas, Department of Psychology, Rutgers University, Busch Campus, 152 Frelinghuysen Road, Piscataway, NJ 08854, USA. Email: kscuevas@eden.rutgers.edu

Charles Dukes, Department of Exceptional Student Education, Florida Atlantic University, Boca Raton, FL 33431, USA. Email: cdukes@fau.edu

Robyn Fivush, Department of Psychology, Emory University, Atlanta, GA 30322, USA. Email: psyrf@emory.edu

Gail S. Goodman, Department of Psychology, University of California, 1 Shields Avenue, Davis, CA 956161, USA. Email: ggoodman@ucdavis.edu

Catherine A. Haden, Department of Psychology, Loyola University of Chicago, 6525 N. Sheridan Road, Chicago, IL 60626, USA. Email: chaden@luc.edu

Harlene Hayne, Psychology Department, University of Otago, Dunedin, New Zealand. Email: hayne@psy.otago.ac.nz

Mark L. Howe, Department of Psychology, Fylde College, Lancaster University, Lancaster LA1 4YF, UK. Email: drmarkl.howe@gmail.com

Judith A. Hudson, Department of Psychology, Rutgers University, 53 Avenue E, Room 425 Tillett Hall, Piscataway, NJ 08854-8040, USA. Email: jhudson@rci.rutgers.edu

Rakel P. Larson, Department of Psychology, University of California, 1 Shields Avenue, Davis, CA 956161, USA. Email: rjlarson@ucdavis.edu

Marianne E. Lloyd, Department of Psychology, Temple University, 1701 N 13th Street, Philadelphia, PA 19122-6085, USA. Email: lloydmar@shu.edu

Estelle M. Y. Mayhew, Department of Psychology, Rutgers University, 53 Avenue E, Room 425 Tillett Hall, Piscataway, NJ 08854-8040, USA. Email: emahyew@rci.rutgers.edu

Nora S. Newcombe, Department of Psychology, Temple University, 1701 N 13th Street, Philadelphia, PA 19122-6085, USA. Email: newcombe@temple.edu

Peter A. Ornstein, Department of Psychology, Davie Hall, University of North Carolina at Chapel Hill, Chapel Hill, NC 27599-3270, USA. Email: pao@unc.edu

Pedro M. Paz-Alonso, Department of Psychology, University of California, 1 Shields Avenue, Davis, CA 956161, USA. Email: ppazalonso@ucdavis.edu

Margaret-Ellen Pipe, Department of Psychology, 3202 James Hall, Brooklyn College, City University of New York, Brooklyn, NY 11210, USA. Email: mepipe@brooklyn.cuny.edu

J. Steven Reznick, Department of Psychology, Davie Hall, University of North Carolina at Chapel Hill, NC 27599-3270, USA. Email: reznick@unc.edu

Maki Rooksby, Department of Psychology, Fylde College, Lancaster University, Lancaster LA1 4YF, UK. Email: m.rooksby@lancaster.ac.uk

Carolyn Rovee-Collier, Department of Psychology, Rutgers University,

Busch Campus, 152 Frelinghuysen Road, Piscataway, NJ 08854, USA. Email: rovee@rci.rutgers.edu

Karen Salmon, School of Psychology, Victoria University of Wellington, P.O. Box 600, Wellington 6140, New Zealand. Email: karen.salmon@vuw.ac.nz

Gabrielle Simcock, School of Psychology, McElwain Building, The University of Queensland, St Lucia, QLD 4072, Australia. Email: simcock@psy.uq.edu.au

1 Introduction

What's new in research on the development of memory in infants and children?

Mary L. Courage
Memorial University, St. John's, Canada

Nelson Cowan
University of Missouri, USA

Memory is not only the food of mental growth; it is the repository of our past that helps shape the essence of who we are. As such, it is of enduring fascination. We marvel at its resilience in some situations and its fragility in others. The origin of this extraordinary cognitive capacity in infancy and childhood is currently the focus of vigorous research and debate as we seek to understand the science of how human memory begins and how it changes with age. The beginning of the scientific study of memory development can be dated to the naturalistic observations of Darwin (1877) and Preyer (1882) whose case studies of their own children provided a database for subsequent experimental scrutiny. However, it was not until the 1970s that research on the development of memory came of age. This progress was due in part to a decline in the behaviorist zeitgeist that had dominated research in the first half of the 20th century and to the subsequent "cognitive revolution" that provided new models of memory based on information processing and neuroscience. Although much of the significant basic research was summarized in the first edition of this book (Cowan, 1997), the remarkable advances that have characterized the field over the past decade compelled us to undertake this thoroughly revised second edition.

With the information-processing metaphor in mind, researchers considered that children's memory (like adults') consisted of three interactive components or phases. First, children encode information from the environment, sometimes the exact details of an event (verbatim) and sometimes the essence of its features (gist). Processes of attention and perception are key facets of encoding. The second component or phase consists of storage of the encoded information. This involves consolidation processes whereby sensory and perceptual aspects of the information are integrated and stabilized into a relatively enduring memory trace. Importantly, storage is a constructive process that organizes information according to our current and past knowledge as well as our emotions, beliefs, and expectations. A host of memory strategies can be used to facilitate the storage of information, including various types of covert or overt rehearsal and the process of binding new stimuli to already-known information. The final phase is the retrieval or accessing of the stored information, perhaps most akin to the commonsense notion of what "memory" really is. As with storage, retrieval involves constructive and reconstructive processes, the nature of which affects the veracity of what is recognized or recalled. Here too, strategies can be deployed. These three phases of memory are not fixed entities that unfold always in the same order and in the same way, as a naïve concept of information processing might imply. Rather, as noted by Bartlett decades ago: "Remembering is not a completely independent function, entirely distinct from perceiving, imaging, or even constructive thinking, but has intimate relations with them all" (Bartlett, 1932, p. 13).

So human memory does not record experience as a video camera would, but rather as an historian would: as a dynamic and inferential process with reconstructions that depend on a variety of sources of information. Memory provides the basic mechanisms or "hardware" whereby information can be stored and retained for future access but the storage is not static. Imagine a filing cabinet in which the entries can be modified when new information is acquired. As the developing child advances in perception, attention, knowledge acquisition, reasoning, and problem solving, there are implications for the retrieval of old information and the storage of new information. Memory processes also vary as a function of the familial, social, and cultural milieu of which the child is a part (Rogoff & Chavajay, 1995; Tulving & Thomson, 1973). Mnemonic processes such as encoding, use of strategies, and autobiographical recall are all embedded in cognitive, affective, and social processes. It is the development that occurs in all of these component processes and in their underlying neural substrates that is the subject of the chapters in this volume.

Research on the development of children's memory has been prolific over the past three decades and we now know a great deal about how memory works and grows. For example, we know that (1) the fundamentals of the human information processing system are in place at least in rudimentary form from birth (or before); (2) if provided with a nonverbal mode of reporting, infants can show robust recognition and recall of stimuli and events; (3) young children show superior recollection of naturally occurring events compared to their apparently poorer recollection of standard laboratory lists of words and pictures; (4) developments in neural structures and processes in the infant and toddler years play a key role in facilitating memory performance; but that (5) as the rapid growth of critical brain structures levels off, subsequent improvements in performance are attributable largely to advances in strategies, knowledge, metamemory (knowledge of one's mnemonic functioning), and also to working memory and the deployment of cognitive resources. We know too, that (6) children's memory reports can be remarkably accurate, but are also vulnerable to the effects of suggestion from others, potentially degrading the veracity of these reports; and (7) memory is not context-free, but operates in part as a function of the world in which we live.

On the theoretical front, we are still engaged in a number of longstanding debates on the nature of memory itself; for example, (1) whether continuity or discontinuity best characterizes the basic processes that govern memory performance from infancy to childhood to adulthood, (2) whether memory is most parsimoniously considered as a single system with multiple routes of access or comprises multiple systems with different operating principles and brain loci, and (3) whether early memories are lost in a process of infantile amnesia or are incorporated into a later form of autobiographical memory.

The authors of the chapters in this volume are internationally known scholars whose established research programs collectively contributed to this extant database on the basic ways that memory develops across the childhood years—from infancy to maturity. As with their early forbears in scientific psychology whose seminal work established many of the basic principles of human memory in adults (e.g., Bartlett, 1932; Ebbinghaus, 1885), their work was driven by two historic and fundamental, though interdependent, sets of questions. The first set concerned the basic science of how human memory (and remembering) evolves across childhood. The second set of questions addressed compelling practical issues about how memory functions in more "ecologically valid" real-world settings and how best to apply knowledge gained from the science of human memory to educational, clinical, and forensic issues and situations. These two themes are evident in the chapters in this volume.

Beyond this matter of content, these researchers are aware of the need for a shift in the direction of their work from the descriptive science of memory development to the more difficult question of how and why memory develops across age. Although Flavell (1971) asked "What develops?" over three decades ago, answering this key question is still a work in progress. Although the issue is being advanced on new empirical (e.g., cognitive neuroscience) and theoretical (e.g., connectionist modeling; non-linear dynamic modeling) fronts, there are those who contend that we are still a long way from identifying the underlying mechanisms and processes that change memory across age (e.g., Neisser, 2004; Ornstein & Haden, 2001). With this overarching issue in mind, certain themes, both classic and new, have enjoyed particular attention over the past decade and are represented in the second edition of the *Development of Memory in Infancy and Childhood*. We provide an outline of some of these research directions below.

The development of long-term memory in infants and toddlers

Chapters 2 and 3 are about the development of long-term memory in infants and toddlers, respectively. This research is reviewed in Chapter 2 by Rovee-Collier and Cuevas, who focus on infants from birth to 18 months, and in Chapter 3 by Hayne and Simcock, who review literature on older infants and toddlers. As these very young children cannot tell us what they remember, progress to date has only been possible through the design and implementation of an array of innovative new tools and techniques (i.e., behavioral, electro-physiological) designed to elicit information from infants and young children for whom verbal reporting on standard laboratory tasks was not a viable option. These have revealed unexpected mnemonic competencies as well as a number of marked limitations that dissipate within the first year or so of life as the baby's brain develops. The implications of these competencies and limitations for basic science questions about the development of memory and the potential impact of early experience on later development are profound. New to this area of research is a greater emphasis on the mechanisms that underlie very early development and an attempt to use the data to address broader theoretical issues on the nature of memory itself and its relationship to the memory processes of verbal children. In particular, researchers are currently debating the role that language plays in the recollection and reporting of events at the transition from infancy to childhood.

Memory for events

In Chapter 4, Hudson and Mayhew provide a review of work on children's memory for the routine and novel events that occur in the natural contexts of their everyday lives, events that contribute to their sense of who they are, what they remember, and how it will be remembered. Memory for events provides a key example of declarative or explicit memory, a "type" of memory that involves the conscious and intentional recollection of previous experience and information. The neural substrates of explicit memory are fairly well understood in adults and are becoming so in infants and young children as well. In this chapter the authors focus on how it is that children develop the cognitive (e.g., general event representations) and neural (e.g., prefrontal cortex) structures that support their memory for routine or recurring events. Important research questions include the processes through which general event knowledge is acquired and develops from infancy through early childhood; the way that general and specific (e.g., autobiographical) event knowledge is organized in memory; the processes that children use to recall single episodes of recurring events; how general event knowledge is used in planning future events; and how memory for recurring events provides a foundation for the development of children's time concepts. The authors note that event knowledge develops with age from simple sequence representations to hierarchical structures that organize many different types of knowledge and can be accessed through pathways as diverse as causal and temporal concepts, the self concept, and concepts of social relationships and behavior.

Implicit memory

Chapter 5 is on the development of implicit memory, or memory without conscious awareness. A familiar example is remembering how to ride a bike, which can persist even following an extended period without practice. Authors Lloyd and Newcombe provide a review of the literature on this topic and reassess its traditional status as perhaps the only aspect of memory that purportedly does *not* develop. The term "implicit memory" encompasses performance on various different tasks including the acquisition of motor skills, perceptual and conceptual priming, and conditioning. Implicit memory stands in contrast to explicit memory or memory for facts and information of which we are consciously aware and about which we can typically provide a verbal report. The authors conclude that in fact there does appear to be developmental invariance in implicit memory when it is assessed with *perceptual* priming tasks (e.g., tasks that are based on physical similarity between prior and subsequent stimulus presentations). In contrast, when implicit memory is assessed with *conceptual* priming tasks (e.g., those based on activation of related concepts shared between prior and subsequent stimulus presentations) developmental changes are clearly apparent. They also discuss the implications of this important finding for false memory reports in children and adults. Finally, they specify a number of definitional and procedural issues that have masked this developmental change in implicit memory, and that have also hindered progress on this very sensitive and understudied aspect of human memory development.

The development of memory and the brain

In Chapter 6, Bauer documents recent advances in research on memory development done from the perspective of cognitive neuroscience, an area that has recently enjoyed a period of rapid growth. This advance reflects our historic interest as behavioral scientists in understanding brain–behavior relationships and the availability of new technologies that have made the examination of brain activity during memory tasks possible. These include the use of technologies that are electrical in nature such as the electroencephalogram and event-related potentials (EEG/ERP), or radiological in nature such as positron emission tomography (PET), and those that are magnetic, such as functional magnetic resonance imaging (fMRI). Bauer discusses the development of memory in terms of the neural systems and basic mnemonic processes that enable memories to be formed, retained, and retrieved. She presents evidence that memory is not a unitary construct but comprises different types of memory that are governed by different neural structures and processes. This position is illustrated with research from adults and non-human animals, and parallels are drawn with recent progress in extending the findings to infants and children. She argues that the biological analysis of memory and its development made possible by new technologies has led to new hypotheses about the source of age-related changes in performance. Moreover, the joint consideration of the processes involved in establishing a memory trace along with the time course of the emergence of the neural structures involved provides the potential to advance the discipline from one of description to one of explanation of underlying causal mechanisms. Additional information on memory development and the brain is included in several of the other chapters in this volume as it pertains to the particular chapter topic.

Memory strategies

Chapter 7 is on the development of memory strategies. One of the ways that both working memory and long-term memory are made to function efficiently is through the use of mental "tricks" or strategies whereby information becomes orderly, familiar, accessible for retrieval, and active in mind during thinking and problem solving. This topic was among the earliest to be addressed by researchers in the 1970s, and is still of enduring interest. This classic literature is reviewed by Bjorklund, Dukes, and Brown, who also provide new insights and perspectives on the acquisition of memory strategies. As a case in point, they discuss recent research in which the use of a microgenetic longitudinal design revealed that the developmental course of strategy acquisition is characteristically more abrupt than gradual, contrary to what had been previously assumed. The authors also highlight the role that advances in knowledge, metamemory, and the deployment of mental resources play in the development and use of memory strategies.

Autobiographical memory

A review of the origin and subsequent development of autobiographical memory is provided by Howe, Courage, and Rooksby in Chapter 8. The fate of our earliest memories has been of interest at least since Henri and Henri (1895) suggested that adults could recall events from about the age of 2 years, but not before, and Freud (1914/1938) decreed that repression of emotionally and sexually charged events was the causal mechanism—one that must be overcome for the good of adult mental health. The inherent and continued interest in this topic has become more intense over the past decade as urgent forensic questions on the accuracy and durability of adults' memories of childhood experiences have required urgent answers. Coincident with these forensic questions (and, to some degree, as a consequence of them), researchers examined the fate of early memory in normally developing children and adults. With this, the emphasis shifted from the offset of infantile amnesia to its converse—the onset of autobiographical memory. The authors maintain that the necessary though not sufficient foundation for this achievement is the emergence of the cognitive self. The cognitive self becomes stable at about 2 years of age and serves as a new organizer around which events can be encoded, stored, and retrieved in memory as personal, or having happened "to me." Subsequent developments in language and other aspects of social cognition serve to elaborate and refine self-characteristics and to affect the nature and durability of event recall.

Social, emotional, and contextual factors in the development of memory

Several chapters in this volume are devoted to this contemporary aspect of memory development research. Much of the early research on memory and its development were undertaken strictly from a behaviorist or an information-processing perspective, in which individual differences and the effects of context, though not denied, were not given the prominence that they currently enjoy. In this volume, the content of Chapters 9, 10, and 11 reflect the fact that much of the current research on the development of memory has been embedded in a much broader framework of what we feel, our sense of self, what we currently experience, what we already know, and what we infer. Context was once considered narrowly to refer to elements of "encoding specificity" (Tulving & Thomson, 1973), the finding that memory retrieval is often better when the retrieval context matches the encoding context. Context is now considered more broadly to include the family, society, and culture in which we live. This prominent trend prompted Kuhn (2000) to reflect on whether "memory development belongs on an endangered topic list" (p. 21). Several chapters in the present volume represent this broader approach. In Chapters 9, Paz-Alonso and colleagues review recent work on emotion, stress, and trauma. Among the topics that they discuss are the implications of using laboratory versus naturalistic methodologies in studying children's memory for emotional, stressful, or traumatic events, and whether or not such memories are encoded, stored, and retrieved by the same principles that govern memory for non-emotional events. In Chapter 10, Pipe and Salmon provide a review of research on children's eyewitness testimony in practical situations in which stress, emotion, and trauma are often important factors that affect memory performance. The primary challenge in these forensic settings has been to elicit the details of traumatic events seen or experienced by young children in a manner that does not compromise their veracity and integrity. In Chapter 11, Fivush reviews the literature that shows how the content of early memory is imbued with the characteristics of the family, society, and culture in which we live. In particular, she contends that the ways in which adults structure their conversations with young children as they reminisce about current and past events have a major impact on how they come to remember, evaluate, and narrate about their own personal past. The importance of language in this process is that it allows children to create more coherent organizational structures for communicating both positive and negative autobiographical memories to others. Consequently, research shows that individual differences in parental conversational style (e.g., high vs. low elaboration) affect the way children in turn report their experiences. Importantly, the effect of conversational style extends beyond exchanges that take place at the individual or family level and is also evident in the cultural differences (e.g., Asian vs. North American) that have been observed in the way children and adults report personally experienced events.

Working memory in infants and young children

Chapter 12, by Cowan and Alloway, is on the development of working memory, the small amount of information that an individual can keep in mind at once in order to complete various cognitive tasks such as language comprehension, reasoning, and problem solving. Considerable advances have been made in determining why there is a progressive improvement in working memory task performance with maturation. It is becoming clear that there actually are multiple mechanisms that improve with development, and it is important for further research to determine the contribution of each mechanism. After explaining how attention-demanding and automatic processes may fit together within a theoretical model of working memory, various sources of developmental change are considered. The changes in working memory processes can include those that correspond metaphorically to increases in the available time, space, or energy devoted to working memory. There also are relevant improvements in children's knowledge and mnemonic strategies with development, and some of the research that is covered illustrates how these various potential factors in working memory development can be investigated. Last, there is a discussion of ways in which working memory processes appear to be involved in various types of learning impairment. In the future, this type of research may lead to better treatment of those impairments. The origins in infancy of working memory and short-term memory, a presumably short-lived type of memory persistence that is the fundamental basis of working memory, are reviewed by Reznick in Chapter 13. He discusses the evidence that infants likely have working memory from about 6 months of age, and the methodological and interpretive challenges of examining its developmental course in a participant who has limited verbal ability and uncertain task motivation. Fundamental steps in overcoming these will be to consider data from multiple procedures, to specify precisely what is meant by "working memory" by identifying its component processes, and to differentiate it from other cognitive processes that it might support.

Memory development research applied to practical issues

Within the field of memory and its development, there is currently a strong emphasis on the importance of applying the information and principles learned to "real-world" situations and settings. To some extent, this is driven by the need to solve "real-world" problems. Lawyers and judges want to understand the issues that affect eyewitness reliability, suggestibility, the impact of stress and trauma on memory, and how to conduct proper interview procedures. Educators want to know how knowledge, strategies, and metamemorial processes can be used to facilitate learning and memory performance in academic settings, especially among children with developmental challenges (e.g., autism, Down syndrome). Psychotherapists and clinicians want to know if early traumatic experiences can continue to affect the lives of individuals even in the absence of overt recall. Parents are eager to know what their babies can learn and remember so that they can understand and facilitate their development. All of the chapters in this volume address some of these practical issues in so far as they relate to their own unique topics. Collectively, they offer relevant commentary on children with math and reading disabilities or attention deficit hyperactivity disorder, on effective strategy acquisition for children in schools, on the formation and identification of false memories and on children's suggestibility to misinformation during forensic interviews, and on a variety of amnesias. They also discuss what and how very young children recall from exposure to television and story books, a powerful source of information in their lives. We hope these comments serve the reader well by putting practical issues in a theoretical context so that the solution does not have to be re-invented for each new situation.

What's next? The state of the science and a look to the future

Finally, this question will be addressed in Chapter 14 in which Ornstein and Haden provide a commentary on some of the work of the last decade and an overview of where the field is (or should be) headed into the future. To anticipate some of their comments, they maintain that the "What develops?" question should not be lost in our enthusiasm to provide ever more data on "memory development" rather than on the "development of memory." Hopefully, the title of this volume will provide a continuous reminder of the need to pursue this course, one that will motivate new research directions into the next decade. As Haith (1993) succinctly noted, we have to "put development back into developmental psychology" (p. 362).

Finally, like the first edition of the *Development of Memory in Childhood*, this revised edition comprises a diverse collection of research. In order to provide each chapter with organizational structure and a common thread of continuity, we asked the contributing authors to consider a series of questions in the context of their particular chapter. So apart from the principal theme of the "development of memory" we asked them to consider the following questions:

1   What is the definition and scope of the chapter's topic?
2   Why is the topic potentially important on theoretical and/or practical grounds?
3   What is currently known about the topic from the literature to date?
4   What are the standard methodologies, paradigms, and measurement issues?
5   Are there studies with adults or non-human species that help explain the key issues?
6   How has cognitive neuroscience research contributed to the current state of knowledge?

7   Are there general principles that hold across the entire developmental lifespan?
8   What is known about individual differences in your topic area?
9   Have there been significant applications of basic principles to "real-world" situations?
10   What remains to be done?

Just as the book was written with these questions in mind, we hope they help readers to adopt an interactive stance and to consider the book as an aid to growth as the field's knowledge accrues and is refined.

REFERENCES

Bartlett, F. C. (1932). *Remembering: A study in experimental and social psychology.* Cambridge, UK: Cambridge University Press.

Cowan, N. (Ed.). (1997). *The development of memory in childhood.* Hove, UK: Psychology Press.

Darwin, C. R. (1877). Biographical sketch of an infant. *Mind, 2,* 285–294.

Ebbinghaus, H. (1885/1964). *Memory: A contribution to experimental psychology* (H. A. Ruger & C. E. Bussenius, Trans.). New York: Dover.

Flavell, J. H. (1971). What is memory development the development of? *Human Development, 14,* 225–286.

Freud, S. (1938). The psychopathology of everyday life. In A. A. Brill (Ed.), *The writings of Sigmund Freud* (pp. 135–178). New York: Modern Library. (Original work published 1914)

Haith, M. M. (1993). Preparing for the 21st century: Some goals and challenges for studies in infant sensory and perceptual development. *Developmental Review, 13,* 354–371.

Henri, V., & Henri, C. (1895). On our earliest recollection of childhood. *Psychological Review, 2,* 215–216.

Kuhn, D. (2000). Does memory development belong on an endangered topics list? *Child Development, 71,* 21–25.

Neisser, U. (2004). Memory development: New questions and old. *Developmental Review, 24,* 154–158.

Ornstein, P. A., & Haden, C. A. (2001). Memory development or the development of memory? *Psychological Science, 10,* 202–205.

Preyer, W. (1882). *The mind of the child.* Leipzig: Grieben.

Rogoff, B., & Chavajay, P. (1995). What's become of research on the cultural bias of cognitive development? *American Psychologist, 50,* 859–877.

Tulving, E., & Thomson, D. M. (1973). Encoding specificity and retrieval processes in episodic memory. *Psychological Review, 80,* 352–373.

2 The development of infant memory

Carolyn Rovee-Collier and Kimberly Cuevas
Rutgers University, New Jersey, USA

To the general public, it seems intuitively unlikely that the memories of pre-verbal human infants could in any way resemble our own. The belief that the memories of infants and adults are fundamentally different is treated as a fact in general psychology and child development texts, in the popular press, and even by well-known scientists. Our common inability to recollect what happened when we were infants ("infantile amnesia") lends credence to this belief—but it is wrong. The present chapter documents why.

INFANT MEMORY: A CLASSIC PARADOX

Human infancy extends from birth through 2 years of age. From the time of Freud (1935), most psychologists have assumed that infants' experiences progressively accrue and form the underpinnings of adult behavior (Stevenson, Hess, & Rheingold, 1967). Implicit in this assumption is the capacity for long-term memory in infancy. If infants' experiences are to affect their later behavior, then infants must possess a relatively enduring record of those experiences—some means of preserving the effects of those experiences until they draw on them in the future. Paradoxically, however, most psychologists also believe that preverbal infants lack the capacity for remembering their experiences over the long term. This belief is bolstered by the phenomenon of infantile amnesia—the common experience that people cannot remember events that occurred before 3–4 years of age (Pillemer & White, 1989). Infantile amnesia is variously attributed to rapid forgetting during infancy, the inability of the immature brain to encode, maintain, and retrieve memories over the long term, infants' exclusive reliance on a primitive memory system, and the onset of language, which blocks retrieval of memories formed preverbally. In what follows, we present research from infants between 2 and 18 months of age (Figure 2.1) that challenges these accounts and suggest alternative explanations for infantile amnesia. First, however, we briefly review the three paradigms that have provided the bulk of what is currently known about infant memory.

Figure 2.1 From left to right, infants are 2, 3, 6, 9, 12, 15, and 18 months of age. Note the dramatic physical and behavioral differences between the youngest and oldest infant.

NOVELTY PREFERENCE PARADIGMS

Visual paired-comparison (VPC) and habituation procedures exploit the tendency of infants older than 8–10 weeks to look longer at a new (novel) stimulus than at an old (familiar) one. In VPC studies, infants are briefly preexposed to a pair of identical stimuli (or occasionally to a single stimulus) and then are simultaneously tested with the preexposed stimulus and a new one. Recognition is inferred if the percentage of total time spent looking at the new stimulus exceeds chance (50%). In habituation studies, infants are repeatedly exposed to a stimulus until the duration of looking at it declines to a criterion value (typically, 50% of looking on Trials 1–3) and then they are tested with a new stimulus. Recognition is inferred if looking at the new stimulus significantly increases, and the longest test delay defines the duration of retention. After one training session, infants typically exhibit retention for 5–10 s at 3–4 months, 1 min at 6 months, and 10 min at 9–12 months (Rose, Feldman, & Jankowski, 2007). After multiple sessions, 5-month-olds recognize achromatic patterns after 48 hr and facial photographs after 2 weeks (Fagan, 1973). Face recognition, however, may be special. Following habituation to faces, newborns exhibit recognition after 2 min (Pascalis & de Schonen, 1994), and 3-month-olds exhibit recognition after 24 hr (Pascalis, de Haan, Nelson, & de Schonen, 1998).

In habituation studies, individual differences in habituation rate are associated with processing speed and later recognition memory, with short lookers (fast habituators) having better recognition memory than long lookers (slow habituators). Evidence of a direct link between infant attention and recognition comes from two sources. First, giving 5-month-old long lookers an experimental treatment that enhanced attention to parts of the target stimulus shortened their looks and improved their recognition to the point that they were indistinguishable from short lookers (for review, see Rose et al., 2007). Second, presenting visual stimuli during periods of "sustained attention" and inattention, as defined by heart-rate change, produced differential changes in the components of evoked-response potentials from scalp electrodes at placements thought to distinguish recognition from attention, respectively (Richards, 2003).

CONDITIONING PARADIGMS

In a review of what was known about memory development in infants and children, Campbell and Coulter (1976, pp. 144–145) concluded:

> Child development psychologists have not yet studied memory over long time intervals. Our best estimates come from retrospective studies of early childhood memories . . . We cannot overemphasize the differences between these indices of long-term memory in man and those used to study memory in the developing rat. The human is asked to recall events of early childhood in the absence of any stimuli associated with that era. The rat, on the other hand, is returned to a highly distinctive setting and asked to reproduce a specific response. If these same procedures were used with man, it seems quite likely that evidence for long-term memory would appear much earlier.

They were right.

In an early classical conditioning study, a 7-month-old infant trained for multiple sessions still exhibited a conditioned galvanic skin response 7 weeks later (Jones, 1930, 1931). More recently, 20-day-olds (but not 10-day-olds) exhibited significant savings 10 days after one session of classical eyeblink conditioning (Little, Lipsitt, & Rovee-Collier, 1984), and 5-month-olds exhibited significant savings 4 weeks afterward (Herbert, Eckerman, & Stanton, 2003). Notably, the optimal interstimulus interval (ISI) for 10- to 30-day-olds (1500 ms) is more than two times longer than the optimal ISI for 5-month-olds (650 ms) and three times longer than the optimal ISI for adults (500 ms; Kimble, 1961).

An operant conditioning study with human infants between 2 and 18 months of age was modeled after Campbell and Campbell's (1962) classical conditioning study of the ontogeny of memory with infant rats. Hartshorn et al. (1998b) found that the duration of long-term memory increased linearly from 1–2 days for infants trained at 2 months to 13–14 weeks for infants trained at 18 months. The retention function (Figure 2.2) provided no hint that long-term memory abruptly improves either at the end of the first year of life, when a qualitatively different memory system is thought to mature (Bauer, DeBoer, & Lukowski, 2007; Mandler, 1990; Nelson, 1997), or during the second year, when infants develop language (K. Nelson, 1993). The duration of deferred imitation also increases linearly from 1 day at 6 months to 4 weeks at 18 months (for review, see Hayne, 2007). The slope of the deferred imitation function (Figure 2.2) is shallower because infants received only one modeling session lasting 30–60 s instead of two conditioning sessions on consecutive days lasting a total of 12–18 min.

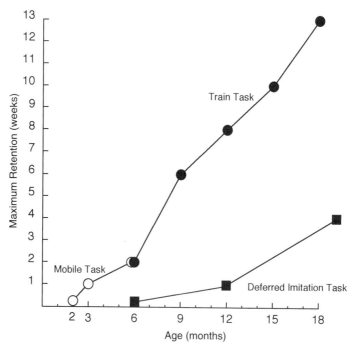

Figure 2.2 Standardized reference functions for the maximum duration of retention (in weeks) of infants who were trained and tested in the operant mobile and train tasks and the deferred imitation (puppet) task using a standardized procedure with age-calibrated parameters. Differences in the slopes of the two functions are due solely to different training parameters. (Reprinted with permission from K. Hartshorn, C. Rovee-Collier, P. Gerhardstein, R. S. Bhatt, T. L. Wondoloski, P. J. Klein, J. Gilch, N. Wurtzel, & M. Campos-de-Carvalhos (1998). The ontogeny of long-term memory over the first year-and-a-half of life. *Developmental Psychobiology, 32*, 69–89. Copyright © 1998, Wiley Periodicals, Inc.).

OPERANT CONDITIONING PROCEDURES

Most of what we currently know about infant long-term memory has been obtained with operant conditioning procedures. The logic of this approach is straightforward: Because preverbal infants cannot say what they recognize, they learn a motoric response (kicking, lever pressing) to use instead. When tested with either the training display or a different one, infants "say" whether they recognize it by responding above baseline.

The mobile conjugate reinforcement task is used with infants from 2 to 6 months of age. Infants are trained in their home cribs for 15 min on each of two successive days. For 3 min at the outset of each session (baseline phase, Session 1), a ribbon connects the infant's ankle to an "empty" mobile stand, while the mobile is suspended from another stand on the opposite crib rail (Figure 2.3b). In this arrangement, the infant can view the mobile but cannot move it. Next, the ankle ribbon is moved to the same stand as the mobile for 9 min (acquisition phase; Figure 2.3a), and kicks conjugately move the mobile. Each session ends with another 3-min nonreinforcement period (immediate retention test, Session 2) when the ankle ribbon is returned to the "empty" stand. Each infant must respond one and a half times above his or her baseline rate (the learning criterion) during an acquisition phase in order to proceed to the memory phase of an experiment. The 3-min long-term retention

(a)   (b)

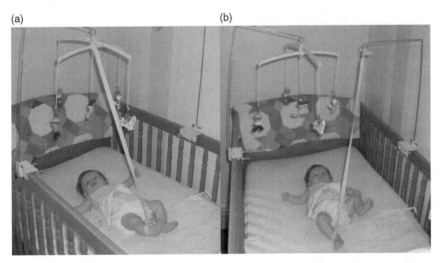

Figure 2.3 The experimental arrangement used with 2- to 6-month-olds in the operant mobile task, shown here with a 3-month-old. From left to right: (a) The experimental arrangement during acquisition. Kicks conjugately move the mobile via an ankle ribbon that is connected to the same stand as the mobile. (b) The experimental arrangement during baseline and the delayed recognition test. The ankle ribbon is attached to an empty mobile stand, while the mobile is suspended from a second stand. In this arrangement, the infant's kicks cannot move the mobile.

test occurs after delays ranging from days to weeks and is procedurally identical to the immediate retention test and the baseline phase. Because responding is not reinforced during the long-term test, infants' performance reflects only what they "bring" to the test session and not new learning at the time of testing. At 6 months, the procedure is the same, but sessions are one third shorter.

Because the mobile task is inappropriate for infants older than 6 months, an operant train task was developed as its upward extension for 6- to 24-month-olds (Figure 2.4). Instead of moving a mobile by kicking, infants move a miniature train around a circular track by lever pressing; each discrete response moves the train for 1 s (2 s at 6 months). At 6 months of age, retention is identical in the mobile and train tasks, confirming that the tasks are equivalent (Hartshorn & Rovee-Collier, 1997). Because baseline rates of unlearned responding can vary widely, we use a relative measure of individual retention, the baseline ratio. Its value is the proportion by which an infant's response rate during the long-term retention test (LRT) exceeds that infant's baseline rate (BASE). A mean baseline ratio (LRT/BASE) significantly exceeding 1.00 indicates retention.

Figure 2.4 The experimental arrangement used with 6- to 24-month-olds in the operant train task, shown here with a 6-month-old. Each lever press moves the
toy train for 2 s (1 s at older ages) during acquisition; the lever is
deactivated during baseline and retention tests.

DEFERRED IMITATION PARADIGM

In the deferred imitation paradigm, the experimenter models the target actions, and infants receive their first opportunity to copy the actions after a delay. Elicited imitation is a variant of the deferred imitation paradigm in which the experimenter provides verbal prompts during modeling, and infants imitate immediately (plus occasionally during the retention interval as well). All of these factors significantly affect deferred imitation: Verbal cues facilitate deferred imitation after long delays and do so differentially at different ages (Hayne, 2007; Hayne & Herbert, 2004), immediate imitation facilitates generalized imitation (Hayne, Barr, & Herbert, 2003; Learmonth, Lamberth, & Rovee-Collier, 2004), and imitation during the retention interval prolongs deferred imitation (Barr, Rovee-Collier, & Campanella, 2005). Piaget (1962) thought that infants younger than 18 months could not exhibit deferred imitation because they could not form mental representations. Meltzoff's (1988) report that 9-month-olds imitated a novel action after 24 hr, however, altered earlier conceptions of infants' representational ability and spawned the current boom of deferred imitation research.

Research on the ontogeny of deferred imitation was made possible when Barr, Dowden, and Hayne (1996) developed a single task that was appropriate for infants from 6 to 24 months. In this task, an experimenter shows infants a hand puppet wearing a mitten of the same color and models a 10-s sequence of three actions—remove the mitten, shake the mitten (which rings a jingle bell pinned inside during the demonstration), and replace the mitten (Figure 2.5). The duration of the demonstration is calibrated to produce 24-hr retention and lasts 60 s for 6-month-olds and 30 s for older infants. An infant's imitation score is the number of target actions (0–3) performed within 90–120 s of touching the puppet. Older infants have higher mean imitation scores and remember progressively longer, but even 6-month-olds occasionally perform most or all of the actions. The mean baserate at which infants spontaneously produce the target actions without seeing them modeled is low (0.13–0.17) between 6 and 24 months.

REINSTATEMENT AND REACTIVATION REMINDERS

Campbell and Campbell (1962) had found that infant rats remembered increasingly longer with age, but even the oldest infants had not remembered long enough for their earlier experience to affect later behavior. Campbell and Jaynes (1966) hypothesized that periodic reinstatement is the mechanism by which early memories are maintained over major developmental periods. The rationale underlying reinstatement is simple: As a memory wanes, intermittent exposure to an abbreviated version of the original event keeps the memory "alive"—like periodically throwing a new log on a fire to prevent it from dying out. In a classic study, they gave rat pups 30 shocks (the unconditional

Figure 2.5 Demonstration of the target actions (top panel) and the deferred imitation
test with a 6-month-old infant (bottom panel).

stimulus, or US) on the black side (the conditioned stimulus, or CS) of a
black-and-white shuttle box, while intermittently placing them on the white
(safe) side. Over the next 3 weeks, they gave pups a weekly shock on the black
side of the box (a reinstatement). When tested 1 month after conditioning,
pups still exhibited fear of the black side. Control groups given either fear
conditioning but no reinstatements or reinstatements but no conditioning exhibited no fear during the 1-month test. This study confirmed that
a periodic partial exposure to the original training event can maintain its
memory for a significant period.

Campbell and Jaynes used the term "reinstatement" to refer to the empirical
fact that the original conditions of training were reintroduced (reinstated)

during reminding. (Today, many researchers use this term incorrectly by referring to reinstating the memory instead of reinstating the training conditions.) Subsequently, Spear and Parsons (1976) found that pups who received a single shock in a different apparatus 24 hr before testing also exhibited conditioned fear during the 1-month test. They called the single-reminder procedure "reactivation" to differentiate it from reinstatement. Presumably, exposure to a fragment of the original event before the test primed (reactivated) the latent memory and increased its accessibility.

In the first reactivation study with human infants, 3-month-olds were trained in the mobile task, allowed to forget it, and then were briefly exposed to a memory prime 13 or 27 days after training. They were tested for retention 24 hr later. During reactivation, infants merely sat under the training mobile (Figure 2.6) while the experimenter moved it for 3 min at the same rate that each infant had kicked to move it at the end of acquisition. Priming alleviated forgetting and restored learned responding to its original level. In addition, the reactivated memory was forgotten at the same rate as the original one (Rovee-Collier, Sullivan, Enright, Lucas, & Fagen, 1980). Both results have now been obtained throughout the infancy period (Hildreth & Rovee-Collier, 2002; Hsu, Rovee-Collier, Hill, Grodkiewicz, & Joh, 2005).

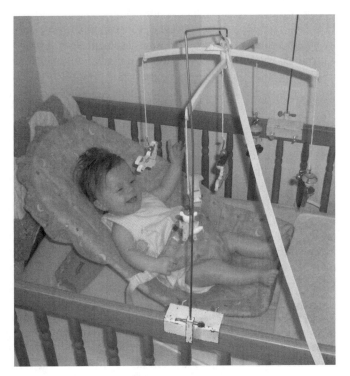

Figure 2.6 The experimental arrangement during reactivation (priming), shown here with a 3-month-old. The infant seat minimizes spontaneous kicking.

In effect, a single prime doubles the "life" of a memory, and multiple primes prolong it even more (Hayne, 1990; Hitchcock & Rovee-Collier, 1996). The possibility that infants' forgotten memories could be recovered without relearning changed the dialog about the lasting impact of infant experiences.

In general, reinstatement has been used with older children (e.g., Howe, Courage, & Bryant-Brown, 1993; Priestley, Roberts, & Pipe, 1999; but see Cornell, 1979), and reactivation has been used with infants (for review, see Rovee-Collier, Hayne, & Colombo, 2001). Most developmental psychologists, however, do not distinguish between reinstatement and reactivation and refer to them interchangeably (e.g., Bauer, Wiebe, Waters, & Bangston, 2001; Howe & O'Sullivan, 1997; Hudson & Sheffield, 1998; Mandler, 1998; K. Nelson, 1990). According to Howe et al. (1993), "the distinction between reinstatement and reactivation is . . . artificial in that both . . . have similar (if not the same) memory-preserving effects." They concluded that "it may be more appropriate to view reinstatement and reactivation as reflecting temporal variations of the same reminding process" (p. 855). Similarly, Richardson, Wang, and Campbell (1993) concluded that "there are some minor procedural differences between reactivation and reinstatement . . . [but] the underlying process is the same in both cases" (p. 2).

Whereas the response-reinforcement contingency is absent during reactivation (e.g., the ankle ribbon is disconnected or the response lever is deactivated), the contingency remains in force during reinstatement. In addition to differing procedurally, however, reinstatement and reactivation differ functionally, raising the prospect that their underlying processes differ also. At both 3 and 6 months of age, for example, reinstatement protracted retention two times longer than reactivation when given halfway through the forgetting function (Adler, Wilk, & Rovee-Collier, 2000; Galluccio & Rovee-Collier, 2006) and 10 times longer when given after the memory was forgotten (Hildreth, Sweeney, & Rovee-Collier, 2003).

There is an upper limit (UL) to how much time can elapse after an event occurred before a reactivation reminder becomes ineffective (Hildreth & Hill, 2003). Between 3 and 12 months, the absolute amount of time that can elapse (the absolute UL of reactivation) increases logarithmically (Figure 2.7, left panel), but the amount of time that can elapse relative to how long the event is initially remembered (the relative UL of reactivation) is constant over age, being four times longer than the duration of original retention (Figure 2.7, right panel). This result raises the possibility that the relative UL of reactivation is constant over a lifetime.

Multiple reminders can maintain memories for very long periods. Two separate studies documented that periodic nonverbal reminders maintained the memories of two overlapping and equivalent tasks from 2 through 24 months of age—the entire period characterized by infantile amnesia. In the first study (Rovee-Collier, Hartshorn, & DiRubbo, 1999), 2-month-olds learned the mobile task. Every 3 weeks thereafter, through 26 weeks of age,

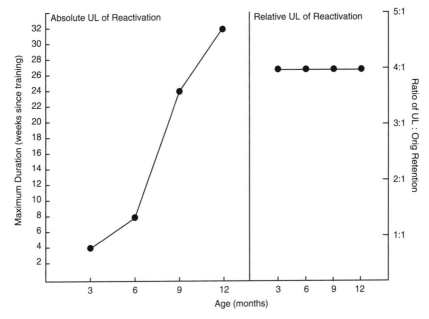

Figure 2.7 The upper limit (UL) of reactivation (the longest delay after training at
which a forgotten memory can be reactivated) at 3, 6, 9, and 12 months of
age. Left panel: The absolute UL, expressed as weeks since original training (3-month point from Greco, Rovee-Collier, Hayne, Griesler, & Earley,
1986). Right panel: The relative UL, expressed as a ratio of the absolute
UL to the maximum duration of original retention. (Reprinted with permission from H. Hildreth, & D. Hill (2003). Retrieval difficulty and retention of reactivated memories over the first year of life. *Developmental
Psychobiology*, *43*, 216–29. Copyright © 2003, Wiley Periodicals, Inc.).

infants received a preliminary retention test (a memory probe) and a 3-min
reminder. During the preliminary test, infants exhibiting retention received
a reinstatement, and those exhibiting no retention received a reactivation
reminder. After a retention test at 29 weeks of age, the experiment was ter-
minated because infants had outgrown the task. A yoked control group that
was not trained but given the same reminders exhibited no retention after any
delay. Although 2-month-olds typically remember for 1–2 days (Figure 2.2),
infants given periodic reminders exhibited significant retention for 4½ months,
and most remembered for 5¼ months!

In the second study (Hartshorn, 2003), 6-month-olds learned the train task.
In three progressive replications, they received a 2-min reinstatement at 7, 8,
9, 12, and 18 months of age and a final retention test at 24 months. Yoked
control groups who were not trained but received the same reminders exhibited no retention after any delay. Although 6-month-olds typically remember
for 2 weeks (Figure 2.2), these infants exhibited significant retention after

1½ years, despite receiving only one brief reminder in the preceding year—at 18 months. Although Hartshorn administered four reinstatements between 7 and 12 months of age, Hildreth et al. (2003) subsequently found that a single reinstatement at 7 months of age maintained retention for another 5 months. This result suggests that Hartshorn could have presented two reinstatements—one at 7 months and another at 12 months—and achieved the same result. Theoretically, if appropriate reminders were periodically encountered, then early experiences could be remembered forever.

Whether infants younger than 6 months could defer imitation was unknown until recently because they lack sufficient motoric competence to perform the target actions. Campanella and Rovee-Collier (2005) overcame this obstacle by using repeated reactivations to maintain the memory of target actions modeled when infants were 3 months old until they were older and capable of performing the actions. Here, the experimenter modeled three target actions for 60 s on a hand puppet for 3-month-olds. Beginning 1 day later and over the next 3 months, she periodically showed infants the stationary puppet for 30–60 s (six times in all). At 6 months of age, infants exhibited significant deferred imitation of the target actions. These infants had not seen the target actions for 3 months nor had previously imitated them. A yoked reactivation control group did not see the actions modeled at 3 months but received the same reminders; it responded at the baserate during the test. The finding that infants imitated what they saw modeled on a single, brief occasion 3 months earlier contradicts the assertion that "priming alone cannot sustain reproduction of observed acts after a delay" (Mandler, 2007, p. 279). Even more importantly, this finding raises questions about the assumption that deferred imitation marks the emergence of a memory system characterized by conscious awareness.

DO INFANTS EXHIBIT RAPID FORGETTING?

Because adult animals remember for so long (Kimble, 1961), animal researchers interested in the process of forgetting had to study infants. Campbell and Campbell (1962) first reported that the rate of forgetting by infant rats was inversely related to age. A parallel operant study with human infants yielded the same result (Hartshorn et al., 1998b): Infants between 2 and 18 months of age exhibited retention after the shortest test delay, but as the retention interval increased, younger infants forgot first (Figure 2.8). The data in Figures 2.2 and 2.8 were obtained after two training sessions separated by 24 hr; after one training session, infants remember approximately half as long (Figure 2.9; Hsu, 2007).

How long individuals remember after two sessions is determined by the interval between Sessions 1 and 2. This spacing effect was predicted by the time window construct (Rovee-Collier, 1995), which states that there is a limited period (a time window) within which successive stimuli or events are

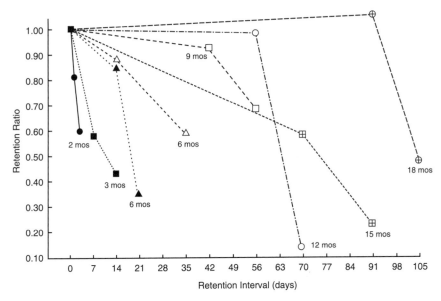

Figure 2.8 Forgetting as a function of infant age. Mean retention ratios of independent groups of infants between 2 and 18 months of age who were trained for 2 consecutive days in the mobile task (2 to 6 months) or the train task (6 to 18 months) and received an immediate retention test after the conclusion of acquisition on day 2. Six-month-olds were trained and tested in both tasks. All infants received a delayed recognition test after different retention intervals until, as shown in the last point on each curve, they exhibited no retention. (Reprinted with permission from K. Hartshorn, C. Rovee-Collier, P. Gerhardstein, R. S. Bhatt, T. L. Wondoloski, P. J. Klein, J. Gilch, N. Wurtzel, & M. Campos-de-Carvalho (1998). The ontogeny of long-term memory over the first year-and-a-half of life. *Developmental Psychobiology*, 32, 69–89. Copyright © 1998, Wiley Periodicals, Inc.).

integrated. A time window opens when an event occurs and shuts when its memory cannot be retrieved. This construct makes three major predictions: (1) Successive events are integrated when the second event occurs inside the time window of the first and retrieves its memory; when the second event occurs outside the time window, it is treated as unique. (2) Each retrieval expands the width of the time window, increasing future retention. (3) The later in the time window a memory is retrieved, the longer it is remembered in the future. Recent data support these predictions throughout the infancy period (Figure 2.10; Hsu, 2007). When operantly trained 3-month-olds received a 3-min reinstatement at the beginning (0 days), mid-point (3 days), or end (5 days) of the time window, for example, retention increased exponentially with the delay, doubling after reinstatement on Day 3 and quadrupling after reinstatement on Day 5 (Galluccio & Rovee-Collier, 2006). This result conforms to the ratio rule (Bjork, 2001), which also describes results in other operant and deferred imitation studies (Barr, Rovee-Collier, & Campanella,

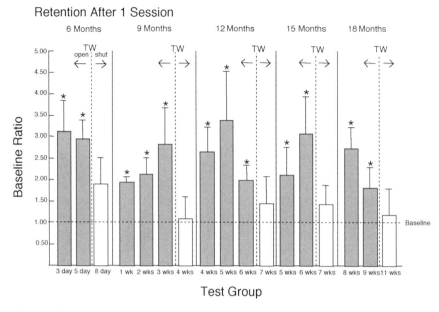

Figure 2.9 Mean baseline ratios of independent groups of 6-, 9-, 12-, 15-, and 18-month-olds who received one training session and a delayed recognition test after various delays. The time window closed when the training memory could no longer be retrieved (white bars).

2005; Hartshorn, Wilk, Muller, & Rovee-Collier, 1998c; Hildreth & Hill, 2003; Rovee-Collier & Barr, 2006).

The nonuniform benefit of a second session at different points within the time window resembles the benefit of distributing the total training time across more sessions. For both adults and infants, distributed training promotes better retention than massed training. Using a VPC procedure, Cornell (1980) simultaneously exposed 5-month-olds to two photographs of the same face for four trials at 3-s (massed training) or 60-s (distributed training) intervals. When tested with the original face and a novel one, both groups recognized the familiar face after 5 s, but only distributed training groups recognized it after 1 min, 5 min, and 1 hr. Similarly, when 2-month-olds were operantly trained for one 18-min session or three 6-min sessions, the distributed training group exhibited near-perfect retention 2 weeks later, but the massed training group exhibited none (Vander Linde, Morrongiello, & Rovee-Collier, 1985). The finding that the impact of distributed training on the retention of 2-month-olds was so profound reveals that their typically poor retention (Figure 2.2) is not due to an encoding or storage failure.

We recently found that 6-month-olds' deferred imitation was prolonged when the demonstration was associated with the memory of the train task. The association was formed when the target actions were modeled on the puppet in the presence of the train. How long imitation was extended

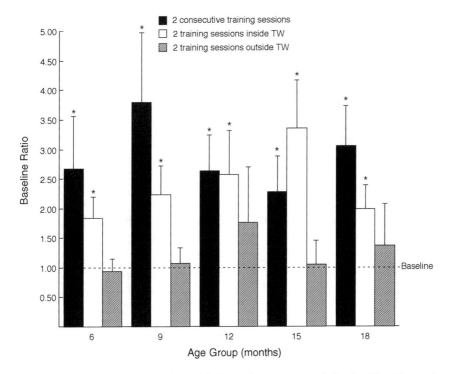

Figure 2.10 Mean baseline ratios of independent groups of 6-, 9-, 12-, 15-, and 18-month-olds who received a second training session either inside (black bars, gray bars) or outside (white bars) the time window (i.e., just before or just after infants forgot the first training session). Infants given Session 2 just inside the time window (gray bars) remembered longer than infants who were given only one session, but infants given Session 2 just outside the time window did not. The dotted line indicates the theoretical baseline ratio of 1.00 (i.e., no retention). An asterisk indicates significant retention. Vertical bars indicate +1 SE.

depended on when the association was formed. When the association was formed immediately after learning the train task, at the beginning of its time window, 6-month-olds exhibited deferred imitation for 2 weeks—the same duration that they remember the train (Barr, Vieira, & Rovee-Collier, 2001). When the association was formed at the midpoint of its time window (7 days), infants exhibited deferred imitation 4 weeks later; and when the association was formed at the end of its time window (14 days), 6-month-olds exhibited deferred imitation 6 weeks later (Rovee-Collier & Barr, 2006). Approximately half of the infants imitated one or two ordered pairs after 4 and 6 weeks. A no-association control group that learned the train task and saw the demonstration 7 days later in a different room with a different experimenter failed to exhibit deferred imitation 1 week after modeling. Thus, despite watching the actions modeled for only 60 s and not imitating them before the long-term test, 6-month-olds exhibited robust and reliable deferred imitation 1½ months later when the demonstration was associated with a stronger memory that was retrieved late in its time window (Figure 2.11).

Citing the original Barr et al. (1996) report that 6-month-olds exhibited deferred imitation for 24 hr, Bauer et al. (2007) observed that the temporally limited imitation at 6 months has "not 'inspired' researchers to examine retention over longer intervals" (p. 246). Because 9-month-olds who saw a two-step sequence modeled in three sessions 2–4 days apart could imitate target actions after 5 weeks, but imitation was neither reliable nor robust before 10 months of age (Bauer et al., 2001), she concluded that the storage and consolidation processes responsible for extended deferred imitation begin to mature at 9 months. This account is obviously inconsistent with the evidence that 3- and 6-month-olds exhibited deferred imitation weeks and months after seeing the target actions modeled in a single, brief session.

The time window construct also predicts that increasing the number of

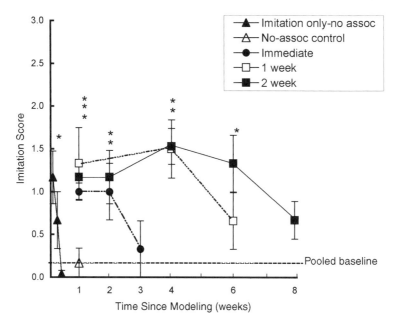

Figure 2.11 The mean imitation scores (±1 SE) of independent groups of 6-month-old infants as a function of the time since modeling (weeks). Six-month-olds originally can exhibit deferred imitation for only 1 day after seeing the target actions modeled (filled triangles; from Barr et al., 2001). For the experimental groups, deferred imitation was mediated by the association that was formed immediately (filled circles), 1 week (open squares), or 2 weeks (filled squares) after operant training. The no-association control group (open triangle) was tested 1 week after session 3. An asterisk indicates that a test group exhibited significant deferred imitation, that is, its mean imitation score was significantly higher than the mean test score of the pooled baseline control group (dashed line).

retrievals prolongs retention. When 6-month-olds imitated the target actions 1 day after the demonstration (the end of the time window) and were retested 10 days later, 100% of them exhibited deferred imitation (Barr et al., 2005). When the retention interval between successive tests was doubled from 10 to 20 days, 100% of the 6-month-olds also exhibited deferred imitation 30 days after the demonstration. And when the retention interval was doubled from 20 to 40 days, infants exhibited significant deferred imitation 70 days (2½ months) after the original demonstration. A replication group that was tested 60 days after the original demonstration also exhibited deferred imitation, but a yoked control group that received the same procedure but no demonstration performed at baseline throughout (Figure 2.12). Infants' deferred imitation was not prolonged because they imitated the actions three times 24 hr later; retention was also prolonged if infants merely watched the actions demonstrated again three times 24 hr later. Rather, the key to their extended imitation was two-fold: (1) the demonstration memory was multiply retrieved, and (2) each retrieval occurred near the end of the expanding time window. These factors undoubtedly had affected the deferred imitation of 9-month-olds too (Bauer et al. 2001; Bauer et al., 2007).

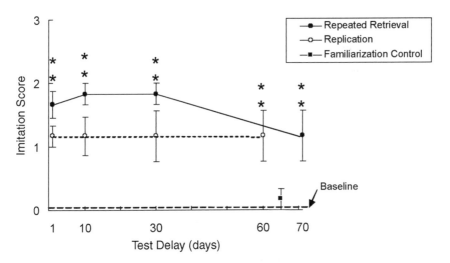

Figure 2.12 The mean imitation scores of the repeated active-retrieval group and the repeated active-retrieval replication group after test delays of 1, 10, 30, and 60 or 70 days. The familiarization control group was tested, on average, after 65 days. The mean test score of the 8-month baseline control group is indicated by the dashed line. An asterisk indicates that a test group exhibited significant deferred imitation (i.e., its mean imitation score was significantly greater than the mean test score of the baseline control group). Vertical bars indicate ±1 standard error. (Reprinted with permission from R. Barr, C. Rovee-Collier, & J. Campanella (2005). Retrieval protracts deferred imitation by 6-month-olds. *Infancy, 7*, 263–83. Copyright © 2005, Lawrence Erlbaum Associates, Inc.)

Thus, although younger infants forget more rapidly, how long they remember is determined experientially, not maturationally. In fact, whether different brain mechanisms have the same functions in adults and infants is unknown (Snyder, 2007). For adults and infants, retention depends on task salience, the number of times the memory was retrieved, when each retrieval occurred within the time window, and the number and strength of the associative links between the target memory and other events. As a reasonable working hypothesis, we propose that younger infants forget more rapidly because they have fewer associations to which the memory can be linked.

DO YOUNG INFANTS RELY EXCLUSIVELY ON A PRIMITIVE MEMORY SYSTEM?

Irrespective of task, young infants encode, store, and retrieve memories after extended periods. Evidence supporting this fact is indisputable. What is in dispute is whether they use a primitive memory system (implicit memory) to do so. Whether adults possess multiple memory systems or only a unitary memory system with different processing operations, however, is also disputed (e.g., Anderson & Bower, 1973; Jacoby, 1991; Johnson & Hirst, 1993; Newcombe & Crawley, 2007; Rabinowitz, 2002; Ratcliff, Van Zandt, & McKoon, 1995; Roediger, Rajaram, & Srinivas, 1990).

In infants, the higher-level memory system (explicit memory) was long believed to emerge late in the first year. This belief was based on evidence that 9-month-olds exhibited deferred imitation, which many view as a marker task for explicit memory, or memory with consciousness (see Chapter 3). The finding that 6-month-olds exhibited deferred imitation 24 hr after modeling (Barr et al., 1996, 2001) lowered that age to 6 months, and the finding that 3-month-olds exhibit deferred imitation of modeled actions 3 months later (Campanella & Rovee-Collier, 2005) lowered that age even more. Today, all sources of evidence indicate that both the implicit and explicit memory systems are functional early in life and develop in parallel, not hierarchically.

In adults, memory dissociations are the hallmark of multiple memory systems. A memory dissociation occurs when an independent variable affects performance on recognition/recall tests but not on priming tests. Although infants as young as 3 months presumably have only an implicit system, they exhibit the same memory dissociations on reactivation (priming) and delayed recognition tests as adults, who presumably have both implicit and explicit systems (Rovee-Collier, 1997). Initially, some questioned whether reactivation and priming were the same automatic process. Amnesics presented with a word fragment (the prime), for example, respond immediately with a word from a study list but cannot recognize the same word (Warrington & Weiskrantz, 1970). In contrast, 3-month-olds take 24 hr to respond to a reactivation reminder that they cannot recognize (Fagen & Rovee-Collier, 1983). Subsequent evidence that infants' response latency decreased with age and became instantaneous by 12 months, however, dispelled this concern (Hildreth & Rovee-Collier, 1999). This evidence was particularly compelling because older infants take increasingly longer to forget, and the reactivation reminder was always presented 1 week after forgetting. Yet, as the interval between training and reactivation increased from 2 weeks to 2¼ months between 3 and 12 months of age, the priming latency decreased logarithmically (Figure 2.13).

EXPLICIT MEMORY HAS BEEN CHARACTERIZED AS CONTEXT-DEPENDENT AND ASSOCIATIVE (TULVING, 1983). WHAT DO DATA FROM YOUNG INFANTS SHOW?

Infant memory is context-dependent

"Context" refers to aspects of the experimental setting, both external (the room, odors, experimenter) and internal (pharmacological state, affective

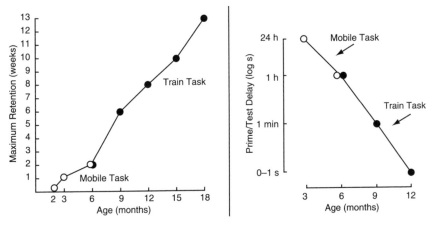

Figure 2.13 Right panel: Decreases in the latency of responding to a memory prime (in log s) over the first year of life. Each data point represents the shortest latency with which infants of a given age exhibited significant retention after exposure to the memory prime. At 6 months, infants were trained, primed, and tested in both the mobile task (open circles) and in the train task (filled circles). The data points represent the first prime/test delay at which infants of a given age demonstrated significant retention. Data for 3-month-olds in the mobile task are from Fagen and Rovee-Collier (1983); data for 6-month-olds in the mobile task are from Boller, Rovee-Collier, Borovsky, O'Connor, and Shyi (1990). Left panel: Increases in the maximum duration of retention over the first year of life (from Hartshorn et al., 1998b). In the present study, the prime was presented 1 week after infants of a given age last exhibited retention. (Reprinted with permission from H. Hildreth, & C. Rovee-Collier (1999). Decreases in the response latency to priming over the first year of life. *Developmental Psychobiology, 35,* 276–89. Copyright © 1999, Wiley Periodicals, Inc.).

state) that do not affect the task demands. Young infants encode numerous aspects of the incidental context. Hartshorn et al. (1998a) found that a change in the external context at the time of testing impaired retention after relatively long delays at 3, 9, and 12 months of age. This effect would have been missed had infants been tested only after short delays. It revealed that infants encode the incidental context and do not configure the training cue and the context. (At 6 months, immediately before the onset of independent locomotion, a context change impaired retention only after short delays.) Hartshorn et al. concluded that once the memory of the training cue becomes fuzzy, the context retrieves the memory of its details, thereby disambiguating the cue and enabling its discrimination from novel test cues (Bouton, 1994). Training in multiple contexts overrides the deleterious impact of a context change on infant retention (Amabile & Rovee-Collier, 1991; Rovee-Collier & DuFault, 1991).

After the mobile memory is forgotten, exposing 3-month-olds to the training context (no mobile present) will reactivate it (Hayne & Findlay, 1995; Rovee-Collier, Griesler, & Earley, 1985). At 6 months, even if the training cue and context successfully reactivate the memory, infants still cannot recognize the cue in a different context 1 day later. By 9 months, they can. At neither age, however, can the original cue reactivate the memory in a different context. By 12 months, it can (DeFrancisco, in press). Thus, infants' memories become less context-dependent with age. The same pattern occurs in studies of deferred imitation. Six-month-olds imitate a sequence of target actions if either the room where modeling occurred or the particular mat they sat on during modeling differs during the 24-hr test, but they fail to exhibit deferred imitation when both differ. By 9 months, infants generalize 24-hr imitation when both the room and mat differ (Learmonth et al., 2004). By 12–18 months, infants generalize deferred imitation across global contextual changes (laboratory vs. home) after 14 days (Hanna & Meltzoff, 1993; Hayne, Boniface, & Barr, 2000). Context effects also accompany changes in the social context (Learmonth, Lamberth, & Rovee-Collier, 2005), olfactory context (Rubin, Fagen, & Carroll, 1998), and auditory context (Fagen, Prigot, Carroll, Pioli, Stein, & Franco, 1997).

In addition to encoding information about the incidental context, young infants can learn to associate an explicit context with a particular experimental contingency. Cuevas, Learmonth, and Rovee-Collier (2005) trained 3-month-olds to kick to move the mobile in context A and extinguished the contingency by disconnecting the ankle ribbon from the mobile in context B. They found that extinction was context-specific. One day later, infants exhibited an extinction effect when tested in the extinction context but exhibited conditioned responding when tested in context A or a neutral context (context C) (Figure 2.14). The renewal effect has been documented in animal and human adults and is attributed to removing the retrieval cues for extinction at the time of testing (Bouton, 1994). It is theoretically important in demonstrating that extinction does not eliminate original learning.

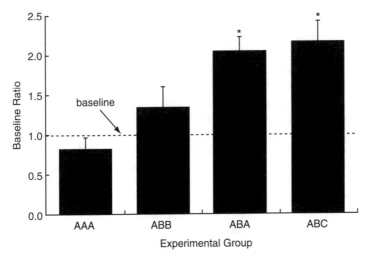

Figure 2.14 The renewal effect in 3-month-olds. All statistical comparisons were against a theoretical baseline ratio of 1.00 (dashed line). In the group labels, the first letter designates the training context, the second letter designates the extinction context, and the third letter designates the test context. Groups AAA and ABB, which were tested in the extinction context, exhibited no retention during the long-term test. Group ABA, which was tested in the acquisition context, and Group ABC, which was tested in a novel context, exhibited significant retention during the long-term test. Asterisks indicate significant retention (M baseline ratio significantly > 1.00); vertical bars indicate +1 SE.

Infant memory is associative

Associations have always played a central role in explanations of memory phenomena. In connectionist models, encountering a retrieval cue activates its concept, which is represented as a node in an associative network. That activation automatically spreads to other nodes that are linked to it and activates them as well (Anderson & Bower, 1973; Collins & Quillian, 1969; Loftus & Loftus, 1974). Activation strengthens the links between nodes the greater the amount of spreading activation. This process occurs without conscious control or awareness.

Timmons (1994) obtained the first evidence that two discrete memories were associatively linked in infancy. In a paired-associate procedure, 6-month-olds learned two cue–response pairs (moving a mobile by kicking, activating a music box by arm-waving or vice versa) 3 days apart in the same context (a red-and-blue striped cloth liner). Twenty days later, when both cue–response pairs were forgotten, infants were reminded with either the mobile or the music box, but all were tested with the mobile 24 hr later. During the test, infants produced a mobile-appropriate response (kicking, arm-waving) of whether the mobile memory was directly reactivated by exposure to the mobile or indirectly reactivated by exposure to the music box. Timmons concluded that when infants had learned the second task, whichever it was, the common training context had activated their memory of the preceding task, associatively linking the coactive representations. Without an associative link, exposure to the music box could not have reactivated the mobile memory 3 weeks later. Similarly, in a reenactment study, directly reactivating the forgotten memories of three of six activities 14- and 18-month-olds had performed in the same session indirectly reactivated the other three (Sheffield & Hudson, 1994).

Cuevas, Rovee-Collier, and Learmonth (2006) demonstrated that 6-month-olds formed an association between two objects that were neither perceptually present nor had ever appeared together when the representations of those objects were simultaneously activated in primary memory by associated retrieval cues. In this study, infants were simultaneously exposed to hand puppets A and B (Phase 1) and, 24 hr later, were trained to kick to move a mobile in a distinctive context (Phase 2). By the end of Phase 2, infants had presumably formed two associations—one between puppet A and puppet B, and one between the mobile and the context. In Phase 3, infants were exposed to puppet A (puppet B not present) in the distinctive context (the mobile not present) to form a new puppet B–mobile association. How? Puppet A presumably activated its associated memory of puppet B, and the distinctive context presumably activated its associated memory of the mobile. If the representations of puppet B and the mobile were simultaneously active in primary memory, then they would be associated, even though neither object was physically present. Finally, the target actions were modeled on puppet B to provide infants with overt behavior for expressing the new association.

Recall that 6-month-olds had exhibited deferred imitation on the puppet for 2 weeks after the demonstration when it was associated with an operant train task that they remembered for 2 weeks (Barr et al., 2001; Figure 2.15, solid circles). Because infants also remember the mobile task for 2 weeks, Cuevas et al. reasoned that if puppet B and the mobile had been associated in absentia, then 6-month-olds would exhibit deferred imitation on puppet B 2 weeks after the demonstration. In fact, the infants successfully imitated the target actions on puppet B after delays up to 2 weeks (Figure 2.15, open circles). Two control groups with no opportunity to form an association failed to imitate on puppet B even 1 week after modeling (Figure 2.15, squares). These findings reveal that young infants form relatively enduring associations between memory representations that are simultaneously activated even in the absence of perceptual support. The memory representations are associatively activated via links to memory representations of physically present objects in the associative network.

Using a sensory preconditioning procedure, a variant of classical conditioning that originated in studies with animals, Townsend (2006) found that 6-month-olds indirectly associated two puppets they had never seen together. In Phase 1, infants were preexposed to either two or three different pairs of

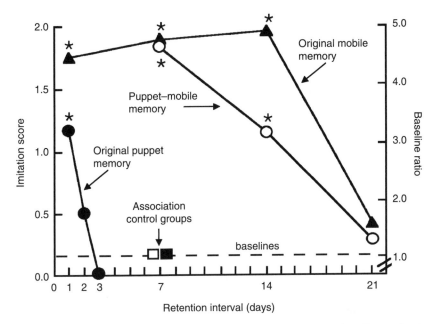

Figure 2.15 Mean deferred imitation score (left *y*-axis) and mean baseline ratio, the index of operant retention (right *y*-axis), as a function of the retention interval. The deferred imitation function of the three experimental groups that associated the memory representations of puppet B and the mobile is presented along with the original deferred imitation function (from Barr et al., 2001) and the forgetting function for the operant mobile task (from Hill, Borovsky, & Rovee-Collier, 1988). Also shown is the test performance of two association control groups. The dotted line indicates the mean baserate (baseline control group) for spontaneous production of the target actions in the deferred imitation task and the theoretical baseline for the mobile task. Asterisks indicate that test performance significantly exceeded the baserate or the theoretical baseline. (Reprinted with permission from K. Cuevas, C. Rovee-Collier, & A. E. Learmonth (2006). Infants form associations between memory representations of stimuli that are absent. *Psychological Science, 17,* 543–549. Copyright © 2006 by the Association for Psychological Science.)

puppets (one pair/day) on 2 or 3 consecutive days (A–B, B–C or A–B, B–C, C–D, respectively). One day following the last preexposure session, he modeled the target actions on the final puppet (C or D; Phase 2) and tested infants with puppet A (the retrieval cue; Phase 3) 24 hr later. Both groups imitated the modeled actions on puppet A, but a group tested with a novel puppet (puppet E) did not. Thus, 6-month-olds had indirectly associated two puppets (A and C or A and D) that were never presented together by means of an associative chain (A→B→C, A→B→C→D); also the associative chain was specific, not generalized. Infants who were preexposed to puppets A and B unpaired or to puppet B alone after the puppet A–B association was formed (an extinction procedure) did not imitate the modeled actions on puppet A, confirming that the A–B link was necessary for imitation. Finally, infants who saw the target actions modeled on puppet A and were tested 24 hr later with puppet C (the retrieval cue) also imitated the actions, indicating that the associative chain was bidirectional. Because transitivity is described as an explicit memory function (Smith & Squire, 2005), these findings are further evidence that explicit memory is not late-maturing.

DOES THE ONSET OF LANGUAGE BLOCK THE RETRIEVAL OF PREVERBAL MEMORIES?

Young children usually cannot report memories of what happened before they were linguistically competent. Their memory failure has been attributed to a "language barrier" that blocks memories acquired preverbally. According to K. Nelson (1990, p. 306), "virtually no early memories slip through the barrier." Because verbal cues are used as retrieval cues for those memories, however, children's memory failure could reflect a mismatch between encoding and retrieval cues. Simcock and Hayne (2002) developed a unique, multistep memory task using the "Magic Shrinking Machine" to examine whether the development of language blocked early memories. In this task, 27-, 33-, and 39-month-old children, trained and tested in their homes, performed a sequence of five actions: (1) pull a lever to activate an array of lights and turn on the machine, (2) select a toy (e.g., ball, teddy bear), (3) drop the toy down a chute on top of the machine, (4) turn the handle on the side of machine (producing music and loud noises), and (5) retrieve a miniature replica of the toy from a side bin on the machine. Either 6 or 12 months later, their memory of the event was assessed with both verbal and nonverbal measures. At all ages, children exhibited retention on both measures after both delays, but their retention on nonverbal measures was consistently superior. During testing, children's verbal reports reflected their verbal competence at the time of encoding, even though words they could have used to report the event were in their vocabularies at the time of testing. Thus, linguistically competent children could remember the event they had encoded preverbally but could not translate what they had encoded preverbally into words—even though the words were at their disposal when they were tested for retention. The finding that infants express their memory in a manner appropriate to the age at encoding rather than the age at testing has also been obtained with rat pups (Richardson & Fan, 2002; Yap & Richardson, 2005).

INFANTILE AMNESIA REDUX

Returning to the issue of infantile amnesia, we can conclude with certainty that it is not caused by (1) immaturity of the brain mechanisms responsible for the encoding, storage, and retrieval of memories, (2) an exclusive reliance on a primitive memory system, (3) rapid forgetting by immature organisms, or (4) the inability of preverbal memories to "break" the language barrier. Because the fundamental principles of memory processing in human infants and adults are the same, the phenomenal experience of infantile amnesia requires no special explanation but can be understood within the framework of normal memory processing.

Consider first that a match between the encoding and retrieval contexts is critical for retrieval, especially after long delays (Hartshorn et al., 1998a). As a result, the shift from nonverbal to verbal retrieval cues dramatically lessens the probability that a memory encoded in infancy would be retrieved later in life. From this perspective, words are retrieval cues whose status is no different than that of other potential retrieval cues. Second, even if an appropriate retrieval cue were to recover an early memory later in life, a person would be unlikely to identify it as such. Because reactivated memories that are older are readily updated, for example, they may be impossible to identify as having originated early on (Galluccio & Rovee-Collier, 2005). Third, as memories of healthy individuals become increasingly remote, they appear to become increasingly disconnected from their original temporal context and more semantic and fact-like (Bayley, Hopkins, & Squire, 2003). Even in infants, specific contextual information is quite fragile and disappears from infants' memories that are older or were previously reactivated (Galluccio & Rovee-Collier, 2005; Hitchcock & Rovee-Collier, 1996). As a result, people might actually remember many early-life events without knowing where or when they occurred.

CONCLUDING REMARKS

A wealth of discoveries over the last decade has changed the face of infant memory research. In addition to expanding the depth and breadth of our knowledge, they have fostered increasingly sophisticated research that has moved us beyond the level of mere description to understanding the mechanisms that underlie memory development. Today, we know that memories are activated both directly and indirectly, that repeated retrievals prolong retention and speed memory processing exponentially, and that periodic reminders maintain early memories over substantial periods of development. The latter discovery revealed how early experience can affect later behavior.

Most important is the discovery that young infants readily form new and relatively permanent associations between (1) objects or events that are physically present, (2) an activated memory representation of an object or event and a physically present object or event, and (3) the activated memory representations between two absent objects or events. Because associations are latent and infants will express only a small fraction of them, it is impossible

to guess how much they know and remember. The strength of a new association is the same whether one or both of its members are present or absent.
The strongest member of the new association determines the retention of the
other member, and operations that prolong the retention of one member of
an association also prolong retention of the other. The members of new
associations can be linked to members of existing associations in a complex
mnemonic network, and the links are strengthened each time activation
spreads through the network. This process is the mechanism by which the
early knowledge base is formed and expanded, but we still have much to learn
about it.

ACKNOWLEDGMENTS

Preparation of this chapter and much of the research described in it were
supported by Grant no. MH32307 from the National Institute of Mental
Health to the first author. We thank Rachel Barr, Sabina Farney, and Maren
Cargill for providing original data and photographs, members of the Rutgers'
Early Learning Project lab for their selfless assistance with this project, and
George Collier for his conceptual contributions and moral support.

REFERENCES

Adler, S. A., Wilk, A., & Rovee-Collier, C. (2000). Reinstatement versus reactivation
    effects on active memory in infants. *Journal of Experimental Child Psychology, 75*,
    93–115.
Amabile, T. A., & Rovee-Collier, C. (1991). Contextual variation and memory
    retrieval at six months. *Child Development, 62*, 1155–1166.
Anderson, J. R., & Bower, G. H. (1973). *Human associative memory*. Washington, DC:
    V. H. Winston.
Barr, R., Dowden, A., & Hayne, H. (1996). Developmental changes in deferred
    imitation by 6- to 24-month-old infants. *Infant Behavior and Development, 19*,
    159–170.
Barr, R., Rovee-Collier, C., & Campanella, J. (2005). Retrieval protracts deferred
    imitation by 6-month-olds. *Infancy, 7*, 263–283.
Barr, R., Vieira, A., & Rovee-Collier, C. (2001). Mediated imitation in 6-month-olds:
    Remembering by association. *Journal of Experimental Child Psychology, 79*,
    229–252.
Bauer, P. J. (2002). Building toward a past: Construction of a reliable long-term recall
    memory system. In N. J. Stein, P. J. Bauer, & M. Rabinowitz (Eds.), *Representation,
    memory, and development* (pp. 17–42). Mahwah, NJ: Lawrence Erlbaum Associates,
    Inc.
Bauer, P. J., DeBoer, T., & Lukowski, A. F. (2007). In the language of multiple mem-
    ory systems. In L. M. Oakes & P. J. Bauer (Eds.), *Short- and long-term memory in
    infancy and early childhood* (pp. 240–270). New York: Oxford University Press.
Bauer, P. J., Wiebe, A., Waters, J. M., & Bangston, S. K. (2001). Reexposure breeds

recall: Effects of experience on 9-month-olds' ordered recall. *Journal of Experimental Child Psychology, 80*, 174–200.

Bayley, P. J., Hopkins, R. O., & Squire, L. R. (2003). Successful recollection of remote autobiographical memories by amnesic patients with medial temporal lobe lesions. *Neuron, 38*, 135–144.

Bjork, R. A. (2001). Recency and recovery in human memory. In H. L. Roediger, III, J. S. Nairne, I. Neath, & A. M. Surprenant (Eds.), *The nature of remembering: Essays in honor of Robert G. Crowder* (pp. 211–232). Washington, DC: American Psychological Association.

Boller, K., Rovee-Collier, C., Borovsky, D., O'Connor, J., & Shyi, G. (1990). Developmental changes in the time-dependent nature of memory retrieval. *Developmental Psychology, 26*, 770–779.

Bouton, M. E. (1994). Context, ambiguity, and classical conditioning. *Current Directions in Psychological Science, 3*, 49–53.

Campanella, J., & Rovee-Collier, C. (2005). Latent learning and deferred imitation at 3 months. *Infancy, 7*, 243–262.

Campbell, B. A., & Campbell, E. H. (1962). Retention and extinction of learned fear in infant and adult rats. *Journal of Comparative and Physiological Psychology, 55*, 1–8.

Campbell, B. A., & Coulter, X. (1976). Neural and psychological processes underlying the development of learning and memory. In T. J. Tighe & R. N. Leaton (Eds.), *Habituation* (pp. 129–157). Hillsdale, NJ: Lawrence Erlbaum Associates, Inc.

Campbell, B. A., & Jaynes, J. (1966). Reinstatement. *Psychological Review, 73*, 478–480.

Collins, A. M., & Quillian, M. R. (1969). Retrieval time from semantic memory. *Journal of Verbal Learning and Verbal Behavior, 8*, 240–247.

Cornell, E. H. (1979). Infants' recognition memory, forgetting, and savings. *Journal of Experimental Child Psychology, 28*, 359–374.

Cornell, E. H. (1980). Distributed study facilitates infants' delayed recognition memory. *Memory and Cognition, 8*, 539–542.

Cuevas, K., Learmonth, A. E., & Rovee-Collier, C. (2005). *Contextual determinants of infant learning: The renewal effect.* Paper presented at the meeting of the Eastern Psychological Association, Boston, MA.

Cuevas, K., Rovee-Collier, C., & Learmonth, A. E. (2006). Infants form associations between memory representations of stimuli that are absent. *Psychological Science, 17*, 543–549.

DeFrancisco, B. S. (in press). The specificity of priming effects over the first year of life. *Developmental Psychobiology.*

Fagan, J. F., III (1973). Infants' delayed recognition memory and forgetting. *Journal of Experimental Child Psychology, 16*, 424–450.

Fagen, J. W., Prigot, J., Carroll, M., Pioli, L., Stein, A., & Franco, A. (1997). Auditory context and memory retrieval in young infants. *Child Development, 68*, 1057–1066.

Fagen, J. W., & Rovee-Collier, C. (1983). Memory retrieval: A time-locked process in infancy. *Science, 222*, 1349–1351.

Freud, S. (1935). *A general introduction to psychoanalysis.* New York: Clarion.

Galluccio, L., & Rovee-Collier, C. (2005). Updating reactivated memories in infancy. II. Time passage and repetition effects. *Developmental Psychobiology, 47*, 18–30.

Galluccio, L., & Rovee-Collier, C. (2006). Nonuniform effects of reinstatement within the time window. *Learning and Motivation, 37*, 1–17.

Greco, C., Rovee-Collier, C., Hayne, H., Griesler, P., & Earley, L. (1986). Ontogeny of early event memory: I. Forgetting and retrieval by 2- and 3-month-olds. *Infant Behavior and Development, 9*, 441–460.

Hanna, E., & Meltzoff, A. N. (1993). Peer imitation by toddlers in laboratory, home, and day-care contexts: Implications for social learning and memory. *Developmental Psychology, 29*, 702–710.

Hartshorn, K. (2003). Reinstatement maintains a memory in human infants for 1½ years. *Developmental Psychobiology, 42*, 269–282.

Hartshorn, K., & Rovee-Collier, C. (1997). Infant learning and long-term memory at 6 months: A confirming analysis. *Developmental Psychobiology, 30*, 71–85.

Hartshorn, K., Rovee-Collier, C., Gerhardstein, P., Bhatt, R. S., Klein, P. J., Aaron, F., et al. (1998a). Developmental changes in the specificity of memory over the first year of life. *Developmental Psychobiology, 33*, 61–78.

Hartshorn, K., Rovee-Collier, C., Gerhardstein, P., Bhatt, R. S., Wondoloski, T. L., Klein, P. J., et al. (1998b). The ontogeny of long-term memory over the first year-and-a-half of life. *Developmental Psychobiology, 32*, 69–89.

Hartshorn, K., Wilk, A., Muller, K., & Rovee-Collier, C. (1998c). An expanding training series protracts retention for 3-month-old infants. *Developmental Psychobiology, 33*, 271–282.

Hayne, H. (1990). The effect of multiple reminders on long-term retention in human infants. *Developmental Psychobiology, 23*, 453–477.

Hayne, H. (2007). Infant memory development. In L. M. Oakes & P. J. Bauer (Eds.), *Short- and long-term memory in infancy and early childhood* (pp. 209–239). New York: Oxford University Press.

Hayne, H., Barr, R., & Herbert, J. (2003). The effect of prior practice on memory reactivation and generalization. *Child Development, 74*, 1615–1627.

Hayne, H., Boniface, J., & Barr, R. (2000). The development of declarative memory in human infants: Age-related changes in deferred imitation. *Behavioral Neuroscience, 114*, 77–83.

Hayne, H., & Findlay, N. (1995). Contextual control of memory retrieval in infancy: Evidence for associative priming. *Infant Behavior and Development, 18*, 195–207.

Hayne, H., & Herbert, J. (2004). Verbal cues facilitate memory retrieval during infancy. *Journal of Experimental Child Psychology, 89*, 127–139.

Herbert, J. S., Eckerman, C. O., & Stanton, M. E. (2003). The ontogeny of human learning in delay, long-delay, and trace eyeblink conditioning. *Behavioral Neuroscience, 117*, 1196–1210.

Hildreth, K., & Hill, D. (2003). Retrieval difficulty and retention of reactivated memories over the first year of life. *Developmental Psychobiology, 43*, 216–229.

Hildreth, K., & Rovee-Collier, C. (1999). Decreases in the response latency to priming over the first year of life. *Developmental Psychobiology, 35*, 276–289.

Hildreth, K., & Rovee-Collier, C. (2002). Forgetting functions of reactivated memories over the first year of life. *Developmental Psychobiology, 41*, 277–288.

Hildreth, K., Sweeney, B., & Rovee-Collier, C. (2003). Differential memory-preserving effects of reminders at 6 months. *Journal of Experimental Child Psychology, 84*, 41–62.

Hill, W. H., Borovsky, D., & Rovee-Collier, C. (1988). Continuities in infant memory development over the first half-year. *Developmental Psychobiology, 21*, 43–62.

Hitchcock, D. F. A., & Rovee-Collier, C. (1996). The effect of repeated reactivations on memory specificity in infants. *Journal of Experimental Child Psychology*, *62*, 378–400.

Howe, M. L., Courage, M. L., & Bryant-Brown, L. (1993). Reinstating preschoolers' memories. *Developmental Psychology*, *29*, 854–869.

Howe, M. L., & O'Sullivan, J. T. (1997). What children's memories tell us about recalling our childhoods: A review of storage and retrieval processes in the development of long-term retention. *Developmental Review*, *17*, 148–204.

Hsu, V. C. (2007). *Time window effects on retention over the first year-and-a-half of life*. Unpublished doctoral dissertation, Rutgers University, New Brunswick, NJ.

Hsu, V. C., Rovee-Collier, C., Hill, D. L., Grodkiewicz, J., & Joh, A. S. (2005). Effects of priming duration on retention over the first 1½ years of life. *Developmental Psychobiology*, *47*, 43–54.

Hudson, J. A., & Sheffield, E. G. (1998). Déjà vu all over again: Effects of reenactment on toddlers' event memory. *Child Development*, *69*, 51–67.

Jacoby, L. L. (1991). A process dissociation framework: Separating automatic from intentional uses of memory. *Journal of Memory and Language*, *30*, 513–541.

Johnson, M. K., & Hirst, W. (1993). MEM: Memory subsystems as processes. In A. F. Collins, S. E. Gathercole, M. A. Conway, & P. E. Morris (Eds.), *Theories of memory* (pp. 241–286). Hillsdale, NJ: Lawrence Erlbaum Associates Inc.

Jones, H. E. (1930). The retention of conditioned emotional reactions in infancy. *Journal of Genetic Psychology*, *37*, 485–498.

Jones, H. E. (1931). The conditioning of overt emotional response. *Journal of Educational Psychology*, *22*, 127–130.

Kimble, G. (Ed.). (1961). *Hilgard & Marquis' conditioning and learning*. New York: Appleton-Century-Crofts.

Learmonth, A. E., Lamberth, R., & Rovee-Collier, C. (2004). Generalization of deferred imitation during the first year of life. *Journal of Experimental Child Psychology*, *88*, 297–318.

Learmonth, A. E., Lamberth, R., & Rovee-Collier, C. (2005). The social context of imitation in infancy. *Journal of Experimental Child Psychology*, *91*, 297–314.

Little, A. H., Lipsitt, L. P., & Rovee-Collier, C. (1984). Classical conditioning and retention of the infant's eyelid response: Effects of age and interstimulus interval. *Journal of Experimental Child Psychology*, *37*, 512–524.

Loftus, G. R., & Loftus, E. F. (1974). The influence of one memory retrieval on a subsequent memory retrieval. *Memory and Cognition*, *2*, 467–471.

Mandler, J. M. (1990). Recall of events by preverbal children. In A. Diamond (Ed.), *Annals of the New York Academy of Sciences: Vol. 608. The development and neural bases of higher cognitive functions* (pp. 485–503). New York: New York Academy of Sciences.

Mandler, J. M. (1998). Representation. In W. Damon (Ed.), *Handbook of child psychology: Cognition, perception, and language* (Vol. 2, pp. 255–308). Hoboken, NJ: Wiley.

Mandler, J. M. (2007). How do we remember? Let me count the ways. In L. M. Oakes & P. J. Bauer (Eds.), *Short- and long-term memory in infancy and early childhood* (pp. 271–239). New York: Oxford University Press.

Meltzoff, A. N. (1988). Infant imitation and memory: Nine-month-olds in immediate and deferred tests. *Child Development*, *59*, 217–225.

Nelson, C. A. (1997). The neurobiological basis of early memory development. In

N. Cowan (Ed.), *The development of memory in early childhood* (pp. 41–82). Hove, UK: Psychology Press.

Nelson, K. (1990). Remembering, forgetting, and childhood amnesia. In R. Fivush & J. A. Hudson (Eds.), *Knowing and remembering in young children* (pp. 301–316). New York: Cambridge University Press.

Nelson, K. (1993). The psychological and social origins of autobiographical memory. *Psychological Science, 4*, 7–14.

Newcombe, N. S., & Crawley, S. L. (2007). To have and have not: What do we mean when we talk about long-term memory development? In L. M. Oakes & P. J. Bauer (Eds.), *Short- and long-term memory in infancy and early childhood* (pp. 291–313). New York: Oxford University Press.

Pascalis, O., de Haan, M., Nelson, C. A., & de Schonen, S. (1998). Long-term recognition memory for faces assessed by visual paired comparison in 3- and 6-month-old infants. *Journal of Experimental Psychology: Learning, Memory, and Cognition, 24*, 249–260.

Pascalis, O., & de Schonen, S. (1994). Recognition memory in 3- to 4-day-old human neonates. *NeuroReport, 5*, 1721–1724.

Piaget, J. (1962). *Play, dreams and imitation in childhood.* New York: Norton.

Pillemer, D. B., & White, S. H. (1989). Childhood events recalled by children and adults. In H. W. Reese (Ed.), *Advances in child development and behavior* (Vol. 21, pp. 297–340). San Diego, CA: Academic.

Priestley, G., Roberts, S., & Pipe, M.-E. (1999). Returning to the scene: Reminders and context reinstatement enhance children's recall. *Developmental Psychology, 35*, 1006–1019.

Rabinowitz, M. (2002). The procedural–procedural knowledge distinction. In N. J. Stein, P. J. Bauer, & M. Rabinowitz (Eds.), *Representation, memory, and development* (pp. 185–198). Mahwah, NJ: Lawrence Erlbaum Associates, Inc.

Ratcliff, R., Van Zandt, T., & McKoon, G. (1995). Process dissociation, single-process theories, and recognition memory. *Journal of Experimental Psychology: General, 124*, 352–374.

Richards, J. E. (2003). Attention affects the recognition of briefly presented visual stimuli in infants: An ERP study. *Developmental Science, 6*, 312–328.

Richardson, R., & Fan, M. (2002). Behavioral expression of conditioned fear in rats is appropriate to their age at training, not their age at testing. *Animal Learning and Behavior, 30*, 394–404.

Richardson, R., Wang, P., & Campbell, B. A. (1993). Reactivation of nonassociative memory. *Developmental Psychobiology, 26*, 1–23.

Roediger, H. L. III., Rajaram, S., & Srinivas, K. (1990). Specifying criteria for postulating memory systems. In A. Diamond (Ed.), *Annals of the New York Academy of Sciences: Vol. 608. The development and neural bases of higher cognitive functions* (pp. 572–589). New York: New York Academy of Sciences.

Rose, S. A., Feldman, J. F., & Jankowski, J. J. (2007). Developmental aspects of visual recognition memory in infancy. In L. M. Oakes & P. J. Bauer (Eds.), *Short- and long-term memory in infancy and early childhood* (pp. 153–178). New York: Oxford University Press.

Rovee-Collier, C. (1995). Time windows in cognitive development. *Developmental Psychology, 51*, 1–23.

Rovee-Collier, C. (1997). Dissociations in infant memory: Rethinking the development of implicit and explicit memory. *Psychological Review, 104*, 467–498.

Rovee-Collier, C., & Barr, R. (2006). *Representation-mediated deferred imitation by 6-month-old infants*. Paper presented at the meeting of the Pavlovian Society, Philadelphia, PA.

Rovee-Collier, C. & DuFault, D. (1991). Multiple contexts and memory retrieval at 3 months. *Developmental Psychobiology*, *24*, 39–49.

Rovee-Collier, C., Griesler, P. C., & Earley, L. A. (1985). Contextual determinants of infant retention. *Learning and Motivation*, *16*, 139–157.

Rovee-Collier, C., Hartshorn, K., & DiRubbo, M. (1999). Long-term maintenance of infant memory. *Developmental Psychobiology*, *35*, 91–102.

Rovee-Collier, C., Hayne, H., & Colombo, M. (2001). *The development of implicit and explicit memory*. Amsterdam: John Benjamins.

Rovee-Collier, C., Sullivan, M. W., Enright, M. K., Lucas, D., & Fagen, J. W. (1980). Reactivation of infant memory. *Science*, *208*, 1159–1161.

Rubin, G. B., Fagen, J. W., & Carroll, M. (1998). Olfactory context and memory retrieval in 3-month-old infants. *Infant Behavior and Development*, *21*, 641–658.

Sheffield, E. G., & Hudson, J. A. (1994). Reactivation of toddlers' event memory. *Memory*, *2*, 447–465.

Simcock, G., & Hayne, H. (2002). Breaking the barrier? Children fail to translate their preverbal memories into language. *Psychological Science*, *13*, 225–231.

Smith, C., & Squire, L. R. (2005). Declarative memory, awareness, and transitive inference. *Journal of Neuroscience*, *25*, 10138–10146.

Snyder, K. A. (2007). Neural mechanisms of attention and memory in preferential looking tasks. In L. M. Oakes & P. J. Bauer (Eds.), *Short- and long-term memory in infancy and early childhood* (pp. 179–208). New York: Oxford University Press.

Spear, N. E., & Parsons, P. J. (1976). Analysis of a reactivation treatment: Ontogenetic determinants of alleviated forgetting. In D. L. Medin, W. A. Roberts, & R. T. Davis (Eds.), *Processes of animal memory* (pp. 135–165). Hillsdale, NJ: Lawrence Erlbaum Associates, Inc.

Stevenson, H. W., Hess, E. H., & Rheingold, H. L. (1967). *Early behavior: Comparative and developmental approaches*. New York: Wiley.

Timmons, C. R. (1994). Associative links between discrete memories in infancy. *Infant Behavior and Development*, *17*, 431–445.

Townsend, D. (2006). *The transitivity of preconditioned infantile associative memories during deferred imitation*. Unpublished doctoral dissertation, Rutgers University, New Brunswick, NJ.

Tulving, E. (1983). *Elements of episodic memory*. New York: Oxford University Press.

Vander Linde, E., Morrongiello, B. A., & Rovee-Collier, C. (1985). Determinants of retention in 8-week-old infants. *Developmental Psychology*, *21*, 601–613.

Warrington, E. K., & Weiskrantz, L. (1970). Amnesic syndrome: Consolidation or retrieval? *Nature*, *228*, 629–630.

Yap, C., & Richardson, R. (2005). Latent inhibition in the developing rat: An examination of context-specific effects. *Developmental Psychobiology*, *47*, 55–65.

3 Memory development in toddlers

Harlene Hayne
University of Otago, New Zealand

Gabrielle Simcock
University of Queensland, Australia

> If any one faculty of our nature may be called more wonderful than the rest, I
> do think it is memory. . . . We are, to be sure, a miracle every way; but our
> powers of recollecting and of forgetting do seem peculiarly past finding out.
>
> (Jane Austen, *Mansfield Park*)

Like Jane Austen, the contributors to this volume are inherently fascinated by
the process of memory—the brain's ability to store virtually endless amounts
of information, retaining it so that we can retrieve, ponder, and use it hours,
days or even decades later. Unlike Jane Austen, however, many of us believe
that scientists will eventually unlock some of the basic secrets to our "powers
of recollecting and forgetting." Furthermore, many of us also believe that
one key to unlocking these secrets will emerge through systematic studies
of memory development. In our view, studies of memory development
yield important information about memory processes in general, including
important lessons for understanding adult memory.

In this chapter, our task is to describe what researchers currently know
about memory during the toddler years. We acknowledge that the term "toddler" is a somewhat colloquial, rather than a scientific, term. Here, we will
use "toddler" to refer to participants who range in age from 1 to 3 years
old. Some of the studies we describe will also include slightly younger (e.g.,
6-month-old) and older (e.g., 4-year-old) participants as well (for additional
studies with preschool-age children, see Chapter 4, this volume). The specific goals of the chapter are four-fold. First, we describe the primary tasks
that have been used to study memory during the toddler period. Second, we
outline some of the major age-related changes in memory that have been
documented using these tasks. Third, we consider the roles of independent
locomotion and language acquisition in memory development during this
period. Finally, we describe some of the implications of these data for practical issues regarding toddlers' ability to learn from television, picture books,
and photographs.

TASKS TO STUDY MEMORY IN TODDLERS

Deferred imitation

What we know about memory development during the toddler period is based largely on research conducted using the deferred imitation paradigm. Although deferred imitation played a central role in Piaget's theory of cognitive development (Piaget, 1962), Meltzoff (1988a) was the first researcher to formalize the task as a tool to study memory. In a standard deferred imitation task, the experimenter performs an action or series of actions with a set of novel objects. The participant is not allowed to touch the objects or practise the actions prior to the test. During the test, the participant is allowed to handle the objects for the first time and his or her ability to imitate the experimenter's actions is measured for a fixed period of time. Each participant is tested only once and the test can be scheduled either immediately after the demonstration or following delays of days, weeks, or months. Memory is inferred if the number of actions that participants imitate during the test exceeds that of age-matched controls who never observe the experimenter model the target actions in the first place.

Tasks of deferred imitation are ideally suited to study memory development in toddlers because they do not require training; participants spontaneously imitate the actions of others both in the laboratory (e.g., Barr, Dowden, & Hayne, 1996; Meltzoff, 1988a; Nielsen, 2006) and in the context of their own home (Barr & Hayne, 2003). Furthermore, the deferred imitation task does not require receptive or productive language skill, which makes it perfect for preverbal or early-verbal children. Finally, given that human children and adults who suffer from amnesia fail on tests of deferred imitation (Adlam, Vargha-Khadem, Mishkin, & de Haan, 2005; McDonough, Mandler, McKee, & Squire, 1995), it is generally assumed that this task requires higher order memory skills (Hayne, 2004; Jones & Herbert, 2006; Meltzoff, 1990; Nelson, 1995). For these reasons, much of what we know about age-related changes in memory between the ages of 1 and 3 years has been learned by studying deferred imitation.

Elicited imitation

The other task that is commonly used to study memory in toddlers is a variant of the deferred imitation task; this task has been referred to as elicited imitation (Bauer, Hertsgaard, & Dow, 1994; Bauer & Mandler, 1989). In the elicited imitation task, the experimenter also models a series of actions with novel objects and the infant is given the opportunity to imitate those actions following a delay. Unlike the deferred imitation task, the demonstration is accompanied by a verbal description of the target actions and the outcome of the event, the infant is allowed the opportunity to practise the target actions briefly prior to the test, and the test typically begins with a verbal cue. In tests of elicited imitation, infants often serve as their own controls; memory is inferred when infants perform more actions from the target sequence than from a sequence that is new to them. Additionally, infants are often tested on multiple occasions (for review, see Bauer, Wenner, Dropik, & Wewerka, 2000).

In the past, the procedural differences between the deferred imitation and elicited imitation tasks have been dismissed as trivial; however, systematic research comparing the two tasks has revealed that they do make a difference to memory performance. For example, Hayne, Barr, and Herbert (2003) examined the effect of practice on memory performance by 18-month-old infants. All of the infants in their study were tested using an imitation paradigm; some infants practised the target actions before the retention interval (elicited imitation) and some did not (deferred imitation). As shown in Figure 3.1, Hayne et al. (2003) found that the opportunity to practise influenced both memory reactivation and generalization. When infants were tested after a 6-week delay, a brief reminder treatment alleviated forgetting by infants who practised prior to the test, but the same reminder failed to alleviate forgetting by infants who did not practise (see Figure 3.1, top panel). Furthermore, infants who practised (albeit only briefly), generalized to a novel test stimulus when they were tested after a 24-hr delay, whereas infants without practice, did not (see Figure 3.1, bottom panel). Thus, the opportunity to practise influenced the long-term accessibility of the memory as well as generalization by toddlers who were tested using these imitation tasks. As we describe below, the addition of language cues, which is typically done in tests of elicited imitation, also influences long-term retention and generalization.

AGE-RELATED CHANGES IN LONG-TERM RETENTION

Research conducted using imitation paradigms has shown that age-related changes in long-term retention that begin during infancy (see Rovee-Collier & Cuevas, Chapter 2, this volume) continue to occur during the toddler period. That is, despite equivalent levels of performance immediately after the demonstration (i.e., equivalent levels of original encoding), older toddlers remember longer. For example, Barr and Hayne (2000) assessed age-related changes in long-term retention between 6 and 12 months of age. In their experiment, an adult demonstrated three target actions using a hand-held puppet. During the demonstration, the experimenter removed a felt mitten that was placed on the puppet's hand, shook the mitten ringing a large jingle bell inside, and then replaced the mitten on the puppet's hand. When tested immediately after the demonstration, 6- and 12-month-olds exhibited the same level of performance; however, the older participants remembered for longer. Following this single demonstration, the maximum duration of retention for the 6-month-olds was 24-hours, while for the 12-month-olds it was 1 week (see Figure 3.2, top panel).

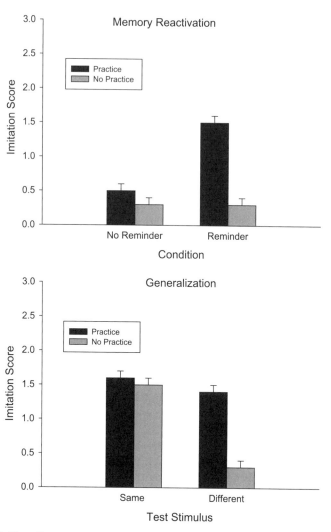

Figure 3.1 The effects of practice on retention and generalization by 18-month-old toddlers (based on data from Hayne, Barr, & Herbert, 2003).

Similarly, Herbert and Hayne (2000a) used a more complex task to study age-related changes in long-term retention by 18- and 24-month-olds. They used two three-step imitation tasks that were adapted from tasks originally developed by Bauer and her colleagues (Bauer, Hertsgaard, & Wewerka, 1995). In one task, the adult model constructed a rattle by placing a wooden block in a jar, placing a stick on the jar that was attached via Velcro and then shaking the stick to make a noise. In the other task, the experimenter created an animal by pulling a lever to raise the ears, placing eyes on the face (attached via Velcro), and "feeding" the animal through a hole in the mouth.

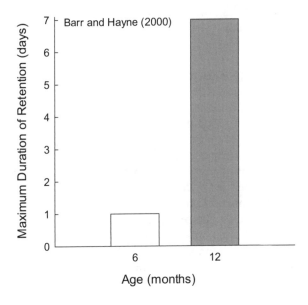

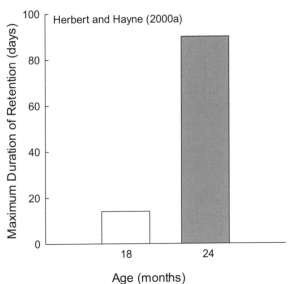

Figure 3.2 Age-related changes in the maximum duration of retention in the deferred imitation paradigm between 6 and 24 months (based on data from Barr & Hayne, 2000 and Herbert & Hayne, 2000a).

Again, when tested immediately after the demonstration, 18- and 24-month-olds exhibited similar levels of imitation performance. When tested after a delay, however, the older participants remembered for longer. Following a single demonstration session, the maximum duration of retention for the

18-month-olds was 14 days, while for the 24-month-olds it was 90 days (see Figure 3.2, bottom panel).

AGE-RELATED CHANGES IN REPRESENTATIONAL FLEXIBILITY

In addition to changes in long-term retention, the other major hallmark of memory development during the toddler period is an age-related increase in *representational flexibility*. As originally described by Eichenbaum (1997), representational flexibility refers to our ability to retrieve and use a memory in situations that differ from those in which the memory was originally encoded. Although human adults can sometimes recall events under conditions that bear little resemblance to the conditions under which the event originally took place, human infants cannot (for review, see Hayne, 2006). In fact, research with young infants has shown that memory retrieval is dependent on an *exact* match between the conditions present at original encoding and the conditions present at memory retrieval. For example, when 2- and 3-month-olds are trained and tested in the mobile conjugate reinforcement paradigm in which they learn to kick their feet to produce movement in an overhead mobile, they exhibit excellent retention when tested after a delay if and only if they are tested with the training mobile in the training context. If either the mobile (Hayne, Greco, Earley, Griesler, & Rovee-Collier, 1986) or the context (Butler & Rovee-Collier, 1989) is altered during the test, then retention suffers. Similarly, when 6-month-olds are tested in the mobile conjugate reinforcement paradigm, the operant train paradigm (see Rovee-Collier & Cuevas, Chapter 2, this volume), or the deferred imitation paradigm, they exhibit excellent retention if and only if the test stimulus is the same as the stimulus that was present during original encoding; if the test stimulus is different, then retrieval is impaired (Hartshorn & Rovee-Collier, 1997; Hayne, Boniface, & Barr, 2000).

Despite the high degree of specificity that characterizes memory retrieval by infants, memory retrieval by toddlers is substantially more flexible, allowing them to profit from their prior experience across a wider range of circumstances. For example, in the operant train paradigm, 9-month-olds exhibit no retention whatsoever if they are tested with a train that differs from the one encountered during original encoding, but 12-month-olds exhibit the same level of performance irrespective of the train present at the time of the test (Hartshorn et al., 1998). Similarly, in the deferred imitation paradigm, changes to the test stimulus eliminate retention by 6- and 12-month-olds, but have no effect on the memory performance of 18-month-olds (Hayne et al., 2000). Using more complex stimuli designed for older toddlers, changes in the test stimuli eliminate retention by 18-month-olds, but 30-month-olds exhibit the same level of performance irrespective of the stimuli present during the test (Herbert & Hayne, 2000b).

Taken together, these studies have clearly shown that the ability to exploit novel retrieval cues increases as a function of age during the toddler period. Research with both operant conditioning and imitation paradigms has confirmed that young infants will only retrieve and express their memories if the conditions of encoding match those of retrieval almost exactly. Given this high degree of specificity, the infants' ability to apply their early experiences to novel situations is quite limited. As a function of age and experience, however, memory retrieval becomes increasingly more flexible, providing toddlers with more opportunity to apply what they have learned to novel circumstances. In fact, there is growing evidence that toddlers can "strike a match" between encoding and retrieval on a conceptual, rather than a strictly perceptual, basis as well, raising even more opportunities for them to apply what they have learned to new problems that they encounter (Chen, Sanchez, & Campbell, 1997; Hayne, 2006).

INDEPENDENT LOCOMOTION FACILITATES MEMORY DEVELOPMENT

One stark difference between infants and toddlers is the emergence of independent locomotion. On average, infants begin to crawl at approximately 8–10 months of age, and they take their first tentative steps sometime close to their first birthday. How might these changes in motor skill influence memory development? For years, Campos and his colleagues have argued that the onset of independent locomotion (i.e., crawling) represents not only a major motor milestone, but a more general cognitive milestone as well (for review, see Campos, Anderson, Barbu-Roth, Hubbard, Hertenstein, & Witherington, 2000); they have shown that the experiences that infants accumulate once they begin to crawl contribute to major changes in perceptual, cognitive, and social development.

In a similar vein, Rovee-Collier (1996) has argued that the onset of independent locomotion plays a particularly important role in memory development. She has hypothesized that once infants begin to crawl they are faced with the ongoing challenge of recognizing old objects in new places, which might make them more resilient to changes in the context. On the basis of her own research, Rovee-Collier has shown that infants begin to generalize across changes in context at about the age of 9 months—the point at which many begin to crawl.

In order to test the hypothesis that motor development might lead to systematic changes in memory development, Herbert, Gross, and Hayne (2007) compared deferred imitation by infants who were crawling with deferred imitation by infants of the same age who were not yet crawling. The infants in their study were all 9 months old (+/– 2 weeks). Half of the infants were crawling and half were not. For all infants, the experimenter demonstrated a single action with a novel object; all infants were tested for imitation 24 hours later. Within each crawling condition, some infants were tested with the demonstration object in the demonstration context and the remaining infants were tested with a novel object in a different context. Although both crawlers and non-crawlers imitated the target action when they were tested with the demonstration object in the demonstration context, only the infants who had already achieved independent locomotion exhibited imitation when tested with a novel object in a different context. In short, infants who were crawling exhibited greater flexibility in memory retrieval than did infants of the same age who were not yet crawling.

In an attempt to replicate and extend the findings reported by Herbert et al. (2007), Gross, Hayne, Perkins, and MacDonald (2006) compared imitation by 9-month-olds who were and were not crawling and then retested these same infants 3 months later when some of them had started to walk. Consistent with the data reported by Herbert et al., only infants who were crawling by 9 months of age imitated the target actions when they were tested under novel conditions. Furthermore, the onset of upright locomotion had exactly the same effect. When 12-month-old walking and non-walking infants were tested using a more complex imitation task, only the infants who were walking exhibited imitation when the object and the context were altered at the time of the test. Clearly, the additional experience afforded by independent locomotion increases the flexibility of memory retrieval by 9- and 12-month-old infants. How long these differences last has yet to be determined.

LANGUAGE ACQUISITION FACILITATES MEMORY DEVELOPMENT

In addition to independent locomotion, the other stark difference between infants and toddlers is the emergence of language. There is a dramatic increase in language comprehension and production between 1 and 4 years of age (Fenson, Dale, Reznick, Bates, Thal, & Pethick, 1994). The acquisition of these language skills provides a new way for toddlers to encode and express their memories. How does toddlers' rapidly emerging language skill influence their memory performance?

Early in development, language comprehension proceeds production. Given this finding, it is possible that toddlers' emerging language comprehension begins to influence their memory performance even before they produce many words themselves. Research using imitation paradigms has shown that adults' verbal cues facilitate memory performance by preverbal and early-verbal children (Hayne & Herbert, 2004; Herbert & Hayne, 2000b). For example, Hayne and Herbert (2004) tested 18-month-olds 4 weeks after the demonstration session. Some infants received empty narration during the demonstration similar to that typically used in studies of deferred imitation (e.g., "Let's have a look at this. Then we have this bit. That was pretty neat, wasn't it?"). Other infants received full narration of the event goal and the target actions at the time of the demonstration (e.g., "We can use these things to make a rattle. Push the ball into the cup. Pick up the stick and put it on the cup. Shake the stick to make a noise."), and during the test, the experimenter provided a verbal cue that described the event goal (e.g., "We can use these things to make a rattle. Can you show me how we can use these things to make a rattle?"). These are the kinds of specific verbal cues that are often used in studies of elicited imitation.

Hayne and Herbert (2004) found that the adult's language cues facilitated performance during the long-term test. Although infants in both conditions exhibited evidence of memory after the 4-week delay, the scores of infants in the full narration condition were superior to those of infants in the empty narration condition. Hayne and Herbert also found that language cues were most effective in enhancing memory performance when they were presented at the time of the test rather than at the time of original encoding (see Figure 3.3). Thus, by the age of 18 months, infants can use verbal retrieval cues to facilitate long-term memory. The finding that adults' verbal cues facilitate toddlers' memory performance has also been obtained in studies of elicited imitation in which infants are allowed to practise the target actions prior to the retention interval (for review, see Bauer et al., 2000).

Adults' language cues do not only facilitate memory retrieval when toddlers are tested after long delays, but they also facilitate generalization to novel test stimuli when toddlers are tested after shorter delays. Herbert and Hayne (2000b), for example, found that when 24-month-olds were given a novel label for an object at the time of the demonstration, they generalized to a novel exemplar that was given the same label during the test 24 hours later. In contrast, 18-month-olds failed to generalize to novel exemplars even when they

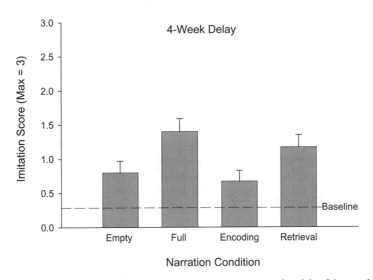

Figure 3.3 The effect of adults' verbal cues on memory retrieval by 24-month-olds (based on data from Hayne & Herbert, 2004).

were provided with the verbal label; they only exhibited imitation when they were tested with objects identical to those that were used during the demonstration.

Given that adults' language facilitates toddlers' memory processes, how does memory change as toddlers begin to express their own memories using words? One approach to this question has been to compare young children's verbal and nonverbal recall for a past event (Bauer & Wewerka, 1995, 1997; Simcock & Hayne, 2002, 2003). Simcock and Hayne (2003), for example, examined 2- to 4-year-olds' memory for a unique event, the Magic Shrinking Machine. In this event, the children were shown how to operate an intriguing machine in order to "shrink" a series of toys. When tested 24 hours later, the 3- to 4-year-olds reported over twice as many items as the 2- to 3-year-olds. However, the oldest children's verbal reports were still particularly sparse given that they knew most of the words required to describe the event. In contrast to their lean verbal reports, most of the children could accurately identify the toys when shown target and non-target photographs and most could successfully reproduce the actions that were required to operate the machine. Thus, as shown in Figure 3.4, young children's verbal recall lagged behind both their verbal skill and their nonverbal measures of memory, suggesting that even as they acquire language, toddlers' continue to rely primarily on their nonverbal representations.

The fact that toddlers continue to rely heavily on their nonverbal memory skills even as they learn to talk, creates yet another memory problem for them. Given that most of what they encode (and express) about the past is retained in some kind of nonverbal format, they would have to translate their preverbal memories into language before they could talk about them. A small body of research has shown that young children find this task difficult (Bauer & Wewerka, 1995, 1997), if not impossible (Simcock & Hayne, 2002). Simcock

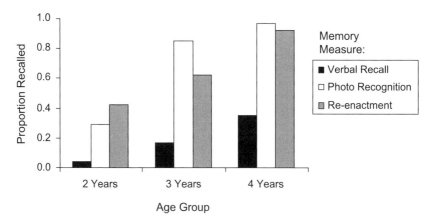

Figure 3.4 Age-related changes in verbal recall, photo recognition, and re-enactment after a 24-hour delay by 2- to 4-year-olds who were tested using the Magic Shrinking Machine (based on data from Simcock & Hayne, 2003).

and Hayne (2002), for example, tested 2- to 4-year-old children's verbal and nonverbal recall for the Magic Shrinking Machine event after delays of 6 months or 1 year. Although there was evidence of forgetting over these long delays, children still exhibited nonverbal recall of the target event as indicated by their photo recognition and re-enactment scores. Some children also exhibited verbal recall, but their reports were very lean. Furthermore, when what each child said during the test was compared to what he or she *could* say at the time of original encoding, Simcock and Hayne found that no child used a word to describe the event that was not part of his or her productive vocabulary at the time of the event. Thus, even though children clearly remembered some aspects of the event and had acquired all of the words necessary to describe it, there was no evidence that they could translate their preverbal memories into language at the time of the test.

Bauer and her colleagues (Bauer, Kroupina, Schwade, Dropik, & Wewerka, 1998; Bauer & Wewerka, 1995, 1997; Cheatham & Bauer, 2005) have also explored children's verbal recall for a preverbal experience. Bauer and Wewerka (1995, 1997), for example, modelled a series of actions for 13- to 20-month-olds and tested their verbal and nonverbal recall 1 to 12 months later (Bauer & Wewerka, 1995) and again 6 to 14 months later (Bauer & Wewerka, 1997). Bauer and Wewerka (1995) reported that children made more mnemonic verbal comments (e.g., named or described an event with the props present) when they were tested with objects they had seen before than they did when they were tested with new objects. On the basis of this finding, Bauer and Wewerka concluded that the children exhibited verbal recall for a preverbal experience.

In hindsight, Bauer and Wewerka may have overestimated children's verbal recall of preverbal information. For example, none of the children exhibited verbal recall in the absence of the familiar objects; furthermore, infants were credited with verbal recall if they narrated their ongoing actions as they interacted with the props. Moreover, as shown in Table 3.1, subsequent studies that did assess the children's verbal comments *prior* to seeing the props yielded next to no spontaneous verbal recall for the past event (Bauer, Wenner, & Kroupina, 2002; Cheatham & Bauer, 2005). Finally, because no measures of task-relevant vocabulary were taken at the time of encoding or at the time of testing, there was no way to determine infants' exhibited verbal recall of events or parts of events that were not initially part of their productive vocabulary. Thus, Bauer and colleagues' conclusion that young children have verbal access to preverbal experiences appears premature. In the end, even if children do gain some verbal access to their preverbal memories, that access is likely to be incomplete and extremely rare.

Table 3.1. The means (and standard deviations) of mnemonic utterances produced by 16- and 20-month-olds for imitated action sequences at delayed recall Test 1 (when the children were aged 17 to 32 months) and delayed recall Test 2 (when the same children were retested at 34 to 41 months) as a function of delay (based on data from Cheatham & Bauer, 2005)

Age (at event) and test	Delay				
	1 month	*3 months*	*6 months*	*9 months*	*12 months*
16 months					
Test 1	0.07 (0.15)	0.07 (0.15)	0.20 (0.42)	0.03 (0.10)	0.36 (0.52)
Test 2	1.27 (0.64)	1.46 (1.26)	1.77 (0.80)	1.33 (0.87)	2.14 (1.13)
20 months					
Test 1	0.00 (0.00)	0.00 (0.00)	0.37 (0.62)	0.06 (0.13)	0.33 (0.47)
Test 2	1.27 (1.04)	1.67 (0.82)	2.43 (1.15)	1.83 (0.78)	2.67 (1.05)

WHAT KIND OF MEMORY DO TODDLERS EXHIBIT?

Over the past 30 years, memory researchers have learned a great deal about the characteristics of memory. Most experts now agree that "memory" is not a single process, but rather is composed of different memory systems that are supported by different neural substrates, serve different functions, and operate according to different principles (Gold, 2004; McDonald, Devan, & Hong, 2004). Although a large number of memory systems have been proposed, one of the most influential dichotomies has been the nondeclarative versus declarative memory dichotomy that was originally proposed by Squire (2004). According to this dichotomy, the nondeclarative memory system supports the retention of skills and habits (e.g., riding a bike, playing the piano), while the declarative memory system is required for the recollection of facts and events. In the context of research, nondeclarative memory is assessed through tasks like classical conditioning and priming, while declarative memory is assessed using tasks like recognition and recall.

Within the declarative memory system, a further distinction has also been made between episodic and semantic memory (Tulving, 1972). Broadly defined, episodic memory refers to the recollection of personal experiences (e.g., what happened last Christmas), while semantic memory involves the recollection of facts (e.g., Christmas falls on December 25). The distinction between semantic and episodic memory is often characterized as the difference between "knowing" and "remembering," respectively. For example, we may know that the capital of Rome is Italy (i.e., semantic memory), but we probably have little or no memory for when and where we learned this information (i.e., episodic memory). If, on the other hand, the acquisition of a particular piece of knowledge was associated with a personally relevant experience (e.g., my 5th grade teacher ridiculed me when I didn't know that the capital of Italy was Rome), then I might also have an episodic memory for the learning episode. For the vast majority of the facts that adults retain, however, there is little or no episodic content to their semantic memory.

The notion that memory consists of multiple, independent processes was originally established through data collected with adults, but the same idea has raised fundamental questions about memory in infants, toddlers, and young children. Initially, researchers assumed that human infants only exhibited nondeclarative memory skills, and that declarative memory emerged later, sometime during the end of the first year of life (Schacter & Moscovitch, 1984). More recent work, however, has shown that this assumption is probably not correct. A number of researchers have shown that infants exhibit at least some rudimentary declarative memory skills very early in development. When tested on tasks that are analogous to those used to test declarative memory in adults, for example, infants show the same pattern of performance (for reviews see Hayne, 2004; Rovee-Collier, Hayne, & Colombo, 2001).

Given that declarative memory emerges very early in human development, the next obvious question is whether infants or toddlers also exhibit episodic memory as well. Using Tulving's terms, do human infants consciously *remember* their past experiences, or do they simply *know* about them? Do they travel back in time, re-experiencing these events in their mind's eye or do they simply acquire new facts that can be applied to similar circumstances in the future? The answer to these questions is much less certain. The problem associated with assessing conscious recollection in preverbal (or nonverbal) organisms is obviously a vexing one (for a full discussion, see Hayne, 2007; Hayne & Colombo, in press). Many researchers have claimed that episodic memory is a uniquely human memory skill, and that even for humans it does not emerge until after the age of 4 years (Perner & Ruffman, 1995; Suddendorf & Busby, 2005; Tulving, 2002). On the basis of our reading of the extant literature, we conclude that toddlers clearly exhibit declarative memory, but we make no claims about the episodic content of their memories. We remain open to the possibility that toddlers may engage in the kind of mental time-travel that characterizes episodic memory in human adults (Tulving, 2005), but at present this possibility has yet to be documented.

PRACTICAL ISSUES

Sometimes in our effort to conduct highly controlled studies of memory development we lose sight of the fact that memory skill plays a key role in toddlers' daily lives as they acquire and retain information about people, objects, and places in their environment. On a daily basis, children are faced with the challenge of learning about their world from a multitude of different sources of information that they then must apply to different problems, in different contexts, and sometimes they must accomplish these memory tasks after considerable delays. Thus, research conducted in the laboratory has important implications for the way in which toddlers might profit from their prior experiences in the course of their daily interactions with the world.

Studies of deferred imitation have shown that toddlers learn and retain a substantial amount of information, simply by watching and repeating the actions of adults, but direct experience observing and interacting with adults is only one way that young children learn about the world. Toddlers, for example, may also learn from interactions with their peers and siblings. In addition to face-to-face interactions, toddlers may also learn about the world around them from various forms of media, such as television programmes designed for their age group, picture-book reading experiences, and even family photographs in the home. The challenge facing young children is to encode information from these different sources and then to retrieve and apply that information in new contexts. Given the age-related changes in representational flexibility that occur during the toddler period, we might expect there to be age-related changes in toddlers' ability to exploit television, picture books, or photographs as sources of information to guide their subsequent behaviour.

Peers and siblings

The vast majority of imitation studies with infants and toddlers have documented learning and memory from *adult* models, but many toddlers spend considerable time interacting with similar-aged peers in preschool settings or with siblings at home. Observation studies have frequently shown that toddlers readily interact with their peers and siblings in these contexts and that they often engage in reciprocal imitative play as a way to sustain these social interactions (Eckerman, Davis, & Didow, 1989; Eckerman, Whatley, & Kutz, 1975; Nadel-Brulfert & Baudonniere, 1982). Piaget's classic example of imitation involving his 1-year-old daughter indicates that toddlers do indeed learn from peer interactions. In this anecdote, Jacqueline observed her playmate scream and stamp his foot in his playpen. The following day, in her own playpen, she replicated this tempter tantrum by screaming and stamping her foot—something she had not done before (Piaget, 1962).

In one of the first experimental studies designed to examine imitation of peers, Hanna and Meltzoff (1993) trained 14-month-old "expert-peers" to produce a novel target action on five objects. The expert-peer demonstrated these actions to an age-matched "novice-peer" whose imitation was assessed after a 5-minute delay. The novice-peers exhibited imitation from the expert-peer by copying 64% of the target actions compared to only 18% produced by age-matched controls who never saw the actions performed by a model. Hanna and Meltzoff (1993) also found that peer imitation can transcend longer delays and changes in contexts. When the expert-peer demonstration occurred in one location (e.g., the laboratory) and the novice-peer test occurred 48 hours later in a novel context (e.g., the child's preschool), the novice-peers exhibited imitation of the target actions by outperforming age-matched controls who were never exposed to the demonstration.

Similarly, Barr and Hayne (2003) examined the frequency with which toddlers learned new actions from their older *siblings*. Barr and Hayne asked parents of 300 12- to 18-month-old toddlers, half with older siblings and half with no siblings, to keep a diary documenting any instances of imitation over a 1-week period. In an orienting session, each parent was trained to identify instances of imitation and was taught how to record these instances using a structured diary. Barr and Hayne (2003) found that, regardless of sibling status, all toddlers learned approximately one to two new behaviours each day simply by observing and repeating the actions of others. Furthermore, although sibling status did not affect the *quantity* of imitation, it did affect the *quality* of the actions that were imitated. For example, toddlers with siblings imitated about half of their new behaviours from other children, whereas toddlers without siblings imitated actions primarily from adults. Moreover, the toddlers with siblings were more likely to imitate spontaneously, whereas toddlers without siblings were more likely to imitate with direct instruction (e.g., "can you do what I'm doing?"). Finally, toddlers with siblings imitated more play acts (rough-and-tumble and pretence) than toddlers with no siblings. For example, toddlers without siblings imitated a large number of cleaning activities (e.g., sweeping, scrubbing), while toddlers with siblings imitated more creative activities like using a box as a space ship or a car. Taken together, both observational and experimental studies have shown that siblings and peers are an important source of new behaviour for toddlers. Furthermore, the information that toddlers learn through these social interactions can be recalled over substantial delays and repeated in contexts that are very different from those in which the behaviour was originally observed.

Television

Clearly, toddlers learn a great deal through interaction with both adults and other children, but what about other sources of information that they encounter in the course of their daily lives? In recent decades, there has been increased experimental interest in the role of television in the lives of toddlers. This increase has been motivated, in part, by a dramatic increase in the number of television programmes and videos that are specifically marketed for very young viewers (e.g., *Blues Clues, Baby Mozart*). These products often include implicit and explicit claims that they are beneficial for toddlers' development—but what do toddlers actually learn from television and video?

The challenge that toddlers face when learning from television is that they must relate the two-dimensional images on television to the corresponding three-dimensional objects in the real world. The 2D images on television may be difficult for toddlers to understand for a number of perceptual reasons: they are smaller in size than real objects, the resolution of the image degrades the representation relative to real objects, and the televised image lacks real-life features such as depth cues (e.g., motion parallax, shadow, and gradients) (Barr & Hayne, 1999; Schmitt & Anderson, 2002; Suddendorf, Simcock, & Nielsen, 2006). The mismatch between the perceptual cues available at encoding the 2D images and the 3D objects present at testing presents a difficult memory retrieval task for toddlers.

Several studies have used imitation paradigms to explore what toddlers learn and remember from television (Barr & Hayne, 1999; Hayne, Herbert, & Simcock, 2003; McCall, Parke, & Kavanaugh, 1977; Meltzoff, 1988b). In one of the first studies of this kind Meltzoff (1988b) found that 14-month-olds imitated actions that they had observed on television. In Meltzoff's study, toddlers watched on closed-circuit television as an experimenter demonstrated a novel one-step action that involved pulling an end off a dumbbell-shaped object. The toddlers' production of this target action was compared to that of two control groups: those who were given the toy to interact with when given no demonstration, and those who observed an adult manipulating the dumbbell without producing the target action. Toddlers who observed the televised demonstration were more likely to produce the target action when tested immediately or after a delay of 24 hours than were the no demonstration and adult manipulation control groups. In a similar study, Barr and Hayne (1999) found age-related changes in imitation from television: 18-month-olds' imitation of a three-step action sequence from television exceeded imitation by 15-month-olds when tested after a 24-hour delay. However, both age groups outperformed age-matched controls who never observed a demonstration, indicating that they were clearly able to learn a multi-step action sequence from television.

Although toddlers can learn and remember what they see on television, their imitation from television is inferior to their imitation of the same actions modelled live. For example, in their study, Barr and Hayne (1999) included a live imitation condition in addition to a video imitation condition. They found that the toddlers' imitation from the live demonstration exceeded imitation from the television demonstration (see also McCall et al., 1977). In similar study, Hayne et al. (2003) found that although 24- and 30-month-olds' imitation from a televised model exceeded the performance of age-matched controls who never saw the target actions modelled, it was inferior to imitation from a live model. Thus, although toddlers can relate the simple actions seen on television to the corresponding 3D objects, it is a more challenging task than imitating from a live model.

The challenging task of understanding the nature of television has also been documented in a number of studies using DeLoache's object-search task (DeLoache, 1991; Troseth, 2003a, 2003b; Troseth & DeLoache, 1998; Schmitt & Anderson, 2002; Suddendorf, 2003). In this task, toddlers watch on closed circuit television as an experimenter enters an adjacent room and hides a toy behind an item of furniture. The child is required to use the information from television to go next door and retrieve the toy from the hiding location. In the original study, Troseth and DeLoache (1998) found that across four search trials, retrieval rates by 30-month-olds were approximately 80%, whereas retrieval rates by 24-month-olds were only approximately 40%.

The low success rate for 24-month-olds originally documented by Troseth and DeLoache (1998) has been replicated a number of times in different laboratories (Agayoff-Deocampo & Hudson, 2005; Schmitt & Anderson, 2002; Suddendorf, 2003). In some circumstances, however, 24-month-olds can use information from television to locate the hidden toy (see Figure 3.5). For example, toddlers of this age pass the task by retrieving the hidden toy if preservative responses on trials 2–4 are precluded by only considering the child's performance on the first search trial rather than averaging across the four trials (Schmitt & Anderson, 2002; Suddendorf, 2003). Successful search rates also increase if toddlers are given experience with live video by having daily opportunities to see themselves live on television in the 2 weeks prior to the experiment (Troseth, 2003a) or if they have a brief period interacting with the researcher over the closed circuit television prior to the experiment (Troseth, Saylor, & Archer, 2006).

Consistent with findings from the imitation literature, toddlers' search performance from television is poorer than when they watch the hiding event live. For example, 24-month-old children perform near ceiling when they observe the hiding event through a window designed to look like a television (Agayoff-Deocampo & Hudson, 2005; Schmitt & Anderson, 2002; Troseth, 2003b). Recently Anderson and Pempek (2005) coined the term *video-deficit* for toddlers' poorer performance on tasks presented on television in

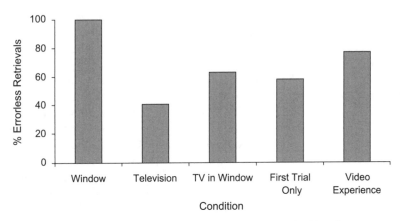

Figure 3.5 Percentage of errorless retrievals made by 2-year-olds who were tested in the object search task in the live window and standard television conditions (based on data from Troseth & DeLoache, 1998) as well as manipulations designed to improve the children's performance, such as the television in window condition (based on data from Troseth & DeLoache, 1998), performance on the first search trial only (based on data from Suddendorf, 2003), and prior experience with live video (based on data from Troseth, 2003a).

comparison to performance on real-life tasks. Thus, toddlers can transfer two-dimensional information from television to the real world, but it is a challenging task that becomes easier across development.

In sum, findings from a small but growing number of imitation and object-search studies indicate that although it is a challenging task, toddlers can indeed learn and remember information presented to them on television. Recently, the American Academy of Paediatrics (1999) has recommended zero television exposure for children under 2 years of age because of potential negative effects on development. Despite these concerns, the empirical evidence reviewed here shows that television can serve as an important learning tool early in development. In fact, experiencing multiple sources of information about objects and events may even facilitate the emergence of some facets of cognitive development, such as representational flexibility. Thus, if used appropriately and in moderation, television may actually have beneficial developmental effects.

Picture books

Unlike the controversy surrounding the potential negative impact that television viewing may have on toddlers and young children, it is generally agreed that picture books are beneficial to their development. At the heart of this view is the assumption that toddlers learn something about the world from joint picture-book interactions with adults (Gelman, Coley, Rosengren, Hartman, & Pappas, 1998; van Kleeck, 2003). Indeed, considerable government funding is spent on developing, promoting, and implementing early-reading initiatives (e.g., Early Head Start in the US and Sure Start in the UK). Despite these funding initiatives, few studies have examined what toddlers under the age of 3 years actually learn and remember from picture books (for review see Fletcher & Reese, 2005).

Several recent studies have begun to explore whether toddlers can learn about objects and events in the real world based on picture-book reading interactions. An initial study by Ganea and DeLoache (2006) found that when 15- and 18-month-old toddlers were taught a label for a novel object that was depicted in a picture book, they extended that label to the real object by correctly identifying it in a two-choice object selection task. Ganea and DeLoache also found that the 18-month-olds, but not the 15-month-olds, successfully generalized the label that they had learned from the picture book to novel real-world exemplars (i.e., objects differing in colour to those depicted in the picture book). Moreover, the iconicity of the pictures affected the children's ability to learn from the book: the children were more successful at selecting the object when the pictures were more realistic (e.g., colour photos) than less realistic (e.g., line drawings).

Similar findings have emerged from two recent studies examining imitation from picture books (Simcock & DeLoache, 2006; Simcock & Dooley, 2006). For example, Simcock and DeLoache (2006) used the rattle stimuli that are often used to study imitation in the Hayne and Bauer laboratories in a short picture book depicting and describing a child constructing a toy rattle in a three-step action sequence. They read 18-, 24- and 30-month-olds the picture book and found that the number of target actions that were performed by the children who saw the book exceeded that of the age-matched controls who did not see the book. Furthermore, the nature of the illustrations in the picture book affected the toddlers' performance: the older children reproduced the target actions regardless of the iconicity of the pictures (e.g., colour photos, drawings, line pictures), whereas the younger children required highly realistic pictures in order to do so (e.g., colour photos). Thus, age-related changes in representational flexibility found in other imitation studies using live models also apply to learning and memory from picture books. That is, older children are more proficient at matching less iconic pictures to 3D objects than are younger children, who only related highly iconic pictures to the corresponding 3D objects.

In a further study, Simcock and Dooley (2006) found similar age-related changes in imitation from a picture book. After the picture-book reading session, the toddlers were either tested in a novel context (e.g., a different room) or with novel stimuli (e.g., a different rattle). As shown in Figure 3.6, Simcock and Dooley found age-related changes in generalization from pictures to the real world. The 24-month-olds, but not 18-month-olds, performed more of the target actions than did their age-matched controls who never saw a demonstration, even when changes were made to the test stimuli or to the text context. Moreover, the 24-month-olds continued to outperform age-matched controls when tested with changes to both the test stimuli *and*

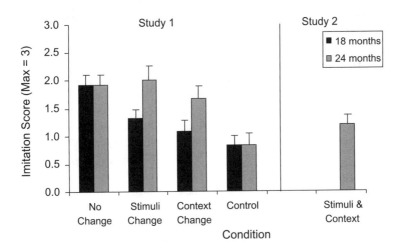

Figure 3.6 Age-related changes in generalization from a picture book when toddlers are tested with no changes, with novel stimuli, or in a novel context (Study 1, left side); 24-month-olds' generalization when tested with novel stimuli in a novel context (Study 2, right side).

the context. Thus, as with changes to the levels of iconicity of the pictures and with studies using live models, generalization from picture books increases across development, reflecting changes in representational flexibility.

In Simcock and colleagues' studies the toddlers clearly transferred information from the book to the corresponding 3D real-world objects. However, imitative performance from the book was not stellar. Thus, in an additional phase, the experimenter modelled the three-step target action to the children and they were given another opportunity to imitate. This phase of the experiment served two functions: it provided an independent measure of children's motivation and ability to perform the target actions, and it provided an estimate of how many actions children perform following a live demonstration of the same sequence. The toddlers' imitation scores following the live demonstration were near ceiling and exceeded their imitation scores from the picture book. Thus, as with the video-deficit effect described by Anderson and Pempek (2005), children's ability to learn and remember from picture books is also more challenging than learning from direct experience.

Photographs

Toddlers' ability to learn from depictions and descriptions in a picture book is consistent with studies showing that toddlers can use a photograph to locate a hidden object (DeLoache, 1991; DeLoache & Burns, 1994). In this variation of the object search task, DeLoache and colleagues showed children a photograph (either a wide-angle view of the room or of the individual item of furniture) of the hiding location of the toy that was concealed behind an item of furniture in an adjacent room. The child was required to use this information to find the toy. Their results mirrored those obtained in the TV search task: 30-month-olds were relatively successful at retrieving the hidden toy (68%) whereas 24-month-olds seldom located the hidden toy (6–27%) (DeLoache & Burns, 1994).

As with the TV version of the task, however, in some circumstances 24-month-olds can use information from a photo to locate the toy. They retrieve the toy, for example, if they are given an easy version of the task that is within their capabilities first (Troseth, 2003b) or if preservative errors across trials are precluded by conducting each of the four hiding and finding trials in a new room (Suddendorf, 2003). The finding that, beginning at approximately 2 years of age, toddlers can relate photos to the real world is consistent with Preissler and Carey's (2004) finding that 18- to 24-month-olds can transfer a verbal label that they learn from a photograph of a novel object to the real-world object itself.

Not only are photographs sources of information about current events in the world, they are also important sources of information about events personally experienced in the past. Photographs of family events and milestones, such as holidays and birthdays, are often salient features of many homes. Can toddlers relate photographs to the past event itself? Simcock and Hayne

(2002, 2003) showed that toddlers can indeed accurately identify photographs of an event they participated in 1 year earlier (see Figure 3.7). In these studies, 2- to 4-year-olds participated in a unique game (the Magic Shrinking Machine, described above) and their memory was assessed 1 day, 6 months, or 1 year later. In the challenging photo recognition test, the children were required to select the target item from among three distracter items from the same category (i.e., select the target ball from a group of four balls). The children's performance on this task after a 24-hour delay approached ceiling, and although some forgetting occurred over the 6-month and 1-year delays, performance by all age-groups remained above chance.

Moreover, photographs can also serve as potent reminders of past events. Several studies have used photographs as reminders to reinstate a memory for a past event during the toddler period (Agayoff-Deocampo & Hudson, 2003; Sheffield & Hudson, 1994, 2006). Agayoff-Deocampo and Hudson (2003), for example, found that 24- and 30-month-olds who saw photos of the target toys just prior to an imitation test performed better than age-matched children who saw photos of unrelated toys and children who did not see any photos prior to the test. However, a recent study with 18-month-olds found that the children in the photograph reminder condition did not outperform age-matched controls, indicating that reinstatement did not occur (Sheffield & Hudson, 2006).

CONCLUSIONS

With only a few, rare exceptions, most of the experiences of toddlerhood will eventually be lost behind the veil of childhood amnesia. Despite the fact that,

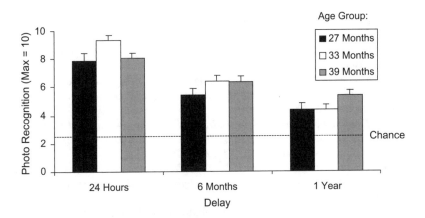

Figure 3.7 Age-related changes in 27-, 33-, and 39-month-old children's recognition of target photographs from the Magic Shrinking Machine event they participated in 24 hours, 6 months, or 1 year earlier.

as adults, we have no recollection of these events, they nonetheless make an important contribution to our cognitive development. The primary purpose of memory during the toddler period is to provide the opportunity for the effects of multiple learning experiences to accumulate and accrue. Given sufficient repetition and memory retrieval, some of the information that toddlers learn may become part of their long-term knowledge base even if the original experiences that contribute to that knowledge base have long been forgotten.

The processes of learning and memory are inextricably linked at all stages of development. In fact, the accumulation of information across successive learning episodes is dependent on two basic memory skills. First, the accumulation of information over time requires the ability to remember from one episode to the next. Second, the integration of information from multiple sources requires the ability to retrieve the representation of relevant prior events when faced with cues that may be similar, but not identical, to cues encountered when those representation(s) were originally established. The data reviewed in this chapter demonstrate that there are age-related changes in both of these basic memory skills during the toddler period. Older toddlers remember longer than younger toddlers, allowing them to use what they learn over increasingly longer delays. Older toddlers also exploit a wider range of potential retrieval cues, allowing them to use what they learn in a wider range of different circumstances. As we have shown here, age-related changes in these basic memory skills are reflected in toddlers' increasing ability to learn from television, picture books and photographs.

REFERENCES

Adlam, A.-L., Vargha-Khadem, F., Mishkin, M., & de Haan, M. (2005). Deferred imitation of action sequences in developmental amnesia. *Journal of Cognitive Neuroscience, 17*, 240–248.

Agayoff-Deocampo, J., & Hudson, J. A. (2003). Reinstatement of 2-year-olds' event memory using photographs. *Memory, 11*, 13–25.

Agayoff-Deocampo, J., & Hudson, J. A. (2005). When seeing is not believing: Two-year-olds' use of video representations to find a hidden toy. *Journal of Cognition and Development, 6*, 229–258.

American Academy of Pediatrics. (1999). Media education. *Pediatrics, 104*, 341–342.

Anderson, D. R., & Pempek, T. A. (2005). Television and very young children. *American Behavioral Scientist, 48*, 505–522.

Barr, R., Dowden, A., & Hayne, H. (1996). Developmental changes in deferred imitation by 6- to 24-month-old infants. *Infant Behavior and Development, 19*, 159–170.

Barr, R., & Hayne, H. (1999). Developmental changes in imitation from television during infancy. *Child Development, 70*, 1067–1081.

Barr, R., & Hayne, H. (2000). Age-related changes in deferred imitation: Implications for memory development. In C. Rovee-Collie, L. P. Lipsitt, & H. Hayne (Eds.),

Progress in infancy research (Vol. 1, pp. 21–67). Mahwah, NJ: Lawrence Erlbaum Associates, Inc.

Barr, R., & Hayne, H. (2003). It's not what you know, it's who you know: Older siblings facilitate imitation during infancy. *International Journal of Early Years Education, 11*, 7–21.

Bauer, P. J., Hertsgaard, L. A., & Dow, G. A. (1994). After 8 months have passed: Long-term recall of events by 1- to 2-year-old children. *Memory, 2*, 353–382.

Bauer, P. J., Hertsgaard, L. A., & Wewerka, S. S. (1995). Effects of experience on long-term recall in infancy: Remembering not to forget. *Journal of Experimental Child Psychology, 59*, 260–298.

Bauer, P. J., Kroupina, M. G., Schwade, J. A., Drpoik, P., & Wewerka, S. S. (1998). If memory serves, will language? Later verbal accessibility of early memories. *Development and Psychopathology, 10*, 655–679.

Bauer, P. J., & Mandler, J. M. (1989). One thing follows another: Effects of temporal structure on 1- to 2-year-olds' recall of events. *Developmental Psychology, 25*, 197–206.

Bauer, P. J., Wenner, J. A., Dropik, P. L., & Wewerka, S. S. (2000). Parameters of remembering and forgetting in the transition from infancy to early childhood. *Monographs of the Society for Research in Child Development, 65*, 1–204.

Bauer, P. J., Wenner, J. A., & Kroupina, M. G. (2002). Making the past present: Later verbal accessibility of early memories. *Journal of Cognition and Development, 3*, 21–47.

Bauer, P. J., & Wewerka, S. S. (1995). One- to two-year-olds' recall of events: The more expressed, the more impressed. *Journal of Experimental Child Psychology, 59*, 475–496.

Bauer, P. J., & Wewerka, S. S. (1997). Saying is revealing: Verbal expression of event memory in the transition from infancy to early childhood. In P. van den Broek, P. J. Bauer, & T. Bourg (Eds.), *Developmental spans in event comprehension and representation: Bridging fictional and actual events*. Hillsdale, NJ: Lawrence Erlbaum Associates, Inc.

Butler, J., & Rovee-Collier, C. (1989). Contextual gating of memory retrieval. *Developmental Psychobiology, 22*, 533–552.

Campos, J. J., Anderson, D. I., Barbu-Roth, M. A., Hubbard, W. M., Hertenstein, M. J., & Witherington, D. (2000). Travel broadens the mind. *Infancy, 1*, 149–219.

Cheatham, C. L., & Bauer, P. J. (2005). Construction of a more coherent story: Prior verbal recall predicts later verbal accessibility of early memories. *Memory, 13*, 516–532.

Chen, Z., Sanchez, R. P., & Campbell, T. (1997). From beyond to within their grasp: The rudiments of analogical problem solving in 10- and 13-month-olds. *Developmental Psychology, 33*, 790–801.

DeLoache, J. S. (1991). Symbolic functioning in very young children: Understanding of pictures and models. *Child Development, 62*, 736–752.

DeLoache, J. S., & Burns, N. M. (1994). Early understanding of the representational function of pictures. *Cognition, 52*(2), 83–110.

Eckerman, C. O., Davis, C. C., & Didow, S. M. (1989). Toddlers' emerging way of developing social coordination with a peer. *Child Development, 60*, 440–453.

Eckerman, C. O., Whatley, J. L., & Kutz, S. L. (1975). Growth of social play with peers during the second year of life. *Developmental Psychology, 11*, 42–49.

Eichenbaum, H. (1997). Declarative memory: Insights from cognitive neurobiology. *Annual Review of Psychology, 48*, 547–572.

Fenson, L., Dale, P. S., Reznick, J. S., Bates, B., Thal, D. J., & Pethick, S. J. (1994). Variability in early communicative development. *Monographs of the Society for Research in Child Development, 59*, 1–189.

Fletcher, K. L., & Reese, E. (2005). Picture book reading with young children: A conceptual framework. *Developmental Review, 25*, 64–103.

Ganea, P. A., & DeLoache, J. S. (2006). *From picture books to the real world: Pictorial realism affects young children's generalization from depicted to real objects.* Unpublished manuscript.

Gelman, S. A., Coley, J. D., Rosengren, K. S., Hartman, E., & Pappas, A. (1998). Beyond labeling: The role of maternal input in the acquisition of richly structured categories. *Monographs of the Society for Research in Child Development, 63* (Serial No. 253).

Gold, P. E. (2004). Coordination of multiple memory systems. *Neurobiology of Learning and Memory, 82*, 230–242.

Gross, J., Hayne, H., Perkins, N. & MacDonald, B. (2006). *Amount of crawling and walking experience has varying effects on cognitive development during infancy.* Paper presented at the International Conference on Infant Studies, Kyoto, Japan.

Hanna, E., & Meltzoff, A. (1993). Peer imitation by toddlers in laboratory, home, and day-care contexts: Implications for social learning and memory. *Developmental Psychology, 29*, 701–710.

Hartshorn, K., & Rovee-Collier, C. (1997). Infant learning and long-term memory at 6 months: A confirming analysis. *Developmental Psychobiology, 30*, 71–85.

Hartshorn, K., Rovee-Collier, C., Gerhardstein, P. C., Bhatt, R. S., Klein, P. J., Aaron, F., et al. (1998). Developmental changes in the specificity of memory over the first year of life. *Developmental Psychobiology, 33*, 61–78.

Hayne, H. (2004). Infant memory development: Implications for childhood amnesia. *Developmental Review, 24*, 33–73.

Hayne, H. (2006). Age-related changes in infant memory retrieval: Implications for knowledge acquisition. In Y. Munakata & M. H. Johnson (Eds.), *Processes of change in brain and cognitive development. Attention and Performance XXI* (pp. 209–231). New York: Oxford University Press.

Hayne, H. (2007). Infant memory development: New questions, new answers. In L. Oakes & P. Bauer (Eds.), *Short- and long-term memory in infancy and early childhood: Taking the first steps toward remembering* (pp. 209–239). New York: Oxford University Press

Hayne, H., Barr, R., & Herbert, J. (2003). The effect of prior practice on memory reactivation and generalization. *Child Development, 74*, 1615–1627.

Hayne, H., Boniface, J., & Barr, R. (2000). The development of declarative memory in human infants: Age-related changes in deferred imitation. *Behavioral Neuroscience, 114*, 77–83.

Hayne, H., & Colombo, M. (in press). Episodic memory: Comparative and developmental issues. In M. S. Blumberg, J. H. Freeman, & S. R. Robinson (Eds.), *Developmental and comparative neuroscience: Epigenesis, evolution, and behavior.* New York: Oxford University Press.

Hayne, H., Greco, C., Earley, L. A., Griesler, P. C., & Rovee-Collier, C. (1986). Ontogeny of early event memory: II. Encoding and retrieval by 2- and 3-month-olds. *Infant Behavior and Development, 9*, 461–472.

Hayne, H., & Herbert, J. (2004). Verbal cues facilitate memory retrieval during infancy. *Journal of Experimental Child Psychology, 89*, 127–139.

Hayne, H., Herbert, J., & Simcock, G. (2003). Imitation from television by 24- and 30-month-olds. *Developmental Science, 6*, 254–261.

Herbert, J., Gross, J., & Hayne, H. (2007). Crawling is associated with more flexible memory retrieval by 9-month-old infants. *Developmental Science, 10*, 183–189.

Herbert, J., & Hayne, H. (2000a). The ontogeny of long-term retention during the second year of life. *Developmental Science, 3*, 50–56.

Herbert, J., & Hayne, H. (2000b). Memory retrieval by 18- to 30-month-olds: Age-related changes in representation flexibility. *Developmental Psychology, 36*, 473–484.

Jones, E. J. H., & Herbert, J. S. (2006). Exploring memory in infancy: Deferred imitation and the development of declarative memory. *Infant and Child Development, 15*, 195–205.

McCall, R. B., Parke, R. D., & Kavanaugh, R. D. (1977). Imitation of live and televised models by children one to three years of age. *Monographs of the Society for Research in Child Development, 42* (5, Serial No. 173).

McDonald, R. J., Devan, B. D., & Hong, N. S. (2004). Multiple memory systems: The power of interactions. *Neurobiology of Learning and Memory, 82*, 333–346.

McDonough, L., Mandler, J. M., McKee, R. D., & Squire, L. R. (1995). The deferred imitation task as a nonverbal measure of declarative memory. *Proceedings of the National Academy of Science, 92*, 7580–7584.

Meltzoff, A. (1988a). Infant imitation after a 1-week delay: Long-term memory for novel acts and multiple stimuli. *Developmental Psychology, 24*, 470–476.

Meltzoff, A. (1988b). Imitation of televised models by infants. *Child Development, 59*, 1221–1229.

Meltzoff, A. N. (1990). The implications of cross-modal matching and imitation for the development of representation and memory in infants. In A. Diamond (Ed.), *Annals of the New York Academy of Sciences: Vol. 608. The development and neural bases of higher cognitive functions* (pp. 1–37). New York: New York Academy of Sciences.

Nadel-Brulfert, J., & Baudonniere, P.-M. (1982). The social function of reciprocal imitation in 2-year-old peers. *International Journal of Behavioral Development, 5*, 95–109.

Nelson, C. A. (1995). The ontogeny of human memory: A cognitive neuroscience perspective. *Developmental Psychology, 31*, 723–738.

Nielsen, M. (2006). Copying actions and copying outcomes: Social learning throughout the second year. *Developmental Psychology, 42*, 555–565.

Perner, J., & Ruffman, T. (1995). Episodic memory and autonoetic consciousness: Developmental evidence and a theory of childhood amnesia. *Journal of Experimental Child Psychology, 59*, 516–548.

Piaget, J. (1962). *Play, dreams and imitation in childhood*. New York: Norton.

Preissler, M. A., & Carey, S. (2004). Do both pictures and words function as symbols for 18- and 24-month-old children? *Journal of Cognition and Development, 5*(2), 185–212.

Rovee-Collier, C. (1996). Shifting the focus from what to why? *Infant Behavior and Development, 19*, 385–400.

Rovee-Collier, C., Hayne, H., & Colombo, M. (2001). The development of implicit and explicit memory. In M. I. Stamenov (Ed.), *Advances in consciousness research* (Vol. 24). Amsterdam/Philadelphia: John Benjamins Publishing Company.

Schacter, D. L., & Moscovitch, M. (1984). Infants, amnesiacs, and dissociable memory systems. In M. Moscovitch (Ed.), *Advances in the study of communication and affect: Vol. 9. Infant memory* (pp. 173–216). New York: Plenum Press.

Schmitt, K. L., & Anderson, D. R. (2002). Television and reality: Toddlers use of visual information from video to guide behavior. *Media Psychology, 4*, 51–76.

Sheffield, E. G., & Hudson, J. A. (1994). Reactivation of toddlers' event memories. *Memory, 2*, 447–465.

Sheffield, E. G., & Hudson, J. A. (2006). You must remember this: Effects of video and photograph reminders on 18-month-olds' event memory. *Journal of Cognition and Development, 7*, 73–93.

Simcock, G., & DeLoache, J. S. (2006). Get the picture? The effects of iconicity on toddlers' re-enactment from picture books. *Developmental Psychology, 42*, 1352–1357.

Simcock G., & Dooley, M. (2006). *Age-related changes in imitation from picture books by toddlers when tested in novel conditions.* Manuscript submitted for review.

Simcock, G., & Hayne, H. (2002). Breaking the barrier? Children fail to translate their preverbal memories into language. *Psychological Science, 13*, 225–231.

Simcock, G., & Hayne, H. (2003). Age-related changes in verbal and nonverbal memory during early childhood. *Developmental Psychology, 39*(5), 805–814.

Squire, L. (2004). Memory systems of the brain: A brief history and current perspective. *Neurobiology of Learning and Memory, 82*, 171–177.

Suddendorf, T. (2003). Early representational insight: Twenty-four-month-olds can use a photo to find an object in the world. *Child Development, 74*(3), 896–904.

Suddendorf, T., & Busby, J. (2005). Making decisions with the future in mind: Developmental and comparative identification of mental time travel. *Learning and Motivation, 36*, 110–125.

Suddendorf, T., Simcock, G., & Nielsen, M. (2006). Visual self-recognition in mirrors and live videos: Evidence for a developmental asynchrony. *Cognitive Development*, available at: doi.10.1016/j.cogdev.2006.09.003.

Troseth, G. L. (2003a). TV guide: Two-year-old children learn to use video as a source of information. *Developmental Psychology, 39*, 140–150.

Troseth, G. L. (2003b). Getting a clear picture: Young children's understanding of a televised image. *Developmental Science, 6*, 247–253.

Troseth, G. L., & DeLoache, J. S. (1998). The medium can obscure the message: Young children's understanding of video. *Child Development, 69*, 950–965.

Troseth, G. L., Saylor, M. M., & Archer, A. H. (2006). Young children's use of video as a source of socially relevant information. *Child Development, 77*, 786–799.

Tulving, E. (1972). Episodic and semantic memory. In E. Tulving & W. Donaldson (Eds.), *Organization of memory* (pp. 381–403). New York: Academic Press.

Tulving, E. (2002). Episodic memory: From mind to brain. *Annual Review of Psychology, 53*, 1–25.

Tulving, E. (2005). Episodic memory and autonoesis: Uniquely human? In H. S. Terrace & J. Metcalfe (Eds.), *The missing link in cognition: Self-knowing consciousness in man and animals* (pp. 3–56). New York: Oxford University Press.

van Kleeck, A. (2003). Research on book sharing: Another critical look. In A. van Kleeck, S. A. Stahl, & E. Bauer (Eds.), *On reading books to children: Parents and teachers* (pp. 271–319). Mahwah, NJ: Lawrence Erlbaum Associates, Inc.

4　The development of memory for recurring events

Judith A. Hudson and Estelle M. Y. Mayhew
Rutgers University, New Jersey, USA

While much of this volume concerns the development of memory for specific experiences, the focus of this chapter is on the development of memory for recurring events. Research from the last 25 years indicates that children and adults organize memory for recurring events in the form of general event schemas, referred to as scripts (Abelson, 1981; Schank & Abelson, 1977) or general event representations (GERs) (Nelson, 1986; Nelson & Gruendel, 1981). GERs are general knowledge structures that specify the sequence of expected actions in everyday events and are used to guide comprehension whenever events are experienced or referred to in discourse or text. GERs also include information about typical locations, people, and objects that are encountered in recurring events. Much of the early research on scripts and GERs focused on how general event knowledge developed in young children (e.g., Bauer & Mandler, 1989; Bauer & Shore, 1987; Nelson, 1986; Nelson & Gruendel, 1981) and how adults and children used scripts in text processing (e.g., Abelson, 1981; Adams & Worden, 1986; Bower, Black, & Turner, 1979; Hudson & Nelson, 1983). Later, researchers examined more closely the process of general knowledge acquisition (Farrar & Goodman, 1990, 1992; Fivush, Kuebli, & Clubb, 1992), infants' and toddlers' event memory (e.g., Bauer, Hertsgaard, Dropik, & Daly, 1998), and effects of general event knowledge on autobiographic memory (Baker-Ward, Gordon, Ornstein, Larus, & Clubb, 1993; Hudson, 1990; Hudson & Nelson, 1986; Myles-Worsley, Cromer, & Dodd, 1986). In the following review, we discuss five currently evolving and emerging areas of research: (1) the development of general event knowledge; (2) the organization of general and specific event knowledge in memory; (3) recall of specific episodes of recurring events; (4) the use of general event knowledge in planning; and (5) the role of general event knowledge in the development of time concepts.

DEVELOPMENT OF GENERAL EVENT KNOWLEDGE

Nelson and Gruendel (1981) first demonstrated that children as young as 3 years had abstract, general, and temporally organized knowledge for recurring events. This discovery was ground-breaking in two ways. First, they challenged the prevailing assumptions that young children's event memories were unorganized, fragmented, and idiosyncratic (Piaget & Inhelder, 1973). In contrast, analysis of children's script reports showed that preschool children's event memories were organized as temporally structured, coherent wholes that included the central aspects of their past experience. Second, they provided evidence that general event knowledge supported children's autobiographic recall, story comprehension, temporal understanding, and conceptual development (Nelson, 1986). Later research has examined the development of general event knowledge from infancy through adulthood.

Event representations in infants and toddlers

Knowledge of sequence—the temporal order in which the components of an event take place—is fundamental to general event knowledge. Bauer and her associates have conducted programmatic research investigating the role of causality and familiarity in young children's event memory (see Chapter 3 by Hayne and Simcock and Chapter 6 by Bauer in this volume for more complete discussions). Because children at this age cannot provide verbal descriptions of events, researchers use an elicited imitation task to examine infants' and toddlers' memory for action sequences that vary in terms of complexity (number of actions and props) and temporal structure (including arbitrary or enabling links between actions). In this procedure, children are presented with some simple props, for an example, a ball and two nesting cups, and are allowed to play with them for an initial baseline exploration phase. Next, an experimenter models simple action sequences such as placing a ball in a cup, covering it with another cup and shaking them to make a "rattle." Children's memory for the sequence is measured by their ability to reproduce the modeled actions when they are given the props again. At 11.5 months infants can immediately imitate both familiar and novel two-step sequences, and at 13.5 months this is extended to three-step sequences (Bauer & Mandler, 1992). It takes much longer for children to imitate arbitrary (as opposed to mixed-up causal) sequences. At 22 months they can imitate a three-step arbitrary sequence if tested immediately, but it is not until 28 months that children can recall an arbitrary sequence after a delay (Bauer et al., 1998; Bauer & Shore, 1987).

Later developments

Event knowledge in older children and in adults is studied by means of tasks in which participants are asked to generate scripts, or sequence pictorial representations of parts of scripts. By 3 years, children are able to provide verbal accounts or script reports for familiar events (Fivush, 1984; Fivush et al., 1992; Hudson & Nelson, 1986; Hudson & Shapiro, 1991; Hudson, Shapiro, & Sosa, 1995). When asked to report "what happens" in familiar events, children from 3 years report general actions using the impersonal pronoun "you" and the timeless present tense, for example, "You buy things" when you go to the grocery store. In addition, the sequence in which children report actions in events tends to be highly accurate. With increasing age, children's script reports include more event components and more optional actions, indicating that children's general event knowledge becomes more complex over time (Hudson & Nelson, 1986; Hudson & Shapiro, 1991; Fivush & Slackman, 1986).

Verbal report measures may underestimate younger children's event knowledge. Using a picture-sequencing task, Fivush and Mandler (1985) found that 4-, 5-, and 6-year-olds easily sequenced six pictures of familiar events (e.g., going grocery shopping) in their correct temporal order. Hudson (1988) asked 4- and 7-year-olds to rate various script actions in terms of their frequency of occurrence and found that children at both ages agreed on how often various script-consistent actions (standing in the check-out line) and script-inconsistent actions (wearing your pajamas to the grocery store) occurred in familiar events. Although 4-year-olds may not mention as many actions as older children in verbal script reports, their knowledge of component events and their ability to sequence actions is equivalent when tested using these alternative methods.

Examining recall of event-based stories has also been used as a method for investigating structural properties of event knowledge. Both children and adults use general event knowledge to guide recall, producing distortions in memory. They produce intrusions in recall, resulting in recall of information that is consistent with general event knowledge, but that was not actually stated in the story (Bower et al., 1979; Hudson & Nelson, 1983; Hudson & Slackman, 1990; Slackman & Nelson, 1984). When actions are presented in a non-canonical order, children tend to re-order the actions in memory, recalling them in a canonical sequence and indicating that their event knowledge is temporally organized (Hudson & Nelson, 1983). Adults and children also recall central script actions better than peripheral actions (Adams & Worden, 1986; Slackman & Nelson, 1984; Smith & Graesser, 1981), indicating that action centrality is a component of general event knowledge representation. In addition, both children's and adults' event representations include information about typicality; in story recall, atypical actions tend to "stand out" in memory and are recalled better than typical actions (Bower et al., 1979; Davidson, 1994; Davidson & Hoe, 1993; Graesser, Woll, Kowalski, & Smith, 1980; Maki, 1990; Smith & Graesser, 1981), especially when the atypical actions are vivid or disrupt the story action (Davidson & Jergovic, 1996; Davidson, Larson, Luo, & Burden, 2000; Galambos, 1983; Hudson, 1988).

Script generation tasks have also been used to examine structural characteristics of general event knowledge. In a study of adults' generation of script-related actions, Barsalou and Sewell (1985) found support for the importance of temporal order in script processing; participants were faster when recalling script items from first to last than when recalling items from most to least central. However, Galambos and Rips (1982) found that more central activity cues provided faster responses than temporal cues in a reaction time recall study.

The lack of developmental differences in the structure and organization of event knowledge from infancy through adulthood is striking. Although general event representations become more complex, temporal sequence is central to event representations at all ages. From early childhood through adulthood, there is evidence that event information is represented in terms of centrality and typicality that affect the processing of information in text comprehension.

Neural correlates of general event knowledge

Script generation and picture sequencing tasks have also been used in research conducted in the last decade that examines the neural correlates of script processing in adults. Some studies compare performance on script tasks by participants with brain lesions to those without lesions, other studies employ imaging during script tasks. Performance on script tasks appears to be dependent on the prefrontal cortex, and differing regions are related to differing characteristics of scripts. Crozier and colleagues (1999) found in an imaging study that a script task in normal subjects activated an area in the dorsolateral prefrontal cortex in both hemispheres, in addition to the left supplementary motor area and left angular gyrus. In a lesion study, subjects with lesions of the prefrontal cortex made more errors in sequencing scripts than those with posterior lesions or no lesions, and took more time to complete the tasks if they were not given activity headers for organizing specific script actions (i.e., indicators of the higher hierarchical level), or were given distractor headers or irrelevant script items (Sirigu, Zalla, Pillon, & Grafman, 1996). Allain and colleagues (Allain, Le Gall, Etcharry-Bouyx, Aubin, & Emile, 1999; Allain, Le Gall, Etcharry-Bouyx, Forgeau, Mercier, & Emile, 2001) found that some subjects with prefrontal lesions had trouble sequencing scripts, but could exclude irrelevant headers and events irrelevant to the script, whereas other subjects with prefrontal lesions could sequence, but could not ignore irrelevant headers or events that did not belong to a particular task script. This suggests that the temporal sequence and the hierarchical connections are processed or represented in different areas of the prefrontal cortex.

It is not only the structural aspects of scripts that are represented or processed in differing regions. When comparing subjects with Parkinson's disease and normal subjects, Zalla, Sirigu, Pillon, Dubois, Agid, and Grafman (2000) found that the subjects with Parkinson's were able to sequence and indicate hierarchy for script activities, but could not indicate how important individual actions were to the overall goal of the script. Patients with prefrontal lesions were not impaired on the evaluation of the script actions, but did poorly on sequencing. This suggests that the basal ganglia are involved in the evaluation of script actions.

The results from lesion studies, as well as the connectivity of various regions in the prefrontal cortex have led Grafman and Wood (Grafman, 2002; Wood & Grafman, 2003) to propose that knowledge is stored in the prefrontal cortex in the form of structured event complexes (SECs). A SEC is "a goal-oriented set of events that is structured in sequence and represents thematic knowledge, morals, abstractions, concepts, social rules, event features, event boundaries and grammars. . . . Aspects of SECs are represented independently but are encoded and retrieved as an episode" (Wood & Grafman, 2003, pp. 142–143). Different types of event knowledge are stored in different regions of the prefrontal cortex, depending on the connectivity with posterior cortical or subcortical regions. This framework is just one of several proposed for the functioning of the human prefrontal cortex, but it is intriguing in light of the importance of general event knowledge in planning (see below).

THE ORGANIZATION OF GENERAL AND SPECIFIC EVENT KNOWLEDGE IN MEMORY

Constructivist accounts of autobiographic memory retrieval maintain that autobiographic memories are constructed in working memory from both general and specific event knowledge stored in long-term memory (Anderson & Conway, 1993; Barsalou, 1988; Conway, 1992; Schank, 1982). The organization of general and specific event knowledge has implications for how event knowledge is accessed and retrieved during recall. There is a widespread view that event knowledge is hierarchically organized in an overall autobiographical memory system (Barsalou, 1988; Conway, 1990, 1992; Conway & Bekerian, 1987; Linton, 1986; Neisser, 1986; Schooler & Herrmann, 1992). Different models, however, place general event knowledge in different levels within the hierarchy (for a review see Lancaster & Barsalou, 1997).

In one view, general event knowledge provides the basis for organizing autobiographic memories (Kolodner, 1983; Reiser, Black, & Abelson, 1985; Schank, 1982). General knowledge of activity types (i.e., GERS and scripts) integrates similar types of event memories. For example, all events involving eating at a restaurant (including Chinese restaurants, Indian food, and so on) are stored together in memory; likewise all events involving going to the movies are stored together, and so on. Specific event memories are organized within the larger general event category and are differentiated by differences among them. In the restaurant example, memories could be organized by different types of restaurants, different participants (family, co-workers, and friends) of other event features. A critical feature of this structure is that activities constitute the highest level of event organization. Although individual events may share common features such as participants, events are not organized by participants. Instead, separate sub-clusters of events for different participants are subsumed under separate activities.

This organization has important implications for retrieving autobiographic memories. Because event memories are organized fundamentally by type of activity, retrieval requires that an activity is identified first, before other event characteristics. This means that a location or participant cue cannot provide direct access to an event memory; an activity cue is required to initiate a search. However, participant or location cues may help to infer a probable activity that can then be used as an effective retrieval cue. For example, if one is trying to remember an event that took place at the beach, it is probable that swimming would be involved. After inferring the activity of swimming, other details may be recalled by searching various sub-clusters of swimming events at the beach (e.g., with family, with friends, at different beaches).

Other proposed frameworks view activity type as only one of many global organizations that are used to simultaneously cross-classify event memories. Lancaster and Barsalou (Barsalou, 1988; Lancaster & Barsalou, 1997) propose that event memories can be cross-classified in terms of other abstract categories such as objects, participants, locations. Event memories can be accessed directly by several types of retrieval cues and no single abstract category has a privileged position at the peak of the hierarchy. For example, memory for a trip to the beach can be accessed by multiple cues such as *family*, *swimming*, *surfboard*, and *sunburn*. Other theorists maintain that non-activity conceptual structures such as goal-derived categories, relationships, emotions, and temporally extended events (e.g., when I was in college) are used at the global level to organize event memories (Anderson & Conway, 1993; Barsalou, 1988; Conway, 1990; Conway & Bekerian, 1987; Conway & Rubin, 1993). Anderson and Conway (1993) argue that the hierarchy of autobiographic memory consists of three levels. At the top level is thematic knowledge that indexes a wide range of general events associated with lifetime periods from an individual's life. General event knowledge forms the inter-mediate level that is more specific than lifetime periods knowledge because it refers to shorter time periods with fewer actors, events, and locations. At the lowest level are specific event memories.

Regardless of whether abstract script-like structures are the most prominent conceptual structure for organizing event memories, most theorists propose that abstract activity knowledge plays a central role in organizing auto-biographic memory. However, it is not known if and when children develop alternative and, perhaps, more global organizational categories in auto-biographic memory (Robinson & Swanson, 1990). Adults' autobiographic memory may be organized in terms of lifetime periods, but when do these emerge in children? Do children organize event memories in terms of emotions? One suspects not, given some clues from research using event categories and emotions as retrieval cues. Hudson and Nelson (1986) found that 3-year-olds could easily retrieve specific memories when given familiar event category cues (e.g., "Tell me about what happened one time when you went to a birthday party.") In contrast, Hudson, Gebelt, Haviland, and Bentivegna (1992) found that 4-year-olds sometimes had difficulty recalling specific events with emotion cues (e.g., "Tell me about what happened one time when you were scared."), suggesting that emotions are not effective retrieval cues for children at this age because their specific event memories are not organized in terms of discrete emotions.

Do children organize event memories in terms of abstract goals? Research does suggest that goal attainment is central to event perception in infants (Meltzoff, 1995; Woodward, 1998) and children (van den Broek, Lorch, & Thurlow, 1996) as well as adults (Abelson, 1981; Bower et al., 1979; Zacks & Tverksy, 2001; Zacks, Tversky, & Iyer, 2001). However, it is not yet known whether explicit references to goals are effective retrieval cues for children's recall of specific event memories.

This is an area where developmental research could inform current debates in the adult literature. Evidence for early formation of global organizational structures in autobiographic memory could provide support for the primacy of one type of organization over another. For example, evidence that children as young as 3 years use familiar event categories as retrieval cues and confuse specific episodes of recurring events suggests that the nesting of specific event memories within general event representations is a developmentally primitive form of event memory organization. In addition, the methods used by developmental researchers may shed light on how global categories are formed. A large literature has examined autobiographic memory in young children by studying parent–child conversations about past events (see Nelson, 1993 and Nelson & Fivush, 2004, for reviews). The kinds of event information that parents discuss with their children during everyday conversations can provide data on how specific events become organized into categories such as goals, emotions, relationships, and lifetime periods. Much of the existing research focuses on preschool-aged children (approximately 2 to 5 years); extended research on memory conversations with older children would be useful for understanding how event memories become reorganized in memory.

RECALL OF SPECIFIC EPISODES OF RECURRING EVENTS

By definition, general event representations are general memory structures that represent the recurring characteristics of familiar events; they are not a collection of autobiographic memories for single occurrences. However, general event schemas can guide the reconstructive processes involved in autobiographic recall. General event knowledge provides a schematic framework for reconstructing memory for single events. The general event schema can provide the main event categories (who, what, when, and so on) that are filled with specific details when recalling a specific instantiation of an event. Because general event knowledge contributes to the construction of specific autobiographic memories, it can both enhance and distort autobiographic recall. Enhanced recall can occur when specific details that are not retrieved in recall are "filled in" with typical slot fillers, for example, recalling that candles were blown out on the birthday cake without actually recollecting the specific action of blowing. On the other hand, when details are filled in incorrectly (perhaps there were no candles on the cake at this particular party), general event knowledge can distort autobiographic recall. Evidence of distortions in children's memory for repeatedly experienced events has received considerable attention not only because it indicates ways in which general and specific event knowledge is organized in memory, but also because these findings have implications for evaluating children's testimony.

Recall of fixed and variable items

In studying children's memory for episodes of repeated events, a distinction is made between fixed items and variable items. Fixed items are actions or objects that are experienced in every encounter with an event, for example, eating cake at a birthday party. Variable items are actions or objects that only occur in some instantiations, for example, having a puppet show at a birthday party. In some events, certain fixed actions occur each time, but the particular details vary. For example, in Hudson's (1990) study of children's recall of a repeated creative music and movement workshop, children sang a song with movements every time, but the particular song was different each time.

A common method for examining children's memory for fixed and variable events has been to provide children with a series of events in which some elements remain constant and others vary. Children's recall, recognition, and susceptibility to suggestion for fixed and variable events are compared, and recall may also be compared to that of children who only experienced a single event. Results indicate that children reliably and accurately report memory for fixed items (Hudson, 1990; Pearse, Powell, & Thomson, 2003; Powell & Thomson, 1996; Powell, Roberts, Ceci, & Hembrooke, 1999). They are more accurate in answering recognition questions regarding fixed items than children who only experienced a single event (Connolly & Lindsay, 2001; Roberts & Powell, 2006); they are more confident in their responses to recognition questions for fixed versus variable items (Roberts & Powell, 2006); and they are less susceptible to false suggestions concerning fixed items as compared to variable items (Connolly & Lindsay, 2001; Powell et al., 1999).

In contrast, children have more difficulty recalling variable items in recurring events. After multiple event experiences, children recall fewer variable instantiations as compared to children who experienced a single event (Pearse et al., 2003; Powell et al., 1999). They are less accurate and less confident in their recall for variable items (Roberts & Powell, 2006) and they may be more susceptible to suggestions regarding variable items as compared to fixed items (Connolly & Lindsay, 2001). However, Powell et al. (1999) did not find differences in susceptibility to misleading questions for children's recall of fixed and variable items. Thus, general event knowledge enhances memory for fixed items, but also produces distortions in recall of variable details.

These effects, although fairly robust, are moderated by age, and timing of recall. In general, children at 3 to 5 years show greater difficulty in distinguishing specific occurrences as compared to children from 6 to 8 years (Powell et al., 1999; Powell & Thomson, 1996, 1997; Powell, Thomson, & Ceci, 2003), and children at all ages are better able to discriminate specific occurrences when questioned soon after their last experience (within 1 week) than when they are questioned after delays of 3 to 6 weeks (Hudson, 1990; Powell & Roberts, 2005; Powell et al., 1999; Powell & Thomson, 1996, 1997; Powell et al., 2003; Roberts & Powell, 2006).

Effects of type of experience and type of questioning

Effects of type of experience on memory for a recurring event were examined by Murachvar, Pipe, Gordon, Owens, and Fivush (1996) in a study of children's event memories acquired through direct experience, observation, or stories. Children at 5 and 6 years received either one or three exposures to a novel event, visiting a pirate room. Children who directly experienced the events produced more complete, organized, and accurate verbal recall a few days later than children who observed the event or heard about it through stories.

Pearse et al. (2003) examined effects of different types of cues on children's ability to discriminate a specific instance of a repeated event. In the temporal cue condition, children were asked to recall the "last time"; in the contextual/temporal cue condition, children were also reminded of a unique feature of the target occurrence. Children from 6 to 7 years recalled more details about a specific occurrence when they were given contextual as well as temporal cues. Roberts and Powell (2006) found that script-consistent suggestions (e.g., children always sat on some kind of mat and the questioning suggested an incorrect mat variation) were falsely recognized more often by 6- and 7-year-olds than script-inconsistent suggestions (e.g., sitting in a chair). They also found that children's source-monitoring ability was positively correlated with resistance to suggestion for both consistent and inconsistent information, when age of the children was controlled.

Most investigations have queried children about the last occurrence of a repeated event that only deviates from the previous experiences in terms of the details of variable items (e.g., the type of mat that children sat on or the specific song that was sung). However, interesting patterns of recall emerge when children are asked to recall the first or middle episodes of a repeated event. Powell, Thomson, and Ceci (2003) asked children from 4 to 8 years to recall various occurrences of a repeated event and to identify the position of the occurrence following delays of either 3 days or 3 weeks after the last occurrence. As in prior research, they found that older children were more accurate than younger children and accuracy decreased over time. More interesting were the effects of position of occurrence on recall of specific episodes. For 6- to 8-year-olds, recall was better for the first and last occurrence when recall was tested after 3 days; after 3 weeks, recall of the last occurrence decreased. For younger children (4 and 5 years), however, no clear position effects were evident.

Recall of naturally occurring events

An alternative to creating novel events for children to experience either repeatedly or on one occasion is to examine children's memory for a specific instance of a naturally occurring recurring event. This is the approach taken by Ornstein, and colleagues who investigated children's memory for specific pediatric examinations (Baker-Ward et al., 1993; Clubb, Nida, Merritt, & Ornstein, 1993; Merritt, Ornstein, & Spicker, 1994; Ornstein, Shapiro, Clubb, Follmer, & Baker-Ward, 1997). Because this is a familiar, scripted event for young children, they exhibit excellent memory retention for delays of 1 to 6 weeks. However, over time (12 weeks), children's recall becomes more reliant on general event knowledge with script-related intrusions emerging. Thus, similar memory effects are found in children's recall of laboratory and naturally occurring events.

Theoretical implications and practical applications

Research indicates that repeated experience with an event can improve children's ability to recall single episodes, but can also reduce children's ability to discriminate between multiple instantiations of variable items. Errors in recall are limited to confusions between script-consistent variations and do not extend to items that are inconsistent with the event. These findings are consistent with both event schema theory and fuzzy-trace theory (e.g., Reyna & Brainerd, 1995). As discussed above, event schema theory predicts that similar episodes of recurring events become merged in memory so that predicable, script-typical items are "absorbed" by general event schemas because general event structures are more efficient representations of recurring events in memory. Details of similar occurrences are therefore difficult to retrieve and become less accessible over time as schematic processing comes into play more (Hudson, 1990; Hudson et al., 1992; Myles-Worsely, Cromer, & Dodd, 1986). Fuzzy-trace theory proposes that two types of memory representations, gist and verbatim, are used to represent event information in memory, and memory distortion effects vary with the relative accessibility of memory representations (Reyna & Brainerd, 1995). Verbatim memory includes information about source and specific surface details; gist memory includes information about general themes or semantic content. Gist representations are accessible for longer periods of time than verbatim representations and are also less susceptible to distortion. In this model, repeated experiences lead to strong gist representations for recurring events (and for fixed items), which are therefore more accessible and less susceptible to distortions from suggestive questioning as compared to the more verbatim-based representations of single occurrences (and variable items) (Connolly & Lindsay, 2001; Pezdek & Roe, 1995; Powell et al., 1999).

Children's recall of specific episodes of repeated events has also been studied to test predictions based on the schema-confirmation–deployment model (Farrar & Goodman, 1990, 1992). According to this model, when children encounter a new event, they try to use an available event schema for comprehension. If none is available (because the event is a novel, first-time experience), all potentially salient event information is retained as a new event representation that does not yet differentiate between typical and atypical components. However, if an appropriate schema is available, children attend to schema-typical information that confirms or identifies the schema to ensure that the appropriate schema is used. This process is the *schema-confirmation* phase. After a schema is confirmed, the *schema-deployment* phase begins. In this phase, schema-consistent information requires less processing (because it can be inferred from the general schema) and attention is directed toward processing new, schema-atypical information. Schema deployment cannot occur until after schema confirmation, and may not occur for newly developed schemas because of the processing demands of attending to all relevant event features. This model, therefore, predicts that the formation of memories of specific episodes of scripted events is dependent on the level of schema deployment and the typicality of new event characteristics that are encountered (schema-consistent or schema-inconsistent).

Support for the schema-confirmation–deployment model comes from studies that find age differences in children's memory for event changes over repeated experiences with novel events. As compared to 7-year-olds, 4-year-old children have greater difficulty in distinguishing atypical variations of repeated events, suggesting that older and younger children are in different phases of schema-confirmation and schema-deployment (Farrar & Boyer-Pennington, 1999; Farrar & Goodman, 1992; Kuebli & Fivush, 1994). Younger children may take longer to establish a new event schema and their attention and memory is directed to schema-consistent information required for schema confirmation after only two or three experiences with an event. In contrast, older children may advance to the schema-deployment phase after two or three experiences and are able to attend to and recall schema-inconsistent information in the third or fourth occurrence. Notably, both increased prior experience (five prior experiences instead of three) and simplified events that facilitated children's advancement to the schema-deployment phase improved 4-year-olds' ability to recall schema-inconsistent information encountered in the final experience (Farrar & Boyer-Pennington, 1999).

The schema-confirmation–deployment model is useful for understanding how and why children of different ages attend to and recall different information from the first encounters with novel, variable events. However, after four experiences with a novel event, even 3-year-olds move to the schema-deployment stage of script processing, and the model does not predict differential processing of event information once schema deployment has been achieved (Hudson et al., 1992). The model is therefore less useful for explaining variations in memory for details of recurring events as a function of age, type of question, and time delay after a general event representation has been constructed.

Event-schema and fuzzy-trace theory perspectives are complementary and make similar predictions regarding children's memory for specific episodes of recurring events. However, because fuzzy-trace theory is concerned with the strength of memory traces for different kinds of event information, it may be more useful for making more fine-grained predictions regarding effects of amount and types of experience; interactions between age, suggestibility and source monitoring; and effects of different types of suggestive questioning in terms of the relative accessibility of gist and verbatim representations over time. This type of analysis has received a great deal of attention in the last decade as researchers have investigated more closely the variables affecting children's testimony about repeated events under different questioning conditions (see also Chapter 10 in this volume by Pipe and Salmon).

USE OF GENERAL EVENT KNOWLEDGE IN PLANNING FUTURE EVENTS

Although planning is an inherently future-oriented mental activity, it relies heavily on knowledge of the past. The ability to plan for the future depends on expectations that past events can be repeated in the future; Haith (1997) proposed that this expectation is the most basic future-oriented process. Although Haith was referring to short-term repetitions such as the successive rings of a telephone, this principle can be applied to repeated events. General event knowledge about what happens in recurring events can therefore form the basis for planning for future occurrences (Hudson & Fivush, 1991; Hudson, Sosa, & Shapiro, 1997).

Research on children's ability to plan from general event knowledge suggests that having relevant event knowledge does not guarantee that children know how to access and use that knowledge to plan for the future. For example, Hudson et al. (1995) observed asymmetries in the length and complexity of children's scripts and verbal plans for familiar events that suggested that planning aloud was more difficult than providing a verbal script. They asked 3-, 4-, and 5-year-olds either to describe what happens in two familiar events, or to plan aloud for future instantiations of going to the beach or going grocery shopping. At all ages, there was considerable overlap in the actions that children mentioned in event scripts and plans, indicating that general event knowledge guided the construction of both types of reports. However, 3-year-olds' event plans were shorter than their script reports for the same events and showed little evidence of planfulness. In contrast, 4- and

5-year-olds differentiated event plans from script reports by including additional planning-related information in their verbal plans. They also focused more on preparation actions occurring at the beginning of the events, such as making a shopping list and getting a shopping cart before going grocery shopping.

Because the process of constructing plans from general event memory involves more than just accessing relevant event knowledge, research has also shown that preschool children benefit considerably when they are provided with support or assistance in constructing and executing plans based on knowledge of routines. Hudson and Fivush (1993) investigated preschool children's ability to plan for future events (a birthday party and breakfast) while shopping for groceries in a pretend grocery store. Three- and 4-year-old children had difficulty keeping a future event goal in mind and using that goal to direct their shopping activities. However, their performance improved when they were provided with external supports for the task, that is, a verbal reminder of the event goal or the opportunity to shop in a store where all the birthday items were placed together and all the breakfast items were placed together in another location. Hudson et al. (1997) examined effects of adult modeling on children's ability to construct plans for making snacks and art projects in their preschool. Children learned novel event sequences involved in making tortillas (the snack project) and puppets (the art project). Some children listened to an adult plan the activities aloud during their training; the other children learned the sequences without exposure to the adult's verbal plan. When asked to plan the activities themselves, children who had heard the adult plan aloud were better able to plan on their own and select the necessary objects to complete the activities from an array of target and distracter items.

Most recently, Shapiro and Hudson (2004) found that preschool children benefited from reminders and prompts in their efforts to carry out plans for familiar events (art projects involving complex events sequences). Interestingly, in this study, children found the task of constructing and executing plans more difficult for more causally constrained event sequences. The art project that included more enabling relationships between actions (e.g., crayon shavings were placed between two pieces of wax paper before ironing the sheets) was more difficult to plan for and execute because the "cost" of temporal errors was greater than for the art project that included more arbitrary relationships between actions (e.g., feathers and glitter were used to decorate a hat, but these could be applied in any order without affecting the outcome). If a child failed to recall the first action in an enabling sequence, the next action could not be performed successfully, but the temporal order of actions arranged in an arbitrary order could be violated with no repercussions. Thus, children benefited from reminders of the overall event goal (viewing a completed project during the planning process), especially when executing complex plans for causally constrained event sequences.

These studies indicate that for preschool children, the task of using event knowledge to plan future events is neither easy nor automatic, but they are more successful when their performance is supported or scaffolded by adult models, reminders, and a structured environment. Nevertheless, the level of planfulness that children demonstrate when planning familiar, recurring events is higher than when they plan in novel contexts, indicating the general event knowledge does support some elements of event planning. For example, 5-year-olds are generally deficient in planning in novel contexts, such as planning a route through a pretend grocery store to select items in the most efficient manner (Gauvain & Rogoff, 1989; Radziszewska & Rogoff, 1991), but 5-year-olds can successfully coordinate two event goals (shopping for birthday party and breakfast items) in planning and executing a pretend grocery shopping activity (Hudson & Fivush, 1991). When they constructed advance verbal plans for going to the beach or going grocery shopping, 5-year-olds frequently mentioned preparations and they could construct plans to remedy and prevent common mishaps (Hudson et al., 1995).

THE ROLE OF GENERAL EVENT KNOWLEDGE IN THE DEVELOPMENT OF TEMPORAL CONCEPTS

Several theorists (Fraisse, 1984; Friedman, 1990, 1992; Nelson, 1996) have proposed that children's early understanding of event sequences in recurring events provides the foundation for the understanding of two fundamental time concepts: succession and duration. Succession refers to the sequential ordering of events, and duration refers to the temporal intervals between events, quantified by conventional measurement systems such as minutes, hours, and days. The conventional units of time used by our culture are based on the division of time into units of years, months, days, hours, and minutes and the regular succession of hours in the day, days in the week, months in the year, and successively dated years.

As discussed above, children can form event representations for enabling and causal sequences from a very early age, suggesting that sequence is central to early event representations. In the preschool years, children often think about time in terms of familiar event sequences. In observations of preschool children's spontaneous use of temporal language, Ames (1946) found that children at 36 months mentioned "lunch time," "juice time," "puzzle time," and "night-time," which appeared to segment their daily routine into sections occupied by activities. Springer (1952) also found that children segmented time in terms of familiar routines in a study in which children were asked at what time school started, at what time the child had lunch, and at what time the child left school. Many 4-year-olds answered these questions by reciting their schedule, essentially providing a script report ("get up, eat breakfast, then school starts" or "I have lunch, then a story, and a nap, then I go home"). By 5 years, a large percentage of the children answered in terms of a 24-hour measurement system instead of schedule recitation. These findings indicate that there is a period during which activities are the indicators as well as the constituents of children's temporal measurement.

To construct conventional time concepts, children not only need to understand sequence, they need to have an understanding of the division of the sequence of their own experience into past, present, and future. Friedman and colleagues have conducted extensive research into children's representations of temporal structure using picture sequencing tasks in which children are asked to order events along a time line relative to the present time or to a designated point within a sequence (e.g., breakfast). By 4 to 5 years, American children can represent the temporal sequence of the main events in their day (Friedman, 1977, 1990, 1992; Freidman & Brudos, 1988); by 6 to 7 years, they can order seasonal events (Friedman, 1977, 1990); and by 7 to 8 years, they can correctly order cards listing the days in the week and months in the year (Friedman, 1977, 1986). Benson (1997) also used a picture sequencing task to test whether 4- and 5-year-olds could correctly sequence 12 daily activities from the past (yesterday), present (today), and future (tomorrow) along a time-line. Children at both ages correctly sequenced these activities, although they were more accurate in sequencing activities from the past than from the future.

What accounts for the emergence of conventional time understanding, as evidenced in sequencing tasks? Nelson (1996) and Friedman (1990, 1992) have proposed that both the regularity of the sequencing of routine events in the real world and social interactions between parent and child that accompany these events provided the basis for young children's understanding of temporal relations. Verbal discussions are critical for the development of conventional time concepts because these concepts must be acquired through language. As Nelson points out, the concept of time is itself a social construction and it is conveyed to children through language (Nelson, 1996). Conversations about past and future events provide children with critical exposure to temporal language while thinking and talking about recurring events. This exposure can provide the basis for children's mapping of the language of conventional temporal measurement onto their memory representations for sequences and cycles of recurring events.

Research on mother–child conversations about past and future events indicates that children are exposed to temporal language in these contexts (Benson, Talmi, & Haith, 1999; Hudson, 2002, 2006; Lucariello & Nelson, 1987). Lucariello and Nelson (1987) examined the temporal language mothers used while talking with 2-year-old children in three event contexts: during a routine event, during unstructured free play, and during thematic play. Both past and future talk were more frequent in the routine event contexts than either of the play contexts, suggesting that shared event knowledge facilitated temporally displaced language use.

Hudson (2002, 2006) found that when mothers discussed events with 2½ and 4-year-old children, they frequently referred to general event knowledge to engage children in talk about the future. References to general event knowledge were greater when discussing future events than when discussing past events. Furthermore, mothers' references to general event knowledge were related to increased participation by 4-year-olds. Mothers also used more temporal language when talking about future events than when discussing past events. This finding suggests that mother–child conversations about future events, framed in terms of children's general event knowledge and memories of recurring events, is a rich context for children to learn about temporal concepts.

These various lines of research all provide evidence that children's memory for routine events provides the foundation for developing temporal concepts. Memory for recurring events provides a basis for understanding of sequence, and later provides a basis for segmenting experience into temporal units that are mapped onto the language of conventional time. Knowledge of familiar event routines is especially important in the development of concepts of future time. Because the future is unknown, it can only be predicted based on past experience (Fraisse, 1963). As shown in the following example of a mother and her 4-year-old child discussing a future event, general event knowledge provides the background for thinking about and planning for the future (from Hudson, 2006):

M: Do you know when your birthday is? Yeah, when is your birthday?
C: July.
M: In July. Yeah, it's in the summer time right?
C: Yeah.
M: And what do you want to do on your birthday?
C: I'm gonna have lots of presents and stuff.
M: What kind of party would you like?
C: A birthday party.
M: Who should come to this birthday party?
C: My friends.
M: Your friends, like who?
C: Amanda, Sarah, Caroline.
M: That sounds like a good list. Should we play some games?
C: Yeah.
M: Yeah, what kind of games should we play?
C: We should play birthday games.
M: How about should we have a cake?
C: I'm gonna have a strawberry.

This excerpt illustrates how conventional temporal language ("In July," "in the summer time") is used to refer to the timing of the occurrence of an annual event. Knowledge of the predictable components of birthday parties (friends, games, presents, birthday cake) is assumed by both participants as they consider possibilities for the next instantiation. Thus, general event knowledge guides the discussion of when future events will occur and what will happen as mothers and children think about and plan for future events.

CONCLUSIONS

Research on children's memory for recurring events has progressed far beyond demonstrations of script knowledge in preschool children. We are cognizant of how event knowledge provides a primary form of mental representation that is used to organize memories of past events, make predictions about future events, and construct fundamental distinctions between past, present, and future events. We also know a great deal about how children remember specific episodes of recurring events and the ways in which different types of event experience, different questioning techniques, and variables such as age and time delay influence this type of recall. This information has been applied to real-world situations in which children are asked to provide testimony regarding specific episodes of recurring events.

Continuities in the structure of event knowledge from infancy through adulthood highlight the centrality of general event knowledge in human memory. Goal-directed, temporally organized actions form the core of event representations from infancy on. At the same time, differences in how general event knowledge coordinates with other knowledge systems in children and adults suggest that adults' memory systems are more elaborated, and that event knowledge becomes coordinated with multiple abstract knowledge structures. With age, event knowledge develops from simple sequence representations to nested, hierarchical structures that organize many types of knowledge and that can be accessed through multiple paths (e.g., causal and temporal concepts, self concepts, concepts of relationships and social behavior). We are in the process of learning how these abstract knowledge structures develop from and are coordinated with general event knowledge during childhood.

Increasingly, the role of social interaction has been emphasized in explaining (1) the emergence of autobiographic memory in young children (Nelson, 1993, Nelson & Fivush, 2004); (2) how children learn how to plan for future events based on memory for recurring events (this chapter) and (3) how abstract concepts of time emerge from children's memory for recurring event sequences (this chapter). This is a promising area of investigation for understanding how children's memory for recurring events is cued and applied to real-world situations involving thinking about the past and planning for the future. Continued discussions of past events between parents and children (and perhaps siblings and peers as well) during middle childhood and adolescence may prompt children to think about the past in terms of multiple categories of information, such as relationships, extended events, and life-time periods. More research that examines the ways in which general event knowledge is accessed and used in everyday interactions is essential for understanding the developmental processes involved in the integration of general event knowledge into more abstract knowledge structures over the life span.

REFERENCES

Abelson, R. P. (1981). Psychological status of the script concept. *American Psychologist, 36*, 715–729.

Adams, L. T., & Worden, P. E. (1986). Script development and organization in preschool and elementary school children. *Discourse Processes, 9*, 149–166.

Allain, P., Le Gall, D., Etcharry-Bouyx, F., Aubin, G., & Emile, J. (1999). Mental representation of knowledge following frontal-lobe lesion: Dissociations on tasks using scripts. *Journal of Clinical and Experimental Neuropsychology, 21*, 643–665.

Allain, P., Le Gall, D., Etcharry-Bouyx, F., Forgeau, M., Mercier, P., & Emile, J. (2001). Influence of centrality and distinctiveness of actions on script sorting and ordering in patients with frontal lobe lesions. *Journal of Clinical and Experimental Neuropsychology, 23*, 465–483.

Ames, L. (1946). The development of the sense of time in the young child. *Journal of Genetic Psychology, 68*, 97–125.

Anderson, S. J., & Conway, M. A. (1993). Investigating the structure of autobiographic memory. *Journal of Experimental Psychology: Learning, Memory, and Cognition, 19*, 1178–1196.

Baker-Ward, L., Gordon, B. N., Ornstein, P. A., Larus, D. M., & Clubb, P. A. (1993). Young children's long-term retention of a pediatric examination. *Child Development, 64*, 1519–1533.

Barsalou, L. S. (1988). The content and organization of autobiographic memories. In U. Neisser & E. Winograd (Eds.), *Real events remembered: Ecological and traditional approaches to the study of memory* (pp. 193–243). Cambridge: Cambridge University Press.

Barsalou, L. W., & Sewell, D. R. (1985). Contrasting the representation of scripts and categories. *Journal of Memory and Language, 24*, 646–665.

Bauer, P. J., Hertsgaard, L. A., Dropik, P., & Daly, B. P. (1998). When even arbitrary order becomes important: Developments in reliable temporal sequencing of arbitrarily ordered events. *Memory, 6*, 165–198.

Bauer, P. J., & Mandler, J. M. (1989). One thing follows another: Effects of temporal structure on 1- to 2-year-olds' recall of events. *Developmental Psychology, 25*, 197–206.

Bauer, P. J., & Mandler, J. M. (1992). Putting the horse before the cart: The use of temporal order in recall of events by one-year-old children. *Developmental Psychology, 28*, 441–452.

Bauer, P. J., & Shore, C. M. (1987). Making a memorable event: Effects of familiarity and organization on young children's recall of action sequences. *Cognitive Development, 2*, 327–338.

Benson, J. B. (1997). The development of planning: It's about time. In S. L. Friedman & E. K. Scholnick (Eds.), *The developmental psychology of planning: Why, how, and when do we plan?* (pp. 43–75). Hillsdale, NJ: Lawrence Erlbaum Associates, Inc.

Benson, J. B., Talmi, A., & Haith, M. M. (April, 1999). *Adult speech about events in time: A replication.* Presented at the meetings of the Society for Research in Child Development, Albuquerque, NM.

Bower, G. H., Black, J. B., & Turner, T. J. (1979). Scripts in memory for text. *Cognitive Psychology, 11*, 177–220.

Clubb, P. A., Nida, R. E., Merritt, K., & Ornstein, P. A. (1993). Visiting the doctor: Children's knowledge and memory. *Cognitive Development, 8*, 361–372.

Connolly, D. A., & Lindsay, D. S. (2001). The influence of suggestions on children's reports of a unique experience versus reporting of a repeated experience. *Applied Cognitive Psychology*, *15*, 205–224.

Conway, M. A. (1990). Autobiographical memory and conceptual representation. *Journal of Experimental Psychology: Learning, Memory, and Cognition*, *16*, 799–812.

Conway, M. A. (1992). A structural model of autobiographical memory. In H. Spinnler & W. A. Wagenaar (Eds.), *Theoretical perspectives on autobiographical memory* (pp. 167–193). Dordrecht, The Netherlands: Kluwer Academic.

Conway, M. A., & Bekerian, D. A. (1987). Organization in autobiographical memory. *Memory and Cognition*, *15*, 119–132.

Conway, M. A., & Rubin, D. C. (1993). The structure of autobiographical memory. In A. E. Collins, S. E. Gathercole, M. A. Conway, & P. E. M. Morris (Eds.), *Theories of memory* (pp. 103–137). Hillsdale, NJ: Lawrence Erlbaum Associates, Inc.

Crozier, S., Sirigu, A., Lehericy, S., van de Moortele, P.-F., Pillon, B., Grafman, J., et al. (1999). Distinct prefrontal activations in processing sequence at the sentence and script level: An fMRI study. *Neuropsychologia*, *37*(13), 1469–1476.

Davidson, D. (1994). Recognition and recall of irrelevant and interruptive actions in script-based stories. *Journal of Memory and Language*, *33*, 757–775.

Davidson, D., & Hoe, S. (1993). Children's recall and recognition memory for typical and atypical actions in script-based stories. *Journal of Experimental Child Psychology*, *55*, 104–126.

Davidson, D., & Jergovic, D. (1996). Children's memory for atypical actions in script-based stories: An examination of the disruption effect. *Journal of Experimental Child Psychology*, *61*, 134–152.

Davidson, D., Larson, S. L., Luo, Z., & Burden, M. J. (2000). Interruption and bizarreness effects in the recall of script-based text. *Memory*, *8*, 217–234.

Farrar, M. J., & Boyer-Pennington, M. E. (1999). Remembering specific episodes of a scripted event. *Journal of Experimental Child Psychology*, *73*, 266–288.

Farrar, M. J., & Goodman, G. S. (1990). Developmental differences in the relation between script and episodic memory: Do they exist? In R. Fivush & J. Hudson (Eds.), *Knowing and remembering in young children* (pp. 30–64). New York: Cambridge University Press.

Farrar, M. J., & Goodman, G. S. (1992). Developmental changes in event memory. *Child Development*, *63*, 1697–1709.

Fivush, R. (1984). Learning about school: The development of kindergartners' school scripts. *Child Development*, *55*, 1697–1709.

Fivush, R., Kuebli, J., & Clubb, P. A. (1992). The structure of events and event representations: A developmental analysis. *Child Development*, *63*, 188–201.

Fivush, R., & Mandler, J. M. (1985). Developmental changes in the understanding of temporal sequence. *Child Development*, *56*, 1437–1446.

Fivush, R., & Slackman, E. (1986). The acquisition and development of scripts. In K. Nelson (Ed.), *Event knowledge: Structure and function in development* (pp. 71–96). Hillsdale, NJ: Lawrence Erlbaum Associates, Inc.

Fraisse, P. (1963). *The psychology of time*. New York: Harper & Row.

Fraisse, P. (1984). Perception and estimation of time. *Annual Review of Psychology*, *35*, 1–36.

Friedman, W. J. (1977). The development of children's knowledge of cyclic aspects of time. *Child Development*, *48*, 1593–1599.

Friedman, W. J. (1986). The development of children's knowledge of temporal structure. *Child Development, 57*, 1386–1400.

Friedman, W. J. (1990). Children representations of the pattern of daily activities. *Child Development, 61*, 1399–1412.

Friedman, W. J. (1992). The development of children's representations of temporal structure. In F. Macar, V. Pouthas, & W. J. Friedman (Eds.), *Time, actions and cognition: Towards bridging the gap* (pp. 67–75). Dordrecht, The Netherlands: Kluwer Academic.

Friedman, W. J., & Brudos, S. L. (1988). On routines and routines: The early development of spatial and temporal representations. *Cognitive Development, 3*, 167–182.

Galambos, J. A. (1983). Normative studies of six characteristics of our knowledge of common activities. *Behavior Research Methods and Instrumentation, 15*(3), 327–340.

Galambos, J. A., & Rips, J. J. (1982). Memories for routines. *Journal of Verbal Learning and Verbal Behavior, 21*, 260–281.

Gauvain, M., & Rogoff, B. (1989). Collaborative problem solving and children's planning skills. *Developmental Psychology, 25*, 139–151.

Graesser, A. C., Woll, S. B., Kowalski, D. J., & Smith, D. A. (1980). Memory for typical and atypical actions in scripted activities. *Journal of Experimental Psychology: Human Learning and Memory, 6*, 503–515.

Grafman, J. (2002). The human prefrontal cortex has evolved to represent components of structured event complexes. In J. Grafman (Ed.), *Handbook of neuropsychology* (Vol. 7, pp. 157–174). Amsterdam: Elsevier.

Haith, M. M. (1997). The development of future thinking as essential for the emergence of skill in planning. In S. L. Friedman & E. K. Scholnick (Eds.), *Why, how, and when do we plan? The developmental psychology of planning* (pp. 25–42). Hillsdale, NJ: Lawrence Erlbaum Associates, Inc.

Hudson, J. A. (1988). Children's memory for atypical actions in script based stories: Evidence for a disruption effect. *Journal of Experimental Child Psychology, 46*, 159–173.

Hudson, J. A. (1990). Constructive processes in children's event memory. *Developmental Psychology, 26*, 180–187.

Hudson, J. A. (2002). "Do you know what we're going to do this summer?" Mothers' talk to preschool children about future events. *Journal of Cognition and Development, 3*, 49–71.

Hudson, J. A. (2006). The development of future time concepts through mother–child conversation. *Merrill Palmer Quarterly, 52*, 70–95.

Hudson, J. A., & Fivush, R. (1991). Planning in the preschool years: The emergence of plans from general event knowledge. *Cognitive Development, 6*, 393–415.

Hudson, J. A., Gebelt, J., Haviland, J., & Bentivegna, C. (1992). Emotion and narrative structure in young children's personal accounts. *Journal of Narrative and Life History, 2*, 129–150.

Hudson, J. A., & Nelson, K. (1983). Effects of script structure on children's story recall. *Developmental Psychology, 19*, 623–635.

Hudson, J., & Nelson, K. (1986). Repeated encounters of a similar kind: Effects of familiarity on children's autobiographic memory. *Cognitive Development, 1*, 253–271.

Hudson, J. A., & Shapiro, L. R. (1991). From knowing to telling: The development of children's scripts, stories, and personal narratives. In A. McCabe & C. Peterson

(Eds.), *Developing narrative structure* (pp. 89–136). Hillsdale, NJ: Lawrence Erlbaum Associates, Inc.

Hudson, J. A., Shapiro, L. R., & Sosa, B. B. (1995). Planning in the real world: Preschool children's scripts and plans for familiar events. *Child Development, 66,* 984–998.

Hudson, J. A., & Slackman, E. A. (1990). Children's use of scripts in inferential text processing. *Discourse Processes, 13,* 375–385.

Hudson, J. A., Sosa, B. B., & Shapiro, L. R. (1997). Scripts and plans: The development of children's event knowledge and event planning. In S. L. Friedman & E. K. Scholnick (Eds.), *Why, how, and when do we plan? The developmental psychology of planning* (pp. 77–102). Hillsdale, NJ: Lawrence Erlbaum Associates, Inc.

Kolodner, J. L. (1983). Maintaining memory organization in dynamic long-term memory. *Cognitive Science, 7,* 260–281.

Kuebli, J., & Fivush, R. (1994). Children's representation and recall of event alternatives. *Journal of Experimental Child Psychology, 58,* 25–45.

Lancaster, J. S., & Barsalou, L. W. (1997). Multiple organisations of events in memory. *Memory, 5,* 569–599.

Linton, M. (1986). Ways of searching and the contents of memory. In D. C. Rubin (Ed.), *Autobiographical memory* (pp. 50–67). Cambridge: Cambridge University Press.

Lucariello, J., & Nelson, K. (1987). Remembering and planning talk between mothers and children. *Discourse Processes, 10,* 219–235.

Maki, R. H. (1990). Memory for script actions: Effects of relevance and detail expectancy. *Memory and Cognition, 18,* 5–14.

Meltzoff, A. N. (1995). Understanding the intentions of others: Reenactment of intended acts by 18-month-old children. *Developmental Psychology, 31,* 838–850.

Merritt, K. A., Ornstein, P. A., & Spicker, B. (1994). Children's memory for a salient medical procedure: Implications for testimony. *Pediatrics, 94,* 17–23.

Murachvar, T., Pipe, M. E., Gordon, R., Owens, J. L., & Fivush, R. (1996). Do, show, and tell: Children's event memories acquired through direct experience, observation, and stories. *Child Development, 67,* 3029–3044.

Myles-Worsley, M., Cromer, C. C., & Dodd, D. H. (1986). Children's preschool script reconstruction: Reliance on general knowledge as memory fades. *Developmental Psychology, 22,* 22–30.

Neisser, U. (1986). Nested structure in autobiographic memory. In D. C. Rubin (Ed.), *Autobiographical memory* (pp. 71–81). Cambridge: Cambridge University Press.

Nelson, K. (1986). *Event knowledge: Structure and function in development.* Hillsdale, NJ: Lawrence Erlbaum Associates, Inc.

Nelson, K. (1993). The psychological and social origins of autobiographical memory. *Psychological Science, 1,* 1–8.

Nelson, K. (1996). *Language in cognitive development: Emergence of the mediated mind.* New York: Cambridge University Press.

Nelson, K. & Fivush, R. (2004). The emergence of autobiographical memory: A social cultural developmental theory. *Psychological Review, 111,* 486–511.

Nelson, K., & Gruendel, J. (1981). Generalized event representations: Basic building blocks of cognitive development. In M. E. Lamb & A. L. Brown (Eds.), *Advances in Developmental Psychology* (Vol. 1, pp. 21–46). Hillsdale, NJ: Lawrence Erlbaum Associates, Inc.

Ornstein, P. A., Shapiro, L. R., Clubb, P. A., Follmer, A., & Baker-Ward, L. (1997).

The influence of prior knowledge on children's memory for salient medical experiences. In N. Stein, P. A. Ornstein, C. J. Brainerd, & B. Tversky (Eds.), *Memory for everyday and emotional events* (pp. 83–111). Hillsdale, NJ: Lawrence Erlbaum Associates, Inc.

Pearse, S. L., Powell, M. B., & Thomson, D. M. (2003). The effect of contextual cues on children's ability to remember an occurrence of a repeated event. *Legal and Criminological Psychology, 8*, 39–50.

Pezdek, K., & Roe, C. (1995). The effect of memory trace strength on suggestibility. *Journal of Experimental Child Psychology, 60*, 116–128.

Piaget, J., & Inhelder, B. (1973). *Mental imagery in the child.* London: Routledge & Kegan Paul.

Powell, K. P., & Roberts, M. B. (2005). Evidence of metacognitive awareness in young children who have experienced a repeated event. *Applied Cognitive Psychology, 19*, 1019–1031.

Powell, M. B., Roberts, K. P., Ceci, S. J., & Hembrooke, H. (1999). The effects of repeated experience on children's suggestibility. *Developmental Psychology, 35*, 1462–1477.

Powell, M. B., & Thomson, D. M. (1996). Children's memory of an occurrence of a repeated event: Effects of age, repetition, and retention interval across three question types. *Child Development, 68*, 1988–2004.

Powell, M. B., & Thomson, D. M. (1997). Contrasting memory for temporal-source and memory for content in children's discrimination of repeated events. *Applied Cognitive Psychology, 11*, 339–360.

Powell, M. B., Thomson, D. M., & Ceci, S. J. (2003). Children's memory of recurring events: Is the first event always the best remembered? *Applied Cognitive Psychology, 17*, 127–146.

Radziszewska, B., & Rogoff, B. (1991). Children's guided participation in planning imaginary errands with skilled adult or peer partners. *Developmental Psychology, 27*, 381–389.

Reiser, B. J., Black, J. B., & Abelson, R. P. (1985). Knowledge structures in the organization and retrieval of autobiographical memories. *Cognitive Psychology, 11*, 107–123.

Reyna, V. F., & Brainerd, C. J. (1995). Fuzzy-trace theory: An interim synthesis. *Learning and Individual Differences, 7*, 1–75.

Roberts, M. B., & Powell, K. P. (2006). The consistency of false suggestions moderates children's reports of a single instance of a repeated event: Predicting increases and decreases in suggestibility. *Journal of Experimental Child Psychology, 94*, 68–89.

Robinson, J. A., & Swanson, K. L. (1990). Autobiographic memory: The next phase. *Applied Cognitive Psychology, 4*, 321–335.

Schank, R. C. (1982). *Dynamic memory: A theory of reminding and learning in computers and people.* New York: Cambridge University Press.

Schank, R. C., & Abelson, R. P. (1995) Knowledge and memory: The real story. In R. S. Wyer, Jr. (Ed.), *Knowledge and memory: The real story* (pp. 1–85). Hillsdale, NJ: Lawrence Erlbaum Associates, Inc.

Schooler, J. W., & Herrmann, D. J. (1992). There is more to episodic memory than just episodes. In M. A. Conway, D. C. Rubin, H. H. Spinnler, & W. A. Wagenaar (Eds.), *Theoretical perspectives on autobiographic memory* (pp. 241–261). Dordrecht, The Netherlands: Kluwer Academic.

Shapiro, L. R., & Hudson, J. A. (2004). Effects of internal and external support on preschool children's event planning. *Journal of Applied Developmental Psychology*, *25*, 49–73.

Sirigu, A., Zalla, T., Pillon, B., & Grafman, J. (1996). Encoding of sequence and boundaries of scripts following prefrontal lesions. *Cortex*, *32*, 297–310.

Slackman, E., & Nelson, K. (1984). Acquisition of an unfamiliar script form by young children. *Child Development*, *55*, 329–340.

Smith, D. A., & Graesser, A. C. (1981). Memory for actions in scripted activities as a function of typicality, retention interval, and retrieval task. *Memory and Cognition*, *9*, 550–559.

Springer, D. (1952). Development in young children of an understanding of time and the clock. *Journal of Genetic Psychology*, *80*, 83–96.

van den Broek, P., Lorch, E. P., & Thurlow, R. (1996). Children's and adults' memory for television stories: The role of causal factors, story-grammar categories, and hierarchical level. *Child Development*, *67*, 3010–3028.

Wood, J. N., & Grafman, J. (2003). Human prefrontal cortex: Processing and representational perspectives. *Nature Reviews Neuroscience*, *4*, 139–147.

Woodward, A. L. (1998). Infants selectively encode the goal object of an actor's reach *Cognition*, *69*, 1–34.

Zacks, J. M., & Tversky, B. (2001). Event structure in perception and conception. *Psychological Bulletin*, *127*, 3–21.

Zacks, J. M., Tversky, B., & Iyer, G. (2001). Perceiving, remembering, and communicating structure in events. *Journal of Experimental Psychology: General*, *120*, 29–58.

Zalla, T., Sirigu, A., Pillon, B., Dubois, B., Agid, Y., & Grafman, J. (2000). How patients with Parkinson's disease retrieve and manage cognitive event knowledge. *Cortex*, *36*, 163–179.

5 Implicit memory in childhood

Reassessing developmental
invariance

Marianne E. Lloyd and Nora S. Newcombe
Temple University, Philadelphia, USA

> It's like riding a bike: once you've learned it, you'll never forget how to do it.

Although it is uncertain whether this adage has been tested empirically, personal experience of the authors suggests that the passage of many years is indeed insufficient to destroy bike-riding ability. Recently, skills such as bike-riding have been termed *implicit memory*, and their retention has been contrasted with what is seen with *explicit memory* tasks, in which participants are aware that they are making a memory decision, as occurs when answering the question, "Who taught you to ride a bike?" Implicit memory has been described as encompassing various tasks, including not only acquisition of motor skill, but also priming (as when something comes quickly and easily to mind because it has been encountered previously) and classical conditioning. (For a typical graphic depiction of these distinctions, see Squire & Zola, 1996.) There has been considerable interest in typologies of this kind as supporting investigations of the architecture of human memory that are informed by combinations of evidence from behavior and neuroscience, and that encompass research with a variety of human and non-human populations.

The terms explicit and implicit memory were proposed by Graf and Schacter (1985; also see Schacter, 1987). In the years since the introduction of these terms, several debates have occurred over the necessity to posit multiple memory systems (e.g., Tulving, 2002) and the possibility that such dissociations are based on tasks rather than processes (Roediger & Blaxton, 1989; Toth & Hunt, 1999). However, the distinction seems to have withstood the test of time, and is in wide use today (e.g., in introductory psychology, physiological psychology, and cognitive psychology texts). Operationally, explicit memory refers to tasks in which people are asked to evaluate their memory, either by saying that they did or did not encounter something before (i.e., recognition test), or by producing a previously encountered stimulus or fact (e.g., autobiographical recollections, free recall, cued recall). In contrast, when the task does not refer to a study episode (e.g., naming tasks, priming measures, stem completion, sequence learning, conditioning), we refer to the results as a measure of implicit memory.

Developmentally, it has been claimed that implicit memory is present robustly from the start of life, and does not undergo the kind of age-related changes that are commonly seen in explicit memory (Reber, 1989). In fact, this theme was the dominant conclusion of the chapter by Alan Parkin (1998) covering implicit memory in the first edition of this volume. The claim has several attractive characteristics. First, explicit memory improves dramatically over the course of childhood (for a review, see Kail, 1990), and many standard explicit tasks such as recall and recognition are simply too difficult to use with children younger than 3 years of age. Although there is increasing recognition that explicit memory is present in infancy (for a review, see Bauer, 2005), implicit memory measures still seem to offer a potentially more sensitive way to determine what information young children have encoded, while still employing measures that can also be used with adults. Second, implicit memory seems to offer a way of understanding a paradox in cognitive development, namely, the fact that early competence is often discerned using looking time measures while, in contrast, studies examining deliberate actions and explicit predictions often show protracted phases of immaturity (see Keen, 2003). That is, perhaps initial knowledge is implicit in nature, but considerable experience with the world is necessary to create explicitly accessible information that can be used to make judgments.

There is actually considerable uncertainty, however, concerning whether implicit memory is as developmentally robust as investigators believed at first. There are several reasons to rethink this position. First, it was based primarily on studies of perceptual priming, without much consideration of other types of implicit memory, or of conceptual priming (Roediger & Blaxton, 1987). Second, it became associated with other propositions that are not logically entailed by it, notably the idea that implicit memory is resistant to decay or interference (as in the bike riding example). Third, it was based on studies of children that began at quite an advanced age from the point of view of discussion of developmental origins of knowledge or invariance over the life span—rarely younger than 3 or 4 years of age.

Our aim in this chapter is to reconsider the development of implicit memory in a more differentiated way than was possible when Parkin's chapter in the first edition was written. However, a complete review of implicit memory development is beyond the scope of one chapter; indeed, an entire book on the topic has been written (Rovee-Collier, Hayne, & Colombo, 2000). We have chosen to restrict our scope in several ways. First, we do not discuss the development of explicit memory except when it is useful to make contrasts with implicit performance, because many other chapters in this book deal with aspects of explicit memory such as autobiographical or source memory. Second, we concentrate on developments in childhood rather than address in detail the issue of which infant memory measures are implicit and which are explicit, as this has a complicated history of its own (see Chapter 2 in this book and also Chapters 5–8 in Oakes and Bauer, 2007).

We first review what the support was for Parkin's (1998) claim that "procedural memory appears age invariant" (p. 124). Most of the evidence for the invariance claim came from studies in which implicit memory was tested using perceptual priming tasks. These findings of equivalent priming effects across childhood have largely been supported subsequently, but there have also been studies showing developmental change in *conceptual* priming tasks that have received much recent attention. We argue, however, that this work entangles issues of priming with issues of conceptual growth and additions to semantic memory, so that the data do not actually challenge the invariance claim in a fundamental way. We then conclude the section on priming with a discussion of what is known about the interplay of implicit with explicit memory, where there does appear to be considerable, and rather late, developmental change. In the second major section, we review findings regarding another kind of implicit memory, different from priming, not covered in the first edition of the book, and for which there is clear evidence that memory *does* change developmentally, namely, sequence learning. We close the chapter with a brief review of some developments in neuroscience, implicit memory in clinical populations, and suggestions for future research.

PRIMING EFFECTS

One of the most striking aspects of the implicit memory construct is that it encompasses many compelling everyday experiences. When a familiar face pops out of a crowd, perceptual priming may be at work. When a seemingly novel idea comes to mind, and we later realize that the idea was proposed by someone else in conversation a few days ago, a different kind of priming is at work—conceptual rather than perceptual (as well as, sadly, an embarrassing rather than an adaptive aspect of priming). In this section, we consider the developmental invariance hypothesis for perceptual priming, followed by an examination of conceptual priming (including its effects on false memory), closing with consideration of how children come to realize that processing fluency (i.e., the speed and ease with which an item is perceived) may be a clue to making explicit memory judgments.

Perceptual priming

Perceptual priming is studied experimentally in situations in which we can be sure that stimuli have been encountered, but in which it is likely that they will not be explicitly remembered. We can then seek evidence that the stimuli are processed more quickly and easily as a function of prior exposure, despite the lack of recall, or even recognition. For example, when participants have recently studied the word "tulip," they can read it faster when it appears on a screen, identify it at a higher level of perceptual masking, or respond to it more quickly on a lexical decision task, compared to a group that has not recently seen the item. Similarly, on a stem completion task, participants are more likely to solve the stem "tu____" with "tulip" than people who have not recently seen the word "tulip." These effects can occur independently of whether they recognize the word on a later recognition test, list it in a recall test, or can accurately remember that the word was viewed as a picture during a source monitoring test (for a review of the effects of encoding and retrieval variables on memory performance, see Richardson-Klavehn & Bjork, 1988; Roediger & McDermott, 1993). Further, unlike explicit tasks such as recall, these priming effects seem to be relatively stable throughout adulthood (e.g., Fleischman, Wilson, Gabrieli, Bienias, & Bennett, 2004).

Much initial work on implicit memory development focused on applying the paradigms typically used with adults to work with children. Some of this work has been verbal (Billingsley, Smith, & McAndrews, 2002; Komatsu, Naito, & Fuke, 1996; Perez, Peynircioglu, & Blaxton, 1998). For example, participants may be asked to complete word stems or fragments after studying a list of items. Some of these may be completed with studied items while others would be completed with novel items. Priming is measured by an increased likelihood of completing items with studied words. Such techniques are not suitable for children who cannot read, however. To modify the methods, studies with children as young as 3 have used pictorial stimuli (Billingsley et al., 2002; Cycowicz, Friedman, Snodgrass, & Rothstein, 2000; Hayes & Hennessey, 1996; Parkin & Streete, 1988; Perez et al., 1998). For example, Billingsley et al. (2002) demonstrated that children and adults perform similarly on two implicit tests: both verbal (category generation) and pictorial (identification) tasks. Working only with pictures, Parkin and Streete (1988) showed common objects to children aged 3, 5, and 7 and later had the children identify distorted pictures that were slowly made clearer. In such a paradigm, priming is represented by faster naming of pictures that have been recently presented. In general, particularly when levels of explicit memory performance were made equivalent (e.g., by reducing the length of the study list for younger children), perceptual priming effects were equivalent across age.

Along the same lines, Drummey and Newcombe (1995) showed pictures to 3- and 5-year-old children as well as adults and later tested their ability to recognize the objects at various degrees of perceptual degradation. The degree of priming (higher masking level for identification for studied versus unstudied pictures) was fairly consistent for the three groups of participants. The participants were also asked for recognition judgments, and this measure of explicit memory showed expected age-related improvement. Similar results were reported by Hayes and Hennessey (1996) who also used implicit (picture identification) and explicit (recognition) memory tasks. In their study, children who were 4, 5, and 10 years of age studied a list of pictures and returned 48 hours later for a memory test. During the test, participants first attempted to identify pictures at varying degrees of blurriness. After identifying a picture, participants made a recognition judgment. There was no difference in the degree of priming among the 4-, 5-, and 10-year-olds. That is, the advantage of having studied a picture on subsequent identification tasks was similar for all three ages. However, recognition memory improved from age 4 to 10. Notably, in both studies, the implicit measure of picture identification was not correlated with the explicit measure of recognition; when there are such correlations, developmental invariance may not be found because explicit memory improvements may create what appear to be implicit memory effects (Parkin, 1998).

As we have seen, evidence that has been accumulating since the first edition of this book continues to suggest that perceptual priming is relatively stable throughout development. One exception is that Cycowicz et al. (2000) have reported evidence for developmental improvements between the ages of 5 and 9 on a picture identification task. However, the task was harder than that used in other studies—participants were under time pressure, and the investigators acknowledge that differences in retrieval speed may have caused the apparent improvement in priming. Further, the youngest children still demonstrated significant priming for the repeated objects.

Findings of equivalent priming rates across age have been taken as evidence that the implicit memory system is older evolutionarily than the explicit system (Reber, 1989) and that it is an independent memory system (e.g., Graf & Schacter, 1985). The idea that perceptual priming is equivalent across the lifespan has not, however, been tested at ages younger than 3 years or so. Although recent data suggest that priming effects exist in infancy (Myers, Clifton, & Clarkson, 1987; Perris, Myers, & Clifton, 1990; Rovee-Collier, 1997; Snyder, 2007; Webb & Nelson, 2001), their magnitude has not been cleanly compared to effects shown by older children, and in fact, such an enterprise is fraught with methodological and conceptual difficulty. For example, work by Clifton and colleagues has shown that infants maintain some memory of motor responses for actions completed in infancy for long periods of time. However, studies with older children and adults rely primarily on verbal or pictorial measures of priming. It is certainly possible that new and more sensitive techniques may show some early changes in the magnitude of perceptual priming. Given the current state of the evidence, it appears that Parkin was correct in his assessment in this book's first edition: perceptual priming effects are similar from the preschool years on, and remain stable throughout normal aging. However, true developmental invariance beginning with infancy has yet to be assessed.

Conceptual priming

Perhaps because the issue of developmental invariance of perceptual priming, at least from 3 years on, seems relatively settled, much recent research in implicit memory development has focused on the contrast between perceptual priming and conceptual priming. Conceptual priming often shows marked improvements with age. For example, although children of different ages show equivalent priming rates for recognizing a picture of a bear that has been presented earlier, young children are often less likely than older children to subsequently complete the stem b___ with the word "bear" (e.g., Komatsu et al., 1996). Similarly, when asked to list words that fit the category "vegetable" older children and adults are more likely to respond with words that were recently presented, relative to younger children (e.g., Billingsley et al., 2002; Perez et al., 1998). Whereas perceptual priming is based on the physical overlap between prior and subsequent presentation, conceptual priming is assumed to be based on the activation of related concepts in memory. Using the example of the category generation task mentioned above, a person who has recently been presented with the words "eggplant" and "corn," should be more likely to include these two items in a task asking for a list of vegetables.

The evidence for developmental invariance of conceptual priming has been mixed. Some work in conceptual priming suggests that it is age invariant while other work suggests developmental changes. A direct comparison between perceptual and conceptual priming was conducted by Perez et al. (1998), who also studied perceptual and conceptual memory of an explicit nature. In their study, preschool and elementary school age children as well as adults participated in four memory tests (perceptual explicit: pictorial cued recall; conceptual explicit: category cued recall; perceptual implicit: picture identification; conceptual implicit: category production). The advantage of the design of this study was having all four measures available for each participant. Perez et al. found that neither the perceptual nor the conceptual implicit tests showed improvement with age. Similarly, Billingsley et al. (2002) found equivalent priming across age with a category generation task. Unfortunately, the youngest group of participants was 8–10 years of age. It may be that younger children would have shown lower performance on the task. However, other researchers do report differences in conceptual priming during development. For example, Perruchet, Frazier, and Lautrey (1995) showed that children improved in measures of conceptual priming when the exemplars were atypical but not when they were typical members of the category. This finding has since been replicated several times (e.g., Mecklenbrauker, Hupbach, & Wippich, 2003; Murphy, McKone, & Slee, 2003).

Although these changes have been argued to be evidence for conceptual priming development, we would argue that perhaps this is an unfair test of priming. That is, it is not priming that is changing, but rather the concepts that these paradigms attempt to test. For example, it has been well documented that the categorical structure of concepts such as animals grows with age. Thus, preschool children may show conceptual and perceptual priming invariance, if tested with suitable materials. Further, we suspect that children may even be able to show *better* conceptual priming than adults when the stimuli are made to be relevant to their lives (e.g., for many toddlers today the popularity of *The Wiggles* probably makes Dorothy a better prime for "Dinosaur" than for "Wizard"). Although many of the papers that find age differences are willing to attribute them to differences in memory, we believe that it is unfair to consider these tasks assessments of conceptual priming capacity.

One line of research that is relevant to developmental changes in category structure is work by Sloutsky and colleagues (Fisher & Sloutsky, 2005; Sloutsky & Fisher, 2004). In this work, an incidental encoding task is used, in which many exemplars of the same animal are presented (e.g., pictures of cats). During a surprise recognition memory test, children outperform adults. That is, they are better able to recognize the pictures of cats that were presented in the study list relative to pictures of other cats that were not presented. The explanation for this pattern is that adults naturally categorize the pictures as "cats" while the children maintain more of the individual features of each item in memory. Contrasts of this kind suggest that changes in conceptual priming ability may be better understood by changes in categorization and semantic organization.

Our point about the role of knowledge in age differences in conceptual priming was also made by Murphy et al. (2003), who argue that conceptual priming reflects changes in knowledge accessibility. Murphy et al. also suggest that priming may be a way to test knowledge levels in children (p. 159). While this is true, an equally important question in studying implicit memory development should be the *capacity* for perceptual and conceptual priming across childhood. That is, is it possible to test conceptual priming in a way that is fair to both adults and children independent of pre-experimental knowledge? We advocate for attention to the basic *mechanisms* supporting priming as well as to the outcome of priming tasks. Given the vast age-related changes in semantic structures and general knowledge, future work aimed at investigating differences in conceptual priming needs to be first concerned with finding measures for which children of different ages have equivalent knowledge for the concept.

One way to achieve this goal would be to look at novel category learning. This would control the level of knowledge for each category for both children and adults. Additionally, this would allow for a paradigm that can test both conceptual and perceptual implicit memory in the same children while controlling exposure duration. To our knowledge, research has not yet been conducted with such a design. Rather, work with novel categories has focused on generalization and reasoning (e.g., Sloutsky, Kloos, & Fisher, 2007). That is, instead of testing for priming effects, these studies have focused on the way that young children learn about classification of novel items. These stimuli should prove very useful in research on priming as well.

Age differences in false memory

Increases in conceptual priming with age are not an unmixed blessing. In the false memory illusion (e.g., Deese, 1959; Roediger & McDermott, 1995; for a review see Gallo, 2006), related lists of words are presented that center around a topic (e.g., bed, rest, dream). The critical theme word that ties the list together is never presented (e.g., sleep). Adults are very likely to falsely recognize or to recall the word "sleep" on a memory test, but children do so to a much lesser degree (e.g., Holliday & Weekes, 2006; Howe, 2006). As in Sloutsky's work on categorization in young children, the false memory effect is an example of children outperforming adults on a memory task. It is assumed that one explanation for this pattern of results is that children do not have the semantic organization that would cause the word "sleep" to be more familiar after presentation of related words (e.g., Brainerd, Forrest, Karibian, & Reyna, 2006).

Another difference between children and adults in false memory may involve a shift from phonological to semantic processing across childhood. In work by Dewhurst and Robinson (2004), children (ages 5, 8, and 11) studied lists of categorized words and were then given a free recall task. The youngest children made significantly more phonological than semantic errors (e.g., were more likely to recall "head" after studying "bed" than to recall "sleep" after studying "bed," "rest," and "dream"). The pattern was the opposite in 11-year-olds: they were more likely to recall the semantically related words. Semantic and phonological errors were balanced for 8-year-olds. These results suggest that the way in which children are storing information shifts from a phonological to a semantic base over time.

Further evidence for links between categorization and false memory has been reported by Holliday and Weekes (2006). In these studies, participants receive lists of categorized words similar to those used in the DRM paradigm described above. Rather than taking a standard recognition test, in which the goal would be to respond "no" to a critical item such as "sleep," participants are asked to take recognition tests that ask them not only to respond positively to items that were presented during the study phase but also to items that are semantically related to those that were studied. Between the ages of 5 and 14 there are dramatic increases in the likelihood of responding positively to words that are highly related (e.g., sleep). This suggests that children are better able to determine how items are related to one other along semantic dimensions with increases in reasoning skills and better semantic knowledge. The finding also supports the possible reason for the equivalent category generation in children between the ages of 8 and 10 that was reported by Billingsley et al. (2002). That is, by middle childhood, there is a better semantic network from which to achieve conceptual priming.

The previous examples using the DRM paradigm highlight measures of memory change in which participants actively generate responses. Such situations are generally conceptualized as belonging to the class of explicit memory, although it is possible that related associates are automatically activated (Underwood & Reichardt, 1975). To date, only one study has looked at memory for critical lures using implicit memory techniques (Diliberto-Macaluso, 2005). In this work, fourth and fifth grade children performed stem completion tasks under either explicit or implicit instructions. That is, participants were either encouraged to complete the lists with words that had been presented earlier, or were simply told to list words that came to mind. The children showed high levels of priming for the critical words in both the explicit and implicit conditions. This result fits nicely with the results of Billingsley et al. (2002), who found intact conceptual priming in 8- to 10-year-old children, and suggests that by age 10, semantic associations are better formed. More work along these lines with younger children would be welcome.

The interaction of priming and explicit memory

Although implicit and explicit memory may be functionally distinct (e.g., Rauch et al., 1997; Grafton, Hazeltine, & Ivry, 1995), in adults there is interplay between the two types of memory. For example, participants may use the experience of priming as a clue for explicit memory decisions. That is, priming leads to an experience of processing fluency (e.g., Jacoby & Dallas, 1981; Murrell & Morton, 1974) in which things that have been experienced recently are perceived quickly and easily relative to novel items. Thus, ease of processing is a cue to recognition memory judgments. Adults readily apply this knowledge to memory decisions (e.g., Jacoby & Whitehouse, 1989; Rajaram, 1993; Unkelback, 2006; Westerman, 2001; Whittlesea & Williams, 1998). The timing of the acquisition of this ability in childhood has yet to be fully determined but a few studies have begun to examine the trajectory of the understanding of the way in which recognition memory works.

Drummey and Newcombe (1995) showed a series of pictures to 3- and 5-year-old children and an adult control group. Three months later, the children participated in both an implicit (identification) and an explicit (recognition memory) task. Pictures were gradually made less blurry until a child recognized the item. At that time, the item was put into full focus and a recognition judgment was made. As mentioned earlier, both the adults and the children showed a priming effect, identifying pictures that had been presented during the study phase at a blurrier state than novel pictures. Only adults, on the other hand, used the priming from the identification task to guide recognition decisions. That is, the children were not more likely to recognize the items they were able to detect at a higher level of blurriness as having been presented. This result suggests the link between perceptual fluency and recognition memory is not evident in children until at least after the age of 5.

More recent research by Guttentag and Dunn (2003) suggests that middle childhood is the time at which the link between fluency and recognition first appears. Similar to the procedure of Drummey and Newcombe (1995), participants (aged 4, 8, and adult) studied pictures during the encoding phase. During the recognition phase, the children had to identify the object as it came into focus. Some of these had been presented during the study phase and others had not. Again, children in both age groups (4 and 8 years of age) showed a priming effect. That is, pictures that had been seen recently could be identified at earlier levels of fragmentation (more degraded). However, only older children were more likely to recognize these items as having been presented earlier. That is, it isn't until later in development that children realize the relationship between implicit memory effects (priming) and prior occurrence. The time of this transition has yet to be fully identified, although it seems to occur between 5 and 8 years of age, and is an important area for future research.

Presumably, the understanding of the relationship between prior exposure and ease of later recognition is an example of metamemory, knowledge of the way that memory works. Middle childhood is the developmental period during which we observe increases in various kinds of metamemory knowledge, such as expectations for the memorability of a stimulus (e.g., Ghetti, 2003; Ghetti, Papini, & Angelini, 2006; see Chapter 7 in this volume). In these studies, participants are given lists of items that are from two categories. One category has many exemplars (e.g., pictures of 20 different animals such as horse, bear, bird), termed "low salience," and the other has few exemplars (e.g., pictures of a car, hammer, house, and shoe), termed "high salience." The idea behind these designations is that items from a category with many exemplars will be less distinct than items from a category with fewer exemplars. Thus, when making a judgment about what has been presented before, participants can use their knowledge about the makeup of the study list to guide their decisions. During a recognition test, participants are better at rejecting lure items from the high salience category (e.g., a screwdriver, which is related to the items on the high-salience list) relative to lure items from the low salience category (e.g., cat). Ghetti and colleagues attribute this ability to a metacognitive knowledge that the unique exemplars are more memorable and thus are easy to reject on the test phase. At the age of 7, participants are in a transition state where they sometimes apply this knowledge and other times do not. By the age of 10, participants perform identically to adults on the recognition test. Thus, a part of memory development is understanding the way that previous experience relates to subsequent memory performance. Although young children are affected by prior exposure, as measured by many implicit tasks, they are not able to use this knowledge to guide memory decisions until several years later.

Summary

In summary, we can draw three conclusions on the development of priming. First, there is consistent evidence for developmental invariance of perceptual priming from 3 years on. However, perceptual priming at younger ages has not been extensively studied, so it is difficult to be sure that the system is as early appearing and evolutionarily basic as has been claimed. Second, performance on conceptual priming tasks clearly changes with age. However, these age differences may derive from changes in conceptual knowledge or language development rather than from changes in the priming mechanism per se; studies using novel materials would be needed to assess this issue. In the case of false memory, perhaps ironically, increases in conceptual know-ledge lead to decreases in accuracy. Finally, development of the relationship between implicit and explicit memory seems to occur in middle childhood, although evidence on this issue is quite sparse.

SEQUENCE LEARNING AND STATISTICAL LANGUAGE LEARNING

There are several other types of implicit memory as well as priming. We have chosen one of these types, sequence learning, as an example of another type of implicit memory measure that should be reviewed for evidence for devel-opmental invariance or change. Statistical learning has received much recent attention in the area of language acquisition, but the paradigms used to investigate it have much in common with sequence learning tasks generally acknowledged to be implicit memory tasks.

Sequence learning refers to research in which the stimuli are presented in a pattern that is based on some sort of statistical regularity or a rule. Typically, these studies train participants on a sequence of events and then test the learning that has occurred. These studies are considered implicit memory tasks because participants typically claim to be ignorant of the rules or regularities guiding the training materials. However, they are able to react more quickly for items that are consistent rather than inconsistent with the training stimuli (e.g., Nissen & Bullemer, 1987; Nissen, Willingham, & Hartman, 1989).

The few developmental studies we have of this kind of sequence learning do show age-related improvement. Thomas et al. (2004; also see Thomas & Nelson, 2001) tested children aged 7–11 and adults using a visual target detection paradigm. Participants were instructed to respond as quickly as possible whenever a target appeared on the screen. During some blocks of trials, stimuli presentation was random. During other critical blocks of train-ing, patterns in the stimuli order were present. Learning these patterns allowed both children and adults to respond more quickly when the target appeared, despite being unable to report the pattern. Thomas et al. collected both behavioral (learning curves and response times) and neurological data (fMRI). Both children and adults learned the sequence during critical trials, but the magnitude and speed of improvement was larger for the adults. This suggests that children are capable of learning the sequence but do not do so as effectively as adults. Interestingly, the fMRI data showed both differences in the regions associated with learning in responses of the motor system. Thus, it may be that the age differences in speed of responding (a measure of priming) were partially a result of differences in motoric responses. However, there may be other causes as well because the effects were still significant after controlling for this variable.

As with conceptual priming, a challenge in examining sequence learning is to devise ways to level the playing field for children and adults by selecting tasks that are equally suitable for each group. One example of a task that is suitable for very young subjects is work by Saffran and colleagues (e.g., Saffran, Aslin, & Newport, 1996; Thiessen, Hill, & Saffran, 2005; Thiessen & Saffran, 2003; also see Johnson & Jusczyk, 2001), who have focused on sensitivity to statistical regularities as a mechanism for understanding the development of language. In these studies, infants listen to a sequence of nonsense syllables governed by underlying statistical regularities. Consider the sequence "bidakupadotigolabubidaku." In this example, "bi" is followed by "da", whereas "pa" is followed by "do." During testing, infants show a novelty preference for those sequences that violate the rules (e.g., "bido" or "pada"). That is, infants will pay attention longer or increase their rate of sucking on a pacifier when sequences are played that violate the rules established during the training phase relative to those that follow the established statistical regularities. This learning happens quickly, with only a few minutes of exposure to the training stimuli.

Such findings are widely viewed as giving insight into the nature of language learning, but they may also be a form of implicit memory (for a similar idea, see Perruchet & Pacton, 2006). Infants appear to be sensitive to the structure of the auditory sequences and use this information to notice violations from what has been previously presented. This form of learning seems to be present from early in development (e.g., 5 months). Further, the sensitivity to statistical regularity is not limited to the auditory domain. Work by Fiser and Aslin (2002) investigated visual sequence learning in infants. Like the work in the auditory modality, the results of these studies have shown that infants are able to detect regularities in their visual environment.

Why is there a difference between the auditory statistical learning data, which do not suggest changes in implicit memory, and the visual sequence learning data, which do suggest changes across childhood? One possible explanation involves a shift from auditory dominance to visual dominance in memory (Napolitano & Sloutsky, 2004; Robinson & Sloutsky, 2004; Sloutsky & Napolitano, 2003). Using a recognition memory paradigm, Sloutsky and colleagues have found that whereas adults show a bias in memory towards visual stimuli (pictures of common objects), children do not show this bias. Rather, they seem to be biased towards the auditory information that was presented. In these studies, participants are presented with pictures of objects that are paired with an auditory stimulus. Participants have to make judgments for later pairings as to whether the object occurred with a certain sound during the study phase. These pairings may contain correct combinations, repairing, or may include a novel portion for the object or the sound. Relative to adults, children around the age of 4 perform better at recognizing when an auditory portion is new. That is, they are less susceptible than adults to falsely recognizing an old object with a new sound. Although this bias seemed to be absent by ages 7–11 (the age groups tested in the 2004 Thomas et al. study), it may be that for a paradigm such as sequence learning, the auditory modality dominance is longer lasting (e.g., Conway & Christiansen, 2005).

A second possibility for the discrepancy between auditory and visual sequence learning with regard to developmental invariance may be the nature of the response. In work in statistical language learning, infants do not have to actively make a response. In contrast, the visual sequence learning study required participants to point to a screen as quickly as possible after the presentation of a target stimulus. Perhaps if a natural response such as eye movements was measured, there may be evidence that adults and children perform equally well. Similarly, if older children were asked to discriminate rule abiding and rule violating sequences in a verbal forced choice discrimination (a task more active and thus more akin to the sequence learning task), it may be that developmental differences would emerge.

In summary, the results of statistical learning studies and of sequence learning studies seem to be in contrast, with early competence in the former and late learning in the latter. However, the claim of developmental invariance requires more than early competence; we need in addition to be concerned with the magnitude of effects. To date, the statistical learning work has not focused much on the issue of comparative magnitude in adults and children. One recent study suggests possible developmental differences: Kam and Newport (2005) found that 5- to 7-year-old children were more likely than adults to regularize input containing inconsistent grammatical morphemes. A possible reason is that adults are striving to probability match their output with the input, while children who have less good sequence memory may simply adopt the predominant pattern. Obviously, however, artificial language learning is importantly different from other statistical learning studies, so it would be nice to have age-comparative studies that used more uniform methodologies and sampled ages more densely.

NEUROSCIENCE AND IMPLICIT MEMORY DEVELOPMENT

Advances in neuroscience have been invaluable in understanding the neuroanatomy of memory systems. The explosion of research using imaging techniques such as fMRI and the wider availability of less expensive measurements such as eye tracking and ERP readings has allowed concrete descriptions of the time course and nature of implicit and explicit memory (e.g., eye tracking: Richardson & Kirkham, 2004; ERP: Reynolds & Richards, 2005). For example, by comparing the fMRI scans of persons with known explicit but not implicit memory deficits (e.g., amnesics) to those with normal functioning in both areas, it may be determined what structures are necessary to support the two types of memory judgments. However, these advances in neuroscience also highlight some of the questions about the implicit/explicit distinction. That is, implicit memory covers several different types of memory judgments including priming, skill learning, and conditioning, and each is generally associated with its own brain structures: neocortex, striatum, and amygdala/cerebellum, respectively (e.g., Squire & Zola, 1996). Perhaps the best opportunity offered by advances in neuroscience is for the memory community to stop lumping all these tasks together and instead look at each category of implicit memory and learning as its own entity.

We have chosen here to discuss the neuroscience of perceptual priming, where given the evidence of developmental invariance at the behavioral level, there is also some evidence for relative equivalence of physiological response in perceptual priming tasks. In a study with older (9- and 10-year-old) participants, Newcombe and Fox (1994) showed photos of preschool classmates and novel children for an autobiographical recognition test. While performing the recognition test, skin conductance responses were measured. In general, participants were only slightly above chance in recognizing their classmates. However, they did show evidence of implicit memory as evidenced by changes in skin conductance to novel and familiar faces. Further, this response was similar regardless of recognition memory performance. That is, whether or not participants were correctly identifying a person as a part of their past, they showed evidence of recognizing the face. Recently, these results have been replicated with younger children (26–48 months) using a similar procedure (Stormark, 2004). In this study, children saw a slideshow containing photos of former nursery school classmates mixed with novel children. Similar to the results of Newcombe and Fox (1994), it was reported that children showed recognition differences in skin conductance and heart rate measures even when they did not do so for explicit recognition judgments. That is, even though participants were unable to recognize their former classmates verbally, they showed physiological signs of recognition.

Evidence of implicit memory through a physiological response has also been reported in infants. Webb and Nelson (2001) collected ERP data from 6-month-old infants while they were viewing a slideshow of upright and inverted faces. Some of these faces were repeated, allowing for an assessment of perceptual priming. Despite a relatively long list of items and a lag of up to 12 faces before repetition, infants still showed sensitivity to repeated stimuli. This is strong evidence for a very early emergence of repetition priming capability. Further, this study represents a gold standard in testing the idea of priming invariance. It demonstrates a method that is suitable across a wide age range and is not dependent on the development of other abilities such as language or semantic knowledge. Thus, we now have the opportunity to evaluate the invariance claim by determining whether adults have a similar magnitude of response as children and even as infants.

All of these studies (Newcombe & Fox, 1994; Stormark, 2004; Webb & Nelson, 2001) are consistent with the idea that perceptual priming is a stable and early developing form of memory (Reber, 1993), whereas explicit memory is prone to significant growth across childhood. These results also fit well with the behavioral data suggesting invariance in perceptual priming as was concluded by Parkin (1998) in the first edition of this book. However, just as implicit memory development work was started after explicit memory development research, the application of cognitive neuroscience techniques to development is still in its earliest stages. We expect that the next decade will show a sharp increase in this research as it becomes clearer what differences in implicit memory are reliable and will be useful for understanding memory development. For example, there is little if any work on several types of implicit memory in children including mere exposure effects, semantic priming, and savings.

BEYOND TYPICAL DEVELOPMENT: IMPLICIT MEMORY IN CLINICAL POPULATIONS

A final contrast between explicit and implicit memory development may be drawn from the results of studies examining memory differences in clinical populations. Although the initial contrast between implicit and explicit memory came from studies demonstrating amnesic patients who had intact implicit, but not explicit, memory (e.g., Graf & Schacter, 1985), recent work has looked at such a dissociation in other populations. In general, the findings both in adult and childhood disorders mirror those of patients with amnesia: a stability in implicit memory performance despite deficits in explicit memory performance (or a larger difference in explicit memory performance than in implicit memory performance). Intact implicit and damaged explicit memory finding has been demonstrated in a variety of populations including autism (Lopez & Leekam, 2003; Renner, Klinger, & Klinger, 2000), Tourette's syndrome (Channon, Pratt, & Robertson, 2003), schizophrenia (Clare, McKenna, Mortimer, & Baddeley, 1993), ADHD (Aloisi, McKone, & Heubeck, 2004), congenital and acquired brain disorder (Yeates & Enrile, 2005), and Down's syndrome (Carlesimo, Marotta, & Vicari, 1997; Vicari, 2001). Like many typical memory development studies, however, there appears to be a focus on implicit memory as defined by priming effects.

There are some exceptions to the focus on perceptual priming measures of implicit memory in clinical populations. One is work on children with Tourette's syndrome. Stebbings, Singh, Weiner, Wilson, Goetz, and Gabrieli (1995) reported that these children had a deficit in rotary pursuit, a type of skill learning. Similarly, work by Vicari (2001) showed that depending on which implicit task was measured, children with Williams syndrome either had spared implicit memory (when measured by a repetition priming task) or were impaired relative to controls (when measured with a skill learning task). This finding continues a theme in the literature that the use of a broad definition of implicit memory may lead to seemingly contradictory conclusions about memory development. Further, it hints to the problem of oversimplification of the simple implicit/explicit distinction especially now that it is clear that different anatomical structures map onto the different types of implicit memory. Additionally, showing these dissociations between different disorders and their impact on implicit memory measures highlights the importance of understanding the way in which different neurological impairments change the type of memory that is impacted. Although this may seem to be an obvious conclusion, that different disorders have different memory outcomes, it is not what would be predicted if implicit memory is viewed as a unitary phenomenon.

Future research should continue to pursue the questions of dissociations of implicit and explicit memory and whether or not the former changes significantly throughout life. If it is the case that perceptual priming is unchanged with development, the question of why such a system has emerged may be important. Is it because perceptual priming is an easier form of memory (e.g., Ratcliff, McKoon, & Verwoerd, 1989)? Or may it be that the current techniques of assessing it are not sophisticated enough to detect subtle changes? A second line of research should be concerned with the parameters of the retention of implicit memory. Perceptual priming effects have been shown to last for as long as 3 years (Lie & Newcombe, 1999) and motor skills may be retained as long or much longer (as was implied by our opening sentence). But are there different time frames for decay as a function of implicit memory divisions? Determining the shape of such functions may also shed light on the issue of developmental invariance for implicit memory. Given the increase in interest in implicit memory development in the past 10 years, we hope that some of these questions will soon be answered.

CONCLUSION

We wish to conclude the second edition of this chapter by noting the advances since the original edition. First, there does seem to be good evidence for developmental invariance in procedural (implicit) memory when it is strictly constrained to perceptual priming. Second, there is promising evidence that at least some kinds of implicit memory exist from the earliest points of life. However, the issue of possible variation in magnitude of effects still awaits full exploration. Finally, the last decade has seen many advances in the neuroanatomical underpinnings of implicit memory, and supports striking differences among the different kinds of implicit memory. We encourage the view that each form of learning and memory operates independently (for a different view, see Gupta & Cohen, 2002), and may have different developmental functions. Relative to Ebbinghaus's groundbreaking work on explicit memory, which has had over 100 years to be fully explained, the work on implicit memory has barely begun. Thus it is not surprising that there is still much work to be done in order to determine the child's path to fully functioning implicit memory.

REFERENCES

Aloisi, B. A., McKone, B., & Heubeck, B. G. (2004). Implicit and explicit memory performance in children with attention deficit/hyperactivity disorder. *British Journal of Developmental Psychology, 22,* 275–292.

Bauer, P. J. (2005). *Remembering the times of our lives: Memory in infancy and beyond.* Mahwah, NJ: Lawrence Erlbaum Associates, Inc.

Billingsley, R. L., Smith, M. L., & McAndrews, M. P. (2002). Developmental patterns in priming and familiarity in explicit recollection. *Journal of Experimental Child Psychology, 81,* 251–277.

Brainerd, C. J., Forrest, T. J., Karibian, D., & Reyna, V. F. (2006). Development of the false-memory illusion. *Developmental Psychology, 42,* 962–979.

Carlesimo, G. A., Marotta, L., & Vicari, S. (1997). Long-term memory in mental retardation: Evidence for a specific impairment in subjects with Down's syndrome. *Neuropsychologica, 35,* 71–79.

Channon, S., Pratt, P., & Robertson, M. M. (2003). Executive function, memory, and learning in Tourette's syndrome. *Neuropsychology, 17,* 247–254.

Clare, L., McKenna, P. J., Mortimer, A. M., & Baddeley, A. D. (1993). Memory in schizophrenia: What is impaired and what is preserved? *Neuropsychologica, 31,* 1225–1241.

Conway, C. M., & Christiansen, M. H. (2005). Modality-constrained statistical learning of tactile, visual, and auditory sequences. *Journal of Experimental Psychology: Learning, Memory, and Cognition, 31,* 24–39.

Cycowicz, Y. M., Freidman, D., Snodgrass, J. G., & Rothstein, M. (2000). A developmental trajectory in implicit memory is revealed by picture fragment completion. *Memory, 8,* 19–35.

Deese, J. (1959). On the prediction of occurrence of particular verbal intrusions in immediate recall. *Journal of Experimental Psychology, 58,* 17–22.

Dewhurst, S. A., & Robinson, C. A. (2004). Evidence for a shift from phonological to semantic associations. *Psychological Science, 15,* 782–785.

Diliberto-Macaluso, K. A. (2005). Priming and false memories from Deese–Roediger–McDermott lists on a fragment completion test with children. *American Journal of Psychology, 118,* 13–28.

Drummey, A. B., & Newcombe, N. (1995). Remembering versus knowing the past: Children's explicit and implicit memories for pictures. *Journal of Experimental Child Psychology, 59,* 549–565.

Fiser, J., & Aslin, R. N. (2002). Statistical learning of new visual feature combinations by infants. *Proceedings of the National Academy of Sciences, 99,* 15822–15826.

Fisher, A. V., & Sloutsky, V. M. (2005). When induction meets memory: Evidence for gradual transition from similarity-based to category-based induction. *Child Development, 76,* 583–597.

Fleischchman, D. A., Wilson, R. S., Gabrieli, J. D. E., Bienias, J. L., & Bennett, D. A. (2004). A longitudinal study of implicit and explicit memory in old persons. *Psychology and Aging, 19,* 617–625.

Gallo, D. A. (2006). *Associatitve illusions in memory: False memory research in DRM and related tasks.* Hove, UK: Psychology Press.

Ghetti, S. (2003). Memory for nonoccurrences: The role of metacognition. *Journal of Memory and Language, 48,* 722–739.

Ghetti, S., Papini, S., & Angelini, L. (2006). The development of the memorability-based strategy: Insights from a training study. *Journal of Experimental Psychology*, *94*, 206–228.

Graf, P., & Schacter, D. L. (1985). Implicit and explicit memory for new associates in normal and amnesic subjects. *Journal of Experimental Psychology: Learning, Memory and Cognition*, *11*, 501–518.

Grafton, S. T., Hazeltine, E., & Ivry, R. (1995). Functional mapping of sequence learning in normal humans. *Journal of Cognitive Neuroscience*, *7*, 497–510.

Gupta, P., & Cohen, N. J. (2002). Theoretical and computational analysis of skill learning, repetition priming, and procedural memory. *Psychological Review*, *109*, 401–448.

Guttentag, R., & Dunn, J. (2003). Judgments of remembering: The revelation effect in children and adults. *Journal of Experimental Child Psychology*, *86*, 153–167.

Hayes, B. K., & Hennessey, R. (1996). The nature and development of nonverbal implicit memory. *Journal of Experimental Child Psychology*, *63*, 22–43.

Holliday, R. E., & Weekes, B. S. (2006). Dissociated developmental trajectories for semantic and phonological false memories. *Memory*, *14*, 624–636.

Howe, M. L. (2006). Developmentally invariant dissociations in children's true and false memories: Not all relatedness is created equal. *Child Development*, *77*, 1112–1123.

Jacoby, L. L., & Dallas, M. (1981). On the relationship between autobiographical memory and perceptual learning. *Journal of Experimental Psychology: General*, *110*, 306–340.

Jacoby, L. L., & Whitehouse, K. (1989). An illusion of memory: False recognition influenced by unconscious perception. *Journal of Experimental Psychology: General*, *118*, 126–135.

Johnson, E. K., & Jusczyk, P. W. (2001). Word segmentation by 8-month-olds: When speech cues count more than statistics. *Journal of Memory and Language*, *44*, 548–567.

Kail, R. V. (1990). *The development of memory in children* (3rd ed.). New York: Freeman.

Kam, C. L. H. & Newport, E. L. (2005). Regularizing unpredictable variation: The roles of adult and child learners in language formation and change. *Language Learning and Development*, *1*, 151–195.

Keen, R. (2003). Representation of objects and events: Why do infants look so smart and toddlers look so dumb? *Current Directions in Psychological Science*, *12*, 79–83.

Komatsu, S., Naito, M., & Fuke, T. (1996). Age-related and intelligence-related differences in implicit memory: Effects of generation on a word-fragment completion test. *Journal of Experimental Child Psychology*, *62*, 151–172.

Lie, E., & Newcombe, N. S. (1999). Elementary school children's explicit and implicit memory for faces of preschool classmates. *Developmental Psychology*, *35*, 102–112.

Lopez, B., & Leekam, S. R. (2003). Do children with autism fail to process information in context? *Journal of Child Psychology and Psychiatry*, *44*, 285–300.

Mecklenbrauker, S., Hupbach, A., & Wippich, W. (2003). Age-related improvements in a conceptual implicit memory test. *Memory and Cognition*, *31*, 1208–1217.

Murphy, K., McKone, E., & Slee, J. (2003). Dissociations between implicit and explicit memory in children: The role of strategic processing and the knowledge base. *Journal of Experimental Child Psychology*, *84*, 124–165.

Murrell, G. A., & Morton, J. (1974). Word recognition and morphemic structure. *Journal of Experimental Psychology*, *102*, 963–968.

Myers, N. A., Clifton, R. K., & Clarkson, M. G. (1987). When they were very young: Almost-threes remember two years ago. *Infant Behavior and Development, 10*, 123–132.

Napolitano, A. C., & Sloutsky, V. M. (2004). Is a picture worth a thousand words? Part II: The flexible nature of modality dominance in young children. *Child Development, 75*(6), 1850–1870.

Newcombe, N., & Fox, N. A. (1994). Infantile amnesia: Through a glass darkly. *Child Development, 65*, 31–40.

Nissen, M. J., & Bullemer, P. (1987). Attentional requirements of learning: Evidence from performance measures. *Cognitive Psychology, 19*, 1–32.

Nissen, M. J., Willingham, D., & Hartman, M. (1989). Explicit and implicit remembering: When is learning preserved in amnesia. *Neuropsychologia, 27*, 341–352.

Oakes, L. M., & Bauer, P. J. (Eds.) (2007). *Short- and long-term memory in infancy and early childhood*. New York: Oxford University Press.

Parkin, A. J. (1998). The development of procedural and declarative memory. In N. Cowan (Ed.), *The development of memory in childhood* (pp. 113–137). Hove, UK: Psychology Press.

Parkin, A. J., & Streete, S. (1988). Implicit and explicit memory in young children and adults. *British Journal of Psychology, 79*, 361–369.

Perez, L. A., Peynircioglu, Z. F., & Blaxton, T. A. (1998). Developmental differences in implicit and explicit memory performance. *Journal of Experimental Child Psychology, 70*, 167–185.

Perris, E. E., Myers, N. A., & Clifton, R. K. (1990). Long-term memory for a single infancy experience. *Child Development, 61*, 1796–1807.

Perruchet, P., Frazier, N., & Lautrey, J. (1995). Conceptual implicit memory: A developmental study. *Psychological Research, 57*, 220–228.

Perruchet, P., & Pacton, S. (2006). Implicit learning and statistical learning: One phenomenon, two approaches. *Trends in Cognitive Sciences, 10*, 233–238.

Rajaram, S. (1993). Remembering and knowing: Two means of access to the personal past. *Memory and Cognition, 21*, 89–102.

Ratcliff, R., McKoon, G., & Verwoerd, M. (1989). A bias interpretation of facilitation in perceptual identification. *Journal of Experimental Psychology: Learning, Memory, and Cognition, 15*, 378–387.

Rauch, S. L., Whaler, P. J., Savage, C. R., Curran, T., Kendrick, A., Brown, H. D., et al. (1997). Striatal recruitment during an implicit sequence learning task as measured by functional magnetic resonance imaging. *Human Brain Mapping, 5*, 124–132.

Reber, A. S. (1989). Implicit learning and tacit knowledge. *Journal of Experimental Psychology: General, 118*, 219–235.

Reber, A. S. (1993). *Implicit learning and tacit knowledge: An essay on the cognitive unconscious*. New York: Oxford University Press

Renner, P., Klinger, L. G., & Klinger, M. R. (2000). Implicit and explicit memory in autism: Is autism an amnesic disorder? *Journal of Autism and Developmental Disorders, 30*, 3–14.

Reynolds, G. D., & Richards, J. E. (2005). Familiarization, attention, and recognition memory in infancy: An event-related potential and cortical source localization study. *Developmental Psychology, 41*, 598–615.

Richardson, D. C., & Kirkham, N. Z. (2004). Multimodal events and moving locations: Eye movements of adults and 6-month-olds reveal dynamic spatial indexing. *Journal of Experimental Psychology: General, 133*, 46–62.

Richardson-Klavehn, A., & Bjork, R. A. (1988). Measures of memory. *Annual Review of Psychology, 39*, 475–543.

Robinson, V. M., & Sloutsky, V. M. (2004). Auditory dominance and its change in the course of development. *Child Development, 75*, 1387–1401.

Roediger, H. L., & Blaxton, T. A. (1987). Effects of varying modality, surface features, and retention interval on priming in word-fragment completion. *Memory and Cognition, 15*, 379–388.

Roediger, H. L., & McDermott, K. B. (1993). Implicit memory in normal human subjects. In F. Boller & J. Grafman (Eds.), *Handbook of neuropsychology* (Vol. 8, pp. 63–131). Amsterdam: Elsevier.

Roediger, H. M., & McDermott, K. B. (1995). Creating false memories: Remembering words not presented in lists. *Journal of Experimental Psychology: Learning, Memory and Cognition, 21*, 803–814.

Rovee-Collier, C. (1997). Dissociations in infant memory: Rethinking the development of implicit and explicit memory. *Psychological Review, 104*, 467–498.

Rovee-Collier, C., Hayne, H., & Colombo, M. (2002). *The development of implicit and explicit memory*. Philadelphia: John Benjamin.

Saffran, J. R., Aslin, R. N., & Newport, E. L. (1996). Statistical learning by 8-month-old infants. *Science, 5294*, 1926–1928.

Schacter, D. L. (1987). Implicit memory: History and current status. *Journal of Experimental Psychology: Learning, Memory, and Cognition, 13*, 501–518.

Sloutsky, V. M., & Fisher, A. V. (2004). When development and learning decrease memory: Evidence against category-based induction in children. *Psychological Science, 15*, 553–558.

Sloutsky, V. M., Kloos, H., & Fisher, A. V. (2007). When looks are everything: Appearance similarity versus kind information in early induction. *Psychological Science, 18*, 179–185.

Sloutsky, V. M., & Napolitano, A. C. (2003). Is a picture worth a thousand words? Preference for auditory modality in young children. *Child Development, 74*, 822–833.

Snyder, K. (2007). Infant memory development—New questions, new answers. In L. M. Oakes & P. J. Bauer (Eds.), *Short- and long-term memory in infancy and childhood: Taking the first steps toward remembering*. Oxford: Oxford University Press.

Squire, L. R., & Zola, S. M. (1996). Structure and function of declarative and non-declarative memory systems. *Proceedings of the National Academy of Sciences, 93*, 13515–13522.

Stebbings, G. T., Singh, J., Weiner, J., Wilson, R. S., Goetz, C. G., & Gabrieli, J. D. E. (1995). Selective impairments of memory functioning in undedicated adults with Gilles de la Tourette's syndrome. *Neuropsychology, 9*, 329–337.

Stormark, K. M. (2004). Skin conductance and heart-rate responses as indices of covert face recognition in preschool children. *Infant and Child Development, 13*, 422–433.

Thiessen, E. D., Hill, E. A., & Saffran, J. R. (2005). Infant-directed speech facilitates word segmentation. *Infancy, 7*, 53–71.

Thiessen, E. D., & Saffran, J. R. (2003). When cues collide: Use of stress and statistical cues to word boundaries by 7- to 9-month-old infants. *Developmental Psychology, 39*, 706–716.

Thomas, K. M., Hunt, R. H., Vizueta, N., Sommer, T., Durston, S., Yang, Y., et al. (2004). Evidence of developmental differences in implicit sequence learning: An fMRI study of children and adults. *Journal of Cognitive Neuroscience, 16,* 1339–1351.

Thomas, K. M., & Nelson, C. A. (2001). Serial reaction time learning in preschool- and school-age children. *Journal of Experimental Child Psychology, 79,* 364–387.

Toth, J. P., & Hunt, R. R. (1999). Not one versus many, but zero versus any: Structure and function in the context of the multiple memory systems debate. In J. K. Foster & M. Jelicic (Eds.), *Memory: Systems, process or function? Debates in psychology* (pp. 232–272). New York: Oxford University Press.

Tulving, E. (2002). Episodic memory: From mind to brain. *Annual Review of Psychology, 53,* 1–25.

Underwood, B. J., & Reichardt, C. S. (1975). Implicit associational responses produced by words in pairs of unrelated words. *Memory and Cognition, 3,* 405–408.

Unkelback, C. (2006). The learned interpretation of cognitive fluency. *Pyschological Science, 17,* 339–345.

Vicari, S. (2001). Implicit versus explicit memory function in children with Down and Williams syndrome. *Down Syndrome Research and Practice, 7,* 35–40.

Webb, S. J., & Nelson, C. A. (2001). Perceptual priming of upright and inverted faces in children and adults. *Journal of Experimental Child Psychology, 79,* 1–22.

Westerman, D. L. (2001). The role of familiarity in item recognition, associative recognition, and plurality recognition on self-paced and speeded tests. *Journal of Experimental Psychology: Learning, Memory, and Cognition, 27,* 723–732.

Whittlesea, B. W. A., & Williams, L. D. (1998). Why do strangers feel familiar, but friends don't? A discrepancy-attribution account of feelings of familiarity. *Acta Psychologica, 98,* 141–165.

Yeates, K. O., & Enrile, B. G. (2005). Implicit and explicit memory in children with congenital and acquired brain disorder. *Neuropsychology, 19,* 618–628.

6 The cognitive neuroscience of the development of memory

Patricia J. Bauer
Duke University, North Carolina, USA

In his *Confessions*, Saint Augustine marveled at everyday mnemonic process, likening memory to a "spacious palace" in which is stored "the treasures of innumerable images, brought into it from things of all sorts perceived by the senses . . . for thought to recall" (Saint Augustine, ~401 C.E.). In the two millennia since Saint Augustine wrote these words our explanations of memory and how it functions have moved beyond the poetic metaphor of a "spacious palace" to the more concrete realities of modern psychological and neural sciences. However, what has not changed is the nature of the phenomenon we are attempting to explain. In his time, Saint Augustine wondered how one "discern(s) the breath of lilies from violets, though smelling nothing . . . but remembering only." Present day psychologists and neuroscientists are asking essentially the same question as we ponder how the roughly 1500 grams (3½ pounds) of tissue that sits in the bony case atop our shoulders manages to vividly re-create—and even allows us to re-live—events and experiences from the past. The modern day developmental scientist further questions how the material substrate and the processes it subserves develops from infancy through childhood.

The purpose of this chapter is to discuss the development of memory in terms of the neural systems and basic mnemonic processes that permit memories to be formed, retained, and later retrieved. This level of analysis is but one of many that ultimately will be required to explain how memory works and how it develops. In addition to the levels of analysis offered in this chapter, a satisfying solution to the puzzle of memory also entails consideration of "higher level" influences such as the social forces that shape what children come to view as important to remember, and even how they express their memories. These far-reaching, complementary, perspectives are necessary because memory is a complex, multidimensional process. Indeed, a guiding assumption of the analysis provided in this chapter is that memory is not even a unitary construct. Rather, there are different types of memory that involve different processes and that are subserved by different neural substrates. Because the most definitive work uniting memory behavior (function) with its underlying neural substrate (structure) has been conducted with adult humans and nonhuman animals, the analysis begins at the end of development (so to speak) rather than at the beginning. After considering the argument for multiple memory systems and the progress that has been made in identifying structure–function relations in adults, the discussion moves to consideration of the emergence of a developmental cognitive neuroscience perspective in development, followed by analysis of structure–function relations in infancy and childhood.

MULTIPLE MEMORY SYSTEMS

The chapter headings in this volume make it clear that there is not one single form or type of memory. Typical divisions of memory are based on the type of content processed (e.g., names, dates, facts, and events or motor procedures and perceptual skills); the rules of operation (conscious access or not); the function served (e.g., rapid vs. gradual learning); and of critical importance to the goals of this chapter, the neural substrates involved (e.g., medial-temporal structures vs. deep nuclei of the brain stem) and their ontogenetic time courses (i.e., early vs. later in development; for discussion, see Schacter & Tulving, 1994; Schacter, Wagner, & Buckner, 2000). Application of these criteria results in identification of no fewer than five memory systems: perceptual representation (a collection of domain-specific stores for the form and structure of words and objects; implicated in perceptual priming), procedural (the products of motor learning), working (specialized for the short-term maintenance and manipulation of information), semantic (general knowledge about the world), and episodic (specific personal experiences located in particular place and time) memory.

Perhaps because, traditionally, they were considered especially late to emerge (see Bauer, 2006b), in the literature on the developmental cognitive neuroscience of memory, most of the attention has been focused on semantic and in particular, episodic, memory. Both of these types of memory fall under the larger rubric of *explicit* or *declarative* memory (e.g., Squire, 1992): memories of names, dates, places, and events, to which one has conscious access. Semantic and episodic memories differ primarily in the type of content processed and the form of consciousness or awareness associated with their retrieval. Specifically, semantic memory is devoted to timeless, placeless world knowledge, retrieval of which is accompanied by *noetic* (knowing) awareness. In contrast, episodic memory is devoted to specific events that are located in a particular place and time, retrieval of which is accompanied by *autonoetic* or self-knowing awareness: a mental re-experience of a previous moment in the past (Wheeler, 2000). Both because some aspect of semantic or episodic memory is the subject of most of the chapters in this volume, and because the development of the neural subtrate subserving these sub-types of declarative memory has received the most research attention, relations between neural structures and mnemonic behavior in the domain of declarative memory are the focus of this chapter.

THE NEURAL BASES OF DECLARATIVE MEMORY IN THE ADULT

The major aim of this chapter is to describe and explain developmental changes in declarative memory by relating age-related changes in the brain with age-related changes in memory. That agenda is furthered by examination of the neural bases of declarative memory in adults: it is in the adult literature that the network of structures that supports explicit recognition and recall is best articlated, owing in part to the long history of the search.

Early investigations of relations between structure and function

A well-known 19th-century approach to linking brain and behavior (including memory) was to examine the correlation between variations in the surface of the skull and profiles of individual differences in abilities (Gall, 1835). The logic of this science of *phrenology* was that distinct psychological functions were localized within the cerebral cortex. Functions that were especially well developed were thought to produce bumps or bulges on the skull. The 20th century brought a different approach to the search for structure–function relations, one exemplified by Kleist's (1934) detailed behavioral examinations of First World War veterans injured by gunshots or shrapnel. Kleist observed that there were systematic relations between the sites of the head wounds the veterans had sustained and the type of impairment they experienced. Kleist's studies supported speculation that different parts of the brain subserve different cognitive functions, including different types of memory.

In the domain of memory, perhaps the single most significant case study of relations between brain and behavior has been patient H. M. In 1953, 27-year-old Henry M. underwent bilateral removal of large portions of his temporal lobes as a treatment for an intractable seizure disorder (Scoville & Milner, 1957). Although the procedure proved a successful treatment for H. M.'s seizures, it produced a devastating impairment in his ability to form new declarative memories (Milner, Corkin, & Teuber, 1968). Critical from the standpoint of the agenda of relating specific neural structures to specific cognitive functions, H. M.'s working memory is intact, as are his perceptual representation (he shows normal priming) and procedural (he shows normal rates of learning of new motor skills, for example) memory systems.

The pattern of deficit and sparing in patient H. M. provided suggestive evidence of a link between medial-temporal lobe structures—and the hippocampus in particular—and the formation of new long-term declarative memories. The link was confirmed by subsequent research with animal models in which the relation could be tested more directly (Mishkin, Spiegler, Saunders, & Malamut, 1982; Squire & Zola-Morgan, 1983). The central role of the hippocampus in memory formation now is supported not only by patient studies and animal models but numerous neuroimaging studies as well (e.g., functional magnetic resonance imaging—fMRI, positron emission tomography—PET; for a review, see Nyberg & Cabeza, 2000). Subsequent studies also have made clear that the hippocampus is necessary, but not sufficient, for the formation, maintenance, and subsequent retrieval of declarative memories. Rather, an entire network of structures is involved.

The temporal–cortical declarative memory network

In adult humans, the formation of new declarative memories depends on a neural network that in addition to the hippocampus includes the medial-emporal cortices as well as neocortical structures (e.g., Eichenbaum & Cohen, 2001; Kandel & Squire, 2000; Zola & Squire, 2000). The network is schematically represented in Figure 6.1. It is best illustrated by a review of each step in the process by which memories are formed and subsequently retrieved.

Encoding

Just as Saint Augustine described, encoding of experience into a memory trace begins with "things of all sorts perceived by the senses." The work of perception is carried out by multiple brain regions distributed across the cortex. For instance, tactile information from the skin and proprioceptive inputs from the muscles and joints register in the primary somatosensory cortex (see Figure 6.2). At the same time, form, color, and motion information registers in the primary visual cortex, and the frequency of associated

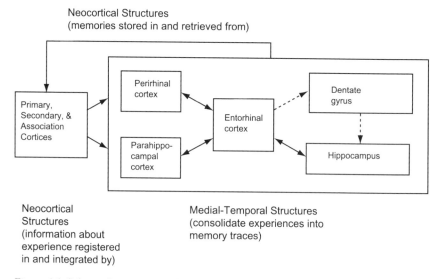

Figure 6.1 Schematic representation of the temporal–cortical declarative memory network. Based on Zola and Squire (2000, Figure 30.1, p. 487).

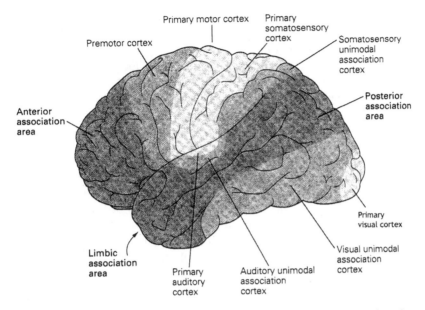

Primary motor cortex
Primary somatosensory cortex
Premotor cortex
Somatosensory unimodal association cortex
Posterior association area
Anterior association area
Primary visual cortex
Limbic association area
Primary auditory cortex
Auditory unimodal association cortex
Visual unimodal association cortex

Figure 6.2 Schematic representation of the association cortices of the brain: Figure 19.1 (p. 350) of Kandel, Schwartz, and Jessell (2000). *Principles of neural science* (4th ed.). Used with permission of McGraw Hill.

sound waves registers in the primary auditory cortex. The primary sensory cortices project the information to unimodal sensory association areas where it is integrated into whole percepts of what objects and events feel like, look like, and sound like, respectively. Unimodal sensory association areas in turn project to polymodal (a.k.a. multimodal) posterior, anterior, and limbic association areas where inputs from the different sense modalities are integrated.

Over the short term (i.e., in the order of 30 seconds), information about a stimulus is maintained in the association areas. For example, electro-physiological examinations have revealed neurons in anterior (prefrontal) association cortex that fire during the delay period between the hiding of a stimulus and a monkey's response to the stimulus (e.g., Fuster & Alexander, 1971). If during the delay the neurons stop firing, the animal "forgets" the location of the stimulus (for reviews, see Eichenbaum & Cohen, 2001; Fuster, 1997). Lesions studies also implicate prefrontal cortex in encoding. They make it difficult for information to be maintained for more than a few seconds (for a review, see Diamond, 2001), and are associated with deficits in memory for temporal order, in particular (e.g., Milner & Petrides, 1984; Petrides, 1995). Neuroimaging studies of intact adults also provide converging evidence: they reliably detect activations in the left prefrontal cortex during memory encoding tasks (for a review, see Schacter et al., 2000).

Consolidation and storage

For information to endure beyond the sensory experience of it, it must undergo additional processing. The processing that turns immediate perceptual experience into an enduring memory trace involves integration and stabilization of the inputs from the different cortical regions. These tasks, collectively termed *consolidation*, are thought to be performed by medial-temporal structures (including the hippocampus), in concert with cortical areas. Whereas consolidation processes begin on registration of a stimulus, they continue for hours, days, months, and even years.

Consolidation originally was hypothesized by Müller and Pilzecker (1900) to explain retroactive interference in list learning experiments. In such experiments, in one condition, subjects studied one list of words, and minutes later they studied a second list, followed by tests of both lists. In another condition, Lists 1 and 2 were separated by seconds rather than minutes. When the study periods were minutes apart, recall of both lists was high. However, when the study periods were spaced closely in time, recall of List 1 was impaired relative to recall of List 2. Müller and Pilzecker suggested that in short-spacing conditions, List 2 retroactively interfered with List 1 because at the time the second list was learned, memory for the first list had not yet consolidated.

Additional evidence that consolidation takes time and that until it is consolidated, newly learned material is vulnerable to forgetting, is apparent in the phenomenon of temporally graded retrograde amnesia. In a pattern precisely the opposite of normal forgetting, memory for recently learned material is impaired, relative to memory for information learned long ago. Temporally graded retrograde amnesia is well documented in humans with lesions and disease of medial-temporal structures (e.g., Brown, 2002), and can be produced in animal models (e.g., Kim & Fanselow, 1992). For example, when they are induced hours to days after training on a hippocampally dependent task (i.e., early in the consolidation period), lesions to the hippocampus produce impaired memory performance. In contrast, when the same lesions are induced 30 days after training (i.e., when learning is more fully consolidated), performance is unimpaired (Takehara, Kawahara, & Kirino, 2003; for reviews, see Eichenbaum & Cohen, 2001; Squire & Alvarez, 1995).

As implied by the association between impairments in consolidation and medial-temporal lobe damage, it is thought that the work of binding a distributed neocortical representation into a single memory trace is performed by medial-temporal structures, including the hippocampus, para-hippocampus, and entorhinal and perirhinal cortices (e.g., Eichenbaum & Cohen, 2001; Kandel & Squire, 2000; Zola & Squire, 2000). Cortical association areas also assume some of the burden of the effort, by associating new learning with the products of earlier experience already stored in the cortex. Specifically, in the early phases of consolidation, information from cortical areas is processed in the hippocampus and other medial-temporal structures.

As illustrated in the schematic diagram of the input and output pathways of the hippocampal formation (see Figure 6.1), the inputs from the unimodal and polymodal cortical association areas project to the perirhinal and parahippocampal cortices in the medial-temporal lobes. These cortices in turn project the information to the entorhinal cortex, which in turn projects to the hippocampus. Processing in these medial-temporal structures creates linkages among the separate elements of the distributed cortical representation, allowing its trace to persist beyond the physical presence of the stimulus.

The means by which the medial-temporal lobe structures create an enduring memory representation is a sort of "neural rehearsal." Within the perirhinal and parahippocampal cortices the patterns of activation associated with experience are maintained through repeated neuronal firing. At the same time, the hippocampus engages in the elaborative processing that encodes conjunctions and relations among the current stimuli (i.e., those being maintained in the medial-temporal cortices), and between current stimuli and those processed previously (i.e., representations of stimuli and events already in long-term neocortical stores). As a result of hippocampal processing, the individual elements of experience become bound into a single event or episode and current episodes are associated with previous episodes (for extended discussion, see Eichenbaum & Cohen, 2001). Eventually, intracortical connections among the different elements of the experience are strengthened to the point that medial-temporal lobe activity is no longer required to maintain the representation. At this point, the representation may be said to be *stored*.

Retrieval

The *raison d'être* for encoding, consolidation, and storage of declarative memories is so that they can be retrieved at a later time. Behavioral and neuroimaging data implicate the prefrontal cortex in the retrieval process. Damage to the prefrontal cortex disrupts retrieval of both pre- and post-morbidly experienced facts and episodes. Deficits are especially apparent in free recall (as opposed to recognition), and for information about the temporal order of events and experiences, and the specific source of experience (i.e., when and where a remembered item was encountered). Imaging studies reveal high levels of activation in the prefrontal cortex during retrieval of memories from long-term stores (for reviews, see Maguire, 2001; Nyberg, 1998).

EMERGENCE OF A DEVELOPMENTAL COGNITIVE NEUROSCIENCE OF DECLARATIVE MEMORY

In contrast to the rich database that has accrued on the neural foundations of declarative memory in adults, in the developmental literature the search is in its infancy. Reasons for the slower rate of progress in the developmental literature, and how they are being addressed, are discussed in turn.

Challenges in the search for relations between structure and function in development

The relative paucity of data on the neural foundations of declarative memory in development is not for lack of research on memory in children. Interest in differences in memory between children and adults dates back to Ebbinghaus (1897), the "father" of the experimental approach to the study of memory in adults. Throughout the 20th century children were often subjects of studies, though the research did not always have a developmental focus (e.g., research in the North American verbal learning tradition that dominated during the middle of the 20th century was decidedly nondevelopmental).

Until late in the 20th century, what was not represented in the literature was research on the neural bases of memory in development. There were both definitional and methodological reasons for the lack of attention. As noted earlier, one of the criteria by which memory systems are differentiated is conscious access to the products of experience. This feature is difficult to evaluate in preverbal infants (see arguments by Nelson, 1997; Rovee-Collier, 1997). Nor has it been easy to investigate links between neural structures and mnemonic functions. Fortunately, human infants and children rarely present with the traumas and diseases that were the source of early hypotheses regarding the neural bases of memory in adults. Those who do suffer neurological insults early in life often have more global lesions, making identification of the role played by specific neural structures difficult to establish. Moreover, animal models tend to be of the mature as opposed to the developing human. Finally, many of the neuroimaging techniques used with adults have been difficult to implement with, or are not appropriate for, infants and young children. For example, MRI and fMRI require that participants remain motionless for long periods of time while being exposed to strong magnetic fields. PET requires injection of radioactive substances, making it unsuitable for use with normally developing infants and young children.

Addressing the challenges

In the late 20th century a number of the difficulties posed by research on the neural base of declarative memory in development were overcome. Although it is a challenge to consider how to apply to preverbal children the criteria of consciousness, the construct does not *require* that it be expressed verbally. Indeed, some scholars have specifically noted that conscious awareness may be expressed through nonverbal behavior (e.g., Köhler & Moscovitch, 1997). Empirically, the concern about application of the criterion of consciousness has been addressed by designing tasks that produce behaviors that look quite different from those exhibited in nondeclarative memory paradigms—such as verbal access to the products of learning. One such task that is increasingly commonly used in research on early developments in declarative memory is elicited or deferred imitation, in which an adult uses props to produce specific actions or sequences of action that the infant or child is encouraged to imitate either immediately (elicited imitation), after a delay (deferred imitation), or both. The products of learning in the task are accessible to language once it is acquired (e.g., for discussion, see Cheatham & Bauer, 2005). Moreover, adults with medial-temporal lobe amnesia are impaired on the task (McDonough, Mandler, McKee, & Squire, 1995; for discussion, see Bauer, 2005b, 2006b).

The methodological challenges of linking age-related changes in memory behavior to developmental changes in the neural substrates of memory are also being addressed. More information about the anatomy and physiology of the developing brain has accrued from increased use of animal models of development (e.g., Benes, 2001) and examination of prenatal and postnatal brains brought to autopsy (e.g., Seress, 2001). High-resolution anatomical images of developmental changes in both gray matter (Sowell, Thompson, Tessner, & Toga, 2001b) and white matter tracts (via diffusion tensor imaging, or DTI: Klingberg, Vaidya, Gabrieli, Moseley, & Hedehus, 1999) are increasingly available. Although the lesion method is not in such wide use in developmental as in adult populations, there is an increasing number of studies in which memory abilities have been examined in samples of children with known (e.g., Adlam, Vargha-Khadem, Mishkin, & de Haan, 2005; Gadian, Aicardi, Watkins, Porter, Mishkin, & Vargha-Khadem, 2000) or suspected (DeBoer, Wewerka, Bauer, Georgieff, & Nelson, 2005) hippocampal lesions. There are also more studies of relations between brain and behavior in developing nonhuman primates (e.g., for a review, see Bachevalier, 2001). Finally, there is increased use of noninvasive neuroimaging techniques such as event-related potentials (ERPs) that allow researchers insights into the timing of neural events in even young infants (for discussion, see Nelson & Monk, 2001). When high-density electrode arrays (e.g., 128 channels) are used, researchers can draw conclusions about the sources of scalp-recorded potentials (e.g., Richards, 2005). As well, reseachers are overcoming the challenges of MR imaging by training children to remain motionless and designing testing protocols that require a minimum amount of time in the scanner. As a result, the number of MR-based studies with children is increasing, and the ages of the participants are decreasing (to as young as 4 years of age: Cantlon, Brannon, Carter, & Pelphrey, 2006).

Although all of the approaches to studying structure–function relations in development have challenges associated with them, with each new piece of the puzzle, the picture has sharpened. Somewhat paradoxically, it is sharper in the infancy literature, relative to the literature with older children. A likely reason is that early in the short history of developmental cognitive neuroscience, there was almost single-minded focus on neural developments in the first 3 years of life, with neglect of later developments (for discussion, see Nelson & Bloom, 1997). Both because of the resulting disparity in the states of the literatures, and because of necessary differences in the methods used to investigate memory behavior itself (with infants, nonverbal methods are used, whereas verbal methods are used with older children), structure–function relations in infancy are discussed separately from those in childhood.

RELATIONS BETWEEN STRUCTURE AND FUNCTION IN INFANCY

Discussion of relations between developmental changes in neural structures and in memonic function in infancy requires an outline of age-related changes in each domain, followed by evaluation of their alignment. Each is discussed in turn. However, because developmental changes in memory behavior in infancy are the subject of other chapters in this volume (see Chapters 2 and 3 by Rovee-Collier and Cuevas, and Hayne and Simcock), proportionally less time is spent on description of behavioral change.

Development of the declarative memory network in infancy

As described earlier, declarative memory depends on a distributed network that includes medial-temporal and cortical structures, as well as connections between them. What is known about developments in each of the components of the network is summarized below (the summary is drawn from Bauer, 2007).

Medial-temporal components

In the human, there are indicators that many of the medial-temporal lobe components of the declarative memory system develop early. First, the neurons in the entorhinal cortex, the cell fields of the hippocampus, and the subiculum, are formed in the first half of gestation and virtually all have migrated prenatally (for discussion, see Seress, 2001). By the 24th gestational week, the cytoarchitecture (i.e., the size, shape, and organization of the cells) of most of the hippocampus is adult-like, and by 32 to 36 weeks gestation, the neurons in the cell fields have matured (Arnold & Trojanowski, 1996). The neurons in most of the hippocampal formation also begin to connect early in development, with synapses present as early as 15 weeks gestational age (Kostovic, Seress, Mrzljak, & Judas, 1989). Spine density and the number of synapses both increase rapidly after birth, with dendritic arborization at adult levels by approximately 6 postnatal months (Paldino & Purpura, 1979).

Studies of glucose utilization also suggest relatively early development of most of the medial-temporal lobe components of the declarative memory system. For example, PET studies show elevated levels of glucose utilization in the temporal cortex by 3 months of age, followed by a gradual decrease to adult levels (Chugani, 1994). There are suggestions that these changes are associated with the acquisition of new abilities and the eventual achievement of adult-levels of functioning, respectively.

In contrast to early maturation of many medial-temporal lobe components, development of the dentate gyrus of the hippocampus is protracted. For instance, the granule cell layer in the dentate gyrus does not begin to form until the 13th to 14th week of gestation; it continues to develop throughout the first postnatal year (Eckenhoff & Rakic, 1991; Seress, 1992). At birth, it includes only about 70% of the adult number of cells (Seress, 2001). This means that roughly 30% of the cells proliferate, migrate, and establish connections post-natally. It is not until 12 to 15 months after birth that the general cytoarchi-tectonic features of the dentate gyrus appear adult-like (Serres, 1992).

Maximum synaptic density in the dentate gyrus also is delayed, relative to that in other medial-temporal regions. In nonhuman primates, there is a period of very rapid accumulation of synapses—or *synaptogenesis*—beginning the 2nd or 3rd postnatal month. Synaptic density reaches its peak in the 4th or 5th month; pruning to adult levels is not accomplished until 10 months of age. In the human, this time frame corresponds to roughly 8 to 12 months for the increase in synaptic density, 16 to 20 months for attainment of peak synaptic density, and 4 to 5 years for achievement of adult levels (Eckenhoff & Rakic, 1991).

Although the functional significance of later development of the dentate gyrus is not clear, there is reason to speculate that it impacts behavior. Infor-mation from distributed regions of the cortex converges on the medial-temporal cortices and from there is projected into the hippocampus either via a "long route" or via a "short route" (see Figure 6.1). The long route (the *hippo-campal trisynaptic circuit*) involves projections from the entorhinal cortex through the dentate gyrus to the cell fields of the hippocampus. The short route involves direct projections from the entorhinal cortex, thereby bypass-ing the dentate gyrus. Although these direct projections may support some forms of memory (Nelson, 1997; Seress, 2001), based on data from rodents, there is reason to believe that the full trisynaptic circuit is critical for adult-like memory function (Nadel & Willner, 1989; Seress, 2001). As such, matur-ation of the dentate gyrus of the hippocampus may be a rate limiting variable in the development of declarative memory early in life (Bauer, 2002, 2004, 2007; Bauer, Wiebe, Carver, Waters, & Nelson, 2003; Nelson, 1997, 2000).

Association cortices

In contrast to relatively early development of major portions of the medial-temporal structures, development in the association areas is more protracted (e.g., Bachevalier & Mishkin, 1994; for a review, see Monk, Webb, & Nelson, 2001). Prenatally, neocortical neurons are formed later than hippocampal neurons (Arnold & Trojanowski, 1996), and neuroblasts migrating to the neocortex have a longer distance to travel, relative to those migrating to the hippocampus (Nowakowski & Rakic, 1981). As a result, even at 20 weeks, the cortex has divided into only three of the six layers of the mature brain. It is not until the 7th prenatal month that all six cortical layers are apparent.

Beginning about midgestation (i.e., 17 to 24 weeks), synaptogenesis begins in the cortex. Whereas the rapid accumulation of synapses begins almost simultaneously across cortical areas, there are regional differences in when it ends and when pruning of unused connections begins (e.g., for a review, see Bourgeois, 2001). For example, as represented in Figure 6.3, in the human primary visual cortex, synaptogenesis ends between 8 and 12 postnatal months and pruning begins at about 2 to 3 years. In contrast, in the prefrontal cortex, synaptic density begins to increase dramatically at 8 postnatal months, peaks between 15 and 24 months, and pruning begins in adolescence (Huttenlocher, 1979; Huttenlocher & Dabholkar, 1997; for discussion, see Bourgeois, 2001). It is not until 24 months that synapses develop adult morphology (Huttenlocher, 1979). There also is an extended period of dendritic change. For example, there is rapid dendritic growth in cortical Layers III and V until about 7½ months and 12 months, respectively. In Layer III, dendrites continue to branch into early adulthood (Koenderink, Uylings, & Mrzljak, 1994). In Layer V, cell body size and the lengths of the dendrites increase until about 5 to 7 years of age (Koenderink & Uylings, 1995). In Layer II of some regions of the dorsolateral prefrontal cortex, the process may continue until 12 to 15 years of age (for discussion, see Benes, 2001).

Studies of blood flow and glucose utilization provide additional evidence of the relatively slow development of the frontal cortex (Chugani, 1994). They peak at higher than adult levels by 8 to 12 and 13 to 14 months of age,

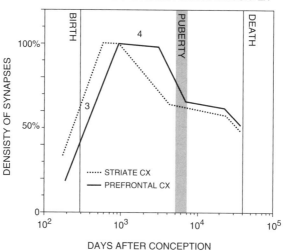

Figure 6.3 A schematic diagram of the relative timing of synaptogenesis in the primary visual cortex (broken line) and prefrontal cortex (solid line) of the human. Figure 2.3 from Bourgeois J.-P. (2001). *Handbook of developmental cognitive neuroscience*, The MIT Press. Copyright © 2001 Massachusetts Institute of Technology. Used with permisson.

respectively. Together with the data on synaptogenesis (Huttenlocher, 1994; Huttenlocher & Dabholkar, 1997), these results suggest that major developments in frontal lobe maturation may take place over the second half of the first year and continue into the second year of life and beyond. Other maturational changes in frontal cortex, such as myelination, continue into adolescence and early adulthood (e.g., Schneider, Il'yasov, Hennig, & Martin, 2004). Adult levels of some neurotransmitters (e.g., acetylcholine and dopamine) are not seen until late childhood and even adulthood (discussed in Benes, 2001).

Network connections

As important as the structures themselves are the connections between them. A case study by Yasuno and colleagues (1999) makes the point: they documented memory deficits associated with disruption of the connections between the hippocampus and the frontal cortex, in the absence of lesions in either of the structures themselves. The study of the development of network connections is virtually synonymous with the study of myelination (the wrapping of oligodendrocytes around axons). Evidence of the progress of myelination has come from histochemical studies and more recently, the imaging methods of MR and DT, which allow for in vivo examination (e.g., Barkovich, Kjos, Jackson, & Norman, 1988; Schneider et al., 2004, respectively). Histochemical analyses make it clear that myelination begins in the second trimester in the spinal cord; the combination of methods documents changes well into the third and even fourth decades of life in cortical fibers. Yet the most pervasive and dramatic changes occur between mid-gestation and the end of the second postnatal year of life (for a review, see Sampaio & Truwit, 2001). During this period throughout the brain there are substantial increases in the volume of white matter (connective tissue) resulting from increases in the number of connections between neurons and the progression of myelination of neuronal axons.

Whereas it is clear that connectivity increases with development, there is little information on age-related change within specific neural networks, such as the temporal–cortical declarative memory network. As already noted, the "short route" connecting the entorhinal cortex directly with the hippocampus develops early. However, the "long route" connecting the entorhinal cortex to the hippocampus via the dentate gyrus develops later. Similarly, the connections from the neocortex to the entorhinal region develop later (Hevner & Kinney, 1996; Seress & Mrzljak, 1992).

Functional maturity of the network

The network that supports declarative memory can be expected to function as an integrated whole only once each of its components, as well as the connections between them, has reached a level of functional maturity that in turn is associated with the rise to peak number of synapses (full maturity is associated with achievement of the adult number of synapses, through synapse elimination: Goldman-Rakic, 1987). This leads to the expectation that the function of the full temporal–cortical network will be apparent by late in the first year of life, with significant development over the course of the second year, and continued development for years thereafter. Specifically, with the exception of the dentate gyrus of the hippocampus, the medial-temporal components of the network would be expected to reach functional maturity between the 2nd and 6th postnatal months (Paldino & Purpura, 1979). Based on increases in synaptogenesis from 8 to 20 months in the dentate gyrus (Eckenhoff & Rakic, 1991), and from 8 to 24 months in the prefrontal cortex (Huttenlocher, 1979; Huttenlocher & Dabholkar, 1997), the network would be expected to reach functional maturity late in the first year and over the course of the second year of life. The network would then be expected to continue to develop, albeit less dramatically, for years thereafter, as a function of the schedule of protracted pruning both in the dentate gyrus (until 4 to 5 years; e.g., Eckenhoff & Rakic, 1991) and in the prefrontal cortex (throughout adolescence; e.g., Huttenlocher & Dabholkar, 1997).

Implications of neural development for changes in behavior in infancy

As discussed elsewhere (e.g., Bauer, 2004, 2006a, 2006b, 2007), the relatively late development of aspects of the temporal–cortical network that supports declarative memory has implications for behavior. The late development of cortical structures is important because they are implicated in all phases of the life of a memory: encoding, consolidation, storage, and retrieval. The late development of the dentate gyrus is critical because in the mature organism it is the major route of communication between the neocortex and hippocampus. It is in the hippocampus that new memory traces are integrated and consolidated for long-term storage. These processes would be challenged by less effective and efficient communication between cortical structures and the hippocampus. Conversely, we would expect to see age-related changes in declarative memory as these structures and connections between them develop.

At a general level, there is correspondence between the time course of changes in behavior in the first months of life and what is known about developments in the temporal–cortical declarative memory network. Because behavioral changes in memory in infancy are the subject of other chapters in this volume (see Chapters 2 and 3 by Rovee-Collier and Cuevas, and Hayne and Simcock), I focus on only one especially salient change, namely, the length of time over which recall is observed. Near the end of the first year of life, coincident with increases in synaptogenesis in the prefrontal cortex and the dentate gyrus of the hippocampus, infants show great strides in recall over long delays, as measured by elicited and deferred imitation. As depicted in Table 6.1, in the first half of the first year of life, the temporal extent of memory seems limited. Six-month-old infants show evidence of recall for only 24 hours (e.g., Barr, Dowden, & Hayne, 1996; though retention can be extended by subsequent reexposure: Barr, Rovee-Collier, & Campanella, 2005). By contrast, 9-month-olds recall multistep sequences over delays of 1 month. Only 1 month later (when infant are 10 months of age), the length of time over which recall is observed has extended to 3 months (Carver & Bauer, 2001). Substantial development in how long infants retain memories continues throughout the second year (e.g., Bauer, Wenner, Dropik, & Wewerka, 2000), coincident with the rise to peak of synaptogenesis and continued morphological development of synapses in the prefrontal cortex and the dentate gyrus.

What underlies these pronounced changes in declarative memory? Perhaps because of the salience of developments in the prefrontal cortex and its well-documented role in retrieval, more effective and efficient retrieval processes have been implicated as a major source of age-related variance in long-term recall (e.g., Liston & Kagan, 2002). However, developmental changes in the prefrontal cortex would be expected to impact all phases of the life of a memory, beginning with encoding. In addition, developments in the dentate gyrus of the hippocampus can be expected to contribute to changes in consolidation in particular. For these reasons, it is important to examine the implications of changes in the temporal–cortical network, starting with the beginning of memory trace formation.

Encoding

We cannot directly observe encoding. Instead, we test for age differences in memory shortly after learning. Both behavioral and electrophysiological measures indicate age-related changes in the first 2 years of life. For example, when they are tested immediately after a single experience of an event in an imitation-based task, 16-month-olds remember fewer actions and less information about temporal order than 20-month-olds (e.g., Bauer & Dow, 1994). Studies in which children are brought to a criterion level of learning—implying complete encoding—reveal that 12-month-olds require

Table 6.1 Lengths of time over which infants exhibit long-term declarative memory

Age group	Length of delay	References
6-month-olds	24 hours	Barr, Dowden, & Hayne (1996)
9-month-olds	1 month	Carver & Bauer (1999, 2001)
10-month-olds	3 months	Carver & Bauer (2001)
13-month-olds	6 months	Bauer, Wenner, Dropik, & Wewerka (2000)
20-month-olds	12 months	Bauer, Wenner, Dropik, & Wewerka (2000)

more learning trials than 15-month-olds, who in turn require more trials than 18-month-olds (Howe & Courage, 1997).

Studies employing electrophysiological measures (event-related potentials; ERPs) indicate changes in encoding late in the first year of life. ERPs are scalp-recorded electrical oscillations associated with excitatory and inhibitory postsynaptic potentials. Because they are noninvasive and require no overt behavior on the part of the participant (e.g., ERPs to auditory stimuli can be recorded while the participant sleeps), they are ideal for use with human infants. Moreover, because they are time locked to a stimulus, differences in the latency and amplitude of the response to different classes of stimuli—familiar and novel, for example—can be interpreted as evidence of differential neural processing.

The combination of ERPs and behavior has revealed age-related changes in encoding in the first year that relate to variability in recall. In a longitudinal study (Bauer et al., 2006), infants were exposed to multistep sequences, and then ERPs were recorded as they viewed photographs of the props used to produce the sequences interspersed with props from novel sequences. Differential responses to the different classes of stimuli indicated recognition, and thus encoding. Infants had more robust ERP responses to sequences encoded at 10 months of age relative to sequences encoded at 9 months. The age-related difference did not extend to responses to novel sequences and thus is specific to mnemonic processes. Differential encoding related to differential recall: Infants had higher levels of recall of sequences encoded at 10 months than of sequences encoded at 9 months.

Consolidation

Although age-related differences in encoding in the first 2 years are apparent, they do not account for all of the age-related variance in long-term recall. With encoding processes controlled statistically (Bauer et al., 2000), by matching (Bauer, 2005a), or by criterion learning (Howe & Courage, 1997), developmental differences in how long-term memory is observed are still apparent. That is, older infants remember more, for longer periods of time, than their younger counterparts. This indicates that a full account of developmental differences in long-term recall will require consideration of post-encoding processes such as consolidation.

A clear indication that consolidation processes are a source of variance in long-term recall comes from another study in which behavior and ERP were combined (Bauer et al., 2003). To minimize encoding as a source of variability, 9-month-olds were exposed to three sequences (Sequences A, B, and C) at each of three sessions. At the third session encoding was tested via ERP (familiar Sequence A vs. novel Sequence D). One week later—as a test of the success of consolidation—another ERP test was administered using different stimuli (Sequences B and E). Long-term recall of the sequences was tested 1 month later (along with three novel sequences as a within-subjects control).

As reflected in Figure 6.4, as a group the infants showed evidence of immediate recognition, and thus encoding (differential responses to Sequences A and D), yet there were differences in the apparent success of consolidation that in turn related to different patterns of long-term recall. Specifically, a subset of the infants failed to recognize the stimuli after 1 week (i.e., similar responses to Sequences B and E) and also failed to recall the sequences after 1 month. A different subset of the infants successfully recognized after 1 week and also recalled the sequences 1 month later. Neither group nor individual variability in encoding was a significant predictor of long-term recall. In contrast, successful consolidation over 1 week accounted for 28% of the variance in recall after 1 month.

Consolidation processes continue to account for variance in the second year. For infants 20 months of age, the amount of information retained 48 hours after exposure to events explains 25% of the variance in their recall 1 month later (Bauer, Cheatham, Cary, & Van Abbema, 2002). Moreover, variability in initial consolidation is observed in populations of infants with suspected hippocampal damage associated with maternal gestational

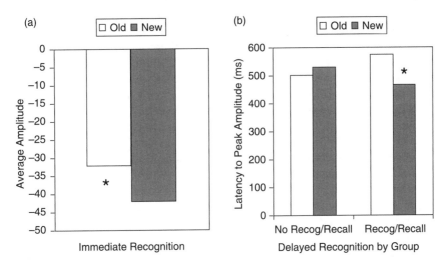

Figure 6.4 Panel (a) reflects the average amplitude at electrode site Fz and provides evidence of differential response to familiar ("Old" sequence) and novel ("New" sequence) stimuli thus indicating successful encoding of the sequences. Panel (b) reflects the 1-week delayed ERP responses (latency to peak amplitude) for infants who failed to show ordered recall after 1 month (left bars). The lack of differentiation of responses to familiar and novel stimuli indicates failed consolidation and storage. The right bars of panel (b) reflect the 1-week delayed ERP responses for infants who later evidenced ordered recall. Differential responses to old and new stimuli indicate successful consolidation and storage. Data from Bauer et al., 2003. Figure 2 from p. 178 in Bauer, P. J. (2006). Constructing a past in infancy: A neuro-developmental account. *Trends in Cognitive Sciences, 10*, 175–181. Copyright © Elsevier (2006). Used with permission.

diabetes (which in animal models impairs hippocampal function as a result of chronic metabolic insults, including iron deficiency, which affects neuro-development: e.g., Georgieff & Rao, 2001). Infants born to mothers with gestational diabetes do not differ from infants from nondiabetic pregnancies at immediate testing. In contrast, after a 10-minute delay, performance by infants of mothers with diabetes is significantly lower than performance of infants of mothers without diabetes. In a longitudinal sample the difference was apparent at 12 months of age (DeBoer et al., 2005) and had not resolved at 24 months (DeBoer, Wewerka, & Fong, 2003). Because differences were not observed at immediate testing, consolidation of information, as opposed to encoding of it, is implicated.

Retrieval

Evidence that encoding and consolidation processes account for age-related and individual variability in long-term recall makes it clear that we cannot explain developmental changes only by examining end-stage processes such as retrieval. In fact, establishing the variance explained by retrieval processes is surprisingly difficult because in most of the empirical literature there is no experimental means of determining whether age effects occur because older infants are more successful at retrieval than younger infants (memory traces are equally intact but differentially accessible: younger infants experience retrieval failure) or because older infants are more successful at maintaining traces in storage (the memory traces that are available for retrieval are differentally intact: younger infants experience storage failure).

One approach to distinguishing storage from retrieval failure is to provide multiple test trials without intervening study trials (Howe & O'Sullivan, 1997). The logic is that since each retrieval attempt entails re-encoding, the associated strengthening of the memory and route to retrieval of it can render an intact trace more accessible on a later trial. Conversely, lack of improvement across trials implies that the trace is not available. Savings in relearning also can distinguish a trace that has disintegrated from one that exists but is inaccessible. Classically, when the number of trials required to relearn a stimulus was smaller than the number required for initial learning, *savings* were said to have occurred (Ebbinghaus, 1885). Savings presumably accrue because the products of relearning are integrated with an existing (though not necessarily accessible) trace. Conversely, the absence of savings is attributed to storage failure: there is no residual trace on which to build. Age-related differences in relearning would suggest that the residual traces available to children of different ages are differentially intact.

Opportunities to evaluate the source of memory failure are rare in the infancy literature. When they are presented, they suggest storage, rather than retrieval, as the major source of age-related change. For example, in Bauer (2005a), 13- to 20-month-olds were matched for levels of encoding prior to imposition of 1- to 6-month delays. In spite of the matching, at the longer delays in particular, younger infants showed more forgetting than older infants; the differences were apparent on two test trials, the second of which also featured additional retrieval cues. Storage processes also were implicated by age-related differences in relearning: older children showed greater savings, relative to younger children. These findings suggest that the memory traces of the younger infants were less well preserved relative to those of the older infants, and thus implicate storage as opposed to retrieval processes as a major source of age-related variance in long-term recall.

RELATIONS BETWEEN STRUCTURE AND FUNCTION IN CHILDHOOD

Although the experimental literature on developmental changes in memory function in childhood is older than that on developmental changes in infancy (the former has a history dating back to the late 1800s, whereas the latter started in the late 1950s), as noted earlier, there has been less attention paid to relations between memory function and neural structure in children than in infants. With the advent of more powerful MR and DT imaging techniques, in particular, there is increasing recognition of the fact of brain development well beyond infancy. Attention to the implications of the changes for function is sure to follow.

Development of the declarative memory network in childhood

As is apparent from earlier sections, in major portions of the temporal–cortical network that supports declarative memory, humans make the transition from infancy to childhood with the largest number of synapses they will ever have: the numbers are well above their adult complements. One of the major changes that takes place in childhood is that the numbers of synapses in these regions are pruned to adult levels. In the dentate gyrus of the hippocampus, adults levels are not reached until the age of 4 to 5 years; in the prefrontal cortex, pruning continues well into adolescence and even early adulthood. It is only once the adult level of synapses is reached that we would expect mature levels of function to be achieved.

Consistent with the evidence of synaptic pruning (which is drawn from postmortem studies), MRI studies have revealed reductions in gray matter density (i.e., cortical thinning) across brain regions between childhood and adulthood (e.g., Giedd et al., 1999; see also Van Petten, 2004). As reflected in Figure 6.5, panel (a), in dorsal parietal regions, gray matter density loss is especially apparent between childhood and adolescence, and in frontal regions, between adolescence and adulthood (e.g., Sowell, Delis, Stiles, & Jernigan, 2001a; Sowell, Thompson, Holmes, Batth, Jernigan, & Toga, 1999; Sowell et al., 2001b). Paradoxically, coincident with cortical thinning are increases in overall brain size. The most likely source of the increase is

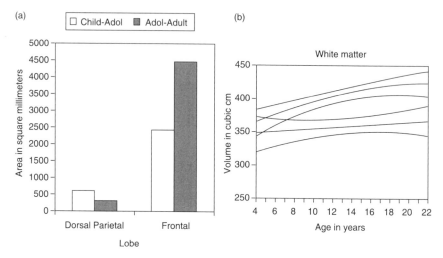

Figure 6.5 Panel (a): Gray matter density reductions (area in square millimeters) in the left dorsal parietal and frontal lobes, between childhood and adolescence (open bars) and between adolescence and adulthood (filled bars). Data from Table 1 in Sowell et al. (2001b). Panel (b): Predicted increase in white matter volume for males (top dark line) and females (bottom dark line) from ages 4 to 22 years, with 95% confidence intervals (in light bars). From Figure 1 in Giedd et al. (1999). Reproduced by permission from Macmillan Publishers Ltd, copyright © 1999.

myelination (myelin consists of space-occupying glial cells: Friede, 1989). As noted earlier, myelination begins prenatally and continues for years thereafter. In the hippocampus it continues throughout childhood and adolescence (e.g., Arnold & Trojanowski, 1996; Schneider et al., 2004). In frontal regions, myelination continues throughout the second decade of life (e.g., Klingberg et al., 1999). Overall, between the ages of 4 and 22 years, there is approximately a 12% increase in white matter volume (see Figure 6.5, panel (b); Giedd et al., 1999).

Myelination is not the only so-called *progressive* event that occurs beyond infancy. As noted earlier, in some cortical layers the childhood years are marked by increases in the size of cells and the lengths and branching of dendrites. More dramatically, in some brain regions new neurons are added. In the dentate gyrus of the hippocampus, as many as 30% of the adult number of granule cells proliferate, migrate, and establish connections postnatally (other areas in which there is postnatal neurogenesis include the cerebellum and olfactory bulb: for discussion, see Tanapat, Hastings, & Gould, 2001). Whereas much of the work is accomplished by the second year of life, there is evidence that neurogenesis continues throughout childhood and adulthood (as it does in the olfactory bulb as well: e.g., Altman & Das, 1965). In short, well beyond infancy, there is continued development in the neural substrate supporting long-term declarative memory. Whereas these later neurodevelopmental changes may not be associated with functional changes as dramatic as those in the first 2 years of life, they nevertheless can be expected to have functional consequences throughout the preschool years.

Implications of neural development for changes in behavior in childhood

Consistent with this suggestion that neurodevelopmental changes in childhood and beyond will have implications for mnemonic function are data from Sowell et al. (2001a). They found that 7- to 16-year-old children with structurally more mature medial-temporal lobes (as assessed by MRI) performed at higher levels on tests of spatial memory. Children with structurally more mature frontal cortices performed at higher levels on verbal as well as spatial memory tasks. The possible implications of age-related changes in these areas for encoding and consolidation, storage, and retrieval processes are discussed in turn.

Encoding

Developmental changes in the prefrontal cortex in particular can be expected to contribute to age-related changes in the efficiency with which preschool-age children encode information. Behavioral evidence of changes in encoding is plentiful. For example, there are changes in short-term memory "span," as measured by tests such as memory for digits or words. Between the ages of 2 years and 5 years, the number of units that children are able to hold in mind changes from two to four; by the age of 7 years, the number of units that children hold in mind has increased to five (for a review, see Cowan and Alloway, Chapter 12 this volume). During this same period of time, children become more effective at keeping task-irrelevant thoughts out of short-term memory, thereby reducing the amount of potentially interfering "cognitive clutter" that otherwise would limit capacity. In addition, during the preschool years there are developmental increases in the use of rehearsal as a means to maintain the accessibility of to-be-remembered material over time. Even more pronounced changes in the use of memory strategies are apparent in the school years (reviewed in Bjorklund, Dukes, and Brown, Chapter 7 this volume). The net result of these changes is that children become increasingly adept not only at maintaining information in temporary registration, but at initiating the type of organizational processing that promotes consolidation of it.

Although there are excellent reasons to expect that developmental changes in encoding over the course of the preschool years might contribute to age-related changes in long-term recall over the same period, there are few studies that can be brought to bear to evaluate the hypothesized relation. A major reason is that researchers interested in long-term memory frequently either have not measured initial encoding or levels of encoding have not been controlled. That is, in many studies, memory is tested only after a delay. In other studies, immediate memory is tested but the impact of age-related differences in initial learning is not assessed. As in the infancy literature, when encoding is controlled by bringing children to a learning criterion, older children reach the criterion faster than younger children, implying age-related differences in encoding. Also as in the infancy period, encoding alone does not explain age-related variance in declarative memory because even with encoding controlled, older children remember more than younger children (for a review, see Howe & O'Sullivan, 1997).

Consolidation, storage, and retrieval

Changes in the processes by which memory representations are consolidated and distributed to long-term memory stores can be expected throughout the preschool years, in association with neurodevelopmental changes within the medial-temporal and prefrontal structures themselves, as well as the connections between them. Changes in prefrontal structures in particular also can be expected to be associated with changes in the efficacy of retrieval processes. Although changes in these processes can be expected, there are few data that can be brought to bear to evaluate whether they are observed. There do not appear to be any studies in which the variance associated with consolidation processes has been evaluated as a determinant of long-term recall. The relative contributions of storage and retrieval processes to age-related differences in long-term recall have been assessed by Brainerd and Reyna and their colleagues (e.g., Brainerd & Reyna, 1990; Brainerd, Reyna, Howe, & Kingma, 1990). The studies imply declines in storage failure rates throughout childhood. In contrast, retrieval failure rates remain virtually unchanged (for a review, see Howe & O'Sullivan, 1997). The field awaits further studies in which a variety of behavioral and neuorimaging methods are brought to bear to evaluate post-encoding processes as determinants of long-term recall throughout childhood and beyond.

ADVANTAGES OF A DEVELOPMENTAL COGNITIVE NEUROSCIENCE OF DECLARATIVE MEMORY

Analysis of the development of declarative memory from a systems neuroscience perspective enhances the description that we have to offer of changes in mnemonic behavior. It also furthers the goal of explanation of age-related change. For example, in the case of early memory development, it leads to identification of medial-temporal structures in general and the dentate gyrus of the hippocampus in particular as a rate limiting variable in long-term recall. As these structures develop, we expect to (and indeed, seem to) see changes in mnemonic behavior. Critically, links across levels of analysis do more than push psychological and behavioral phenomena into biology. They also lead to new hypotheses regarding the sources of age-related change.

As discussed in Bauer (2006a), an implicit assumption in the literature on memory development is that there is age-related variability in retention of memory traces *over the long term*. That is, there is an assumption that as time goes by, the memory representations of younger children begin to fade, whereas those of older children remain robust. Differential loss of information over time seems consistent with this suggestion. In Bauer (2005a), for example, 16- and 20-month-old infants were matched for levels of encoding prior to imposition of delays ranging from 1 to 6 months. At the shortest delay of 1 month, the amount of information forgotten by the younger and older infants did not differ. At both the 3- and 6-month delay tests, however, the age groups differed. At both time points the 16-month-olds showed more forgetting than the 20-month-olds. The findings thus seemed consistent with the suggestion that age effects set in "as time goes by."

The notion that age effects set in with time implies that memories are most vulnerable or more fragile when they are "old." A logically related assumption is that memories are less vulnerable or more robust when they are "new." However, consideration of the processes that occur to make new memories, and of the time course of development of some of the structures and the network involved in their creation, leads to a different conclusion. The revised conclusion is that memories are most vulnerable as they are being translated from immediate experience into enduring traces (Bauer, 2006a). The process of translation is especially challenging for younger infants and children because of the late development of portions of the responsible neural network. Thus, at least early in development, early-stage, rather than later-stage, processes are a major source of age-related differences in long-term recall. Regardless of age, early vulnerability of traces is critical because information that is not successfully encoded is not available for consolidation. In turn, information that escapes consolidation is not available for storage. And of course, information that is not stored cannot be retrieved. This analysis suggests that memories become fragile as they age not because of end-stage processes but because they were fragile in the early stages of their development. In effect, early vulnerability confers later vulnerability. The behavioral profiles outlined earlier are consistent with the suggestion that development is associated with more robust initial processes (i.e., more effective and efficient encoding and consolidation).

Another assumption that stems from this neurodevelopmental perspective is that with age, the locus of maximum vulnerability of a memory trace shifts from encoding and consolidation to storage and retrieval (Bauer, 2006a). This assumption follows from the expectation that as the medial-temporal components of the temporal-cortical network reach maturity, encoding and consolidation processes will become more effective and efficient. As a result, more and more memories will survive the initial stages of trace formation, thus reducing the variance in long-term recall explained by these processes. Conversely, the proportion of variance accounted for by the later-stage processes of storage and retrieval should increase with age. Ultimately, whether these specific hypotheses are supported is not what is most important. What is critical is that a biological analysis of memory and its development leads to new hypotheses about the sources of age-related change. Tests of the hypotheses will provide new data that ultimately will aid in the description as well as the explanation of age-related change.

CONCLUSIONS

The study of the neurobiology of memory has a long history. Based on research with patients with specific lesions and disease, animal models, and neuroimaging studies, the neural substrate that supports declarative memory in adults has been relatively well articulated. By contrast, studies of the neural bases of memory in development are in their infancy. Developmental cognitive scientists and neuroscientists are just beginning to trace the age-related changes that result in a competent mnemonist.

Although the subfield of the cognitive neuroscience of memory development is young, it already bears one of the marks of a mature discipline, namely, movement beyond description to explanation. Novel predictions regarding the sources of age-related change have arisen from joint consideration of the processes involved in building a memory trace, and of the time course of development of the neural structures involved. Specifically, relatively protracted developments in the prefrontal cortex and in the dentate gyrus of the hippocampus lead to the expectation that early in development, encoding and consolidation processes account for significant age-related variance in long-term declarative memory. Further, although the suggestion has yet to be tested empirically, there is reason to believe that with development, the locus of maximum vulnerability for memory traces shifts from the early-stage processes of encoding and consolidation to the later-stage processes of memory storage and retrieval. Whereas these insights may have come about by focus on overt behavior alone, it is likely that their generation was facilitated by consideration of the biological bases of behavior. Ultimately, the neurodevelopmental window on mnemonic behavior is one of many that allows for the full light of explanation of it.

ACKNOWLEDGMENTS

Much of the author's work discussed was supported by the National Institute of Child Health and Human Development (HD-28425, HD-42483). The author also thanks the many colleagues who have helped to shape her thinking on memory and its development; and the infants, children, and families who make our work possible.

REFERENCES

Adlam, A.-L. R., Vargha-Khadem, F., Mishkin, M., & de Haan, M. (2005). Deferred imitation of action sequences in developmental amnesia. *Journal of Cognitive Neuroscience, 17*, 240–248.

Altman, J., & Das, G. D. (1965). Autoradiographic and histological evidence of postnatal hippocampal neurogenesis in rats. *Journal of Comparative Neurology, 124*, 319–335.

Arnold, S. E., & Trojanowski, J. Q. (1996). Human fetal hippocampal development: I. Cytoarchitecture, myeloarchitecture, and neuronal morphologic features. *Journal of Comparative Neurology, 367*, 274–292.

Augustine, A. (~401/1999). *The confessions of Saint Augustine.* Book X, Chapter VIII. (Edward B. Pusey, Trans.). Grand Rapids, MI: Christian Classics Ethereal Library.

Bachevalier, J. (2001). Neural bases of memory development: Insights from neuropsychological studies in primates. In C. A. Nelson & M. Luciana (Eds.), *Handbook of developmental cognitive neuroscience* (pp. 365–379). Cambridge, MA: MIT Press.

Bachevalier, J., & Mishkin, M. (1994). Effects of selective neonatal temporal lobe lesions on visual recognition memory in rhesus monkeys. *Journal of Neuroscience, 14*, 2128–2139.

Barkovich, A. J., Kjos, B. O., Jackson, D. E., & Norman, D. (1988). Normal maturation of the neonatal and infant brain: Mr imaging at 1.5 T. *Neuroradiology, 166*, 173–180.

Barr, R., Dowden, A., & Hayne, H. (1996). Developmental change in deferred imitation by 6- to 24-month-old infants. *Infant Behavior and Development, 19*, 159–170.

Barr, R., Rovee-Collier, C., & Campanella, J. (2005). Retrieval protracts deferred imitation by 6-month-olds. *Infancy, 7*, 263–283.

Bauer, P. J. (2002). Long-term recall memory: Behavioral and neurodevelopmental changes in the first 2 years of life. *Current Directions in Psychological Science, 11*, 137–141.

Bauer, P. J. (2004). Getting explicit memory off the ground: Steps toward construction of a neuro-developmental account of changes in the first two years of life. *Developmental Review, 24*, 347–373.

Bauer, P. J. (2005a). Developments in declarative memory: Decreasing susceptibility to storage failure over the second year of life. *Psychological Science, 16*, 41–47.

Bauer, P. J. (2005b). New developments in the study of infant memory. In D. M. Teti (Ed.), *Blackwell handbook of research methods in developmental science* (pp. 467–488). Oxford: Blackwell Publishing.

Bauer, P. J. (2006a). Constructing a past in infancy: A neuro-developmental account. *Trends in Cognitive Sciences, 10*, 175–181.

Bauer, P. J. (2006b). Event memory. In W. Damon & R. M. Lerner (Eds.-in-chief), D. Kuhn & R. Siegler (vol. Eds.), *Handbook of child psychology: Vol. 2. Cognition, perception, and language* (6th ed., pp. 373–425). Hoboken, NJ: John Wiley & Sons, Inc.

Bauer, P. J. (2007). *Remembering the times of our lives: Memory in infancy and beyond.* Mahwah, NJ: Lawrence Erlbaum Associates, Inc.

Bauer, P. J., Cheatham, C. L., Cary, M. S., & Van Abbema, D. L. (2002). Short-term forgetting: Charting its course and its implications for long-term remembering. In S. P. Shohov (Ed.), *Advances in psychology research* (Vol. 9, pp. 53–74). Huntington, NY: Nova Science Publishers.

Bauer, P. J., & Dow, G. A. A. (1994). Episodic memory in 16- and 20-month-old children: Specifics are generalized, but not forgotten. *Developmental Psychology, 30*, 403–417.

Bauer, P. J., Wenner, J. A., Dropik, P. L., & Wewerka, S. S. (2000). Parameters of remembering and forgetting in the transition from infancy to early childhood. *Monographs of the Society for Research in Child Development, 65* (4, Serial No. 263).

Bauer, P. J., Wiebe, S. A., Carver, L. J., Lukowski, A. F., Haight, J. C., Waters, J. M., et al. (2006). Electrophysiological indices of encoding and behavioral indices of recall: Examining relations and developmental change late in the first year of life. *Developmental Neuropsychology, 29*, 293–320.

Bauer, P. J., Wiebe, S. A., Carver, L. J., Waters, J. M., & Nelson, C. A. (2003). Developments in long-term explicit memory late in the first year of life: Behavioral and electrophysiological indices. *Psychological Science, 14*, 629–635.

Benes, F. M. (2001). The development of prefrontal cortex: The maturation of neurotransmitter systems and their interaction. In C. A. Nelson & M. Luciana (Eds.), *Handbook of developmental cognitive neuroscience* (pp. 79–92). Cambridge, MA: MIT Press.

Bourgeois, J.-P. (2001). Synaptogenesis in the neocortex of the newborn: The ultimate frontier for individuation? In C. A. Nelson & M. Luciana (Eds.), *Handbook of developmental cognitive neuroscience* (pp. 23–34). Cambridge, MA: MIT Press.

Brainerd, C. J., & Reyna, V. F. (1990). Gist is the grist: Fuzzy-trace theory and the new intuitionism. *Developmental Review, 10*, 3–47.

Brainerd, C. J., Reyna, V. F., Howe, M. L., & Kingma, J. (1990). The development of forgetting and reminiscence. *Monographs of the Society for Research in Child Development, 55* (3–4, Serial No. 222).

Brown, A. S. (2002). Consolidation theory and retrograde amnesia in humans. *Psychonomic Bulletin and Review, 9*, 403–425.

Cantlon, J. S., Brannon, E. M., Carter, E. J., & Pelphrey, K. A. (2006). Functional imaging of numerical processing in adults and 4-y-old children. *PloS Biology, 4*, e125.

Carver, L. J., & Bauer, P. J. (1999). When the event is more than the sum of its parts: 9-month-olds long-term ordered recall. *Memory, 7*, 147–174.

Carver, L. J., & Bauer, P. J. (2001). The dawning of a past: The emergence of long-term explicit memory in infancy. *Journal of Experimental Psychology: General, 130*, 726–745.

Cheatham, C. L., & Bauer, P. J. (2005). Construction of a more coherent story: Prior verbal recall predicts later verbal accessibility of early memories. *Memory, 13*, 516–532.

Chugani, H. T. (1994). Development of regional blood glucose metabolism in relation to behavior and plasticity. In G. Dawson & K. Fischer (Eds.), *Human behavior and the developing brain* (pp. 153–175). New York: Guilford.

DeBoer, T., Wewerka, S., Bauer, P. J., Georgieff, M. K., & Nelson, C. A. (2005). Explicit memory performance in infants of diabetic mothers at 1 year of age. *Developmental Medicine and Child Neurology, 47*, 525–531.

DeBoer, T. L., Wewerka, S. M., & Fong, S. S. (2003, April). *Elicited imitation as a tool to investigate the impact of abnormal prenatal environments on memory development.* Paper presented at the 70th Biennial Meeting of the Society for Research in Child Development, Tampa, Florida.

Diamond, A. (2001). A model system for studying the role of dopamine in the prefrontal cortex during early development in humans: Early and continuously treated phenylketonuria. In C. A. Nelson & M. Luciana (Eds.), *Handbook of developmental cognitive neuroscience* (pp. 433–472). Cambridge, MA: MIT Press.

Ebbinghaus, H. (1897). Über eine neue Methode zur Prüfung geistiger Fähigkeiten and ihre Anwendung bei Schulkindern [About a new method for testing intellectual abilities and its application with school children]. *Zeitschrift für Psychologie und Physiologie der Sinesorgane, 13*, 401–457.

Eckenhoff, M., & Rakic, P. (1991). A quantitative analysis of synaptogenesis in the molecular layer of the dentate gyrus in the rhesus monkey. *Developmental Brain Research, 64*, 129– 135.

Eichenbaum, H., & Cohen, N. J. (2001). *From conditioning to conscious recollection: Memory systems of the brain.* New York: Oxford University Press.

Friede, R. L. (1989). Gross and microscopic development of the central nervous system. In R. L. Friede (Ed.), *Developmental neuropathology* (2nd ed., pp. 2–20). Berlin: Springer.

Fuster, J. M. (1997). Network memory. *Trends in Neuroscience, 20*, 451–459.

Fuster, J. M., & Alexander, G. E. (1971). Neuron activity related to short-term memory. *Science, 173*, 652–654.

Gadian, D. G., Aicardi, J., Watkins, K. E., Porter, D. A., Mishkin, M., & Vargha-Khadem, F. (2000). Developmental amnesia associated with early hypoxic-ischaemic injury. *Brain, 123*, 499–507.

Gall, F. J. (1835). *The influence of the brain on the form of the head* (W. Lewis, Trans.). Boston: Marsh, Capen & Lyon.

Georgieff, M. K., & Rao, R. (2001). The role of nutrition in cognitive development. In C. A. Nelson & M. Luciana (Eds.), *Handbook of developmental cognitive neuroscience* (pp. 491–504). Cambridge, MA: MIT Press.

Giedd, J. N., Blumenthal, J., Jeffries, N. O., Castellanos, F. X., Lui, H., Zijdenbos, A., et al. (1999) Brain development during childhood and adolescence: A longitudinal MRI study. *Nature Neuroscience, 2*, 861–863.

Goldman-Rakic, P. S. (1987). Circuitry of primate prefrontal cortex and regulation of behavior by representational memory. In F. Plum (Ed.), *Handbook of physiology, the nervous system, higher functions of the brain* (Vol. 5, pp. 373–417). Bethesda, MD: American Physiological Society.

Hevner, R. F., & Kinney, H. C. (1996). Reciprocal entorhinal–hippocampal connections established by human fetal midgestation. *Journal of Comparative Neurology, 372*, 384–394.

Howe, M. L., & Courage, M. L. (1997). Independent paths in the development of infant learning and forgetting. *Journal of Experimental Child Psychology, 67*, 131–163.

Howe, M. L., & O'Sullivan, J. T. (1997). What children's memories tell us about recalling our childhoods: A review of storage and retrieval processes in the development of long-term retention. *Developmental Review, 17*, 148–204.

Huttenlocher, P. R. (1979). Synaptic density in human frontal cortex: Developmental changes and effects of aging. *Brain Research, 163*, 195–205.

Huttenlocher, P. R. (1994). Synaptogenesis in human cerebral cortex. In G. Dawson & K. Fischer (Eds.), *Human behaviour and the developing brain.* New York: Guilford Press.

Huttenlocher, P. R., & Dabholkar, A. S. (1997). Regional differences in synaptogenesis in human cerebral cortex. *Journal of Comparative Neurology*, *387*, 167–178.

Kandel, E. R., Schwartz, J. H., & Jessell, T. M. (2000). *Principles of neural science* (4th ed.). New York: McGraw-Hill.

Kandel, E. R., & Squire, L. R. (2000). Neuroscience: Breaking down scientific barriers to the study of brain and mind. *Science*, *290*, 1113–1120.

Kim, J. J., & Fanselow, M. S. (1992). Modality-specific retrograde amnesia of fear. *Science*, *256*, 675–677.

Kleist, K. (1934). Kriegsverletzungen des Gehirns in inrher Bedeutung fur die Hirnlokalisation and Hirnpathologie. In K. Bonhoeffer (Ed.), *Handbuch der Aerztlichen Erfahrungen im Weltkriege 1914/1918, Vol. 4: Geistes- und Nervenkrankheiten* (pp. 343–360). Leipzig: Barth.

Klingberg, T., Vaidya, C. J., Gabrieli, J. D. E., Moseley, M. E., & Hedehus, M. (1999). Myelination and organization of the frontal white matter in children: A diffusion tensor MRI study. *Neuroreport*, *10*, 2817–2821.

Koenderink, M. J. T., & Uylings, H. B. M. (1995). Postnatal maturation of layer V pyramidal neurons in the human prefrontal cortex. A quantitative Golgi analysis. *Brain Research*, *678*, 233–243.

Koenderink, M. J. T., Uylings, H. B. M., & Mrzljak, L. (1994). Postnatal maturation of the layer III pyramidal neurons in the human prefrontal cortex: A quantitative Golgi study. *Brain Research*, *653*, 173–182.

Köhler, S., & Moscovitch, M. (1997). Unconscious visual processing in neuropsychological syndromes: A survey of the literature and evaluation of models of consciousness. In M. D. Rugg (Ed.), *Cognitive neuroscience* (pp. 305–373). London: UCL Press.

Kostovic, I., Seress, L., Mrzljak, L., & Judas, M. (1989). Early onset of synapse formation in the human hippocampus: A correlation with Nissl-Golgi architectonics in 15- and 16.5-week-old fetuses. *Neuroscience*, *30*, 105–116.

Liston, C., & Kagan, J. (2002). Memory enhancement in early childhood. *Nature*, *419*, 896.

Maguire, E. A. (2001). Neuroimaging studies of autobiographical event memory. *Philosophical Transactions of the Royal Society of London*, *356*, 1441–1451.

McDonough, L., Mandler, J. M., McKee, R. D., & Squire, L. R. (1995). The deferred imitation task as a nonverbal measure of declarative memory. *Proceedings of the National Academy of Sciences*, *92*, 7580–7584.

Milner, B., Corkin, S., & Teuber, H. L. (1968). Further analysis of the hippocampal amnesic syndrome: 14-year followup study of H. M. *Neuropsychologia*, *6*, 215–234.

Milner, B., & Petrides, M. (1984). Behavioural effects of frontal-lobe lesions in man. *Trends in Neuroscience*, *7*, 403–407.

Mishkin, M., Spiegler, B. J., Saunders, R. C., & Malamut, B. J. (1982). An animal model of global amnesia. In S. Corkin, K. L. Davis, J. H. Growdon, E. J. Usdin, & R. J. Wurtman (Eds.), *Toward a treatment of Alzheimer's disease* (pp. 235–247). New York: Raven Press.

Monk, C. S., Webb, S. J., & Nelson, C. A. (2001). Prenatal neurobiological development: Molecular mechanisms and anatomical change. *Developmental Neuropsychology*, *19*, 211–236.

Müller, G. E., & Pilzecker, A. (1900). Experimentalle Beitrage zur Lehre vom Gedachtnis. *Zeitschrift fur Psychologie*, *1*, 1–300.

Nadel, L., & Willner, J. (1989). Some implications of postnatal maturation of the hippocampus. In V. Chan-Palay & C. Köhler (Eds.), *The hippocampus—new vistas* (pp. 17–31). New York: Alan R. Liss.

Nelson, C. A. (1997). The neurobiological basis of early memory development. In N. Cowan (Ed.), *The development of memory in childhood* (pp. 41–82). Hove, UK: Psychology Press.

Nelson, C. A. (2000). Neural plasticity and human development: The role of early experience in sculpting memory systems. *Developmental Science, 3,* 115–136.

Nelson, C. A., & Bloom, F. E. (1997). Child development and neuroscience. *Child Development, 68,* 970–987.

Nelson, C. A., & Monk, C. S. (2001). The use of event-related potentials in the study of cognitive development. In C. A. Nelson & M. Luciana (Eds.), *Handbook of developmental cognitive neuroscience* (pp. 125–136). Cambridge, MA: MIT Press.

Nowakowski, R. S., & Rakic, P. (1981). The site of origin and route and rate of migration of neurons to the hippocampal region of the rhesus monkey. *Journal of Comparative Neurology, 196,* 129–154.

Nyberg, L. (1998). Mapping episodic memory. *Behavioral Brain Research, 90,* 107–114.

Nyberg, L., & Cabeza, R. (2000). Brain imaging of memory. In E. Tulving and F. I. M. Craik (Eds.), *The Oxford handbook of memory* (pp. 501–519). New York: Oxford University Press.

Paldino, A., & Purpura, D. (1979). Quantitative analysis of the spatial distribution of axonal and dendritic terminals of hippocampal pyramidal neurons in immature human brain. *Experimental Neurology, 64,* 604–619.

Petrides, M. (1995). Impairments on nonspatial self-ordered and externally ordered working memory tasks after lesions of the mid-dorsal part of the lateral frontal cortex in monkeys. *The Journal of Neuroscience, 15,* 359–375.

Richards, J. E. (2005). Localizing cortical sources of event-related potentials in infants' covert orienting. *Developmental Science, 8,* 255–278.

Rovee-Collier, C. (1997). Dissociations in infant memory: Rethinking the development of implicit and explicit memory. *Psychological Review, 104,* 467–498.

Sampaio, R. C., & Truwit, C. L. (2001). Myelination in the developing human brain. In C. A. Nelson & M. Luciana (Eds.), *Handbook of developmental cognitive neuroscience* (pp. 35–44). Cambridge, MA: MIT Press.

Schacter, D. L., & Tulving, E. (1994). What are the memory systems of 1994? In D. L. Schacter & E. Tulving (Eds.), *Memory systems* (pp. 1–38). Cambridge, MA: MIT Press.

Schacter, D. L., Wagner, A. D., & Buckner, R. L. (2000). Memory systems of 1999. In E. Tulving and F. I. M. Craik (Eds.), *The Oxford handbook of memory* (pp. 627–643). New York: Oxford University Press.

Schneider, J. F. L., Il'yasov, K. A., Hennig, J., & Martin, E. (2004). Fast quantitative diffusion-tensor imaging of cerebral white matter from the neonatal period to adolescence. *Neuroradiology, 46,* 258–266.

Scoville, W. B., & Milner, B. (1957). Loss of recent memory after bilateral hippocampal lesions. *Journal of Neurological and Neurosurgical Psychiatry, 20,* 11–12.

Seress, L. (1992). Morphological variability and developmental aspects of monkey and human granule cells: Differences between the rodent and primate dentate gyrus. *Epilepsy Research, 7* (Supplement), 3–28.

Seress, L. (2001). Morphological changes of the human hippocampal formation from midgestation to early childhood. In C. A. Nelson & M. Luciana (Eds.), *Handbook of developmental cognitive neuroscience* (pp. 45–58). Cambridge, MA: MIT Press.

Seress, L., & Mrzljak, L. (1992). Postnatal development of mossy cells in the human dentate gyrus: A light microscopic Golgi study. *Hippocampus, 2*, 127–142.

Sowell, E. R., Delis, D., Stiles, J., & Jernigan, T. L. (2001a). Improved memory functioning and frontal lobe maturation between childhood and adolescence: A structural MRI study. *Journal of the International Neuropsychological Society, 7*, 312–322.

Sowell, E. R., Thompson, P. M., Holmes, C. J., Batth, R., Jernigan, T. L., & Toga, A. W. (1999). Localizing age-related changes in brain structure between childhood and adolescence using statistical parametric mapping. *NeuroImage, 9*, 587–597.

Sowell, E. R., Thompson, P. M., Tessner, K. D., & Toga, A. W. (2001b). Mapping continued brain growth and gray matter density reduction in dorsal frontal cortex: Inverse relationships during postadolescent brain maturation. *The Journal of Neuroscience, 21*, 8819–8829.

Squire. L. R. (1992). Memory and the hippocampus: A synthesis from findings with rats, monkeys, and humans. *Psychological Review, 99*, 195–231.

Squire, L. R., & Alvarez, P. (1995). Retrograde amnesia and memory consolidation: A neurobiological perspective. *Current Opinion in Neurobiology, 5*, 169–177.

Squire, L. R., & Zola-Morgan, S. (1983). The neurology of memory: The case for correspondence between the findings for human and nonhuman primate. In J. A. Deutsch (Ed.), *The physiological basis of memory* (pp. 199–268). New York: Academic Press.

Takehara, K., Kawahara, S., & Kirino, Y. (2003). Time-dependent reorganization of the brain components underlying memory retention in trace eyeblink conditioning. *The Journal of Neuroscience, 23*, 9897–9905.

Tanapat, P., Hastings, N. B., & Gould, E. (2001). Adult neurogenesis in the hippocampal formation. In C. A. Nelson & M. Luciana (Eds.), *Handbook of developmental cognitive neuroscience* (pp. 93–105). Cambridge, MA: MIT Press.

Van Petten, C. (2004). Relationship between hippocampal volume and memory ability in healthy individuals across the lifespan: Review and meta-analysis. *Neuropsychologia, 42*, 1394–1413.

Wheeler, M. A. (2000). Episodic memory and autonoetic awareness. In E. Tulving and F. I. M. Craik (Eds.), *The Oxford handbook of memory* (pp. 597–608). New York: Oxford University Press.

Yasuno, F., Hirata, M., Takimoto, H., Taniguchi, M., Nakagawa, Y., Ikerjiri, Y., et al. (1999). Retrograde temporal order amnesia resulting from damage to the fornix. *Journal of Neurology, Neurosurgery, and Psychiatry, 67*, 102–105.

Zola, S. M., & Squire, L. R. (2000). The medial-temporal lobe and the hippocampus. In E. Tulving and F. I. M. Craik (Eds.), *The Oxford handbook of memory* (pp. 485–500). New York: Oxford University Press.

7 The development of memory strategies

David F. Bjorklund and Charles Dukes
Florida Atlantic University, USA

Rhonda Douglas Brown
Teachers College, Cincinnati, Ohio, USA

Sometimes memory is easy, like when you're driving down the road and recognize a street corner and just "know" that there's a Starbucks on the next block, or when you're watching *Jeopardy* and you call out "Who was Captain Cook?" to the clue "He was the first European explorer to set foot on Hawaii," and being surprised that you knew that piece of trivia. Other times memory is difficult, like when you're trying to learn and later recall the causes and consequences of the French Revolution, or when, while walking up and down the aisles of the supermarket, you try to reconstruct the grocery list you left on the kitchen table. It is the development of the latter type of explicit, often difficult, memory that is the focus of this chapter, specifically children's use of *strategies*, or *mnemonics*, to acquire and later retrieve information.

STRATEGIES: THEIR DEFINITION, IMPORTANCE TO MEMORY DEVELOPMENT, AND HISTORY

Strategies as effortful and controllable processes

Memory strategies are a particular type of cognitive process. Although different researchers have defined strategies slightly differently, they are generally conceived as mentally effortful, goal-directed processes that are adopted to enhance memory performance. Strategies are controllable and are implemented deliberately by the individual and are potentially available to consciousness (see Harnishfeger & Bjorklund, 1990; Pressley & Hilden, 2006). Strategies co-exist with other cognitive operations and are influenced by many factors. And, above all, strategies develop. Age differences are observed both in the number of strategies children of different ages have available to them and in the efficiency with which they use those strategies.

Geary (1995) suggested that cognitive processes can be classified into one of two broad categories: *biologically primary abilities* and *biologically secondary abilities*. Biologically primary abilities are those that have been selected in evolution and are found in similar forms across cultures. Biologically secondary abilities are those that are shaped by one's particular culture, especially formal schooling. The memory strategies discussed in this chapter are clearly biologically secondary abilities. They are not found universally but are acquired through practice, and some may develop only as a result of formal schooling. In fact, high levels of performance in some school tasks can only be achieved when children use memory strategies. Nonetheless, although we would not expect children to spontaneously use most memory strategies without some instruction, we can expect children to sometimes *discover* strategies while solving certain problems.

Understanding strategy development is important for understanding memory development. The lives of many children, especially those growing up in information-age societies such as ours, require the deliberate acquisition, retention, and retrieval of information, and memory strategies play an important role in such information processing. The number of studies published on this topic over the past four decades in general reflects the significance of strategy development to memory development. Beginning in the 1960s and continuing into the 1990s, research in memory strategy development was predominant in the field of cognitive development. This research focus has waned in the last decade, in large part because of the great amount learned about strategy development in over 30 years of research (Pressley & Hilden, 2006). Despite a shift in research interest from children's strategic (and metastrategic) memory to investigations of children's recollections of real-world events (e.g., Fivush & Hudson, 1990; Ornstein, Haden, & Hedrick, 2004) and memory in preverbal infants (e.g., Bauer, 2006; Rovee-Collier, 1999), the study of memory strategies remains an important topic. Understanding the development of memory strategies is central to one of the principal issues of cognitive development: How do children gain control over their own behavior? Not all important aspects of cognition are controllable by the individual or subject to conscious evaluation; but much of what we consider to be central to human intelligence is intentionally implemented and available to self-awareness, and a look at children's strategies provides a window to this important aspect of cognitive development.

A little history

The modern era of memory development research can trace its beginnings to a paper published in 1966 by Flavell, Beach, and Chinsky. (For a more in-depth review of the history of strategy development research, see Harnishfeger & Bjorklund, 1990.) In this study, Flavell and his colleagues noted that older children who rehearsed sets of pictures during an interval between studying and recalling the pictures, named the pictures to themselves more so than did younger children. This led to research examining the role of *rehearsal* in children's memory development. It also led to questions about why children, who obviously *can* rehearse words, do not do so spontaneously. From this beginning, research in strategy development focused as much on what children *cannot* do as what they *can* do.

Strategy deficiencies: mediation, production, and utilization deficiencies

Even prior to the publication of the work by Flavell and his colleagues on children's rehearsal, it was recognized that, for some problem-solving tasks, many young children could not benefit from a strategy even when one was demonstrated to them. Reese (1962) originally described this as a *mediation deficiency*. The implication was that children do not have the conceptual ability to use a strategy (i.e., strategies fail to mediate, or facilitate, task performance). Most research in memory strategy development, however, has not been concerned with mediation deficiencies, but rather with *production deficiencies* (Flavell, 1970). A production deficiency is inferred when children who do not spontaneously use a strategy can do so when instructed and experience some benefit from its use. That is, their "deficiency" is in terms of producing the strategy, not in benefiting from its use.

A relative newcomer to the "strategy deficiency" list is *utilization deficiency*. Miller (1990) suggested that a utilization deficiency represents an early phase in strategy acquisition when children spontaneously acquire a strategy but experience little or no benefit from it. Unlike mediation deficiencies, children produce the strategy themselves; and unlike production deficiencies, when they use the strategy they experience little or no enhancement of their task performance (see Bjorklund & Coyle, 1995; Miller & Seier, 1994). Miller and Seier (1994) reported strong or partial evidence of utilization deficiencies in more than 90% of all experiments examining children's spontaneous use of memory strategies. Similarly, utilization deficiencies were found in more than 50% of memory training studies conducted over a 30-year period (Bjorklund, Miller, Coyle, & Slawinski, 1997).

Although there seems to be little question that children display utilization deficiencies in their memory performance, there has been substantial debate about their frequency and meaning (e.g., Schlagmüller & Schneider, 2002; Schneider, Kron, Hünnerkopf, & Krajewski, 2004; Waters, 2000). Recent research has concluded that utilization deficiencies are context dependent and only one of several patterns of recall/strategy-use relations that children show. For example, Schwenck, Bjorklund, and Schneider (2007) administered a series of sort-recall trials to first- and third-grade children. Some children were given instructions in strategy use on some trials whereas others were not. A utilization deficiency would be indicated if children's strategy use increased over trials but their levels of recall did not. This pattern was observed for many first- and third-grade children following training or on an immediate transfer trial, in which children maintained a high level of strategy use but did not experience a corresponding improvement in recall. Other children showed increases in both strategy use and recall on adjacent trials, as would be expected if strategies have a direct impact on memory performance. And still other children showed an increase in recall in the absence of an increase in strategy use. This typically happened when children were given the same set of items on consecutive trials. The repetition of the words facilitated the memory for those words without the need of strategies. In general, this research shows that utilization deficiencies are real, but only one of several patterns of recall/strategy-use relations that children show that are influenced by a variety of child and task variables.

The training study

With the emphasis that researchers placed on strategy "deficiencies," it should not be surprising that the principal research paradigm has involved training children to use strategies. Many studies of strategy development follow a three-step process: (1) find a strategy that older children use but younger children do not; (2) train young children to use the strategy and assess the effects of training; and (3) evaluate the extension, or transfer, of training by letting children perform a similar memory task again "any way they want."

Following this paradigm, successful training implies a production deficiency. However, most training studies are done not just to demonstrate that training is possible (that is, to illustrate a production deficiency), but are theoretically motivated. Experimental manipulations are performed to provide some insight into the mechanisms that underlie normal development. When training "works," one can infer something about the processes of natural development. If the experiment was designed to manipulate children's metacognitive awareness, background knowledge, or processing load, the results of the study suggest how these factors may contribute to age differences in memory performance in groups of nontrained children. Similar inferences are made when evaluating transfer of training. Unsuccessful training and transfer can also be informative. For example, if children's memory performance increases during training but falls back to baseline levels on a transfer task, what does it say about the role of the factors being trained?

In the remainder of this chapter, we look at research and theory into children's strategy development. We first look at their existence in young children and pose the question, "What are production deficient children doing?" This is followed by a section examining the development over childhood of some of the different memory strategies that have been studied over the past 40 years. We then review some of the factors that have been shown to influence both developmental and individual differences in children's strategy use. Included in this section are the factors of processing efficiency, the knowledge base, and metamemory. We then take a look at how memory strategies are taught in school and at home and conclude the chapter with a brief overview of where strategy development research has been and where it is likely to be going in the future.

STRATEGIC BEHAVIOR IN YOUNG CHILDREN (OR, WHAT ARE PRODUCTION-DEFICIENT CHILDREN DOING?)

Young children do not display the array of memory strategies that older children do. It is likely inappropriate, however, to call these children astrategic, for a closer examination of their behavior indicates that, at least in some situations, they actually *are* using strategies, just not the ones we think they should be using. The strategies they use are often simple and frequently not very effective, but preschool children do do things to help them remember, and we feel comfortable calling these things strategies (see Wellman, 1988).

A simple strategy used by some 3- and 4-year-olds involves selectively attending to items that they are trying to remember (e.g., Baker-Ward, Ornstein, & Holden, 1984; Wellman, Ritter, & Flavell, 1975). This includes frequently re-attending to the stimuli, which is a form of visual rehearsal. Preschool children have also been observed to spontaneously name items they are asked to remember, but this strategy, although associated with higher levels of memory performance for school-aged children, is ineffective for 4-year-olds (Baker-Ward et al., 1984), reflective of a utilization deficiency.

In other research, Blumberg and Torenberg (2005; Blumberg, Torenberg, & Randall, 2005) showed 3- and 4-year-old children a miniature room containing two classes of objects (e.g., animals and chairs). Children were told that one set of items was "special" ("It's very important that the animals get fed regularly"), and the children's job was to help the experimenter take care of these special things. They were then told to remove all the objects (relevant and irrelevant) from the room. After an intervening task (for example, "feeding" the animals), children were asked to put the objects back in the room where they had been before. Blumberg and Torenberg examined the extent to which children removed and then replaced the objects according to their category membership (e.g., all the animals together, followed by all the chairs together). They reported that about 70% of the preschoolers used a selective removal or replacement strategy. However, use of these strategies was not related to correct relocation of the items, indicative of a utilization deficiency.

One potentially useful strategy involves the use of external memory cues. For example, Heisel and Ritter (1981) asked 3- to 9-year-old children to hide an object in one of 196 containers, arranged in a 14×14 grid, so that they could remember the location. An effective strategy would be to hide objects in distinctive positions, such as the corners of the display, which is what children 5 years of age and older did. The youngest children, however, did not use such techniques, although some attempted to hide the objects in the same location on all trials. This is a good idea and reflects a controllable behavior executed to facilitate performance (that is, a strategy). Unfortunately, 3-year-olds rarely chose distinctive locations to hide objects, making the strategy an ineffective one.

One reason why strategies are rarely observed in young children may be because they perceive the memory tasks they are asked to perform as being irrelevant and meaningless. By the time children from our culture are in first grade, they have learned that many of the tasks adults ask them to do may have no immediate consequences to their lives. That is, these tasks are performed "out of context." Formal schooling in general takes education out of the homes, streets, and fields, where children in more traditional societies are educated, and moves it into the classroom. Perhaps preschool children will show more goal-directed and strategic behavior when the task is embedded in a more relevant context.

This was the approach taken by DeLoache and Brown (DeLoache & Brown, 1983; DeLoache, Cassidy, & Brown, 1985), who investigated young children's memory for the location of hidden objects in a naturalistic setting—their homes. These experimenters used a hide-and-seek-game format, something that even the 18- to 24-month-old children in their studies were familiar with. A toy (Big Bird) was hidden in one of several locations in a child's home, and children were told to remember the location so they could find the toy later. After waiting several minutes, children were permitted to search for the hidden toy. Despite being distracted during the waiting interval, many children showed signs of mnemonic activity. For example, children sometimes checked the hiding place to see if the toy was indeed still hidden there, stated the name of the hidden toy, or stared or pointed at the hiding location during the delay interval.

As this brief overview indicates, it is not appropriate to classify preschool children as astrategic. Under highly constrained, highly motivated, and naturalistic conditions, they do indeed implement what appear to be intentional, goal-directed behaviors. Sometimes these strategies work, and other times they are what Wellman (1988) described as "faulty strategies"—strategic behaviors that do not help remembering—or what Miller (1990) would describe as utilization deficiencies. Wellman (1988) went so far as to claim that preschoolers' strategies are every bit as goal-directed and influential as are the strategies of older children. We make a more cautious interpretation of the research findings. Young children's memory activities tend to be fragile and restricted to limited domains. There has been a tendency in developmental psychology over the past several decades to redress previous overstatements about what infants and young children *cannot do* and instead emphasize what they *can do*. However, while noting that preschoolers are not as deficient in strategic abilities as we once believed they were, we should not overlook the fact that their mnemonic abilities are substantially less than those of older schoolaged children, who display strategies in a wide range of situations, including school-like and laboratory tasks.

AGE CHANGES IN THE USE OF MEMORY STRATEGIES

In the following sections we discuss specific types of memory strategies that have been frequently investigated in developmental psychology. These include *rehearsal, organization,* and *retrieval.* Other, less frequently investigated but often powerful strategies are also examined.

Rehearsal

In 1966, the publication of an innovative study conducted by John Flavell and his colleagues (discussed briefly earlier in the chapter) described the development of rehearsal in children between the ages of 5 and 10. Kindergarten, second-, and fifth-grade children were asked to play some games, during which they wore space helmets with translucent visors. The children observed a set of pictures of familiar objects as an experimenter pointed to three of the pictures in succession. Immediately after presentation and following a 15-second delay, children viewed the set of pictures arranged in a different, random order and were asked to point to the three pictures in the sequence that had been demonstrated earlier by the experimenter (a serial recall task). The children pulled their space helmet visors down during the 15-second delay so they could not see the to-be-remembered items (or the experimenter) during the study period. An experimenter, who was trained to identify lip movements corresponding to the target words, then observed the children's mouths in order to record frequency of rehearsal.

Flavell et al. (1966) reported age-related increases in both the amount of rehearsal and levels of recall. More specifically, 85% of fifth-graders produced some spontaneous rehearsal in comparison to only 10% of kindergartners. Furthermore, within each grade, levels of recall for children who exhibited more rehearsal were generally higher than those of children who rehearsed less. Based on these results, Flavell and his colleagues concluded that verbal rehearsal serves to mediate memory and that the more children rehearse, the more they remember.

This study served as a catalyst for developmental psychologists, and several experiments on children's rehearsal were published in the following years (e.g., Hagen, Hargrave, & Ross, 1973; Kingsley & Hagen, 1969). However, it was not until almost a decade later that Flavell's frequency hypothesis was seriously questioned (Cuvo, 1975; Ornstein, Naus, & Liberty, 1975). For example, in a study by Ornstein and his colleagues, third-, sixth-, and eighth-grade children were presented a series of words for recall with an interval of several seconds between each successive word. Children were instructed to repeat aloud the last word presented at least once and were told that they may repeat any of the other words as well during each rehearsal set. Thus, in this *overt-rehearsal procedure,* rehearsal was mandatory, and the experimenters were able to determine the exact nature of their rehearsal.

In contrast to Flavell's study, the overt-rehearsal procedure did *not* reveal age-related differences in the frequency of rehearsal. Younger children rehearsed just as much as older children, although they recalled fewer items. Ornstein and his colleagues explained these findings in terms of differences in the quality, or style, of rehearsal. More specifically, younger children's rehearsal was characterized as *passive* because they repeated each word starting with only one or two other words during the interstimulus interval. In contrast, the older children rehearsed the target word with many other words during the interstimulus interval, a style labeled *active*, or *cumulative*. This led Ornstein and his colleagues to conclude that the primary developmental change in rehearsal concerns style rather than frequency (see also Cuvo, 1975; Guttentag, Ornstein, & Siemens, 1987).

Training studies provided additional evidence for a causal relationship between rehearsal style and memory performance. For example, young children trained to use a cumulative rehearsal style exhibit increased levels of recall, especially for items presented early in lists (e.g., Cox, Ornstein, Naus, Maxfield, & Zimler, 1989; Ornstein, Naus, & Stone, 1977). Thus, although age differences are rarely eliminated, training young children to use a more effective rehearsal strategy benefits their memory performance. These findings led to the conclusion that a critical developmental difference concerns children's inclination to implement a particular strategy rather than their ability to use it (i.e., they are production deficient).

Organization

One of the most frequently studied strategies involves the organization of stimulus materials into meaningful categories. For example, memory for items that must be purchased at the grocery store is enhanced if the shopper organizes the items into categories (dairy products, meats, or vegetables) or meals (breakfast, lunch, or dinner items).

Studies examining the effects of organization on recall usually involve the random presentation of items that can be organized into categories, such as animals, tools, or fruits. Such studies are designed to detect whether or not children remember items from the same category together even though they were presented randomly, a phenomenon referred to as *clustering*. Results indicate that adults who demonstrate high levels of clustering in their recall generally remember more than adults who demonstrate lower levels of clustering (e.g., Bower, 1970). Developmental trends in clustering and recall indicate that preschoolers perform at chance levels and that clustering and recall increase with age (e.g., Bjorklund, Coyle, & Gaultney, 1992; Lange & Jackson, 1974).

A more direct measurement of organization in memory is obtained through the use of *sort-recall tasks*, in which children are provided with the opportunity to sort items into categories prior to recall. Similar to findings of clustering studies, sort-recall experiments demonstrate that younger children rarely organize (that is, sort) information by meaning spontaneously; however, older children are more likely to do so and experience greater memory performance as a result (e.g., Best & Ornstein, 1986; Hasselhorn, 1992; Schneider, 1986).

Young children's reluctance to use an organizational strategy in sort-recall tasks is illustrated in a study by Salatas and Flavell (1976). First-grade children were given 16 pictures that could be organized into four distinct categories (animals, clothing, toys, and tools). After naming each picture and each of the four categories, the experimenter placed the pictures randomly on a table in front of the children. The children were then told that they would be asked to remember the pictures later and that they should put the pictures together in a way that would help them remember. Free recall was tested 90 seconds later. Despite instructions that would seemingly lead children to physically sort the pictures into categories, only 27% did so.

However, even preschoolers use organizational strategies and demonstrate enhanced levels of memory performance when instructions are modified to emphasize the importance of grouping items according to their meaning (e.g., Lange & Jackson, 1974; Sodian, Schneider, & Perlmutter, 1986), when slight changes in stimulus presentation procedures are made (e.g., Guttentag & Lange, 1994), or when children are explicitly trained to use organizational strategies (e.g., Carr & Schneider, 1991; Lange & Pierce, 1992). In other words, the organizational abilities of preschoolers, kindergartners, and young elementary school children resemble their rehearsal abilities in that they demonstrate a production deficiency. Young children are capable of organizing information for recall, but they typically fail to do so without prompting. Additionally, training rarely eliminates age differences, and young children transfer organizational strategies to new situations only after extensive training (e.g., Carr & Schneider, 1991; Cox & Waters, 1986). Even so, higher levels of organization do not necessarily lead to high levels of recall, providing evidence for utilization deficiencies in organization for preschoolers and elementary school children (e.g., Bjorklund et al., 1992; Lange & Pierce, 1992; Schwenck et al., 2007).

Retrieval

Retrieval strategies can be described as deliberate operations individuals perform in order to access information from long-term memory. A classic demonstration of age differences in retrieval and younger children's deficiencies in using external memory cues was provided by Kobasigawa (1974). First-, third-, and sixth-grade children were presented with sets of categorizable pictures to remember and with cue cards for classifying the pictures. For example, a picture of a zoo served as the cue card for classifying pictures of animals. This procedure required the children to use categorical information as they encoded the items. There were three retrieval conditions in this experiment: *free recall*, in which children were asked to remember the items in any order; *available cue*, in which children were asked to recall the items in any order using the cue cards that had been paired with the items earlier, if they wished; and *directive cue*, in which children were shown each cue card one at a time, told how many items had been paired with it, and then asked to recall as many of those items as they could before going on to the next category.

Results from the experiment are illustrated in Figure 7.1. Levels of performance were generally low in the free-recall condition, with the sixth-graders recalling more than the first- and third-grade children. Recall was elevated in the available-cue condition only for the sixth-graders, who made use of the cues to guide their recall. Only very few first-graders used the available cues to guide their recall, although 75% of the third-graders did so. However, many third-graders who used the cue cards did so poorly, and their recall was not significantly higher than for children in the free-recall condition. The directive-cue condition produced high levels of performance for all children and minimized age differences. This finding indicates that first- and third-graders stored just as much information about the stimuli as sixth-graders; their difficulty was getting it out of memory.

Other studies using similar procedures have also reported considerable reductions in younger children's recall deficits under directive-cue conditions (e.g., Kee & Bell, 1981), and when children are asked to recall information from stories or personal experiences (e.g., Fivush & Hamond, 1990; Hudson, 1990). These studies suggest that younger children benefit more from the presentation of retrieval cues than older children, who may spontaneously generate retrieval plans (e.g., Hasselhorn, 1990; Mistry & Lange, 1985).

Other strategies

In sort-recall tasks, where children have the opportunity to prepare for recall, they can, and often do, use a variety of other strategies to aid their recall. For instance, children can *self-test*, studying the items and then looking away, and practice recall before the "real" test. This is a sophisticated study behavior and is low in frequency among young elementary school children and

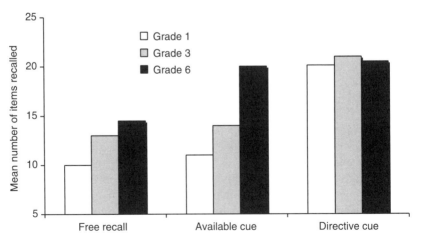

Figure 7.1 Children's mean level of recall by grade and retrieval condition (based on data from Kobasigawa, 1974).

increases in incidence for older schoolage children (e.g., Coyle & Bjorklund, 1997; Shin, Bjorklund, & Beck, 2007). Similarly, children can engage in *category naming* (e.g., "those are vegetable, those are tools"). This is also a low-frequency behavior, especially for young elementary school children, but like self-testing, increases with age (e.g., Shin et al., 2007). Other studies have examined children's *allocation of study time*, evaluating the amount of time children take to prepare for a memory test (e.g., Dufresne & Kobasigawa, 1989; O'Sullivan, 1993). Generally, older (9- and 10-year-olds) relative to younger (6- to 8-year-olds) children allocate more time to studying sets of to-be-remembered items and tend to study "harder" items more than "easier" items (e.g., Dufresne & Kobasigawa, 1989).

One late-developing strategy is *elaboration*. Elaboration is similar to organization in that both strategies involve the imposition of semantic relations on to-be-remembered items. More specifically, in elaboration an association between two or more items is formed by the creation of a representation, such as an image, sentence, or word, that links the items. For example, if you needed to remember to pick up your dry cleaning on the way home from work, you could imagine your car wearing a sports coat. When you saw your car, the ridiculous image of it wearing a coat would increase your chances of stopping at the cleaners.

Elaboration research has typically used the *paired-associate task*, in which participants learn pairs of unrelated items and are later given one item and asked to recall its mate. Children do not spontaneously generate elaborations until adolescence (e.g., Pressley & Levin, 1977; Rohwer, Raines, Eoff, & Wagner, 1977), and even adults often need instructions to elaborate on paired-associate tasks (Rohwer, 1980). Schoolage children can be trained to form elaborations, reflecting a production deficiency (Pressley, 1982; Siaw & Kee, 1987). However, when younger children generate elaborations, they tend to be less effective in aiding performance than those produced by older children, indicative of a utilization deficiency (Reese, 1977).

Another late-developing strategy is the use of external symbols as a memory aid. For instance, Eskritt and Lee (2002) played a memory card game (Concentration, or Memory) with children in grades 1, 3, 5, and 7, in which cards were laid on a table and they had to find pairs that matched, turning over one card at a time. Children were allowed to make notes to aid their performance. Even the first- and third-grade children made notes, but they were generally not helpful in remembering the location of previously seen cards. For example, these young children would sometimes draw pictures unrelated to the memory game. In contrast, the older children's notes aided their performance, for example, by writing the name of a card on the table in its corresponding position on a sheet of paper. In fact, when the notes were unexpectedly taken away, fifth- and seventh-grade children's performance decreased, indicating that the notes were serving as effective memory cues.

Other late-developing memory strategies include those used to remember complex material, such as material from text. These include ways of identifying, underlining, and summarizing the main ideas of text passages, and they typically develop during the high school years and usually only with explicit instruction (see Brown, Bransford, Ferrara, & Campione, 1983; Pressley & Hilden, 2006). (It also seems that these strategies are not being taught in school as frequently or effectively as they should be, see Pressley, Wharton-McDonald, Mistretta-Hampston, & Echevarria, 1998.) As with the previous strategies discussed, production deficiencies and poor performance characterize children's initial use of strategies for understanding and remembering texts. Proficient strategy use can be observed only after extensive practice.

Training experiments reveal that complicated text processing strategies can be taught to normal elementary school children (e.g., Gaultney, 1995; Pressley, Forrest-Pressley, & Elliot-Faust, 1988). Instructional programs that include reading strategy components are beneficial for poor readers as well (Palincsar & Brown, 1984; Short & Ryan, 1984). However, although training promotes the use of complicated text processing strategies, their spontaneous production is the exception rather than the rule. Thus, traditional accounts of strategy development that focus on rote recall seem to underestimate age-related variability in natural strategic competence. That is, although simple strategies can be observed in early childhood, more complex strategies are often not observed even in adults (Pressley & Van Meter, 1993).

One line of recent research has investigated the strategies children use in remembering events, and particularly in rejecting false memories (e.g., Ghetti & Alexander, 2004; Ghetti, Papini, & Angelini, 2006; Roebers & Schneider, 2005). For example, Ghetti and her colleagues investigated what they term the *memorability-based strategy*. When people are asked whether they recall a specific event, they rely, in part, on their expectation of the memorability of that event. Some events, if they happened, would surely be recalled ("Do I remember being chased by a bear? No, and if I had been, I'm sure I would remember it!"), whereas others may be less salient ("Did I eat cornflakes for breakfast last week? Maybe.") In a study by Ghetti and Alexander (2004), 5-, 7-, and 9-year-old children were told of possible events that may have happened to them, some being of high memorability (e.g., taking a trip to the Grand Canyon) and others of low memorability (e.g., wearing a bandage after getting hurt on an eye). The investigators then explained to the children that people typically remember high-memorability events whereas they are more apt to forget low-memorability events. When then asked whether they had experienced certain events, only the 9-year-olds rejected the high-memorability events more than the low-memorability events. In a subsequent training study, 6- and 7-year-old children rejected bizarre (high-memorability) events, suggesting that young schoolage children under some conditions can use a memorability-based strategy (Ghetti et al., 2006).

Table 7.1 presents the typical age of appearance of various memory strategies for children in schooled cultures.

Table 7.1 Approximate ages by which most children display spontaneously various memory strategies effectively for children in schooled cultures[1] (adapted from Schneider & Bjorklund, 2003)

	6–7 years	8–10 years	11–14 years
Single-item rehearsal	X		
Cumulative rehearsal			X
Organization with highly associated items	X		
Organization with less highly associated items		X	
Self-testing/category naming		X	
Effective allocation of study time		X	
Retrieval strategies		X	
Memorability-based strategy		X	
Elaboration[2]			X
Strategies for remembering complex text[2]			X

Notes:
[1] Younger children than listed often display effective strategies when prompted.
[2] These strategies may not be displayed until later, and many adults fail to use these strategies effectively.

Multiple and variable strategy use

Not only are there developmental differences in children's use of individual strategies, but children are also more likely to use multiple strategies with age (e.g., Coyle, 2001; Coyle & Bjorklund, 1997; DeMarie, Miller, Ferron, & Cunningham, 2004; Schwenck et al., 2007). For example, Coyle and Bjorklund (1997) gave second-, third-, and fourth-grade children a series of sort-recall trials and assessed the strategies they used on each trial (sorting, category naming, and rehearsal, and showing high levels of clustering at recall). They reported that the average number of strategies children used per trial increased with age, although even the youngest children used more than one strategy per trial (mean number of strategies per trial = 1.61, 1.91, and 2.40 for children in grades, 2, 3, and 4, respectively). Moreover, the number of strategies children use on a memory task is correlated with amount recalled (e.g., Coyle & Bjorklund, 1997; DeMarie et al., 2004). In other work, second- and fourth-grade children were found to organize different strategies into coherent patterns (Hock, Park, & Bjorklund, 1998). For example, children would sort items into groups and identify categories early in a trial and rehearse or self-test later in a trial. Such patterns were more apparent in fourth-grade than second-grade children.

The nature of developmental changes in memory strategies

The impression one gets when looking at memory strategy research is that children show regular and gradual changes in strategy use over time. However, most studies that have examined age-related changes in strategy use have been cross-sectional—assessing different children at different ages. True patterns of change can only be assessed using longitudinal methods, and until recently few such studies were available. Wolfgang Schneider and his colleagues have conducted two independent longitudinal studies of children's strategic memory development, the Munich Longitudinal Study on the Genesis of Individual Competencies (LOGIC) (Sodian & Schneider, 1999), which followed children between the ages of 4 and 18 years, and the Würzburg Longitudinal Memory Study (Schneider, Kron, Hünnerkopf, & Krajewski, 2004; Schneider, Kron-Sperl, & Hünnerkopf, in press), which has followed children aged between 6 and 9 years, and is continuing. Children's strategic memory was observed at intervals ranging from 6 months to 2 years. Schneider and his colleagues found that very few children displayed gradual changes in strategic memory over time. Rather, when children became strategic it often occurred between consecutive testing intervals, with their performance going from chance to near-perfect levels. Figure 7.2 shows the patterns of strategy change in the two longitudinal studies (from Schneider et al., in press).

As can be seen, a handful of children were nonstrategic at all times tested (most from the Würzburg study that tested younger children), whereas a small

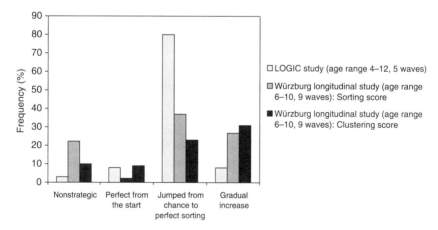

Figure 7.2 Percentage of children in each of the four strategy-change groups from the LOGIC and Würzburg Longitudinal Studies. As can be seen, most children showed abrupt jumps from being nonstrategic to being strategic. (From Schneider, W., Kron-Sperl, V., & Hünnerkopf, M. (in press). The development of young children's memory strategies: Evidence from the Würzburg Longitudinal Memory Study. *European Journal of Developmental Psychology*.) Reproduced by permission of Taylor & Francis Group, LLC., http://www.taylorandfrancis.com.

percentage of other children were strategic from the first time they were tested. Most children in both studies, however, displayed substantial improvement in strategy use over time, with more children in both studies (but especially the LOGIC study with older children) demonstrating "jumps" rather than gradual increases. Thus, although cross-sectional data can give the impression of a gradual change in strategic functioning over childhood, longitudinal data indicate that, for most children, the transition from astrategic to strategic occurs relatively quickly, and at different ages for different children.

A drawback of longitudinal studies for assessing patterns of strategy change is that a lot can happen in 6 months (and even more in 2 years), and it may be that strategy change is happening gradually between the time children are being tested, making the abrupt change more apparent than real (Ornstein, 1999). This was addressed in a *microgenetic study* by Schlagmüller and Schneider (2002). Microgenetic studies assess changes in behaviors that occur over relatively short intervals by testing children repeatedly. In the Schlagmüller and Schneider study, 8- to 12-year-old children performed a series of sort-recall tasks over 11 consecutive weeks. Patterns of change in their recall and strategy use were then assessed, much as was done in the longitudinal studies. Consistent with the findings of the longitudinal studies, they reported that the transition from nonstrategic to strategic functioning occurred quickly, not gradually, and that once children started to use an organizational strategy, they experienced corresponding improvements in their recall.

FACTORS THAT INFLUENCE CHILDREN'S USE OF MEMORY STRATEGIES

From the research presented in the previous sections, it is clear that strategies develop. After describing some of these changes, the next question is, "How?", or more precisely, "What are the factors that contribute to developmental differences in memory strategies?" The list of contributing factors can become quite long, and, of course, any factor does not have its effect independent of others. Moreover, although some of these factors may have a greater influence than others, it is not possible to point to any single factor as "the" principal cause of strategy development. Any factor may have a different effect on strategy performance as a function of the age, background knowledge, and ability level of the child, as well as the strategy in question. In this section, we examine three of the most important and most studied influences on children's memory strategies. Included in our survey are efficiency of cognitive processing, knowledge base, and metamemory.

Efficiency of cognitive processing: Strategies and mental effort

By definition, strategies are effortful mental processes, consuming some portion of a person's limited mental resources for their execution. One hypothesis concerning age differences in strategy use revolves around age differences in the efficiency of cognitive processing. Younger children process information more slowly (e.g., Kail & Miller, 2006) and less efficiently (Case, 1985) than older children. As a result, they are less likely to use a strategy spontaneously and less likely to benefit from the imposition of a strategy (Bjorklund, 1987; Kee, 1994). That is, strategy use has a cost in terms of mental effort. Young children use so much of their limited cognitive resources executing the strategy that they do not retain sufficient mental capacity to perform other aspects of the task efficiently (Case, 1985; Cowan et al. 2005).

How can one test this hypothesis? One technique that has been used is the *dual-task paradigm*, which is based on the simple idea that it is difficult to do two things at once. The degree of this difficulty is reflected in the amount of interference that doing one task has on doing the other. For example, Bjorklund and Harnishfeger (1987) used a dual-task paradigm to assess the degree of mental effort required to execute a memory strategy for third- and seventh-grade children. In their study (Experiment 2), children tapped the space bar of a computer as rapidly as they could: (a) alone (baseline); (b) during a free-recall task with categorically related words (free recall); and (c) during a free-recall task in which they were trained to use an organizational memory strategy (trained recall). Changes in tapping rate between the free- and trained-recall sessions, all relative to baseline tapping rate, reflect the differences in the mental effort requirements of the two tasks. It was expected that the trained task, on which children were required to use an organizational strategy, would be more effortful than the free-recall task. Also assessed were changes in levels of recall and clustering, the latter of which served as the measure of strategy use.

Levels of recall, clustering, and percentage interference in tapping rate for the third- and seventh-graders on the free- and trained-recall tasks are shown in Table 7.2. As can be seen, both the third- and the seventh-graders

Table 7.2 Mean recall, clustering, and percentage interference scores for free recall (baseline) and trained recall for third- and seventh-grade children. (From Bjorklund, D. F., & Harnishfeger, K. K. (1987). Developmental differences in the mental effort requirements for the use of an organizational strategy in free recall. *Journal of Experimental Child Psychology, 44,* 109–125; Experiment 2.)

	Free recall	*Trained recall*
Third grade		
Percent interference	17.31	21.29 ($p < .01$)
Clustering (ARC)	.14	.53 ($p < .001$)
Recall	4.60	5.07 (ns)
Seventh grade		
Percent interference	18.07	23.53 ($p < .01$)
Clustering (ARC)	.09	.80 ($p < .001$)
Recall	5.89	7.73 ($p < .01$)

experienced more interference in tapping rate for the trained- than for the free-recall task, and both demonstrated significant improvements in clustering. These findings indicate that both groups of children learned the instructed organizational strategy and that using this strategy was significantly more effortful than not using it. However, only the older children also experienced a significant increase in recall on the trained trial. The third-grade children, despite successfully using the trained strategy (as reflected by the higher clustering scores), did not show a corresponding increase in recall (i.e., they displayed a utilization deficiency). Bjorklund and Harnishfeger interpreted these findings as reflecting the fact that the younger children expended too much of their limited mental resources executing the strategy and thus had too few resources remaining to devote to retrieving individual items.

Similar findings and interpretations have been reported in other free-recall tasks (Guttentag, 1984), for simpler attentional strategies (Miller, Seier, Probert, & Aloise, 1991), and for elaboration (Kee & Davies, 1990). In other studies, individual differences in working memory, a measure of mental capacity, predicted the efficiency of strategy use for kindergarten and first-grade children (Woody-Dorning & Miller, 2001) and adults (Gaultney, Kipp, & Kirk, 2005). Children and adults with greater working memory demonstrated more benefit in task performance from using a strategy than did those with lesser working memory.

Other researchers have developed models to describe how capacity and other factors interact to influence children's memory performance (e.g., DeMarie & Ferron, 2003; DeMarie et al., 2004). For example, DeMarie and her colleagues (2004) administered a series of capacity (such as working memory), metamemory, intelligence, and strategic memory tasks to children between the ages of 5 and 11 years. They performed a series of path analyses to describe the data. The model that best described the results consisted of two parts, the first focusing on *strategy production* (which is influenced by capacity and metamemory), and the second focusing on *strategy effectiveness*. Important for our discussion here is the significant role that capacity had in interaction with strategy use in influencing memory performance. This model, which they referred to as the Utilization Deficiency Model because it predicted the incidence of utilization deficiencies in their participants, is schematically displayed in Figure 7.3.

Knowledge base

Differences in efficiency of cognitive processing certainly have a profound effect on strategic memory. Moreover, because speed of processing, which is the single best indicator of efficiency of processing, varies reliably with age and is presumably under endogenous control (Kail & Miller, 2006), it is tempting to think that cognitive efficiency is therefore under strict maturational control and is relatively uninfluenced by other factors. This is not the

Utilization Deficiency

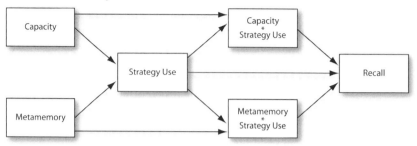

Figure 7.3 The Utilization Deficiency Model of children's memory development. (Adapted from DeMarie, D., Miller, P. H., Ferron, J., & Cunningham, W. R. (2004). Path analysis tests of theoretical models of children's memory performance. *Journal of Cognition and Development, 5*, 461–492.)

case, however. Speed and efficiency of processing are also influenced by one's *knowledge base*—the background information a person has about a particular topic. For instance, memory span and working-memory span, which are often used as measures of information-processing capacity (see Chapter 12 in this volume, by Cowan & Alloway), are influenced by a child's knowledge base for the to-be-remembered information (Chi, 1978; Dempster, 1978; Schneider, Gruber, Gold, & Opwis, 1993). For example, in the classic study by Chi (1978), the memory span of chess-expert children for chess pieces on a chessboard was superior to that of a group of nonchess-expert adults. The pattern was reversed when digits were used as stimuli. Do these children have greater *capacity* for chess pieces than for digits? Yes and no. Although it seems that there are indeed some age differences in the *actual capacity* of working memory, as assessed by span of apprehension tests (Cowan, Nugent, Elliott, Ponomarev, & Saults, 1999; see Cowan & Alloway, Chapter 12, this volume), perhaps more important are difference in *functional capacity* of working memory; people use their limited information-processing capacity more efficiently when dealing with information for which they have detailed knowledge (see Bjorklund, 1987; Kee, 1994).

How does knowledge influence children's use of memory strategies? Most researchers believe that having a detailed, or elaborated, knowledge base results in faster processing, which in turn results in more efficient processing. According to Bjorklund, Muir-Broaddus, and Schneider (1990, p. 95):

> the primary effect that an elaborated knowledge base has on cognitive processing is to increase speed of processing for domain-specific information. Individual items can be accessed more quickly from the long-term store, as can relations among related items in the knowledge base . . . [F]aster processing is equated with more efficient processing, which results in greater availability of mental resources. These mental resources

can then be applied to retrieving specific items (item specific effects . . .), to domain-specific strategies, or to metacognitive processes.

There have been many demonstrations of both developmental and individual differences in strategy use and memory performance as a function of knowledge base. For example, when children are given sets of category typical items to remember (e.g., for CLOTHING, *shirt, dress, coat*) as opposed to sets of category atypical items (e.g., for CLOTHING, *hat, socks, belt*), levels of both strategy use (usually clustering) and memory performance are greater for the category typical sets of items (e.g., Bjorklund, 1988; Rabinowitz, 1984; Schwenck et al., 2007). In other research, young children perform well when sets of highly associated items serve as stimuli (e.g., *dog, cat, horse, cow*), but not when equally familiar but less strongly associated category items are used as stimuli (e.g., *tiger, elephant, cow, pig*). Older children perform well for both sets of materials (e.g., Bjorklund & Jacobs, 1985; Schneider, 1986). The apparent reason for this pattern is that highly associated words become well established early in life (Bjorklund & Jacobs, 1984), whereas relations among the less strongly related category items are not established until later in development. Other research has shown that children acquire strategies more readily, both spontaneously and through training, and generalize a learned strategy to new contexts more successfully when familiar and well-integrated sets of items (such as highly associated words or category typical items), as opposed to less familiar and well integrated sets of items (such as low associated words or category atypical items), are used as stimuli (e.g., Best, 1993; Schneider, 1986; Schwenck et al., 2007).

Although the impact of knowledge base on children's strategic memory seems incontrovertible, there is one peculiar finding that deserves attention. When comparing the memory performance on strategic memory tasks of experts and novices on materials in the experts' area of specialty, the experts always remember more than the novices. The surprising finding, however, is that this memory advantage is not always mediated by strategies. For example, several free- and sort-recall experiments have contrasted the memory performance of expert children (in soccer or baseball) with those of novices. The typical result is significantly greater memory performance for the experts when the list consists of categories and items from the experts' area of expertise (e.g., baseball equipment, types of baseball plays). Yet few or no differences are found between the experts and novices for strategy use (e.g., clustering or sorting) (Gaultney, Bjorklund, & Schneider, 1992; Schneider & Bjorklund, 1992; Schneider, Bjorklund, & Maier-Brücker, 1996). These findings suggest that the enhanced performance on strategic tasks for expert children is primarily mediated by item-specific effects associated with their more elaborated knowledge base rather than through more effective use of strategies.

In some cases, children may have such well-developed knowledge bases that organized retrieval can be achieved without the need of a deliberate strategy. For example, Bjorklund and Zeman (1982, 1983) reported that first-through fifth-grade children recalled the names of their current school class-mates in highly organized orders (e.g., by seating arrangement, reading groups, or sex), yet seemed unaware that they were following any particular scheme. Rather, because their classmates' names constituted a well-established knowledge base, the recall of one name automatically activated the recall of another, without the need of a deliberate plan. They speculated that this process of nonstrategic organization could sometimes lead to strategic organ-ization. In the process of retrieving names via the relatively automatic acti-vation of semantic-memory relations, children may reflect on what they have done and discover a strategy in the process ("Hey, all these kids sit together. Maybe I'll remember the rest of the class that way."). In this case, an elaborated knowledge base might indirectly lead to better strategy use (see Bjorklund & Jacobs, 1985 for a demonstration of this).

The evidence for a potent role of knowledge base in children's strategic memory cannot be denied. In fact, it seems that there is no other single factor that has such an effect on children's memory performance. In studies that have assessed the impact of a variety of factors on children's free recall, including intelligence, metamemory, and knowledge base, more of the differences in memory performance can be attributed to differences in knowledge base than to any other factor (Alexander & Schwanenflugel, 1994; Hasselhorn, 1992).

Metamemory

Metamemory can be described as knowledge an individual possesses regard-ing the functioning and contents of his or her memory. Although the rela-tionship is far from perfect, high levels of metamemory are usually associated with high levels of memory performance (see Schneider & Lockl, 2002; Schneider & Pressley, 1997).

What do children know about memory strategies? To find out, Justice (1985) showed children videotaped examples of other children using different strat-egies (e.g., looking, naming, rehearsing, and grouping). Children were then presented with each strategy paired with each other one, one pair at a time, and asked which of the two strategies was better suited for remembering. This and similar studies (e.g., Justice, 1986; Schneider, 1986) produced a consistent picture of children's developing strategy knowledge. Kindergarten and young elementary-school children recognized differential effectiveness only when strategies produced substantial differences in performance (e.g., grouping versus looking), whereas older children were more likely to detect subtle differences in strategy effectiveness.

Memory monitoring is an important aspect of metamemory that has been found to be related to children's strategy use and effectiveness. Memory (or self-) monitoring can be described as a bottom-up process that involves keep-ing track of one's progress towards goals concerning understanding and remembering (Schneider & Bjorklund, 1998, 2003). Several researchers have provided evidence that training in memory-monitoring enhances the effectiveness and maintenance of strategy training (e.g., Ghatala, Levin, Pressley, & Goodwin, 1986; Ringel & Springer, 1980). For example, Ringel and Springer (1980) trained first-, third-, and fifth-graders in the use of an organizational strategy. In comparison to a baseline phase, all participants demonstrated increases in memory performance as a result of training. After completing training, some participants were given explicit feedback regarding their improved performance on the task and others were not. Fifth-graders demonstrated successful transfer of the organizational strategy in both conditions, whereas first-graders failed to demonstrate any significant transfer. However, third-graders who received feedback generalized the organizational strategy to a transfer task, whereas those who did not receive feedback failed to demonstrate any significant transfer. Thus, information regarding their memory performance affected third-graders' generalization of a strategy. The older children did not appear to need feedback, presumably because they were capable of assessing their own progress, and the younger children were either incapable of transferring the strategy or insufficiently trained. This study is consistent with the findings of other researchers who note that transfer of strategy training is most effective when the training includes a significant metamemory component (e.g., Ghatala et al., 1986; Lodico, Ghatala, Levin, Pressley, & Bell, 1983).

Metamemory was one of the factors that DeMarie and her colleagues included in their evaluations of models of memory development (DeMarie & Ferron, 2003; DeMarie et al., 2004; see also Pierce & Lange, 2000). As you can see in Figure 7.3, metamemory played a major role in the Utilization Deficiency Model that best described 5- to 11-year-old children's memory behavior. They further reported that individual differences in metamemory appear to have a greater impact on the performance of older relative to younger children (DeMarie & Ferron, 2003), and influence both the number of strategies children are apt to use and the effectiveness of those strategies (DeMarie et al., 2004).

There is one aspect of metamemory that may be inversely related to strategic memory, and that is memory estimation. Young children consistently overestimate their memory abilities (e.g., Schneider, 1998; Shin et al., 2007; Yussen & Levy, 1975). However, rather than being a deficit, such overestimation of one's abilities may serve to protect children's self-efficacy with respect to memory performance. Children whose memory performance is relatively low should benefit from believing that they are doing better than they actually are, and as a result maintain high levels of motivation and persist at the task at hand more so than poor-performing children who are more in touch with their cognitive abilities. Shin and her colleagues (2007) investigated this on a multi-trial sort-recall task with kindergarten, first-, and third-grade children, and reported that children who overestimated how many items they thought they would remember on earlier trials showed greater memory gains (or smaller losses) on subsequent trials than more accurate children. Shin et al. argued that the children who were more out of touch with their abilities were not discouraged by their initially poor memory performance and persevered more on later trials than their more in-touch peers.

There are many factors that influence children's memory strategies, and we have examined here only the three that have garnered the most research attention. Other basic-level cognitive factors, such as how children encode, or represent, the information they are trying to remember (e.g., Ackerman, 1987), influence children's use of memory strategies, as do a myriad of other factors including intelligence (e.g., Bjorklund & Schneider, 1996; Pressley & Hilden, 2006) and motivation (e.g., Guttentag, 1995; Pierce & Lange, 2000). However, as recent models of strategic memory development reveal (e.g., DeMarie et al., 2004), these effects are interactive, and researchers study the influence on memory development of one or two factors at a time, not because they believe that memory is influenced only by a small number of factors, but because of practical considerations of testing both children and theoretical models.

Although the field of strategy development has relied on training experiments, most of the interventions have been brief and generalization of the strategies limited to laboratory contexts. Memory strategies are relevant in the real world, however, especially for children in schooled cultures such as ours. In the next section we examine the relation between schooling and children's memory strategies.

SCHOOLING AND STRATEGIES

We noted at the beginning of this chapter that, following Geary's (1995) classification, memory strategies are biologically secondary abilities in that they are highly dependent on cultural experience. In fact, some of the memory strategies discussed in this chapter are likely found almost exclusively in schooled cultures. This is not to say that people from more traditional cultures do not use memory strategies, merely that the intellectual demands of their environment are different from those of us growing up in information-age societies, and that the out-of-context-type of memory strategies that develop so predictably in our culture may not develop in the same manner in theirs.

Moely and her colleagues conducted several studies examining strategy instruction in American schools, and they report that there is substantial variability among teachers in the degree to which they teach strategies (Moely et al., 1992; Moely et al., 1986; Moely, Santulli, & Obach, 1995). Specific strategy instruction was generally low in most classrooms they observed, with instruction varying with subject matter (for example, strategies were more likely to be taught for solving math problems). Children from classrooms where strategies were taught more often seemed to garner some advantage from their experience, showing higher levels of achievement (Moely et al., 1995).

In an ongoing longitudinal study, Ornstein, Coffman, and McCall (2005) evaluated first-grade teachers' use of "mnemonic orientation" in their classroom and related it to children's strategic memory behavior. Teachers with a high mnemonic orientation emphasized strategy instruction, provided metacognitive information (e.g., "How did you study those words?"; "If you make a picture in your mind, it will help you to remember"), made memory requests, and structured cognitive activities more so than teachers with a low mnemonic orientation. They reported that children with teachers with a high mnemonic orientation displayed higher levels of strategy use on memory tasks than children with teachers with a low mnemonic orientation, and that this difference was maintained at least into the second grade, when children were in new classrooms with different teachers.

Differences in strategy instruction in school and in the home may also account for some cross-cultural differences in memory performance. For example, research comparing German and American children on sets of strategic memory tasks reported a consistent advantage for the German children as young as 7 years of age (e.g., Carr, Kurtz, Schneider, Turner, & Borkowski, 1989; Kurtz, Schneider, Carr, Borkowski, & Rellinger, 1990). The apparent reason for the German children's superior performance was found in instructional practices in their schools and homes. Questionnaires completed by children's teachers and parents revealed that the German teachers taught more strategies in schools than the American teachers, and that the German parents engaged in more games requiring strategies with their children than the American parents.

CONCLUSION

The modern era of memory development began with the study of strategies. Strategies develop, with children using a larger variety of effective strategies as they age. Our view of the role of strategies has changed somewhat since the early days of memory development research. Strategies are still important, especially for people growing up in information-age societies. But much of what is important and interesting in memory development is not highly effortful or planful, and this volume represents many other aspects of memory development that deserve serious attention. Moreover, memory strategies do not develop in as straightforward a way as we once thought. Instead, there is evidence that strategies do not develop gradually but may actually increase abruptly and in combination with other strategies. Strategies do not always help performance, at least not immediately, and simple and inefficient strategies reside alongside more sophisticated and efficient ones, competing for use. The process of strategy development is not one of simply replacing the ineffective with the effective (see Siegler, 1996).

What is the future of strategy research? First, we expect that the issue of strategy variability will become more important (see Coyle, 2001). For example, what is the relation between strategy variability, age, and strategy effectiveness? Are children who show more variability in strategy use different in any important way from less variable children? Second, we expect that researchers will take closer looks at strategies that develop in more naturalistic contexts, that is, not in school and for school-specific tasks. What role do parents and peers play in fostering children's use of simple learning and memory strategies? Do these real-world strategies generalize to school? Third, as we learn more about the processes of strategy development, researchers will be asking themselves what is universal and typical of all members of the species with respect to strategy development and what is tied to specific cultural contexts. Cross-cultural studies, examining both developmental and individual differences, will need to be done in order to answer these questions. And fourth, more still needs to be learned about school-type strategies. When is the best time to teach various strategies to children? Is earlier always better, or might it be desirable to wait until children's general cognitive abilities are better developed before beginning some instruction? How can we best teach strategies, especially to low-achieving children?

Research into memory strategies has changed over the decades, as any vital research topic must change. The questions scientists are now asking reflect the diversity of factors that affect children's strategy use and the insight that there is no single developmental pathway that all children in a culture must follow to become effective rememberers.

REFERENCES

Ackerman, B. P. (1987). Descriptions: A model of nonstrategic memory development. In H. W. Reese (Ed.), *Advances in child development and behavior* (Vol. 20, pp. 143–183). Orlando, FL: Academic Press.

Alexander, J. M., & Schwanenflugel, P. J. (1994). Strategy regulation: The role of intelligence, metacognitive attributes, and knowledge base. *Developmental Psychology, 30*, 709–723.

Baker-Ward, L., Ornstein, P. A., & Holden, D. J. (1984). The expression of memorization in early childhood. *Journal of Experimental Child Psychology, 37*, 555–575.

Bauer, P. (2006). *Remembering the times of our lives: Memory in infancy and beyond.* Mahwah, NJ: Lawrence Erlbaum Associates, Inc.

Best, D. L. (1993). Inducing children to generate mnemonic organizational strategies: An examination of long-term retention and materials. *Developmental Psychology, 29*, 324–336.

Best, D. L., & Ornstein, P. A. (1986). Children's generation and communication of mnemonic organizational strategies. *Developmental Psychology, 22*, 845–853.

Bjorklund, D. F. (1987). How age changes in knowledge base contribute to the development of children's memory: An interpretive review. *Developmental Review, 7*, 93–130.

Bjorklund, D. F. (1988). Acquiring a mnemonic: Age and category knowledge effects. *Journal of Experimental Child Psychology*, *45*, 71–87.

Bjorklund, D. F., & Coyle, T. R. (1995). Utilization deficiencies in the development of memory strategies. In F. E. Weinert & W. Schneider (Eds.), *Memory performance and competencies: Issues in growth and development* (pp. 161–180). Hillsdale, NJ: Lawrence Erlbaum Associates, Inc.

Bjorklund, D. F., Coyle, T. R., & Gaultney, J. F. (1992). Developmental differences in the acquisition and maintenance of an organizational strategy: Evidence for the utilization deficiency hypothesis. *Journal of Experimental Child Psychology*, *54*, 434–448.

Bjorklund, D. F., & Harnishfeger, K. K. (1987). Developmental differences in the mental effort requirements for the use of an organizational strategy in free recall. *Journal of Experimental Child Psychology*, *44*, 109–125.

Bjorklund, D. F., & Jacobs, J. W. (1984). A developmental examination of ratings of associative strengths. *Behavior Research Methods, Instruments and Computers*, *16*, 568–569.

Bjorklund, D. F., & Jacobs, J. W. (1985). Associative and categorical processes in children's memory: The role of automaticity in the development of organization in free recall. *Journal of Experimental Child Psychology*, *39*, 599–617.

Bjorklund, D. F., Miller, P. H., Coyle, T. R., & Slawinski, J. L. (1997). Instructing children to use memory strategies: Evidence of utilization deficiencies in memory training studies. *Developmental Review*, *17*, 411–442.

Bjorklund, D. F., Muir-Broaddus, J. E., & Schneider, W. (1990). The role of knowledge in the development of strategies. In D. F. Bjorklund (Ed.), *Children's strategies: Contemporary views of cognitive development* (pp. 93–128). Hillsdale, NJ: Lawrence Erlbaum Associates, Inc.

Bjorklund, D. F., & Schneider, W. (1996). The interaction of knowledge, aptitudes, and strategies in children's memory performance. In H. W. Reese (Ed.), *Advances in child development and behavior* (Vol. 25, pp. 59–89). San Diego: Academic Press.

Bjorklund, D. F., & Zeman, B. R. (1982). Children's organization and metamemory awareness in the recall of familiar information. *Child Development*, *53*, 799–810.

Bjorklund, D. F., & Zeman, B. R. (1983). The development of organizational strategies in children's recall of familiar information: Using social organization to recall the names of classmates. *International Journal of Behavioral Development*, *6*, 341–353.

Blumberg, F. C., & Torenberg, M. (2005). The effects of spatial configuration on preschoolers' attention strategies, selective attention, and incidental learning. *Infant and Child Development*, *14*, 243–258.

Blumberg, F. C., Torenberg, M., & Randall, J. D. (2005). The relationship between preschoolers' selective attention and memory for location strategies. *Cognitive Development*, *20*, 242–255.

Bower, G. H. (1970). Organizational factors in memory. *Cognitive Psychology*, *1*, 18–46.

Brown, A. L., Bransford, J. D., Ferrara, R. A., & Campione, J. C. (1983). Learning, remembering, and understanding. In J. H. Flavell & E. M. Markman (Eds.), *Handbook of child psychology* (Vol. 3, pp. 77–166). New York: Wiley.

Carr, M., Kurtz, B. E., Schneider, W., Turner, L. A., & Borkowski, J. G. (1989). Strategy acquisition and transfer among American and German children: Environmental influences on metacognitive development. *Developmental Psychology*, *25*, 765–771.

Carr, M., & Schneider, W. (1991). Long-term maintenance of organizational strategies in kindergarten children. *Contemporary Educational Psychology, 16*, 61–72.

Case, R. (1985). *Intellectual development: Birth to adulthood*. New York: Academic Press.

Chi, M. T. H. (1978). Knowledge structure and memory development. In R. Siegler (Ed.), *Children's thinking: What develops?* (pp. 73–96). Hillsdale, NJ: Lawrence Erlbaum Associates, Inc.

Cowan, N., Elliott, E. M., Saults, J. S., Morey, C. C., Mattox, S., Hismjatullino, A., et al. (2005). On the capacity of attention: Its estimation and its role in working memory and cognitive aptitudes. *Cognitive Psychology, 51*, 42–100.

Cowan, N., Nugent, L. D., Elliott, E. M., Ponomarev, I., & Saults, J. S. (1999). The role of attention in the development of short-term memory: Age differences in the verbal span of apprehension. *Child Development, 70*, 1082–1097.

Cox, B. D., Ornstein, P. A., Naus, M. J., Maxfield, D., & Zimler, J. (1989). Children's concurrent use of rehearsal and organizational strategies. *Developmental Psychology, 25*, 619–627.

Cox, D., & Waters, H. S. (1986). Sex differences in the use of organization strategies: A developmental analysis. *Journal of Experimental Child Psychology, 41*, 18–37.

Coyle, T. R. (2001). Factor analysis of variability measures in eight independent samples of children and adults. *Journal of Experimental Child Psychology, 78*, 330–358.

Coyle, T. R., & Bjorklund, D. F. (1997). Age differences in, and consequences of, multiple- and variable-strategy use on a multitrial sort-recall task. *Developmental Psychology, 33*, 372–380.

Cuvo, A. J. (1975). Developmental differences in rehearsal and free recall. *Journal of Experimental Child Psychology, 19*, 265–278.

DeLoache, J. S., & Brown, A. L. (1983). Very young children's memory for the location of objects in a large scale environment. *Child Development, 54*, 888–897.

DeLoache, J. S., Cassidy, D. J., & Brown, A. L. (1985). Precursors of mnemonic strategies in very young children's memory. *Child Development, 56*, 125–137.

DeMarie, D., & Ferron, J. (2003). Capacity, strategies, and metamemory: Tests of a three-factor model of memory development. *Journal of Experimental Child Psychology, 84*, 167–193.

DeMarie, D., Miller, P. H., Ferron, J., & Cunningham, W. R. (2004). Path analysis tests for theoretical models of children's memory performance. *Journal of Cognition and Development, 5*, 461–492.

Dempster, F. N. (1978). Memory span and short-term memory capacity: A developmental study. *Journal of Experimental Child Psychology, 26*, 419–431.

Dufresne, A., & Kobasigawa, A. (1989). Children's spontaneous allocation of study time: Differential and sufficient aspects. *Journal of Experimental Child Psychology, 47*, 274–296.

Eskritt, M., & Lee, K. (2002). "Remember where you last saw that card": Children's production of external symbols as a memory aid. *Developmental Psychology, 38*, 254–266.

Fivush, R., & Hamond, N. R. (1990). Autobiographical memory across the preschool years: Toward reconceptualizing childhood amnesia. In R. Fivush & J. A. Hudson (Eds.), *Knowing and remembering in young children* (pp. 223–248). Cambridge: Cambridge University Press.

Fivush, R., & Hudson, J. A. (1990). *Knowing and remembering in young children.* Cambridge: Cambridge University Press.

Flavell, J. H. (1970). Developmental studies of mediated memory. In H. W. Reese & L. P. Lipsitt (Eds.), *Advances in child development and behavior* (pp. 181–211). New York: Academic Press.

Flavell, J. H., Beach, D. H., & Chinsky, J. M. (1966). Spontaneous verbal rehearsal in a memory task as a function of age. *Child Development, 37,* 283–299.

Gaultney, J. F. (1995). The effect of prior knowledge and metacognition on the acquisition of a reading comprehension strategy. *Journal of Experimental Child Psychology, 59,* 142–163.

Gaultney, J. F., Bjorklund, D. F., & Schneider, W. (1992). The role of children's expertise in a strategic memory task. *Contemporary Educational Psychology, 17,* 244–257.

Gaultney, J. F., Kipp, K., & Kirk, G. (2005). Utilization deficiency and working memory capacity in adult memory performance: Not just for children anymore. *Cognitive Development, 20,* 205–213.

Geary, D. C. (1995). Reflections of evolution and culture in children's cognition: Implications for mathematical development and instruction. *American Psychologist, 50,* 24–37.

Ghatala, E. S., Levin, J. R., Pressley, M., & Goodwin, D. (1986). A componential analysis of the effects of derived and supplied strategy-utility information on children's strategy selection. *Journal of Experimental Child Psychology, 41,* 76–92.

Ghetti, S., & Alexander, K. W. (2004). "If it happened, I would remember it": Strategic use of event memorability in the rejection of false autobiographical events. *Child Development, 75,* 542–561.

Ghetti, S., Papini, S., & Angelini, L. (2006). The development of the memorability-based strategy: Insight from a training study. *Journal of Experimental Child Psychology, 94,* 206–228.

Guttentag, R. E. (1984). The mental effort requirement of cumulative rehearsal: A developmental study. *Journal of Experimental Child Psychology, 37,* 92–106.

Guttentag, R. E. (1995). Mental effort and motivation: Influences on children's memory strategy use. In F. E. Weinert & W. Schneider (Eds.), *Research on memory development: State of the art and future directions* (pp. 207–224). Hillsdale, NJ: Lawrence Erlbaum Associates, Inc.

Guttentag, R. E., & Lange, G. (1994). Motivational influences on children's strategic remembering. *Learning and Individual Differences, 6,* 309–330.

Guttentag, R. E., Ornstein, P. A., & Siemens, L. (1987). Children's spontaneous rehearsal: Transitions in strategy acquisition. *Cognitive Development, 2,* 307–326.

Hagen, J. W., Hargrave, S., & Ross, W. (1973). Prompting and rehearsal in short-term memory. *Child Development, 44,* 201–204.

Harnishfeger, K. K., & Bjorklund, D. F. (1990). Children's strategies: A brief history. In D. F. Bjorklund (Ed.), *Children's strategies: Contemporary views of cognitive development* (pp. 1–22). Hillsdale, NJ: Lawrence Erlbaum Associates, Inc.

Hasselhorn, M. (1990). The emergence of strategic knowledge activation in categorical clustering during retrieval. *Journal of Experimental Child Psychology, 50,* 59–80.

Hasselhorn, M. (1992). Task dependency and the role of category typicality and metamemory in the development of an organizational strategy. *Child Development, 63,* 202–214.

Heisel, B. E., & Ritter, K. (1981). Young children's storage behavior in a memory for location task. *Journal of Experimental Child Psychology, 31*, 350–364.

Hock, H. S., Park, C. L., & Bjorklund, D. F. (1998). Temporal organization in children's strategy formation. *Journal of Experimental Child Psychology, 70*, 187–206.

Hudson, J. A. (1990). The emergence of autobiographical memory in mother–child conversation. In R. Fivush & J. A. Hudson (Eds.), *Knowing and remembering in young children* (pp. 166–196). Cambridge: Cambridge University Press.

Justice, E. M. (1985). Categorization as a preferred memory strategy: Developmental changes during elementary school. *Developmental Psychology, 21*, 1105–1110.

Justice, E. M. (1986). Developmental changes in judgements of relative strategy effectiveness. *British Journal of Developmental Psychology, 4*, 75–81.

Kail, R. V., & Miller, C. A. (2006). Developmental change in processing speed: Domain specificity and stability during childhood and adolescence. *Journal of Cognition and Development, 7*, 119–137.

Kee, D. W. (1994). Developmental differences in associative memory: Strategy use, mental effort, and knowledge access interactions. In H. W. Reese (Ed.), *Advances in child development* (Vol. 25, pp. 7–32). San Diego, CA: Academic Press.

Kee, D. W., & Bell, T. S. (1981). The development of organizational strategies in the storage and retrieval of categorical items in free-recall learning. *Child Development, 52*, 1163–1171.

Kee, D. W., & Davies, L. (1990). Mental effort and elaboration: Effects of accessibility and instruction. *Journal of Experimental Child Psychology, 49*, 264–274.

Kingsley, P. R., & Hagen, J. W. (1969). Induced versus spontaneous rehearsal in short-term memory in nursery school children. *Developmental Psychology, 1*, 40–46.

Kobasigawa, A. (1974). Utilization of retrieval cues by children in recall. *Child Development, 45*, 127–134.

Kurtz, B. E., Schneider, W., Carr, M., Borkowski, J. G., & Rellinger, E. (1990). Strategy instruction and attributional beliefs in West Germany and the United States: Do teachers foster metacognitive development? *Contemporary Educational Psychology, 15*, 268–283.

Lange, G., & Jackson, P. (1974). Personal organization in children's free recall. *Child Development, 45*, 1060–1067.

Lange, G., & Pierce, S. H. (1992). Memory-strategy learning and maintenance in preschool children. *Developmental Psychology, 28*, 453–462.

Lodico, M. G., Ghatala, E. S., Levin, J. R., Pressley, M., & Bell, J. A. (1983). The effects of strategy-monitoring on children's selection of effective memory strategies. *Journal of Experimental Child Psychology, 35*, 263–277.

Miller, P. H. (1990). The development of strategies of selective attention. In D. F. Bjorklund (Ed.), *Children's strategies: Contemporary views of cognitive development* (pp. 157–184). Hillsdale, NJ: Lawrence Erlbaum Associates, Inc.

Miller, P. H., & Seier, W. L. (1994). Strategy utilization deficiencies in children: When, where, and why. In H. W. Reese (Ed.), *Advances in child development and behavior* (Vol. 25, pp. 107–156). New York: Academic Press.

Miller, P. H., Seier, W. L., Probert, J. S., & Aloise, P. A. (1991). Age differences in the capacity of a strategy among spontaneously strategic children. *Journal of Experimental Child Psychology, 52*, 149–165.

Mistry, J. J., & Lange, G. W. (1985). Children's organization and recall of information in scripted narratives. *Child Development, 56*, 953–961.

Moely, B. E., Hart, S. S., Leal, L., Santulli, K. A., Rao, N., Johnson, T., et al. (1992). The teacher's role in facilitating memory and study strategy development in the elementary school classroom. *Child Development, 63,* 653–672.

Moely, B. E., Hart, S. S., Santulli, K., Leal, L., Johnson, T., Rao, N., et al. (1986). How do teachers teach memory skills? *Educational Psychologist, 21,* 55–71.

Moely, B. E., Santulli, K. A., & Obach, M. S. (1995). Strategy instruction, meta-cognition, and motivation in the elementary school classroom. In F. E. Weinert & W. Schneider (Eds.), *Memory performance and competencies: Issues in growth and development* (pp. 301–321). Hillsdale, NJ: Lawrence Erlbaum Associates, Inc.

Ornstein, P. A. (1999). Comments: Toward an understanding of the development of memory. In F. E. Weinert & W. Schneider (Eds.), *Individual development from 3 to 12: Findings from the Munich Longitudinal Study* (pp. 94–105). Cambridge: Cambridge University Press.

Ornstein, P. A., Coffman, J., & McCall, L. (April, 2005). *Linking teachers' memory-relevant language and children's memory performance.* Paper presented at meeting of Society for Research in Child Development, Atlanta, GA.

Ornstein, P. A., Haden., C. A., & Hedrick, A. M. (2004). Learning to remember: Social-communicative exchanges and the development of children's memory skills. *Developmental Review, 24,* 374–395.

Ornstein, P. A., Naus, M. J., & Liberty, C. (1975). Rehearsal and organizational processes in children's memory. *Child Development, 46,* 818–830.

Ornstein, P. A., Naus, M. J., & Stone, B. P. (1977). Rehearsal training and developmental differences in memory. *Developmental Psychology, 13,* 15–24.

O'Sullivan, J. T. (1993). Preschoolers' beliefs about effort, incentives, and recall. *Journal of Experimental Child Psychology, 55,* 396–414.

Palincsar, A. S., & Brown, A. L. (1984). Reciprocal teaching of comprehension-fostering and comprehension-monitoring activities. *Cognition and Instruction, 1,* 117–175.

Pierce, S. H., & Lange, G. (2000). Relationships among metamemory, motivation and memory performance in young school-age children. *British Journal of Developmental Psychology, 18,* 121–135.

Pressley, M. (1982). Elaboration and memory development. *Child Development, 53,* 296–309.

Pressley M., Forrest-Pressley D., & Elliot-Faust, D. J. (1988). What is strategy instructional enrichment and how to study it: Illustrations from research on children's prose memory and comprehension. In F. E. Weinert & M. Perlmutter (Eds.), *Memory development: Universal changes and individual differences* (pp. 101–130). Hillsdale, NJ: Lawrence Erlbaum Associates, Inc.

Pressley, M., & Hilden, K. R. (2006). Teaching reading comprehension. In A. McKeough, L. M. Phillips, V. Timmons, & J. L. Lupart (Eds.), *Understanding literacy development: A global view* (pp. 49–64). Mahwah, NJ: Lawrence Erlbaum Associates, Inc.

Pressley, M., & Levin, J. R. (1977). Task parameters affecting the efficacy of a visual imagery learning strategy in younger and older children. *Journal of Experimental Child Psychology, 24,* 53–59.

Pressley, M., & Van Meter, P. (1993). Memory strategies: Natural development and use following instruction. In R. Pasnak & M. L. Howe (Eds.), *Emerging themes in cognitive development: Vol. II. Competencies* (pp. 128–165). New York: Springer.

Pressley, M., Wharton-McDonald, R., Mistretta-Hampston, J., & Echevarria, M.

(1998). Literacy instruction in 10 fourth- and fifth-grade classrooms in upstate New York. *Scientific Studies in Reading*, *2*, 159–194.

Rabinowitz, M. (1984). The use of categorical organization: Not an all-or-none situation. *Journal of Experimental Child Psychology*, *38*, 338–351.

Reese, H. W. (1962). Verbal mediation as a function of age level. *Psychological Bulletin*, *59*, 502–509.

Reese, H. W. (1977). Imagery and associative memory. In R. V. Kail & J. W. Hagen (Eds.), *Perspectives on the development of memory and cognition* (pp. 113–175). Hillsdale, NJ: Lawrence Erlbaum Associates, Inc.

Ringel, B. A., & Springer, C. J. (1980). On knowing how well one is remembering: The persistence of strategy use during transfer. *Journal of Experimental Child Psychology*, *29*, 322–333.

Roebers, C. M., & Schneider, W. (2005). The strategic regulation of children's memory performance and suggestibility. *Journal of Experimental Child Psychology*, *91*, 24–44.

Rohwer, W. D., Jr. (1980). An elaborative conception of learner differences. In R. E. Snow, P. A. Federico, & W. E. Montague (Eds.), *Aptitude, learning, and instruction: Vol. 2. Cognitive process analyses of learning and problem* (pp. 23–46). Hillsdale, NJ: Lawrence Erlbaum Associates, Inc.

Rohwer, W. D., Jr., Raines, J. M., Eoff, J., & Wagner, M. (1977). The development of elaborative propensity during adolescence. *Journal of Experimental Child Psychology*, *23*, 472–492.

Rovee-Collier, C. (1999). The development of infant memory. *Current Directions in Psychological Science*, *8*, 80–85.

Salatas, H., & Flavell, J. H. (1976). Behavioral and metamnemonic indicators of strategic behaviors under remember instructions in first grade. *Child Development*, *47*, 81–89.

Schlagmüller, M., & Schneider, W. (2002). The development of organizational strategies in children: Evidence from a microgenetic longitudinal study. *Journal of Experimental Child Psychology*, *81*, 298–319.

Schneider, W. (1986). The role of conceptual knowledge and metamemory in the development of organizational processes in memory. *Journal of Experimental Child Psychology*, *42*, 218–236.

Schneider, W. (1998). Performance prediction in young children: Effects of skill, metacognition, and wishful thinking. *Developmental Science*, *1*, 291–297.

Schneider, W., & Bjorklund, D. F. (1992). Expertise, aptitude, and strategic remembering. *Child Development*, *63*, 461–473.

Schneider, W., & Bjorklund, D. F. (1998). Memory. In W. Damon (Series Ed.), and R. S. Siegler & D. Kuhn (Vol. Eds.), *Handbook of child psychology*: *Vol. 2. Cognitive, language, and perceptual development* (pp. 467–521). New York: Wiley.

Schneider, W., & Bjorklund, D. F. (2003). Memory and knowledge development. In J. Valsiner & K. Connolly (Eds.), *Handbook of developmental psychology* (pp. 370–403). London: Sage.

Schneider, W., Bjorklund, D. F., & Maier-Brücker, W. (1996). The effects of expertise and IQ on children's memory: When knowledge is, and when it is not enough. *International Journal of Behavioral Development*, *19*, 773–796.

Schneider, W., Gruber, H., Gold, A., & Opwis, K. (1993). Chess expertise and memory for chess positions in children and adults. *Journal of Experimental Child Psychology*, *56*, 328–349.

Schneider, W., Kron, V., Hünnerkopf, M., & Krajewski, K. (2004). The development of young children's memory strategies: Findings from the Würzburg Longitudinal Memory Study. *Journal of Experimental Child Psychology, 88,* 193–209.

Schneider, W., Kron-Sperl, V., & Hünnerkopf, M. (in press). The development of young children's memory strategies: Evidence from the Würzburg Longitudinal Memory Study. *European Journal of Developmental Psychology.*

Schneider, W., & Lockl, K. (2002). The development of metacognitive knowledge in children and adolescents. In T. Perfect & B. Schwartz (Eds.), *Applied metacognition* (pp. 224–257). Cambridge: Cambridge University Press.

Schneider, W., & Pressley, M. (1997). *Memory development between 2 and 20* (2nd ed.). Mahwah, NJ: Lawrence Erlbaum Associates, Inc.

Schwenck, C., Bjorklund, D. F., & Schneider, W. (2007). Factors influencing the incidence of utilization deficiencies and other patterns of recall/strategy-use relations in a strategic memory task. *Child Development, 78,* 1771–1787.

Shin, H.-E., Bjorklund, D. F., & Beck, E. F. (2007). The adaptive nature of children's overestimation in a strategic memory task. *Cognitive Development, 22,* 197–212.

Short, E. J., & Ryan, E. B. (1984). Metacognitive differences between skilled and less skilled readers: Remediating deficits through story grammar and attribution training. *Journal of Educational Psychology, 76,* 225–235.

Siaw, S. N., & Kee, D. W. (1987). Development of elaboration and organization in different socioeconomic-status and ethnic populations. In M. A. McDaniel & M. Pressley (Eds.), *Imagery and related mnemonic processes: Theories, individual differences, and applications* (pp. 237–273). New York: Springer-Verlag.

Siegler, R. S. (1996). *Emerging minds: The process of change in children's thinking.* New York: Oxford University Press.

Sodian, B., & Schneider, W. (1999). Memory strategy development: Gradual increase, sudden insight, or roller coaster? In F. E. Weinert & W. Schneider (Eds.), *Individual development from 3 to 12: Findings from the Munich Longitudinal Study* (pp. 61–77). Cambridge: Cambridge University Press.

Sodian, B., Schneider, W., & Perlmutter, M. (1986). Recall, clustering, and meta-memory in young children. *Journal of Experimental Child Psychology, 41,* 395–410.

Waters, H. S. (2000). Memory strategy development: Do we need yet another deficiency? *Child Development, 71,* 1004–1012.

Wellman, H. M. (1988). The early development of memory strategies. In F. E. Weinert & M. Perlmutter (Eds.), *Memory development: Universal changes and individual differences* (pp. 3–29). Hillsdale, NJ: Lawrence Erlbaum Associates, Inc.

Wellman, H. M., Ritter, K., & Flavell, J. H. (1975). Deliberate memory behavior in the delayed reactions of very young children. *Developmental Psychology, 11,* 780–787.

Woody-Dorning, J., & Miller, P. H. (2001). Children's individual differences in capacity: Effects on strategy production and utilization. *British Journal of Developmental Psychology, 19,* 543–557.

Yussen, S. R., & Levy, V. M. (1975). Developmental changes in predicting one's own span of short-term memory. *Journal of Experimental Child Psychology, 19,* 502–508.

8 The genesis and development of autobiographical memory

Mark L. Howe
Fylde College, Lancaster University, UK

Mary L. Courage
Memorial University, St. John's, Newfoundland, Canada

Maki Rooksby
Fylde College, Lancaster University, UK

Autobiographical memory has been defined as "memory for the events of one's life" (Conway & Rubin, 1993) and can be considered to be a special case of explicit or declarative memory. Phenomenologically, autobiographical memory forms our "personal life history". Such memories involve the who, what, where, and when of personalized events that collectively form a vital part of our knowledge about who we are. Critically, the loss of this important self-memory relationship that occurs in amnesic conditions has devastating consequences for the individual affected (Conway & Fthenaki, 2000). Although there is a large literature on the characteristics and function of autobiographical memory in later childhood and adulthood (for reviews, see Conway, 2005; Fivush, Chapter 11, this volume; Rubin, 1996), considerably less is known about its genesis and early development. Although it is clear that factors such as language, culture, belief, understanding of others, one's own life history, and our current perceptions and expectations can all influence our ability to remember the events of our lives and, importantly, the way in which we remember them, these variables do not contribute directly to the nascence of autobiographical memory (e.g., see Howe, 2004). Rather, we contend that the factor that is most important to the emergence of autobiographical memory (Howe & Courage, 1993, 1997; Howe, Courage, & Edison, 2003) as well as to autobiographical memory throughout the lifespan is the self (e.g., Conway, 2005). Without a well-articulated sense of self, there can be no autobiography. Before we examine the critical role of the self in the origins of human autobiographical memory we provide a brief overview of what memory is like prior to the onset of autobiographical memory and of the dynamic forces that change simple event memories into memories that happened to "me".

EARLY MEMORY FOR EVENTS IN HUMAN INFANTS

To begin, it is well known that the neural "hardware" necessary to encode, store, and retrieve information is present at birth or before (albeit in rudimentary form) and that infants can retain an impressive array of information encoded through all modalities (for a review, see Courage & Howe, 2004). However, it is equally very clear that infant memory is markedly immature compared to that of older children and adults, and does not typically retain detailed information over protracted periods of time (see Chapters 2 and 3 by Rovee-Collier & Cuevas, and Hayne & Simcock, this volume). Experiments that have employed a diverse array of memory measures and procedures (e.g., conjugate reinforcement, Rovee-Collier, Hayne, & Colombo, 2001; novelty preference, Courage & Howe, 1998; Courage, Howe, & Squires, 2004; deferred imitation, Hayne, 2004; Meltzoff, 1995; elicited imitation, Bauer, 2004; and behavioural re-enactment, McDonough & Mandler, 1994; Sheffield & Hudson, 1994) have shown that when the initial level of learning or acquisition of information is equated across age, infant age and memory longevity are positively correlated. That is, older infants retain information about objects, people, and events over longer intervals than do younger infants. Although long-term retention can be extended by manipulating factors such as the amount and distribution of practice with the task or material, matching proximal and distal context cues at the study session with those at the test session, and using reinstatement or reminder techniques, infant memory is fundamentally very fragile. As the neural structures that subserve memory mature (see Bauer, 2004, and Chapter 6, this volume) and as knowledge structures and information gathering strategies develop (see Chapters 4 and 7 by Hudson & Mayhew, and Bjorklund, Dukes, & Brown, this volume) memories become more durable and less vulnerable to decay and interference.

   The case can be made that this very frailty of early memory is an important factor underlying the phenomenon of infantile amnesia, a term first used by Freud (1905/1953) to describe the fact that adults seem unable to recall events that happened to them during their infant and toddler years, as though experiences before 2 years of age are somehow "time-locked" and inaccessible to conscious recall. This amnesia is especially puzzling given adults' excellent recall of events that happened to them just beyond this "barrier" in the preschool years. Moreover, infant and toddler memory for concurrent events is quite good, albeit less robust than that of older children who have passed the infantile amnesia barrier (Bruce, Wilcox-O'Hearn, Robinson, Phillips-Grant, Francis, & Smith, 2005), though these early memories may never be readily verbalizable (Simcock & Hayne, 2002; but see Bauer, Kroupina, Schwade, Dropik, & Wewerka, 1998; Bauer, van Abbema, Wiebe, Cary, Phill, & Burch, 2004; Bauer, Wenner, & Kroupina, 2002; Morris & Baker-Ward, 2007).

   Contemporary theorists and researchers have debated the underlying source of the fragility of infant memory, and the nature of its relationship to infantile amnesia, for decades (for a review, see Howe & Courage, 1993). This issue is an important one because it goes to the heart of the question of what actually happens to information in long-term memory, an issue of both scientific and practical (e.g., forensic) importance (see Pipe & Salmon, Chapter 10, this volume). Traditional explanations have targeted either storage or retrieval limitations (see Howe, 2000). Specifically, if storage of information and experience is permanent, then the inability to recall early experiences may be a matter of retrieval failure that in theory should be alleviated by reinstating the appropriate testing conditions. In this view, early memories are available but cannot be accessed because the context in which they were laid down in infancy is too discrepant from the one in which it is being retrieved (see Hayne, 2004; Rovee-Collier et al., 2001). However, strictly retrieval-based explanations have been ruled out by a variety of other empirical findings (for a review, see Howe, 2007). Alternatively, explanations that focus on storage-failure have faired somewhat better (Bauer, 2005; Rovee-Collier et al., 2001). In that view, if storage is labile and not permanent or if events were not properly encoded initially (as might be expected in the neurologically and perceptually immature infant), then recall of early experiences may be impossible and infantile amnesia may be a result of storage limitations (e.g., failure of encoding or consolidation processes) (see also Nelson, 1997, 2000). Finally, and perhaps most likely, the possibility remains that elements of both storage and retrieval may be involved in forgetting.

EARLY MEMORY FOR EVENTS IN NONHUMAN SPECIES

Though infantile amnesia has been traditionally cast as a uniquely human phenomenon, Arnold and Spear (1997) contend that it has been observed in every altricial species in which it has been tested. They define infantile amnesia as the rapid forgetting of events during infancy relative to that of events occurring later in life—a definition that parallels but is not identical to the classic definition of human infantile amnesia. The crux of their argument is that many of the common features of childhood memories (e.g., their transient character, susceptibility to distortion, potential for reactivation) represent basic and ubiquitous biological processes and that human infantile amnesia (and forgetting in general) would most productively and parsimoniously be examined from a biological perspective. Moreover, they contend that it is only by using nonhuman species that the proper experimental questions can be both asked and answered. To illustrate, they reference a large number of studies (primarily with rodent species) that show the applicability of these memory phenomena to nonhuman species in general. For example, research that has employed a variety of both associative and non-associative learning tasks indicates that younger animals forget faster than do older animals despite equated levels of initial learning (see also Campbell & Spear, 1972). The mechanisms and processes proposed to underlie this accelerated forgetting in juveniles include greater susceptibility to interference, irrelevant stimulus attribute selection during encoding, the alteration of contextual cues or the physiological state of the animal from training to test, and to a lesser degree, brain maturation. The argument for examining the continuity of memory processes (including those that underlie infantile amnesia) across age and species, and the formulation and use of animal models to interpret and explain data and to make predictions, is compelling and will likely inform this enduring debate. However, aspects of the infantile amnesia and auto-biographical memory phenomena are rooted firmly in, and perhaps driven by processes that many would argue are uniquely human (e.g., the self, language, culture) (but see Clayton and Dickinson, 1998; Eacott, Easton, & Zinkivskay, 2006; Hampton & Schwartz, 2004; Schwartz, Hoffman, & Evans, 2005 for examples of event-like memories in nonhuman species). Importantly, whether these event or event-like memories in nonhuman species are ever "auto-biographical" is a far more complex question yet to be resolved (see Howe, 2007).

Before turning to a consideration of these higher-level cognitive processes, it is of more than passing interest to note that Tulving (1993) has argued that autobiographical memory also includes "autonoetic" consciousness (the personal awareness of remembering). That is, autobiographical remembering implies conscious awareness of a particular experience that occurred in a past context. Tulving contends that nonhuman animals and very young children do not code temporal information that allows them to travel back and re-experience past episodes—that is, they do not have autonoetic consciousness and in his view, autobiographical memory. It is extremely unlikely that we will ever establish whether nonhuman animals or preverbal humans have autonoetic consciousness (although there are some promising electro-physiological techniques that may change this, see Conway, Pleydell-Pearce, Whitecross, & Sharpe, 2002). As noted by researchers who examine episodic memory in nonhuman animals, this problem exists in part because there are no agreed *behavioural* (i.e., nonverbal) markers of conscious experience (Griffiths, Dickinson, & Clayton, 1999). Hence any model of episodic memory that requires conscious awareness must apply solely to language-using organisms. As Clayton, Bussey, and Dickinson (2003) point out, without language, there is no test that establishes whether an organism re-experienced the past during episodic recall.

Recognizing the futility of using phenomenological criteria in language-challenged organisms, researchers focus on behavioural criteria in an attempt to establish that nonhuman animals (and preverbal humans) do have episodic (autobiographical) memory. Perhaps more germane to this controversy is the recent acknowledgement that the anatomical details of the hippocampus and parahippocampal regions of the brain are conserved across (human and nonhuman) mammals (Manns & Eichenbaum, 2006). To the extent that the hippocampus and parahippocampal regions are critical for declarative, episodic memory (e.g., de Hoz & Wood, 2006; Tulving & Markowitsch, 1998), these across-species similarities are consistent with the claim that episodic (and perhaps autobiographical) memory may exist in a variety of mammalian species and is not special to humans. Because of this it may be that the autonoetic component of human conscious recollection is neither necessary not sufficient but rather epiphenomenal and not a requirement of autobiographical memory itself. Similarly, Ferbinteanu, Kennedy, and Shapiro (2006) argue that autonoetic experience may simply be a byproduct of human consciousness and is not an aspect of episodic memory per se. Hence, episodic memory may exist in many species, including preverbal humans, and can be measured behaviourally in human and nonhuman species alike. It is clear that differences exist across species in the psychological properties of episodic memories (perhaps including autonoetic experiences), but these may arise because of differences in neocortical inputs to the hippocampus and parahippocampal regions, as well as their outputs, rather than to differences in the hippocampal and parahippocampal regions themselves (see Howe, 2007; Manns & Eichenbaum, 2006).

We argue here that the waning of infantile amnesia and the onset of autobiographical memory is the result of advances in cognitive structures that optimize and build on an organism's basic memory processes. Specifically, we argue for developmental continuity at the level of basic memory processes, and that what brings about the personalization of early memory in humans is the advent of the cognitive self. This self serves to organize event information as something that happened to "me" and like other cognitive advances (e.g., concepts, categories), occurs prior to other changes (e.g., language) that emerge around the end of the second year of life (for a review of these and other achievements at this transition point, see Courage & Howe, 2002). Moreover, these changes have established neurological correlates, ones that can be seen primarily at the cortical level (e.g., see Levine, 2004; Pfefferbaum, Mathalon, Sullivan, Rawles, Zipursky, & Lim, 1994). Although no direct link between these neurobiological changes and the offset of infantile amnesia has been established, the cognitive advances that generate autobiographical memory (i.e., the advent of the cognitive self) may have their neural correlates in early changes in the prefrontal cortex. We will return to this point below.

In what follows, we elaborate this theory of the genesis of autobiographical memory and start by reviewing the literature on early neurological developments that are linked to memory in infancy. We then provide an overview of the literature on the development of the self and how this shapes the changes in memory that result in the advent of autobiographical memory. We will also examine the neurological correlates of these cognitive changes and speculate about how these and other maturation- and environmental-based changes are linked to subsequent advances in autobiographical recall.

THE ROLE OF NEUROLOGICAL CHANGES IN EARLY MEMORY DEVELOPMENT

How does neurological maturation impact memory development? As noted (and consistent with the biological/process continuity perspective adopted here), there is a considerable degree of overlap between human and nonhuman animals in the development, anatomy, and function of the hippocampus (and parahippocampal regions; e.g., Ferbinteanu et al., 2006; Manns & Eichenbaum, 2006), a network of structures critical to the encoding, storage, and retrieval of information in memory. Here we provide a brief overview of the neural underpinnings of memory development in so far as they relate to autobiographical memory (see Bauer, Chapter 6, this volume; Gogtay et al., 2006; Serres, 2001).

In a seminal review of the literature drawn from research with human infants, lesioned and normally developing nonhuman primates, and clinical cases of brain-injured human patients, Nelson (1995, 1997) argued that certain neurological structures that develop early in postnatal life (e.g., the hippocampus, striatum, cerebellum, olivary–cerebellar complex) are sufficient to sustain a "pre-explicit" or procedural memory system that makes possible the types of recognition memory performance expressed by infants in novelty preference, habituation, instrumental and classical conditioning, and visual expectancy tasks. In contrast, performance on certain other "explicit" memory tasks (e.g., delayed non-match to sample, cross-modal recognition, deferred and elicited imitation) and working memory tasks (e.g., A-not-B, delayed response) depend, in addition, on later developing structures of the medial temporal lobe (e.g., the amygdala), inferior temporal cortical regions, and regions of the prefrontal cortex, which do not become stable in human infants until the latter half of the first year of life. Though incomplete, these structures continue to mature across infancy and childhood, and along with other cognitive and linguistic achievements, underlie the significant and robust improvements in memory performance that have been observed in this time frame. Nelson proposed that the last half of the first postnatal year marks a qualitative shift in the development of early memory that is coincident with (or perhaps enabled by) qualitative changes in neurological maturation in regions of the developing brain. This shift from early functioning based on a "pre-explicit" memory system to the onset of an "explicit" memory system that occurs between 6 and 12 months of age, supposedly signals (among other things) the onset of recall in infancy. Although there is strong evidence to support this brain–behaviour transition (see Bauer, Chapter 6, this volume; Bauer et al., 2006), other evidence indicates that explicit memory is robust at least from 6 months of age (see Barr, Dowden, & Hayne, 1996; Barr, Rovee-Collier, & Campanella, 2005, Hayne & Simcock, Chapter 3, this volume). The research needed to clarify and refine these discrepant timelines is ongoing.

Clearly, although some of the neural structures related to declarative memory develop early, others are more protracted in their developmental course with critical changes culminating near the end of the first postnatal year and the beginning of the second year (Serres, 2001). Consistent with this, key developments occur in the dentate gyrus of the hippocampus (an area that serves as a critical link in the circuitry that connects the parahippocampal structures to the hippocampus), the frontal cortex, and reciprocal connections between the neocortex and the hippocampus (Serres, 2001). Although development continues for some time, the network necessary to sustain declarative memory reaches functional maturity (in humans) late in the first year of life. Thus, by the beginning of the second year of postnatal life, humans are capable of sustaining declarative recollection.

The timing of these neurological changes is at odds with data that show autobiographical memories are available from around the end of the second (not first) year of life (for reviews, see Howe & Courage, 1993, 1997). For this reason, neurobiological constraints may not lie at the source of infantile amnesia (see Howe, 2007). Despite other advances that occur in neocortical structures during subsequent maturation, we have argued previously (Howe & Courage, 1993, 1997) that neither age nor neurological development can account for the timing of the genesis of autobiographical memory. Rather, the emergence of autobiographical memory, like other advances in memory development, is controlled by changes that occur in the underlying processes of encoding, storage, and retrieval. These changes may have neurobiological correlates, but their origins are more parsimoniously localized in developments occurring in the organism's knowledge (cognitive) structures.

EMERGENCE OF THE SELF AND THE GENESIS OF AUTOBIOGRAPHICAL MEMORY

We have argued (e.g., Howe & Courage, 1997; Howe et al., 2003) that the necessary (though not sufficient) condition for the onset of autobiographical memory is the emergence of the cognitive self late in the second year of life. This achievement sets the lower limit on the age at which memories can be encoded, stored, and retrieved as personal—something that happened to "me". This fledgling cognitive self enables a new knowledge structure whereby information and experience can be organized as personal. Prior to the articulation of the self, infants learn and remember but their experiences will not be recognized as specific events that happened to "me". After the onset of the cognitive self, adults' recollection of childhood events become more numerous and as with advances in memory more generally, are a result of increases in storage maintenance and to strategic retrieval processes. Importantly, the onset of the cognitive self coincides roughly with the point at which studies have dated the onset of adults' earliest memories for significant life events (e.g., Crawley & Eacott, 2006; Eacott & Crawley, 1998; Usher & Neisser, 1993).

Research and theory on the nature and early development of the cognitive self have a long history that has been reviewed elsewhere (e.g., Courage & Howe, 2002; Howe, 2004; Howe & Courage, 1997). Here we provide a brief overview of the emergence of the objective, categorical (i.e., cognitive) aspect of the self described by William James (1890) as the "me" component of the self—and the one that we contend forms the cornerstone of autobiographical memory. Empirically, the first unambiguous sign of the emergent cognitive self has been regarded as the point at which the child recognizes that his or her mirror image is "me". This is assessed with a "mark" or "rouge" test during which face paint is surreptitiously placed on the child's nose. The child who recognizes the marked image as "me" will touch his or her own nose as opposed to other mirror-directed reactions. Since the beginning of its use as a tool for studying infants' emerging self-knowledge, this mirror self-recognition (MSR) task has provided valuable insights into this important aspect of social cognitive development.

Mirrors provide a powerful visual stimulus for infants and the consensus of the early research (e.g., see Amsterdam, 1972; Bertenthal & Fischer, 1978; Bullock & Lutkenhaus, 1990; Dickie & Strader, 1974; Lewis & Brooks-Gunn, 1979; Loveland, 1987; Mitchell, 1993; Pipp, Fischer, & Jennings, 1987; Schulman & Kaplowitz, 1977) indicates that from at least 3 months of age infants are both attentive and positive toward their mirror images and by 8 to 9 months they show awareness of the contingency cues provided by the tandem movement of the image with themselves and they can use these cues for play, imitation, and object location. Full self-recognition of a mirror image as their own occurs unambiguously in most infants at about 18 months of age (but see Mitchell, 1993). Coincident with the onset of MSR, infants begin to show embarrassment (shy smiling, gaze aversion, and self touching) when confronted with their images and subsequently, at about 22 months of age, will provide a correct verbal label of the image (see also Courage, Edison, & Howe, 2004). Collectively, these behaviours provide confirmation that the infant recognizes the mirror image as "me". Although there is evidence from research with photo and video material that infants can discriminate their facial and other body features from those of another infant from about 4 or 5 months (Bahrick, Moss, & Fadil, 1996; Legerstee, Anderson, & Schaffer, 1998; Rochat & Striano, 2002; Schmuckler, 1995), the level of self-knowledge inherent in these discriminations is unclear (but see Nielsen, Suddendorf, & Slaughter, 2006).

However, the significance of MSR as a marker of the objective sense of self has been debated. At issue has been the question of what it actually means, or more specifically, what prerequisite cognitive-developmental achievements (e.g., understanding the reflective properties of mirrors; visual–proprioceptive matching; motivation to explore the spot) in addition to self-awareness might mediate (or mask) successful task performance (e.g., Loveland, 1987; Michiko & Hiraki, 2006; Robinson, Connell, & McKenzie, 1990). An implication of this is that the objective sense of self might already be under way by the time the infant can successfully perform the MSR task, perhaps rooted in the early perception, learning, and social exchanges that provide infants with the information they need to differentiate their own characteristics from the physical and social environment (e.g., see Bahrick et al., 1996; Butterworth, 1995; Gibson, 1995; Meltzoff & Moore, 1994; Mitchell, 1993; Neisser, 1993; Rochat, 1995, 2001). We contend that this earlier developing sense of self-awareness is akin to what James (1890) referred to as the "I" aspect of the self, a subjective, implicit sense of self as the subject of experience that does not require the explicit idea of "me". In this view, the development of the self is an incremental process and MSR is a step along the path in which "me" evolves from "I". Alternatively, the case has been made that MSR onset indicates the emergence of a new level of conscious awareness and self-reflection, one that is unique to humans and a few of the higher nonhuman primates (Gallup, 1979; Kagan, 1981, 1998; Lewis, 1994). Consistent with this view is the fact that MSR is coincident with (and perhaps a part of) a number of other cognitive changes that emerge in the same time frame (e.g., language, symbolic play, deferred imitation, empathy, self-evaluation), and which collectively enable the infant to represent various sources of information simultaneously, to formulate "testable" hypotheses about the way the world operates, and to evaluate and modify these until they "get it right" (see Courage & Howe, 2002; Gopnik & Meltzoff, 1997).

Recently we (Courage, Edison, & Howe, 2004) used a microgenetic approach to assess the development of MSR in toddlers from 15 to 23 months of age. Although data taken from cross-sectional samples showed the typical abrupt onset of MSR at about 18 months, longitudinal data indicated that intra-individual MSR emerged more gradually and showed wide variability in expression prior to becoming stable, a finding masked in the cross-sectional data. In any event, these two perspectives are not mutually exclusive and both concur that the onset of MSR is an important milestone in social cognition, though one whose developmental course remains unclear.

Regardless of whether the self develops continuously or emerges abruptly, the fact remains that at about the age of 2 years the cognitive self, a new organizer of information and experience, becomes available and facilitates the grouping and personalization of memories for events into what will become autobiographical memory. That childhood memories become more numerous after the onset of the self is expected given that (1) features associated with the self grow and expand, providing a larger base that encoding processes can reference, (2) improvements in the basic processes that drive memory (encoding, storage, and retrieval) that occur across development (attention, strategy use, knowledge, and metamemory) facilitate memory functioning in general, and (3) certain neurocognitive developments relevant to this expanding knowledge base about the self occur in this time frame. For example, functional neuroimaging studies with adults have shown that the processing of self-related information and autobiographical recall depend in part on regions of the prefrontal cortex (Levine, 2004), a brain area that undergoes marked developmental change across the preschool years. Consistent with this, Ottinger-Alberts and Newcombe (1999) reported that 4-year-olds' recall of real events was significantly predicted from other measures of prefrontal functioning.

Alternative views of the onset and development of autobiographical memory set a very different time course for this achievement. For example, K. Nelson, Fivush and their colleagues (e.g., K. Nelson, 1996; Fivush, 1997; Fivush, Haden, & Reese, 1996; Fivush & Reese, 1992; K. Nelson & Fivush, 2004), adopting a sociolinguistic perspective, contend that autobiographical memory follows from the child's ability to establish a "personal life story" in memory. This achievement occurs largely through conversations with adults and significant others in which personal events and experiences are shared (see Fivush, Chapter 11, this volume). However, this view of the emergence of autobiographical memory presupposes linguistic and narrative competence that is not strong until the preschool years, thus precluding the infant and toddler periods (see also Pillemer & White, 1989). A related position has been taken by Perner and Ruffman (1995), who tied the emergence of autobiographical memory to general advances in metacognition, specifically to children's emerging theory of mind. They argue that event memory in very young children is based on "noetic" awareness or "knowing" something happened rather than on "autonoetic" awareness or "remembering" something happened (see Tulving, 1989). In this view the transition from one to the other at about the age of 4 marks the beginning of autobiographical memory. Consistent with the sociolinguistic perspective, they believe that children's conversations with others (mothers in particular) serve as an important source of data for the development of their theory of the mind, in turn promoting the establishment of autobiographical memory.

What does the evidence indicate? Only fairly recently has there been any empirical research in which roles of the cognitive self and early language in the development of autobiographical memory have been examined conjointly. In one study, Harley and Reese (1998) repeatedly examined mother–child dyads when the children were between 19 and 32 months old. The toddlers were tested on language, self-recognition, deferred imitation, and verbal memory for events. For this latter measure, children's memory and maternal reminiscing style (low or high elaboration) for unique past events were evaluated. The results showed that both self-recognition and maternal reminiscing style contributed independently to verbal memory, with self-recognition emerging as a stronger predictor. Interestingly, follow-up research (Cleveland & Reese, 2005; Farrant & Reese, 2000; Reese, 2002) revealed that what was remembered over the long haul was related to maternal reminiscing styles. However, for several reasons in the broader context this is not surprising—some related to measurement (e.g., use of verbal recall measures), some related to rehearsal (e.g., more repetition of shared information), and some related to changes in self and memory at the level of storage (e.g., alterations in knowledge and its organization).

Recently we (Courage et al., 2004; Howe et al., 2003) showed in both cross-sectional and longitudinal data that MSR was the earliest precursor of several indices of self-recognition (e.g., self affect, self-referent language) to emerge late in the second year of life. Moreover, long-term retention of a unique toy play event was contingent on the children having had a cognitive self at the time of the event, but was unrelated to the affective and language measures of self. More recently, Prudhomme (2005) found that the cognitive self was essential for early declarative, autobiographical memory. Children classed as early recognizers were not only better than those classed as late recognizers on an elicited imitation test of recall memory, but they also had more advanced representational skills that enabled greater flexibility in retrieving information.

AFTER THE COGNITIVE SELF: FURTHER DEVELOPMENTS IN AUTOBIOGRAPHICAL MEMORY

As noted earlier, alternative hypotheses about the onset of autobiographical memory set a later beginning and a developmental course rooted in language and social cognition. One of these perspectives has focused on the role of social interaction in the emergence of the autobiographical memory system, in particular, the sharing of experiences with others linguistically (for reviews see K. Nelson & Fivush, 2004; Reese, 2002). As young children learn to talk about the past with adults, they begin to organize these events autobiographically (especially in terms of time lines) in memory. The primary *function* of autobiographical memory then, is to develop a life history in time and to do that by telling others what one is like through narrating the events of the past. In this way children learn both about the form of reporting about past events and the social functions that talking about the past provides.

However, the functional aspects of memory should not be identified with its representational structure. As Damasio (1999, p. 108) has pointed out (see also Conway, 2005):

> language is a translation of something else, a conversion from nonlinguistic images which stand for entities, events, relationships, and inferences. If language operates for the self and for consciousness in the same way it operates for everything else, that is, by symbolizing in words and sentences what exists first in nonverbal form, then there must be a nonverbal self and a nonverbal knowing for which the words "I" and "me" or the phrase "I know" are the appropriate translations in any language.

In any event, research indicates that at about the age of 2.5 years most children begin to talk about specific events, although these early conversations are heavily "scaffolded" by adults (e.g., Hudson, 1990; Hudson & Mayhew, Chapter 4, this volume). By about 3 years of age, children assume more responsibility for talking about past events and begin to use the story or narrative form in these conversational exchanges. Although some of these advances begin to occur as early as 3 to 4 years of age, K. Nelson (1996) has maintained that "true" autobiographical memory is quite late to develop and may not be complete until the end of the preschool years or later. According to this sociolinguistic view, then, autobiographical memory depends on the development of fairly sophisticated language-based representational skills, ones that do not emerge until children are about 5 or 6 years old. Once these skills are established, memories can be retained and organized around a life history, one that extends in time. Povinelli and his colleagues (Povinelli, Landau, & Perilloux, 1996; Povinelli, Landry, Theall, Clarke, & Castile, 1999; Povinelli & Simon, 1998) also contend that a sense of continuity must be linked with our knowledge of our personal history. As it is this "life history" component that ostensibly makes a memory autobiographical, very young children's reports of personally experienced events are precluded, a judgement that is not consistent with many findings in the empirical literature on young children's memory for personally experienced events.

Because this sociolinguistic perspective places considerable importance on children's conversations about the past, particularly with their parents (and especially mothers), it is important to see what validation exists for the role of these conversations in children's autobiographical memory. Research conducted within this framework reveals that individual differences in the way that parents talk to their children about the past leads to individual differences in children's reporting of their own past experiences. In particular, two different parent conversational styles of talking with children have been identified. "High-elaborative" parents provide a large amount of detailed information about past events. They elaborate and expand on the child's partial recall, ask further questions to enhance event detail, and correct the child's memory if necessary. In contrast, "low-elaborative" parents tend to repeat their questions over and over in an attempt to get a specific answer from the child, switch topics more frequently, and do not seek elaborative detail from the child's report. Importantly, the high-elaborative style is associated with children's provision of more elaborative narratives, both concurrently and longitudinally (Cleveland & Reese, 2005; Haden, Haine, & Fivush, 1997; Harley & Reese, 1998, 1999; Reese, Haden, & Fivush, 1993). Although adult conversational style does appear to facilitate the richness and narrative organization of children's memory talk and in so doing plays an important role in children's developing ability to *report* autobiographical memories, it does not necessarily determine the *content* or *accuracy* of children's memory reports (see Fivush, 1994; Goodman, Quas, Batterman-Faunce, Riddlesberger, & Kuhn, 1994). In fact, reconstruction of events through conversations with others can lead to systematic distortions of memory details, ones that are consistent with the current beliefs and expectations of the narrator and the listener (e.g., Ross & Wilson, 2000). Thus, as with the well-replicated finding in the memory literature more generally, the strategy of verbal rehearsal (elaborative or non-elaborative) can serve not only to reinforce and reinstate memories, but can also lead to a number of errors or distortions in recall.

From the sociolinguistic perspective then, parents are actively engaged in teaching their children how to remember and also the techniques of sharing memories with others through narrative reports. In the bigger picture, in which our culture is our teacher, recent research shows that like the individual differences in children's conversational styles and the memory reports that correlate with parent talk, children in other cultures exposed to different conversational styles differ in memory reporting (see Fivush, Chapter 11, this volume). For example, some research shows that American mothers talk to their 3-year-olds about past events three times as often as do Korean mothers. Further, American children talk about past events more than do Korean children and American adults report earlier autobiographical memories than do Korean adults (Han, Leichtman, & Wang, 1998; Mullen, 1994; Mullen & Yi, 1995). Similar relationships were found between age of earliest memory, culture, and conversational interactions in a comparison of Maori, Pakeha, and Asian adults living in New Zealand (MacDonald, Uesiliana, & Hayne, 2000). Interestingly, culture appears to affect not only the linguistic expression of event memories but also the perspective from which events are encoded. In a recent study with Asian and American adults, Cohen and Gunz (2002) found that the contents of their memories of events were influenced by their phenomenological experiences as members of these two cultures, with Asians being more likely than Americans to experience the self in memory from the perspective of the generalized other (e.g., to have more third-person memories).

As mentioned earlier, another view of the development of autobiographical memory in which language plays a more ancillary role is one in which children's own self-awareness or autonoetic consciousness is the critical necessary ingredient. For example, Perner and Ruffman (1995) argue that autobiographical memory follows achievements in metacognition in which children begin to have recollective experiences of remembering (as opposed to simply knowing about) past events, experiences that are unlikely to occur before the age of 3 to 5 years. They contend that young children's need for scaffolding and prompting in order to elicit recollections means that their memories are dominated by the contents of adults' questions and suggests a noetic rather than an autonoetic form of remembering. Like the sociolinguistic model, mothers' elaborated talk about past episodes is thought to play a significant role in the evolution of autonoetic consciousness as well as in children's theory of the mind (see Perner & Ruffman, 1995). Although conscious awareness of oneself and one's experiences may be a component of episodic memory more generally, and may play a role in the accumulation of autobiographical memories throughout childhood, it does not appear to be necessary for the initial onset of autobiographical memory. That is, although the *experience* of remembering often accompanies autobiographical recall (e.g., see Conway, 1996), the existence of personalized memories is not contingent on such experiencing.

What these language-based theories of the development of autobiographical memory contribute to the debate is that the language environment of the child, whether it is familial or cultural, serves to teach children that *reporting* memories is important, and that such reports have a particular *narrative structure*, and a particular *social and cognitive function*. Further, language can serve to strengthen (or alter) the content of events to be preserved over time. The importance of this role for language and language interactions in autobiographical memories is not a matter of debate. What is controversial is the role of language in the initial onset of autobiographical memory. We have argued here and elsewhere (Howe, 2000, 2004, 2007; Howe & Courage, 1997) that its role is negligible, with the critical event being the onset of the cognitive self. Once this latter event has occurred, the foundation for autobiographical memory has been laid and only then can the variety of other (experiential) factors (including language) and individual differences come into play to shape and sculpt our autobiographies and to permit us to reflect on them.

CONCLUSIONS

The conclusions from this review of the genesis of autobiographical memory are clear. First, neural structures related to declarative memory (particularly the hippocampus and parahippocampal regions) are operational early in life and prior to the offset of infantile amnesia and the genesis of autobiographical memory. Indeed, there is considerable evidence attesting to the continuity of basic memory processes across development (see Bauer, 2004, 2005; Howe, 2000, 2004; Howe & Courage, 1993, 1997). The capacity to organize information more coherently in memory is critical to most, if not all, memory advances throughout childhood. Advances in children's knowledge base, whether they have to do with the self or other constructs (e.g., animals, food), afford greater integration and more resistance to forgetting for information that is stored in memory. As we have seen in this chapter, the genesis of autobiographical memory is driven by the advent of one particular knowledge structure, the cognitive self.

Second, the debate over the relative importance of cognitive self versus sociolinguistic factors in the development of autobiographical memory may be more apparent than real. We maintain that it is the emergence of the cognitive self late in the second year of life that enables the *onset* of autobiographical memory. However, there is no doubt that *subsequent* advances in language and social cognition are extremely important as they provide an expressive outlet for those recollections (and reflections on those recollections) as autobiographical memory continues to evolve and mature into the childhood years. In that capacity, conversational exchanges not only provide a narrative structure for reporting events, but also serve to preserve (e.g., through rehearsal, reinstatement) though potentially alter (e.g., through reconstruction) memory records of personally experienced events.

REFERENCES

Amsterdam, B. (1972). Mirror self-image reactions before age two. *Developmental Psychobiology, 5,* 297–305.

Arnold, H. M., & Spear, N. E. (1997). Infantile amnesia: Using animal models to understand forgetting. In P. J. B. Slater, J. S. Rosenblatt, C. T. Snowden, & M. Milinski (Eds.), *Advances in the study of behavior* (Vol. 26, pp. 251–284). New York: Academic Press.

Bahrick, L. E., Moss, L., & Fadil, C. (1996). The development of visual self-recognition in infancy. *Ecological Psychology, 8,* 189–208.

Barr, R., Dowden, A., & Hayne, H. (1996). Developmental change in deferred imitation by 6- to 24-month-old infants. *Infant Behavior and Development, 19,* 159–170.

Barr, R., Rovee-Collier, C., & Campanella, J. (2005). Retrieval protracts deferred imitation by 6-month-old infants. *Infancy, 7,* 263–283.

Bauer, P. J. (2004). Getting explicit memory off the ground: Steps toward construction of a neuro-developmental account of changes in the first two years of life. *Developmental Review, 24,* 347–373.

Bauer, P. J. (2005). Developments in declarative memory: Decreasing susceptibility to storage failure over the second year of life. *Psychological Science, 16,* 41–47.

Bauer, P. J., Kroupina, M. G., Schwade, J. A., Dropik, P. L., & Wewerka, S. S. (1998). If memory serves, will language? Later verbal accessibility of early memories. *Development and Psychopathology, 10,* 655–679.

Bauer, P. J., van Abbema, D. L., Wiebe, S. A., Cary, M. S., Phill, C., & Burch, M. M. (2004). Props, not picture, are worth a thousand words: Verbal accessibility of early memories under different conditions of contextual support. *Applied Cognitive Psychology, 18,* 373–392.

Bauer, P. J., Wenner, J. A., & Kroupina, M. G. (2002). Making the past present: Verbal reports of preverbal memories. *Journal of Cognition and Development, 3,* 21–47.

Bauer, P. J., Wiebe, S. A., Carver, L. J., Lukowski, A. F., Haight, J. C., Waters, J. M., et al. (2006). Electrophysiological indices of encoding and behavioral indices of recall: Examining relations and developmental change in the first year of life. *Developmental Neuropsychology, 29,* 293–320.

Bertenthal, B., & Fischer, K. W. (1978). Development of self-recognition in the infant. *Developmental Psychology, 14,* 44–50.

Bruce, D., Wilcox-O'Hearn, L. A., Robinson, J. A., Phillips-Grant, K., Francis, L., & Smith, M. C. (2005). Fragment memories mark the end of childhood amnesia. *Memory and Cognition, 33,* 567–576.

Bullock, M., & Lutkenhaus, P. (1990). Who am I? Self-understanding in toddlers. *Merrill-Palmer Quarterly, 36,* 217–238.

Butterworth, G. E. (1995). The self as an object of consciousness in infancy. In P. Rochat (Ed.), *The self in infancy: Theory and research* (pp. 35–51). Amsterdam: Elsevier.

Campbell, B. A., & Spear, N. E. (1972). Ontogeny of memory. *Psychological Review, 79,* 215–236.

Clayton, N. S., Bussey, T. J., & Dickinson, A. (2003). Can animals recall the past and plan for the future? *Nature Reviews Neuroscience, 4,* 685–691.

Clayton, N. S., & Dickinson, A. (1998). Episodic-like memory during cache recovery by scrubjays. *Nature, 395,* 272–274.

Cleveland E. S., & Reese, E. (2005). Maternal structure and autonomy support in conversations about the past: Contributions to children's autobiographical memory. *Developmental Psychology*, *41*, 376–388.

Cohen, D., & Gunz, A. (2002). As seen by the other: Perspectives on the self in the memories and perceptions of Easterners and Westerners. *Psychological Science*, *13*, 55–59.

Conway, M. A. (1996). Autobiographical knowledge and autobiographical memories. In D. Rubin (Ed.), *Remembering our past: Studies in autobiographical memory* (pp. 67–93). New York: Cambridge University Press.

Conway, M. A. (2005). Memory and the self. *Journal of Memory and Language*, *53*, 594–628.

Conway, M. A., & Fthenaki, A. (2000). Disruption and loss of autobiographical memory. In L. S. Cermak (Ed.), *Handbook of neuropsychology: Memory and its disorders* (2nd ed., pp. 281–312). Amsterdam: Elsevier.

Conway, M. A., Pleydell-Pearce, C. W., Whitecross, C. W., & Sharpe, H. (2002). Brain imaging autobiographical memory. *The Psychology of Learning and Motivation*, *41*, 229–264.

Conway, M. A., & Rubin, D. C. (1993). The structure of autobiographical memory. In A. F. Collins, S. E. Gathercole, M. A. Conway, & P. E. Morris (Eds.), *Theories of memory* (pp. 103–137). Hillsdale, NJ: Lawrence Erlbaum Associates, Inc.

Courage, M. L., Edison, S. E., & Howe, M. L. (2004). Variability in the early development of visual self-recognition. *Infant Behavior and Development*, *27*, 509–532.

Courage, M. L., & Howe, M. L. (1998). The ebb and flow of infant attentional preferences: Evidence for long-term recognition memory in 3-month-olds. *Journal of Experimental Child Psychology*, *70*, 26–53.

Courage, M. L., & Howe, M. L. (2002). From infant to child: The dynamics of cognitive change in the second year of life. *Psychological Bulletin*, *128*, 250–277.

Courage, M. L., & Howe, M. L. (2004). Advances in early memory development research: Insights about the dark side of the moon. *Developmental Review*, *24*, 6–32.

Courage, M. L., Howe, M. L., & Squires, S. E. (2004). Individual differences in 3.5-month-olds' visual attention: What do they predict at 1 year? *Infant Behavior and Development*, *27*, 19–30.

Crawley, R. A., & Eacott, M. J. (2006). Memories of early childhood: Qualities of the experience of recollection. *Memory and Cognition*, *34*, 287–294.

Damasio, A. (1999). *The feeling of what happens: Body and emotion in the making of consciousness*. New York: Harcourt Brace & Company.

de Hoz, L., & Wood, E. R. (2006). Dissociating the past from the present in the activity of place cells. *Hippocampus*, *16*, 704–715.

Dickie, J. R., & Strader, W. H. (1974). Development of mirror responses in infancy. *Journal of Psychology*, *88*, 333–337.

Eacott, M. J., & Crawley, R. A. (1998). The offset of childhood amnesia: Memory for events that occurred before age 3. *Journal of Experimental Psychology: General*, *127*, 22–33.

Eacott, M. J., Easton, A., & Zinkivskay, A. (2006). Recollection in an episodic-like memory task in the rat. *Learning and Memory*, *12*, 221–223.

Farrant, K., & Reese, E. (2000). Maternal reminiscing style and dyadic quality: Stepping stones in children's autobiographical memory development. *Journal of Cognition and Development*, *1*, 193–225.

Ferbinteanu, J., Kennedy, P. J., & Shapiro, M. L. (2006). Episodic memory—From brain to mind. *Hippocampus, 16*, 691–703.

Fivush, R. (1994). Young children's event recall: Are memories constructed through discourse? *Consciousness and Cognition, 3*, 356–373.

Fivush, R. (1997). Event memory in early childhood. In N. Cowan (Ed.), *The development of memory in childhood* (pp. 139–161). Hove, UK: Psychology Press.

Fivush, R., Haden, C. A., & Reese, E. (1996). Remembering, recounting, and reminiscing: The development of autobiographical memory in social context. In D. Rubin (Ed.), *Remembering our past: Studies in autobiographical memory* (pp. 341–359). Cambridge, MA: Cambridge University Press.

Fivush, R., & Reese, E. (1992). The social construction of autobiographical memory. In M. A. Conway, D. C. Rubin, H. Spinnler, & W. A. Wagenaar (Eds.), *Theoretical perspectives on autobiographical memory* (pp. 115–132). Dordrecht, The Netherlands: Kluwer Academic.

Freud, S. (1953). Three essays on the theory of sexuality. In J. Strachey (Ed.), *The standard edition of the complete psychological works of Sigmund Freud* (Vol. 7, pp. 135–243). London: Hogarth Press. (Original work published 1905.)

Gallup, G. G. (1979). Self-recognition in chimpanzees and man: A developmental and comparative perspective. In M. Lewis & L. Rosenblum (Eds.), *The child and its family: The genesis of behavior* (Vol. 2, pp. 107–126). New York: Plenum.

Gibson, E. J. (1995). Are we automata? In P. Rochat (Ed.), *The self in infancy: Theory and research* (pp. 3–15). Amsterdam: Elsevier.

Gogtay, N., Nugent, T. F., III, Herman, D. H., Ordonez, A., Greenstein, D., Hayashi, K. M., et al. (2006). Dynamic mapping of normal human hippocampal development. *Hippocampus, 16*, 664–672.

Goodman, G. S., Quas, J. A., Batterman-Faunce, J. M., Riddlesberger, M. M., & Kuhn, J. (1994). Predictors of accurate and inaccurate memories of traumatic events experienced in childhood. *Consciousness and Cognition, 3*, 269–294.

Gopnik, A., & Meltzoff, A. N. (1997). *Words, thoughts, and theories.* Cambridge, MA: MIT Press.

Griffiths, D. P., Dickinson, A., & Clayton, N. S. (1999). Declarative and episodic memory: What can animals remember about their past? *Trends in Cognitive Sciences, 3*, 74–80.

Haden, C. A., Haine, R. A., & Fivush, R. (1997). Developing narrative structure in parent–child reminiscing across the preschool years. *Developmental Psychology, 33*, 295–307.

Hampton, R. R., & Schwartz, B. L. (2004). Episodic memory in nonhumans: What, and where, is when? *Current Opinion in Neurobiology, 14*, 192–197.

Han, J. J., Leichtman, M. D., & Wang, Q. (1998). Autobiographical memory in Korean, Chinese, and American Children. *Developmental Psychology, 34*, 701–713.

Harley, K., & Reese, E. (1998). Origins of autobiographical memory. *Developmental Psychology, 35*, 1338–1348.

Hayne, H. (2004). Infant memory development: Implications for childhood amnesia. *Developmental Review, 24*, 33–73.

Howe, M. L. (2000). *The fate of early memories: Developmental science and the retention of childhood experiences.* Washington, DC: American Psychological Association.

Howe, M. L. (2004). Early memory, early self, and the emergence of autobiographical memory. In D. Beike, J. M. Lampinen, & D. A. Behrend (Eds.), *The self and memory* (pp. 45–72). New York: Psychology Press.

Howe, M. L. (2007). The nature of infantile amnesia. In J. H. Byrne (Ed. in Chief) & R. Menzel (Vol. Ed.), *Learning and memory—a comprehensive reference: Vol. 1. Learning theory and behavior*. San Diego, CA: Academic Press/Elsevier.

Howe, M. L., & Courage, M. L. (1993). On resolving the enigma of infantile amnesia. *Psychological Bulletin, 113*, 305–326.

Howe, M. L., & Courage, M. L. (1997). The emergence and early development of autobiographical memory. *Psychological Review, 104*, 499–523.

Howe, M. L., Courage, M. L., & Edison, S. E. (2003). When autobiographical memory begins. *Developmental Review, 23*, 471–494.

Hudson, J. A. (1990). The emergence of autobiographical memory in mother–child conversation. In R. Fivush & J. Hudson (Eds.), *Knowing and remembering in young children* (pp. 166–196). New York: Cambridge University Press.

James, W. (1890). *The principles of psychology* (Vol. 1). New York: Holt.

Kagan, J. (1981). *The second year*. Cambridge, MA: Harvard University Press.

Kagan, J. (1998). Is there a self in infancy? In M. Ferrari & R. Sternberg (Eds.), *Self awareness: Its nature and development*. New York: Guilford Press.

Legerstee, M., Anderson, D., & Schaffer, A. (1998). Five- and eight-month-old infants recognize their faces and voices as familiar and social stimuli. *Child Development, 69*, 37–50.

Levine, B. (2004). Autobiographical memory and the self in time: Brain lesion effects, functional neuroanatomy, and lifespan development. *Brain and Cognition, 55*, 54–68.

Lewis, M. (1994). Myself and me. In S. Parker, R. Mitchell, & M. Boccia (Eds.), *Self-awareness in animals and humans: Developmental perspectives* (pp. 20–34). Cambridge, MA: Cambridge University Press.

Lewis, M., & Brooks-Gunn, H. (1979). *Social cognition and the acquisition of self*. New York: Plenum Press.

Loveland, K. A. (1987). Behavior of young children with Down syndrome before the mirror: Finding things reflected. *Child Development, 58*, 928–936.

MacDonald, S., Uesiliana, K., & Hayne, H. (2000). Cross-cultural and gender differences in childhood amnesia. *Memory, 8*, 365–376.

Manns, J. R., & Eichenbaum, H. (2006). Evolution of declarative memory. *Hippocampus, 16*, 795–808.

McDonough, L., & Mandler, J. M. (1994). Very long-term recall in infants: Infantile amnesia reconsidered. *Memory, 2*, 339–352.

Meltzoff, A. N. (1995). What infant memory tells us about infantile amnesia: Long-term recall and deferred imitation. *Journal of Experimental Child Psychology, 59*, 497–515.

Meltzoff, A. N., & Moore, M. K. (1994). Imitation, memory, and the representation of persons. *Infant Behavior and Development, 17*, 83–100.

Michiko, M., & Hiraki, K. (2006). Delayed intermodal contingency affects young children's recognition of their current self. *Child Development, 77*, 736–750.

Mitchell, R. W. (1993). Mental models of mirror self-recognition: Two theories. *New Ideas in Psychology, 11*, 295–325.

Morris, G., & Baker-Ward, L. (2007). Fragile but real: Children's capacity to use newly acquired words to convey preverbal memories. *Child Development, 78*, 448–458.

Mullen, M. K. (1994). Earliest recollections of childhood: A demographic analysis. *Cognition, 52*, 55–79.

Mullen, M. K., & Yi, S. (1995). The cultural context of talk about the past: Implications for the development of autobiographical memory. *Cognitive Development, 10*, 407–419.

Neisser, U. (Ed.). (1993). *The perceived self. Ecological and interpersonal sources of self-knowledge*. New York: Cambridge University Press.

Nelson, C. A. (1995). The ontogeny of human memory: A cognitive neuroscience perspective. *Developmental Psychology, 31*, 723–738.

Nelson, C. A. (1997). The neurobiological basis of early memory development. In N. Cowan (Ed.), *The development of memory in early childhood* (pp. 41–82). Hove, UK: Psychology Press.

Nelson, C. A. (2000). Neural plasticity in human development: The role of early experience in sculpting memory systems. *Developmental Science, 3*, 115–130.

Nelson, K. (1996). *Language in cognitive development: The emergence of the mediated mind*. New York: Cambridge University Press.

Nelson, K., & Fivush, R. (2004). The emergence of autobiographical memory: A social cultural developmental theory. *Psychological Review, 111*, 486–511.

Nielsen, M., Suddendorf, T., & Slaughter, V. (2006). Mirror self-recognition beyond the face. *Child Development, 77*, 1176–1185.

Ottinger-Alberts, W., & Newcombe, N. (1999). *Retrieval effort, source monitoring, and childhood amnesia: A new look at an old problem*. Paper presented at the biennial meeting of the Society for Research in Child Development, Albuquerque, MN.

Perner, J., & Ruffman, T. (1995). Episodic memory and autonoetic consciousness: Developmental evidence and a theory of childhood amnesia. *Journal of Experimental Child Psychology, 59*, 516–548.

Pfefferbaum, A., Mathalon, D. H., Sullivan, E. V., Rawles, J. M., Zipursky, R. B., & Lim, K. O. (1994). A quantitative magnetic resonance imaging study of changes in brain morphology from infancy to late adulthood. *Archives of Neurology, 51*, 874–887.

Pillemer, D. B., & White, S. H. (1989). Childhood events recalled by children and adults. In H. W. Reese (Ed.), *Advances in child development and behavior* (Vol. 21, pp. 297–340). San Diego, CA: Academic Press.

Pipp, S., Fischer, K. W., & Jennings, S. (1987). Acquisition of self and mother knowledge in infancy. *Developmental Psychology, 23*, 86–96.

Povinelli, D. J., Landau, K. R., & Perilloux, H. K. (1996). Self-recognition in young children using delayed versus live feedback: Evidence of a developmental asynchrony. *Child Development, 67*, 1540–1554.

Povinelli, D., Landry, A. M., Theall, L. A., Clarke, B. R., & Castile, C. M. (1999). Development of young children's understanding that the recent past is causally bound to the present. *Developmental Psychology, 35*, 1426–1439.

Povinelli, D. J., & Simon, B. B. (1998). Young children's understanding of briefly versus extremely delayed images of the self: Emergence of the autobiographical stance. *Developmental Psychology, 34*, 188–194.

Prudhomme, N. (2005). Early declarative memory and self-concept. *Infant Behavior and Development, 28*, 132–144.

Reese, E. (2002). Social factors in the development of autobiographical memory: The state of the art. *Social Development, 11*, 124–142.

Reese, E., Haden, C. A., & Fivush, R. (1993). Mother–child conversations about the past: Relationships of style and memory over time. *Cognitive Development*, *8*, 403–430.

Robinson, J. A., Connell, S., & McKenzie, B. E. (1990). Do infants use their own images to locate objects reflected in a mirror? *Child Development*, *61*, 1558–1568.

Rochat, P. (1995). Early objectification of the self. In P. Rochat (Ed.), *The self in infancy: Theory and research* (pp. 53–71). Amsterdam: Elsevier.

Rochat, P. (2001). Origins of self-concept. In J. G. Bremner & A. Fogel (Eds.), *Blackwell handbook of infant development*. Oxford: Basil Blackwell.

Rochat, P., & Striano, T. (2002). Who is in the mirror? Self–other discrimination in specular images by four- and nine-month-old infants. *Child Development*, *73*, 35–46.

Ross, M., & Wilson, A. E. (2000). Constructing and appraising past selves. In D. L. Schacter & E. Scarry (Eds.), *Memory, brain, and belief* (pp. 231–259). Cambridge, MA: Harvard University Press.

Rovee-Collier, C., Hayne, H., & Colombo, M. (2001). *The development of implicit and explicit memory*. Amsterdam: John Benjamins Publishing Company.

Rubin, D. C. (Ed.). (1996). *Remembering our past: Studies in autobiographical memory*. Cambridge: Cambridge University Press.

Schmuckler, M. A. (1995). Self-knowledge of body position: Integration of perceptual and action system information. In P. Rochat, (Ed.), *The self in infancy: Theory and research* (pp. 221–242). Amsterdam: North Holland/Elsevier.

Schulman, A., & Kaplowitz, C. (1977). Mirror image response during the first two years of life. *Developmental Psychobiology*, *10*, 133–142.

Schwartz, B. L., Hoffman, M. L., & Evans, S. (2005). Episodic-like memory in a gorilla: A review and new findings. *Learning and Motivation*, *36*, 226–244.

Serres, L. (2001). Morphological changes of the human hippocampal formation from midgestation to early childhood. In C. A. Nelson & M. Luciana (Eds.), *Handbook of developmental cognitive neuroscience* (pp. 45–58). Cambridge, MA: MIT Press.

Sheffield, E. G., & Hudson, J. A. (1994). Reactivation of toddlers' event memory. *Memory*, *2*, 447–465.

Simcock, G., & Hayne, H. (2002). Breaking the barrier? Children fail to translate their preverbal memories into language. *Psychological Science*, *13*, 225–231.

Tulving, E. (1989). Remembering and knowing the past. *American Scientist*, *77*, 361–367.

Tulving, E. (1993). What is episodic memory? *Current Directions in Psychological Science*, *2*, 67–70.

Tulving, E., & Markowitsch, H. J. (1998). Episodic and declarative memory: Role of the hippocampus. *Hippocampus*, *8*, 198–204.

Usher, J. N., & Neisser, U. (1993). Childhood amnesia and the beginnings of memory for four early life events. *Journal of Experimental Psychology: General*, *122*, 155–165.

9 Memory development: emotion, stress, and trauma

**Pedro M. Paz-Alonso, Rakel P. Larson,
Paola Castelli, Deborah Alley,
and Gail S. Goodman**
University of California, Davis, USA

That future is mine. And I have every hope that it will be a peaceful one, even if one can never forget the unforgettable.

(Sabine Dardenne, from: *I was 12 years old, I took my bike and I left for school*; Dardenne & Cuny, 2004, p. 00)

The author of this quotation survived one of the world's most despised serial rapists and murderers, Marc Dutroux, who abducted and kept Sabine locked in a basement for 80 days. He subjected her to repeated sexual abuse. During her captivity, she wrote a journal and letters to her parents, and she used symbols such stars or crosses to mark on a calendar certain events, for example, when she saw Dutroux or was raped by him. After Dutroux kidnapped a 14-year-old girl who was then also held captive and sexually abused in the basement with Sabine, the police were able to locate both girls. Once they were set free by the police, investigators discovered some of Sabine's letters under a carpet, as well as the buried bodies of several victims—two of them as young as 8 years old—who did not survive in Dutroux's deadly dungeon. In 2004, Dutroux was sentenced to life imprisonment for the kidnapping and rape of six young girls and the murder of four of them. Sabine and the 14-year-old testified against him at the trial. Dardenne's account of her abduction and its aftermath are documented in her memoir, *J'avais douze ans, j'ai pris mon vélo et je suis partie à l'école* (*I was twelve years old, I took my bike and I left for school*), published following the trial and that has became a bestseller in Europe.

This real case captures some of the research questions, as well as challenges, in investigating the effects of emotion, stress, and trauma on childhood memory. For example, how can developmental psychologists study, in a scientifically sound fashion, memory for the kinds of traumatic experiences Sabine unfortunately experienced? How does trauma affect children's memory, and do such effects differ depending on a child's age (e.g., if the two 8-year-olds had survived, how accurately and completely could they, compared to the older girls, have recounted what happened)? Are such terrible and traumatic events "unforgettable" and therefore remembered in vivid detail, or are they sometimes lost from memory? When Sabine was later interviewed, she stated: "I'm very strong-willed. I know what I want and I know what's important for me. I won't ever give up if that's what's at stake. In his cellar, I knew what was important for me was to see my family again, my parents, my sisters. So I didn't give up; I kept going." In such circumstances, not everyone would be as resilient as Sabine. Are there individual differences (e.g., in mental health, attachment style) that affect emotional reactions to and memory accuracy for distressing information?

The aim of the present chapter is to review research that has addressed questions such as these, which abound because of their theoretical and applied significance. In doing so, we first describe the main methodological procedures employed by researchers to investigate the effects of emotion, stress, and trauma on children's memory. This is of special importance because the use of different methodological approaches, ranging from laboratory-based experiments (i.e., on memory for emotional words and stories) to naturalistic studies (i.e., on memory for natural disasters, violent events, documented cases of child abuse), may determine some of the inconsistent findings within this area of research. Also, the pros and cons of each of these methodological approaches in studying emotion, stress, trauma, and memory development are discussed.

Second, we review mechanisms such as selective attention and post-stimulus elaboration, involved at different stages (encoding, retention, and retrieval) of information processing of distressing events. Third, we also discuss whether or not memory for emotional/stressful/traumatic events is governed by the same principles that apply to memory for non-emotional events. Moreover, trauma and memory research (which largely focuses on child sexual abuse), and some of the theoretical models of trauma memory, are described. Research on memory for childhood sexual trauma is of special importance to debates about normal versus special memory mechanisms relevant to trauma. Child sexual abuse often involves situations where children experience chronic exposure to traumatic and shameful events, and may differ substantially from the one-time exposure to events often studied in research on emotion and memory. Fourth, we then review empirical findings from research investigating children's false memories and misinformation effects for emotional experiences.

Fifth, we consider the possible contribution of several cognitive and individual difference factors to children's memory for emotional, stressful, and traumatic information. Factors such as age, delay, distinctiveness, personal relevance, personal participation, and parenting variables have been shown to play a critical role in how accurately emotion-arousing information is recollected. Finally, we conclude with questions that still need to be addressed by future research.

RESEARCH ON CHILDREN'S MEMORY FOR EMOTIONAL STIMULI, STRESSFUL EVENTS, AND TRAUMATIC EXPERIENCES

In this section, we introduce some of the main findings from research on children's memory for emotional, stressful, and traumatic events and the diversity of research methods investigators employ to examine children's memory for such information. The different methods are organized under two broad categories: (1) Laboratory research, which includes several approaches used in scientific studies of children's memories for emotional materials, such as word lists and stories; and (2) Naturalistic research, which includes examining memory for naturally occurring, real-life stressful and traumatic experiences, such as doctor visits, emergency room treatments, natural disasters, and child abuse.

Laboratory research

Because of obvious ethical concerns, laboratory studies of children's memories for emotional materials mainly rely on relatively mild stimuli, such as word lists and stories (e.g., Bartlett, Burleson, & Santrock, 1982; Forgas, Burnham, & Trimboli, 1988; Moradi, Taghavi, Neshat-Doost, Yule, & Dalgleish, 2000; Neshat-Doost, Taghavi, Moradi, Yule, & Dalgleish, 1998), or on videotaped or staged events where children watch but do not directly experience a somewhat stressful incident (e.g., Bugental, Blue, Cortez, Fleck, & Rodriguez, 1992). In the following subsections, we briefly describe a few of the laboratory procedures frequently utilized.

Memory for emotional stimuli

Measuring children's memory for specific emotional and/or non-emotional story content is a common method utilized by investigators. Davidson, Luo, and Burden (2001), for example, studied 6- to 11-year-old children's memory for emotional behaviors (e.g., "Her dad gave her a beautiful present") and non-emotional behaviors (e.g., "Maria watched television with her brothers") in stories about everyday family life. Children recalled more of the emotional behaviors as compared to the non-emotional behaviors, suggesting that emotion (both positive and negative) can have a facilitative effect on recall. Other studies of children's memory for stories have also revealed that the distinctiveness of the to-be-remembered materials (which is often hard to separate from emotional impact) may facilitate recall (e.g., Davidson & Jergovic, 1996; see Howe, 1997, for a review). One frequent methodological problem in such research is that the stimuli differ not only in emotional valence but also in content. In the example above, for instance, perhaps it is easier to remember getting a present than watching TV for reasons other than emotion. Overall, however, laboratory studies of children's memories for word lists and stories suggest that emotional material is better remembered than neutral material.

Eyewitness memory for emotional events

Children are often required to give eyewitness accounts of stressful and traumatic events during investigations and legal proceedings (see Pipe & Salmon, Chapter 10 this volume); therefore, studies of children's eyewitness memory and suggestibility have important forensic implications (e.g., Goodman, Batterman-Faunce, Schaaf, & Kenney, 2002; Ornstein, Baker-Ward, Gordon, & Merritt, 1997; Saywitz & Nathanson, 1993).

A common procedure for examining children's eyewitness memory and suggestibility in the laboratory is to have children view emotionally arousing videos (e.g., Bugental et al., 1992; Roebers & Schneider, 2002; Roebers, Schwartz, & Neumann, 2005), or witness a live staged event (e.g., Poole & White, 1991). Roebers and Schneider (2002), for instance, examined the consistency of 6-, 8-, and 10-year-olds' memories of a video depicting a theft and one of a treasure hunt. After a delay, the children were prompted by free recall (e.g., "Tell me everything you remember about the videos"), cued recall (e.g., "How much money was in the wallet?"), and misleading questions (e.g., "The boy had blond hair, didn't he?"). Across age groups, memory for the details of both videos was generally accurate; however, older children provided more units of information and were less suggestible to the misleading questions.

Pros and cons of laboratory research

Laboratory studies usually have the advantage of internal validity, allowing researchers to manipulate a variable (i.e., independent variable) to examine if it has a causal relation to another variable, in particular, to memory (i.e., dependent variable). Additionally, the accuracy of children's memories can be directly and precisely measured against objective records (e.g., videotapes) of a specific stressful event. However, as mentioned earlier, sometimes both content and emotion are confounded in such studies. Moreover, a particularly important disadvantage is that arousal may not reach levels necessary to detect effects of stress and trauma on memory (see Deffenbacher, Bornstein, Penrod, & McGorty, 2004). To illustrate how researchers have dealt with the later limitation of laboratory studies, we now turn our attention to methodologies that involve examining children's memories for real-life events— events ranging from mildly stressful experiences to ones that are highly traumatic and potentially life threatening.

Naturalistic research

Developmentalists have become increasingly creative in their efforts to find ethical methods to study children's memory for real-life emotional, stressful, and traumatic events. Such studies have the advantages of "external validity," which refers to how well a study's results generalize to the real-world situation of interest. In this effort, investigators take advantage of naturally occurring stressful experiences in young children's lives, such as emergency medical procedures and natural disasters (e.g., Bahrick, Parker, Fivush, & Levitt, 1998; Hamond & Fivush, 1991; see also Gordon, Baker-Ward, & Ornstein, 2001). Events of personal importance that children experience provide investigators with the means to examine the effects of stress and arousal levels on memory. Some of the important methods in the naturalistic study of stress and trauma are briefly described in the following subsections.

Memory for medical procedures

Typically, medical procedures are salient personal experiences that can elicit distress. Children are required to undergo doctor-ordered medical procedures for health reasons. Memory researchers take advantage of that fact to study memory for mildly stressful (e.g., well-child checkups) to highly stressful (e.g., emergency room visits, surgery, cancer treatments) medical procedures (Baker-Ward, Gordon, Ornstein, Larus, & Clubb, 1993; Burgwyn-Bailes, Baker-Ward, Gordon, & Ornstein, 2001; Chen, Zeltzer, Craske, & Katz, 2000; Goodman, Hirschman, Hepps, & Rudy, 1991; Goodman, Quas, Batterman-Faunce, Riddlesberger, & Kuhn, 1997; Peterson & Bell, 1996; Shrimpton, Oates, & Hayes, 1998).

A common approach in medical procedure studies is to assess the child's distress level and obtain an objective record of the medical procedure through videotaping what happened (e.g., Goodman, Hirschman, et al., 1991). In other studies, what occurred is documented via parental statements or medical records (e.g., Burgwyn-Bailes et al., 2001; Peterson & Bell, 1996). An important goal is to have a detailed and accurate account of the stressful event. Peterson and colleagues, for example, conducted an important longitudinal study of children's memories for various traumatic injuries requiring emergency treatment (e.g., broken bones, burns, dog bites, crushed fingers, and lacerations requiring stitches). Children (2 to 13 years old) receiving treatment were recruited from a hospital waiting room and interviewed a few days after the injury about the experience. Retesting of memory occurred at 6 months (Peterson & Bell, 1996) and also 5 years after the event (Peterson & Whalen, 2001). At each subsequent interview, children who were at least 3 years old at the time of the injury were able to recall remarkable amounts of information concerning the central components of what occurred; however, reports of the hospital treatment were less complete, suggesting that the nature of the event and the centrality of the information influences recall of stressful and traumatic experiences (e.g., Quas, Goodman, Bidrose, Pipe, Craw, & Ablin, 1999; see also Christianson, 1992; Christianson & Lindholm, 1998, for reviews).

Another medical procedure studied by memory researchers is called voiding cystourethrogram fluoroscopy (VCUG). VCUG is a painful and potentially embarrassing procedure involving genital penetration. It permits researchers to interview children about information that could be of concern in child sexual abuse investigations (e.g., Goodman et al., 1997; Merritt, Ornstein, & Spicker, 1994; Quas et al., 1999; Salmon, Price, & Pereira, 2002). Results from VCUG studies reveal that stress does not necessarily have a facilitative or deleterious effect on memory and that young children can accurately report details of the procedure during free recall, although more distressed children may report fewer details (Merritt et al., 1994). However, when presented with specific or misleading questions, older children are quite consistently more accurate and less suggestible than younger children (see Sjöberg & Lindholm, 2005, for a review).

Although the gist of stressful medical procedures is often retained well by children, errors in memory for such experiences are not uncommon. For example, young children may misidentify who was present when shown photo line-ups (especially line-ups that do not include the medical staff who were actually seen) or when intentionally misled about what occurred (e.g., Bruck, Ceci, Francouer, & Barr, 1995; Goodman, Bottoms, Schwartz-Kenney, & Rudy, 1991).

Thus, medical procedures have proven to be effective tools for researchers who examine the effects of stress and trauma on memory. The results are not entirely consistent, however, in finding that higher levels of distress are associated with better memory. Moreover, there are limitations in using this methodology. In particular, most of the injuries studied to date were not life threatening, and medical procedures are socially indicated with the intent to help the child, not cause further injury. Therefore, arousal levels may not be commensurate with those elicited by events where severe physical danger, even death, is more likely (e.g., Bahrick et al., 1998; Fivush, Sales, Goldberg, Bahrick, & Parker, 2004).

Memory for traumatic experiences—flashbulb memories, violent events, and natural disasters

Memories for the details of a single distinctive, consequential, and distressing public event, such as the September 11th terrorist attacks, were coined "flashbulb" memories by Brown and Kulik (1977). Flashbulb memories are believed to form as a result of an event's unexpectedness, emotional content, personal consequences, and importance (e.g., Conway, 1995; Er, 2003). Examining children's memories for events that may give rise to flashbulb memories (e.g., natural disasters and violent events) provides another approach for investigating the effects of stressful and traumatic experiences on memory. For example, Terr, Bloch, Michel, and Shi (1996) examined 8- to 15-year-old children's memories for the *Challenger* explosion. Children who watched the explosion (i.e., high involvement group) produced more clear, consistent, and detailed accounts about the explosion itself and their surrounding personal circumstances (e.g., personal placement, incidents, other people who were there) than those children who just heard about the event (i.e., low involvement group), at both 5–7 weeks and 14 month retention intervals. However, 30% of the study participants misunderstood some details of the event and incorporated these misunderstandings into their memory reports. (Note that, although we focus on accuracy of memory in this chapter, consistency in reporting is another important factor because it allows for the examination of the endurance of specific types of memories; e.g., Berntsen & Rubin, 2006; Er, 2003; Peace & Porter, 2004; see van Giezen, Arensman, Spinhoven, & Wolters, 2005, for a review.)

Other methods for examining traumatic memories include comparing children's memories to public reports of an event and/or comparing memory accounts across repeated questionings. Terr (1981), for instance, did both when she examined victims' memories of the Chowchilla school-bus kidnapping, a highly publicized crime in which children 5 to 14 years old were abducted and subsequently buried alive. This study was based on Terr's clinical interviews of victims during psychological treatment, which occurred approximately 5 to 23 months after the event. Overall, children exhibited vivid memories of the experience immediately, and retained accurate memory for the gist of the incident 1 and 5 years after the kidnapping (Terr, 1983; see also Pynoos & Eth, 1984; Pynoos & Nader, 1989). However, children also showed persistent memory inaccuracies involving peripheral details such as the date, time, and duration of the event.

Natural disasters have also been utilized as target events to examine the influence of stress on children's memory. Bahrick et al.'s (1998) study concerned the memories of 3- and 4-year-old children who experienced Hurricane Andrew, a strong category 4 storm that devastated the Florida coast in 1992. Children were categorized into low, medium, or high stress groups depending on the severity of the storm damage they experienced. When interviewed a few weeks after the event, all children provided detailed accounts of the disaster; however, children who experienced moderate to high levels of stress recalled more than those in the low stress group. When Fivush and colleagues (2004) conducted follow-up interviews 6 years after the hurricane, they found that children in all three stress groups recalled twice the information originally recounted, which could be a result of increased verbal abilities at retest and extensive rehearsal of the event with friends and family (see Fivush, 1998, for a review). Of importance, this longitudinal study suggests that the details of stressful and traumatic experiences can be well remembered over relatively long periods of time.

Researchers are also interested in how enduring and vivid memories remain into adulthood (e.g., Winograd & Killinger, 1983). Berntsen and Rubin (2006) interviewed Danish Second World War survivors between the ages of 59 and 90 years old about their childhood memories of the German invasion of 1940 and subsequent surrender 5 years later. Results showed that respondents who were 7 years old at the time of the invasion or the surrender had vivid, extensive memories of these events. This finding suggests that childhood traumatic memories can be maintained into adulthood (e.g., Reviere & Bakeman, 2001).

Overall, evidence from research using naturalistic events suggests that detailed memories of highly salient and personally consequential experiences are relatively well retained over long periods of time. Nevertheless, it is important to note that even with high personal involvement and report of strong emotion during the incident, these traumatic memories are not immune from forgetting or distortion (e.g., Terr et al., 1996; see also Neisser & Harsch, 1992; Nourkova, Bernstein, & Loftus, 2004; Pezdek, 2003). Moreover, because public events are often involved, children and adults may have opportunities to discuss their experiences socially, which may help explain the endurance of these memories in some instances (e.g., Fivush et al., 2004). Therefore, it is possible that memory for events that take place in private and involve secrecy and possibly shame, may be recalled differently. This brings us to the study of memory for child sexual abuse. Although child sexual abuse involves assault and therefore is often of a violent nature, we devote a separate section to research on this topic because of the controversial nature of children's memory for sexual abuse and because of the special emotions that may arise in remembering such experiences.

Memory for childhood sexual abuse

Documented cases of child abuse provide a means to examine how real-life traumatic events may be represented in children's and adults' memory. In doing so, an individual's memories may be compared to existent information in legal, research, and medical records (e.g., Goodman et al., 2003; Williams, 1994) and, if any, to records of the actual abusive events (e.g., photographs, video, and audio tapes; Bidrose & Goodman, 2000; Leander, Granhag, & Christianson, 2005; Orbach & Lamb, 1999). For example, Williams (1994) interviewed young adult women who previously were victims of documented childhood sexual abuse (e.g., documented through hospital medical records). The abuse occurred when the victims were between 10 months and 12 years old, and the follow-up interviews were conducted 17 years later. Despite the long delay, Williams found that a majority of victims recalled the documented abuse; however, 38% failed to disclose. In contrast, Goodman et al.'s (2003) prospective study, modeled after William's research, showed that only 15% of the adults failed to report their documented cases of childhood sexual abuse, and that older age when the abuse ended, maternal support following disclosure of the abuse, and more severe abuse were associated with an increased likelihood of disclosure.

Another instance of utilizing documented sexual abuse to assess memory comes from a study conducted by Bidrose and Goodman (2000). The case involved four 8- and 15-year-old girls who had been sexually victimized. The researchers were able to compare the girls' forensic interviews and court testimonies to photographs and audiotapes, made by the perpetrator and confiscated by the police, of the actual crimes that had been committed. Using this method, Bidrose and Goodman found that almost 86% of the alleged sexual acts were corroborated by the existent objective records. Further, consistent with other memory studies, omission errors were more prevalent than commission ones (e.g., Leander et al., 2005).

Pros and cons of naturalistic research

The methods described in this subsection have been instrumental in adding to scientific knowledge of children's memory of emotional, stressful, and traumatic events. The findings generally suggest that individuals can recall the details of traumatic experiences even after long delays; however, a certain percentage of individuals may fail to disclose their traumatic experiences, which may be a result of such factors as forgetting and/or embarrassment. Memories for stressful and traumatic events are neither indelible (e.g., Goodman et al., 2003; Williams, 1994), nor immune to distortion (Bruck et al., 1995), and memory inaccuracies may persist over time (Terr, 1983).

However, it is important to appreciate the limitations of naturalistic research. Although the real-life events studied are often emotionally gripping and socially consequential, the quality of the science behind the research is important for drawing firm conclusions about the effects of emotion, stress, and trauma on children's memory. First, a methodological limitation of naturalistic research is that often a complete objective record of the event is unobtainable. For instance, most child sexual abuse occurs in private, and what happens comes down to the child's word versus that of the accused. Unless an objective record of the event exists, it is difficult to evaluate children's memory accuracy with precision. Note that in some cases, an objective record of traumatic events does exist (e.g., when a perpetrator records the assaults, as in the Bidrose and Goodman, 2000, study); however, the availability of such recordings for research is rare. In the Sabine Dardenne case mentioned at the start of this chapter, Sabine recorded some of the events in a journal that she wrote. Such recordings could be invaluable for evaluating her latter memory, but with the caveat that only a subset of the terrible things she experienced was described and in unknown detail, and that the events were recorded from her own perspective. A second limitation of naturalistic research is that researchers cannot randomly assign children to groups, one that experiences trauma and one that does not. Such random assignment is key to drawing causal inferences. A third limitation of naturalistic studies is that a small number of children at each age may experience the event, which may differ considerably for each child. This makes it difficult to conduct *developmental* research on the effects of stress and trauma on memory.

Summary

This overview of the different methodologies employed to examine the influence of stress and trauma on memory reveals the creativity of scientific inquiry. Because stressful events cannot be ethically simulated in laboratory studies, researchers turn to naturally occurring events in their efforts to find more externally valid and forensically relevant approaches for examining the effects of emotional arousal on memory. Overall, despite the methodological variations between studies, evidence from research reviewed in this section shows that stress per se does not have a deleterious effect on children's memory (but see Deffenbacher et al., 2004). In fact, for central information, it more likely has a facilitative effect. However, as we will see later in this chapter, individual differences among children in their reactions and memory can also be profound. Next, we turn to memory mechanisms that underlie whether emotional, stressful, and traumatic events are successfully retained and accurately recalled over time.

MECHANISMS INVOLVED IN MEMORY FOR EMOTIONALLY AROUSING AND TRAUMATIC INFORMATION

As indicated earlier, emotional stimuli are often remembered better than non-emotional stimuli both by adults (e.g., Buchanan & Lovallo, 2001; Payne, Jackson, Ryan, Hoscheidt, Jacobs, & Nadel, 2006) and children (e.g., Davidson et al., 2001; Fivush et al., 2004; Goodman, Hirschman, et al., 1991). This general finding has led scholars to speculate whether or not memory for emotional/stressful events is governed by the same principles that apply to memory for non-emotional events. Brown and Kulik (1977), for example, hypothesized the existence of a special "Now Print!" mechanism, that was assumed to automatically register the surrounding circumstances (e.g., where, when, with whom) of emotionally arousing events that were experienced as surprising and that entailed some personal consequences, producing flashbulb memories that were assumed to be particularly accurate and long lasting. Their idea came from the observation that the concomitant circumstances of public tragedies (e.g., President John F. Kennedy's assassination) were generally remembered particularly vividly, leading the authors to speculate that high levels of arousal likely produced physiological changes that would permanently imprint memories (see also Conway, Anderson, Larsen, & Donnelly, 1994; Er, 2003; Yarmey & Bull, 1978; for a developmental account of flashbulb memories, see Pillemer, 1992; Warren & Swartwood, 1992).

Other researchers, however, have challenged the existence of special memory mechanisms, such as the "Now Print!" mechanism, devoted to the elaboration of emotional stimuli (e.g., Christianson, 1989, 1992; McCloskey, Wible,

& Cohen, 1988; Neisser & Harsch, 1992; Talarico & Rubin, 2003), suggesting that the memory enhancement effect often observed in relation to emotionally charged events could simply be related to the higher likelihood of such events being also meaningful, distinctive, and salient, and could thus be explained by ordinary memory mechanisms (Schooler & Eich, 2000; Shobe & Kihlstrom, 1997; Talarico & Rubin, 2003; see Howe, 1997, for a review). It is clear that distinctiveness is often one component inherent in emotionally arousing events that enhances individuals' memory. Research shows, for example, that distinct (e.g., unique, salient) negative events are particularly well remembered and retained over time by children as young as 3 years of age (e.g., Peterson & Rideout, 1998; Pynoos & Nader, 1989).

Distinctiveness alone, however, cannot account for the enhanced memory performance often observed for emotional over neutral information. When non-emotional events are considered, for example, research shows that after multiple occurrences an event may lose its distinctiveness and become part of a script (see Fivush, 1997, for a review). Once memory assumes this more schematic "script-like" form, it becomes more difficult to distinguish and report specific details related to any single instance of the recurring experience (see Fivush, 2002), especially at younger ages (Farrar & Goodman, 1992). This doesn't seem to always hold true when the event (or series of events) in question is emotional in nature. It is not arguable that scripts may also be created for emotional events; however, the few studies that specifically compared children's memory for single versus recurrent stressful events, show no difference in accuracy between these two classes of events (e.g., Chen et al., 2000; Goodman, Quas, Batterman-Faunce, Riddlesberger, & Kuhn, 1994; Howard, Osborne, & Baker-Ward, 1997). Although these studies often failed to analyze the level of specificity of the information recalled, they still seem to suggest that memory for highly emotional experiences may actually maintain its salience even after repetition. Further research is needed, however.

In the following subsections, we review some of the "normal" memory mechanisms indicated in the encoding, retention, and retrieval of emotional stimuli. Research that emphasizes the effects of traumatization on memory, and that has explored situations in which special memory mechanisms might be more likely to come into play, is also addressed.

Emotional valence and appraisals

When considering the specific processes involved in memory for emotionally arousing stimuli, it is important to consider that emotional valence can in principle be separated from arousal (Lang, Greenwald, Bradley, & Hamm, 1993). Emotional valence concerns whether an event is positive or negative. Arousal concerns the intensity or provocativeness of the event. Often, however, these two dimensions are not separated in studies of memory development.

As mentioned previously, studies examining memory accuracy often highlight emotional valence and find an advantage of negative events over positive events in adults (e.g., Christianson & Fällman, 1990; Kern, Libkuman, Otani, & Holmes, 2005), and children (e.g., Fivush et al., 2004; Paz-Alonso, Goodman, Ibabe, & DePaul, 2003), although some exceptions exist (e.g., Reisberg, Heuer, McLean, & O'Shaughnessy, 1988; Talarico, LaBar, & Rubin, 2004). Research investigating children's narratives of experienced events also indicates that emotional valence may influence the way an event is encoded and retained. Narratives of past negative events (e.g., losing a soccer game) are usually found to include more emotional appraisals and interpretations compared to narratives of positive events (e.g., winning a soccer game; Baker-Ward, Eaton, & Banks, 2005). Emotional appraisals, in addition to comprehension of the event, are believed to control the flow of attention, and the encoding process during an emotional experience (e.g., Stein, Trabasso, & Liwag, 1994).

Similarly, after the event, emotional valence also affects such processes as rehearsal of the information. For instance, parent–child conversations, which in effect constitute a form of rehearsal, differ substantially in their qualities and content depending on the valence of the emotionally arousing event discussed (Bohanek, Fivush, & Walker, 2005; Lagattuta & Wellman, 2002; Sales, Fivush, Parker, & Bahrick, 2005; Sales, Fivush, & Peterson, 2003), suggesting that emotionally arousing stimuli may be processed differently depending on valence (e.g., Bluck & Li, 2001; Kern et al., 2005).

Emotional valence, however, does not directly specify a specific emotion that is elicited during an experience, and the specific emotion matters. For instance, events that make one mad versus sad are both negative, but they may have quite different consequences for memory. Appraisal theories suggest that each emotional state is associated with specific goals and motivations, and that different information-processing strategies are adopted according to the goals and motivations related to the particular emotion being elicited (e.g., Stein, 2002; Stein & Levine, 1990; Stein, Trabasso, & Liwag, 2000).

Nevertheless, positive (e.g., joy, pride) and negative (e.g., disgust, fear) emotions can, for present purposes, be roughly categorized together. Such events likely educe different information-processing strategies, which in turn may affect their being differently remembered. In conditions of positive arousal, for example, no immediate threat to goal achievement is perceived. Thus individuals are likely motivated to preserve their emotional state. To this end, reliance on "script" knowledge (i.e., knowledge of the typical components and sequences of routine events) may be adequate, even though such reliance may lead to greater likelihood of memory intrusions if such knowledge is used to fill in gaps in one's memory (Bless, Clore, Schwarz, & Golisano, 1996; Levine & Bluck, 2004). Negative emotions, on the other hand, are generally associated with a perceived threat to the attainment of a goal. Individuals are, therefore, more likely to engage in effortful processing and to evaluate information in a systematic way to avoid goal failure. Such effortful processing and systematic evaluation may be particularly important when dealing with traumatic events, given that such experiences are often linked with the obstruction of an entire system of meaningful goals (Stein, 2002). Even though children may have more limited knowledge than adults regarding possible obstacles to goal attainment, research suggests that stressful and traumatic events are often likely to elicit the same kind of appraisals observed in adults, which may explain some of the similarities found in memory for emotional events across the life span (see Stein, 2002, for a review).

Selective attention

Appraisal theories suggest that emotions work as organizational principles for directing attention to information that is relevant to the specific emotional state elicited (see Levine & Pizarro, 2004, for a review). Selective attention toward information that elicits emotional states is indeed one of the important mechanisms leading to enhanced memory for emotionally charged material. In his "cue-utilization hypothesis," Easterbrook (1959) proposed that under conditions of arousal, attention becomes more and more narrowed. Specifically, he argued that conditions of high arousal cause a decrease in the number of cues to which individuals attend. Although Easterbrook's ideas have been interpreted to imply that under extremely high levels of arousal, narrowing of attention is so severe as to interfere with memory, according to appraisal theory such narrowing would lead individuals to focus on details particularly relevant to the emotional state evoked, while not attending well to information "peripheral" to the emotional state.

More recently, Christianson (1992) similarly proposed that conditions of negative emotional arousal are especially likely to produce a narrowing of attention. However, he concluded that such narrowing mainly interferes with memory for peripheral information, not for information of high relevance to the stressor. Following the observation that humans may be evolutionarily predisposed to retain negative emotional information so as to avoid the aversive stimulus in the future, Christianson (1992) speculated that, when facing a negatively arousing situation, the "core" emotional aspects of the event are automatically targeted by a pre-attentive mechanism (see also Kern et al., 2005; Öhman, Flykt, & Esteves, 2001), which directs attention to these specific details. Later, when more volitional, controlled processing of the emotional event takes place, resources have already been allocated to the emotionally relevant details that were the earlier focus of attention, which will be therefore preferentially processed. Such preferential processing of the core details favors memory for them (which is evolutionarily adaptive) and compromises memory for details that are peripheral relative to the source of the emotional arousal.

Although data from adults are relatively consistent in highlighting the heightened advantage of central over peripheral details for negatively arousing versus more neutral stimuli (e.g., Berntsen, 2002; Christianson, 1992; Christianson & Loftus, 1987, 1991; Schmidt, 2004), data from children are more mixed. Nevertheless, overall, studies with children tend to confirm that details "central" to negatively arousing stimuli are better retained than peripheral information (e.g., Howe, Courage, & Peterson, 1994; Terr, 1983; but see Eisen, Goodman, Qin, & Davis, 2007; Merritt et al., 1994). Moreover, even for children, central versus peripheral information is less likely to be affected by misinformation (e.g., Goodman, Hirschman et al., 1991; Paz-Alonso & Goodman, 2008; Paz-Alonso et al., 2003; Roebers & Schneider, 2000), thus supporting the idea that under negatively arousing conditions, the core details of the arousing events may, at least at times, receive preferential processing by children.

Differential recall of central and peripheral details, however, is not a completely stable finding, even with adults. This variability may depend in part on the diverse materials and methodologies employed in different studies (e.g., Laney, Campbell, Heuer, & Reisberg, 2004; Laney, Heuer, & Reisberg, 2003; Wessel, van der Kooy, & Merckelbach, 2000), and also on the dissimilar criteria adopted to define the "central" and "peripheral" information that is used for comparisons across studies (e.g., Christianson & Lindholm, 1998; Paz-Alonso, Goodman, & Ibabe, under review; Reisberg & Heuer, 2004). Some researchers have utilized a perceptual/spatial definition, wherein central details are those associated with the central character of the plot (even if they are irrelevant to the plot) or are central to the emotional event (e.g., Christianson, 1992; Christianson & Loftus, 1991). Other researchers have adopted more of a conceptual definition, in which any element of the story that could not be omitted without changing the basic plot is considered central (e.g., Heuer & Reisberg, 1992; see also Heath & Erickson, 1998; Ibabe & Sporer, 2004, for additional centrality criteria).

Also in developmental studies, researchers have varied in the criteria used to define information centrality. Goodman, Hirschman, et al. (1991), for example, defined central and peripheral details according to ratings provided by adults. Howe and colleagues (1994) mainly relied on Christianson's criteria. Finally, Peterson and Bell (1996) adopted a combination of the perceptual/spatial criteria advocated by Christianson (1992) and the plot-relevant/irrelevant criteria proposed by Heuer and Reisberg (1992). In many developmental studies, however, central and peripheral details were not even systematically assessed, as researchers simply focused on the sheer amount of information recalled, or discussed the distinction post hoc (e.g., Baker-Ward et al., 1993).

These discrepancies in the operational definition of centrality adopted across different studies make it difficult to reach any lasting conclusions regarding the accuracy of the narrowing of attention model as, for example, proposed by Christianson. Moreover, researchers generally failed to consider the impact of discrete emotions when defining their centrality criteria. As appraisal theories suggest, information that is considered "central" in one emotional state (e.g., fear) may not be considered central in another emotional state (e.g., sadness), which may also account for some of the divergent findings emergent in the literature. The difficulty in finding an adequate operational definition of centrality is further aggravated in developmental studies by the inability to clearly establish whether the criteria adopted with adults are applicable to children (see Peterson & Bell, 1996). That is, what is central to adults may not be central to children. Also, children focus at times on details of traumatic/ stressful events that are relevant to them for idiosyncratic reasons. Thus, to clearly understand whether the encoding processes operative for emotionally arousing information in children are truly comparable to those operative for adults, future research should address whether an advantage for central information would be confirmed in studies with children in which "centrality" is defined from a child's perspective.

Post-stimulus elaboration

Evidence reviewed so far suggests that attentional mechanisms elicited under conditions of negative emotional arousal lead to memory improvement in adults and children. The observed memory advantage for negatively arousing events, however, may not only be a result of factors facilitating the encoding of negative, emotionally arousing information, such as pre-attentive process-ing, but also of the further conceptual processing devoted to this type of stimuli, which may facilitate its accessibility at retrieval (Christianson, 1992). Rehearsal is one such process.

The emotional character of certain events may make them more likely to be discussed with others, and thus rehearsed, and consequently better remem-bered. In the case of flashbulb memories, the media coverage that usually accompanies public events may contribute to the reinstatement and vividness of the memories (e.g., Fivush et al., 2004; Winograd & Killinger, 1983). It is important to note, however, that although rehearsal contributes to slowing down the normal progress of forgetting (e.g., Bjork, 1988; Dunning & Stern, 1992), it does not always protect against memory intrusion (e.g., Cassel, Roebers, & Bjorklund, 1996). Warren and Swartwood (1992), for example, in their investigation of children's memory for the *Challenger* explosion, highlighted that rehearsal influenced the amount of information children reported over time, but not its accuracy. Overt rehearsal, however, is not the only process influencing the persistence of memory for emotionally arousing stimuli.

Research suggests that arousing negative events may be better remembered not only because they are more likely to be shared, but also because they are more likely to be ruminated on, evaluated, and interpreted in an attempt to understand the emotion-evoking situation and to cope with negative feelings (Levine & Pizarro, 2004). This additional cognitive processing of negative emotional stimuli is typically reflected in individuals' narratives of their nega-tive experiences (e.g., use of words such as *understand, realize*). Comparing children's narratives for positive and negative events, for example, Fivush and colleagues (Fivush, Hazzard, Sales, Sarfati, & Brown, 2003) reported that narratives of negative compared to positive events were more likely to contain information about thoughts and feelings and less likely to contain descriptive details (see also Baker-Ward et al., 2005). Children's elaboration of negative arousing events may also be facilitated by their shared parent–child conversations. Mothers are indeed found to be more likely to ask open-ended questions and to provide more causal explanation when discussing negative compared to positive events with their children (e.g., Ackil, Van Abbema, & Bauer, 2003; Bauer, Stark, Lukowski, Rademacher, Van Abbema, & Ackil, 2005; Sales et al., 2003), thus influencing (and "scaffolding"; Vygotsky, 1978; Wood, Bruner, & Ross, 1976) their children's memory by encouraging them to reflect and elaborate on the event.

Summary

In summary, negatively arousing events are often likely to elicit the same kind of appraisals in children as found in adults. Specifically, when facing negative situations, children may be as likely as adults to focus on the source of the emotional arousal and evince better memory for central details related to the event. That said, it is also possible that children's more limited knowledge base and more limited cognitive processing abilities will at times result in developmental differences in appraisals and attentional focus. Moreover, children are at times also likely to engage in cognitive elaborations and rehearsals similar to those responsible for the memory enhancement effects generally found in adults, although children's cognitive elaborations and rehearsals may be less spontaneous and involve more adult "scaffolding" than do those of adults.

We can now ask a crucial question: Are the same mechanisms operative for highly traumatic events as well? We turn to this question next.

TRAUMATIZATION AND MEMORY

Memory for traumatic events in many ways appears to follow the same cognitive principles as memory for distinctive non-traumatic events (e.g., Goodman & Paz-Alonso, 2006; Howe, Toth, & Cicchetti, 2006; Pezdek & Taylor, 2002). However, in some cases, other mechanisms may also be involved. Many of the previously described studies examined memory for one-time exposures to distressing events, and to stimuli that may be more accurately described as "stressful" rather than as "traumatic." Although definitions of what constitutes a traumatic experience vary considerably (American Psychiatric Association, 1994; Cordón, Pipe, Sayfan, Melinder, & Goodman, 2004; Eisen & Goodman, 1998; Fivush, 1998; Freyd, 1996), much of the current debate around trauma and memory has focused on child sexual abuse, which often involves situations where children experience chronic exposure to stressful events.

When exposure to traumatic events starts in childhood, individuals may especially come to focus on threat or trauma-associated cues as a general personality or information-processing strategy. The person is, in effect, in a chronic fear state, or at least is more easily transformed into a state of fear than is a non-traumatized person. This fear state should result in what Foa and her colleagues have termed "fear networks," as described within the emotional processing theory framework (Foa, Feske, Murdock, Kozak, & McCarthy, 1991; Foa & Kozak, 1986; Foa & Rothbaum, 1992). Fear networks are semantic/episodic mental structures for storing trauma-related information, which guide both attention and memory. When something in the environment matches one or more of the fear structure elements, it is activated and the activation spreads throughout the network. These fear networks are associated with the development and maintenance of post-traumatic stress disorder (PTSD), which is prevalent in both adults (i.e., 25–30%; Green, 1994) and children (i.e., 36%; Fletcher, 1996) who have experienced traumatic events (Foa & Rothbaum, 1998). For most trauma survivors, these pathological structures are corrected through engagement in daily activities that disconfirm them. However, traumatized individuals who develop PTSD and under-engage or over-engage trauma-related thoughts and activities do not have the opportunity to incorporate disconfirming information and thus maintain these pathological elements (Rauch & Foa, 2006). Overall, the central abnormality in PTSD has been conceptualized as the nature of the underlying memory representation of the traumatic event and its link to other autobiographical memories (e.g., Brewin, Dalgleish, & Joseph, 1996; Ehlers & Clark, 2000).

Consistent with the idea of fear networks, research indicates that traumatized individuals over-focus on trauma cues and have difficulty ignoring trauma stimuli (e.g., McNally, Metzger, Lasko, Clancy, & Pitman, 1998). These individuals appear to show hypersensitivity and enhanced perceptual priming to traumatic or threatening stimuli (e.g., Michael, Ehlers, & Halligan, 2005; see also Ehlers, Michael, Chen, Payne, & Shan, 2006). Thus traumatized individuals' knowledge base for trauma-related information might well be more elaborated than that of someone who has never experienced trauma. This line of research suggests that traumatized individuals are more likely to remember their abuse experiences, and to remember them particularly accurately. Thus, according to this view, abuse tends not to be forgotten, but rather remembered, perhaps all too well. (Recall Sabine Dardenne's statement that "one can never forget the unforgettable.")

This evidence contrasts with some of the trauma and memory theories that suggest trauma victims, such as incest survivors, may experience amnesia for the trauma (e.g., Freyd, 1996; Freyd, DePrince, & Zubriggen, 2001), and that children who have suffered a larger number of traumatic events tend to forget or remember more poorly those experiences compared to children who have been exposed to a single traumatic event (Terr, 1988, 1994; see also Howe, 2000, for a review). These theoretical accounts suggest the possibility that certain "special memory mechanisms" like repression and/or dissociation may come into play (e.g., Freyd, 1996; Terr, 1990; van der Kolk, 1997). Repression is a Freudian concept, according to which a traumatic event *that has negative implications for the self* can become completely inaccessible to conscious recollection, even though the memory remains in detail within the recesses of the mind and eventually might become accessible once the individual feels safe enough ("recovered memory"). Dissociation is a related concept, harkening back to the time of Freud, in which specific anxiety-provoking thoughts, emotions, or physical sensations are believed to be experienced and/or stored separately from the rest of the psyche. These "defense mechanisms" are believed to result in temporary or permanent loss of memory of trauma experiences, especially when such experiences are associated with self-blame, helplessness, and/or repeated trauma. Child sexual abuse is often characterized by feelings of self-blame and helplessness among victims, and by repeated assaults. Thus child sexual abuse is a prime possible candidate for repression and/or dissociation.

Goodman et al.'s (2003) prospective study on child sexual abuse and memory in adults examined the predictors of lost memory/lack of disclosure. As mentioned before, individuals who were younger when the abuse occurred and who had less maternal support were less likely to disclose. Also, individuals who experienced more severe child sexual abuse were more likely to disclose than were individuals who experienced less severe child sexual abuse. Findings such as these can be largely explained by normal memory mechanisms (e.g., "infantile amnesia," that is, the inability to remember specific events from early childhood, is common for memory generally; maternal support is associated with discussing the event, which is a form of rehearsal; and, greater stress is often associated with better memory for main stressors). However, one finding was consistent with the special memory mechanism point of view: Individuals who scored higher on a measure of dissociation (i.e., Dissociative Experiences Scale; DES) were less likely to disclose than were their less dissociative counterparts. Dissociation has been considered as a mental process that produces a lack of connection in a person's thoughts, memories, feelings, actions, and/or sense of identity. Thus, if a person is dissociative during a traumatic event, certain information about that traumatic event will not be associated with other information about the event as would normally occur. If dissociation becomes a part of a person's personality structure, it might also interfere with retrieval. Dissociation has been mentioned by clinicians as a "special memory mechanism," and specifically as a response to the trauma of child sexual abuse that could create holes in memory for the traumatic experience. However, results of the Goodman et al. research indicated overall that lost memory or failing to report the abuse was not as common (i.e., 15%) as that indicated in Williams' study (i.e., 38%).

Nevertheless, if one believes that memory for childhood trauma can be lost from consciousness, there is still the question of whether such memories can be recovered back into awareness. Therefore, in the Goodman et al. study, individuals who disclosed the target child sexual abuse case were asked if there was ever a time during which they had forgotten the abusive incidents

(Ghetti et al., 2006). Williams (1995) had asked a similar question in her study. Clearly, the findings are important in relation to the "repressed/ recovered memory" controversy. Ghetti et al.'s results were quite comparable to those of Williams. In their study, 14% reported periods of having forgotten the abuse; Williams reported that about 10% of her sample had done so. However, it was unclear how the respondents interpreted the question about forgetting. For instance, did they think the interviewer was just trying to ask if there had ever been a time when they were not thinking about the abuse, even though they could have easily retrieved the memory, if only they had tried? Fortunately, Ghetti et al. posed a second question: During the time when you had no memory for the child sexual abuse, if someone had directly asked you about it, would you have remembered it? To this question, virtually everyone said "yes." Thus most of the individuals who were candidates for repressed and then recovered memory indicated that the lost memory really had not been lost at all, at least not in the Freudian sense of a repressed and, therefore, consciously inaccessible memory. Instead, it appeared that the respondents did not interpret the initial question as implying total amnesia for the child sexual abuse.

In the same study by Goodman and her colleagues, the accuracy of the victims' long-term memories of the child sexual abuse was examined (Alexander et al., 2005). Although it had been 12 to 21 years since the abuse had occurred, on average the victims' memories were fairly accurate (e.g., 72% correct, with 14% commission errors and another 14% omission errors). Moreover, the more traumatic the child sexual abuse was, the better was the victims' memory. For instance, child sexual abuse victims who said that this abuse was the worst thing that had ever happened to them, or who had more PTSD symptoms, had particularly accurate memories. Why? Possibly the more traumatized individuals had developed "fear networks" (e.g., Foa & Kozak, 1991; Foa & Rothbaum, 1998) that maintained accurate memory for the abuse. These fear networks arguably reflect the workings of normal and special memory mechanisms. They are normal in the sense of being semantic/ episodic memory stores. But they are also special in the sense that they reflect the effects of psychopathology and traumatization.

Post-event elaboration or avoidant coping strategies that children and adults often use after traumatic experiences may also substantially affect the memory representations of those events, as well as the individuals' psychological adjustment. Post-event elaboration may happen through conversations between children and their parents (e.g., Stallard, Velleman, Langsford, & Baldwin, 2001), or by children's own rumination about the experience (e.g., Ehlers et al., 2003). In fact, constructing and repeating a verbal account of the experienced traumatic event has been successfully used in therapy with PTSD patients (see Foa & Meadows, 1997), to overcome an over-focus on trauma-related information (e.g., Mattia, Heimberg, & Hope, 1993; McNally, Riemann, & Kim, 1990), and to reduce disorganized thoughts and improve individuals' psychological functioning (e.g., Alvarez-Conrad, Zoellner, &

Foa, 2001; Foa, Molnar, & Cashman, 1995; van Minnen, Wessel, Dijkstra, & Roelofs, 2002).

In contrast, avoidant coping strategies lead children to try to evade thoughts, conversations, or reminders about the traumatic experiences (e.g., Aaron, Zaglul, & Emery, 1999; Briere & Conte, 1993; Pynoos & Nader, 1990; Stallard et al., 2001; see also Koutstaal & Schacter, 1997, for a review). Other factors, however, may also facilitate this type of avoidance, such as parents' attempts to minimize their own or their children's distress (e.g., Claflin & Barbarin, 1991; Kazak et al., 1997), children's attempts to maintain secrecy, or children's feelings about the event and its disclosure (e.g., Fivush, 2004; Fivush, Pipe, Murachver, & Reese, 1997; Lawson & Chaffin, 1992; Smith, Letourneau, Saunders, Kilpatrick, Resnick, & Best, 2000). Post-event avoidance processes may prevent the creation of a complete, detailed, and verbally accessible account of the traumatic experience, as well as prevent the integration of these memories with the individual's other autobiographical memories (e.g., Brewin et al., 1996; Ehlers & Clark, 2000). This fragmentation in memory representations is believed to make the individual more vulnerable to develop PTSD, and is also associated with impairments in psychological functioning (Foa et al., 1995; van Minnen et al., 2002).

Now that neuroscientists can, in effect, look inside the brain to see its structure and function, through magnetic resonance imaging (MRI) and functional magnetic resonance imaging (fMRI), scientists have examined the possible effects of traumatization on the brain. Adults who have PTSD secondary to child sexual abuse have smaller hippocampal volumes (e.g., Bremner & Narayan, 1998) than do adults without PTSD, perhaps as a result of dysregulation of their hypothalamic pituitary axis (HPA), which can produce a flood of cortisol. Cortisol is known to cause hippocampal cell death (Sapolsky, 1996), and the hippocampus is crucial for consolidation of explicit (consciously accessible) memories. Although such findings could underlie lost memory of trauma, the results across studies are not entirely consistent. Moreover, in developmental studies of children who had suffered abuse, reduced hippocampal volumes were not detected (e.g., De Bellis, 2001).

Finally, several experimental paradigms where participants try to forget or suppress memories of previously encountered information (i.e., *retrieval-induced forgetting*; *directed forgetting*; *memory suppression*; see Anderson, 2005, for a review) have been used to examine the effects of avoidance of information processing for emotional and neutral information in adults (e.g., DePrince & Freyd, 2001, 2004; Depue, Banich, & Curran, 2006; McNally, Clancy, & Schacter, 2001; McNally et al., 1998; Moulds & Bryant, 2002). For example, using a directed-forgetting task where participants were asked to forget several words but also to remember several other words, DePrince and Freyd (2001, 2004) found that under divided-attention demands (i.e., to attend simultaneously to more than one source of information), people who scored high in dissociation recalled fewer trauma-related and more neutral to-be-remembered words than those who scored low in dissociation (but see

McNally et al., 2001; McNally et al., 1998; Wessel & Merckelbach, 2006). Also, Depue et al.'s (2006) study has recently shown that suppression of emotional information through executive control was more effective than suppression of non-emotional information (but see Hertel & Gerstle, 2003). However, results from these experimental paradigms using emotional and neutral stimuli are mixed, and there are few developmental studies that have examined these forms of avoidant processing.

In sum, debates about the effects of trauma on memory have waged for years, but without sufficient empirical evidence to constrain theory and speculation. To date, there is some empirical support to suggest that trauma victims who develop PTSD may encode, retain, and retrieve trauma-related information somewhat differently from those who do not. However, there is little scientific evidence indicating that the basic memory processes of traumatized individuals are different from those of non-traumatized individuals (e.g., Eisen et al., 2007; Howe et al., 2006). Although normal memory mechanisms can explain much of the memory and forgetting results obtained with adults who were sexually abused as children, some of whom were traumatized to the point of having PTSD symptoms even many years later, a few "special memory mechanisms" (e.g., dissociative processes) might also be involved. Even these "special memory mechanisms" may have normal memory mechanisms at their base, such as activation of semantic networks (albeit ones that revolve around fear) and avoidance of trauma memories.

FALSE MEMORIES, MISINFORMATION EFFECTS, AND EMOTIONAL EVENTS

A growing body of research shows that emotion does not necessarily protect against memory distortion, and that false information may be incorporated into children's and adults' memory accounts for emotional events. For example, in certain circumstances, children and adults can be led to report entirely fictitious events that never actually occurred (e.g., Loftus & Pickrell, 1995; Pezdek, Finger, & Hodge, 1997; Pezdek & Hodge, 1999; see also Bottoms, Shaver, & Goodman, 1996, for a description of questionable evidence of alleged satanic and ritualistic child sexual abuse). Such "implanted memories," as well as other memory errors, may depend in part on the salience and plausibility of the events suggested (Ghetti & Alexander, 2004; Mazzoni, Loftus, & Kirsch, 2001; Pezdek et al., 1997). Pezdek and Hodge (1999) found that a plausible false event such having been lost in a shopping mall was more likely to be falsely acknowledged by both children and adults as a real memory than was an implausible episode about receiving a rectal enema (see also Pezdek et al., 1997). Also, it seems easier to obtain memory malleability effects about a plausible change in an action that did occur than to suggest an entirely new action that did not occur (Gobbo, 2000; Pezdek & Roe, 1997). However, research has also shown developmental differences in

218 Paz-Alonso et al.

the ability to use memorability-based strategies to resist false information (e.g., in trying to remember if one received an enema in childhood, the memorability-based strategy would lead one to think "If that had happened, I would remember it"). Compared to younger children (5- to 7-year-olds), older children and adults appear to be able to use such "metacognitive" strategies to reject false information based on an event's salience and plausibility (see Ghetti & Alexander, 2004; Pezdek & Hodge, 1999).

Additionally, an event's emotional valence may also affect children's acceptance of false information. Ceci, Loftus, Leichtman, and Bruck (1994), for example, observed that children's false assent rates were higher for positive (e.g., birthday party) and neutral events (e.g., going to school with a blue sweater) than for negative ones (e.g., the death of a pet). In a recent developmental study (Paz-Alonso & Goodman, 2008), children's memory, suggestibility, and compliance (i.e., tendency to agree) about central versus peripheral false information were investigated, as a function of an event's emotional valence (negative vs. positive). Children watched either a negative or positive version of a film, and then half of the children were given misinformation about the film before their memory was tested. When their memory was tested, additional misinformation was intermittently provided in specific misleading questions (e.g., "Did the boy get the ball out of the girl's hand?", when in fact, the boy played with the ball himself). Results showed that, compared to older children (i.e., 10- to 12-year-olds), 8- to 9-year-olds were more suggestible in terms of misinformation effects and complied more with false information embedded in the specific misleading questions. Moreover, children who did not receive misinformation (i.e., control group) were more correct responding to central versus peripheral misinformation questions. Control participants who watched the negative event were less compliant with false information than those who watched the positive event. These effects, however, did not emerge for the misinformation group, suggesting that the expected memory advantages for emotional events regarding information centrality and event valence may be substantially reduced by the influence of misinformation.

CONTRIBUTIONS OF COGNITIVE AND INDIVIDUAL DIFFERENCE FACTORS TO CHILDREN'S MEMORY FOR EMOTIONAL STIMULI, STRESSFUL EVENTS, AND TRAUMATIC EXPERIENCES

As previously indicated, memory for highly emotional experiences may be *relatively* stable over time (see Ackil et al., 2003), but still dynamic and subject to forgetting, interference, and distortion (e.g., Courage & Howe, 2004; Howe et al., 1994; Loftus, 2003, 2005; van Giezen et al., 2005). Moreover, cognitive and individual difference factors influence memory for emotional events. Next, we review how age, delay, distinctiveness, personal relevance, personal participation, and parenting variables, including attachment, may affect children's recollection of emotional, stressful, and traumatic experiences.

Age

Age is a crucial variable in predicting accurate memory of emotional stimuli and past experiences (for reviews, see Baker-Ward, Gordon, & Ornstein, 2001; Cordón et al., 2004; Peterson, 2002). Clear developmental trends have emerged, suggesting that compared to older children (i.e., school-aged), younger children (i.e., preschoolers) tend to provide less detailed, complete, and consistent reports of emotional (Gobbo, Mega, & Pipe, 2002; Goodman & Reed, 1986; Pillemer, Picariello, & Pruett, 1994; Rudy & Goodman, 1991) and stressful events (Ghetti, Goodman, Eisen, Qin, & Davis, 2002; Leippe, Manion, & Romanczyk, 1991; Merritt et al., 1994), as is true for non-emotional events as well (e.g., Fivush, 1998; Goodman & Reed, 1986).

Further, young children are particularly susceptible to suggestion, are more likely to make errors on specific and misleading questions, and are more prone to forgetting over time than are older children (e.g., Eisen, Qin, Goodman, & Davis, 2002; see Bruck & Ceci, 1999; Gordon et al., 2001; Sjöberg & Lindholm, 2005, for reviews). Ornstein and colleagues (Ornstein, Baker-Ward, Gordon, Pelphrey, Tyler, & Gramzow, 2006), for example, found age differences between 4- to 7-year-olds' memory for a physical examination over a 6-month interval. Specifically, older children as compared with younger children recalled more overall information and reported more details when questioned. Similar developmental patterns have been found in studies assessing children's memory for medical procedures up to a 3- to 12-week delay and even longer (Baker-Ward et al., 1993; Goodman et al., 1994; Ornstein et al., 1997; Quas et al., 1999; Salmon & Pipe, 1997). However, although marked age differences typically appear, even very young children (e.g., 2- and 3-year-olds) are capable of providing fairly rich memory accounts of stressful events under certain conditions (Howe, 1997; Peterson & Whalen, 2001).

Age differences in memory performance may reflect developmental changes in cognitive functioning, such as improvements in processing speed and language acquisition, the formation of and increased ability to effectively use complex mental strategies, and the accumulation of prior event knowledge (Imhoff & Baker-Ward, 1999; Ornstein et al., 1997). Children, for example, who have pre-event knowledge may recall more information and have increased resistance to suggestion than those who do not (Elischberger, 2005; Goodman et al., 1997; Salmon, McGuigan, & Pereira, 2006; Sutherland, Pipe, Schick, Murray, & Gobbo, 2003); however, having a strong knowledge base may also have negative effects under certain conditions. For example, a child who has come to expect particular characteristics of an event may use selective attention during the experience and thus reduce the chance for proper encoding (Ornstein et al., 1997).

Delay

It is also important to note that, even within an age group, there can be dramatic individual differences. Some 3-year-olds are remarkably verbal and resistant to misinformation; some adults make memory errors. Understanding such individual differences is an important challenge within memory development research. The literature regarding children's accuracy for emotional stimuli following extended delays (e.g., 1 to 12 years) is mixed. On the one hand, children may experience significant memory decay after long delays (e.g., Goodman et al., 2002). On the other hand, those experiences associated with more emotional intensity and salience tend to be less likely forgotten (see Cordón et al., 2004, for a review) and can be relatively well-retained even after extended periods of time (Alexander et al., 2005; Peterson, 1999; Peterson & Whalen, 2001; see also Brainerd & Poole, 1997, for a fuzzy-trace account regarding the long-term persistence of true and false memories). Children may forget aspects of distant memories, but the proportion of information remembered can be remarkably accurate and detailed even years after the event's occurrence (e.g., Hudson & Fivush, 1991; Van Abbema & Bauer, 2005). Moreover, there is even evidence to suggest that memory reports of stressful events may actually increase in detail over long delays (Fivush et al., 2004). Further research utilizing longitudinal designs is needed to assess possible differential effects between age at occurrence versus age at retrieval. Such research would help to disentangle developmental changes in the ability to store as opposed to retrieve emotional childhood memories, and help to identify potential memory decay and distortion over time (e.g., Peterson & Parsons, 2005; see also Van Abbema & Bauer, 2005, for suggestions for future research).

Distinctiveness and personal relevance

The distinctiveness and personal relevance of an event may be important—and often intertwined—predictors of children's ability to consistently and accurately report recollections concerning a past experience. Distinctiveness is characterized by personal salience or a violation of one's expectations, and is unique relative to one's other experiences and knowledge (e.g., Howe, 1997, 2000). Distinctiveness may also help people discriminate between highly similar memory traces, as well as help reduce interference from other information in memory (e.g., Ghetti, Qin, & Goodman, 2002; Howe, 2006). Children may find these "unusual" characteristics of an event to be emotionally arousing, or attention grabbing. Both non-traumatic and highly emotional events can be distinctive; however, traumatic events are often relatively unique and personally salient, and perhaps therefore are recalled with greater vividness over short and long retention intervals than less emotional experiences (Ackil et al., 2003; Berliner, Hyman, Thomas, & Fitzgerald, 2003; Cordón et al., 2004).

Evaluating events as personally significant and distinctive may lead to superior encoding and rehearsal of the events' central details (see Westmacott & Moscovitch, 2003). However, superior memory for distinctive events can still occur even without conscious recollection (Geraci & Rajaram, 2004). Moreover, evaluation of event or stimulus characteristics as distinctive can change with an individual's increasing age and vary over time (e.g., Howe, Courage, Vernescu, & Hunt, 2000). For example, an event that may be unique for a child (e.g., going to a movie) may not be special as an adult (but see Howe, 2006). This change in distinctiveness may also occur for traumatic events as well. Maltreated children may no longer view abusive events as distinctive after repeated exposure.

Personal participation

Moreover, children's personal involvement in an experience may affect memory accuracy. Individuals who directly experience an event provide more accurate memory accounts than those who merely watch the event's occurrence (e.g., Roebers, Gelhaar, & Schneider, 2004; Rudy & Goodman, 1991; Thierry & Spence, 2004; van Giezen et al., 2005). Shrimpton and colleagues (1998) evaluated 4- to 12-years-olds' memories of a medical procedure involving venipuncture that was either observed or directly experienced by the participants after a short (i.e., 2–7 days) or a long (i.e., 6–8 weeks) delay. Children who directly experienced the event, compared to those who did not, were more likely to provide accurate information during free recall and less likely to provide incorrect responses to misleading questions (see also Gobbo et al., 2002; Lindberg, Jones, Collard, & Thomas, 2001). In cases of severe trauma, however, children who observe a highly stressful or traumatic event (e.g., sexual, physical, or emotional abuse of a family member) may encode and retain memories similar to those who directly experience it (see Howe, 1997, for a review).

Parenting variables

Parenting variables such as parent–child interaction, parenting styles, and parental responsiveness have been shown to play a critical role in children's memories for emotional and stressful experiences. Parent–child interactions provide an opportunity for rehearsal and reactivation of event details that may help maintain and strengthen memory traces (e.g., Howe, Courage, & Bryant-Brown, 1993), thus reducing the effects of decay, while enhancing long-term retention. However, when parents avoid discussion of emotional events, this may contribute to forgetting or memory error (e.g., Goodman et al., 1994). Next we review research relevant to parental variables as they may affect children's memory for emotional events.

Parent–child interaction may influence how children communicate and rehearse emotional events with others. For example, parents who highly elaborate in conversation may do so as a means to bond with their children (Fivush & Vasudeva, 2002) by asking them to expand on questions and by offering numerous event details and information during discussion. In contrast, parents who employ low elaboration tend to use conversation as a method to examine memory accuracy by asking few, specific questions that are often repeated (Reese, Haden, & Fivush, 1993; Wareham & Salmon, 2006). Parents who tend to talk more about past emotional events are likely to have children who provide more information when recounting their memories than are parents who are less communicative (e.g., Burch, Austin, & Bauer, 2004; see also McGuigan & Salmon, 2004). Furthermore, caregivers with an elaborative interaction style tend to have more secure attachment relationships with their children than those classified as low on elaboration (Fivush & Reese, 2002). To recollect the experiences of their past, children must be willing and able to express their thoughts. Evaluating parents' readiness to discuss stressful experiences with their offspring may help shed light on children's willingness to communicate with other people within and outside their family about their emotions and emotional experiences (Alexander, Quas, & Goodman, 2002).

Parenting styles play a role in children's memory accuracy for stressful and highly emotional events. Styles associated with openness to and respect for others' ideas and future directions may be related to children's enhanced ability to provide accurate accounts of an emotional event after a delay (e.g., Burgwyn-Bailes et al., 2001), whereas authoritarian parenting focused on traditional values (i.e., obedience to and respect of authority figures) may enhance young children's suggestibility to misleading information (e.g., Clarke-Stewart, Malloy, & Allhusen, 2004; see also Bruck & Melnyk, 2004). Thus, rehearsal of event details may be more likely to occur within a parent–child relationship that is characterized by willingness to discuss emotions openly. Future research is needed to determine the relation between parenting style and children's memory for emotional experiences.

Another key factor influencing rehearsal of emotional stimuli is *parental responsiveness*. For example, children who received maternal support after disclosure of child sexual abuse provided more accurate reports of their maltreatment experiences years after the abuse reportedly ended, compared to those who do not (e.g., Alexander et al., 2005). Moreover, children whose mothers provided physical comfort (e.g., hugs) after a stressful experience and who discussed the event with them provided more accurate details and fewer omission errors than those whose mothers did not (e.g., Goodman et al., 1994).

Attachment

Attachment theory, which concerns parent–child interactions, may provide a useful framework to examine children's reactions to and memory for emotional, stressful, and traumatic events (e.g., Goodman & Quas, 1997;

Goodman et al., 1997; Quas, Qin, Schaaf, & Goodman, 1997). This theory was originally developed to describe parent–child interactions (Ainsworth, Blehar, Waters, & Wall, 1978; Bowlby, 1969, 1973), but more recently it has been extended to describe adult interpersonal relationships as well (e.g., Fraley & Shaver, 2000; Hazan & Shaver, 1987). According to this theoretical account, infants form internal working models (IWM) based partially on their perceptions of their caregivers' ability and willingness to satisfy their basic needs, protect them from harm, and provide them with emotional and physical support. Children use these IWM representations to interpret and predict future behaviors, responses, and outcomes for themselves and others (Bowlby, 1969). IWMs are activated particularly in times of distress during which a child may feel threatened and need protection (Bowlby, 1958). Over time, individuals develop attachment styles (i.e., secure, insecure–avoidant, insecure–anxious/ambivalent, or disorganized) consistent with, and representative of, their IWMs (Ainsworth et al., 1978).

The *Strange Situation*, an experimental procedure in which children are briefly separated from and reunited with their caregivers, may provide a method to observe how IWMs influence behavior and social interactions during stressful experiences (Ainsworth et al., 1978; see Alexander et al., 2002, for a review). Children with secure attachment styles (i.e., Type B) tend to play independently in the presence of a caregiver (because the caregiver provides a "secure base" for playful exploration) and may experience a reasonable amount of distress when the parent is not nearby. However, these children tend to be easily comforted by their caregivers on return and are able to restore their independent play by quickly reengaging in their previous activities. Through repeated exposure and past experience, these children may have developed secure IWMs and come to anticipate that their caregiver will be a source of comfort and support, thus enabling them to manage their emotions effectively during a stressful situation.

In contrast, children with an insecure–avoidant attachment style (i.e., Type A) may not show any external reaction when separated from their parent and may appear distracted on their caregiver's return. These children may have learned over time that their caregiver is not supportive during stress situations and, thus, the children do not seek their comfort. These children may, therefore, experience a greater amount of distress than children with secure attachments, as the former will not expect to be comforted by others. Children with insecure–anxious/ambivalent attachment styles (i.e., Type C) appear unusually distressed when their caregiver is absent and are preoccupied with their return. These children may seek comfort from their caregiver, but may not anticipate support because of IWMs that were developed through past discrepancies in their caregiver's responsiveness (e.g., caregiver alternates between providing support versus withdrawing from their child during times of stress). Thus, although children with insecure–anxious/ambivalent attachment styles may hope to be comforted by others, their caregivers' responsiveness will vary and cannot be relied on (Ainsworth et al.,

1978). Finally, children with disorganized attachment styles (i.e., Type D) exhibit disoriented or strange behaviors on return of their parent (e.g., Main & Hesse, 1990; Main & Solomon, 1990). A high percentage of children who have suffered maltreatment have disorganized attachment styles. Moreover, these children tend to have parents with unresolved grief or trauma histories.

Recent research on adult (as opposed to parent–child) attachment suggests that IWMs may affect social interaction patterns and behaviors across the lifespan (Hazan & Shaver, 1987; see Alexander et al., 2002, for a review). Adult attachment styles may influence, for example, caregivers' relationships with their children in terms of parental responsiveness (e.g., Edelstein et al., 2004) and use of effective communication during discussion of emotional or stressful experiences (Goodman et al., 1997). More specifically, adults with secure attachments tend to exhibit more parental responsiveness and tend to discuss stressful events more than those with insecure attachments.

Children who form avoidant attachment styles may use strategies that interfere with encoding of distressing information so as not to have their attachment system activated (Alexander et al., 2002). Bowlby (1980, 1987) termed this "defensive exclusion." For example, children with an insecure–avoidant attachment style are likely to use distraction in an attempt to escape from emotionally distressing situations (e.g., ones that activate the attachment system), thus reducing the likelihood that they will encode specific target event information (Kirsh & Cassidy, 1997). Further, survivors of child sexual abuse who are classified as having an avoidant attachment style, and who do not receive maternal support following disclosure, may be less likely to discuss their trauma with others (e.g., Edelstein et al., 2005). This has potential personal and forensic implications as there may be a reduced willingness to rehearse the details of the event, thereby limiting the opportunity to strengthen the memory traces, to report the alleged crime, and to openly talk about their trauma in the presence of others.

Parents' attachment style and responsiveness may also affect children's memory for emotional experiences. Using a self-report measure of adult attachment, Edelstein and colleagues (2004) found that parents scoring high on avoidance were less responsive when their children exhibited high levels of distress during an inoculation than parents scoring low on avoidance. Parents scoring high on avoidance measures also became less responsive as their child's level of stress increased, whereas caregivers scoring low on avoidance became more responsive. Children of parents with avoidant attachment styles tend to be more distressed during emotional events, as well as more suggestible and less accurate in their memory reports, than children of parents with secure attachment styles (e.g., Goodman et al., 1997; Quas et al., 1999). Overall, attachment theory may provide memory development researchers with important insights into parental influences on children's memory for emotional, stressful, and traumatic events.

Summary

Children's memory for emotional stimuli may be influenced by a variety of cognitive and individual factors. Developmental differences are typically evident such that, compared to younger children, older children tend to be more accurate and complete in their memory reports for non-stressful and stressful events. Memory distortion and decay tend to occur over time; however, distinctiveness, personal relevance, and personal participation may maintain and enhance memory strength over extended time delays. Parent–child interactions (e.g., elaborative communication by parents, parental responsiveness) may lead to rehearsal of event details that supports accurate memory. Children's and parents' attachment styles may affect the children's coping with and thus their memory for stressful experiences.

CONCLUSIONS

Researchers of emotion, stress, trauma, and memory development have studied a variety of events and capitalized on numerous methodological procedures to examine children's memory. Despite these variations, all of the approaches have been useful for addressing a complex area of study. However, further laboratory-based and naturalistic studies in this scientific arena are needed. For example, developmental studies examining the role of executive control in forgetting and/or suppressing of previously encountered emotional and non-emotional information are of importance to shed light on the possible developmental and cognitive memory processes that may operate in helping people to avoid unwanted memories. And, conducting ethical and externally valid studies that allow scientists to examine children's memory for events with high emotional intensity, and that have been experienced repeatedly, is still of special importance theoretically and forensically.

Future research may help elucidate the effects of stress and trauma on memory and its development and, more specifically, the nature and extent to which normal and special memory mechanisms may be involved in processing trauma-related information. Although a few "special memory mechanisms" (e.g., dissociative processes) might be involved in the memories of trauma survivors who developed PTSD, even such special memory mechanisms may have normal memory mechanisms at their base (i.e., activation of semantic networks, avoidance of trauma memories).

Children's coping strategies to deal with stressful or traumatic situations may often depend on caregivers' communication and parenting styles. The attachment styles of both parents and children may partly determine communication. Such communication may affect children's memory. Further research on topics like these will advance scientific understanding of children's memory of emotional, stressful, and traumatic events. Such research, it is hoped, will lead to theoretical and applied advances. These advances may help child victims cope with and overcome traumatic experiences like the one described at the beginning of this chapter that Sabine Dardenne endured when she was 12 years old, took her bike, and left for school.

ACKNOWLEDGMENTS

This chapter is based in part on work supported by the National Science Foundation under Grant No. 0004369 to Dr. Gail S. Goodman, and by a grant from the Program for Research Training (Department of Education, Universities, and Research) of the Basque Government to Dr. Pedro M. Paz-Alonso. Any opinions, findings, conclusions, or recommendations expressed in this article are those of the authors and do not necessarily reflect the views of the National Science Foundation. Address correspondence to: Dr. Gail S. Goodman or Dr. Pedro M. Paz-Alonso at the Department of Psychology, University of California, 1 Shields Avenue, Davis, CA 95616 (emails: ggoodman@ucdavis. edu; ppazalonso@ucdavis.edu).

REFERENCES

Aaron, J., Zaglul, H. F., & Emery, R. E. (1999). Posttraumatic stress in children following acute physical injury. *Journal of Pediatric Psychology*, *24*, 335–343.

Ackil, J. K., Van Abbema, D. L., & Bauer, P. J. (2003). After the storm: Enduring differences in mother–child recollections of traumatic and nontraumatic events. *Journal of Experimental Child Psychology*, *84*, 286–309.

Ainsworth, M. D. S., Blehar, M. C., Waters, E., & Wall, S. (1978). *Patterns of attachment: A psychology study of the strange situation*. Hillsdale, NJ: Lawrence Erlbaum Associates, Inc.

Alexander, K. W., Quas, J. A., Ghetti, S., Goodman, G. S., Edelstein, R. S., Redlich, A. D., et al. (2005). Traumatic impact predicts long-term memory for documented child sexual abuse. *Psychological Science*, *16*, 33–40.

Alexander, K. W., Quas, J. A., & Goodman, G. S. (2002). Theoretical advances in understanding children's memory for distressing events: The role of attachment. *Developmental Review*, *22*, 490–519.

Alvarez-Conrad, J. A., Zoellner, L. A., & Foa, E. B. (2001). Linguistic predictors of trauma pathology and perceived health status. *Applied Cognitive Psychology*, *15*, S159–S170.

American Psychiatric Association (1994). *Diagnostic and statistical manual of mental disorders (4th ed.; DSM-IV)*. Washington, DC: American Psychiatric Association.

Anderson, M. C. (2005). The role of inhibitory control in forgetting unwanted memories: A consideration of three methods. In C. MacLeod & B. Uttl (Eds.), *Dynamic cognitive processes* (pp. 159–190). Tokyo: Springer-Verlag.

Bahrick, L. E., Parker, J. F., Fivush, R., & Levitt, M. (1998). The effects of stress on young children's memory for a natural disaster. *Journal of Experimental Psychology: Applied*, *4*, 308–331.

Baker-Ward, L. E., Eaton, K. L., & Banks, J. B. (2005). Young soccer players' reports of a tournament win or loss: Different emotions, different narratives. *Journal of Cognition and Development, 6*, 507–527.

Baker-Ward, L., Gordon, B. N., & Ornstein, P. A. (2001). Children's testimony: A review of research on memory for past experiences. *Clinical Child and Family Psychology, 4*, 157–181.

Baker-Ward, L., Gordon, B. N., Ornstein, P. A., Larus, D. M., & Clubb, P. A. (1993). Young children's long-term retention of a pediatric examination. *Child Development, 64*, 1519–1533.

Bartlett, J. C., Burleson, G., & Santrock, J. W. (1982). Emotional mood and memory in young children. *Journal of Experimental Child Psychology, 34*, 59–76.

Bauer, P. J., Stark, E. N., Lukowski, A. F., Rademacher, J., Van Abbema, D. L., & Ackil, J. K. (2005). Working together to make sense of the past: Mothers' and children's use of internal states language in conversations about traumatic and nontraumatic events. *Journal of Cognition and Development, 6*, 463–488.

Berliner, L., Hyman, I., Thomas, A., & Fitzgerald, M. (2003). Children's memory for traumatic and positive experiences. *Journal of Traumatic Stress, 16*, 229–236.

Berntsen, D. (2002). Tunnel memories for autobiographical events: Central details are remembered more frequently from shocking than from happy experiences. *Memory and Cognition, 30*, 1010–1020.

Berntsen, D., & Rubin, D. C. (2006). Flashbulb memories and posttraumatic stress reactions across the life span: Age-related effects of the German occupation of Denmark during World War II. *Psychology and Aging, 21*, 127–139.

Bidrose, S., & Goodman, G. S. (2000). Testimony and evidence: A scientific case study of memory for child sexual abuse. *Applied Cognitive Psychology, 14*(3), 197–213.

Bjork, R. A. (1988). Retrieval practice and the maintenance of knowledge. In M. M. Gruneberg, P. E. Morris, & R. N. Sykes (Eds.), *Practical aspects of memory: Current research and issues: Vol. 1. Memory in everyday life* (pp. 396–401). Oxford: Wiley.

Bless, H., Clore, G. L., Schwarz, N., & Golisano, V. (1996). Mood and the use of scripts: Does a happy mood really lead to mindlessness? *Journal of Personality and Social Psychology, 71*, 665–679.

Bluck, S., & Li, K. Z. H. (2001). Predicting memory completeness and accuracy: Emotion and exposure in repeated autobiographical recall. *Applied Cognitive Psychology, 15*, 145–158.

Bohanek, J. G., Fivush, R., & Walker, E. (2005). Memories of positive and negative emotional events. *Applied Cognitive Psychology, 19*, 51–66.

Bottoms, B. L., Shaver, P. R., & Goodman, G. S. (1996). An analysis of ritualistic and religion-related child abuse allegations. *Law and Human Behavior, 20*, 1–34.

Bowlby, J. (1958). The nature of the child's tie to his mother. *International Journal of Psychoanalysis, 39*, 350–373.

Bowlby, J. (1969). *Attachment and loss: Vol. 1. Attachment.* New York: Basic Books.

Bowlby, J. (1973). *Attachment and loss: Vol. 2. Separation.* New York: Basic Books.

Bowlby, J. (1980). *Attachment and loss: Vol. III. Loss, sadness and depression.* New York: Basic Books.

Bowlby, J. (1987). Defensive processes in the light of attachment theory. In J. L. Sacksteder, D. P. Schwartz, & Y. Akabane (Eds.), *Attachment and the therapeutic process: Essays in honor of Otto Allen Will, Jr.* (pp. 63–79). Madison, CT: International Universities Press.

Brainerd, C. J., & Poole, D. A. (1997). Long-term survival of children's false memories: A review. *Learning and Individual Differences, 9*, 125–151.

Bremner, J. D., & Narayan, M. (1998). The effects of stress on memory and the hippocampus throughout the life cycle: Implications for childhood development and aging. *Developmental Psychopathology, 10,* 871–886.

Brewin, C. R., Dalgleish, T., & Joseph, S. (1996). A dual representation theory of posttraumatic stress disorder. *Psychological Review, 103,* 670–686.

Briere, J. N., & Conte, J. (1993). Self-reported amnesia for abuse in adults molested as children. *Journal of Traumatic Stress, 6,* 21–31.

Brown, R., & Kulik, J. (1977). Flashbulb memories. *Cognition, 5,* 73–99.

Bruck, M., & Ceci, S. J. (1999). The suggestibility of children's memory. *Annual Review of Psychology, 50,* 419–439.

Bruck, M., Ceci, S. J., Francoeur, E., & Barr, R. (1995). "I hardly cried when I got my shot": Influencing children's reports about a visit to their pediatrician. *Child Development, 66,* 193–208.

Bruck, M., & Melnyk, L. (2004). Individual differences in children's suggestibility: A review and synthesis. *Applied Cognitive Psychology, 18,* 947–996.

Buchanan, T. W., & Lovallo, W. R. (2001). Enhanced memory for emotional material following stress-level cortisol treatment in humans. *Psychoneuroendocrinology, 26,* 307–317.

Bugental, D. B., Blue, J., Cortez, V., Fleck, K., & Rodriguez, A. (1992). Influences of witnessed affect on information processing in children. *Child Development, 63,* 774–786.

Burch, M. M., Austin, J., & Bauer, P. J. (2004). Understanding the emotional past: Relations between parent and child contributions in emotionally negative and non-negative events. *Journal of Experimental Child Psychology, 89,* 276–297.

Burgwyn-Bailes, E., Baker-Ward, L., Gordon, B. N., & Ornstein, P. A. (2001). Children's memory for emergency medical treatment after one year: The impact of individual difference variables on recall and suggestibility. *Applied Cognitive Psychology, 15,* S25–S48.

Cassel, W. S., Roebers, C. M., & Bjorklund, D. F. (1996). Developmental patterns of eyewitness responses to repeated and increasingly suggestive questions. *Journal of Experimental Child Psychology, 61,* 116–133.

Ceci, S. J., Loftus, E. F., Leichtman, M. D., & Bruck, M. (1994). The possible role of source misattributions in the creation of false beliefs among preschoolers. *International Journal of Clinical and Experimental Hypnosis, 42,* 304–320.

Chen, E., Zeltzer, L. K., Craske, M. G., & Katz, E. R. (2000). Children's memories for painful cancer treatment procedures: Implications for distress. *Child Development, 71,* 933–947.

Christianson, S. Å. (1989). Flashbulb memories: Special, but not so special. *Memory and Cognition, 17,* 435–443.

Christianson, S. Å. (1992). Emotional stress and eyewitness memory: A critical review. *Psychological Bulletin, 112,* 284–309.

Christianson, S. Å., & Fällman, L. (1990). The role of age on reactivity and memory for emotional pictures. *Scandinavian Journal of Psychology, 31,* 291–301.

Christianson, S. Å., & Lindholm, T. (1998). The fate of traumatic memories in childhood and adulthood. *Development and Psychopathology, 10,* 761–780.

Christianson, S. Å., & Loftus, E. F. (1987). Memory for traumatic events. *Applied Cognitive Psychology, 1,* 225–239.

Christianson, S. Å., & Loftus, E. F. (1991). Remembering emotional events: The fate of detailed information. *Cognition and Emotion, 5,* 81–108.

Claflin, C. J., & Barbarin, O. A. (1991). Does "telling" less protect more? Relationships among age, information disclosure, and what children with cancer see and feel. *Journal of Pediatric Psychology, 16,* 169–191.

Clarke-Stewart, K. A., Malloy, L. C., & Allhusen, V. D. (2004). Verbal ability, self-control, and close relationships with parents protect children against misleading suggestions. *Applied Cognitive Psychology, 18,* 1037–1058.

Conway, M. A. (1995). *Flashbulb memories.* Hove, UK: Lawrence Erlbaum Associates Ltd.

Conway, M. A., Anderson, S. J., Larsen, S. F., & Donnelly, C. M. (1994). The formation of flashbulb memories. *Memory and Cognition, 22,* 326–343.

Cordón, I. M., Pipe, M.-E., Sayfan, L., Melinder, A., & Goodman, G. S. (2004). Memory for traumatic experiences in early childhood. *Developmental Review, 24,* 101–132.

Courage, M. L., & Howe, M. L. (2004). Advances in early memory development research: Insights about the dark side of the moon. *Developmental Review, 24,* 6–32.

Dardenne, S., & Cuny, M.-T. (2004). *J'avais douze ans, j'aipris mon vélo et je suis partie à l'école* [I was 12 years old, I took my bike and I left for school]. Paris, France: OH! Editions.

Davidson, D., & Jergovic, D. (1996). Children's memory for atypical actions in script-based stories: An examination of the disruption effect. *Journal of Experimental Child Psychology, 61,* 134–152.

Davidson, D., Luo, Z., & Burden, M. J. (2001). Children's recall of emotional behaviours, emotional labels, and nonemotional behaviours: Does emotion enhance memory? *Cognition and Emotion, 15,* 1–26.

De Bellis, M. D. (2001). Developmental traumatology: The psychobiological development of maltreated children and its implications for research, treatment, and policy. *Development and Psychopathology, 13,* 537–561.

Deffenbacher, K. A., Bornstein, B. H., Penrod, S. D., & McGorty, E. K. (2004). A meta-analytic review of the effects of high stress on eyewitness memory. *Law and Human Behavior, 28,* 687–706.

DePrince, A. P., & Freyd, J. J. (2001). Memory and dissociative tendencies: The roles of attentional context and word meaning in a directed forgetting task. *Journal of Trauma and Dissociation, 2,* 67–82.

DePrince, A. P., & Freyd, J. J. (2004). Forgetting trauma stimuli. *Psychological Science, 15,* 488–492.

Depue, B. E., Banich, M. T., & Curran, T. (2006). Suppression of emotional and nonemotional content in memory. *Psychological Science, 17,* 441–447.

Dunning, D., & Stern, L. B. (1992). Examining the generality of eyewitness hypermnesia: A close look at time delay and question type. *Applied Cognitive Psychology, 6,* 643–657.

Easterbrook, J. A. (1959). The effect of emotion on cue utilization and the organization of behavior. *Psychological Review, 66,* 183–201.

Edelstein, R. S., Alexander, K. W., Shaver, P. R., Schaaf, J. M., Quas, J. A., Lovas, G. S., et al. (2004). Adult attachment style and parental responsiveness during a stressful event. *Attachment and Human Development, 6*(1), 31–52.

Edelstein, R. S., Ghetti, S., Quas, J. A., Goodman, G. S., Alexander, K. W., Redlich, A. D., et al. (2005). Individual differences in emotional memory: Adult attachment and long-term memory for child sexual abuse. *Personality and Social Psychology Bulletin, 31*(11), 1537–1548.

230   *Paz-Alonso et al.*

Ehlers, A., & Clark, D. M. (2000). A cognitive model of posttraumatic stress disorder. *Behaviour Research and Therapy, 38*, 319–345.

Ehlers, A., Clark, D. M., Hackmann, A., McManus, F., Fennell, M., Herbet, C., et al. (2003). A randomized controlled trial of cognitive therapy, a self-help booklet, and repeated assessments as early interventions for posttraumatic stress disorder. *Archives of General Psychiatry, 60*, 1024–1032.

Ehlers, A., Michael, T., Chen, Y. P., Payne, E., & Shan, S. (2006). Enhanced perceptual priming for neutral stimuli in traumatic context: A pathway to intrusive memories? *Memory, 143*, 316–328.

Eisen, M. L., & Goodman, G. S. (1998). Trauma, memory and suggestibility in children. *Development and Psychopathology, 10*, 717–738.

Eisen, M. L., Goodman, G. S., Qin, J., & Davis, S. L. (2007). Maltreated children's memory: Accuracy, suggestibility, and psychopathology. *Developmental Psychology, 43*, 1275–1294.

Eisen, M. L., Qin, J., Goodman, G. S., & Davis, S. L. (2002). Memory and suggestibility in maltreated children: Age, stress arousal, dissociation, and psychopathology. *Journal of Experimental Child Psychology, 83*, 167–212.

Elischberger, H. B. (2005). The effects of prior knowledge on children's memory and suggestibility. *Journal of Experimental Child Psychology, 92*, 247–275.

Er, N. (2003). A new flashbulb memory model applied to the Marmara earthquake. *Applied Cognitive Psychology, 17*, 503–517.

Farrar, M. J., & Goodman, G. S. (1992). Developmental changes in event memory. *Child Development, 63*, 173–187.

Fivush, R. (1997). Event memory in early childhood. In N. Cowan (Ed.), *The development of memory in childhood* (pp. 139–161). Hove, UK: Psychology Press.

Fivush, R. (1998). Children's recollections of traumatic and nontraumatic events. *Development and Psychopathology, 10*, 699–716.

Fivush, R. (2002). Scripts, schemas, and memory of trauma. In N. L. Stein, P. J. Bauer, & M. Rabinowitz (Eds.), *Representation, memory, and development: Essays in honor of Jean Mandler* (pp. 53–74). Mahwah, NJ: Lawrence Erlbaum Associates, Inc.

Fivush, R. (2004). The silenced self: Constructing self from memories spoken and unspoken. In D. Beike, J. Lampien, & D. Behrand (Eds.), *The self and memory* (pp. 75–93). New York: Psychology Press.

Fivush, R., Hazzard, A., Sales, J. M., Sarfati, D., & Brown, T. (2003). Creating coherence out of chaos? Children's narratives of emotionally positive and negative events. *Applied Cognitive Psychology, 17*, 1–19.

Fivush, R., Pipe, M.-E., Murachver, T., & Reese, E. (1997). Events spoken and unspoken: Implications of language and memory development for the recovered memory. In M. Conway (Ed.), *Recovered memories and false memories: Debates in psychology* (pp. 34–62). New York: Oxford University Press.

Fivush, R., & Reese, E. (2002). Reminiscing and relating: The development of parent–child talk about the past. In J. D. Webster & B. K. Haight (Eds.), *Critical advances in reminiscence work* (pp. 109–122). New York: Springer.

Fivush, R., Sales, J. M., Goldberg, A., Bahrick, L., & Parker, J. (2004). Weathering the storm: Children's long-term recall of Hurricane Andrew. *Memory, 12*(1), 104–118.

Fivush, R., & Vasudeva, A. (2002). Remembering to relate: Socioemotional correlates of mother–child reminiscing. *Journal of Cognition and Development, 3*, 73–90.

Fletcher, K. E. (1996). Childhood posttraumatic stress disorder. In E. J. Mash & R. A. Barkley (Eds.), *Child psychopathology* (pp. 242–276). New York: Guilford.

Foa, E. B., Feske, U., Murdock, T., Kozak, M. J., & McCarthy, P. R. (1991). Processing of threat-related information in rape victims. *Journal of Abnormal Psychology*, *100*, 156–162.

Foa, E. B., & Kozak, M. J. (1986). Emotional processing of fear: Exposure to corrective information. *Psychological Bulletin*, *99*, 20–35.

Foa, E. B., & Kozak, M. J. (1991). Emotional processing: Theory, research, and clinical implications for anxiety disorders. In J. D. Safran & L. S. Greenberg (Eds.), *Emotion, psychotherapy, and change* (pp. 21–49). New York: Guilford.

Foa, E. B., & Meadows, E. A. (1997). Psychosocial treatments for posttraumatic stress disorder: A critical review. *Annual Review of Psychology*, *48*, 449–480.

Foa, E. B., Molnar, C., & Cashman, L. (1995). Change in rape narratives during exposure therapy for posttraumatic stress disorder. *Journal of Traumatic Stress*, *8*, 675–690.

Foa, E. B., & Rothbaum, B. O. (1992). Post-traumatic stress disorder: Clinical features and treatment. In R. D. Peters & R. J. McMahon (Eds.), *Aggression and violence throughout the life span* (pp. 155–170). Thousand Oaks, CA: Sage.

Foa, E. B., & Rothbaum, B. O. (1998). *Treating the trauma of rape: Cognitive-behavioral therapy for PTSD*. New York: Guilford.

Forgas, J. P., Burnham, D. K., & Trimboli, C. (1988). Mood, memory, and social judgments in children. *Journal of Personality and Social Psychology*, *54*, 697–703.

Fraley, R. C., & Shaver, P. R. (2000). Adult romantic attachment: Theoretical developments, emerging controversies, and unanswered questions. *Review of General Psychology*, *4*, 132–154.

Freyd, J. (1996). *Betrayal trauma*. Cambridge, MA: Harvard University Press.

Freyd, J., DePrince, A. P., & Zubriggen, E. L. (2001). Self-reported memory for abuse depends upon victim–perpetrator relationship. *Journal of Trauma and Dissociation*, *2*, 5–16.

Geraci, L., & Rajaram, S. (2004). The distinctiveness effect in the absence of conscious recollection: Evidence from conceptual priming. *Journal of Memory and Language*, *51*, 217–230.

Ghetti, S., & Alexander, K. W. (2004). "If it happened, I would remember it": Strategic use of event memorability in the rejection of false autobiographical events. *Child Development*, *75*, 542–561.

Ghetti, S., Edelstein, R. S., Goodman, G. S., Cordon, I., Quas, J. A., Alexander, K. W., et al. (2006). What can subjective forgetting tell us about memory for childhood trauma? *Memory and Cognition*, *34*, 1011–1025.

Ghetti, S., Goodman, G. S., Eisen, M. L., Qin, J., & Davis, S. L. (2002). Consistency in reports of sexual and physical abuse. *Child Abuse and Neglect*, *26*, 977–995.

Ghetti, S., Qin, J., & Goodman, G. S. (2002). False memories in children and adults: Age, distinctiveness, and subjective experience. *Developmental Psychology*, *38*, 705–718.

Gobbo, C. (2000). Assessing the effects of misinformation on children's recall: How and when makes a difference. *Applied Cognitive Psychology*, *14*, 163–182.

Gobbo, C., Mega, C., & Pipe, M.-E. (2002). Does the nature of the experience influence suggestibility? A study of children's event memory. *Journal of Experimental Child Psychology*, *81*, 502–530.

Goodman, G. S., Batterman-Faunce, J. M., Schaaf, J. M., & Kenney, R. (2002). Nearly 4 years after an event: Children's eyewitness memory and adults' perception of children's accuracy. *Child Abuse and Neglect*, *26*, 849–884.

Goodman, G. S., Bottoms, B. L., Schwartz-Kenney, B. M., & Rudy, L. (1991). Children's testimony about a stressful event: Improving children's reports. *Journal of Narrative and Life History, 1*, 69–99.

Goodman, G. S., Ghetti, S., Quas, J. A., Edelstein, R. S., Alexander, K. W., Redlich, A. D., et al. (2003). A prospective study of memory for child sexual abuse: New findings relevant to the repressed-memory controversy. *Psychological Science, 14*, 113–118.

Goodman, G. S., Hirschman, J. E., Hepps, D., & Rudy, L. (1991). Children's memory for stressful events. *Merrill-Palmer Quarterly, 37*, 109–157.

Goodman, G. S., & Paz-Alonso, P. M. (2006). Trauma and memory: Normal versus special memory mechanisms. In B. Uttl, N. Ohta, & A. L. Siegenthaler (Eds.), *Memory and emotion: Interdisciplinary perspectives*. Oxford: Blackwell Publishing.

Goodman, G. S., & Quas, J. A. (1997). Trauma and memory: Individual differences in children's recounting of a stressful experience. In N. L. Stein, P. A. Ornstein, B. Tversky, & C. Brainerd (Eds.), *Memory for everyday and emotional events* (pp. 267–294). Mahwah, NJ: Lawrence Erlbaum Associates, Inc.

Goodman, G. S., Quas, J. A., Batterman-Faunce, J. M., Riddlesberger, M. M, & Kuhn, J. (1994). Predictors of accurate and inaccurate memories of traumatic events experienced in childhood. *Consciousness and Cognition, 3*, 269–294.

Goodman, G. S., Quas, J. A., Batterman-Faunce, J. M., Riddlesberger, M. M., & Kuhn, J. (1997). Children's reactions to and memory for a stressful event: Influences of age, anatomical dolls, knowledge, and parental attachment. *Applied Developmental Science, 1*, 54–75.

Goodman, G. S., & Reed, R. S. (1986). Age differences in eyewitness testimony. *Law and Human Behavior, 10*, 317–332.

Gordon, B. N., Baker-Ward, L., & Ornstein, P. A. (2001). Children's testimony: A review of research on memory for past experiences. *Clinical Child and Family Psychology Review, 4*(2), 157–181.

Green, B. (1994). Psychosocial research in traumatic stress: An update. *Journal of Traumatic Stress, 7*, 341–362.

Hamond, N. R., & Fivush, R. (1991). Memories of Mickey Mouse: Young children recount their trip to Disneyworld. *Cognitive Development, 6*, 433–448.

Hazan, C., & Shaver, P. (1987). Romantic love conceptualized as an attachment process. *Journal of Personality and Social Psychology, 52*, 511–524.

Heath, W. P., & Erickson, J. R. (1998). Memory for central and peripheral actions and props after varied post-event presentation. *Legal and Criminological Psychology, 3*, 321–346.

Hertel, P. T., & Gerstle, M. (2003). Depressive deficits in forgetting. *Psychological Science, 14*, 573–578.

Heuer, F., & Reisberg, D. (1992). *Emotion, arousal, and memory for detail*. Hillsdale, NJ: Lawrence Erlbaum Associates, Inc.

Howard, A. N., Osborne, H. L., & Baker-Ward, L. (1997, April). *Childhood cancer survivors' memory of their treatment after long delays*. Paper presented at the meeting of the Society for Research on Child Development, Washington, DC.

Howe, M. L. (1997). Children's memory for traumatic experiences. *Learning and Individual Differences, 9*, 153–174.

Howe, M. L. (2000). *The fate of early memories: Developmental science and the retention of childhood experiences*. Washington, DC: American Psychological Association.

Howe, M. (2006). Developmental invariance in distinctiveness effects in memory. *Developmental Psychology, 42,* 1193–1205.

Howe, M. L., Courage, M. L., & Bryant-Brown, L. (1993). Reinstating children's memories. *Developmental Psychology, 26,* 292–303.

Howe, M. L., Courage, M. L., & Peterson, C. (1994). How can I remember when "I" wasn't there: Long-term retention of traumatic experiences and emergence of cognitive self. *Consciousness and Cognition, 3,* 327–355.

Howe, M. L., Courage, M. L., Vernescu, R., & Hunt, M. (2000). Distinctiveness effects in children's long-term retention. *Developmental Psychology, 36,* 778–792.

Howe, M. L., Toth, S. L., & Cicchetti, D. (2006). Memory and developmental psychopathology. In D. Cicchetti & D. J. Cohen (Eds.), *Developmental psychopathology* (pp. 629–655). Hoboken, NJ: Wiley.

Hudson, J. A., & Fivush, R. (1991). As time goes by: Sixth graders remember a kindergarten experience. *Applied Cognitive Psychology, 5,* 347–360.

Ibabe, I., & Sporer, S. L. (2004). How you ask is what you get: On the influence of question form on accuracy and confidence. *Applied Cognitive Psychology, 18,* 711–726.

Imhoff, M. C., & Baker-Ward, L. (1999). Preschoolers' suggestibility: Effects of developmentally appropriate language and interviewer supportiveness. *Applied Developmental Psychology, 20,* 407–429.

Kazak, A. E., Barakat, L. P., Meeske, K., Christakis, D., Meadows, A. T., Casey, R., et al. (1997). Posttraumatic stress, family functioning, and social support in survivors of childhood leukemia and their mothers and fathers. *Journal of Consulting and Clinical Psychology, 65,* 120–129.

Kern, R. P., Libkuman, T. M., Otani, H., & Holmes, K. (2005). Emotional stimuli, divided attention, and memory. *Emotion, 5,* 408–417.

Kirsh, S. J., & Cassidy, J. (1997). Preschoolers' attention to and memory for attachment-relevant information. *Child Development, 68,* 1143–1153.

Koutstaal, W., & Schacter, D. L. (1997). Intentional forgetting and voluntary thought suppression: Two potential methods for coping with childhood trauma. In L. J. Dickstein, M. B. Riba, & J. M. Oldham (Eds.), *American Psychiatric Press review of psychiatry* (Vol. II, pp. 79–121). Washington, DC: American Psychiatric Association.

Lagattuta, K. H., & Wellman, H. M. (2002). Differences in early parent–child conversations about negative versus positive emotions: Implications for the development of psychological understanding. *Developmental Psychology, 38,* 564–580.

Laney, C., Campbell, H. V., Heuer, F., & Reisberg, D. (2004). Memory for thematically arousing events. *Memory and Cognition, 32,* 1149–1159.

Laney, C., Heuer, F., & Reisberg, D. (2003). Thematically induced arousal in naturally occurring emotional memories. *Applied Cognitive Psychology, 17,* 995–1004.

Lang, P. J., Greenwald, M. K., Bradley, M. M., & Hamm, A. O. (1993). Looking at pictures: Affective, facial, visceral, and behavioral reactions. *Psychophysiology, 30,* 261–273.

Lawson, L., & Chaffin, M. (1992). False negatives in sexual abuse disclosure interviews. *Journal of Interpersonal Violence, 7,* 532–42.

Leander, L., Granhag, P. A., & Christianson, S. Å. (2005). Children exposed to obscene phone calls: What they remember and tell. *Child Abuse and Neglect, 29,* 871–888.

Leippe, M. R., Manion, A. P., & Romanczyk, A. (1991). Eyewitness memory for a touching experience: Accuracy differences between child and adult witnesses. *Journal of Applied Psychology, 76*, 367–379.

Levine, L. J., & Bluck, S. (2004). Painting with broad strokes: Happiness and the malleability of event memory. *Cognition and Emotion, 18*, 559–574.

Levine, L. J., & Pizarro, D. A. (2004). Emotion and memory research: A grumpy overview. *Social Cognition, 22*, 530–554.

Lindberg, M. A., Jones, S., Collard, L. M., & Thomas, S. W. (2001). Similarities and differences in eyewitness testimonies of children who directly versus vicariously experience stress. *Journal of Genetic Psychology, 162*, 314–333.

Loftus, E. F. (2003). Make-believe memories. *American Psychologist, 58*, 867–873.

Loftus, E. F. (2005). Planting misinformation in the human mind: A 30-year investigation of the malleability of memory. *Learning and Memory, 12*, 361–366.

Loftus, E. F., & Pickrell, J. E. (1995). The formation of false memories. *Psychiatric Annals, 25*, 720–725.

Main, M., & Hesse, E. (1990). Parents' unresolved traumatic experiences are related to infant disorganized attachment status: Is frightened and/or frightening parental behavior the linking mechanism? In M. T. Greenberg, D. Cicchetti, & M. E. Cummings (Eds.), *Attachment in the preschool years: Theory, research, and intervention* (pp. 161–182). Chicago, IL: University of Chicago Press.

Main, M., & Solomon, J. (1990). Procedures for identifying infants as disorganized/disoriented during the Ainsworth Strange Situation. In M. T. Greenberg, D. Cicchetti, & M. E. Cummings (Eds.), *Attachment in the preschool years: Theory, research, and intervention* (pp. 121–160). Chicago, IL: University of Chicago Press.

Mattia, J. I., Heimberg, R. G., & Hope, D. A. (1993). The revised Stroop color-naming task in social phobics. *Behaviour Research and Therapy, 31*, 305–313.

Mazzoni, G., Loftus, E. F., & Kirsch, I. (2001). Changing beliefs about implausible autobiographical events: A little plausibility goes a long way. *Journal of Experimental Psychology: Applied, 7*, 51–59.

McCloskey, M., Wible, C. G., & Cohen, N. J. (1988). Is there a special flashbulb-memory mechanism? *Journal of Experimental Psychology: General, 117*, 171–181.

McGuigan, F., & Salmon, K. (2004). The time to talk: The influence of the timing of adult–child talk on children's event memory. *Child Development, 75*, 669–686.

McNally, R. J., Clancy, S. A., & Schacter, D. L. (2001). Directed forgetting of trauma cues in adults reporting repressed or recovered memories of childhood sexual abuse. *Journal of Abnormal Psychology, 110*, 151–156.

McNally, R. J., Metzger, L. J., Lasko, N. B., Clancy, S. A., & Pitman, R. K. (1998). Directed forgetting of trauma cues in adult survivors of childhood sexual abuse with and without posttraumatic stress disorder. *Journal of Abnormal Psychology, 107*, 596–601.

McNally, R. J., Riemann, B. C., & Kim, E. (1990). Selective processing of threat cues in panic disorder. *Behaviour Research and Therapy, 28*, 407–412.

Merritt, K. A., Ornstein, P. A., & Spicker, B. (1994). Children's memory for a salient medical procedure: Implications for testimony. *Pediatrics, 94*, 17–23.

Michael, T., Ehlers, A., & Halligan, S. L. (2005). Enhanced priming for trauma-related material in posttraumatic stress disorder. *Emotion, 5*, 103–112.

Moradi, A. R., Taghavi, M. R., Neshat-Doost, H. T., Yule, W., & Dalgleish, T. (2000). Memory bias for emotional information in children and adolescents with post-traumatic stress disorder: A preliminary study. *Journal of Anxiety Disorders, 14*, 521–534.

Moulds, M. L., & Bryant, R. A. (2002). Directed forgetting in acute in stress disorder. *Journal of Abnormal Psychology*, *111*, 175–179.

Neisser, U., & Harsch, N. (1992). Phantom flashbulbs: False recollections of hearing the news about challenger. In E. Winograd & U. Neisser (Eds.), *Affect and accuracy in recall: Studies of "flashbulb" memories. Emory symposia in cognition* (Vol. 4, pp. 9–31). New York: Cambridge University Press.

Neshat-Doost, H. T., Taghavi, M. R., Moradi, A. R., Yule, W., & Dalgleish, T. (1998). Memory for emotional trait adjectives in clinically depressed youth. *Journal of Abnormal Psychology*, *107*, 642–650.

Nourkova, V., Bernstein, D. M., & Loftus, E. F. (2004). Altering traumatic memory. *Cognition and Emotion*, *18*, 575–585.

Öhman, A., Flykt, A., & Esteves, F. (2001). Emotion drives attention: Detecting the snake in the grass. *Journal of Experimental Psychology: General*, *130*, 466–478.

Orbach, Y., & Lamb, M. E. (1999). Assessing the accuracy of a child's account of sexual abuse: A case study. *Child Abuse and Neglect*, *23*, 91–98.

Ornstein, P. A., Baker-Ward, L., Gordon, B. N., & Merritt, K. A. (1997). Children's memory for medical experiences: Implications for testimony. *Applied Cognitive Psychology*, *11*, 87–104.

Ornstein, P. A., Baker-Ward, L., Gordon, B. N., Pelphrey, K. A., Tyler, C. S., & Gramzow, E. (2006). The influence of prior knowledge and repeated questioning on children's long-term retention of the details of a pediatric examination. *Developmental Psychology*, *42*, 332–344.

Payne, J. D., Jackson, E. D., Ryan, L., Hoscheidt, S., Jacobs, W. J., & Nadel, L. (2006). The impact of stress on neutral and emotional aspects of episodic memory. *Memory*, *14*, 1–16.

Paz-Alonso, P. M., & Goodman, G. S. (2008). Children eyewitness memory and compliance: Effects of post-event misinformation on memory for negative and positive events. *Memory*, *16*, 58–75.

Paz-Alonso, P. M., Goodman, G. S., & Ibabe, I. (under review). Adult eyewitness memory and compliance: Effects of post-event misinformation on memory for a negative event. *Memory*.

Paz-Alonso, P. M., Goodman, G. S., Ibabe, I., & DePaul, J. (2003, July). *The influence of emotion on children eyewitness suggestibility*. Poster presented at the 2nd International Psychology and Law Interdisciplinary Conference, Edinburgh, UK.

Peace, K. A., & Porter, S. (2004). A longitudinal investigation of the reliability of memories for trauma and other emotional experiences. *Applied Cognitive Psychology*, *18*, 1143–1159.

Peterson, C. (1999). Children's memory for medical emergencies: 2 years later. *Developmental Psychology*, *35*, 1493–1506.

Peterson, C. (2002). Children's long-term memory for autobiographical events. *Developmental Review*, *22*, 370–402.

Peterson, C., & Bell, M. (1996). Children's memory for traumatic injury. *Child Development*, *67*, 3045–3070.

Peterson, C., & Parsons, B. (2005). Interviewing former 1- and 2-year-olds about medical emergencies 5 years later. *Law and Human Behavior*, *29*, 743–754.

Peterson, C., & Rideout, R. (1998). Memory for medical emergencies experienced by 1- and 2-year-olds. *Developmental Psychology*, *34*, 1059–1072.

Peterson, C., & Whalen, N. (2001). Five years later: Children's memory for medical emergencies. *Applied Cognitive Psychology*, *15*, S7–S24.

Pezdek, K. (2003). Event memory and autobiographical memory for the events of September 11, 2001. *Applied Cognitive Psychology, 17*, 1033–1045.

Pezdek, K., Finger, K., & Hodge, D. (1997). Planting false childhood memories: The role of event plausibility. *Psychological Science, 8*, 437–441.

Pezdek, K., & Hodge, D. (1999). Planting false childhood memories in children: The role of event plausibility. *Child Development, 70*, 887–895.

Pezdek, K., & Roe, C. (1997). The suggestibility of children's memory for being touched: Planting, erasing, and changing memories. *Law and Human Behavior, 21*, 95–106.

Pezdek, K., & Taylor, J. (2002). Memory for traumatic events in children and adults. In M. L. Eisen, J. A. Quas, & G. S. Goodman (Eds.), *Memory and suggestibility in the forensic interview* (pp. 165–183). Mahwah, NJ: Lawrence Erlbaum Associates, Inc.

Pillemer, D. B. (1992). Preschool children's memories of personal circumstances: The fire alarm study. In E. Winograd & U. Neisser (Eds.), *Affect and accuracy in recall: Studies of "flashbulb" memories* (pp. 121–137). New York: Cambridge University Press.

Pillemer, D. B., Picariello, M. L., & Pruett, J. C. (1994). Very long term memories of a salient preschool event. *Journal of Applied Cognitive Psychology, 8*, 95–106.

Poole, D. A., & White, L. T. (1991). Effects of question repetition on the eyewitness testimony of children and adults. *Developmental Psychology, 27*, 975–986.

Pynoos, R. S., & Eth, S. (1984). The child as witness to homicide. *Journal of Social Issues, 40*, 87–108.

Pynoos, R. S., & Nader, K. (1989). Children's memory and proximity to violence. *Journal of the American Academy of Child and Adolescent Psychiatry, 28*, 236–241.

Pynoos, R. S., & Nader, K. (1990). Children's exposure to violence and traumatic death. *Psychiatric Annals, 20*, 334–344.

Quas, J. A., Goodman, G. S., Bidrose, S., Pipe, M.-E., Craw, S., & Ablin, D. (1999). Emotion and memory: Children's long-term remembering, forgetting, and suggestibility. *Journal of Experimental Child Psychology, 72*, 235–270.

Quas, J. A., Qin, J., Schaaff, J. M., & Goodman, G. S. (1997). Individual differences in children's and adults' suggestibility and false event memory. *Learning and Individual Differences, 9*, 359–390.

Rauch, S., & Foa, E. (2006). Emotional processing theory (EPT) and exposure therapy for PTSD. *Journal of Contemporary Psychotherapy, 36*, 61–65.

Reese, E., Haden, C. A., & Fivush, R. (1993). Mother–child conversations about the past: Relationships of style and memory over time. *Cognitive Development, 8*, 403–430.

Reisberg, D., & Heuer, F. (2004). Memory for emotional events. In D. Reisberg, & P. Hertel (Eds.), *Memory and emotion* (pp. 3–41). New York: Oxford University Press.

Reisberg, D., Heuer, F., McLean, J., & O'Shaughnessy, M. (1988). The quantity, not the quality, of affect predicts memory vividness. *Bulletin of the Psychonomic Society, 26*, 100–103.

Reviere, S. L., & Bakeman, R. (2001). The effects of early trauma on autobiographical memory and schematic self-representation. *Applied Cognitive Psychology, 15*, 89–100.

Roebers, C. M., Gelhaar, T., & Schneider, W. (2004). "It's magic!" The effects of presentation modality on children's event memory, suggestibility, and confidence judgments. *Journal of Experimental Child Psychology, 87*, 320–335.

Roebers, C. M., & Schneider, W. (2000). The impact of misleading questions on eyewitness memory in children and adults. *Applied Cognitive Psychology, 14*, 509–526.

Roebers, C. M., & Schneider, W. (2002). Stability and consistency of children's event recall. *Cognitive Development, 17*, 1085–1103.

Roebers, C. M., Schwartz, S., & Neumann, R. (2005). Social influence and children's event recall and suggestibility. *European Journal of Developmental Psychology, 2*, 47–69.

Rudy, L., & Goodman, G. S. (1991). Effects of participation on children's reports: Implications for children's testimony. *Developmental Psychology, 27*, 527–538.

Sales, J. M., Fivush, R., Parker, J., & Bahrick, L. (2005). Stressing memory: Long-term relations among children's stress, recall and psychological outcome following hurricane Andrew. *Journal of Cognition and Development, 6*, 529–545.

Sales, J. M., Fivush, R., & Peterson, C. (2003). Parental reminiscing about positive and negative events. *Journal of Cognition and Development, 4*, 185–209.

Salmon, K., McGuigan, F., & Pereira, J. K. (2006). Brief report: Optimizing children's memory and management of an invasive medical procedure: The influence of procedural narration and distraction. *Journal of Pediatric Psychology, 31*, 522–527.

Salmon, K., & Pipe, M.-E. (1997). Props and children's event reports: The impact of a 1-year delay. *Journal of Experimental Child Psychology, 65*, 261–292.

Salmon, K., Price, J., & Pereira, J. K. (2002). Factors associated with young children's long-term recall of an invasive medical procedure: A preliminary investigation. *Developmental and Behavioral Pediatrics, 23*, 347–352.

Sapolsky, R. M. (1996). Why stress is bad for your brain. *Science, 273*, 749–750.

Saywitz, K. J., & Nathanson, R. (1993). Children's testimony and their perceptions of stress in and out of the courtroom. *Child Abuse and Neglect, 17*, 613–622.

Schmidt, S. R. (2004). Autobiographical memories for the September 11th attacks: Reconstructive errors and emotional impairment of memory. *Memory and Cognition, 32*, 443–454.

Schooler, J. W., & Eich, E. (2000). Memory for emotional events. In E. Tulving & F. I. M. Craik (Eds.), *The Oxford handbook of memory* (pp. 379–392). New York: Oxford University Press.

Shobe, K. K., & Kihlstrom, J. F. (1997). Is traumatic memory special? *Current Directions in Psychological Science, 6*, 70–74.

Shrimpton, S., Oates, K., & Hayes, S. (1998). Children's memory of events: Effects of stress, age, time delay and location of interview. *Applied Cognitive Psychology, 12*, 133–143.

Sjöberg, R. L., & Lindholm, T. (2005). A systematic review of age-related errors in children's memories for voiding cystourethrograms (VCUG). *European Child and Adolescent Psychiatry, 14*, 104–105.

Smith, D. W., Letourneau, E. J., Saunders, B. E., Kilpatrick, D. G., Resnick, H. S., & Best, C. L. (2000). Delay in disclosure of childhood rape: Results from a national survey. *Child Abuse and Neglect, 24*, 273–287.

Stallard, P., Velleman, R., Langsford J., & Baldwin, S. (2001). Coping and psychological distress in children involved in road traffic accidents. *British Journal of Clinical Psychology, 40*, 197–208.

Stein, N. L. (2002). Memories for emotional, stressful, and traumatic events. In N. L.

Stein, P. J. Bauer, & M. Rabinowitz (Eds.), *Representation, memory, and development: Essays in honor of Jean Mandler* (pp. 247–265). Mahwah, NJ: Lawrence Erlbaum Associates, Inc.

Stein, N. L., & Levine, L. J. (1990). Making sense out of emotion: The representation and use of goal-structured knowledge. In N. L. Stein, B. Leventhal, & T. Trabasso (Eds.), *Psychological and biological approaches to emotion* (pp. 45–73). Hillsdale, NJ: Lawrence Erlbaum Associates, Inc.

Stein, N. L., Trabasso, T., & Liwag, M. D. (1994). The Rashomon phenomenon: Personal frames and future-oriented appraisals in memory for emotional events. In M. M. Haith, J. B. Benson, R. Roberts, & B. F. Pennington (Eds.), *The development of future-oriented processes* (pp. 409–435). Chicago, IL: University of Chicago Press.

Stein, N. L., Trabasso, T., & Liwag, M. D. (2000). A goal appraisal theory of emotional understanding: Implications for development and learning. In M. Lewis & J. M. Haviland-Jones (Eds.), *Handbook of emotions* (pp. 436–457). New York: Guilford.

Sutherland, R., Pipe, M.-E., Schick, K., Murray, J., & Gobbo, C. (2003). Knowing in advance: The impact of prior event information on memory and event knowledge. *Journal of Experimental Child Psychology, 84*, 244–263.

Talarico, J. M., LaBar, K. S., & Rubin, D. C. (2004). Emotional intensity predicts autobiographical memory experience. *Memory and Cognition, 32*, 1118–1132.

Talarico, J. M., & Rubin, D. C. (2003). Confidence, not consistency, characterizes flashbulb memories. *Psychological Science, 14*, 455–461.

Terr, L. C. (1981). Psychic trauma in children: Observations following the Chowchilla school-bus kidnapping. *American Journal of Psychiatry, 138*, 14–19.

Terr, L. C. (1983). Chowchilla revisited: The effects of psychic trauma four years after a school-bus kidnapping. *American Journal of Psychiatry, 140*, 1543–1550.

Terr, L. C. (1988). What happens to early memories of trauma? A study of twenty children under age five at the time of documents events. *Journal of the American Academy of Child and Adolescent Psychiatry, 27*, 96–104.

Terr, L. C. (1990). *Too scared to cry: Psychic trauma in childhood*. New York: Harper & Row.

Terr, L. C. (1994). *Unchained memories: True stories of traumatic memories, lost and found*. New York: Basic Books.

Terr, L. C., Bloch, D. A., Michel, B. A., & Shi, H. (1996). Children's memories in the wake of *Challenger*. *American Journal of Psychiatry, 153*, 618–625.

Thierry, K. L. & Spence, M. J. (2004). A real-life event enhances the accuracy of preschoolers' recall. *Applied Cognitive Psychology, 18*, 297–309.

Van Abbema, D. L., & Bauer, P. J. (2005). Autobiographical memory in middle childhood: Recollections of the recent and distant past. *Memory, 13*, 829–845.

van der Kolk, B. A. (1997). Traumatic memories. In P. S. Applebaum & L. A. Uyehara (Eds.), *Trauma and memory: Clinical and legal controversies* (pp. 243–260). New York: Oxford University Press.

van Giezen, A. E., Arensman, E., Spinhoven, P., & Wolters, G. (2005). Consistency of memory for emotionally arousing events: A review of prospective and experimental studies. *Clinical Psychology Review, 25*, 935–953.

van Minnen, A., Wessel, I., Dijkstra, T., & Roelofs, K. (2002). Changes in PTSD patients' narratives during prolonged exposure therapy: A replication and extension. *Journal of Traumatic Stress, 15*, 255–258.

Vygotsky, L. (1978). *Mind in society*. Cambridge, MA: Harvard University Press.

Wareham, P., & Salmon, K. (2006). Mother–child reminiscing about everyday experiences: Implications for psychological interventions in the preschool years. *Clinical Psychology Review, 26*, 535–554.

Warren, A. R., & Swartwood, J. N. (1992). Developmental issues in flashbulb memory research: Children recall the *Challenger* event. In E. Winograd & U. Neisser (Eds.), *Affect and accuracy in recall: Studies of "flashbulb" memories* (pp. 95–120). New York: Cambridge University Press.

Wessel, I., & Merckelbach, H. (2006). Forgetting "murder" is not harder than forgetting "circle": Listwise-directed forgetting of emotional words. *Cognition and Emotion, 20*, 129–137.

Wessel, I., van der Kooy, P., & Merckelbach, H. (2000). Differential recall of central and peripheral details of emotional slides is not a stable phenomenon. *Memory, 8*, 95–100.

Westmacott, R., & Moscovitch, M. (2003). The contribution of autobiographical significance to semantic memory. *Memory and Cognition, 31*, 761–774.

Williams, L. M. (1994). Recall of childhood trauma: A prospective study of women's memories of child sexual abuse. *Journal of Consulting and Clinical Psychology, 62*, 1167–1176.

Williams, L. M. (1995). Recovered memories of abuse in women with documented child sexual victimization histories. *Journal of Traumatic Stress, 8*, 649–673.

Winograd, E., & Killinger, W. A. (1983). Relating age at encoding in early childhood to adult recall: Development of flashbulb memories. *Journal of Experimental Psychology: General, 112*, 413–422.

Wood, D., Bruner, J. S., & Ross, G. (1976). The role of tutoring in problem solving. *Journal of Child Psychology and Psychiatry, 17*, 89–100.

Yarmey, A. D., & Bull, M. P. (1978). Where were you when President Kennedy was assassinated? *Bulletin of the Psychonomic Society, 11*, 133–135.

10 Memory development and the forensic context

Margaret-Ellen Pipe
City University of New York, USA

Karen Salmon
*Victoria University of Wellington,
New Zealand*

Defendant kidnapped little 5-year-old Samantha Runnion who was playing
with her friend Sarah just several yards away from her condominium complex.
He drove by them in his green Thunderbird and asked whether they had seen a
puppy. When Samantha leaned down and asked whether he was about this
big, Avila snatched her up. Samantha bravely screamed, kicked and fought.
The last thing Sarah saw was Samantha looking toward her from Avila's car.
She told her friend to get her grandmother. Sarah immediately went to
Samantha's grandmother who called the police. Sarah articulately gave a
detailed description to the police which initiated a massive, televised manhunt.
A day later, Samantha's nude and battered body was found on a deserted trail
overlooking Lake Elsinore. A few days later, Avila was arrested by police who
acted on a tip from the mother of one of Avila's prior sexual victims.

(People v Alejandro Avila, Office of the District Attorney,
Orange County)[1]

Of great interest to me, several years earlier this same man had been accused
of child sexual abuse by two 9-year-old girls. The case went to trial, but the
jurors did not believe the children, and the man was acquitted.

(Goodman, 2006, p. 824)

When a child is the primary source of information in a forensic investigation,
how do we know whether or when we can trust his or her testimony? In many
cases, such as when sexual abuse is suspected or alleged, or when a child has
been the only witness to a crime such as an assault, abduction, or homicide,
the child's memory and reporting of the experienced or witnessed events are
critical and their memorial abilities inevitably come under intense scrutiny.
The reasons for the scrutiny are obvious and understandable: The consequences of errors can be far reaching for an accused person, particularly if
a child's erroneous account contributes to a conviction; even without conviction, an unfounded allegation, for example, of sexual abuse, can be extremely
damaging. On the other hand, if we fail to believe children or mistrust their
accounts inappropriately, the consequences can also be far from trivial,

resulting in the failure to protect not only the particular child misjudged, but others as well, as the case above so tragically demonstrates. The question of what we know and believe about children's ability to remember and report their experiences in forensic settings may thus have profound consequences for both child victims and those suspected of crimes alike.

Memory is not, of course, the only determinant of children's ability to recount forensically relevant experiences and to give testimony, but it is central and has been the focus of our understanding of what we can and cannot expect of child witnesses. The very earliest studies of children's abilities as witnesses, soon after the turn of the 20th century, were concerned with the susceptibility of children to suggestive questioning (e.g., Binet, 1900; Stern, 1910; Varendonck, 1911; see Bruck, Ceci, & Principe, 2006; Ceci & Bruck, 1993; Goodman, 1984, for reviews). These early demonstrations that children can be misled were informative but far from definitive, because they told us almost nothing about what children are capable of when *not* misled, such as when children are given the opportunity to provide free narrative accounts or are asked more open-ended questions. Nonetheless, these early demonstrations of the fallibility of children's memories were followed by a long dormant period during which there was almost no research concerned with children's competencies as witnesses. As a result, when Goodman and Michelli asked the question "Would you believe a child witness?" some 25 years ago, there was scant evidence for an informed answer (Goodman, 2006). Since that time the situation has changed drastically. This is in part as a result of the more basic memory research described throughout this volume, and in part the increased awareness of sexual abuse and the need to rely on children's accounts when, as is the norm, there is no corroborative evidence. Consequently, research examining children's forensically relevant competencies, as well as their frailties, has burgeoned during the last three decades.

Before turning to the contemporary research, we must first consider what is expected of children undergoing forensic investigations. Forensic interviews are particularly challenging in several respects. First, there is a premium on accuracy, as already noted. Importantly, in the forensic context not only the "gist" or generalities of children's accounts must be accurate, but also critical details that would implicate the accused person in specific criminal acts. Second, and related, children must recall and recount specific episodes in detail, including when they are describing recurring instances of abuse. That is, the emphasis is on *episodic memory*, with children recalling the who, what, where and when of the experienced or witnessed episode(s). Detailed accounts relating, for example, to temporal information (How many times? How long ago? How often?) may be particularly challenging for young children (see Orbach & Lamb, 2007), yet if children do not provide such information they may be perceived as less credible (see Lyon & Saywitz's, 2006, discussion of the Alejandro Avila case, for example).

Third, children are often required to recall events they had experienced or witnessed months or even years before; in cases of sexual abuse, in particular, children often do not disclose abuse immediately or even within weeks or months of when it (last) occurred (see London, Bruck, Ceci, & Shuman, 2005, 2007; Pipe, Lamb, Orbach, & Cederborg, 2007). Thus, even when formal investigative interviews promptly follow an allegation or suspicion, children may be reporting events that occurred much earlier in time, and delays because of legal processes inevitably compound the problem.

Fourth, we must consider the nature of the event itself. The effects of trauma on memory are discussed elsewhere in this volume (see Chapter 9 by Paz-Alonso and colleagues), and while many of the events children recall as witnesses may be traumatic, this is by no means always the case. For example, a child may not perceive abuse as abuse (see for example, Cederborg, Lamb, & Laurel, 2007), at least not at the time. Moreover, forensic investigations may relate to a range of experienced and witnessed events, other than sexual abuse, events experienced only once or on multiple occasions, involving known people or strangers, and so on. The influence of these event-related characteristics on children's memory reports also needs to be considered.

Fifth, in forensic interviews, the interviewer has a critical influence on how much and how accurately information is retrieved from memory. Children's accounts of past experiences must be elicited with as little interviewer input that might be interpreted as potentially contaminating as possible, while at the same time effectively eliciting the requisite details. The challenge here is one of facilitating accurate and detailed retrieval of forensically relevant information.

Finally, all of these requirements have to be considered in the context of the developmental abilities that the child brings to the interview. Although thus far we have simply referred to children, without specifying age, children's memorial abilities do, of course, change as the chapters in this volume attest, and what we can expect of a young, 5- to 6-year-old witness might be expected to differ substantially from that of an older, say 12- to 13-year-old child. Moreover, even within general age groups there are likely to be individual differences, for example relating to language and social competencies, that moderate children's ability to provide detailed accounts for forensic purposes; for example, a child who has experienced maltreatment may function at a lower level in these domains than their age-peers.

In sum, forensic interviewers face a somewhat daunting task, eliciting a detailed account, not only of what happened, but also of the temporal and spatial context in which it happened and the people involved, and, as we shall see, in many cases from the very children who may be ill-prepared to provide this information. Moreover, we also need to keep in mind that children may sometimes be less than willing informants, for example, because of the nature of the events, evoking feelings of shame, responsibility, or embarrassment, because they are motivated to protect a loved suspect, or because they have been threatened or cajoled to maintain secrecy (Pipe, Sternberg, Lamb, Orbach, Stewart, & Esplin, 2007).

Before we turn to the research that has informed and shaped forensic interviews with children, we want to emphasize that sexual abuse is not the only context in which children are interviewed about their experiences. As Chaffin (2006) has pointed out, sexual abuse comprises less than 10% of all instances of child maltreatment. More frequently, children who have experienced physical maltreatment and neglect, and/or who have witnessed parental violence or other crimes, are interviewed about their experiences in the context of Family or Children's Court, and here the primary question is "What does this child need?" (Chaffin, 2006; Lyon & Saywitz, 2006). In these settings, also, children's perceptions of their circumstances are a vital part of assessment, and clinicians must be adept at eliciting reliable information.

Nonetheless, in part because of the much higher probability that allegations of sexual abuse will lead to criminal proceedings, and hence forensic investigation including formal interviews, attention has focused on sexual abuse. Concerns about the reliability of children's allegations of sexual abuse, in turn reflect concerns that some children may be motivated to make false allegations or that their memories may be contaminated either intentionally or inadvertently (see Bruck & Ceci, 1999; Bruck et al., 2006). We touch on some of these issues, particularly when discussing sources of contamination of children's accounts; however, a full review of the false memory/reporting (i.e., false positives) research is outside the scope of the current chapter and has been amply reviewed elsewhere (see Bruck et al., 2006, for review). Similarly, although attention has recently turned to the other side of the coin, the possibility that a small but significant number of children may remember, but be motivated to *not* report abuse, or minimize it, and even falsely deny abuse even when interviewed (false negatives), again we touch on these motivational issues only briefly (see London, Bruck, Ceci, & Shuman, 2005; 2007; Lyon, 2007; Pipe, Lamb, Orbach, & Cederborg, 2007, for reviews of these and related topics).

CONTEMPORARY RESEARCH ON CHILDREN'S MEMORY REPORTS IN FORENSIC INTERVIEWS

Paradigms

Studies examining children's memory for forensically relevant information, and the best ways to elicit this in forensic interviews, have typically used one of two approaches. In laboratory-style *analog* and *event memory studies*, researchers examine the quantity and quality of the information children report about staged or naturally occurring events. Because the event is known, often contrived for the study and/or videotaped for later examination, the particular strength of this approach is, of course, that we can assess not only the content and amount of detail in children's memory reports, but also its accuracy. Thus we can draw conclusions about the influence of variables of interest on both how complete the account is, as well as how accurate it is.

Further, because researchers have control over many of these variables, such as the ages of the children studied, the nature of the event, and the ways in which children are interviewed, much stronger conclusions about their effects can be drawn than in the field studies described next.

In *field studies*, interviews with children undergoing forensic interviews, conducted by police or specialist interviewers (e.g., at child advocacy centers), are examined. Because the child is typically the only source of information about what happened, with rare exceptions (see, for example, Bidrose & Goodman, 2000; Cederborg et al., 2007; Orbach & Lamb, 1999), accuracy cannot be assessed in these studies. Nonetheless, the ecological validity of field studies is indisputable, and it is possible to determine whether theory and research about memory development based on laboratory and analog studies generalize to the real-world setting of forensic interviews, at least with respect to the quantity and quality of the information children of different ages report.

As we have argued elsewhere, the convergence of findings from these two approaches provides the most robust basis for recommendations from the lab to the field as how best to elicit children's accounts of their experiences (Pipe, Lamb, Orbach, & Esplin, 2004; Pipe, Thierry, & Lamb, 2007). Not only has laboratory-style research been important in informing practice, but consideration of children's developing memory abilities as they are reflected in performance in challenging real-world situations has, in turn, influenced the direction of more basic research, generating questions of both practical and theoretical importance.

Children's memory of forensically relevant information

How accurate and detailed can we expect children to be in forensic interviews? The answers are not simple, and the determinants of amount and accuracy, respectively, turn out to be quite different.

Children's free-recall narratives

From an applied perspective, the distinction between recall and recognition memory is crucial. One of the most consistent findings from studies of children's event memory, whether of contrived events or of events in naturalistic settings, is that when very general prompts such as "Tell me what happened" are the means of eliciting an account, young children typically recall significantly less information than older children, and frequently omit much information that adults consider important (see Ornstein, Baker-Ward, Gordon, & Merritt, 1997; Saywitz, Goodman, Nicholas, & Moan, 1991; and Pipe et al., 2004; Pipe, Thierry, & Lamb, 2007; Schneider & Pressley, 1997, for reviews). Such general, open-ended prompts attempt to elicit a narrative in the child's own words, free of interviewer input, and tap into recall memory.

These developmental differences in children's recall emerge not only when children recall neutral or even pleasant experiences, but also when they are interviewed about painful, distressing, and traumatic experiences, such as accidental injuries and intrusive medical procedures (e.g., Goodman, Quas, Batterman-Faunce, Riddlesberger, & Kuhn, 1994; Howe, Courage, & Peterson, 1994, 1996; McDermott Sales, Rees, & Fivush, 2007; Merritt, Ornstein, & Spicker, 1994; O'Kearney, Speyer, & Kenardy, 2007; Peterson, 1999; Peterson & Bell, 1996; Peterson & Whalen, 2001; Salmon, Price, & Pereira, 2002; see Cordón, Pipe, Sayfan, Melinder, & Goodman, 2004, for review). Similar age differences are evident in field studies of children's accounts of abusive experiences (Lamb, Sternberg, & Esplin, 2000; Sternberg, Lamb, Orbach, Esplin, & Mitchell, 2001). Although younger children are likely to provide less complete narrative accounts than older children, field studies also show that the proportion of the information that can be elicited through free-recall prompting remains constant, at least from age 4 to age 13 (Lamb, Sternberg, Orbach, Esplin, Stewart, & Mitchell, 2003).

How, then, can we elicit from the youngest children the kind of detail required in the forensic context, without putting accuracy at risk? Additional open-ended invitations asking for elaboration of information the child has already reported can be very effective in eliciting more detailed accounts from even the youngest children likely to be interviewed for forensic purposes. For example, field studies show that when interviewers refocus children on details they had provided earlier, and at the same time invite them to elaborate further (e.g., "You said [. . .]. Tell me more about that" or "And then what happened?"), children are able to provide significantly more information than in the original narrative (e.g., Lamb et al., 2000, 2003; Orbach, Hershkowitz, Lamb, Sternberg, Esplin, & Horowitz, 2000; Orbach & Lamb, 2000; Sternberg et al., 2001; Sternberg, Lamb, Esplin, Orbach, & Hershkowitz, 2002). Consistent with this, in an analog study, Evans, Roberts, and Beaupre (2007) have shown that paraphrasing information the child has provided paired with an invitation to elaborate further similarly elicits significantly more detail. The paraphrasing alone was insufficient, but when paired with the invitation, children recounted more information and, importantly, accuracy remained high (Evans et al., 2007). Such open-ended cuing procedures do not eliminate developmental differences in recall (Lamb et al., 2003), but may help some of the youngest children, in particular, to provide a "threshold" of forensically relevant information in their own words.

The primary advantage of obtaining free recall accounts of what happened—accounts in the child's own words—is that such accounts are likely to be highly accurate (e.g., Cole & Loftus, 1987; Dent & Stephenson, 1979; Gee & Pipe, 1995; Goodman & Reed, 1986; Lieppe, Romanczyk, & Manion, 1991; Poole & White, 1991; Salmon, Bidrose, & Pipe, 1995), with errors tending to be those of omission rather than errors of commission (Steward, Bussey, Goodman, & Saywitz, 1993). In fact, in several studies, young children's free recall accounts have been found to be as accurate as those of older children (e.g., Goodman & Aman, 1990; Goodman & Reed, 1986; Johnson &

Foley, 1984; Oates & Shrimpton, 1991) and adults (e.g., King & Yuille, 1987), as the relatively greater amounts of correct information reported by older children and adults may be compromised by a concurrent increase in errors (e.g., Cole & Loftus, 1987; Goodman & Reed, 1986; Marin, Holmes, Guth, & Kovac, 1979; Poole & White, 1991).

Recall memories are not always accurate, of course, especially when there is pressure on children to provide information that they have not encoded or have encoded poorly, when the events occurred long before the interview, or there have been repeated opportunities for pre- (Leichtman & Ceci, 1995) or post-event contamination (Leichtman & Ceci, 1995; Poole & Lindsay, 1995, 1996; Poole & White, 1993; Warren & Lane, 1995). Moreover, recall memory is not immune to source-monitoring errors, or confusion of details from separate instances of similar experiences, as discussed in more detail later in the chapter. Nonetheless, accounts based on open-ended prompts are much more likely to be accurate than those elicited using recognition cues or more focused prompts (Lamb, Orbach, Hershkowitz, Horowitz, & Abbott, 2006); as we shall see in the next section, more focused questioning may have detrimental effects on the reports of younger children, in particular.

Focused questions and prompts

Because children do not always report the level of detail required in forensic contexts, or information critical to the investigation, interviewers often turn to more focused questions, many of which tap into recognition memory rather than recall memory. Laboratory research suggests that developmental differences in memory performance are much smaller in recognition than in recall memory tasks (e.g., Mandler & Stein, 1974) and hence their appeal. However, recognition prompts that take the form of yes–no or multiple choice questions, such as "Did he have a beard?" or "Did this happen in the day or in the night?" risk reducing the accuracy of the additional information elicited (Dale, Loftus, & Rathbun, 1978; Dent, 1982, 1986; Dent & Stephenson, 1979; Gee, Gregory, & Pipe, 1999; Goodman, Hirschman, Hepps, & Rudy, 1991; Hutcheson, Baxter, Telfer, & Warden, 1995; Lamb & Fauchier, 2001; Oates & Shrimpton, 1991; Orbach & Lamb, 2001), particularly if such questions are asked repeatedly within an interview (see also Howie, Sheehan, Mojarrad, & Wrzesinska, 2004; Poole & White, 1991).

Young children are particularly vulnerable to being misled when the question is phrased to elicit agreement with the interviewer, such as when asked a misleading tag question (e.g., "He asked you to go with him, didn't he?") (Cassel, Roebers, & Bjorklund, 1996; Greenstock & Pipe, 1996; Peterson, Dowden, & Tobin, 1999; Walker, 1997; Walker & Hunt, 1998). Focused questions can also be posed as open-ended recall questions (e.g., "What color was the hat he was wearing?"), but these too can be misleading and hence risky. For example, if the suspect was not wearing a hat, as with the tag questions noted above, the child must disagree with the interviewer to make a correct response, and this may be a tall order for a young child. Thus the advantages of focused questions, from the perspective of eliciting details from memory, can very quickly turn to disadvantages in the forensic context. As a result, several protocols and guidelines for forensic interviews recommend what is sometimes called the funnel approach, and that these more focused questions should be delayed until towards the end of interviews, when information elicited by free recall prompts and requests for elaboration have been exhausted (see, for example, Yuille, Hunter, Joffe, & Zaparniuk, 1993).

Temporal information

An example of the kind of specific detail the interviewer may wish to pursue relates to the temporal attributes of an event, such as the number, timing, and sequence of event occurrences. In the forensic context this information can be particularly important, yet there has been surprisingly little research examining children's ability to provide it (Lyon & Saywitz, 2006). In a recent field study, Orbach and Lamb (2007) highlighted developmental improvements in 4- to 10-year-olds' ability to report temporal information, both spontaneously and in response to interviewers' temporal requests, about alleged abusive incidents. The findings were consistent with previous laboratory and event memory studies examining the development of temporal concepts (e.g., Friedman, 1978, 1992); some types of temporal information, for example sequencing, are used by children at a much earlier age than predicted by Piaget, and their use increases gradually (Brown & French, 1976; Fivush & Haden, 1997; Strube & Weber, 1988), whereas the appropriate use of other types of temporal information, such as dating and frequency, increases more dramatically around 8 to 10 years of age, as predicted by Piaget (Droit-Volet, Clement, & Wearden, 2001; Friedman, 1978, 1992; McCormack, Brown, Smith, & Brock, 2004). If children do not have the appropriate knowledge base or conceptual understanding, pressure to provide the information will at best draw a blank and at worst lead to inconsistencies and inaccuracies in children's accounts, and undermine the credibility of their recall of features they *do* remember (see Lyon & Saywitz, 2006). Interestingly, Orbach and Lamb found that nearly three-quarters of the temporal information was reported in response to free recall prompts, rather than in response to more specific questioning.

Event-related characteristics affecting memory

Children are interviewed about a wide range of experiences, including those that have been traumatic or distressing; events they have witnessed, or alternatively have experienced perhaps many times over long durations; recent events, and commonly also those from months or even years earlier; experiences that others may have known about, and hence discussed with the child, and those that the child kept secret and seldom discussed, to name but a few of the relevant dimensions. Both event memory studies and those conducted in the field attest to the sometimes marked effects that these variables have on children's memory. Because the effects of trauma on memory have been discussed extensively by Paz-Alonso et al. (Chapter 9, this volume), they will not be discussed in detail here.

Recalling one of several occurrences

Children interviewed about abuse, both sexual and physical, must often recount multiple abusive incidents that took place over a prolonged time period. From a legal perspective, however, details of exactly what happened on particular occasions at specific times are critically important. How reasonable is it to expect children to provide accurate accounts of specific instances when abuse has been ongoing? Analog studies suggest that this is not an easy task, particularly for younger children.

Although repeated experience of an event generally results in better recall of the common features (i.e., what "usually" occurs) (Fivush, Kuebli, & Clubb, 1992; Murachver, Pipe, Gordon, Fivush, & Owens, 1996; Powell, Roberts, Ceci, & Hembrooke, 1999), recall of details that are unique to an occurrence or that only sometimes happen may be particularly difficult (see Roberts, 2002; Roberts & Powell, 2001, for review). Details that change across experiences are less likely to be recalled, and may be more vulnerable to suggestion, at least under some conditions (Connolly & Lindsay, 2001; Gobbo, Mega, & Pipe, 2002; McNichol, Shute, & Tucker, 1999; but see Powell et al., 1999; Powell, Roberts, & Thomson, 2000). Furthermore, confusion about when these changing details occurred is common. That is, although children often accurately remember the details of what happened, even when they change, they confuse when they happened, and thus details "migrate" across instances of the experience in children's reports (Hudson, 1990; Powell & Thomson, 1997; Roberts & Powell, 2001, 2007; Slackman & Nelson, 1984).

Powell and Thomson (1997), for example, examined how well children could recall specific details about an event that was experienced six times, with minor variations in some details but the same basic event structure. When the 4- to 5- and 6- to 8-year-old children were asked to recall the final instance of the event, they frequently recalled details from the earlier instances, rather than the final instance (see also Farrar & Goodman, 1990, 1992; Fivush et al., 1992; Hudson, 1990). The migration of details across episodes and confusion regarding source are more likely among younger than older children, particularly over time (Myles-Worsley, Cromer, & Dodd, 1986; Slackman & Nelson, 1984).

Particularly problematic is the possibility that details from other sources might similarly be confused with the child's account of their own experience and that these details might also "migrate" into children's accounts. Children acquire knowledge about events not only from their own unique or repeated personal experiences, but also from vicarious sources such as conversations, television, and books (Roberts & Powell, 2001; Sutherland, Pipe, Schick, Murray, & Gobbo, 2003). As a result, children's event accounts could reflect confusion not only among repeated, similar experiences, but also among similar events experienced personally and vicariously. The relevant analog studies have generally used recognition procedures, and these show that children can confuse episodes they experienced as well as episodes they experienced and heard about (Poole & Lindsay, 2001) or experienced and observed (Roberts & Blades, 2000; Thierry, Spence, & Memon, 2001). Few studies have examined whether these confusions occur in children's open-ended or spontaneous narratives, and from a forensic perspective further research is clearly needed.

Several researchers have attempted to improve children's source monitoring performance and their ability to recall specific experienced events accurately and without intrusion of information from other similar experiences. Saywitz and Snyder (1993), for example, showed that script-based errors can be reduced by pre-interview counseling or instruction and Thierry et al. (2001) found that children monitored the source of their memories better when asked misleading questions after they had been trained to monitor the source of information actively. Poole and Lindsay (2002) likewise found that having children monitor the source of seen and heard events in a training phase helped 7- to 8-year-olds (but not 3- to 4-year-olds) to distinguish between activities. Conversely, asking children to recall experiences regardless of source and then asking for source attributions does not help reduce confusion (Powell & Thomson, 1997; Priestley & Pipe, 1997). Moreover, *repeatedly* recalling seen and imagined objects without regard to their source leads adults to be more confused and to make more source monitoring errors in subsequent memory tests (Henkel, 2004). This appears to be true of children, too (Thierry, Goh, Pipe, & Murray, 2005).

Experiencing vs. witnessing

In general, directly participating in an event is likely to result in stronger and/or more accessible memories, for both adults and children, than being a bystander or observer, or learning about the same event second hand (Murachver et al., 1996; Roediger, McDermott, Pisoni, & Gallo, 2004; Rudy & Goodman, 1991; Tobey & Goodman, 1992). Tobey and Goodman (1992), for example, found that 4-year-old children who participated in a real-life event (a Simon Says game) freely recalled central actions more accurately than children who merely observed the same event on video, and Rudy and Goodman (1991) found that 4-year-olds who were direct participants in a real-life event were less susceptible to misleading questions than children who observed the real-life event. Similarly, Murachver et al. (1996) found that children who participated in a contrived interaction with an adult "pirate" recalled more information than those who read a story about "visiting the pirate." Their free recall was also more accurate than that of children who only watched the event or heard about the event. However, ethical considerations limit the kinds of witnessed events that can be studied in analog research and in the real world witnessed events are likely to vary substantially in terms of salience and significance to the child, and hence their memorability. Thus while participation generally leads to better recall and reporting, witnessed events may nonetheless be very well remembered in some circumstances.

Delays

In forensic interviews many children are asked to recount experiences or events they witnessed that took place weeks, months, or even years earlier; in cases of abuse, in particular, delayed reporting is as much the norm as the exception (see London et al., 2007; Lyon, 2007). Can we reasonably expect children to be able to provide detailed and comprehensive accounts over such long delays?

Some event memory studies suggest that forgetting is often quite marked following such forensically relevant delays (e.g., Flin, Boon, Knox, & Bull, 1992; Goodman, Batterman-Faunce, Schaaf, & Kenney, 2002; Hudson & Fivush, 1991; Jones & Pipe, 2002; Ornstein et al., 1997; Salmon & Pipe, 2000; but see Fivush & Schwarzmueller, 1998). Jones and Pipe (2002), for example, found that 5- to 6-year-old children recalled significantly less about an analog event, visiting the pirate, when interviewed 6 months later than those children interviewed soon after the event, although the most rapid forgetting occurred in the weeks immediately following the event. Other studies, however, suggest that memories of even quite young children may be resilient and show little change over periods of several years (e.g., Burgwyn-Bailes, Baker-Ward, Gordon, & Ornstein, 2001; Fivush, Sales, Goldberg, Bahrick, & Parker, 2004; Merritt et al., 1994; Peterson, 1999; Peterson & Whalen, 2001). Peterson and colleagues found, for example, that children showed little change in their recall of an injury requiring outpatient treatment at a hospital when interviewed 2 and 5 years later. Interestingly, children younger than age 5 at the time of injury appeared to remember slightly more over time, whereas those who had been older than 5 showed some forgetting (Cordón et al., 2004).

Generalization from these analog studies to the forensic context is not straightforward, however. Studies finding some memories to be resilient over time have often involved distressing or painful experiences, suggesting they have been better encoded than more neutral or pleasant experiences, and perhaps in part because event distinctiveness is likely to lead to better long-term recall (Howe, 1997). But as noted earlier, the events about which children are interviewed as part of forensic investigations are not always salient or significant to them at the time. Moreover, in many of the studies showing good retention, children were probably reminded of their experiences (for example, an injury or a hurricane) by family members, friends, interviewers, and even by the media. Sexual abuse, in contrast, is a very private experience, rarely discussed with others (see, for example, London et al., 2005, 2007), which may affect the memorability of abusive experiences (Fivush, 1997, 2004; Fivush, Pipe, Murachver, & Reese, 1997).

In the only published field study examining the effects of delay on children's recall of alleged sexual abuse, Lamb et al. (2000) reported that children interviewed within a month of the alleged abuse were more likely to provide information in response to the interviewers' open-ended prompts and questions than children interviewed following long (5- to 14-month) delays, although children interviewed early provided no more details in total than those interviewed following the longest delay. That is, detailed open-ended prompting was effective in eliciting details that might otherwise not have been reported over the long delays.

HELPING CHILDREN RETRIEVE AND REPORT DETAILED INFORMATION

Although verbal prompts have been the mainstay of the forensic interview, a number of other techniques and training procedures have been explored, to help children remember and/or report their experiences, and it is to these that we now turn. Generally the focus of these techniques has been younger children, but often they have been useful across a broad age range, with the associated risks greatest when used with the youngest age groups.

The use of non-verbal techniques for helping children to remember and talk about their experiences has a long history, particularly in clinical settings. While the emphasis in the clinical literature has been on their role as aids to communication, in forensic contexts the virtue of non-verbal techniques may lie in their effects on memory. Techniques that have been examined under controlled conditions include revisiting the environmental context in which the event occurred (Pipe & Wilson, 1994; Priestley, Roberts, & Pipe, 1999; Wilkinson, 1988), providing children with either items (Gee & Pipe, 1995; Smith, Ratner, & Hobart, 1987) or representations of items (Goodman & Aman, 1990; Price & Goodman, 1990; Priestley & Pipe, 1997; Salmon et al., 1995) associated with the to-be-remembered event, human figure drawings, or drawing during interviews (Brennan & Fisher, 1998; Butler, Gross, & Hayne, 1995; Gross & Hayne, 1998).

In general, props may serve to compensate for some of the developmental limitations that constrain young children's accounts of their experiences. For example, they may enable the demonstration of information (by pointing or re-enactment) that children find difficult to talk about because of its distressing or traumatic nature or because their language skill is insufficiently developed (e.g., Sattler, 2002). Props may also facilitate memory processes, potentially provide concrete external retrieval cues, and extend the child's memory search because they remain physically present during questioning (Goodman & Aman, 1990; Pipe & Wilson, 1994; Price & Goodman, 1990; see Pipe, Salmon, & Priestley, 2002; Salmon, 2001, for reviews). Research investigating the influence of props on children's recall in analog studies shows that their effectiveness is determined not only by the type of props and the child's age and associated cognitive development, but also by the degree to which the props are specific to the event and the ways in which they are presented to the child. We now turn, more specifically, to some of these key findings relating to the use of props in forensic (rather than clinical) contexts.

Reinstating the context and real props

The rationale for "returning to the scene of the crime", or providing prop items as contextual cues at the time of interview, is based on Tulving's encoding specificity principle, whereby retrieval cues that were present during memory encoding help to bring into consciousness details of an event that might not have been retrieved without such cues (Tulving, 1983). Thus children interviewed in the presence of contextual cues should show better memory performance.

Consistent with these theoretical predictions, analog studies show that children recall more information, without adverse effects on accuracy, if they are interviewed where an event occurred (Gee & Pipe, 1995; Pipe & Wilson, 1994; Price & Goodman, 1990; but see La Rooy, Pipe, & Murray, 2005). These findings that have been supported by field studies in which children interviewed back in the context in which the alleged incidents had occurred were able to report additional information (Hershkowitz, Orbach, Lamb, Sternberg, Horowitz, & Hovav, 1998; Orbach, Hershkowitz, Lamb, Sternberg, & Horowitz, 2000). Similarly, having prop items from the event present at the time of the interview increases the amount of correct information recalled by children aged between 3 and 10 years (e.g, Gee & Pipe, 1995; Pipe & Wilson, 1994; Salmon et al., 1995; Steward & Steward, 1996; see Salmon, 2001, for review).

Moreover, consistent with the extensive research on reminders conducted with young infants, and non-human animals (see Chapter 2 in this volume by Rovee-Collier and Cuevas), even brief exposure to the event context may be sufficient to make an event memory more accessible for subsequent recall. Priestley et al. (1999) found that taking children back into the event context as a reminder of the experience 24 hours *before* the interview—without allowing children the opportunity to interact with the prop items—increased the amount of information that 5- to 7-year-old children reported about a staged event. The "reminder" exposure was just as effective in increasing detailed reporting as interviewing children back in the event context with prop items present throughout the interview. One of the advantages of the reminder procedure is that it potentially decreases the risk of errors that can be introduced via re-enactment.

Finally, mental context reinstatement, a component of the cognitive interview developed to elicit more detailed reports from adult witnesses (e.g., Fisher & Geiselman, 1992), has also been effective with children (see Bowen & Howie, 2002; Geiselman & Padilla, 1988; Memon, Cronin, Eaves, & Bull, 1993; see Köhnken, Milne, Memon, & Bull, 1999, for a review). For example, in a field study, Hershkowitz, Orbach, Lamb, Sternberg, and Horowitz (2001) also showed that 4- to 13-year-olds who were required to mentally reinstate the context of an alleged sexual abuse incident (children were instructed to "close your eyes and think about that time . . . think about sounds or voices you could hear . . . smells you could smell") produced proportionally more details in response to open-ended invitations than children who were not instructed to reinstate the context mentally.

There are qualifications to the effectiveness of real props, however, and several problems arise when applying these memory techniques in the real world. Although they may be useful over long delays (Salmon & Pipe, 1997, 2000), repeated interviews with the props in the interim may compromise the accuracy of children's memory reports (Pipe, Gee, Wilson, & Egerton, 1999). Moreover, the availability of "foils" or distracter props results in a dis-proportionate number of errors, particularly when children use the props to demonstrate their experience.

Interviewing at the scene of the crime is also likely to be logistically dif-ficult, particularly when forensic interviews are conducted following an inter-disciplinary model, and are observed "on-line" by police, child protection, district attorneys, and so on. Also of concern, it will not always be possible to return to the exact context in which the event occurred, and distortions potentially lead to errors in children's accounts. In this respect, mental con-text reinstatement may have an advantage, at least insofar as the child is able to generate the effective contextual cues. Indeed, many abusive experiences occur in very familiar contexts, such as the home, and laboratory research suggests contextual cues with many associations ("cue overload") may fail to be effective retrieval cues for specific events. Finally, the potential emotional consequences for the child in some instances will also constrain the usefulness of these techniques; although Hershkowitz et al. reported that none of the children in their study were distressed by the interview conducted in context, nonetheless, there may be situations where it is emotionally distressing and therefore inappropriate.

These various constraints notwithstanding, there may be circumstances in which revisiting the event context provides an important opportunity to "remind" the child of details he or she might otherwise not remember and report, or when prop items help focus the investigation and serve as effective retrieval tools. Given that in investigative interviews children are often recall-ing experiences or witnessed events from months or years earlier, the accessi-bility of the information may indeed be an issue.

Dolls, toys, and models

In real-world contexts, of course, toys are much more readily available than are the real objects present during the child's experience of abuse and have the added advantage of intuitive appeal; given their ubiquity in children's play it seems obvious that props such as dolls, toys, drawings, and so on, can put children at ease in the interview. Anatomically detailed dolls have been the most controversial of these props, although much of the controversy has focused on whether the dolls can help "diagnose" sexual abuse, rather than on their use in facilitating children's reports of abuse already disclosed. Concerns about the inaccuracy of doll-associated reports have prompted recommendations of caution in the forensic use of dolls, especially when young children are involved (Bruck, Ceci, Francouer, & Renick, 1995; Poole & Lamb, 1998). However, their use during interviews with allegedly abused children, particularly when interviewers follow professional guidelines (Everson & Boat, 2002), or protocols in which the dolls are used for very specific purposes, such as clarification when the child has already made a verbal allegation in the interview, is still relatively widely advocated (American Professional Society on the Abuse of Children, 2002; CornerHouse, 1990, 2003; Everson & Boat, 2002; Koocher, Goodman, White, Friedrich, Sivan, & Reynolds, 1995).

Given their generic nature and availability in play settings, most toys will provide little specificity, potentially compromising their effectiveness as retrieval cues. Additionally, for preschoolers, whose ability to appreciate the dual nature of symbols is relatively immature, understanding the relation between the toy and the item it represents is likely to be problematic in the absence of a high degree of similarity. This is especially so if the toy is a doll that the child is asked to use to represent the self to demonstrate where she or he was touched (DeLoache, 2004; DeLoache & Burns, 1993; DeLoache & Marzolf, 1995).

It is not surprising, then, that analog studies have found that dolls, either alone or with other toys, are not helpful for children under age 5 years; they increase the number of errors that children make, especially when suggestive questions are also posed, and they fail to elicit additional correct information (e.g., Bruck, Ceci, & Francoeur, 2000; DeLoache & Marzolf, 1995; Goodman & Aman, 1990; Goodman, Quas, Batterman-Faunce, Riddlesberger, & Kuhn, 1997; Gordon, Ornstein, Nida, Follmer, Crenshaw, & Albert, 1993), although they may help older children (aged 5 to 7 years) report information that would otherwise not be reported because shame or embarrassment (e.g., genital touch, Saywitz et al., 1991).

Toys or models (other than dolls) that are similar to the items in the event can also increase the amount of correct information that 3- and 5-year-old children report about a staged event. However, the accuracy of the information that is *re-enacted* using the items is compromised (Priestley & Pipe, 1997; Salmon et al., 1995). Further, permitting children to interact with toys before using them to report specific event information also dramatically increases the risk of errors (Nigro & Wolpow, 2004; Priestley & Pipe, 1997). Children appear to be drawn to the toys; Nigro and Wolpow (2004) commented, for example, that toys "stimulate behavioural activity" (p. 562). The result may be that the additional information elicited is not necessarily related to the events under inquiry.

Research conducted in the field extends findings from analog studies. Thierry, Lamb, Orbach, and Pipe (2005) analyzed 173 forensic interviews, comparing information elicited with and without the dolls present, in a within-subject design. They found that the information obtained was of poorer quality with dolls than without them. Younger children (aged 3 to 6 years) were more likely to re-enact information with the dolls and to engage in exploratory and speculative play using the dolls than were the older children (aged 7 to 12 years). Even the older children did not benefit greatly from the dolls, as they provided most information verbally, and children of both age groups provided proportionately more fantastic details with dolls than without them. These findings generally paint a negative picture of the effects of dolls on children's accounts. It must be noted, however, that the use of the dolls did not conform to current practice guidelines and recommended use (American Professional Society on the Abuse of Children (APSAC), 2002; CornerHouse, 1990, 2003), in that not all children had disclosed abuse prior to the introduction of the dolls, and children could interact with both the dolls and other toys present, a practice which, as noted earlier, leads to errors in children's accounts.

Human figure diagrams

Interviewer-provided line drawings are also sometimes used in forensic interviews to elicit children's names for body parts and/or to enable them to indicate or clarify where they have been touched. In a field study, Aldridge and colleagues (Aldridge, Lamb, Sternberg, Orbach, Esplin, & Bowler, 2004) found that alleged child abuse victims (aged 4 to 13 years) reported additional, new information about touch in response to human figure drawings provided at the end of an exhaustive verbal interview using the National Institute of Child Health and Human Development (NICHD) protocol (Orbach, Hershkowitz, Lamb, Sternberg, & Horowitz, 2000). The cost was, however, that the interviewers used more focused questions, potentially compromising accuracy (Aldridge et al., 2004). In a direct analog of Aldridge et al.'s field study, Brown, Pipe, Lewis, Lamb, and Orbach (2007) similarly found that 5- to 6-year-old children provided new information about touch that had occurred during a staged event (visiting the photographer) in response to human figure drawings, although asking children about touch (without the drawings) was just as effective. Compared to children questioned about touch without drawings, however, children provided with the drawings reported more incorrect touches.

Willcock, Morgan, and Hayne (2006) also found that 5- to 6-year-old children's indications of innocuous touch from a scripted event tended to be inaccurate; only half of the reported touches had actually occurred and, of particular concern, errors included indications of touches to the genital and breast areas. In Brown et al.'s (2007) study, such forensically relevant errors were much less frequent, perhaps because of methodological differences in the actual drawings and their use. Importantly, in Brown et al.'s study, errors were rarely elaborated on when children were prompted for verbal clarification. Thus, while several children indicated, either non-verbally or with a simple yes/no answer, that they had been touched in a way that could easily have been interpreted as inappropriate, asking for elaboration dispelled any concerns, almost immediately (Brown et al., 2007).

These findings highlight the risks inherent in interpreting non-verbal responses, or simple verbal responses, without clarification (Brown et al., 2007), and mirror our earlier concerns in relation to non-verbal demonstrations using dolls and other prop items. Several forensic interview protocols recommend that human figure drawings are introduced only to clarify verbal reports of touches, during the verbal interview (e.g., Home Office, 2002; American Professional Society on the Abuse of Children (APSAC), 2002; Poole & Lamb, 1998) and their use in this way has yet to be evaluated in either analog or field studies.

Drawing

Are there strategies that enhance memory and reporting without involving externally provided props? Some researchers have speculated that asking children to draw their experience may circumvent the difficulties associated with interacting with props. There is considerable debate concerning whether the child's drawing itself provides forensically important information (e.g., Burkitt, Barrett, & Davis, 2003; Dunn, O'Connor, & Levy, 2002; Gross & Hayne, 1998; Thomas & Jolley, 1998). Nonetheless, drawing an experience while talking about it may have advantages, independent of content, because, for example, it prolongs the interview, provides a series of self-generated retrieval cues, or structures the child's narrative account, and as a result, the child's verbal account may benefit.

Analog studies have shown that asking children older than age 5 to draw and talk about their experience can improve their verbal recall, particularly for more able drawers and when drawing is used in combination with direct questions (Butler et al., 1995; Gross & Hayne, 1998). But drawing, too, may have limitations as an effective tool in the real world. For example, the reports of preschool children are not improved (Bruck, Melnyk, & Ceci, 2000; Butler et al., 1995); even with the older children, drawing may not always elicit additional information (Salmon & Pipe, 2000), or the effects may be specific to the number of objects reported, with no difference in actions from the number reported verbally, yet it could well be argued that actions are critical in forensic contexts (Gross & Hayne, 1998; Wesson & Salmon, 2001). Further, as with dolls, discussed earlier, asking children to draw also results in less accurate reports under suggestive interviewing conditions (Bruck et al., 2000) and increases the likelihood that they subsequently report false events (Strange, Garry, & Sutherland, 2003).

Rapport building and practice

Forensic interviews typically involve an initial phase prior to any attempt to elicit an account of the event of interest. This is often referred to as the rapport-building phase, although in actuality it may serve multiple functions. Indeed, while rapport building may be particularly important when investigating sensitive topics, or when children have been threatened or coerced into secrecy, as Lyon and Saywitz (2006) point out, attempts to build trust and rapport are often somewhat cursory in analog studies, and there is a paucity of research on effective "rapport-building" strategies. More is known about some of the other benefits of this initial phase, however, including the effects of explaining the ground rules for the interview, and giving children practice, for example, in correcting the interviewer, saying "I don't know" (Gee et al., 1999; Saywitz & Moan-Hardie, 1994) or "I don't understand" (Peters & Nunez, 1999; Saywitz, Snyder, & Nathanson, 1999), and/or in providing detailed narrative responses to open-ended prompting.

Saywitz and her colleagues (e.g., Camparo, Wagner, & Saywitz, 2001; Saywitz & Snyder, 1996), for example, developed a memory training technique, known as the narrative elaboration technique (NET), which helps to structure children's recall by providing external visual cues to aid retrieval of event details. Children are trained with cards that cue their memories of various event components (participants, settings, actions, and affective states) associated with the experienced events, and are given feedback as to the level of detail expected in their responses. Seven- to 8- and 10- to 11-year-olds trained using the NET produced more accurate details about an event than children in control groups (Saywitz & Snyder, 1996). Subsequent studies suggest that simply cuing the categories of information (verbally) may be just as effective, at least with neutral or pleasant experiences (Brown & Pipe, 2003b).

The "pre-substantive phase" of the NICHD interview protocol is similarly designed to enhance narrative elaboration using somewhat similar techniques. Whereas in the NET, the interviewer provides category cues, the child's own narrative provides cues to prompt further recall in the NICHD interview protocol. Sternberg and her colleagues (1997, 2001) showed that practice responding to such open-ended prompts about neutral experienced events in the initial ("pre-substantive") phase of forensic interviews indeed allowed children to produce more information from recall memory in response to the first prompt relating to the alleged event. That is, children who were questioned using closed questions during the pre-substantive phase reported much less information. The purpose of these practice and feedback procedures is to make the expectations of the interview clear, given they may be in conflict with children's prior socialization about their conversations with adults.

Summary

In sum, extant studies provide some support for the use of non-verbal props and other techniques, including practice narratives, in aiding the retrieval and reporting of more detailed information about past experiences. The findings outlined above also highlight the risks to the accuracy of children's reports that may ensue when interviewers provide props and use other techniques, such as human figure drawings. Clearly it is important to consider both the age of the child being interviewed and how the prop items are introduced and used within the interview. While existing studies have clearly demonstrated that there are ways of using these techniques that put accuracy at risk, particularly with pre-school age children, analog studies have generally not addressed whether accuracy is similarly compromised when used for more limited purposes and/or following strict professional guidelines. This is an area in which a closer association between researchers and professionals in the field is imperative if more basic research is to continue to have a positive influence on practice.

INDIVIDUAL DIFFERENCES IN RECALL

Within age groups, children vary considerably in the amount of information that they correctly report about their experiences and the extent to which they are influenced by misleading or inaccurate information provided after the event or during the interview. Age is an imperfect guide to what we might expect of children "on the witness stand." Moreover, in most of the studies reviewed thus far, the children studied have not been maltreated or from otherwise vulnerable populations, such as children with learning disabilities. As we shall see, these and other sources of individual difference may significantly influence children's memory reports.

Although many factors, demographic, cognitive, and socioemotional, have been investigated (see, for example, Bruck & Melnyk, 2004; Pipe & Salmon, 2002, for reviews), in this section we consider cognitive and socioemotional factors that are likely to have the greatest relevance to the populations of children who present in forensic contexts.

Precursors and sequelae of child maltreatment

In considering the characteristics of children who might be interviewed in forensic settings, it is important to note that there is much overlap in the sequelae of subtypes of maltreatment. This is perhaps unsurprising, as the majority of children experience more than one type (e.g., Azar & Wolfe, 2006; Briere & Elliott, 2003; McMahon, Grant, Compas, Thurm, & Ey, 2003); indeed, childhood physical abuse is a risk factor for sexual abuse (Gladstone Parker, Mitchell, Malhi, Wilhelm, & Austin, 2004). Hence, many children interviewed about their experience of sexual abuse will also manifest the cognitive and emotional sequelae of physical and emotional maltreatment. Some child characteristics may also confer vulnerability. For example, children with intellectual disabilities are more than twice as likely to experience maltreatment of all subtypes (Ford et al., 2003; Kendall-Tackett, Lyon, Taliaferro, & Little, 2005).

Despite preliminary findings suggesting that the chronic stress or trauma induced by maltreatment does not negatively influence children's memory processes (Howe, Cicchetti, & Toth, 2006), it is too soon to conclude that maltreatment has no enduring effects on children's memory performance. Although some children are relatively resilient, many experience significant difficulties that are highly likely to have indirect effects on their recall and reporting of their experiences. One of the very few studies investigating maltreated children's recall of an event found that despite more similarities than differences in their recall, when compared to nonmaltreated children matched with respect to age, gender, and SES status, maltreated children answered fewer questions correctly, provided less complete free recall accounts (particularly young boys), and were less likely to correctly identify a confederate from an array of photographs (Goodman, Bottoms, Rudy, Davis, & Schwartz-Kenney, 2001).

Underlying many of the difficulties in socioemotional and cognitive functioning experienced by many maltreated children are the negative and impoverished interactions between parent and child. As Cicchetti and Toth (2005) note, "maltreating families do not provide many of the experiences that the existing theories of normal development postulate are necessary for facilitating competent adaptation" (p. 414). Compromised functioning can occur with respect to the ability to recognize, express, understand, and regulate emotion (Cicchetti & Toth, 2005; Pollak, Vardi, Bechner, & Curtin, 2005), and maltreated children have been reported to exhibit controlling behavior and role reversal with caregivers and assessors (Stovall-McClough & Cloitre, 2006; Toth, Cicchetti, MacFie, & Emde, 1997). Maltreated children manifest negative representations of the self and, girls, in particular, experience greater shame and less pride (Kim & Cicchetti, 2006; Stuewig & McCloskey, 2005). Difficulties across childhood are evident in the syntactic (less complex language, less advanced vocabulary) and pragmatic (e.g., more repetitive, less self-descriptive) aspects of language development relative to control children matched for socioemotional status and maternal intellectual functioning (Beeghly, 2006; Eigsti & Cicchetti, 2004; McFadyen & Kitson, 1996). These and other developmental difficulties occur in the context of the insecure attachment relationships experienced by the majority of maltreated children and their parent (Toth, Maughan, Manly, Spagnola, & Cicchetti, 2002). Across subtypes, therefore, it is not surprising that maltreated children experience externalizing (conduct problems; inattention and behavioral disinhibition), and internalizing problems (anxiety, PTSD, depression) (McMahon et al., 2003; Saywitz, Mannarino, Berliner, & Cohen, 2000; Wekerle & Wolfe, 2003).

Individual differences and event memory: Research findings

In recent reviews of the influence of individual factors on children's recall and reporting of their experiences, several factors have been consistently implicated; these include intellectual functioning, language and conversation, and attachment (Bruck & Melnyk, 2004; Pipe & Salmon, 2002). In the following section, we review the evidence for each of these factors, and consider the implications for interviewing maltreated children.

Intellectual functioning

A child's intellectual functioning influences all aspects of information processing, including understanding of an experience and the concomitant strength and organization of the event representation as well as the efficiency with which the information may be retrieved (Brown & Pipe, 2003a). Consistent with this premise, the relatively few extant studies have shown that children with an intellectual disability (ID) report less information and are more vulnerable to misleading information on eyewitness memory tasks than are their chronological age (CA) peers, and that this difference is more marked for moderate than mild ID. In contrast, children with an ID can perform similarly to children matched for mental age (MA) (e.g., Gordon, Jens, Hollings, & Watson, 1994; Henry & Gudjonsson, 2003, 2005; Michel, Gordon, Ornstein, & Simpson, 2000), although they do not always. For example, Agnew and Powell (2004) found that, relative to both CA- and MA-matched control groups, children with an ID (aged 9 to 12 years) reported less correct information about a staged event, with less clarity and accuracy, required greater specificity of questioning to elicit information, and were less accurate in their responses. Nonetheless, even children with a moderate ID were able to provide accurate information that could potentially lead to corroborative evidence in a forensic context, and free narrative prompts were effective in eliciting this information.

Very little research has investigated the associations between intellectual functioning and recall in maltreated children. An exception is a study by Eisen, Qin, Goodman, and Davis (2002), who found significant, albeit low, associations in predicted directions between children's performance and their responses to direct questions and errors made when interviewed about a physical examination.

With respect to typically developing children, findings indicate that higher rather than lower IQ is associated with reporting more information (Brown & Pipe, 2003a; Roebers & Schneider, 2001), although there is some evidence that this pattern occurs only when large differences are considered (Roebers & Schneider, 2001). Lower IQ has also been found to be associated with greater suggestibility. The lack of association when IQ is greater than 105 raises the possibility, requiring replication, of a nonlinear association (Gignac & Powell, 2006).

Language

That language ability influences children's memory for and reporting of their experiences is intuitively evident, and despite earlier inconsistencies in findings (e.g., Baker-Ward, Gordon, Ornstein, Larus, & Clubb, 1993; Gordon et al., 1993; Greenhoot, Ornstein, Gordon, & Baker-Ward, 1999), recent studies demonstrate significant associations. For example, having subdivided preschool children according to language skill, Boland, Haden, and Ornstein (2003) found that children in the former group provided more elaborations in their recall of a staged event. The association between language skill and suggestibility is not necessarily straightforward, however. Clarke-Stewart, Malloy, and Allhusen (2004) found that lower language ability was one of three factors that independently predicted 5-year-old children's suggestibility with respect to a visit to the laboratory 9 months previously (see also Burgwyn-Bailes et al., 2001; Imhoff & Baker-Ward, 1999, for related findings). In contrast, Roebers and Schneider (2005) reported that 4-year-old children with better language skill were more vulnerable to misleading information than those with poorer skill, perhaps because they were better able to recall the misleading information.

That, as for intellectual functioning, language might have a greater influence on recall for younger and therefore less linguistically able children is suggested by two recent findings. McGuigan and Salmon (2004) reported that, whereas for 3-year-old children there were significant positive correlations between both expressive and receptive language and total recall of a staged event, for 5-year-olds the relationship held only for expressive language. Similarly, Burgwyn-Bailes et al. (2001) found that increases in receptive language skill were associated with concomitant increases in recall only for younger children in a sample of 3- to 7-year-old children undergoing an invasive medical procedure and interviewed following delays of up to 1 year; for the older children, language was not helpful in predicting recall.

While findings to date do indicate a positive association between language skill and children's recall, gaps in our understanding remain. Most studies have been conducted with very young children and there is a need to include a wider age range in future work. Moreover, no research has yet been conducted with children with specific language impairments, who manifest pragmatic language difficulties in response to adult questioning and constitute between 2% and 8% of preschool-aged children (Beeghly, 2006; Bishop, Chan, Adams, Hartley, & Weir, 2000).

Adult–child conversation

Over and above the influence of language ability, the nature and extent of parent–child discussion about children's experiences is likely to have a significant influence on how they recount their experiences. There is now a convergence of research indicating that conversation between parents and children about the child's experiences shapes children's autobiographical memory and is also a rich source of information about the self and one's own and others' minds and emotions, as well as facilitating language development and emergent literacy (see Carpendale & Lewis, 2004; Fivush, Haden, & Reese, 2006; Wareham & Salmon, 2006, for reviews).

With respect to memory, it is in conversations with their parents that young children learn how to organize their recall and reporting of their personal experiences in narrative form. Much of the research to date has focused on reminiscing between mothers and their young children. Findings show that mothers manifest stable reminiscing styles, differing with respect to the scaffolding provided: high-elaborative mothers engage their children in detailed conversations, expanding and encouraging the child's contribution, whereas, at the other end of a continuum, low-elaborative mothers tend to ask repeated closed questions to elicit an apparently desired response. By age 5 or 6, children have internalized their mother's reminiscing style, including her tendency to use narrative devices such as orienting, temporal, and evaluative information (Fivush et al., 2006; Nelson & Fivush, 2004; Reese, 2002). Peterson et al. (2007) have recently shown that parental style of talking about events was related to young children's memory of an injury requiring outpatient treatment, both soon after and 2 years later.

Experimental and naturalistic paradigms also show an influence of adult–child discussion, either as the experience unfolds or afterwards, with respect to children's recall of a specific event (e.g., Boland et al., 2003; Conroy & Salmon, 2006; Goodman et al., 1997; Haden, Ornstein, Eckerman, & Didow, 2001; McGuigan & Salmon, 2004). Discussion after an event has been shown to have a stronger effect on young children's recall than talk at other times because it effectively reinstates the information in memory, although further research on the relative effects of timing is required (Howe, Courage, & Bryant-Brown, 1993; McGuigan & Salmon, 2004; Ornstein & Haden, 2006).

Reminiscing about an experience does not guarantee that an event will be well recalled over time, however; indeed, in some circumstances, post-event discussion or review can have a negative influence. Specifically, post-event discussion that consistently focuses on some aspects of an experience but not on others can impair memory of the information not discussed. This phenomenon, known as "retrieval induced forgetting (RIF)," has been demonstrated in research with adults and children (e.g., Anderson, 2003; Conroy, 2005; Conroy & Salmon, 2006; MacLeod & Saunders, 2005). In the context of children's recall of their experience, it is conceivable that RIF may occur when parents or evidential interviewers repeatedly ask a child about some aspects of an experience at the expense of others. Scheeringa and Zeanah (2001), for example, described the case of a mother who persistently prompted her child to tell her only certain details of a sexual molestation episode, at the expense of others.

These findings, supported by longitudinal, experimental, and intervention paradigms, have a number of important implications for child witnesses.

First, and most obvious, when the interactions between parent and child have been infrequent and impoverished, the child is likely to have limited ability to recall his or her experiences in an organized and coherent manner, because of limitations in both language and narrative skill. In this regard, Westcott and Kynan (2004) examined videotaped statements of 70 children aged up to 12 years suspected of having been sexually abused, and found that "although, superficially, the accounts adhered to a story structure, they were often incomplete, ambiguous, and disordered to a degree which would impact on understanding" (p. 37) (see also Snow & Powell, 2005).

Further, impoverished discussion between parents and their young children is likely to have implications for their comprehension of other aspects of their experiences – for example, the emotional impact. Shipman and Zeman (1999) observed maltreating mothers and controls in discussions of past emotional events with their children (aged 6 to 12 years). Maltreating mothers were less likely to engage in discussion that included the causes and consequences of emotion, and significant relations were found between maternal discussion and children's emotion understanding skills. Perhaps not surprisingly, relative to their nonmaltreated peers, maltreated children use restricted emotion language and demonstrate less advanced emotion understanding (see Cicchetti & Lynch, 1995, for review).

We note, in passing, that much remains to be understood about the effective elements of maternal reminiscing style for both typical and atypical populations, and their implications for interviewing children in forensic contexts. Interestingly, caregivers of children with an ID used a relatively direct and controlling style with limited use of open-ended questions when asked to discuss a staged past event with their child, and the children in turn provided less information to their parent than to an unknown interviewer (Agnew, Powell, & Snow, 2006). This raises the possibility that, over and above the child's level of intellectual functioning, maternal style of reminiscing contributes to their children's relatively skeletal memory reports. Indeed, it raises the further possibility that some children, because of their particular socialization into conversation, may be more in need, and benefit from techniques such as narrative practice or NET. Researchers have observed considerable variability in children's response to NET, although significant predictors of the variation have generally remained elusive (Brown & Pipe, 2003b). Whether such techniques are more (or indeed, less) useful with children who have had a long history of providing relatively brief responses is an important issue for future research.

Coping strategies

Children's coping strategies during or after an emotionally laden, stressful, or traumatic experience, whether or not they're intentional, may also influence how and how well the child remembers the experience. Effective coping involves the ability to regulate or modulate emotion or arousal, and processes involving the deployment of attention (effortful control) appear to be integral to this (Saarni, Mumme, & Campos, 1998; see Pipe & Salmon, 2002). Although very little research has focused on the influence of specific cognitive strategies on children's recall of their experiences, it is likely that while some forms of coping that involve focusing on the experience may facilitate recall (e.g., cognitive reframing and other forms of self talk), others, such as avoidance, will contribute to poorer recall by precluding its reinstatement in memory. Thus, Conroy, Salmon, and O'Meara (2007) found that children (aged 7 to 12 years) who reported that they avoided emotions, activities, and conversations associated with an emergency hospital visit following injury provided less information in their accounts of the experience than did children who reported using avoidance to a lesser extent. Of course, the coping strategies available to the child are influenced by his or her developmental stage, but by early to middle childhood, with increasing linguistic and metacognitive maturity, children become able to invoke cognitive strategies in addition to the behavioral strategies used by younger children (Compas, Connor-Smith, Saltzman, Thomsen, & Wadsworth, 2001).

Cognitive theories of the development and maintenance of PTSD, bolstered by findings with adults, highlight associations among cognitive avoidance, memory of a traumatic experience, and posttraumatic symptomatology. For example, recent findings show that adults with PTSD provide less coherent and more repetitious, poorly sequenced narratives than do those without, although the findings require replication with children (Jones, Harvey, & Brewin, 2007). Nonetheless, recent research suggests that in children, as in adults (e.g., Halligan, Michael, Clark, & Ehlers, 2003; Jones et al., 2007; Stovall-McClough & Cloitre, 2006), avoidant coping is associated with greater levels of posttraumatic stress, and it is quite possible that a cycle of avoidance and increased symptomatology similarly has negative implications for children's recall (Conroy, 2005; Lengua, Long, & Meltzoff, 2006; Salmon & Bryant, 2002; see also O'Kearney et al., 2007).

Other forms of post-event processing may also influence memory of the kinds of experiences children are interviewed about for forensic purposes (Conroy, 2005). To take one example, rumination, repeatedly focusing on only some aspects of a traumatic event (such as its causes and consequences) and a core feature of depression, may impair an individual's recall of the "non-ruminated on" aspects of an experience or related experiences. For example, in attempting to account for an individual who "remembered" sexual abuse she had disclosed as a child after many years of apparent forgetting, Schooler (1997) suggested that her "exclusive searches for memories of physical abuse may have reduced the accessibility of the memory for sexual abuse" (p. 132). Rumination and avoidance are also associated with an impaired ability to retrieve specific event memories and a tendency, instead, to retrieve "overgeneral" memories (e.g., "I used to do x . . ." rather than "I did x on that day . . .") in both adults and children (Vrielynck, DePlus, & Philippot, 2007; see Williams et al., 2007, for review of research with adults). Cognitive coping strategies such as thought suppression (Wenzlaff & Wegner, 2000) and thought substitution (Anderson & Green, 2001; Hertel & Calcaterra, 2005) are likely to differ in their effects on memory but have received scant experimental focus with children.

Implications

Together, the findings we have reviewed in this section indicate that in establishing rapport and eliciting information from children manifesting the cognitive and emotional sequelae of maltreatment, demands are imposed over and above the effective strategies for developing rapport and eliciting information that we discussed earlier in this chapter. There is limited guidance in the literature on strategies that might engage children who have difficulty cooperating during the interview. As Lyon and Saywitz (2006) note, "efforts to develop rapport in child studies are cursory interchanges that are not designed to overcome high levels of fear or inordinate concerns about safety, trust, embarrassment, or betrayal" (p. 844). The clinical literature can point to some potentially useful strategies, but these require empirical evaluation in studies involving maltreated participants.

For example, for all children but particularly those whose demeanor during the interview is characterized by attempts to control the interviewer, non-compliance, distractibility associated with ADHD, PTSD, and/or misinterpretation of neutral cues in favor of threat, and a desire to avoid the high levels of anxiety associated with discussion of traumatic experiences, the behavioral principles from the parent training literature are likely to be helpful. These include assertive language to communicate clear and specific instructions (even at a very specific level such as asking the child to keep his or her feet on the floor (Prifitera, Saklofske, & Weiss, 2005)); use of encouragers accompanied by immediate and descriptive praise (e.g., "you're thinking really hard about my questions – that's great"); and brief planned ignoring for inappropriate but nonharmful behaviors (e.g., Dadds & Hawes, 2006). Permitting the child to make decisions such as where to sit, when to take a break, and what to discuss first may serve to circumvent a cycle whereby interviewer and child attempt to control the behavior of the other, or may help decrease the child's avoidance. Excessive feelings of shame, likely to be accompanied by low mood, may also be attenuated if the young person is provided with the opportunity to sit beside rather than opposite the adult, reducing "the intrusion of the interviewer into the child's world" (Steward & Steward, 1996, p. 33). A similar function may be served by empathic comments that normalize feelings of ambivalence (e.g., "people often have mixed feelings – part of you wants to talk about something and part doesn't") (Lyon & Saywitz, 2006, p. 844).

With respect to eliciting the child's account, taking particular care to ensure that the language used by the interviewer is developmentally appropriate will optimize the likelihood that the message received by the child and that intended by the adult are congruent. In this regard, Imhoff and Baker-Ward (1999) showed that simple strategies such as using short and unambiguous sentences and indicating topic changes by transitional statements reduced 3.5-year-old children's suggestibility. Other findings also suggest that some interview conditions may moderate the effect of language and intellectual functioning. For example, Brown and Pipe (2003a) reported that the differences in recall between low and high IQ groups (less or more than 100, WISC-short form) disappeared when children were interviewed using the Narrative Elaboration Technique (Saywitz & Snyder, 1996; see also Salmon, Roncolato, & Gleitzman, 2003).

CONCLUDING COMMENTS

The foregoing review, while far from exhaustive, illustrates the healthy discourse that is now well established between researchers pursuing more theoretically driven questions about memory development, and those whose concerns focus on the real-world context of forensic investigations involving children. We have known for some time that simple conclusions about whether or at what age children are likely to make reliable informants are untenable. As our review illustrates, our understanding of the range of variables (and the interactions among them) that determine just how accurate and informative a child will be when interviewed, has increased dramatically during the last three decades. Yet our understanding of the complexities of children's memory in the real world of the forensic investigation is by no means complete, and many questions of practical importance remain. There is every reason to be optimistic that the productive dialog between memory researchers and those in the field will continue.

NOTE

1   Tom Lyon first brought this case to our attention as part of a joint presentation (Lyon, Pipe, Stewart, & Steele, 2005).

REFERENCES

Agnew, S. E., & Powell, M. B. (2004). The effect of intellectual disability on children's recall of an event across different question types. *Law and Human Behavior, 28,* 273–294.
Agnew, S. E., Powell, M. B., & Snow, P. C. (2006). An examination of the questioning styles of police officers and caregivers when interviewing children with intellectual disabilities. *Legal and Criminological Psychology, 11,* 35–53.
Aldridge, J., Lamb, M. E., Sternberg, K. J., Orbach, Y., Esplin, P. W., & Bowler, L. (2004). Using a human figure drawing to elicit information from alleged victims

of child sexual abuse. *Journal of Consulting and Clinical Psychology*, *72*, 304–316.

American Professional Society on the Abuse of Children. (1990, 1997, 2002). *Guidelines for psychosocial evaluation of suspected sexual abuse in young children* (Rev. ed.). Chicago, IL: APSAC.

Anderson, M. C. (2003). Rethinking interference theory: Executive control and the mechanisms of forgetting. *Journal of Memory and Language*, *49*(4), 415–445.

Anderson, M. C., & Green, C. (2001). Suppressing unwanted memories by executive control. *Nature*, *410*, 366–369.

Azar, S. T., & Wolfe, D. A. (2006). Child physical abuse and neglect. In E. J. Mash and R. A. Barkley (Eds.), *Treatment of childhood disorders* (3rd ed., pp. 595–646). New York: Guilford Press.

Baker-Ward, L., Gordon, B. N., Ornstein, P. A., Larus, D. M., & Clubb, P. A. (1993). Young children's long-term retention of a pediatric examination. *Child Development*, *64*, 1519–1533.

Beeghly, M. (2006). Translational research on early language development: Current challenges and future directions. *Development and Psychopathology*, *18*, 737–757.

Bidrose, S., & Goodman, G. S. (2000). Testimony and evidence: A scientific case study of memory for child sexual abuse. *Applied Cognitive Psychology*, *14*(3), 197–213.

Binet, A. (1900). *La suggestibilite*. Paris: Schleicher Freres.

Bishop, D. V. M., Chan, J., Adams, C., Hartley, J., & Weir, F. (2000). Conversational responsiveness in specific language impairment: Evidence of disproportionate pragmatic difficulties in a subset of children. *Development and Psychopathology*, *12*, 177–199.

Boland, A. M., Haden, C. A., & Ornstein, P. A. (2003). Boosting children's memory by training mothers in the use of an elaborative conversational style as an event unfolds. *Journal of Cognition and Development*, *4*, 39–65.

Bowen, C. J., & Howie, P. M. (2002). Context and cue cards in young children's testimony: A comparison brief narrative elaboration and context reinstatement. *Journal of Applied Psychology*, *87*, 1077–1085.

Brennan, K. H., & Fisher, R. P. (1998). *Drawing as a technique to facilitate children's recall*. Unpublished manuscript.

Briere, J., & Elliott, D. M. (2003). Prevalence and psychological sequelae of self-reported childhood physical and sexual abuse in a general population sample of men and women. *Child Abuse and Neglect*, *27*, 1205–1222.

Brown, A. L., & French, L. A. (1976). Construction and regeneration of logical sequences using causes or consequences as the point of departure. *Child Development*, *47*, 930–940.

Brown, D., & Pipe, M.-E. (2003a). Individual differences in children's event memory reports and the narrative elaboration technique. *Journal of Applied Psychology*, *88*, 195–206.

Brown, D., & Pipe, M.-E. (2003b). Variations on a technique: Enhancing children's recall using narrative elaboration training. *Applied Cognitive Psychology*, *17*, 377–399.

Brown, D. A., Pipe, M.-E., Lewis, C., Lamb, M., & Orbach, Y. (2007). Supportive or suggestive: Do human figure drawings help 5- to 7-year-old children to report touch? *Journal of Consulting and Clinical Psychology*, *75*, 33–42.

Bruck, M., & Ceci, S. J. (1999). The suggestibility of children's memory. *Annual Review of Psychology, 50*, 419–439.

Bruck, M., Ceci, S. J., & Francouer, E. (2000). Children's use of anatomically detailed dolls to report genital touching in a medical examination: Developmental and gender comparisons. *Journal of Experimental Psychology: Applied, 6*(1), 74–83.

Bruck, M., Ceci, S. J., Francouer, E., & Renick, A. (1995). Anatomically detailed dolls do not facilitate preschoolers' reports of a pediatric examination involving genital touching. *Journal of Experimental Psychology: Applied, 1*, 95–109.

Bruck, M., Ceci, S. J., & Principe, G. (2006). The child and the law. In K. Anne Reninger & R. Lerner (Eds.), *Handbook of child psychology* (Vol. 4, 6th ed.). New York: Wiley.

Bruck, M., & Melnyk, L. (2004). Individual differences in children's suggestibility: A review and synthesis. *Applied Cognitive Psychology, 18*, 947–996.

Bruck, M., Melnyk, L., & Ceci, S. J. (2000). Draw it again Sam: The effect of drawing on children's suggestibility and source monitoring ability. *Journal of Experimental Child Psychology, 77*, 169–196.

Burgwyn-Bailes, E., Baker-Ward, L., Gordon, B. N., & Ornstein, P. A. (2001). Children's memory for emergency medical treatment after one year: The impact of individual difference variables on recall and suggestibility. *Applied Cognitive Psychology, 15*, S25–S48.

Burkitt, E., Barrett, M., & Davis, A. (2003). Children's colour choices for completing drawings of affectively characterised topics. *Journal of Child Psychology and Psychiatry, 44*, 445–455.

Butler, S., Gross, J., & Hayne, H. (1995). The effect of drawing on memory performance in young children. *Developmental Psychology, 31*, 597–608.

Camparo, L. B., Wagner, J. T., & Saywitz, K. J. (2001). Interviewing children about real and fictitious events: Revisiting the narrative elaboration procedure. *Law and Human Behavior, 25*, 63–80.

Carpendale, J. I. M., & Lewis, C. (2004). Constructing an understanding of mind: The development of children's social understanding within social interaction. *Behavioral and Brain Sciences, 27*, 79–151.

Cassel, W. S., Roebers, C. E. M., & Bjorklund, D. F. (1996). Developmental patterns of eyewitness responses to repeated and increasingly suggested questions. *Journal of Experimental Child Psychology, 61*, 116–133.

Ceci, S. J., & Bruck, M. (1993). Suggestibility of the child witness: A historical review and synthesis. *Psychological Bulletin, 113*, 403–439.

Cederborg, A. C., Lamb, M. E., & Laurel, O. (2007). Delay of disclosure, minimization, and denial of abuse when the evidence is unambiguous: A multivictim case. In M.-E. Pipe, M. E. Lamb, Y. Orbach, & A.-C. Cederborg (Eds.), *Child sexual abuse: Disclosure, delay and denial* (pp. 159–173). Mahwah, NJ: Lawrence Erlbaum Associates, Inc.

Chaffin, M. (2006). The changing focus of child maltreatment research and practice within psychology. *Journal of Social Issues, 62*(4), 663–684.

Cicchetti, D., & Lynch, M. (1995). Failures in expectable environment and their impact on individual development: The case of child maltreatment. In D. Cicchetti & D. Cohen (Eds.), *Developmental psychopathology* (Vol. 2, pp. 32–71). New York: John Wiley and Sons.

Cicchetti, D., & Toth, S. L. (2005). Child maltreatment. *Annual Review of Clinical Psychology, 1*, 409–438.

Clarke-Stewart, K. A., Malloy, L. C., & Allhusen, V. D. (2004). Verbal ability, self-control, and close relationships with parents protect children against misleading suggestions. *Applied Cognitive Psychology, 18*, 1037–1058.

Cole, W. E., & Loftus, E. F. (1987). Incorporating new information into memory. *American Journal of Psychology, 92*(3), 413–425.

Compas, B. E., Connor-Smith, J. K., Saltzman, H., Thomsen, A. H., & Wadsworth, E. (2001). Coping with stress during childhood and adolescence: Problems, progress, and potential in theory and research. *Psychological Bulletin, 127*, 87–127.

Connolly, D. A., & Lindsay, D. S. (2001). The influence of suggestions on children's reports of a unique experience versus an instance of a repeated experience. *Applied Cognitive Psychology, 15*, 205–223.

Conroy, R. (2005). *Post-event processing and children's memory for traumatic events.* Unpublished doctoral dissertation, University of New South Wales, Sydney, Australia.

Conroy, R., & Salmon, K. (2006). Talking about parts of a past experience: The influence of elaborative discussion and event structure on children's recall of nondiscussed information. *Journal of Experimental Child Psychology, 95*, 278–297.

Conroy, R., Salmon, K., & O'Meara, M. (2007). *Attachment, avoidance, and children's recall of a stressful medical experience.* Manuscript in preparation.

Cordón, I. M., Pipe, M.-E., Sayfan, L., Melinder, A., & Goodman, G. S. (2004). Memory for traumatic experiences in early childhood. *Developmental Review, 24*, 101–132.

CornerHouse Interagency Child Abuse Evaluation and Training Center. (1990). *Child sexual abuse forensic interview training manual.* Minneapolis, MN: Author.

CornerHouse Interagency Child Abuse Evaluation and Training Center. (2003). *Child sexual abuse forensic interview training manual.* Minneapolis, MN: Author.

Dadds, M. R., & Hawes, D. (2006). *Integrated family intervention for child conduct problems: A behaviour attachment systems intervention for parents.* Sydney: Australian Academic Press.

Dale, P. S., Loftus, E. F., & Rathbun, L. (1978). The influence of the form of the question of the eyewitness testimony of preschool children. *Journal of Psycholinguistic Research, 74*, 269–277.

DeLoache, J. S. (2004). Scale errors by very young children: A dissociation between action planning and control. *Behavioral and Brain Sciences, 27*, 32–33.

DeLoache, J. S., & Burns, N. M. (1993). Symbolic development in young children: Understanding models and pictures. In C. Pratt & A. F. Garton (Eds.), *Systems of representation in children: Development and use* (pp. 91–112). Chichester: John Wiley & Sons.

DeLoache, J. S., & Marzolf, D. P. (1995). The use of dolls to interview young children: Issues of symbolic representation. *Journal of Experimental Child Psychology, 60*, 155–173.

Dent, H. R. (1982). The effects of interviewing strategies on the results of interviews with child witnesses. In A. Trankell (Ed.), *Reconstructing the past: The role of psychologists in criminal trials* (pp. 279–297). Stockholm: Norstedt.

Dent, H. R. (1986). Experimental study of the effectiveness of different techniques of questioning mentally handicapped child witnesses. *British Journal of Clinical Psychology, 25*, 13–17.

Dent, H. R., & Stephenson, G. M. (1979). An experimental study of the effectiveness of different techniques of questioning child witnesses. *British Journal of Social and Clinical Psychology*, *18*, 41–51.

Droit-Volet, S., Clement, A., & Wearden, J. (2001). Temporal generalizations in 3- to 8-year-old children. *Journal of Experimental Child Psychology*, *80*, 271–288.

Dunn, J., O'Connor, T. G., & Levy, I. (2002). Out of the picture: A study of family drawings by children from step-, single-parent and non-step families. *Journal of Clinical Child and Adolescent Psychology*, *31*, 505–512.

Eigsti, I., & Cicchetti, D. (2004). The impact of child maltreatment on expressive syntax at 60 months. *Developmental Science*, *7*, 88–102.

Eisen, M. L., Qin, J., Goodman, G. S., & Davis, S. L. (2002). Memory and suggestibility in maltreated children: Age, stress arousal, dissociation, and psychopathology. *Journal of Experimental Child Psychology*, *83*, 167–212.

Evans, A. D., Roberts, K. P., & Beaupre, J. (2007, March). Testing the effects of paraphrasing on children's event reports. In paper presented in the symposium: The Effects of the Spacing of Events and the Timing of Retrieval on Children's Event Memory and Source Monitoring (K. L. Thierry & K. P. Roberts, organizers) at the biennial meeting of the Society for Research on Child Development, Boston, MA.

Everson, M. D., & Boat, B. W. (2002). The utility of anatomical dolls and drawings in child forensic interviews. In M. L. Eisen, J. A. Quas, & G. S. Goodman (Eds.), *Memory and suggestibility in the forensic interview* (pp. 383–408). Mahwah, NJ: Lawrence Erlbaum Associates, Inc.

Farrar, M. J., & Goodman, G. S. (1990). Developmental differences in the relation between scripts and episodic memory: Do they exist? In R. Fivush & J. A. Hudson (Eds.), *Emory symposia in cognition: Vol. 3. Knowing and remembering in young children* (pp. 30–64). New York: Cambridge University Press.

Farrar, M. J., & Goodman, G. S. (1992). Developmental changes in event memory. *Child Development*, *63*, 173–187.

Fisher, R. P., & Geiselman, R. E. (1992). *Memory-enhancing techniques for investigating interviewing: The cognitive interview*. Springfield, IL: Charles C. Thomas.

Fivush, R. (1997). Event memory in early childhood. In C. Nelson (Ed.), *The development of memory in childhood. Studies in developmental psychology* (pp. 139–161). Hove, UK: Psychology Press.

Fivush, R. (2004). The silenced self: Constructing self from memories spoken and unspoken. In D. Beike, J. Lampinen, & D. Behrand (Eds.), *The self and memory*. Hove, UK: Psychology Press.

Fivush, R., & Haden, C. A. (1997). Narrating and representing experience: Preschoolers' developing autobiographical accounts. In P. W. van den Broek, P. J. Bauer & T. Bourg (Eds.), *Developmental spans in event comprehension and representation: Bridging fictional and actual events* (pp. 169–198). Mahwah, NJ: Lawrence Erlbaum Associates, Inc.

Fivush, R., Haden, C., & Reese, E. (2006). Elaborating on elaborations: The role of maternal reminiscing style in cognitive and socioemotional development. *Child Development*, *77*, 1568–1588.

Fivush, R., Kuebli, J., & Clubb, P. A. (1992). The structure of events and event representations: A developmental analysis. *Child Development*, *63*, 188–201.

Fivush, R., Pipe, M.-E., Murachver, T., & Reese, E. (1997). Events spoken and unspoken: Implications of language and memory development for the recovered memory debate. In M. A. Conway (Ed.), *Recovered memories and false memories. Debates in psychology* (pp. 34–62). Oxford: Oxford University Press.

Fivush, R., Sales, J. M., Goldberg, A., Bahrick, L., & Parker, J. (2004). Weathering the storm: Children's long-term recall of Hurricane Andrew. *Memory*, *12*, 104–118.

Fivush, R., & Schwarzmueller, A. (1998). Children remember childhood: Implications for childhood amnesia. *Applied Cognitive Psychology*, *12*, 455–473.

Flin, R., Boon, J., Knox, A., & Bull, R. (1992). The effect of a five month delay on children's and adults' eyewitness memory. *British Journal of Psychology*, *83*, 323–336.

Ford, J. D., Racusin, R., Ellis, C. G., Daviss, W. B., Reiser, J., Fleischer, M., et al. (2000). Child maltreatment, other trauma exposure, and posttraumatic symptomatology among children with oppositional defiant and attention deficit hyperactivity disorder. *Child Maltreatment*, *5*, 205–217.

Friedman, W. J. (1978). Development of time concepts in children. In H. W. Reese & L. P. Lipsitt (Eds.), *Advances in child development and behavior* (Vol. 12, pp. 267–298). New York: Academic Press.

Friedman, W. J. (1992). Children's time memory: The development of a differentiated past. *Cognitive Development*, *7*, 171–187.

Gee, S., Gregory, M., & Pipe, M.-E. (1999). "What colour is your pet dinosaur?" The impact of pre-interview training and question type on children's answers. *Legal and Criminological Psychology*, *4*, 111–128.

Gee, S., & Pipe, M.-E. (1995). Helping children to remember: The influence of object cues on children's accounts of a real event. *Developmental Psychology*, *31*, 746–758.

Geiselman, R. E., & Padilla, J. (1988). Cognitive interviewing with child witnesses. *Journal of Police Science and Administration*, *16*, 236–242.

Gignac, G. E., & Powell, M. B. (2006). A direct examination of the nonlinear (quadratic) association between intelligence and suggestibility in children. *Applied Cognitive Psychology*, *20*, 617–623.

Gladstone, G. L., Parker, G. B., Mitchell, P. B., Malhi, G. S., Wilhelm, K., & Austin, M. (2004). Implications of childhood trauma for depressed women: An analysis of pathways from childhood sexual abuse to deliberate self-harm and revictimization. *American Journal of Psychiatry*, *161*, 1417–1425.

Gobbo, C., Mega, C., & Pipe, M.-E. (2002). Does the nature of the experience influence children's suggestibility? A study of children's event memory. *Journal of Experimental Child Psychology*, *81*, 502–530.

Goodman, G. S. (1984). Children's testimony in historical perspective. *Journal of Social Issues*, *40*(2), 9–31.

Goodman, G. S. (2006). Children's eyewitness memory: A modern history and contemporary commentary. *Journal of Social Issues*, *62*, 811–832.

Goodman, G. S., & Aman, C. (1990). Children's use of anatomically detailed dolls to recount an event. *Child Development*, *61*, 1859–1871.

Goodman, G. S., Batterman-Faunce, J. M., Schaaf, J. M., & Kenney, R. (2002). Nearly 4 years after an event: Children's eyewitness memory and adults' perceptions of children's accuracy. *Child Abuse and Neglect*, *26*, 849–884.

Goodman, G. S., Bottoms, B. L., Rudy, L., Davis, S. L., & Schwartz-Kenney, B. M. (2001). Effects of past abuse experiences on children's eyewitness memory. *Law and Human Behavior*, *25*, 269–298.

Goodman, G. S., Hirschman, J., Hepps, D., & Rudy, L. (1991). Children's memory for stressful events. *Merrill-Palmer Quarterly*, *37*, 109–158.

Goodman, G. S., Quas, J. A., Batterman-Faunce, J. M., Riddlesberger, M. M., &

Kuhn, J. (1994). Predictors of accurate and inaccurate memories of traumatic events experienced in childhood. *Consciousness and Cognition, 3*, 269–294.

Goodman, G. S., Quas, J. A., Batterman-Faunce, J. M., Riddlesberger, M. M., & Kuhn, J. (1997). Children's reactions to and memory for a stressful event: Influences of age, anatomical dolls, knowledge, and parental attachment. *Applied Developmental Science, 1*, 54–75.

Goodman, G. S., & Reed, D. S. (1986). Age differences in eyewitness testimony. *Law and Human Behavior, 10*, 317–332.

Gordon, B. N., Jens, K. G., Hollings, R., & Watson, T. E. (1994). Remembering activities performed versus those imagined: Implications for testimony of children with mental retardation. *Journal of Clinical Child Psychology, 23*, 239–248.

Gordon, B. N., Ornstein, P. A., Nida, R. E., Follmer, A., Crenshaw, M. C., & Albert, G. (1993). Does the use of dolls facilitate children's memory of visits to the doctor? *Applied Cognitive Psychology, 7*, 459–474.

Greenhoot, A. F., Ornstein, P. A., Gordon, B. N., & Baker-Ward, L. (1999). Acting out the details of a pediatric check-up: The impact of interview condition and behavioral style on children's memory reports. *Child Development, 70*, 363–380.

Greenstock, J., & Pipe, M.-E. (1996). Interviewing children about past events: The influence of peer support and misleading questions. *Child Abuse and Neglect, 20*, 69–80.

Gross, J., & Hayne, H. (1998). Drawing facilitates children's verbal reports of emotionally laden events. *Journal of Experimental Psychology: Applied, 4*, 163–179.

Haden, C. A., Ornstein, P. A., Eckerman, C. O., & Didow, S. M. (2001). Mother–child conversational interactions as events unfold: Linkages to subsequent remembering. *Child Development, 72*(4), 1016–1031.

Halligan, S. L., Michael, T., Clark, D. M., & Ehlers, A. (2003). Posttraumatic stress disorder following assault: The role of cognitive processing, trauma memory, and appraisals. *Journal of Consulting and Clinical Psychology, 71*, 419–431.

Henkel, L. A. (2004). Erroneous memories arising from repeated attempts to remember. *Journal of Memory and Language, 50*, 26–46.

Henry, L. A., & Gudjonsson, G. H. (2003). Eyewitness memory, suggestibility, and repeated recall sessions in children with mild and moderate intellectual disabilities. *Law and Human Behavior, 27*, 481–505.

Henry, L. A., & Gudjonsson, G. L. (2005). The effects of memory trace strength on eyewitness recall in children with and without intellectual disabilities. *Journal of Experimental Child Psychology, 98*, 53–71.

Hershkowitz, I., Orbach, Y., Lamb, M. E., Sternberg, K. J., & Horowitz, D. (2001). The effects of mental context reinstatement on children's accounts of sexual abuse. *Applied Cognitive Psychology, 15*, 235–248.

Hershkowitz, I., Orbach, Y., Lamb, M. E., Sternberg, K. J., Horowitz, D., & Hovav, M. (1998). Visiting the scene of the crime: Effects on children's recall of alleged abuse. *Legal and Criminological Psychology, 3*, 195–207.

Hertel, P. T., & Calcaterra, G. (2005). Intentional forgetting benefits from thought substitution. *Psychonomic Bulletin and Review, 12*, 484–489.

Home Office. (2002). *Achieving best evidence in criminal proceedings: Guidance for vulnerable or intimidated witnesses, including children.* London: Home Office.

Howe, M. L. (1997). Children's memory for traumatic experiences. *Learning and Individual Differences, 9*, 153–174.

Howe, M. L., Cicchetti, D., & Toth, S. (2006). Children's basic memory processes, stress, and maltreatment. *Development and Psychopathology, 18*, 759–769.

Howe, M. L., Courage, M. L., & Bryant-Brown, L. (1993). Reinstating preschoolers' memories. *Developmental Psychology, 29*, 854–869.

Howe, M. L., Courage, M. L., & Peterson, C. (1994). How can I remember when "I" wasn't there: Long-term retention of traumatic experiences and emergence of the cognitive self. *Consciousness and Cognition, 3*, 327–355.

Howe, M. L., Courage, M. L., & Peterson, C. (1996). How can I remember when "I" wasn't there: Long-term retention of traumatic experiences and emergence of the cognitive self. In K. Pezdek & W. P. Banks (Eds.), *The recovered memory/false memory debate* (pp. 121–149). San Diego, CA: Academic Press.

Howie, P., Sheehan, M., Mojarrad, T., & Wrzesinska, M. (2004). Undesirable and desirable shifts in children's responses to repeated questions: Age differences in the effect of providing a rationale for repetition. *Applied Cognitive Psychology, 18*, 1161–1180.

Hudson, J. A. (1990). Constructive processing in children's event memory. *Developmental Psychology, 26*, 180–187.

Hudson, J. A., & Fivush, R. (1991). As time goes by: Sixth graders remember a kindergarten experience. *Applied Cognitive Psychology, 5*, 347–360.

Hutcheson, G. D., Baxter, J. S., Telfer, K., & Warden, D. (1995). Child witness statement quality: Question type and errors of omission. *Law and Human Behavior, 19*, 631–648.

Imhoff, M. C., & Baker-Ward, L. (1999). Preschoolers' suggestibility: Effects of developmentally appropriate language and interviewer supportiveness. *Journal of Applied Developmental Psychology, 20*, 407–429.

Johnson, M. K., & Foley, M. A. (1984). Differentiating fact from fantasy: The reliability of children's memory. *Journal of Social Issues, 40*, 33–50.

Jones, C., Harvey, A. G., & Brewin, C. R. (2007). The organisation and content of trauma memories in survivors of road traffic accidents. *Behaviour Research and Therapy, 45*, 151–162.

Jones, C. H., & Pipe, M.-E. (2002). How quickly do children forget events? A systematic study of children's event reports as a function of delay. *Applied Cognitive Psychology, 16*, 755–768.

Kendall-Tackett, K., Lyon, T., Taliaferro, G., & Little, L. (2005). Why child maltreatment researchers should include children's disability status in their maltreatment studies. *Child Abuse and Neglect, 29*, 147–151.

Kim, J., & Cicchetti, D. (2006). Longitudinal trajectories of self-system processes and depressive symptoms among maltreated and nonmaltreated children. *Child Development, 77*, 624–639.

King, M. A., & Yuille, J. C. (1987). Suggestibility and the child witness. In S. J. Ceci, D. F. Ross, & M. P. Toglia (Eds.), *Children's eyewitness memory* (pp. 24–35). New York: Springer-Verlag.

Köhnken, G., Milne, R., Memon, A., & Bull, R. (1999). The cognitive interview: A meta-analysis. *Psychology, Crime and Law, 5*, 3–27.

Koocher, G. P., Goodman, G. S., White, C. S., Friedrich, W. N., Sivan, A. B., & Reynolds, C. R. (1995). Psychological science and the use of anatomically detailed dolls in child sexual-abuse assessments. *Psychological Bulletin, 118*, 199–222.

La Rooy, D., Pipe, M.-E., & Murray, J. E. (2005). Reminiscence and hypermnesia in children's eyewitness memory. *Journal of Experimental Child Psychology, 90,* 235–254.

Lamb, M. E., & Fauchier, A. (2001). The effects of question type on self-contradiction by children in the course of forensic interviews. *Applied Cognitive Development, 15,* 483–491.

Lamb, M. E., Orbach, Y., Hershkowitz, I., Horowitz, D., & Abbott, C. B. (2006). Does the type of prompt affect the accuracy of information provided by alleged victims of abuse in forensic interviews? *Applied Cognitive Psychology, 20,* 1–14.

Lamb, M. E., Sternberg, K. J., & Esplin, P. W. (2000). Effects of age and delay on the amount of information provided by alleged sexual abuse victims in investigative interviews. *Child Development, 71,* 1589–1596.

Lamb, M. E., Sternberg, K. J., Orbach, Y., Esplin, P. W., Stewart, H., & Mitchell, S. (2003). Age differences in young children's responses to open-ended invitations in the course of forensic interviews. *Journal of Consulting and Clinical Psychology, 71,* 926–934.

Leichtman, M. D., & Ceci, S. J. (1995). The effects of stereotypes and suggestions on preschoolers' reports. *Developmental Psychology, 31,* 568–578.

Lengua, L. J., Long, A. C., & Meltzoff, A. N. (2006). Pre-attack stress-load, appraisals, and coping in children's responses to the 9/11 terrorist attacks. *Journal of Child Psychology and Psychiatry, 47,* 1219–1227.

Lieppe, M. R., Romanczyk, A., & Manion, A. P. (1991). Eyewitness memory for a touching experience: Accuracy differences between child and adult witnesses. *Journal of Applied Psychology, 76*(3), 367–379.

London, K., Bruck, M., Ceci, S. J., & Shuman, D. W. (2005). Disclosure of child sexual abuse: What does the research tell us about the ways that children tell? *Psychology, Public Policy, and Law, 11,* 194–196.

London, K., Bruck, M., Ceci, S. J., & Shuman, D. W. (2007). Disclosure of child sexual abuse: A review of the contemporary empirical literature. In M.-E. Pipe, M. E. Lamb, Y. Orbach, & A.-C. Cederborg (Eds.), *Child sexual abuse: Disclosure, delay and denial.* Mahwah, NJ: Lawrence Erlbaum Associates, Inc.

Lyon, T. D. (2007). False denials: Overcoming methodological biases in abuse disclosure research. In M.-E. Pipe, M. E. Lamb, Y. Orbach, & A.-C. Cederborg (Eds.), *Child sexual abuse: Disclosure, delay and denial* (pp. 41–62). Mahwah, NJ: Lawrence Erlbaum Associates, Inc.

Lyon, T. D., Pipe, M.-E., Stewart, H., & Steele, L. (2005). *Interviewing children about maltreatment.* Full day workshop presented at the National Symposium on Child Abuse, Huntsville, AL.

Lyon, T. D., & Saywitz, K. J. (2006). From post-mortem to preventive medicine: Next steps for research on child witnesses. *Journal of Social Issues, 62,* 833–861.

MacLeod, M. D., & Saunders, J. (2005). The role of inhibitory control in the production of misinformation effects. *Journal of Experimental Psychology: Learning, Memory and Cognition, 31,* 964–979.

Mandler, J. M., & Stein, N. L. (1974). Recall and recognition of pictures by children as a function of organization and distractor similarity. *Journal of Experimental Psychology, 102*(4), 657–669.

Marin, B. V., Holmes, D. L., Guth, M., & Kovac, P. (1979). The potential of children as eyewitnesses. *Law and Human Behavior, 3,* 295–305.

McCormack, T., Brown, G. D. A., Smith, M. C., & Brock, J. (2004). A timing-specific memory distortion effect in young children. *Journal of Experimental Child Psychology*, *87*, 33–56.

McFadyen, R. G. & Kitson, W. J. H. (1996). Language comprehension and expression among adolescents who have experienced childhood physical abuse. *Journal of Child Psychology and Psychiatry*, *37*, 551–562.

McGuigan, F., & Salmon, K. (2004). The time to talk: The influence of adult–child talk on children's event memory. *Child Development*, *75*, 669–686.

McMahon, S. D., Grant, K. E., Compas, B. E., Thurm, A. E., & Ey, S. (2003). Stress and psychopathology in children and adolescence: Is there evidence of specificity? *Journal of Child Psychology and Psychiatry*, *44*, 107–133.

McNichol, S., Shute, R., & Tucker, A. (1999). Children's eyewitness memory for a repeated event. *Child Abuse and Neglect*, *23*, 1127–1139.

Memon, A., Cronin, O., Eaves, R., & Bull, R. (1993). The cognitive interview and child witnesses. *Issues in Criminological and Legal Psychology*, *20*, 3–9.

Merritt, K. A., Ornstein, P. A., & Spicker, B. (1994). Children's memory for a salient medical procedure: Implications for testimony. *Pediatrics*, *94*, 17–23.

Michel, M. K., Gordon, B. N., Ornstein, P. A., & Simpson, M. A. (2000). The abilities of children with mental retardation to remember personal experiences: Implications for testimony. *Journal of Clinical Child Psychology*, *29*, 453–463.

Murachver, T., Pipe, M.-E., Gordon, R., Fivush, R., & Owens, J. L. (1996). Do, show, and tell: Children's event memories acquired through direct experience, observation, and stories. *Child Development*, *67*, 3029–3044.

Myles-Worsley, M., Cromer, C., & Dodd, D. (1986). Children's preschool script reconstruction: Reliance on general knowledge as memory fades. *Developmental Psychology*, *22*, 2–30.

Nelson, K., & Fivush, R. (2004). The emergence of autobiographical memory: A social cultural developmental theory. *Psychological Review*, *111*, 486–511.

Nigro, G. N., & Wolpow, S. I. (2004). Interviewing young children with props: Prior experience matters. *Applied Cognitive Psychology*, *18*, 549–565.

Oates, K., & Shrimpton, S. (1991). Children's memories for stressful and non-stressful events. *Medical Science and Law*, *31*, 4–10.

O'Kearney, R., Speyer, J., & Kenardy, J. (2007). Children's narrative memory for accidents and their post-traumatic distress. *Applied Cognitive Psychology*, *21*(7), 821–838.

Orbach, Y., Hershkowitz, I., Lamb, M. E., Sternberg, K. J., Esplin, P. W., & Horowitz, D. (2000). Assessing the value of structured protocols for forensic interviews of alleged child abuse victims. *Child Abuse and Neglect*, *24*, 733–752.

Orbach, Y., Hershkowitz, I., Lamb, M. E., Sternberg, K. J., & Horowitz, D. (2000). Interviewing at the scene of the crime: Effects on children's recall of alleged abuse. *Legal and Criminological Psychology*, *5*, 135–147.

Orbach, Y., & Lamb, M. E. (1999). Assessing the accuracy of a child's account of sexual abuse: A case study. *Child Abuse and Neglect*, *23*, 91–98.

Orbach, Y., & Lamb, M. E. (2000). Enhancing children's narratives in investigative interviews. *Child Abuse and Neglect*, *24*, 1631–1648.

Orbach, Y., & Lamb, M. E. (2001). The relationship between within-interview contradictions and eliciting interviewer utterances. *Child Abuse and Neglect*, *25*, 323–333.

Orbach, Y., & Lamb, M. E. (2007). Young children's references to temporal attributes of allegedly experienced events in the course of forensic interviews. *Child Development, 78,* 1100–1120.

Ornstein, P. A., Baker-Ward, L., Gordon, B. N., & Merritt, K. A. (1997). Children's memory for medical experiences: Implications for testimony. *Applied Cognitive Psychology, 11,* S87–S104.

Ornstein, P. A., & Haden, C. A. (2006, July). *Adult–child conversational interactions and the development of children's mnemonic skills.* Paper presented at the Fourth International Conference on Memory, Sydney, Australia.

Peters, W. W., & Nunez, N. (1999). Complex language and comprehension monitoring: Teaching child witnesses to recognize linguistic confusion. *Journal of Applied Psychology, 84,* 661–669.

Peterson, C. (1999). Children's memory for medical emergencies: 2 years later. *Developmental Psychology, 35,* 1493–1506.

Peterson, C., & Bell, M. (1996). Children's memory for traumatic injury. *Child Development, 67,* 3045–3070.

Peterson, C., Dowden, C., & Tobin, J. (1999). Interviewing preschoolers: Comparisons of yes/no and wh- questions. *Law and Human Behavior, 23,* 539–555.

Peterson, C., McDermott Sales, J., Rees, M., & Fivush, R. (2007). Parent–child talk and children's memory for stressful events. *Applied Cognitive Psychology, 21*(8), 1057–1075.

Peterson, C., & Whalen, N. (2001). Five years later: Children's memory for medical emergencies. *Applied Cognitive Psychology, 15,* S7–S24.

Pipe, M.-E., Gee, S. J., Wilson, J. C., & Egerton, J. M. (1999). Children's recall 1 or 2 years after an event. *Developmental Psychology, 35,* 781–789.

Pipe, M.-E., Lamb, M. E., Orbach, Y., & Cederborg, A. C. (Eds.). (2007). *Child sexual abuse: Disclosure, delay and denial.* Mahwah, NJ: Lawrence Erlbaum Associates, Inc.

Pipe, M.-E., Lamb, M. E., Orbach, Y., & Esplin, P. W. (2004). Recent research on children's testimony about experienced and witnessed events. *Developmental Review, 24,* 440–468.

Pipe, M.-E., & Salmon, K. (2002). What children bring to the interview context: Individual differences in children's event reports. In M. L. Eisen, J. A. Quas, & G. S. Goodman (Eds.), *Memory and suggestibility in the forensic interview* (pp. 235–261). Mahwah, NJ: Lawrence Erlbaum Associates, Inc.

Pipe, M.-E., Salmon, K., & Priestley, G. (2002). Enhancing children's accounts: How useful are non-verbal techniques? In H. L. Westcott, G. M. Davies, & R. H. C. Bull (Eds.), *Children's testimony: A handbook of psychological research and forensic practice* (pp. 161–174). New York: John Wiley & Sons.

Pipe, M.-E., Sternberg, K., Lamb, M. E., Orbach, Y., Stewart, H., & Esplin, P. (2007). Non-disclosures and alleged abuse in forensic interviews. In M.-E. Pipe, M. E. Lamb, Y. Orbach, & A.-C. Cederborg (Eds.), *Child sexual abuse: Disclosure, delay and denial.* Mahwah, NJ: Lawrence Erlbaum Associates, Inc.

Pipe, M.-E., Thierry, K., & Lamb, M.-E. (2007). The development of event memory: Implications for child witness testimony. In M. P. Toglia, J. D. Read, D. F. Ross, & R. C. L. Lindsay (Eds.), *Handbook of eyewitness psychology: Vol 1. Memory for events.* Mahwah, NJ: Lawrence Erlbaum Associates, Inc.

Pipe, M.-E., & Wilson, C. (1994). Cues and secrets: Influences on children's event reports. *Developmental Psychology, 30,* 515–525.

Pollak, S. D., Vardi, S., Bechner, A. M. P., & Curtin, J. J. (2005). Physically abused children's regulation of attention in response to hostility. *Child Development, 76,* 968–977.

Poole, D. A., & Lamb, M. E. (1998). *Investigative interviews of children: A guide for helping professionals.* Washington, DC: American Psychological Association.

Poole, D. A., & Lindsay, D. S. (1995). Interviewing preschoolers: Effects of non-suggestive techniques, parental coaching, and leading questions on reports of nonexperienced events. *Journal of Experimental Child Psychology, 60,* 129–154.

Poole, D. A., & Lindsay, D. S. (1996, June). *Effects of parental suggestions, interviewing techniques, and age on young children's event reports.* Paper presented to the NATO Advanced Study Institute on Recollections of Trauma, Port de Bourgenay, France.

Poole, D. A., & Lindsay, D. S. (2001). Children's eyewitness reports after exposure to misinformation from parents. *Journal of Experimental Psychology: Applied, 7,* 27–50.

Poole, D. A., & Lindsay, D. S. (2002). Reducing child witnesses' false reports of misinformation from parents. *Journal of Experimental Child Psychology, 81,* 117–140.

Poole, D. A., & White, L. T. (1991). Effects of question repetition on the eyewitness testimony of children and adults. *Developmental Psychology, 27,* 975–986.

Poole, D. A., & White, L. T. (1993). Two years later: Effects of question repetition and retention intervals on the eyewitness testimony of children and adults. *Developmental Psychology, 29,* 844–853.

Powell, M. B., Roberts, K. P., Ceci, S. J., & Hembrooke, H. H. (1999). The effects of repeated experience on children's suggestibility. *Developmental Psychology, 35,* 1462–1477.

Powell, M. B., Roberts, K. P., & Thomson, D. M. (2000). The effect of a suggestive interview on children's memory of a repeated event: Does it matter whether suggestions are linked to a particular incident? *Psychiatry, Psychology, and Law, 7,* 182–191.

Powell, M. B., & Thomson, D. M. (1997). Contrasting memory for temporal-source and memory for content in children's discrimination of repeated events. *Applied Cognitive Psychology, 11,* 339–360.

Price, D. W. W., & Goodman, G. S. (1990). Visiting the wizard: Children's memory of a recurring event. *Child Development, 61,* 664–680.

Priestley, G., & Pipe, M.-E. (1997). Using toys and models in interviews with young children. *Applied Cognitive Psychology, 11,* 69–87.

Priestley, G., Roberts, S., & Pipe, M.-E. (1999). Returning to the scene: Reminders and context reinstatement enhance children's recall. *Developmental Psychology, 35,* 1006–1019.

Prifitera, A., Saklofske, D. H., & Weiss, L. G. (2005). *WISC-IV clinical use and inter-pretation: Scientist-practitioner perspectives.* San Diego, CA: Elsevier Academic Press.

Reese, E. (2002). Social factors in the development of autobiographical memory: The state of the art. *Social Development, 11,* 125–142.

Roberts, K. P. (2002). Children's ability to distinguish between memories from multiple sources: Implications for the quality and accuracy of eyewitness statements. *Developmental Review, 22,* 403–435.

Roberts, K. P., & Blades, M. (2000). *Children's source monitoring.* Mahwah, NJ: Lawrence Erlbaum Associates, Inc.

Roberts, K. P., & Powell, M. B. (2001). Describing individual incidents of sexual abuse: A review of research on the effects of multiple sources of information on children's reports. *Child Abuse and Neglect, 25,* 1643–1659.

Roberts, K. P., & Powell, M. (2007). The roles of prior experience and the timing of misinformation presentation on young children's event memories. *Child Development, 78,* 1137–1152.

Roebers, C. M., & Schneider, W. (2001). Individual differences in children's eyewitness recall: The influence of intelligence and shyness. *Applied Developmental Science, 5,* 9–20.

Roebers, C. M., & Schneider, W. (2005). Individual differences in young children's suggestibility: Relations to event memory, language abilities, working memory, and executive functioning. *Cognitive Development, 20,* 427–447.

Roediger, H. L., McDermott, K. B., Pisoni, D. B., & Gallo, D. A. (2004). Illusory recollection of voices. *Memory, 12,* 586–602.

Rudy, L., & Goodman, G. S. (1991). Effects of participation on children's reports: Implications for children's testimony. *Developmental Psychology, 27*(4), 527–538.

Saarni, C., Mumme, D. L., & Campos, J. J. (1998). Emotional development: Action, communication, and understanding. In W. Damon (Ed.-in-Chief) & N. Eisenberg (Vol. Ed.), *Handbook of child psychology: Vol. 3. Social, emotional and personality development* (5th ed., pp. 237–310). New York: John Wiley & Sons.

Salmon, K. (2001). Remembering and reporting by children: The influence of cues and props. *Clinical Psychology Review, 21,* 267–300.

Salmon, K., Bidrose, S., & Pipe, M.-E. (1995). Providing props to facilitate children's reports: A comparison of toys and real items. *Journal of Experimental Child Psychology, 60,* 174–194.

Salmon, K., & Bryant, R. A. (2002). Posttraumatic stress disorder in children: The influence of developmental factors. *Clinical Psychology Review, 22,* 163–188.

Salmon, K., & Pipe, M.-E. (1997). Props and children's event reports: The impact of a 1-year delay. *Journal of Experimental Child Psychology, 65,* 261–292.

Salmon, K., & Pipe, M.-E. (2000). Recalling an event one year later: The impact of props, drawing and a prior interview. *Applied Cognitive Psychology, 14,* 99–120.

Salmon, K., Price, M., & Pereira, J. K. (2002). Factors associated with young children's long-term recall of an invasive medical procedure: A preliminary investigation. *Journal of Developmental and Behavioral Pediatrics, 23,* 347–352.

Salmon, K., Roncolato, W., & Gleitzman, M. (2003). Children's reports of emotionally laden events: Adapting the interview to the child. *Applied Cognitive Psychology, 17,* 65–67.

Sattler, J. (2002). *Assessment of children: Behavioral and clinical applications.* La Mesa, CA: Jerome Sattler.

Saywitz, K. J., Goodman, G. S., Nicholas, E., & Moan, S. F. (1991). Children's memories of a physical examination involving genital touch: Implications for reports of child sexual abuse. *Journal of Consulting and Clinical Psychology, 59,* 682–691.

Saywitz, K. J., Mannarino, A. P., Berliner, L., & Cohen, J. A. (2000). Treatment for sexually abused children and adolescents. *American Psychologist, 55,* 1040–1049.

Saywitz, K. J., & Moan-Hardie, S. (1994). Reducing the potential for distortion of childhood memories. *Consciousness and Cognition, 3,* 408–425.

Saywitz, K. J., & Snyder, L. (1993). Improving children's testimony with preparation. In G. S. Goodman & B. L. Bottoms (Eds.), *Child victims, child witnesses: Understanding and improving testimony* (pp. 117–146). New York: Guilford.

Saywitz, K. J., & Snyder, L. (1996). Narrative elaboration: Test of a new procedure for interviewing children. *Journal of Consulting and Clinical Psychology*, *64*, 1347–1357.

Saywitz, K. J., Snyder, L., & Nathanson, R. (1999). Facilitating the communicative competence of the child witness. *Applied Developmental Science*, *3*, 58–68.

Scheeringa, M. S., & Zeanah, C. H. (2001). A relational perspective on PTSD in early childhood. *Journal of Traumatic Stress*, *14*, 799–815.

Schneider, W., & Pressley, M. (1997). *Memory development between two and twenty* (2nd ed.). Mahwah, NJ: Lawrence Erlbaum Associates, Inc.

Schooler, J. W. (1997). Reflections on a memory discovery. *Child Maltreatment: Journal of the American Professional Society on the Abuse of Children*, *2*, 126–133.

Shipman, K., & Zeman, J. (1999). Emotional understanding: A comparison of physically maltreating and nonmaltreating mother–child dyads. *Journal of Clinical Child Psychology 28*, 407–417.

Slackman, E., & Nelson, K. (1984). Acquisition of an unfamiliar script in story form by young children. *Child Development*, *55*, 329–340.

Smith, B. S., Ratner, H. H., & Hobart, C. J. (1987). The role of cueing and organization in children's memory for events. *Journal of Experimental Child Psychology*, *44*, 1–24.

Snow, P. C., & Powell, M. B. (2005). What's the story? An exploration of narrative language abilities in male juvenile offenders. *Psychology, Crime and Law*, *11*, 239–253.

Stern, W. (1910). Abstracts of lectures on the psychology of testimony and on the study of individuality. *American Journal of Psychology*, *21*, 270–282.

Sternberg, K. J., Lamb, M. E., Esplin, P. W., Orbach, Y., & Hershkowitz, I. (2002). Using a structured protocol to improve the quality of investigative interviews. In M. Eisen, J. A. Quas, & G. S. Goodman (Eds.), *Memory and suggestibility in the forensic interview* (pp. 409–436). Mahwah, NJ: Lawrence Erlbaum Associates, Inc.

Sternberg, K. J., Lamb, M. E., Hershkowitz, I., Yudilevitch, L., Orbach, Y., Esplin, P. W., et al. (1997). Effects of introductory style on children's abilities to describe experiences of sexual abuse. *Child Abuse and Neglect*, *21*, 1133–1146.

Sternberg, K. J., Lamb, M. E., Orbach, Y., Esplin, P. W., & Mitchell, S. (2001). Use of a structured investigative protocol enhances young children's responses to free recall prompts in the course of forensic interviews. *Journal of Applied Psychology*, *86*, 997–1005.

Steward, M. S., Bussey, K., Goodman, G. S., & Saywitz, S. J. (1993). Implications of developmental research for interviewing children. *Child Abuse and Neglect*, *17*, 25–37.

Steward, M. S., & Steward, D. S. (with L. Farquhar, J. E. B. Myers, M. Reinhart, J. Welker, N. Joye, J. Driskill, et al.). (1996). Interviewing young children about body touch and handling. *Monographs of the Society for Research in Child Development*, *61* (4–5, Serial No. 248).

Stovall-McClough, K. C., & Cloitre, M. (2006). Unresolved attachment, PTSD, and dissociation in women with childhood abuse histories. *Journal of Consulting and Clinical Psychology*, *74*, 219–228.

Strange, D., Garry, M., & Sutherland, R. (2003). Drawing out children's false memories. *Applied Cognitive Psychology*, *17*, 607–619.

Strube, G., & Weber, A. (1988). Die Entwicklung der zeitlichen Einordnung und Datierung von Ereignissen [The development of temporal ordering and dating of events]. *Zeitschrift Fuer Entwicklungspsychologie und Paedagogische Psychologie*, *20*, 225–238.

Stuewig, J., & McCloskey, L. A. (2005). The relation of child maltreatment to shame and guilt among adolescents: Psychological routes to depression and delinquency. *Child Maltreatment*, *10*, 324–336.

Sutherland, R., Pipe, M.-E., Schick, K., Murray, J., & Gobbo, C. (2003). Knowing in advance: The impact of prior event information on memory and event knowledge. *Journal of Experimental Child Psychology*, *84*, 244–263.

Thierry, K. L., Goh, C. L., Pipe, M.-E., & Murray, J. (2005). Source recall enhances children's discrimination of seen and heard events. *Journal of Experimental Psychology: Applied*, *11*, 33–44.

Thierry, K. L., Lamb, M. E., Orbach, Y., & Pipe, M.-E. (2005). Developmental differences in the function and use of anatomically detailed dolls during interviews with alleged sexual abuse victims. *Journal of Counselling and Clinical Psychology*, *73*, 1125–1134.

Thierry, K. L., Spence, M. J., & Memon, A. (2001). Before misinformation is encountered: Source monitoring decreases child witness suggestibility. *Journal of Cognition and Development*, *2*, 1–26.

Thomas, G., & Jolley, J. P. (1998). Drawing conclusions: A re-evaluation of the psychological and conceptual bases for psychological evaluation of children from their drawings. *British Journal of Clinical Psychology*, *37*, 127–139.

Tobey, A. E., & Goodman, G. S. (1992). Children's eyewitness memory: Effects of participation and forensic context. *Child Abuse and Neglect*, *16*, 779–796.

Toth, S. L., Cicchetti, D., MacFie, J., & Emde, R. (1997). Representations of self and other in the narratives of neglected, physically abused, and sexually abused preschoolers. *Development and Psychopathology*, *9*, 781–796.

Toth, S. L., Maughan, A., Manly, J. T., Spagnola, M., & Cicchetti, D. (2002). The relative efficacy of two interventions in altering maltreated preschool children's representational models: Implications for attachment theory. *Development and Psychopathology*, *14*, 877–908.

Tulving, E. (1983). *Elements of episodic memory*. Oxford: Clarendon Press.

Varendonck, J. (1911). Les temoignages d'enfants dans un process retentissant [The testimony of children in a famous trial]. *Archives de Psycholgie*, *11*, 129–171.

Vrielynck, N., DePlus, S., & Philippot, P. (2007). Overgeneral autobiographical memory and depressive disorder in children. *Journal of Clinical Child and Adolescent Psychology*, *36*, 95–105.

Walker, N. E. (1997). Should we question how we question children? In J. D. Read & D. S. Lindsay (Eds.), *NATO ASI Series: Series A: Life Sciences: Vol. 291. Recollections of trauma: Scientific evidence and clinical practice* (pp. 517–521). Dordrecht, Netherlands: Kluwer Academic/Plenum.

Walker, N. E., & Hunt, J. S. (1998). Interviewing child victim-witnesses: How you ask is what you get. In C. R. Thompson, D. Herrman, J. D. Read, D. Bruce, D. Payne, & M. P. Toglia (Eds.), *Eyewitness memory: Theoretical and applied perspectives* (pp. 55–87). Mahwah, NJ: Lawrence Erlbaum Associates, Inc.

Wareham, P., & Salmon, K. (2006). Mother–child reminiscing about everyday experiences: Implications for clinical interventions in the preschool years. *Clinical Psychology Review*, *26*, 535–554.

Warren, A. R., & Lane, P. (1995). Effects of timing and type of questioning on eyewitness accuracy and suggestibility. In M. S. Zaragoza, J. R. Graham, G. C. N.

Hall, R. Hirschman, & Y. S. Ben-Porath (Eds.), *Memory and testimony in the child witness* (pp. 44–60). Thousand Oaks, CA: Sage.

Wekerle, C., & Wolfe, D. A. (2003). Child maltreatment. In E. J. Mash & R. A. Barkley (Eds.), *Child psychopathology* (2nd ed., pp. 632–684). New York: Guilford Press.

Wenzlaff, R. M., & Wegner, D. M. (2000). Thought suppression. *Annual Review of Psychology, 51*, 59–91.

Wesson, M., & Salmon, K. (2001). Showing and telling: The use of drawing and re-enactment to enhance children's reports of their emotional experiences. *Applied Cognitive Psychology, 15*, 301–319.

Westcott, H. L., & Kynan, S. (2004). The application of a "story-telling" framework to investigate interviews for suspected child sexual abuse. *Legal and Criminological Psychology, 9*, 37–56.

Wilkinson, J. (1988). Context effects in children's event memory. In M. M. Gruneberg, P. E. Morris, & R. N. Sykes (Eds.), *Practical aspects of memory: Vol. 1. Current research issues* (pp. 107–111). New York: Wiley.

Willcock, E., Morgan, K., & Hayne, H. (2006). Body maps do not facilitate children's reports of touch. *Applied Cognitive Psychology, 20*, 607–615.

Williams, J. M. G., Barnhofer, T., Crane, C., Hermans, D., Raes, F., Watkins, E., et al. (2007). Autobiographical memory specificity and emotional disorder. *Psychological Bulletin, 133*, 122–148.

Yuille, J. C., Hunter, R., Joffe, R., & Zaparniuk, J. (1993). Interviewing children in sexual abuse cases. In G. S. Goodman & B. L. Bottoms (Eds.), *Child victims, child witnesses: Understanding and improving testimony* (pp. 95–115). New York: Guilford.

11 Sociocultural perspectives on autobiographical memory

Robyn Fivush
Emory University, Atlanta, USA

We all talk about the events of our lives. Beginning in early childhood and continuing throughout the lifespan, over the dinner table, on the telephone, catching up with old friends or meeting new acquaintances, we talk about what happened and what it means. And, importantly, it is as we share our experiences with others that these experiences take on meaning for the self. Particularly from a developmental perspective, the ways in which adults reminisce with young children has a profound influence on how young children come to remember and evaluate their personal past. Whereas many of the chapters in this book focus on the role of biological and cognitive changes in the ability to encode, consolidate and retrieve information, the research reviewed in this chapter expands the horizons of memory development to include the social and cultural values and behaviors that influence how children come to narrate their personal experiences and construct an autobiography that relates their past to their present, and their selves to others.

More specifically, this body of research explores the early emergence of autobiographical memory in parent-guided reminiscing from a sociocultural perspective that focuses on how parents structure reminiscing with their preschool children, and how these parental differences relate to children's emerging abilities to construct coherent elaborated autobiographical narratives. To place this research in context, I first describe the development of verbal recall and discuss the critical role of language and narrative in the development of autobiographical memory. I then describe the research on parent-guided reminiscing in detail, highlighting individual, gender and cultural differences throughout.

THE EMERGENCE OF TALK ABOUT THE PAST

The development of verbal recall

Intriguingly, children begin to talk about the past virtually as soon as they begin talking. At about 16 to 18 months of age, children begin to make references to past events, although at this early point these references are fleeting, just a word or two, and tend to refer to recent events of the past minutes or hours (Nelson & Ross, 1980). Children quickly begin to refer to past events in more elaborated ways, although these early conversations about the past are heavily guided, or scaffolded, by adults (see Hudson & Mayhew, Chapter 4, this volume; Eisenberg, 1985). Between 24 and 36 months of age, children will respond to parental questions about past events with a simple word or two, or by confirming or repeating what the parent says (Hudson, 1990). By age 3, most children are able to participate more fully in these conversations, providing more detailed answers to parental questions, but much of the structure and content of these conversations is still scaffolded by the parent. Essentially, as children contribute more information to the memory conversation, parents weave this information into a structured, coherent narrative. By the end of the preschool years, most children are able to give reasonably coherent and detailed narratives of personally experienced events (see Fivush, 1993, 2002, for reviews).

The developmental progression from heavy reliance on parentally scaffolded narratives to the ability to provide an independent autobiographical narrative suggests that children are learning the forms and functions of narrating the past by participating in parent-scaffolded reminiscing. This argument follows from Vygotsky's (1978) sociocultural theory, which posits that children are learning the skills necessary to become competent members of their culture through participating in adult structured activities that highlight specific skills and how to perform them (Rogoff, 1990). In the domain of autobiographical memory, cultures differ in the value of having and telling a life story, and children are learning both the cultural values associated with, and the narrative form of, constructing and telling life stories, or autobiographical narratives, through participating in parent-scaffolded reminiscing.

Language, narrative, and autobiographical memory

Following from this approach, differences in the ways in which parents structure early autobiographical narratives with their young children should be reflected in individual differences in children's developing autobiographical narrative skills. More specifically, parents who engage in highly elaborative reminiscing, talking about the past in rich detail and weaving highly descriptive stories of what occurred, will have children who themselves come to tell more detailed and more coherent narratives of their personal past than children of parents who engage in less elaborated reminiscing. Note that this argument centers on autobiographical *narratives*; narratives are culturally canonical linguistic structures for organizing and communicating events (Bruner, 1990; Labov & Waletzky, 1967). Thus language-based narratives are a fundamental tool for autobiographical memory.

This is certainly not to argue that autobiographical memory is language based; it is not. Autobiographical memories are multifaceted and encoded in multiple sensory forms. Moreover, recent empirical evidence indicates that infants are able to recall specific episodes from their past by the latter half of the first year of life (see Bauer, Chapter 6, this volume, and Howe, Courage, & Rooksby, Chapter 8, this volume), and there is abundant evidence that 1- and 2-year-olds are able to recall specific episodes over delays of many months, developments that are linked to both neurological and cognitive developments (see Bauer, 2005, Chapter 6, this volume; Howe et al., Chapter 8, this volume). However, language is critical for *autobiographical* memory, memory of the self engaged in the past, in that, first, it helps to create more coherently organized memory structures and, second, it allows us to communicate our autobiographical experiences to others, as discussed in more detail below (Fivush & Nelson, 2004; Nelson, 1996; Nelson & Fivush, 2004).

Narrative organization

Language-based narratives move beyond a simple description of what happened to place the event in spatial and temporal context, to include background information, and, most importantly, to include evaluative information; information about why this event is interesting, important, noteworthy (Labov & Waletzky, 1967). Evaluative information can be communicated through linguistic devices that emphasize or mark aspects of the external event (e.g., "It was *really really* cold" or "It was the *biggest meanest* dog I had ever seen"), or through linking external events to what Bruner (1990) has called the "landscape of consciousness," information about the inner thoughts, feelings, desires, beliefs of the event participants (e.g., "I had never been so *angry*" or "I *wanted* that pink dress so badly").

Through canonical narrative structure, events come to take on a particular organizational story-like form, with a beginning, middle, and end linked together through human intentions and motivations. Events do not simply happen in the world; they happen to people for a reason and have specific consequences. In this way, narratives transform memories of specific episodes in the world into memories of self and other engaging in events together through time. It is in this way that memories become autobiographical; this is what happened and this is what it *means* to *me*.

Narrative communication

Further, it is only through language that memories of the past can be communicated to others. Through language, we can talk about what happened, but even more important, it is only through language that we can talk about how we felt and thought about the past, and how that might be the same or different from what others thought or felt. Without language, we could not discuss, compare, and negotiate thoughts and feelings about the past with others. Through conversations in which past events are communicated, evaluated, and negotiated, we come to re-interpret and re-represent these events for ourselves. Thus language allows us to express, to share, to negotiate, and ultimately to interpret and evaluate past events, and it is this process that makes episodic memories truly autobiographical memories (Fivush, 2001; Fivush & Nelson, 2006). Given these arguments, it is even more intriguing that there are individual differences in how parents co-construct narratives about the past with their young children.

INDIVIDUAL DIFFERENCES IN PARENT–CHILD REMINISCING

Methodological approaches

Over the past 20 years, research has amply demonstrated individual differences in how parents reminisce with their preschool children. The majority of this research is semi-naturalistic in method, in that families are visited in their homes and parent–child reminiscing is tape recorded and the resulting transcripts are coded and analyzed. Virtually all of the research has focused on mothers with their preschool children, with only a small number of studies examining fathers as well. For the most part, mothers and fathers show similar variability in their reminiscing styles, but differ depending on whether they are reminiscing with daughters or with sons, an issue I return to later. Because most of the research has examined mothers, I review this research in detail, referring to fathers when data are available.

In some research, mothers are simply given a tape recorder and asked to record conversations during particular times of day, such as meal time or bedtime (Lucariello & Nelson, 1987; Miller, 1994; Peterson & McCabe, 1994) and references to past events are identified and examined. In most of the research, however, mothers are explicitly asked to select specific past events that they have shared with their child, such as a family outing to a museum or amusement park, or a special family event such as a wedding or a reunion, and then to talk about this event as they normally would with their preschooler. Again, the conversations are tape recorded and the transcripts are coded and analyzed. Although somewhat different methodologies and coding schemes have been used across studies, the results are remarkably consistent.

Maternal reminiscing style

Elaborative reminiscing

One of the most robust findings is that mothers vary along a dimension of elaboration (see Fivush, Haden, & Reese, 2006, and Nelson & Fivush, 2004, for reviews), such that some mothers reminisce in highly elaborated ways, talking a great deal about the past, asking many questions, with each question providing more and more information about the event under discussion, as illustrated in this excerpt of an conversation between a highly elaborative mother and her 40-month-old son:

Mother: Remember when we first came in the aquarium? And we looked down and there were a whole bunch of birdies . . . in the water? Remember the name of the birdies?
Child: Ducks!
Mother: Nooo! They weren't ducks. They had on little suits. (pause) Penguins. Remember what did the penguins do?
Child: I don't know.
Mother: You don't remember?
Child: No.
Mother: Remember them jumping off the rocks and swimming in the water?
Child: Yeah.
Mother: Real fast. You were watching them jump in the water, hmm?
Child: Yeah.

Here we see that the child is engaged in the conversation although not recalling any accurate information. With each additional question, the mother provides additional information such that by the end of this excerpt, there is a sense of story, a coherent account of seeing the penguins at the aquarium. In contrast, other mothers are less elaborative; they do not talk about the past as frequently, and when they do, they tend to ask few, sparse and redundant questions, as this excerpt of a low elaborative mother and her 40-month-old child reminiscing about a visit to the zoo illustrates:

Mother: What kind of animals did you see, do you remember?
Child: Lollipops.
Mother: Lollipops aren't animals, are they? Who, what kind of animals did you see?
Child: Giraffe.
Mother: You saw giraffes? And what else?
Child: RRROAR!
Mother: What's roar?
Child: Lion.
Mother: What else did you see?
Child: ROAR!
Mother: What else did you see?

As can be seen, when the child first gives an inaccurate response, the mother simply repeats her initial question. Then when the child does provide some bits of accurate information, the mother does not elaborate on the information the child provided, for example by talking about the noises the lion made or what the lion looked like. Instead, this mother simply keeps repeating the same question, seemingly in order to get a list of animals seen. There is no sense of story or shared experience here.

As these examples illustrate, highly elaborative mothers both invite their children's participation and follow in on and elaborate on their children's contributions to a greater extent than less elaborative mothers. Some researchers have labeled this difference as high versus low elaborative (Hudson, 1990), elaborative versus repetitive (Fivush & Fromhoff, 1988), or as topic-extending versus topic-switching (McCabe & Peterson, 1991), but the critical difference is that highly elaborative mothers keep the conversation going by providing additional information with each additional question, essentially telling a story of what occurred, and weaving their children's contributions into this emerging story, whereas low elaborative mothers simply ask their children to provide a specific piece of information and either repeat the question if the child does not respond or switch to a new aspect of the event if the child does respond, thus not constructing a coherent narrative of the past.

Gender and culture in autobiographical narratives

Interestingly, elaborative reminiscing varies as a function of gender of the child and of culture. Although not all studies find gender differences, when they do emerge, it is the case that both mothers and fathers are more elaborative with daughters than with sons (Fivush, Berlin, Sales, Mennuti-Washburn, & Cassidy, 2003; Reese, Haden, & Fivush, 1996). In a provocatively parallel fashion, as adults, females tell longer, more detailed, and more vivid narratives of their past experiences than do males, at least in Euro-American cultures (see Fivush & Buckner, 2003, for a review), suggesting that gendered ways of thinking about and narrating the past may be socialized.

Similarly, Euro-American mothers are more elaborative in reminiscing than are Asian mothers in several Asian cultures studied, including middle-class Maori (Hayne & MacDonald, 2003; MacDonald, Uesiliana, & Hayne, 2000), Korean (Mullen & Yi, 1995), Indian (Leichtman, Wang, & Pillemer, 2003), and Chinese (Wang, 2001) families (see Fivush & Haden, 2003, for a review). And as adults, Asians tend to have fewer autobiographical memories than Euro-American adults, especially of childhood, and these memories tend to be narrated in spare and skeletal form (Pillemer, 1998). Theorists have argued that Euro-American cultures are more independently oriented (Oyserman & Markus, 1993), focusing on self as an active agent in construct-ing one's life, which would be reflected in more self-focused and elaborated autobiographical memories. In contrast, Asian cultures are more inter-dependently oriented, focusing on self as a member of a community, which would be expressed in fewer memories focused on self (Wang, 2003). Findings from parent–child reminiscing suggest that the values associated with gender and culture are expressed in autobiographical narratives, and that individuals are learning how to think about their lives and their selves through early parent-scaffolded reminiscing. If this is the case, then differences in parental reminiscing style should be systematically related to differences in children's developing autobiographical narratives.

MATERNAL REMINISCING AND CHILDREN'S AUTOBIOGRAPHICAL NARRATIVES

Maternal reminiscing over time

More highly elaborative mothers have children who contribute more to the ongoing memory conversation (Bauer & Burch, 2004; Fivush & Fromhoff, 1988; Hudson, 1990; Reese, Haden, & Fivush, 1993). Moreover, maternal elaborative reminiscing is consistent over time; mothers who are highly elaborative when their children are just entering the preschool years remain highly elaborative compared to their counterparts even as their children enter the early school years (Farrant & Reese, 2000; Reese et al., 1993; Reese & Farrant, 2003), although the type of elaborations mothers are most likely to use changes as their children become more competent participants in reminiscing, as discussed below. Critically, however, maternal elaborative reminiscing is not related to maternal education, or to general level of maternal talkativeness (see Fivush et al., 2006, for a review). Mothers who are highly elaborative during reminiscing are not necessarily more talkative during story book reading, free play, or caregiving routines (Haden & Fivush, 1996; Hoff-Ginsburg, 1991; Lucariello, Kyratzis, & Engel, 1986), although mothers are consistent in their level of elaborative reminiscing across siblings (Haden, 1998). These findings suggest that reminiscing is a unique conversational context that might uniquely predict children's developing autobiographical memory skills.

Indeed, several longitudinal studies have now demonstrated that children of more highly elaborative mothers come to tell more coherent and elaborated autobiographical narratives, both in reminiscing with their mothers as well as in their independent autobiographical narratives told to an unfamiliar adult, even when controlling for children's general language skills (e.g., Bauer & Burch, 2004; Farrant & Reese, 2000; Fivush, 1991; Fivush & Vasudeva, 2002; Flannagan, Baker-Ward, & Graham, 1995; Haden, 1998; Harley & Reese, 1999; Hudson, 1990; Leichtman, Pillemer, Wang, Koreishi, & Han, 2000; Low & Durkin, 2001; Peterson, Jesso, & McCabe, 1999; Reese et al., 1993; Welch-Ross, 1997, 2001). Moreover, regression analyses in these studies indicate that the direction of effect is more from mother to child than from child to mother. That is, highly elaborative maternal reminiscing early in development is strongly and consistently related to children's autobiographical narratives later in development, but children's early skills are not as predictive of later maternal reminiscing style.

Determining causal relations

Longitudinal studies support the supposition that children are learning how to narrate their personal experiences through participating in parent-guided reminiscing, but the semi-naturalistic correlational methodology does not allow causal interpretations. A few studies have used an intervention methodology, training a group of mothers to use specific elaborative devices and comparing children's narratives before and after maternal training in comparison to a control group of mothers who receive no training. These studies converge on finding that training mothers to increase their elaborative questions subsequently results in children providing more elaborated narratives of their personal past, both in co-constructing narratives with their mother and narrating independently with an unfamiliar adult (Boland, Haden, & Ornstein, 2003; Peterson et al., 1999).

In addition to training mothers, some studies have also used an experimental approach, assigning some children to a high elaborative condition in which they experience a structured event (e.g., visiting the pirate) and then interact with an experimenter who reminisces about the event in a highly elaborative way, whereas other children experience the same event but the experimenter reminisces about it using a low elaborative style. Children who reminisce with a highly elaborative experimenter subsequently recall more about the event and recall the event more accurately than children who reminisce about the same event with a low elaborative experimenter (Conroy, 2006; McGuigan & Salmon, 2004; Tessler & Nelson, 1994). These experimental findings confirm that a highly elaborative reminiscing style facilitates children's recall. They further suggest that children who experience a high elaborative style on a regular basis in their natural environment will have more elaborated memories in general (Tessler & Nelson, 1994).

STRUCTURE AND CONTENT OF MATERNAL ELABORATIONS

Developmental changes

A closer examination of maternal elaborations reveals even more specific relations between maternal reminiscing style and child outcome. Returning to the theoretical framework guiding this research, Vygotskian theory posits that adults who are sensitive to children's developmental capabilities, and provide the right amount of structure, not too much and not too little, best facilitate children's developing skills. In essence, adults guide children to the next level by helping them to perform at a level just beyond their ability to perform on their own. Consistent with this formulation, mothers change in their type of elaboration as their children become more skilled at participating in reminiscing. Early in development, when children are just beginning to be able to participate in reminiscing, mothers ask mainly close-ended yes/no elaborative questions ("Remember when we went to the zoo? Did we see a giraffe there?") only requiring children to confirm or repeat what the mother says. As children become more capable participants, mothers "up the ante" by asking more open-ended, wh- questions ("Remember when we went to the zoo? What animals did we see there?) that require the child to provide a new piece of information.

In line with Vygotsky's theoretical postulates, it is the use of close-ended elaborations early in development, but open-ended elaborations later in development, that best facilitate children's developing autobiographical memory skills (Haden, Ornstein, Rudek, & Branstein, 2006; Farrant & Reese, 2000). Thus it seems that a maternal elaborative style that is sensitive to the child's developmental capabilities and needs, and changes accordingly, is most predictive of positive outcome.

Narrative structure

Mothers also vary on what aspects of the narrative they choose to elaborate on. Some mothers include and elaborate on orienting information that places the event in time and space, as well as background information that places this event in a larger context of other people and events (Peterson & McCabe, 1996). And some mothers provide a great deal of evaluative information, emphasizing noteworthy aspects of the event, and especially focusing on thoughts and emotions about the event, which provides explicit meaning and significance to what occurred (Fivush & Haden, 2005; Haden, Haine, & Fivush, 1997). Importantly, mothers who provide more context early in development have children who include more of this kind of information in their independent autobiographical narratives later in development, and mothers who provide more evaluative information similarly have children who begin to include more of this kind of information in their independent autobiographical narratives by the end of the preschool years (Fivush, 1991; Haden et al., 1997; Peterson & McCabe, 1992, 2004).

The specificity of relations between what mothers focus on in co-constructed narratives early in development and what children focus on in their narratives later in development provides additional evidence that children are learning the forms and functions of talking about the past in early mother-guided reminiscing. It is not simply that mothers who elaborate more have children who elaborate more, but rather it is the specific narrative forms that mothers elaborate on that predict what children will later incorporate in their independent narratives, indicating that children's autobiographical narrative skills emerge from participating in specific forms of narrative interaction with their mothers.

Provocatively, however, whereas maternal reminiscing style predicts children's emerging autobiographical memory skills, no such relations have been found for fathers. That is, fathers' use of orientations or evaluations in early father–child reminiscing is not related to how children subsequently use orientations and evaluations in their independent narratives (Haden et al., 1997). Thus mothers seem to be a more powerful influence on their children's emerging autobiographical memory skills than are fathers.

Internal state language in autobiographical narratives

The findings on narrative evaluations are particularly intriguing as it is this aspect of autobiographical narratives that gives the event its personal meaning. It is what we thought and felt about an event that link that event most closely to self, and through using this kind of internal state language in autobiographical narratives, mothers and children are providing specific links between the past and the present (this is what happened; this is what I thought and felt about it at the time and this what I think and feel about it now) as well as specific links between self and other (this is what happened, and this is what I thought and felt about in contrast to what you thought and felt about it). It is internal state language, and the discussion of thoughts and feelings, that provides a subjective perspective on what happened and makes an event uniquely one's own experience (Fivush, 2001; Fivush & Haden, 2005; Fivush & Nelson, 2006).

Understanding of mind through time

Developing use of internal state language is also related to children's developing understanding of mind, that individuals have thoughts, emotions, beliefs, and desires that underlie and motivate their behavior, and that different individuals can have different internal states even about the same object or event (Wellman, 2002). Understanding of mind develops gradually across the preschool years, and is clearly related to language (Astington, 1993) and, more specifically, to mother–child conversations. Mothers who use more internal state language in their everyday talk have children who both use more of this kind of language and display a better understanding of self, mind, and other on a variety of standardized tasks that assess these abilities (Carpendale & Lewis, 2004; Symons, 2004). Talk about the past may be particularly influential in children's developing understanding of self, mind, and other, because talk about the past requires the mother and child to explicitly link mental states from the past to the present, thus focusing on the continuity of mind over time (Fivush & Nelson, 2006; Perner & Ruffman, 1995).

Indeed, mothers who use more language reflecting mental states, using words such as *know*, *understand*, *believe*, during reminiscing, have children who use more of this kind of language in their autobiographical narratives both concurrently and longitudinally (Rudek & Haden, 2005). Regression analyses suggest that mothers influence children's concurrent use of this kind of language, which, in turn, predicts children's later use of mental state terms in autobiographical reminiscing. There is also some suggestion that use of mental state language in mother–child reminiscing is related to children's ability to perform on standardized tasks assessing understanding of mind (Welch-Ross, 1997).

Emotional content of autobiographical narratives

A critical aspect of mental state language is emotion. Discussion of emotions of self and other provides evaluation and perspective on an event. In general, families that talk more about emotion, and especially the causes and consequences of emotional experience, have children who not only talk more about emotion but also display higher levels of emotional understanding and regulation (Denham, Zoller, & Couchoud, 1994; Dunn, Bretherton, & Munn, 1987; Dunn, Brown, & Beardsall, 1991).

Once again, talk about emotions associated with past events may be particularly important for several reasons. First, when discussing a past event, mothers and children are not in the heat of the emotional moment and may be better able to reflect on and evaluate the emotional experiences. Second, in reminiscing, specific types of emotional experience may be focused and elaborated on to a greater extent than other types of emotional experiences (e.g., elaborations on sadness versus anger), perhaps leading to a more nuanced understanding of some emotions over others. Finally, in reminiscing, different aspects of emotional experience can be elaborated on, including the experience itself, the causes and consequences of the emotion, or the resolutions, especially for negative emotions, again leading to differing abilities to regulate different kinds of emotional experiences (Fivush, 1998; Fivush, Brotman, Buckner, & Goodman, 2000).

Positive versus negative events

In most of the research, mothers are asked to reminisce about special events they shared with their children, and thus not surprisingly, the majority of research has focused on mothers and children reminiscing about positive child-centered events, such as family outings and visits to and from friends and family. When reminiscing about positive events, mothers may be particularly interested in creating a shared history in the service of strengthening emotional bonds (Fivush, Haden, & Reese, 1996). In support of this interpretation, mothers of children who have a more secure attachment relationship are more elaborative (Fivush & Vasudeva, 2002; Laible, 2004; Laible & Thompson, 2000). Creating more elaborated narratives of the shared past may both emerge from and contribute to the mother–child emotional relationship (Fivush & Reese, 2002).

But the goal of creating a shared history may be specific to sharing emotionally positive events, events that are recounted again and again because they contribute to an ongoing sense of enjoyment in each other's company. This would most likely not be the goal of talking about highly stressful events. Rather, in this situation, mothers may be trying to help their children to understand this event in the service of emotional regulation and life lessons. Only a few studies have compared highly positive and highly negative events, but it appears that mother–child reminiscing does differ as a function of the valance of the event. When discussing positive events, mothers ask more close-ended elaborative questions (essentially yes/no questions that simply require the child to confirm the mother's rendering of the event), but when discussing negative events, mothers ask more open-ended elaborative questions (essentially wh- questions, asking the child to supply the asked for information) (Sales, Fivush, & Peterson, 2003). This difference supports the idea that mothers are trying to create a shared history when discussing positive events. By providing most of the narrative themselves and asking only for confirmation, mothers may be focusing on creating a shared understanding of what happened about positive events, a narrative that will function to bond the participants together through a shared past that is mutually understood.

In contrast, in reminiscing about negative experiences, mothers may be more concerned with helping their children understand how and why such aversive events occur. Adults who are better able to provide coherent explanatory narratives of stressful events subsequently show higher levels of well-being (Pennebaker, 1997). By trying to elicit more of the memory information from the child, mothers may be trying to help their children to focus on and recall critical aspects of the event that may better help them to individually understand what happened. In line with this interpretation, mothers focus on the causes of negative events to a greater extent than positive events (Ackil, Van Abbema, & Bauer, 2003; Fivush et al., 2003; Sales et al., 2003), suggesting that mothers may be concerned with helping their children understand how and why negative experiences occurred, perhaps in the service of helping children to understand and cope with aversive experiences (Sales & Fivush, 2005).

Gender and culture in the emotional content of autobiographical narratives

Parent–child reminiscing also differs as a function of the type of negative experience being discussed, and these differences are a function of both gender and culture. Both mothers and fathers discuss and elaborate about sadness more with daughters than with sons. Parents also elaborate on the causes of sadness more with daughters than with sons (see Fivush, 1998; Fivush et al., 2000; Fivush & Buckner, 2003, for reviews). In contrast, mothers reminisce about anger more with sons than with daughters (Bird & Reese, 2006; Fivush, 1989, 1998). These differences obviously reflect cultural stereotypes about gender and emotion, with females stereotypically experiencing and expressing sadness more than males and males stereotypically experiencing and expressing anger more than females (Basow, 1992), and may reflect one way in which these stereotyped emotional experiences are conveyed and socialized. Across gender, mothers are more likely to try to resolve feelings of sadness when reminiscing with their children than feelings about anger

(Fivush et al., 2003), although they are more likely to try to resolve anger with daughters than with sons (Fivush, 1989).

Parents also place past emotional experiences in a more relational context with daughters than with sons. For example, daughters are sad because they could not play with a special friend, whereas boys are sad because they lost a favorite toy. Finally, parents talk more about other people and relationships when reminiscing with daughters than with sons (Buckner & Fivush, 2000). In all of these ways, parent–daughter reminiscing is more detailed, more emotional, and more relationally oriented than is parent–son reminiscing.

Early in the preschool years, there are no gender differences in children's reminiscing skills. Boys and girls contribute equally, and are equally engaged and on task during parent-scaffolded reminiscing. By the end of the preschool years, however, girls are contributing more, and especially more emotional, information to parent-scaffolded reminiscing (Reese et al., 1996), and when asked to narrate their experiences to an unfamiliar adult, 6- to 8-year-old girls are providing more detailed, more emotional, and more relationally oriented autobiographical narratives than are boys (Buckner & Fivush, 1998; Haden et al., 1997). And as adults, females tell more detailed, more vivid, more emotional, and more relationally oriented autobiographical narratives than do males (Bauer, Stennes, & Haight, 2003; Fivush & Buckner, 2003). Females include more references to specific emotional states and reactions and more references to people and to affiliations in their autobiographical narratives than males. This pattern suggests a socialization process whereby girls are coming to narrate, and quite likely represent and understand, their past experiences, and perhaps themselves, in more elaborated, emotional and relational ways through participating in more elaborated, more emotional parent-scaffolded reminiscing.

There are also cultural differences in the emotional content of auto-biographical reminiscing. Euro-American mothers elaborate more about emotions when reminiscing than do Asian mothers and, in particular, they focus on the causes and consequences of emotions (Fivush & Wang, 2005; Wang, 2001, 2003; Wang & Fivush, 2005). Asian mothers, in contrast, focus on moral lessons to be learned from emotional experiences (Wang, 2001). Perhaps surprisingly, Asian mothers discuss sadness less and anger more than do Euro-American mothers (Fivush & Wang, 2005). Possibly because anger can be highly disruptive to smooth social functioning, Asian mothers may see a greater need to socialize their children about anger, and ways to resolve this emotion, than do Euro-American mothers. Sadness, on the other hand is a more ruminative emotion, focusing on one's own internal emotional experience, and thus Asian mothers may be less likely to discuss this emotion than are Euro-American mothers. By middle childhood, Euro-American children are providing more elaborated autobiographical narratives than Asian children (Han, Leichtman, & Wang, 1998) and they demonstrate a more complex level of emotional understanding on standardized developmental tasks (Wang, 2003).

These findings suggest that the values cultures place on the expression and understanding of emotion are reflected in the emotional content of autobiographical narratives. Females are stereotypically more emotional than men, at least in Euro-American cultures (Basow, 1992), and beginning in middle childhood and throughout adulthood, females report feeling more emotions, feeling emotions more intensely, and valuing emotional experiences more so than males (Fischer, 2000). In terms of culture, the more independent autonomous self valued by Euro-American cultures focuses more on individual experiences, and thus would focus more on individual emotions, whereas the interdependent relational self valued by Asian cultures would focus more on emotions as moral and communal guidelines, and thus the way in which personal emotional experience is construed and evaluated would fall along these lines. Parent-scaffolded reminiscing may be one important avenue for communicating to children the emotion values that they will have to adopt in order to become competent members of their culture. Even more, the ways in which emotions are understood and integrated into autobiographical narratives will play a major role in how individuals of different genders and in different cultures come to understand and evaluate their past experiences and their selves.

CONCLUSIONS

How we represent the events of our lives is clearly a social process that begins early in development. The research reviewed in this chapter places memory in a larger social and cultural context within which the experiences of our lives are embedded and evaluated. Differences in the ways in which mothers structure reminiscing with their preschool children are related to differences in children's emerging abilities to narrate their personal past. More highly elaborative mothers facilitate children's developing autobiographical memory skills, such that children of highly elaborative mothers come to tell more elaborated, detailed and coherent autobiographical narratives. Moreover, differences in maternal reminiscing style are systematically related to gender and culture in ways that inform the values we place on personal memory, and the ways in which these values are expressed and communicated in everyday interactions in which self and memory are integrated.

ACKNOWLEDGMENTS

This chapter was written while the author was a senior fellow in the Center for the Interdisciplinary Study of Law and Religion at Emory University, sponsored by a grant from the Pew Charitable Trusts. The opinions expressed here are those of the author and do not necessarily reflect the views of The Pew Charitable trusts. Please address all correspondence to Robyn Fivush,

Department of Psychology, Emory University, Atlanta, GA 30322, USA, or through email to Robyn Fivush at psyrf@emory.edu

REFERENCES

Ackil, J. K., Van Abbema, D. L., & Bauer, P. J. (2003). After the storm: Enduring differences in mother–child recollections of traumatic and nontraumatic events. *Journal of Experimental Child Psychology*, *84*, 286–309.

Astington, J. (1993). *The child's discovery of mind*. Cambridge, MA: Harvard University Press.

Basow, S. A. (1992). *Gender stereotypes and roles*. Belmont, CA: Brooks-Cole.

Bauer, P. J. (2005). Developments in declarative memory: Decreasing susceptibility to storage failure over the second year of life. *Psychological Science*, *16*, 41–47.

Bauer, P. J., & Burch, M. M. (2004). Developments in early memory: Multiple mediators of foundational processes. In J. M. Lucariello, J. A. Hudson, R. Fivush, & P. J. Bauer (Eds.), *The development of the mediated mind* (pp. 101–125). Mahwah, NJ: Lawrence Erlbaum Associates, Inc.

Bauer, P., Stennes, L., & Haight, J. (2003). Representation of the inner self in autobiography: Women's and men's use of internal states language in personal narratives. *Memory*, *11*, 27–42.

Bird, A., & Reese, E. (2006). Emotional reminiscing and the development of an autobiographical self. *Developmental Psychology*, *42*, 613–626.

Boland, A. M., Haden, C. A., & Ornstein, P. A., (2003). Boosting children's memory by training mothers in the use of an elaborative conversational style as an event unfolds. *Journal of Cognition and Development*, *4*, 39–65.

Bruner, J. (1990). *Acts of meaning*. Cambridge, MA: Harvard University Press.

Buckner, J. P., & Fivush, R. (1998). Gender and self in children's autobiographical narratives. *Applied Cognitive Psychology*, *12*, 407–429.

Buckner, J. P., & Fivush, R. (2000). Gendered themes in reminiscing. *Memory*, *8*, 401–412.

Carpendale, J. I. M., & Lewis, C. (2004). Constructing an understanding of mind: The development of children's social understanding within social interactions. *Brain and Behavior Sciences*, *27*, 79–151.

Conroy, R. (2006). *Children's memory for traumatic events: The influence of post-event avoidance and elaboration*. Unpublished dissertation, University of New South Wales, Australia.

Denham, S. A., Zoller, D., & Couchoud, E. A. (1994). Socialization of preschoolers' emotion understanding. *Developmental Psychology*, *30*, 928–936.

Dunn, J., Bretherton, I., & Munn, P. (1987). Conversations about feeling states between mothers and their young children. *Developmental Psychology*, *23*, 132–139.

Dunn, J., Brown, J., & Beardsall, L. (1991). Family talk about feeling states and children's later understanding of others' emotions. *Developmental Psychology*, *27*, 448–455.

Eisenberg, A. (1985). Learning to describe past experience in conversation. *Discourse Processes*, *8*, 177–204.

Farrant, K., & Reese, E. (2000). Maternal style and children's participation in reminiscing: Stepping stones in children's autobiographical memory development. *Journal of Cognition and Development, 1*, 193–225.

Fischer, A. H. (2000). *Gender and emotion: Social psychological perspectives.* New York: Cambridge University Press.

Fivush, R. (1989). Exploring sex differences in the emotional content of mother–child talk about the past. *Sex Roles, 20*, 675–691.

Fivush, R. (1991). The social construction of personal narratives. *Merrill-Palmer Quarterly, 37*, 59–82.

Fivush, R. (1993). Developmental perspectives on autobiographical recall. In G. Goodman & B. Bottoms (Eds.), *Child victims, child witnesses: Understanding and improving testimony* (pp. 1–24). New York: Guilford Press.

Fivush, R. (1998). Gendered narratives: Elaboration, structure and emotion in parent–child reminiscing across the preschool years. In C. P. Thompson, D. J. Herrmann, D. Bruce, J. D. Read, D. G. Payne, & M. P. Toglia (Eds.), *Auto-biographical memory: Theoretical and applied perspectives* (pp. 79–104). Mahwah, NJ: Lawrence Erlbaum Associates, Inc.

Fivush, R. (2001). Owning experience: The development of subjective perspective in autobiographical memory. In C. Moore & K. Lemmon (Eds.), *The self in time: Developmental perspectives* (pp. 35–52). Mahwah, NJ: Lawrence Erlbaum Associates, Inc.

Fivush, R. (2002). The development of autobiographical memory. In H. Westcott, G. Davies, & R. Bull (Eds.), *Children's testimony in context* (pp. 55–68). New York: John Wiley & Sons.

Fivush, R., Berlin, L., Sales, J. M., Mennuti-Washburn, J., & Cassidy, J. (2003). Functions of parent–child reminiscing about emotionally negative events. *Memory, 11*, 179–192.

Fivush, R., Brotman, M., Buckner, J. P., & Goodman, S. (2000). Gender differences in parent–child emotion narratives. *Sex Roles, 42*, 233–254.

Fivush, R., & Buckner, J. (2003). Constructing gender and identity through autobiographical narratives. In R. Fivush & C. Haden (Eds.), *Auto-biographical memory and the construction of a narrative self: Developmental and cultural perspectives* (pp. 149–167). Hillsdale, NJ: Lawrence Erlbaum Associates, Inc.

Fivush, R., & Fromhoff, F. (1988). Style and structure in mother–child conversations about the past. *Discourse Processes, 11*, 337–355.

Fivush, R., & Haden, C. A. (Eds.). (2003). *Autobiographical memory and the construction of a narrative self: Developmental and cultural perspectives.* Mahwah, NJ: Lawrence Lawrence Erlbaum Associates, Inc.

Fivush, R., & Haden, C. A. (2005). Parent–child reminiscing and the construction of a subjective self. In B. D. Homer & C. S. Tamis-LeMonda (Eds.), *The development of social cognition and communication* (pp. 315–335). Mahwah, NJ: Lawrence Erlbaum Associates, Inc.

Fivush, R., Haden, C. A., & Reese, E. (2006). Elaborating on elaborations: Maternal reminscing style and children's socioemotional outcome. *Child Development, 77*, 1568–1588.

Fivush, R., Haden, C. A., & Reese, E. (1996). Remembering, recounting and reminiscing: The development of autobiographical memory in social context. In D. Rubin (Ed.), *Reconstructing our past: An overview of autobiographical memory* (pp. 341–359). New York: Cambridge University Press.

Fivush, R., & Nelson, K. (2004). Culture and language in the emergence of autobiographical memory. *Psychological Science, 15*, 573–577.

Fivush, R., & Nelson, K. (2006). Parent–child reminiscing locates the self in the past. *British Journal of Developmental Psychology, 24*, 235–251.

Fivush, R., & Reese, E. (2002). Origins of reminiscing. In J. Webster and B. Haight (Eds.), *Critical advances in reminiscence work* (pp. 109–122). New York: Springer.

Fivush, R., & Vasudeva, A. (2002). Remembering to relate: Socioemotional correlates of mother–child reminiscing. *Journal of Cognition and Development, 3*, 73–90.

Fivush, R., & Wang, Q. (2005). Emotion talk in mother–child conversation of the shared past: The effects of culture, gender, and event valence. *Journal of Cognition and Development, 6*, 489–506.

Flannagan, D., Baker-Ward, L., & Graham, L. (1995). Talk about preschool: Patterns of topic discussion and elaboration related to gender and ethnicity. *Sex Roles, 32*, 1–15.

Haden, C. A. (1998). Reminiscing with different children: Relating maternal stylistic consistency and sibling similarity in talk about the past. *Developmental Psychology, 34*, 99–114.

Haden, C. A., & Fivush, R. (1996). Contextual variation in maternal conversational styles. *Merrill-Palmer Quarterly, 42*, 200–227.

Haden, C. A., Haine, R., & Fivush, R. (1997). Developing narrative structure in parent–child conversations about the past. *Developmental Psychology, 33*, 295–307.

Haden, C. A., Ornstein, P. A., Rudek, D. J., & Branstein, D. (2006). *Reminiscing in the early years: Patterns of maternal elaborativeness and children's remembering.* Manuscript under review.

Han, J. J., Leichtman, M. D., & Wang, Q. (1998). Autobiographical memory in Korean, Chinese, and American children. *Developmental Psychology, 34*, 701–713.

Harley, K., & Reese, E. (1999). Origins of autobiographical memory. *Developmental Psychology, 35*, 1338–1348.

Hayne, H., & MacDonald, S. (2003). The socialization of autobiographical memory in children and adults: The roles of culture and gender. In R. Fivush & C. A. Haden (Eds.), *Autobiographical memory and the construction of a narrative self: Developmental and cultural perspectives* (pp. 99–120). Mahwah, NJ: Lawrence Lawrence Erlbaum Associates, Inc.

Hoff-Ginsburg, E. (1991). Mother–child conversations in different social classes and communicative settings. *Child Development, 62*, 782–796.

Hudson, J. A. (1990). The emergence of autobiographic memory in mother–child conversation. In R. Fivush & J. A. Hudson (Eds.), *Knowing and remembering in young children* (pp. 166–196). New York: Cambridge University Press.

Labov, W., & Waletzky, J. (1967). Narrative analysis: Oral versions of personal experiences. In J. Helm (Ed.), *Essays on the verbal and visual arts* (pp. 12–44). Seattle: University of Washington Press.

Laible, D. (2004). Mother–child discourse in two contexts: Links with child temperament, attachment security, and socioemotional competence. *Developmental Psychology, 40*, 979–992.

Laible, D., & Thompson, R. (2000). Mother–child discourse, attachment security, shared positive affect, and early conscience development. *Child Development, 71*, 1424–1440.

Leichtman, M., Wang, Q., & Pillemer, D. B. (2003). Cultural variation in interdependence and autobiographical memory. In R. Fivush & C. Haden (Eds.),

Autobiographical memory and the construction of a narrative self: Developmental and cultural perspectives. Mahwah, NJ: Lawrence Erlbaum Associates, Inc.

Leichtman, M. D., Pillemer, D. B., Wang, Q., Koreishi, A., & Han, J. J. (2000). When baby Maisy came to school: Mothers' interview styles and preschoolers' event memories. *Cognitive Development, 15*, 99–114.

Low, J., & Durkin, K. (2001). Individual differences and consistency in maternal talk style during joint story encoding and retrospection: Associations with children's long-term recall. *International Journal of Behavioral Development, 25*, 27–36.

Lucariello, J., Kyratzis, A., & Engel, S. (1986). Event representations, context, and language. In K. Nelson (Ed.), *Event knowledge: Structure and function in development* (pp. 137–160). Hillsdale, NJ: Lawrence Erlbaum Associates, Inc.

Lucariello, J., & Nelson, K. (1987). Remembering and planning talk between mothers and children. *Discourse Processes, 10*, 219–235.

MacDonald, S., Uesiliana, K., & Hayne, H. (2000). Cross-cultural and gender differences in childhood amnesia. *Memory, 8*, 365–376.

McCabe, A., & Peterson, C. (1991). Getting the story: A longitudinal study of parental styles in eliciting narratives and developing narrative skill. In A. McCabe & C. Peterson (Eds.), *Developing narrative structure* (pp. 217–253). Hillsdale, NJ: Lawrence Erlbaum Associates, Inc.

McGuigan, F., & Salmon, K. (2004). The time to talk: The influence of the timing of adult–child talk on children's event memory. *Child Development, 75*, 669–686.

Miller, P. J. (1994). Narrative practices: Their role in socialization and self-construction. In U. Neisser & R. Fivush (Eds.), *The remembering self: Construction and accuracy in the life narrative* (pp. 158–179). New York: Cambridge University Press.

Mullen, M., & Yi, S. (1995). The cultural context of talk about the past: Implications for the development of autobiographical memory. *Cognitive Development, 10*, 407–419.

Nelson, K. (1996). *Language in cognitive development*. Mahwah, NJ: Lawrence Erlbaum Associates, Inc.

Nelson, K., & Fivush, R. (2004). The emergence of autobiographical memory: A social cultural developmental theory. *Psychological Review, 111*, 486–511.

Nelson, K., & Ross, G. (1980). The generalities and specifics of long-term memory in infants and young children. In M. Perlmutter (Ed.), *New directions for child development: Children's memory* (pp. 87–101). San Francisco, CA: Jossey-Bass.

Oyserman, D., & Markus, H. (1993). The sociocultural self. In J. Suls (Ed.), *Psychological perspectives on the self: The self in social perspective* (Vol. 4, pp. 187–220). Mahwah, NJ: Lawrence Erlbaum Associates, Inc.

Pennebaker, J. W. (1997). *Opening up*. New York: Guilford.

Perner, J., & Ruffman, T. (1995). Episodic memory and autonoetic consciousness: Developmental evidence and a theory of childhood amnesia. *Journal of Experimental Child Psychology, 59*, 516–548.

Peterson, C., Jesso, B., & McCabe, A. (1999). Encouraging narratives in preschoolers: An intervention study. *Journal of Child Language, 26*, 49–67.

Peterson, C., & McCabe, A. (1992). Parental styles of narrative elicitation: Effect on children's narrative structure and content. *First Language, 12*, 299–321.

Peterson, C., & McCabe, A. (1994). A social interactionist account of developing decontextualized narrative skill. *Developmental Psychology, 30*, 937–948.

Peterson, C., & McCabe, A. (1996). Parental scaffolding of context in children's narratives. In C. E. Johnson & J. H. V. Gilbert (Eds.), *Children's language* (Vol. 9, pp. 183–196). Hillsdale, NJ: Lawrence Erlbaum Associates, Inc.

Peterson, C., & McCabe, A. (2004). Echoing our parents: Parental influences on children's narration. In M. W. Pratt & B. H. Fiese (Eds.), *Family stories and the life course: Across time and generations* (pp. 27–54). Mahwah, NJ: Lawrence Erlbaum Associates, Inc.

Pillemer, D. (1998). *Momentous events, vivid memories*. Cambridge, MA: Harvard University Press.

Reese, E., & Farrant, K. (2003). Origins of reminiscing in parent–child relationships. In R. Fivush & C. A. Haden (Eds.), *Autobiographical memory and the construction of a narrative self: Developmental and cultural perspectives* (pp. 29–48). Mahwah, NJ: Lawrence Erlbaum Associates, Inc.

Reese, E., Haden, C. A., & Fivush, R. (1993). Mother–child conversations about the past: Relationships of style and memory over time. *Cognitive Development, 8*, 403–430.

Reese, E., Haden, C. A., & Fivush, R. (1996). Mothers, fathers, daughters, sons: Gender differences in reminiscing. *Research on Language and Social Interaction, 29*, 27–56.

Rogoff, B. (1990). *Apprenticeship in thinking*. New York: Oxford University Press.

Rudek, D., & Haden, C. A. (2005). Mothers' and preschoolers' mental state language during reminiscing over time. *Merrill-Palmer Quarterly, 51*, 557–583.

Sales, J. M., & Fivush, R. (2005). Social and emotional functions of mother–child reminiscing about stressful events. *Social Cognition, 23*, 70–90.

Sales, J. M., Fivush, R., & Peterson, C. (2003). Parental reminiscing about positive and negative events. *Journal of Cognition and Development, 4*, 185–209.

Symons, D. K. (2004). Mental state discourse, theory of mind, and an internalization of self–other understanding. *Developmental Review, 24*, 159–188.

Tessler, M., & Nelson, K. (1994). Making memories: The influence of joint encoding on later recall by young children. *Consciousness and Cognition, 3*, 307–326.

Vygotsky, L. S. (1978). *Mind in society: The development of higher psychological processes*. Cambridge, MA: Harvard University Press.

Wang, Q. (2001). "Did you have fun?" American and Chinese mother–child conversations about shared emotional experiences. *Cognitive Development, 16*, 693–715.

Wang, Q. (2003). Emotion situation knowledge in American and Chinese preschool children and adults. *Cognition and Emotion, 17*, 725–746.

Wang, Q., & Fivush, R. (2005). Mother–child conversations of emotionally salient events: Exploring the functions of reminiscing in Euro-American and Chinese families. *Social Development, 14*, 473–495.

Welch-Ross, M. K. (1997). Mother–child participation in conversation about the past: Relationship to preschoolers' theory of mind. *Developmental Psychology, 33*, 618–629.

Welch-Ross, M. K. (2001). Personalizing the temporally extended self: Evaluative self-awareness and the development of autobiographical memory. In C. Moore & K. Skene (Eds.), *The self in time: Developmental issues* (pp. 97–120). Hillsdale, NJ: Lawrence Erlbaum Associates, Inc.

Wellman, H. M. (2002). Understanding the psychological world: Developing a theory of mind. In U. Goswami (Ed.), *Blackwell handbook of childhood cognitive development* (pp. 167–187). Malden, MA: Blackwell.

12 Development of working memory in childhood

Nelson Cowan
University of Missouri, USA

Tracy Alloway
Child Development Research Unit,
Durham University, UK

Working memory is the small amount of information that can be kept accessible or "kept in mind" in the service of ongoing cognitive activity. It is of key importance in language comprehension and all sorts of problem-solving. We discuss what working memory means, what is special about it, and how it might be understood within models of cognition and human information processing. Then we examine various types of specific processes within working memory that may undergo developmental improvement. Given limited space, we do not cover working memory in infancy, for which a different set of experimental techniques is needed (see Diamond, 1985; Oakes & Bauer, 2007; Rovee-Collier & Cuevas, Chapter 2, this volume; Reznick, Chapter 13, this volume), or in non-human animals. Finally, we consider some practical consequences of working memory in cognitive disorders relevant to education.

WHAT IS WORKING MEMORY?

William James (1890, p. 403) said "Every one knows what attention is." Maybe so but, for a related concept, working memory, researchers disagree on what it is. Miyake and Shah (1999) asked the authors of various chapters in their book to define working memory and the definitions differed considerably. Some (e.g., Cowan, 1999) took a rather a priori approach and described it as the ensemble of mental mechanisms that allow information to be held in a temporarily accessible form to allow thinking. Others included in the definition the specific mechanisms or structures that they thought to be part of working memory, such as automatic storage mechanisms dedicated to a particular kind of information such as speech sounds, or a central attention mechanism that controls cognitive performance. One way to approximate a consensus is to use the definition from Wikipedia, an on-the-web encyclopedia allowing readers to edit the entry. On 30 August 2006, the definition at the website (http://en.wikipedia.org/wiki/Working_memory) was as follows: "In cognitive psychology, working memory is a theoretical framework that refers to structures and processes used for temporarily storing and manipulating information." The term dates back to a book by Miller, Galanter, and Pribram (1960) theorizing that, in carrying out a complex behavior (e.g., comprehending a written paragraph, completing a math problem, or packing a suitcase), an individual has to remember the overall goal memory as well as the data, an overall plan, and various sub-plans necessary to reach the goal. This information that is only temporarily appropriate to guide action is saved in what they called working memory.

Many other related terms have cropped up in the psychological literature, such as James's (1890) distinction between primary memory, comprising limited information in conscious awareness, and secondary memory, comprising the information learned over a lifetime. In the dawning of cognitive psychology in the late 1950s and 1960s, the terms short-term and long-term memory often served a similar purpose (e.g., Atkinson & Shiffrin, 1968). However, Baddeley and Hitch (1974) returned the field to the term working memory for several reasons. First, they wished to emphasize the use of this memory for carrying out cognitive operations; it is primarily from their influence that the Wikipedia definition of working memory includes not only holding information, but also manipulating it. Second, whereas primary or short-term memory was typically conceived as a single component of the mind, evidence by Baddeley and Hitch suggested that the concept had to be fractionated into several components, including separate phonological and visuospatial storage mechanisms that hold special information for a short time effortlessly, and a central processing unit that could hold various information while changing or manipulating it as the problem required (e.g., remembering numbers while adding them together). Third, they found that, although one could impede working memory by adding a demanding secondary task to be carried out along with the memory task, it did not affect some aspects of memory that other researchers attributed to primary memory; it did not quash the especially good recall of the most recent items in the list, or recency effect. Therefore, they came to see working memory as something different from what other people were calling primary or short-term memory. Nevertheless, all three terms—primary, short-term, or working memory—included a component of the mind that is very much like a focus of attention, a mindful, general-purpose entity that could deal with only a limited amount of information at once but could do wonders with it. Some have defined working memory as the active, attention-related part of temporary memory, and short-term memory as the passive part (e.g., Engle, Tuholski, Laughlin, & Conway, 1999); others have defined working memory as the entire ensemble of mechanisms that includes both the active and passive parts (e.g., Baddeley, 1986; Cowan, 1988, 1999).

WHAT IS SPECIAL ABOUT WORKING MEMORY?

Ordinarily, what is special about a mental process is what it is capable of doing. However, to understand working memory, one must also consider what its limits are, as they distinguish it from the rest of the cognitive system. Working memory is capable of making certain ideas more readily accessible to ongoing thinking and actions (e.g., items, words, concepts, visual representations). However, it can do so only for a limited number of ideas at a time, and only for a limited time per idea. Therefore, there is an important process of selecting the ideas to be included in working memory. For example, if the goal of an action is lost from working memory, the action is not likely to be completed successfully until it is recovered. (Have you ever entered a room wondering, "Why did I come in here again?") If the part of the present sentence that precedes the comma is lost from working memory, then the part of the sentence after the comma will have no particular meaning for you.

Working memory limits

One can draw an analogy between the limits of working memory and limits of physical objects or events (see Kail & Salthouse, 1994). The latter are limited in time, space, and/or energy, which are described below in turn. Although these may encompass the basic working-memory mechanisms, there are other, more general processes that also influence performance on working memory tasks, and these too are explained.

Time-related limits

In working memory, a time limit would indicate that any active idea in working memory stays active or accessible only for a short time, unless something is done to reactivate it, such as actively devoting attention to it anew or saying it to oneself (rehearsing it). This source of forgetting from working memory (or from short-term memory) is termed decay. In the early days of cognitive psychology, one could find evidence seeming to confirm decay (e.g., Baddeley, Thomson, & Buchanan, 1975; Peterson & Peterson, 1959) or seeming to disconfirm it (e.g., Keppel & Underwood, 1962; Waugh & Norman, 1965). Today, despite considerable additional research, one still can find recent evidence seeming to confirm decay (e.g., Barrouillet, Bernardin, & Camos, 2004; Cowan, Nugent, Elliott, & Geer, 2000; Mueller, Seymour, Kieras, & Meyer, 2003) or seeming to disconfirm it (e.g., Cowan, Elliott, Saults, Nugent, Bomb, & Hismjatullina, 2006; Lewandowsky, Duncan, & Brown, 2004; Lovatt, Avons, & Masterson, 2002). A challenge for this research is to be sure that rehearsal is not taking place. One can insert a distracting task to prevent rehearsal, but the distracting task may displace the memoranda in working memory, a mechanism different from decay. So, today, the proposition that there is forgetting of unrehearsed items in working memory as a function of time in the absence of interference (i.e., decay) is still quite controversial.

A corollary to the decay hypothesis is that the speed of processing should make a difference. For example, if items from a list are being forgotten while an individual is recalling them from working memory, then faster recall should allow more items to be recalled before they become unavailable for recall because of decay. Lewandowsky et al. (2004, Experiment 2) slowed down recall by having participants insert a spoken word (super) once, twice, or thrice in each gap between letters from a list as it was recalled, but no effect of the amount of delay on recall was observed. Nevertheless, some would argue that when a single word is to be repeated like this, the repetition becomes routine enough that some attention is freed up and is used to reactivate the items to be recalled, which obscures the process of memory loss (Baddeley, 1986; Barrouillet et al., 2004).

Space-related limits

The relevance of space in working memory applies if one thinks of each idea as a physical object, in which case a metaphor for working memory is a box that holds the currently active objects. The number of objects that can be held depends on the space taken up by the box (i.e., its volume). This approach was advanced by one of the best-known articles in the field of psychology (Miller, 1956), in which it was suggested that adults seem to be able to remember lists of about seven items. According to a previous approach, it could have been expected that what is important for memorability of a list is the amount of information that each item carries, in addition to the number of items in the list. For example, there are 26 English letters so, to identify any letter, up to five binary (yes-or-no) questions must be answered (because $2^5 > 26 > 2^4$). If we learn that a letter is after m, it can be any of 13 letters; if is also before t, any of 6 letters; if also after p, any of 3 letters (q, r, or s); if also before s, either of 2 letters (q or r); and if it is also after q, it can only be r. There are only 10 digits (carrying less information per item than letters) and there are thousands of words (carrying much more information per item than letters); yet, we can remember lists of about seven items no matter whether they are digits, letters, or words.

What increases this limit is grouping items together to form larger meaningful items, as in the acronym IBM, which includes three letters but forms a single meaningful unit representing a corporation in the United States (International Business Machines). Miller (1956) called this grouping process chunking. It is difficult to remember a list of nine random letters, but it is easy when the letters form a much smaller number of meaningful chunks (as in the list IBM-NBC-RCA, representing three well-known corporations). Now, one could ask whether it is possible to remember lists of seven of these acronyms, or, say, seven idiomatic expressions or phrases, and the answer appears to be "no" (Glanzer & Razel, 1974; Simon, 1974; Tulving & Patkau, 1962).

However, it has been argued that the ordinary limit of seven is possible only because some special processes enhance working memory capability. Participants may group items together rapidly to form new chunks, or they may engage in silent, covert rehearsal of short verbal items (e.g., Baddeley, 1986). When those processes are prevented, participants more typically recall three or four chunks (Broadbent, 1975; Cowan, 2001) and this appears to be true not only for short chunks such as digits, letters, or words, which can be articulated quickly, but also for longer chunks such as phrases, or for chunks that cannot be articulated at all (e.g., Glanzer & Razel, 1974; Gobet & Clarkson, 2004).

Can these findings be accommodated with the space metaphor? Probably so. A box can hold only a fixed number of objects of a certain size, but the density of the objects does not matter. Chunking may be compared to taking objects of a standard size and compacting two or more of them together until they take up the same space that a single standard object took before the compression. By doing so, more objects can fit in the same box. Although there have been recent studies showing that capacity limits provide an excellent account of performance (Chen & Cowan, 2005; Cowan, Chen, & Rouder, 2004), the generality of this conclusion remains unknown.

Energy-related limits

The energy metaphor takes into account that information does not just enter working memory automatically and then leave it automatically. A person's goals make him or her strive to put certain items in working memory and to remove other, irrelevant items to make room for those relevant to the task at hand, whatever it may be. Yet these goals can conflict with other mental tendencies that have to be suppressed or overridden. For example, in the classic procedure of Stroop (1935), the participant must name an ink color as quickly as possible instead of reading aloud the conflicting color word that the ink forms (e.g., the word "blue" written in yellow ink). Given that the conversion from print to speech is automatic in normal adults, the printed word must be inhibited to prevent errors in this task. Individuals with less working memory have a difficult time suppressing the word-reading response and can be more often lulled into reading the word instead of naming the ink color, especially if the word matches the ink color on most trials (Kane & Engle, 2003). Low-span individuals may have less of the relevant type of energy to control attention. In daily life, considerable energy must be exerted to maintain working memory, as when one waits patiently for a turn to say something without either interrupting or forgetting what one wanted to say. This general concept of working memory limits in energy (i.e., control of attention) may be less controversial than limits in time (decay) and space (capacity). However, in any particular situation, it is difficult to identify exactly which of these limits applies. For example, the inability to remove irrelevant items from working memory could deflate the estimate of how many relevant items can be held at once (May, Hasher, & Kane, 1999; Vogel, McCollough, & Machizawa, 2005).

Other limits affecting working memory

Last, a number of other factors may influence how well one performs a working memory task. Knowledge of the material being tested makes a difference (Chi, 1978), and its influence can be separated from those of other factors, such as recall speed (Hulme, Maughan, & Brown, 1991) or working memory for less familiar materials (Hambrick & Engle, 2001). The ability to use particular mnemonic strategies, such as types of rehearsal and grouping, makes a difference (Budd, Whitney, & Turley, 1995; McNamara & Scott, 2001), as does one's knowledge of what strategies would or would not be feasible or helpful, termed metamemory (Bunnell, Baken, & Richards-Ward, 1999). With all of these possible factors, it is actually quite difficult to conclude that a particular age difference in memory definitely is caused by one particular factor.

With these ideas and cautions in mind, we now introduce some conceptions of the working memory system and then examine evidence of developmental change.

MODELS OF WORKING MEMORY

Why models are helpful

It might be possible to test each proposition about working memory and its development separately. Is there decay? Is there a capacity limit? Is control of attention an issue? Which of these changes with development? In practice, though, it is difficult to do this. For example, if one wants to examine age differences in decay, one must explore the possibility that the combination of capacity and control-of-attention factors might produce results that look like decay. In exploring any one factor, it helps to keep in mind one's conception of the processing system as a whole. In any case, an important goal of research is to refine our understanding of the system as a whole. At least partly for these reasons, considerable effort has gone into the development of models of working memory. What is meant by this is a simplified conception of the parts of working memory and how they operate together, a bundle of hypotheses about working memory that all fit a logically consistent system leading to testable predictions.

Types of models

One can distinguish at least four types of models of working memory. They can be classified as cognitive versus neural on one hand, and as conceptual versus computational on the other hand. In cognitive, conceptual models, the aim appears to be to take into consideration all that is known about working-memory performance and to describe a plausible system of mechanisms that could produce the data. The predictions based on this sort of model are primarily ordinal; performance is predicted to be higher in one particular condition than in another. In cognitive computational models, additional assumptions are made explicit so that the model can yield predictions about the mathematical form of results. This generally can be done only by adopting some assumptions that cannot presently be checked, and only by limiting the scope of evidence that can be taken into consideration. In neural models, statements are made about the neural activities underlying working memory performance. Neural models also can be of either the conceptual or the computational variety although, at present, to create a neural, computational model one generally has to go "far out on a limb" with unsubstantiated assumptions. We do not advocate the use of any one type of model alone; they are not mutually exclusive, and there is a need for all of them until such time as a grand, unifying, conceptually and computationally explicit model of performance on both the cognitive and neural levels can be developed and verified. For now, though, we emphasize one model type.

Cognitive, conceptual models

Figure 12.1 summarizes three models of this type. The first model is a rough sketch of the entire human information processing system offered by Broadbent (1958) in a footnote within his book. (The terminology is modified here, as Broadbent's original terms conflict with more recent usage.) Coming at the awakening of the field of cognitive psychology, Broadbent distinguished between two types of temporary memory: a sensory memory that contains traces from sensory experience in all modalities and channels at once, but not for long; and a central processing unit that can accept only a small fraction of the information present in sensory memory and is, in that way, limited in capacity. These ultimately contribute to a long-term memory of experience. According to Broadbent's conception, the higher-level stores could feed information back to the lower-level stores to help encode and interpret information within them. In most subsequent models there is a level of sensory memory that is not interpreted on the basis of categorical knowledge. Atkinson and Shiffrin (1968) refined this model to make it more computational and to give a more vivid account of control processes, such as covert rehearsal, that presumably are involved in cycling information from one phase of storage to another.

   The middle panel shows the model of Baddeley (2000). An earlier version by Baddeley (1986) has been probably the most influential model in the field of working memory per se. The newer version shown in the figure differs from the earlier version only in that the former model did not include the box labeled the episodic buffer. The original model was designed to explain why a

Modal Model (after Broadbent, 1958)

Working-Memory Model (after Baddeley, 2000)

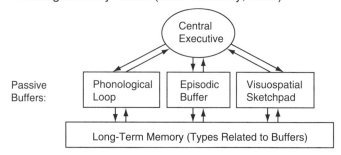

Embedded-Processes Model (after Cowan, 1988)

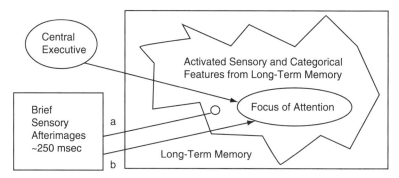

Figure 12.1 Three conceptual, behavioral models of working memory. From Cowan, N. (2005). *Working memory capacity.* New York: Psychology Press (p. 18, Figure 1.2).

single capacity-limited store, such as that of Broadbent (1958), cannot account for all of the working memory results. The idea of a capacity-limited region of memory implies that keeping in mind one type of information impairs memory for another kind of information. In reality, though, Baddeley and colleagues found little interference between verbal materials, on one hand, and visual-spatial materials, on the other hand, so separate types of memory storage were advocated for these two types of materials. Although

Baddeley and Hitch (1974) considered that there also might be a capacity-limited, general type of memory storage running across domains, Baddeley (1986) did away with that type of storage for the sake of parsimony and suggested that every type of memory of interest could rely on phonological and/or visuospatial memory, with central executive processes that manipulate and process information, controlling its flow, but do not store it per se. Phonological and visuospatial memory were said to be limited by decay, for reasons we will explore later. Baddeley (2000) reconsidered the need for a more general type of memory storage, for various reasons. For example, one must often temporarily remember the links between verbal and visual sources of information, or a new arrangement of abstract ideas that are neither phonological nor visuospatial in form. To account for these types of memory, Baddeley (2000) added the episodic buffer to the model.

The bottom panel of Figure 12.1 shows a model proposed by Cowan (1988) and elaborated in later writing (Cowan, 1995, 1999, 2001). It was suggested as a general processing model, taking into account the role of attention processes in storage more than did the model of Baddeley (1986). It can be contrasted to the other two models in several ways. Broadbent's (1958) model includes the notion of an attention filter limiting how much information can be transferred from the sensory store to the capacity-limited store at any moment; it is generally limited to a single stream of input. In contrast, Cowan (1988) considered that there must be some way for at least sensory information from multiple streams of input to be transferred. In evidence that Broadbent summarized, when individuals attend selectively to one of several channels (such as one ear's message in a dichotic listening situation with different messages to the two ears) they remember little or nothing of the material in the unattended channel. However, they do notice when an unattended message changes abruptly in its physical properties (such as a switch from a male voice to a female voice in the unattended message). They sometimes also notice their own names in the message to be ignored (Moray, 1959), although this can be explained on the basis that some individuals' attention wanders from the assigned channel, allowing attention to a channel that was supposed to be ignored (Conway, Cowan, & Bunting, 2001). Cowan's (1988) model postulates that all incoming stimulation has some influence on the processing system, activating parts of long-term memory. For unattended stimuli, this activated information may or may not be limited to the gross physical features of the stimuli. If these features change abruptly, the stimuli not only activate long-term memory features, but also recruit attention. This in turn results in a deeper, more complete analysis of the changed stimuli. The assumption is that a mnemonic representation of the environment is built up and that orienting of attention (Sokolov, 1963) occurs after an individual processes stimuli that produce a discrepancy from that representation. As the representation is modified to reflect the change, the orienting response dies down as the individual habituates to the new status quo.

Cowan's (1988) model also can be compared to Baddeley (2000). One difference is that Cowan's model is less modular. In place of the phonological and visuospatial stores, it depicts activated portions of long-term memory. The intent was not to deny a difference between phonological and visuospatial representations. However, at present it is not clear how memory should be divided up. Perhaps the phonological store also works for nonverbal sounds. Perhaps there is a representation that is auditory and spatial, or tactile and spatial. Therefore, Cowan simply stated the hypothesis that the amount of interference between one stimulus and another depends on the similarity in the features of the two stimuli; it was thought that positing a specific taxonomy of the varieties of activated memory, or the exact nature and number of buffers, would be premature.

In addition to activated elements of long-term memory, Cowan supposed that a subset of that activated memory is in the focus of attention. Later work suggested that the focus typically includes three to five meaningful chunks of information in normal adults (Cowan, 2001, 2005). It may also include new associations between elements. In fact, all items present in the focus of attention at once may become inter-associated. If one pays attention while two people are being introduced, for example, then the focus of attention may hold information about which name goes with which person. Whether all of this information is successfully transferred to long-term memory is a question that probably cannot yet be answered. The focus of attention functions in a manner that may be similar to Baddeley's (2000, 2001) episodic buffer, except that Baddeley has not taken a definitive stand on the attention requirements of that buffer. Overall, there is a lot of similarity between the revised Baddeley model and the Cowan model. According to one use of terminology, the activated memory can be called short-term memory and the focus of attention can be called working memory (Engle et al., 1999).

Other types of models

Other varieties of models aside from the cognitive, conceptual ones are important but have perhaps only just begun to make an impact on developmental research. Cognitive, computational models include many models specific to serial recall processes (for a summary see Farrell & Lewandowsky, 2004). A few models of short-term working memory more generally are conceptually quite similar to the Cowan (1999) model, but in a computationally explicit way (Anderson, Bothell, Lebiere, & Matessa, 1998; Davelaar, Goshen-Gottstein, Ashkenazi, Haarman, & Usher, 2005; Oberauer & Kliegl, 2006). In neural, conceptual models of working memory, areas of the brain have begun to be identified with particular processes related to working memory, providing important clues to guide future investigations even though we do not yet know much about each of these brain areas. In particular, emphasis has been placed on frontal lobe systems as a basis of the control of attention (e.g., Cowan, 1995; Kane & Engle, 2002) as well as parietal lobe systems as an important part of the seat of attention, or its focus (Cowan, 1995, 1999). The intraparietal and intraocular sulci have been found to respond to visual arrays in a working memory task in a manner that mirrors performance. Todd and Marois (2004) found these areas to increase in activity as the visual working memory load increased, and to reach an asymptotic level of activity when the behaviorally defined memory capacity was reached. Xu and Chun (2006) replicated this and showed that some of the sub-areas respond to the number of objects regardless of their complexity; but they also found related areas that are influenced by the level of complexity in the stimuli, which also affects working memory capacity. This leads to the notion that there is a limit to how many objects can be represented (about four at most) and another limit to the total amount of complexity (with the capacity lowered for complex objects), all in keeping with behavioral results (Alvarez & Cavanagh, 2004). Finally, neural, computational models have suggested why working memory capacity is limited. The suggestion is basically that the multiple features of several items can be represented at the same time if the neural substrates of the features of a given object all fire in unison and, within a short, fixed cycle, all items have a turn. If more than a few objects enter working memory, there is an increasing danger that the features of different items will be confused with one another (Lisman & Idiart, 1995). For example, one may forget whether the items included a red square and a green triangle or a green square and a red triangle, if several other items also were included in the set.

In practice, the division between model types is not so clean because, for example, some conceptual models may appeal to neural-like principles without including many actual neural details, computational models may have a conceptual wing that is not modeled, broad conceptual models may have a computational component that is itself not very broad or comprehensive, and so on. All of the models may be viewed as theoretical tools to guide empirical investigations.

Distinguishing between models based on mechanisms

Although it is difficult to determine which model is correct, mechanisms help to distinguish between models. In some models, time-related decay of memory is postulated (e.g., Baddeley, 1986; Broadbent, 1958; Cowan, 1999), whereas, in other models, time-related decay is not part of the model at all (e.g., Lewandowsky et al., 2004; Waugh & Norman, 1965). According to some models there should be a general capacity that is shared between different types of materials (Baddeley, 2001; Broadbent, 1958; Cowan, 1999) but, according to other models, there is no such capacity because retention is accomplished entirely in domain-specific stores (e.g., Baddeley, 1986). Also, in some models (e.g., Engle et al., 1999; Kane & Engle, 2003) the ability to control attention might entirely explain individual differences in capacity, whereas, according to other models, more emphasis is placed on working memory storage limits as being separate from these attention-control differences (Cowan, 1999, 2001). Addressing the fundamental mechanisms is probably an efficient way to guide the selection among models.

DEVELOPMENT OF WORKING MEMORY

No doubt working memory improves with development but it is difficult to determine what basic mechanisms account for this improvement with maturation. Here we consider the role of mechanisms we have already introduced. Given that mechanisms help to distinguish between models of working memory, it seems likely that developmental evidence on the role of these mechanisms in turn can help guide the selection of models. Thus the relation between cognitive psychology and cognitive development is a two-way street.

Time-related (decay and speed) factors

The examination of time-related factors has involved experimental methods in which a list of items is presented and the task is to recall the list in its presented order (in developmental studies, orally or by pointing to items). Sometimes, fixed list lengths are used and, other times, the list length is variable and the question is the length of list that can be recalled without error (a memory span task).

Speed–memory correlation

Traditionally, investigations of decay and speed co-occur. According to the logic developed by Baddeley et al. in understanding the word length effect, individuals could remember lists of about as many words as they could pronounce in 2 seconds. The maximal speed of pronunciation of a few words was assumed to provide an estimate of the speed of covert rehearsal, perhaps not a bad assumption inasmuch as covert and overt varieties of speech do seem to proceed at comparable rates (Landauer, 1962). The data suggested that the speed of rehearsal could account for memory span. The assumption was that the phonological memory trace is lost if it is not refreshed soon enough through covert verbal rehearsal, in a repeating phonological loop. On the assumption that everyone has the same decay rate and loses an unrehearsed memory trace in about 2 seconds, individual differences in memory can be accounted for by differences in the speed of covert rehearsal. This logic was later extended to account for developmental differences in span, the finding being that younger children speak more slowly and recall commensurately less than older children or adults (Hulme, Thomson, Muir, & Lawrence, 1984; Hulme & Tordoff, 1989; Kail, 1992; Kail & Park, 1994). An example of this relationship is shown in Figure 12.2.

Similar arguments had been made regarding the relation between other

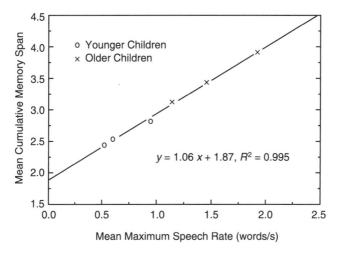

Figure 12.2 The relation between speech rate and memory span in 4-year-old and 8-year-old children. From Cowan, N., Keller, T., Hulme, C., Roodenrys, S., McDougall, S., & Rack, J. (1994). Verbal memory span in children: Speech timing clues to the mechanisms underlying age and word length effects. *Journal of Memory and Language, 33*, 234–250 (p. 240, Figure 1). Copyright © Elsevier (1994). Used with permission.

sorts of short-term memory and processing speed, as well (Case, Kurland, & Goldberg, 1982).

A problem with the phonological loop interpretation was that other research suggests that young (e.g., 4-year-old) children, whose data fit the nice linear relation between speech rate and memory span, cannot carry out useful rehearsal (Flavell, Beach, & Chinsky, 1966), suggesting that the rate of rehearsal cannot be a determining factor. A slight modification of the theory still could work. Whether the phonological memory trace lasts long enough to result in successful recall should depend not only on the speed of covert rehearsal, but on the speed of overt, spoken responses. Specifically, memory can be lost during the response period. If the first item in the response is articulated too slowly or if the pause after it is too slow, memory for the second and following items can fade during that time; and so on. Evidence does suggest that the overt response speed is of interest, in that (1) young children show effects of speech rate on memory span, such as a word length effect, only when there is a spoken response, whereas older children show these effects even when the response is nonverbal (Henry, 1991); and (2) the speed of spoken responses in memory span tasks does dramatically increase with age in childhood (Cowan, Keller, Hulme, Roodenrys, McDougall, & Rack, 1994; Cowan, Wood, Wood, Keller, Nugent, & Keller, 1998).

Speed–memory path of causation?

A critical question that still needs to be examined is whether the chain of causation suggested by the phonological loop model really holds. Recall the Lewandowsky et al. (2004) finding that, in adults, response speed in a serial recall task could be slowed without impairing span. Of course, their use of repetitions of a single word to slow down recall may have been inadequate to stop rehearsal during that delay (see Barrouillet et al., 2004). However, discouraging results also have been obtained in studies designed with the intent of speeding up children's recall, to see if span increases in the expected manner. Hulme and Muir (1985) tried to train children to learn to produce words at a faster rate to see whether that would result in an increase in memory span, presumably by allowing the children to rehearse more quickly. They were unable to train children reliably so it was not possible to test the hypothesis. Cowan, Elliott, et al. (2006, Experiment 2) took a slightly different approach, with second-grade children (most of whom were 8 years old) recalling lists of digits. Instead of trying to increase the maximum rate of rehearsal, this study concentrated on the usual rate of recall. A baseline digit span measurement was obtained in every child and then, in a second phase of the experiment, half of the children were simply instructed to speak as quickly as possible without making errors. In a third phase, they could again determine their own speed (but generally chose to remain fast). In a control group, no speed instruction was given in any phase. Each phase also included some post-span trials with lengths adjusted relative to span, to equalize the difficulty level. The results are shown in Figure 12.3.

Even though children in the experimental group increased their speech rate to one faster than the usual adult rate (as measured in a first experiment), there was absolutely no improvement in memory in any part of the experiment.

Caution is still in order. It is possible that each person's memory response occurs at some sort of ideal rate for that individual. He or she might find through experience that slower speeds cause memory loss whereas faster speeds require so much effort that there is no benefit to memory, because of mechanisms outside of the phonological loop. It is also possible that second-grade children engage in some sort of rehearsal between items in their responses, and that different results would be obtained if even younger children were instructed to recall quickly. However, an alternative account would state that the correlation between speech rate and memory span, or even between speed and memory more generally (Kail & Salthouse, 1994), occurs for some other reason. It could be that the memory requirement of saying things quickly plays a role. It also could be that both speed and memory are independent indices of some general neural efficiency and that neither one really influences the other. This issue is difficult to resolve but we look forward to interesting research to resolve it.

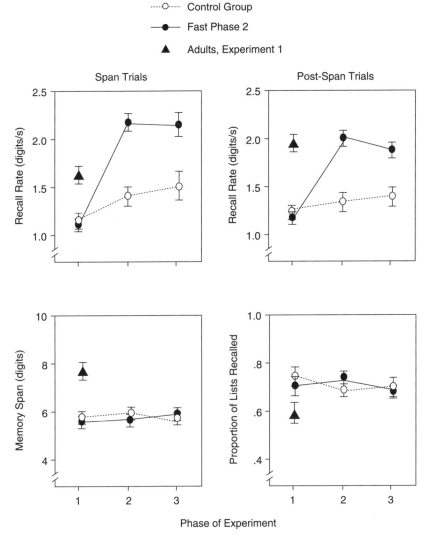

Figure 12.3 Span and post-span (ability-adjusted) trials within three phases of an experiment in which one of two groups of children received instructions to speak quickly in Phase 2. Top panels show speech rates and bottom panels show memory scores. From Cowan, N., Elliott, E. M., Saults, J. S., Nugent, L. D., Bomb, P., & Hismjatullina, A. (2006). Rethinking speed theories of cognitive development: Increasing the rate of recall without affecting accuracy. *Psychological Science*, *17*, 67–73 (p. 70, Figure 2). Reproduced with the permission of Blackwell Publishing.

Decay differences with age

Another important question is whether an untested simplifying assumption is valid. According to the usual phonological-loop-based account of age differences, the rate of decay does not change with age but the rate of rehearsal and speech does change. It is difficult actually to measure decay (if, in fact, it exists) because it is difficult to separate decay from interference effects. In a working memory task, if one does not include a distracting stimulus during a retention interval, one cannot rule out the possibility that the participant rehearsed the stimuli. Yet, such distracting stimuli may cause interference. A couple of studies addressed this issue by engaging children in a silent computer game that involved silently looking for pictures with names that rhyme (Cowan, Nugent, Elliott, & Saults, 2000; Saults & Cowan, 1996). Most stimuli were to be ignored but, once in a while, the computer game would be replaced with a request to name the last spoken word (Saults & Cowan) or digit list (Cowan et al.). Attention and mnemonic strategies would be prevented both during the presentation of the auditory stimuli, so that spoken stimuli could not be memorized, and during a retention interval of 1, 5, or 10 seconds, so that spoken stimuli could not be rehearsed. If the silent computer game caused interference, we might expect that it could impair performance for digits in all serial positions within the study of Cowan et al. However, what actually was found, for lists adjusted to each individual's span, was a pronounced difference between the rates of decay in second- versus fifth-grade children at the final serial position and no difference at any previous position (see Figure 12.4).

This suggests that there may be an age difference in decay of an uninterrupted sensory memory but that it applies only to the last item spoken. Each item may interrupt sensory memory for previous items so that only the last list item benefits much from that sort of memory (see Balota & Engle, 1981). For the sake of phonological loop explanations, this finding only suggests a small modification. Again, more research is needed.

Space-related (capacity) factors

Working memory capacity limits in terms of units, increasing in number with maturation, form the fundamental basis of cognitive development according to the neo-Piagetian school of thought (Burtis, 1982; Case, 1972; Pascual-Leone, 1970, 2005; Weiss, 1995). This type of hypothesis applies across child development. There are still few studies of the development of the capacity of working memory in chunks, mainly because the field is still uncertain how these chunks should be identified. Cowan et al. (2005) examined several working memory tasks across the elementary school years and in adulthood, and several of the tasks were selected to minimize the role of mnemonic strategies so the role of capacity could be observed. In those tasks, the assumption was that each presented item was recalled as a separate chunk of information. One task was the array-comparison task of Luck and Vogel

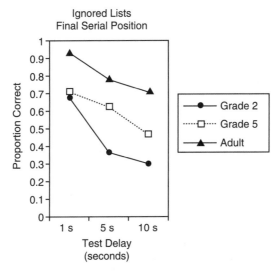

Figure 12.4 In three age groups, decay of memory in the final serial position of lists unattended during their presentation. The lists were adjusted based on span for attended lists and no decay differences were found elsewhere in the lists. From Cowan, N., Nugent, L. D., Elliott, E. M., & Saults, J. S. (2000). Persistence of memory for ignored lists of digits: Areas of developmental constancy and change. *Journal of Experimental Child Psychology*, *76*, 151–172 (p. 164, Figure 3 top panel). Copyright © Elsevier (2000). Used with permission.

(1997), in which the presentation is generally too brief and arbitrary to allow much of a role of grouping or covert rehearsal (on the latter see Morey & Cowan, 2004, 2005). Another was a running memory span task with a very fast, four-items-per-second presentation rate. A list of digits of an unpredictable length (12 to 20 items) was presented and then the participant was to recall as many items as possible from the end of the list. Because it was not possible to rehearse, the only way to accomplish the task was to wait until the list ended and then load as many items as possible from a passive sensory or phonological store into working memory. A third measure involved memory for spoken lists that were unattended at the time they were presented, as the participant was busy with a silent computer game, ignoring most lists until an occasional recall cue was presented just after a list ended. These measures suggested that the capacity increases with child development, from just over two items in the early elementary school years toward an adult capacity of about four items on average (generally ranging from two to six in adults). This is shown for one such measure, memory for spoken lists that were ignored during their presentation, in the solid lines of Figure 12.5. (The dashed lines show how much was added by attention at the time of presentation; a bit more in older participants.)

It is not yet clear whether Cowan et al. have fair measures of capacity or

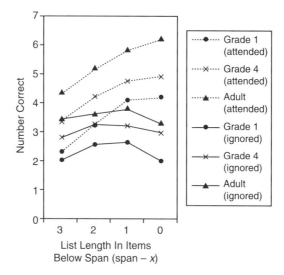

Figure 12.5 Memory for speech that was attended (dashed lines) or ignored (solid lines) during its presentation, for three age groups. From Cowan, N., Elliott, E. M., Saults, J. S., Morey, C. C., Mattox, S., Hismjatullina, A., et al. (2005). On the capacity of attention: Its estimation and its role in working memory and cognitive aptitudes. *Cognitive Psychology, 51,* 42–100 (p. 55, Figure 1). Copyright © Elsevier (2005). Used with permission.

whether the critical difference is the development of the ability to use attention to load working memory and use it at the time of recall (see Vogel et al., 2005). Therefore, it is not yet known whether capacity truly increases with age, or whether the apparent increase is a byproduct of an increase in the efficiency of loading and using of working memory.

Another type of capacity is not measured in meaningful chunks per se, but in phonological segments. Gathercole and Baddeley (1989) presented children with nonsense words of varying numbers of syllables (e.g., prug, mulfost) and found that children who could repeat longer nonwords had larger vocabularies. Nonword repetition at 4 years of age predicted vocabulary a year later (Gathercole, Willis, Emslie, & Baddeley, 1992), whereas the reverse was not true in that age range, although vocabulary became a predictor of nonword repetition at an older age. Later work showed that children who were able to repeat longer nonwords also went on to excel at reading, and the trend was especially strong when the least word-like nonwords were considered (Gathercole, 1995). A reasonable interpretation is that some children have a higher capacity for phonological information than others do. Still, it is not clear just how to think about this ability; is it a matter of longer or more detailed phonological representations in some children than in others, or less decay in some than in others? That is not clear, nor is the reason for developmental improvements in this task.

In sum, then, we actually know very little about whether capacity, narrowly defined as the number of chunks or other basic units that can be kept active at once, increases with age. We certainly know that working memory increases with age, but there is still a lot of work left to do to understand how basic capacity contributes to that improvement.

Energy-related (attention control) factors

If one thing is clear from the last few decades of cognitive development research, it is that there is a developmental improvement in the ability to control attention. This has been demonstrated in a wide variety of behavioral research (e.g., for a summary see Bjorklund & Harnishfeger, 1990) and, increasingly, in neuroimaging research (e.g., for a summary see Posner, 2004). The frontal lobes of the brain have a long course of maturation throughout childhood, and their ability to help control attention (e.g., Kane & Engle, 2002) improves accordingly. Several central executive functions involved in what is commonly termed working memory are thought to depend on this control of attention, such as maintaining a goal (Kane, Bleckley, Conway, & Engle, 2001), updating working memory (Oberauer, 2005), switching attention from one task to another, and inhibiting irrelevant information (Friedman, Miyake, Corley, Young, DeFries, & Hewitt, 2006; May et al., 1999). This topic has been of great interest medically, given the epidemic of attention deficit disorder in children (Barkley, 2003). The brevity of our coverage of the control of attention in children occurs not for a lack of information, but because it would require a whole book. We focus on one germane question: What specific effect does this development have on working memory performance?

The work leading to an understanding of the effects of attention on working memory in childhood has largely adapted procedures used to study individual differences in adults. Daneman and Carpenter (1980) developed a technique combining the storage of information with processing episodes so as to tie up both storage and processing, which, according to early views of working memory, shared resources (Baddeley & Hitch, 1974). The sentence span procedure is depicted on the left-hand side of Figure 12.6.

A sentence is presented, and the participant is required to comprehend the sentence and then also retain the last word in the sentence for later recall. The measure of span is how many sentence-final words can be recalled in order while the sentences are adequately comprehended, as measured by a later test. Case, Kurland, and Goldberg (1982) reported on a related procedure in which fields of dots are counted and the count for each field is then reported (counting span, middle of Figure 12.6). Later, Turner and Engle (1989) extended this procedure to cases in which the processing episode was arithmetic and a word to be recalled was presented after each problem (operation span, right side of Figure 12.6). These tasks all are sometimes referred to as complex span tasks for lack of a better term. (Operation span might have been a good

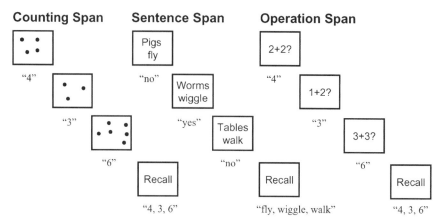

Figure 12.6 Modified versions of three complex span tasks: the counting span (Case et al., 1982), sentence span (Daneman & Carpenter, 1980), and operation span (Turner & Engle, 1989) tasks. Note that Engle and colleagues have promoted a version in which the item to be recalled is a word presented after each processing episode that did not come from it.

general term but it has come to refer only to the arithmetic version.) Complex span tasks typically produce very high correlations with intellectual aptitude tasks, much higher than the digit span task that is part of most intelligence tests, and the complex span tasks together have become the gold standard for the measurement of working memory (Conway, Kane, Bunting, Hambrick, Wilhelm, & Engle, 2005). Adults with higher working memory spans are better able to ignore an irrelevant channel in selective listening (Conway et al., 2001), avoid looking at a suddenly appearing object when the assigned task is to look away from it (Kane et al., 2001), and avoid naming an irrelevant color word in the Stroop task (Kane & Engle, 2003).

There is controversy about why complex span correlates well with aptitudes. Is it because of the contribution of all central executive functions to intelligence, or only because of the contribution of the process of updating working memory, as Friedman et al. (2006) found? Cowan et al. (2005) found that complex span tasks correlated well with working memory tasks that did not include a dual task, but still discouraged mnemonic strategies, such as running span with a fast presentation rate and two-array comparisons. Both predicted aptitudes well. Cowan et al. suggested that complex spans are effective because mnemonic strategies are impeded by the processing episodes, allowing the task to measure a core capacity (see Barrouillet et al., 2004).

Various researchers have stated different opinions as to why complex working memory span increases with age in childhood. Towse, Hitch, and Hutton (1998) carried out a counting span task in which the order of displays varied. They found that scores were lowest when the largest displays occurred at the beginning of the list rather than the end, presumably because, with the largest displays at the beginning, the counts that were to be recalled had to be maintained for a longer time while subsequent displays were presented. Similar results were obtained in operation and reading span tasks. However, for the age range tested (8–11 years), the delay manipulation hurt all age groups about equally. Therefore, this delay effect does not seem to be the basis of the development of working memory performance, which was robust under both short-processing-first or long-processing-first conditions.

According to Cowan et al. (2005), complex spans work by preventing mnemonic strategies. In adults, they provide a much higher correlation with aptitude tests than does a simple digit span, which freely allows grouping and rehearsal processes. However, in children too young to engage in these mnemonic processes, even a simple digit span task should work well and correlate highly with aptitudes. That is exactly what Cowan et al. found. Converging on their interpretation, other recent developmental studies have found that in children, as in adults, performance on complex span tasks correlates with aptitudes better when the span task is conducted with a time limit rather than according to the participant's chosen speed, which further takes up attention and thereby prevents mnemonic strategies from being sneaked into the task (Conlin, Gathercole, & Adams, 2005; Friedman & Miyake, 2004; Lépine, Barrouillet, & Camos, 2005).

If this last conjecture is correct, the implication is that the developmental difference observed in complex span tasks may not result from age differences in the control of attention as one might assume, but rather from age differences in the scope of attention, which may be synonymous with working memory capacity in chunks. Scope and control of attention seem to be partly independent and partly overlapping in terms of individual and developmental differences (Cowan, Fristoe, Elliott, Brunner, & Saults, 2006). This is not to say that developmental differences in the control of attention are unimportant in development generally, but that their importance can be seen more clearly in working memory tasks for which the use of strategies is critical and can make use of that control of attention, not in complex span tasks in which strategies may be curbed. The contribution of strategies is discussed shortly. The control of attention also can be seen to influence development in working memory tasks for which it is necessary to inhibit irrelevant information. For example, the detrimental effect of irrelevant speech on serial recall of a printed list is larger in younger children (Elliott, 2002).

When an individual, including a child, is off-task (e.g., Gathercole & Alloway, 2005) it is difficult to distinguish between a failure of capacity or the scope of attention, so that the instructions were forgotten, versus a failure of the control of attention, so that the individual was unable to exert the energy necessary to avoid distraction. We believe that, in principle, this question can be resolved but, in practice, it is still unresolved.

Unsworth and Engle (2007) argued that the control of attention is important in working memory tasks not only to hold information in primary or short-term memory, but also to guide the retrieval of information from secondary or long-term memory. This proposal includes the common assumption that no task is pure in terms of the processes tapped, and that the tasks termed complex working memory span tasks often benefit from some role of memorization in the task, just as in a long-term memory task. Cowan et al. (2003) showed one way in which it may play a role. They measured the silent time preceding recall in several types of span task and found that these are much longer in sentence span tasks than in counting span or digit span tasks, and that the time difference is greater in younger children (Figure 12.7).

One account of these results is that, in sentence spans, it is possible to try to reinstate sentences from long-term memory to provide a context for recalling the sentence-final words. That strategy takes a fair amount of time, especially in younger children. With Unsworth and Engle, we can speculate that this age difference may be the result of older children's and adults' more effective use of attention in long-term retrieval.

Other factors

In addition to the basic properties of time (speed and decay), space (capacity), and energy (attention control), the remaining factors to be considered are quite important and include things that are not part of working memory strictly speaking but that, in practice, help performance considerably. These include knowledge of the stimuli to be remembered in working memory tasks and strategies for carrying out those tasks. Knowledge and strategies are

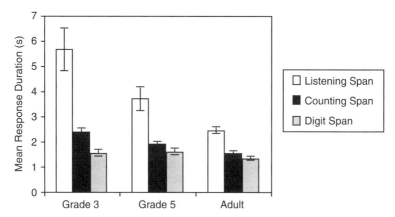

Figure 12.7 Mean response durations for three working memory tasks in three age groups. From Cowan, N., Towse, J. N., Hamilton, Z., Saults, J. S., Elliott, E. M., Lacey, J. F., et al. (2003). Children's working-memory processes: A response-timing analysis. *Journal of Experimental Psychology: General*, *132*, 113–132 (p. 124, Figure 3). Copyright © (2003) by the American Psychological Association. Reproduced with permission.

covered at length by Bjorklund et al. (Chapter 7, this volume) but here we briefly consider their relation to the development of working memory.

Knowledge

Disentangling multiple processes in working memory requires caution. For example, suppose one presented to children of different ages both words and nonwords and found that the advantage of words over nonwords (there is one) was larger in older children. One might be tempted to conclude that this difference is a result of greater lexical knowledge in the older children. However, this result alone would not be sufficient to specify the mechanism involved. It could be that words are pronounced more quickly than nonwords and that this difference in pronunciation speed underlies the word–nonword difference and is greater in more mature individuals.

Hulme et al. (1991) showed how effects of lexical information and pronunciation speed can be dissociated. They presented lists of short, medium, and long words and nonwords; each list was homogeneous in both lexical status and length. Word length and lexical status operate in different ways, as Figure 12.8 shows.

Word length affected recitation speed (which also was measured) and

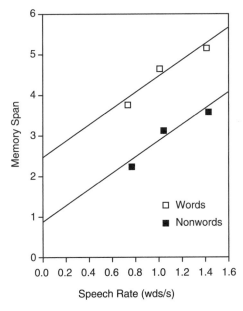

Figure 12.8 The relation between the rate of speech and memory span for words and nonwords. From Hulme, C., Maughan, S., & Brown, G. D. A. (1991). Memory for familiar and unfamiliar words: Evidence for a long-term memory contribution to short-term memory span. *Journal of Memory and Language, 30*, 685–701 (p. 690, Figure 1). Copyright © Elsevier (1991) Used with permission.

resulted in a linear relation between speed and span. Lexical status did not change the slope of that linear relation, but strongly affected the intercept. Roodenrys, Hulme, and Brown (1993) carried out a similar study developmentally. They found that there was a large speed difference between 6- and 10-year-olds; the older group's data points were higher up on the regression line relating speech rate to memory span, indicating both faster speaking capability and better span. However, older children also showed a slightly larger benefit with the presentation of words as opposed to nonwords, and this does indicate a contribution of children's growing lexical knowledge to memory span. Another example was described above for the use of linguistic knowledge to aid sentence span (Cowan et al., 2003). It is likely that many other examples exist in which knowledge is important for a particular working memory task.

Strategies

There is something special about strategies. For the other possible mechanisms of developmental change we have discussed, the proposal was one of a quantitative change: Older children have less decay, faster processing, more capacity, better control of attention, and more knowledge. For strategies, we are in a different position because the proposed change is qualitative. Strategies begin in later childhood that apparently are not used at all in early childhood (see Bjorklund et al., Chapter 7, this volume; Miller & Seier, 1994; Siegler, 1996).

Strategies that can apply to working memory tasks vary depending on the task. Two of the most common are verbal rehearsal (e.g., Flavell et al., 1966; Ornstein & Naus, 1978) and sorting items by some category such as meaning or appearance to assist recall (e.g., Schneider, Kron, Hunnerkopf, & Krajewski, 2004). One issue is whether the child produces a certain strategy and another issue is whether that strategy is used effectively. In a longitudinal study, Schneider et al. reported that children actually change from non-strategic to strategic performers rather quickly across tasks. A utilization deficiency seems uncommon but, when it appears, it seems to persist in the individual for long after strategies are first used, and correlates with poor working memory.

Two studies illustrate the great importance of strategies, at least in working memory tasks that allow strategy use. Cowan, Cartwright, Winterowd, and Sherk (1987) examined adults' serial order memory for lists of phonologically dissimilar spoken words, such as fish, hat, and spoon, as well as lists of phonologically similar words, such as bat, cat, and rat. The phonologically dissimilar words are recalled better from at least 4 years of age, but previous work showed that the magnitude of this phonological similarity effect increased markedly with age. A simple explanation is that, as older children and adults learn to use covert verbal rehearsal, this improves their serial order memory for dissimilar lists but does little for the similar lists, which are easily confused with one another during the rehearsal process. Verifying this theoretical account, Cowan et al. found that the pattern was changed in adults when they were required to whisper the alphabet while listening to the stimuli through headphones. This task can be assumed to suppress covert verbal rehearsal. The adults under articulatory suppression yielded results similar to 5-year-old children in both level and pattern.

A more elaborate study with a similar outcome was conducted by Cowan, Saults, and Morey (2006). The question was how verbal–spatial associations are saved. In a task administered to third- and sixth-grade children and adults, an array of three to seven line-drawing "houses" was presented. Then an equal number of names was presented, one at a time, with each name centered in a house and then disappearing, with 1-second presentations and 1-second inter-word intervals. Then a probe word was presented centrally and the task was to use the mouse to drag it to the house in which it had appeared. We considered that there are two ways to accomplish this task. One way is to store the verbal–spatial associations; that kind of storage of abstract information may be attention-demanding, however (Baddeley, 2000; Cowan, 1999). Another way would be to rehearse the list of names while, in parallel, retaining the visual path of houses assigned to those names. After the probe name was presented, the two types of information would be used together. For example, if the probe was the second name in the list, then the response is the second house in the spatial path. Thus, by exploiting something like what Baddeley (1986) termed passive phonological and visuospatial buffers together, it might be possible to exert less effort in this task.

We examined this issue by constructing two versions of the verbal–spatial mapping task. In a 1-to-1 version, each house was assigned to a single name. In an alternative, uneven version, this was not the case. At least one house was left empty, while at least one house was assigned to two, non-adjacent names in the list. By making the spatial path confusing, this uneven condition discourages the parallel use of phonological and visuospatial stores (see Figure 12.9).

The finding was that third-grade children showed a significant advantage for the uneven condition, the sixth-grade children showed no advantage at all, and the adults showed a significant advantage for the 1-to-1 condition. This is to be expected if the third-grade children cannot rehearse and therefore must use the verbal–spatial associative process to retain the items; in the uneven condition, there are fewer houses per trial to remember. The adults, who can rehearse, use the parallel method that is easier to carry out in the 1-to-1 condition. Finally, the pattern of performance of adults who repeated the word "the" as an articulatory suppression task was nearly identical to that of third-grade children (see Figure 12.10).

Presumably, suppression knocked out rehearsal and what was left over was similar to the mental apparatus that the third-grade children were able to bring to bear in this task. This study illustrates that developing strategies comprise a very important aspect of working memory development.

1-to-1 Condition

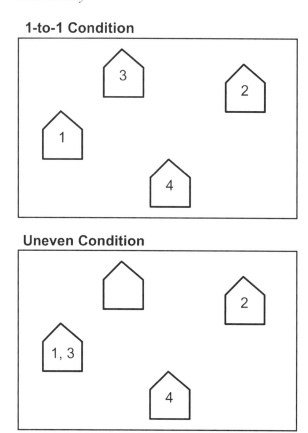

Uneven Condition

Figure 12.9 An illustration of the two presentation conditions of Cowan, Saults, and Morey (2006). Each number represents the serial order of a name presented within the location shown by a stylized house. There could be three to seven items per trial and there were always the same number of names and locations. In the uneven condition (bottom panel), at least one location was used twice, decreasing the number of locations used but adding to the spatial path recursion, and therefore confusion. The 1-to-1 condition produced better performance in adults with no dual task; the uneven condition produced better performance in third-grade children, and also in adults carrying out articulatory suppression during the task.

Development and models of working memory

The developmental research we have reviewed seems to demonstrate change in multiple mechanisms, with no mechanism ruled out. Still, it can help to distinguish between models of working memory, in at least two ways. One way is by demonstrating developmental changes in memory stemming from a mechanism that should not be important according to the model. For example, given that only some models include decay of working memory

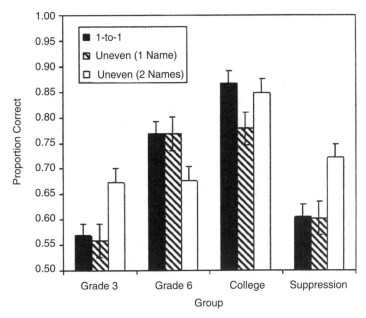

Figure 12.10 Pattern of performance on 1-to-1 trials and on uneven trials for which 1 versus 2 names were assigned to the house that serves as the correct answer. Adults with articulatory suppression perform almost exactly like third-grade children. From Cowan, N., Saults, J. S., & Morey, C. C. (2006). Development of working memory for verbal–spatial associations. *Journal of Memory and Language, 55,* 274–289 (p. 282, Figure 3). Copyright © Elsevier (2006). Used with permission.

representations as a function of time over a few seconds (see above), only those models can account for developmental differences in decay rates (e.g., Figure 12.4). This seems particularly important given how difficult it has been to observe decay conclusively in standard adult procedures. Another way development can help is by demonstrating a mechanism more clearly in children than in adults, given that the mechanism may be obscured by the sophisticated strategies that adults use. Thus, given that some models do not include a type of storage that cuts across specific domains, it would be hard for them to explain the pattern of results shown in Figure 12.10 by young children and by adults in a condition in which rehearsal is suppressed. As discussed above, that pattern suggests that verbal–spatial associations are saved in working memory, but only when a serial rehearsal strategy is not possible (in young children) or is difficult to apply (when the spatial path is convoluted). In all, the results of these studies seem consistent with the types of models offered by Baddeley (2000, 2001) and Cowan (1999, 2001), which allow for a general, cross-domain type of storage, more domain-specific interference mechanisms of storage (through either separate stores or separate types of interference effects), decay over time, and attention-demanding executive processes as possible sources of developmental change. However, these conclusions are still tentative.

PRACTICAL IMPLICATIONS

Research on the development of working memory, aside from clarifying a key part of normal cognitive development, may be helpful in education and medicine. Klingberg et al. (2005) have suggested that training with working memory tasks can improve a child's performance and adjustment across a wide range of tasks, although we believe that this finding must be further explored. Gathercole and Alloway (2004, 2005) have shown that poor class-room adjustment in children often is an effect of an undiscovered working memory deficit preventing the child from remembering and following instructions as well as carrying out assignments. Below, we provide further detail about some of the implications of working memory for cognitive impairments of childhood. Notice how the models and mechanisms of working memory we have discussed selectively come into play in these disorders, providing guidance to research on the causes of, and treatments for, these disorders.

Working memory and language disorders

There are strong links between short-term memory and language impairments. Tasks involving immediate recall of short sequences are among the best indicators of language deficits, such as specific language impairment (Gathercole & Baddeley, 1990). When asked to repeat nonwords such as "woogalamic" and "blonterstapping," children with this impairment perform at a level 2 years behind their peers (Archibald & Gathercole, 2006). The novelty of the phonological forms of nonwords prevents participants from using lexical knowledge to support recall as they could do in recalling words they know. As a result, this task appears to mimic how children learn vocabulary.

Some have suggested that, the greater the processing load in a task, the more children with language impairments will struggle. For example, Montgomery (2000) found that children with specific language impairment were more impaired on a condition in which they were to repeat a sequence of words in order of their physical size (e.g., hearing nut, head, cow, thumb and producing nut, thumb, head, cow), compared to simply recalling the words in any order. Yet, children with specific language impairment may perform at levels comparable to age-matched controls on visuospatial working memory measures (Archibald & Gathercole, 2006). The working memory deficit in this group appears specific to the verbal domain.

Working memory and reading

Reading disabilities include difficulties in word recognition, spelling, and reading comprehension. It has often been suggested that phonological short-term or working memory deficits cause reading disabilities. The idea would be that it is difficult to read if one cannot remember the string of phonemes that result from sounding out the word. Oddly, though, this hypothesis has not proved to be true. Tasks that require memory of nonwords or short series of randomly arranged words have been used. Children with reading disabilities do show problems on such tasks, but the phonological memory at one age does not seem to predict reading performance at an older age (Wagner & Muse, 2006; Wagner et al., 1997).

Other tasks also were examined in this sort of study, such as phonological awareness tasks in which the child must dissect a word into its parts, such as rhyming words or words with the same initial sounds, and the ability to name pictures rapidly. In a 5-year longitudinal study of several hundred children who were followed from kindergarten through fourth grade, the measures were correlated but a key difference between them was that, at three different time periods, only phonological awareness skills predicted individual differences in reading words (Wagner, Torgesen, & Rashotte, 1999). The phonological awareness tasks probably require phonological memory, but they also require other skills that are essential for reading, such as letter-to-sound correspondences. Indeed, illiterate adults cannot do these tasks well (Morais, Bertelson, Luz, & Alegria, 1986) because the sounds of speech are quite entangled acoustically, and rudimentary reading skills are therefore needed to understand that each syllable can be further decomposed into its sounds.

Complex working memory tasks that combine storage and processing are more predictive of reading. Children with reading disabilities show significant and marked decrements on such tasks (Siegel & Ryan, 1989). In typically developing children, scores on working memory tasks predict reading achievement independently of measures of phonological short-term memory (e.g., Swanson, 2003) or phonological awareness (e.g., Swanson & Beebe-Frankenberger, 2004). This special contribution of complex working memory tasks has been explained as the result of limited capacity for processing and storage together in children with reading disabilities (De Jong, 1998). It may take considerable working memory capacity to keep in mind at once the relevant speech sounds and concepts necessary for successfully identifying words and comprehending text.

Working memory and mathematics

There is also a close relationship between mathematical skills and working memory but this is mediated by the age of the child as well as the task. Verbal working memory plays a strong role in math skills in 7-year-olds (Bull & Scerif, 2001; Gathercole & Pickering, 2000) and is also a reliable indicator of mathematical disabilities in the first year of formal schooling (Gersten, Jordan, & Flojo, 2005). However, once children reach adolescence, working memory is no longer significantly linked to mathematical skills (e.g., Reuhkala, 2001). One explanation for this change is that verbal working memory plays a crucial role for basic arithmetic (both to learn arithmetic facts and to retain relevant data such as carried digits) but that as children get older other factors, such as number knowledge and strategies, play a greater role (e.g., Thevenot & Oakhill, 2005). Low working memory scores have been found to be closely related to poor computational skills (Bull & Scerif, 2001; Geary, Hoard, & Hamson, 1999) and poor performance on arithmetic word problems (Swanson & Sachse-Lee, 2001).

Visuospatial memory is also closely linked with mathematical skills. It has been suggested that visuospatial memory functions as a mental black-board, supporting number representation, such as place value and alignment in columns, in counting and arithmetic (D'Amico & Guarnera, 2005; Geary, 1990; McLean & Hitch, 1999). Specific associations have been found between visuospatial memory and encoding in problems presented visually (e.g., Logie, Gilhooly, & Wynn, 1994), and in multi-digit operations (e.g., Heath-cote, 1994). Visuospatial memory skills also uniquely predict performance in nonverbal problems, such as sums presented with blocks, in preschool children (Rasmussen & Bisanz, 2005). In contrast, the role of verbal short-term memory is restricted to temporary number storage during mental calculation (Fürst & Hitch, 2000; Hecht, 2002), rather than general mathematical skills (McLean & Hitch, 1999; Reuhkala, 2001).

A key question regarding the relationship between working memory and learning disabilities is whether working memory is simply a proxy for IQ. There is evidence that working memory tasks measure something different from general intelligence tests (e.g., Cain, Oakhill, & Bryant, 2004; Siegel, 1988). While IQ tests measure knowledge that the child has already learned, working memory tasks are a pure measure of a child's learning potential. Thus working memory skills are able to predict a child's performance in both literacy and numeracy, even after a child's general abilities have been taken into account (Gathercole, Alloway, Willis, & Adams, 2006; Nation, Adams, Bowyer-Crane, & Snowling, 1999; Stothard & Hulme, 1992; for a review see Swanson & Saez, 2003).

Working memory and attention disorders

Could working memory impairments be explained by attention problems? The standard manual of clinical psychology, DSM-IV, describes attention deficit and hyperactivity disorders (ADHD) as including three subtypes: (1) hyperactive-impulsive behavior or ADHD-H, (2) inattention and distract-ibility or ADHD-I, and (3) a combination of these behaviors or ADHD-C. There is widespread agreement that individuals with ADHD-H have marked impairments in one particular aspect of central executive function, namely the ability to inhibit responses that have been overlearned, becoming what is known as prepotent (e.g., Barkley, 1997; Sonuga-Barker, Dalen, Daley, & Remington, 2002). An example is performance in the Stroop (1935) procedure, in which one must suppress a known color word in order to name the conflicting color of print in which it is written. Impairments of advanced executive functions such as organization and planning may be found in the later childhood years (Barkley, 2003; Brown, 2002). Crucially, though, children with ADHD-H do not consistently show impairments in working memory. In an influential review, Pennington and Ozonoff (1996) concluded that there was no evidence of general working memory deficits in such children, a claim that has been borne out also in more recent studies (e.g., Adams & Snowling, 2001; Kerns, McInerney, & Wilde, 2001; Ruckridge & Tannock, 2002). There is, however, evidence that ADHD groups including ADHD-I may be impaired on tasks involving memory for visual or spatial information (e.g., Geurts, Vertie, Oosterlaan, Roeyers, & Sergeant, 2004; Mehta, Goodyer, & Sahakian, 2004).

Barkley (2003) has suggested that, in contrast to ADHD-H, pervasive working memory deficits are a hallmark of the other major subtype of ADHD, which include inattentivity and distractibility. Behaviors associated with working memory failures (such as having trouble remembering what they are doing) have been found to be significantly higher than normal in children with these subtypes of ADHD (Gioia, Isquith, Guy, & Kenworthy, 2000). They also may be impaired in the coordination of dual tasks (Karatekin, 2004), which require both retention of information and executive function to coordinate the retained information.

Is it possible that working memory deficits underlie inattentive behavior in ADHD? A recent observational study of children with very poor verbal working memory skills but otherwise normal cognitive profiles shed light on this question (Gathercole, Lamont, & Alloway, 2006). The children's behavior was observed during normal classroom activities. The behavioral characteristics of this group appear to be very similar to those of children with ADHD-I. However, three types of error were very common: forgetting complex instructions, failing to cope with tasks that impose significant processing and storage loads, and losing their place in complex tasks. Interestingly, the teachers failed to identify the children as having poor memory skills, attributing their poor classroom performance instead to either lack of attention or poor motivation. There is not yet enough evidence to determine whether children diagnosed with inattentivity and those with impairments of verbal working memory represent a single group or separate groups. Based on the available data we speculate that the ADHD-I and memory-impaired groups both have deficits of verbal working memory, whereas children with ADHD-H are deficient in inhibitory processing and, possibly, planning and visuospatial working memory, but not in verbal working memory. More work is needed on the group with combined symptoms, ADHD-C.

We have shown that children with various deficits in learning and cognitive performance show different types of working memory impairment; they can be impaired on verbal retention, spatial retention, and/or executive function, mirroring three main parts of the working memory model of Baddeley (1986). However, the evidence on children with working memory impairment is not yet sufficient to indicate which theoretical model of working memory is correct. In the model of Cowan (1988, 1999), for example, the activated portions of long-term memory are allowed to be divisible into different modalities and codes. Such divisions include, but are not necessarily limited to, the division between verbal and visuospatial information (see Alloway, Gathercole, & Pickering, 2006). Theoretically, for example, it might be possible to find an individual with an inability to retain the spatial arrangement of sounds. It seems likely that there are also deficits related to other aspects of working memory, including improper functioning of the focus of attention (Cowan, 1988, 2005) or episodic buffer (Baddeley, 2000, 2001), which may result in abnormal development in the ability to retain associations between features of an object (e.g., Cowan, Naveh-Benjamin, Kilb, & Saults, 2006). It is not clear if the latter deficits are part of ADHD. Developmental deficits in specific mechanisms such as decay, speed, and chunk capacity warrant further research.

CONCLUDING OBSERVATIONS

Working memory is central to all of cognition. It is definite that working memory improves with age in childhood, but that is not a very specific statement. We have considered possible developmental changes in decay, speed, chunk capacity, control of attention, knowledge, and mnemonic strategies. It remains to be determined whether the number of causal concepts can be reduced in further work; perhaps, for example, age differences in speed are a result, rather than a cause, of age difference in capacity. Strategic change is probably the strongest example of developmental change, reflecting an actual qualitative change in the nature of mnemonic processing rather than just a quantitative change. Still, we do not yet know if that type of change is the most fundamental or results from sufficient resources to allow the strategy to be carried out, as a neo-Piagetian approach might suggest. It is clear that working memory is important not only theoretically, for an understanding of the development of the mind, but also for the practical understanding of developmental and educational disorders. When we understand what is fundamental in working memory, we will better understand how to treat the disorders, too.

REFERENCES

Adams, J. W., & Snowling, M. J. (2001). Executive function and reading impairments in children reported by their teachers as "hyperactive". *British Journal of Developmental Psychology, 19*, 293–306.

Alloway, T. P., Gathercole, S. E., & Pickering, S. J. (2006). Verbal and visuospatial short-term and working memory in children: Are they separable? *Child Development, 77,* 1698–1716.

Alvarez, G. A., & Cavanagh, P. (2004). The capacity of visual short-term memory is set both by visual information load and by number of objects. *Psychological Science, 15,* 106–111.

Anderson, J. R., Bothell, D., Lebiere, C., & Matessa, M. (1998). An integrated theory of list memory. *Journal of Memory and Language, 38,* 341–380.

Archibald, L. M., & Gathercole, S. E. (2006). Short-term and working memory in specific language impairment. *International Journal of Language and Communication Disorders, 41,* 675–693.

Atkinson, R. C., & Shiffrin, R. M. (1968). Human memory: A proposed system and its control processes. In K. W. Spence & J. T. Spence (Eds.), *The psychology of learning and motivation: Advances in research and theory* (Vol. 2, pp. 89–195). New York: Academic Press.

Baddeley, A. D. (1986). *Working memory* (Oxford Psychology Series No. 11). Oxford: Clarendon Press.

Baddeley, A. D. (2000). The episodic buffer: A new component of working memory? *Trends in Cognitive Sciences, 4,* 417–423.

Baddeley, A. D. (2001). The magic number and the episodic buffer. *Behavioral and Brain Sciences, 24,* 117–118.

Baddeley, A. D., & Hitch, G. (1974). Working memory. In G. Bower (Ed.), *The psychology of learning and motivation, 8* (pp. 47–90). New York: Academic Press.

Baddeley, A. D., Thomson, N., & Buchanan, M. (1975). Word length and the structure of short-term memory. *Journal of Verbal Learning and Verbal Behavior, 14,* 575–589.

Balota, D. A., & Engle, R. W. (1981). Structural and strategic factors in the stimulus suffix effect. *Journal of Verbal Learning and Verbal Behavior, 20,* 346–357.

Barkley, R. A. (1997). *ADHD and the nature of self-control.* New York: Guilford.

Barkley, R. A. (2003). Issues in the diagnosis of attention-deficit/hyperactivity disorder in children. *Brain and Development, 25,* 77–83.

Barrouillet, P., Bernardin, S., & Camos, V. (2004). Time constraints and resource sharing in adults' working memory spans. *Journal of Experimental Psychology: General, 133,* 83–100.

Bjorklund, D. F., & Harnishfeger, K. K. (1990). The resources construct in cognitive development: Diverse sources of evidence and a theory of inefficient inhibition. *Developmental Review, 10,* 48–71.

Broadbent, D. E. (1958). *Perception and communication.* New York: Pergamon Press.

Broadbent, D. E. (1975). The magic number seven after fifteen years. In A. Kennedy & A. Wilkes (Eds.), *Studies in long-term memory* (pp. 3–18). New York: Wiley.

Brown, T. E. (2002). DSM-IV: ADHD and executive function impairment. *Proceedings of the Annual Meeting of the American Psychiatric Association, 2,* 910–914.

Budd, D., Whitney, P., & Turley, K. J. (1995). Individual differences in working memory strategies for reading expository text. *Memory and Cognition, 23,* 735–748.

Bull, R., & Scerif, G. (2001). Executive functioning as a predictor of children's mathematics ability. Shifting, inhibition and working memory. *Developmental Neuropsychology, 19,* 273–293.

Bunnell, J. K., Baken, D. M., & Richards-Ward, L. A. (1999). The effect of age on metamemory for working memory. *New Zealand Journal of Psychology, 28,* 23–29.

Burtis, P. J. (1982). Capacity increase and chunking in the development of short-term memory. *Journal of Experimental Child Psychology*, *34*, 387–413.

Cain, K., Oakhill, J., & Bryant, P. (2004). Children's reading comprehension ability: Concurrent prediction by working memory, verbal ability and component skills. *Journal of Educational Psychology*, *96*, 31–42.

Case, R. (1972). Validation of a neo-Piagetian mental capacity construct. *Journal of Experimental Child Psychology*, *14*, 287–302.

Case, R., Kurland, D. M., & Goldberg, J. (1982). Operational efficiency and the growth of short-term memory span. *Journal of Experimental Child Psychology*, *33*, 386–404.

Chen, Z., & Cowan, N. (2005). Chunk limits and length limits in immediate recall: A reconciliation. *Journal of Experimental Psychology: Learning, Memory, and Cognition*, *31*, 1235–1249.

Chi, M. T. H. (1978). Knowledge structures and memory development. In R. Siegler (Ed.), *Children's thinking: What develops?* Hillsdale, NJ: Lawrence Erlbaum Associates, Inc.

Conlin, J. A., Gathercole, S. E., & Adams, J. W. (2005). Children's working memory: Investigating performance limitations in complex span tasks. *Journal of Experimental Child Psychology*, *90*, 303–317.

Conway, A. R. A., Cowan, N., & Bunting, M. F. (2001). The cocktail party phenomenon revisited: The importance of working memory capacity. *Psychonomic Bulletin and Review*, *8*, 331–335.

Conway, A. R. A., Kane, M. J., Bunting, M. F., Hambrick, D. Z., Wilhelm, O., & Engle, R. W. (2005). Working memory span tasks: A methodological review and user's guide. *Psychonomic Bulletin and Review*, *12*, 769–786.

Cowan, N. (1988). Evolving conceptions of memory storage, selective attention, and their mutual constraints within the human information processing system. *Psychological Bulletin*, *104*, 163–191.

Cowan, N. (1995). *Attention and memory: An integrated framework* (Oxford Psychology Series, No. 26). New York: Oxford University Press.

Cowan, N. (1999). An embedded-processes model of working memory. In A. Miyake & P. Shah (Eds.), *Models of working memory: Mechanisms of active maintenance and executive control* (pp. 62–101). Cambridge: Cambridge University Press.

Cowan, N. (2001). The magical number 4 in short-term memory: A reconsideration of mental storage capacity. *Behavioral and Brain Sciences*, *24*, 87–185.

Cowan, N. (2005). *Working memory capacity*. Hove, UK: Psychology Press.

Cowan, N., Cartwright, C., Winterowd, C., & Sherk, M. (1987). An adult model of preschool children's speech memory. *Memory and Cognition*, *15*, 511–517.

Cowan, N., Chen, Z., & Rouder, J. N. (2004). Constant capacity in an immediate serial-recall task: A logical sequel to Miller (1956). *Psychological Science*, *15*, 634–640.

Cowan, N., Elliott, E. M., Saults, J. S., Morey, C. C., Mattox, S., Hismjatullina, A., et al. (2005). On the capacity of attention: Its estimation and its role in working memory and cognitive aptitudes. *Cognitive Psychology*, *51*, 42–100.

Cowan, N., Elliott, E. M., Saults, J. S., Nugent, L. D., Bomb, P., & Hismjatullina, A. (2006). Rethinking speed theories of cognitive development: Increasing the rate of recall without affecting accuracy. *Psychological Science*, *17*, 67–73.

Cowan, N., Fristoe, N. M., Elliott, E. M., Brunner, R. P., & Saults, J. S. (2006). Scope of attention, control of attention, and intelligence in children and adults. *Memory and Cognition, 34,* 1754–1768.

Cowan, N., Keller, T., Hulme, C., Roodenrys, S., McDougall, S., & Rack, J. (1994). Verbal memory span in children: Speech timing clues to the mechanisms underlying age and word length effects. *Journal of Memory and Language, 33,* 234–250.

Cowan, N., Naveh-Benjamin, M., Kilb, A., & Saults, J. S. (2006). Life-span development of visual working memory: When is feature binding difficult? *Developmental Psychology, 42,* 1089–1102.

Cowan, N., Nugent, L. D., Elliott, E. M., and Geer, T. (2000). Is there a temporal basis of the word length effect? A response to Service (1998). *Quarterly Journal of Experimental Psychology, 53A,* 647–660.

Cowan, N., Nugent, L. D., Elliott, E. M., & Saults, J. S. (2000). Persistence of memory for ignored lists of digits: Areas of developmental constancy and change. *Journal of Experimental Child Psychology, 76,* 151–172.

Cowan, N., Saults, J. S., & Morey, C. C. (2006). Development of working memory for verbal–spatial associations. *Journal of Memory and Language, 55,* 274–289.

Cowan, N., Towse, J. N., Hamilton, Z., Saults, J. S., Elliott, E. M., Lacey, J. F., et al. (2003). Children's working-memory processes: A response-timing analysis. *Journal of Experimental Psychology: General, 132,* 113–132.

Cowan, N., Wood, N. L., Wood, P. K., Keller, T. A., Nugent, L. D., & Keller, C. V. (1998). Two separate verbal processing rates contributing to short-term memory span. *Journal of Experimental Psychology: General, 127,* 141–160.

D'Amico, A. & Guarnera, M. (2005). Exploring working memory in children with low arithmetic achievement. *Learning and Individual Differences, 15,* 189–202.

Daneman, M., & Carpenter, P. A. (1980). Individual differences in working memory and reading. *Journal of Verbal Learning and Verbal Behavior, 19,* 450–466.

Davelaar, E. J., Goshen-Gottstein, Y., Ashkenazi, A., Haarman, H. J., & Usher, M. (2005). The demise of short-term memory revisited: Empirical and computational investigations of recency effects. *Psychological Review, 112,* 3–42.

De Jong, P. F. (1998). Working memory deficits of reading disabled children. *Journal of Experimental Child Psychology, 70,* 75–96.

Diamond, A. (1985). Development of the ability to use recall to guide action, as indicated by infants' performance on AB. *Child Development, 56,* 868–883.

Elliott, E. M. (2002). The irrelevant-speech effect and children: Theoretical implications of developmental change. *Memory and Cognition, 30,* 478–487.

Engle, R. W., Tuholski, S. W., Laughlin, J. E., & Conway, A. R. A. (1999). Working memory, short-term memory, and general fluid intelligence: A latent-variable approach. *Journal of Experimental Psychology: General, 128,* 309–331.

Farrell, S., & Lewandowsky, S. (2004). Modelling transposition latencies: Constraints for theories of serial order memory. *Journal of Memory and Language, 51,* 115–135.

Flavell, J. H., Beach, D. H., & Chinsky, J. M. (1966). Spontaneous verbal rehearsal in a memory task as a function of age. *Child Development, 37,* 283–299.

Friedman, N. P., & Miyake, A. (2004). The reading span test and its predictive power for reading comprehension ability. *Journal of Memory and Language, 51,* 136–158.

Friedman, N. P., Miyake, A., Corley, R. P., Young, S. E., DeFries, J. C., & Hewitt, J. K. (2006). Not all executive functions are related to intelligence. *Psychological Science, 17,* 172–179.

Fürst, A. J., & Hitch, G. J. (2000). Different roles for executive and phonological components of working memory in mental arithmetic. *Memory and Cognition, 28*, 774–782.

Gathercole, S. E. (1995). Is nonword repetition a test of phonological memory or long-term knowledge? It all depends on the nonwords. *Memory and Cognition, 23*, 83–94.

Gathercole, S. E., & Alloway, T. P. (2004). Working memory and classroom learning. *Dyslexia Review, 15*, 4–9.

Gathercole, S. E., & Alloway, T. P. (2005). *Understanding working memory: A classroom guide*. London: Medical Research Council.

Gathercole, S. E., Alloway, T. P., Willis, C., & Adams, A. M. (2006). Working memory in children with reading disabilities. *Journal of Experimental Child Psychology, 93*, 265–281.

Gathercole, S. E., & Baddeley, A. (1989). Evaluation of the role of STM in the development of vocabulary of children: A longitudinal study. *Journal of Memory and Language, 28*, 200–213.

Gathercole, S. E., & Baddeley, A. D. (1990). Phonological memory deficits in language disordered children: Is there a causal connection? *Journal of Memory and Language, 29*, 336–360.

Gathercole, S. E., Lamont, E., & Alloway, T. P. (2006). Working memory in the classroom. In S. Pickering (Ed.), *Working memory and education* (pp. 219–240). Oxford: Elsevier Press.

Gathercole, S. E., & Pickering, S. J. (2000). Assessment of working memory in six- and seven-year old children. *Journal of Educational Psychology, 92*, 377–390.

Gathercole, S. E., Willis, C., Emslie, H., & Baddeley, A. (1992). Phonological memory and vocabulary development during the early school years: A longitudinal study. *Developmental Psychology, 28*, 887–898.

Geary, D. C. (1990). A componential analysis of an early learning deficit in mathematics. *Journal of Experimental Child Psychology, 49*, 363–383.

Geary, D. C., Hoard, M. K., & Hamson, C. O. (1999). Numerical and arithmetical cognition: Patterns of functions and deficits in children at risk for a mathematical disability. *Journal of Experimental Child Psychology, 74*, 213–239.

Gersten, R., Jordan, N. C., & Flojo, J. R. (2005). Early identification and interventions for students with mathematics difficulties. *Journal of Learning Disabilities, 38*, 293–304.

Geurts, H. M., Vertie, S., Oosterlaan, J., Roeyers, H., & Sergeant, J. A. (2004). How specific are executive functioning deficits in attention deficit hyperactivity disorder and autism? *Journal of Child Psychology and Psychiatry, 45*, 836–854.

Gioia, G. A., Isquith, P. K., Guy, S. C., & Kenworthy, L. (2000). *Behavior rating inventory of executive function*. London: Harcourt Assessment.

Glanzer, M., & Razel, M. (1974). The size of the unit in short-term storage. *Journal of Verbal Learning and Verbal Behavior, 13*, 114–131.

Gobet, F., & Clarkson, G. (2004). Chunks in expert memory: Evidence for the magical number four . . . or is it two? *Memory, 12*, 732–747.

Hambrick, D. Z., & Engle, R. W. (2001). Effects of domain knowledge, working memory capacity, and age on cognitive performance: An investigation of the knowledge-is-power hypothesis. *Cognitive Psychology, 44*, 339–387.

Heathcote, D. (1994). The role of visuospatial working memory in the mental addition of multi-digit addends. *Current Psychology of Cognition, 13*, 207–245.

Hecht, S. A. (2002). Counting on working memory in simple arithmetic when counting is used for problem solving. *Memory and Cognition, 30*, 447–455.

Henry, L. A. (1991). The effects of word length and phonemic similarity in young children's short-term memory. *Quarterly Journal of Experimental Psychology, 43A*, 35–52.

Hulme, C., Maughan, S., & Brown, G. D. A. (1991). Memory for familiar and unfamiliar words: Evidence for a long-term memory contribution to short-term memory span. *Journal of Memory and Language, 30*, 685–701.

Hulme, C., & Muir, C. (1985). Developmental changes in speech rate and memory span: A causal relationship? *British Journal of Developmental Psychology, 3*, 175–181.

Hulme, C., Thomson, N., Muir, C., & Lawrence, A. (1984). Speech rate and the development of short-term memory span. *Journal of Experimental Child Psychology, 38*, 241–253.

Hulme, C., & Tordoff, V. (1989). Working memory development: The effects of speech rate, word length, and acoustic similarity on serial recall. *Journal of Experimental Child Psychology, 47*, 72–87.

James, W. (1890). *The principles of psychology.* New York: Henry Holt.

Kail, R. (1992). Processing speed, speech rate, and memory. *Developmental Psychology, 28*, 899–904.

Kail, R., & Park, Y.-S. (1994). Processing time, articulation time, and memory span. *Journal of Experimental Child Psychology, 57*, 281–291.

Kail, R., & Salthouse, T. A. (1994). Processing speed as a mental capacity. *Acta Psychologica, 86*, 199–255.

Kane, M. J., Bleckley, M. K., Conway, A. R. A., & Engle, R. W. (2001). A controlled-attention view of working-memory capacity. *Journal of Experimental Psychology: General, 130*, 169–183.

Kane, M. J., & Engle, R. W. (2002). The role of prefrontal cortex in working-memory capacity, executive attention, and general fluid intelligence: An individual-differences perspective. *Psychonomic Bulletin and Review, 9*, 637–671.

Kane, M. J., & Engle, R. W. (2003). Working-memory capacity and the control of attention: The contributions of goal neglect, response competition, and task set to Stroop interference. *Journal of Experimental Psychology: General, 132*, 47–70.

Karatekin, C. (2004). A test of the integrity of the components of Baddeley's model of working memory in attention-deficit/hyperactivity disorder (ADHD). *Journal of Child Psychology and Psychiatry, 45*, 912–926.

Keppel, G., & Underwood, B. J. (1962). Proactive inhibition in short-term retention of single items. *Journal of Verbal Learning and Verbal Behavior, 1*, 153–161.

Kerns, K. A., McInerney, R. J., & Wilde, N. J. (2001). Time reproduction, working memory, and behavioural inhibition in children with ADHD. *Child Neuropsychology, 7*, 21–31.

Klingberg, T., Fernell, E., Olesen, P. J., Johnson, M., Gustafsson, P., Dahlstrom, K., et al. (2005). Computerized training of working memory in children with ADHD—A randomized, controlled trial. *Journal of the American Academy of Child and Adolescent Psychiatry, 44*, 177–186.

Landauer, T. K. (1962). Rate of implicit speech. *Perceptual and Motor Skills, 15*, 646.

Lépine, R., Barrouillet, P., & Camos, V. (2005). What makes working memory spans so predictive of high level cognition? *Psychonomic Bulletin and Review, 12*, 165–170.

Lewandowsky, S., Duncan, M., & Brown, G. D. A. (2004). Time does not cause forgetting in short-term serial recall. *Psychonomic Bulletin and Review, 11*, 771–790.

Lisman, J. E., & Idiart, M. A. P. (1995). Storage of 7 + 2 short-term memories in oscillatory subcycles. *Science, 267*, 1512–1515.

Logie, R. H., Gilhooly, K. J., & Wynn, V. (1994). Counting on working memory in arithmetic problem solving. *Memory and Cognition, 22*, 395–410.

Lovatt, P., Avons, S. E., & Masterson, J. (2002). Output decay in immediate serial recall: Speech time revisited. *Journal of Memory and Language, 46*, 227–243.

Luck, S. J., & Vogel, E. K. (1997). The capacity of visual working memory for features and conjunctions. *Nature, 390*, 279–281.

May, C. P., Hasher, L., & Kane, M. J. (1999). The role of interference in memory span. *Memory and Cognition, 27*, 759–767.

McLean, J. F., & Hitch, G. H. (1999). Working memory impairments in children with specific mathematics learning difficulties. *Journal of Experimental Child Psychology, 74*, 240–260.

McNamara, D. S., & Scott, J. L. (2001). Working memory capacity and strategy use. *Memory and Cognition, 29*, 10–17.

Mehta, M. A., Goodyer, I. M., & Sahakian, B. J. (2004). Methylphenidate improves working memory and set-shifting in AD/HD: Relationships to baseline memory capacity. *Journal of Child Psychology and Psychiatry, 45*, 292–305.

Miller, G. A. (1956). The magical number seven, plus or minus two: Some limits on our capacity for processing information. *Psychological Review, 63*, 81–97.

Miller, G. A., Galanter, E., & Pribram, K. H. (1960). *Plans and the structure of behavior*. New York: Holt, Rinehart & Winston.

Miller, P. H., & Seier, W. L. (1994). Strategy utilization deficiencies in children: When, where, and why. In H. W. Reese (Ed.), *Advances in child development and behavior* (Vol. 25, pp. 107–156). San Diego: Academic Press.

Miyake, A., & Shah, P. (Eds.). (1999). *Models of working memory: Mechanisms of active maintenance and executive control*. Cambridge: Cambridge University Press.

Montgomery, J. (2000). Verbal working memory in sentence comprehension in children with specific language impairment. *Journal of Speech, Language, and Hearing Research, 43*, 293–308.

Morais, J., Bertelson, P., Luz, C., & Alegria, J. (1986). Literacy training and speech segmentation. *Cognition, 24*, 45–64.

Moray, N. (1959). Attention in dichotic listening: Affective cues and the influence of instructions. *Quarterly Journal of Experimental Psychology, 11*, 56–60.

Morey, C. C., & Cowan, N. (2004). When visual and verbal memories compete: Evidence of cross-domain limits in working memory. *Psychonomic Bulletin and Review, 11*, 296–301.

Morey, C. C., & Cowan, N. (2005). When do visual and verbal memories conflict? The importance of working-memory load and retrieval. *Journal of Experimental Psychology: Learning, Memory, and Cognition, 31*, 703–713.

Mueller, S. T., Seymour, T. L., Kieras, D. E., & Meyer, D. E. (2003). Theoretical implications of articulatory duration, phonological similarity, and phonological complexity in verbal working memory. *Journal of Experimental Psychology: Learning, Memory, and Cognition, 6*, 1353–1380.

Nation, K., Adams, J. W., Bowyer-Crane, C. A., & Snowling, M. J. (1999). Working memory deficits in poor comprehenders reflect underlying language impairments. *Journal of Experimental Child Psychology, 73*, 139–158.

Oakes, L. M., & Bauer, P. J. (Eds.). (2007). *Short- and long-term memory in infancy and early childhood*. New York: Oxford University Press.

Oberauer, K. (2005). Control of the contents of working memory—A comparison of two paradigms and two age groups. *Journal of Experimental Psychology: Learning, Memory, and Cognition, 31*, 714–728.

Oberauer, K., & Kliegl, R. (2006). A formal model of capacity limits in working memory. *Journal of Memory and Language, 55*, 601–626.

Ornstein, P. A., & Naus, M. J. (1978). Rehearsal processes in children's memory. In P. A. Ornstein (Ed.), *Memory development in children* (pp. 69–99). Hillsdale, NJ: Lawrence Erlbaum Associates, Inc.

Pascual-Leone, J. A. (1970). Mathematical model for the transition rule in Piaget's developmental stages. *Acta Psychologica, 32*, 301–345.

Pascual-Leone, J. (2005). A neoPiagetian view of developmental intelligence. In O. Wilhelm & R. W. Engle (Eds.), *Understanding and measuring intelligence* (pp. 177–201). London: Sage.

Pennington, B. F., & Ozonoff, S. (1996). Executive functions and developmental psychopathology. *Journal of Child Psychology and Psychiatry, 37*, 51–87.

Peterson, L. R., & Peterson, M. J. (1959). Short-term retention of individual verbal items. *Journal of Experimental Psychology, 58*, 193–198.

Posner, M. I. (Ed.). (2004). *Cognitive neuroscience of attention.* New York: Guilford Press.

Rasmussen, C., & Bisanz, J. (2005). Representation and working memory in early arithmetic. *Journal of Experimental Child Psychology, 91*, 137–157.

Reuhkala, M. (2001). Mathematical skills in ninth-graders: Relationship with visuospatial abilities and working memory. *Educational Psychology, 21*, 387–399.

Roodenrys, S., Hulme, C., & Brown, G. (1993). The development of short-term memory span: Separable effects of speech rate and long-term memory. *Journal of Experimental Child Psychology, 56*, 431–442.

Ruckridge, J. R., & Tannock, R. (2002). Neuropsychological profiles of adolescents with ADHD: Effects of reading difficulties and gender. *Journal of Child Psychology and Psychiatry, 43*, 988–1003.

Saults, J. S., & Cowan, N. (1996). The development of memory for ignored speech. *Journal of Experimental Child Psychology, 63*, 239–261.

Schneider, W., Kron, V., Hunnerkopf, M., & Krajewski, K. (2004). The development of young children's memory strategies: First findings from the Würzburg Longitudinal Memory Study. *Journal of Experimental Child Psychology, 88*, 193–209.

Siegel, L. S. (1988). Evidence that IQ scores are irrelevant to the definition and analysis of reading-disability. *Canadian Journal of Psychology, 42*, 201–215.

Siegel, L. S., & Ryan, E. B. (1989). The development of working memory in normally achieving and subtypes of learning disabled children. *Child Development, 60*, 973–980.

Siegler, R. S. (1996). *Emerging minds: The process of change in children's thinking.* New York: Oxford University Press.

Simon, H. A. (1974). How big is a chunk? *Science, 183*, 482–488.

Sokolov, E. N. (1963). *Perception and the conditioned reflex.* New York: Pergamon Press.

Sonuga-Barker, E. J. S., Dalen, L., Daley, D., & Remington, B. (2002). Are planning, working memory, and inhibition associated with individual differences in preschool ADHD symptoms? *Developmental Neuropsychology, 21*, 255–272.

Stothard, S. E., & Hulme, C. (1992). Reading comprehension difficulties in children. *Reading and Writing: An Interdisciplinary Journal, 4*, 245–256.

Stroop, J. R. (1935). Studies of interference in serial verbal reactions. *Journal of Experimental Psychology, 18*, 643–662.

Swanson, H. L. (2003). Age-related differences in learning disabled and skilled readers' working memory. *Journal of Experimental Child Psychology, 85*, 1–31.

Swanson, H. L. & Beebe-Frankenberger, M. (2004). The relationship between working memory and mathematical problem solving in children at risk and not at risk for math disabilities. *Journal of Education Psychology, 96*, 471–491.

Swanson, H. L., & Sachse-Lee, C. (2001). Mathematical problem solving and working memory in children with learning disabilities: Both executive and phonological processes are important. *Journal of Experimental Child Psychology, 79*, 294–321.

Swanson, H. L. & Saez, L. (2003). Memory difficulties in children and adults with learning disabilities. In H. L. Swanson, S. Graham, & K. R. Harris (Eds.), *Handbook of learning disabilities* (pp. 182–198). New York: Guilford Press.

Thevenot, C., & Oakhill, J. (2005). The strategic use of alternative representations in arithmetic word problem solving. *Quarterly Journal of Experimental Psychology, 58A*, 1311–1323.

Todd, J. J., & Marois, R. (2004). Capacity limit of visual short-term memory in human posterior parietal cortex. *Nature, 428*, 751–754.

Towse, J. N., Hitch, G. J., & Hutton, U. (1998). A reevaluation of working memory capacity in children. *Journal of Memory and Language, 39*, 195–217.

Tulving, E., & Patkau, J. E. (1962). Concurrent effects of contextual constraint and word frequency on immediate recall and learning of verbal material. *Canadian Journal of Psychology, 16*, 83–95.

Turner, M. L., & Engle, R. W. (1989). Is working memory capacity task dependent? *Journal of Memory and Language, 28*, 127–154.

Unsworth, N., & Engle, R. W. (2007). The nature of individual differences in working memory capacity: Active maintenance in primary memory and controlled search from secondary memory. *Psychological Review, 114*, 104–132

Vogel, E. K., McCollough, A. W., & Machizawa, M. G. (2005). Neural measures reveal individual differences in controlling access to working memory. *Nature, 438*, 500–503.

Wagner, R. K., & Muse, A. (2006). Short-term memory deficits in developmental dyslexia. In T. P. Alloway & S. E. Gathercole (Eds.), *Working memory in neuro-developmental conditions* (pp. 41–57). Hove, UK: Psychology Press.

Wagner, R. K., Torgesen, J., & Rashotte, C. (1999). *Comprehensive test of phono-logical processing*. Austin, TX: Pro-Ed.

Wagner, R. K., Torgesen, J. K., Rashotte, C. A., Hecht, S. A., Barker, T. A., Burgess, S. R., et al. (1997). Changing relations between phonological processing abilities and word-level reading as children develop from beginning to skilled readers: A 5-year longitudinal study. *Developmental Psychology, 33*, 468–479.

Waugh, N. C., & Norman, D. A. (1965). Primary memory. *Psychological Review, 72*, 89–104.

Weiss, V. (1995). Memory span as the quantum of action of thought. *Cahiers de Psychologie Cognitive, 14*, 387–408.

Xu, Y., & Chun, M. M. (2006). Dissociable neural mechanisms supporting visual short-term memory for objects. *Nature, 440*, 91–95.

13 Working memory in infants and toddlers

J. Steven Reznick
University of North Carolina at Chapel Hill, USA

DEFINITION AND SIGNIFICANCE OF WORKING MEMORY

For over a century, psychologists have amassed empirical research on phenomena that can be labeled "memory." For better or worse, the constraints on the phenomena that are labeled "memory" are as broad as the wide boundaries that define the term in standard lexical use, which has a wide enough focus to include memory process, content, and product. Leading theoreticians have long recognized the need to parse memory into specific constructs. Efforts to organize the abundance of potentially relevant empirical phenomena that could be called memory have not generated an inclusive overarching taxonomy but have at least provided many meaningful dimensions and distinctions. For example, if memory is defined as a process, theoretical accounts suggest that the process must include sub-processes that support representation, storage, and retrieval. Or, if memory is defined as the specific content of the information stored, we know that there is some utility in distinguishing between stored information that is more or less a direct representation of the event (i.e., episodic memory) and stored information that describes or categorizes the event (i.e., semantic memory). Finally, if memory refers to the duration of storage, there is an obvious distinction between information stored briefly and then discarded versus information stored for a long period of time. Obvious? Well, not exactly. The leitmotif of this chapter is that researchers who study short-term memory are focusing on several different processes and that any hope of a cumulative science of memory development requires that we pay more attention to specific procedures of measurement and the extent to which our constructs are yoked to these procedures.

Sperling (1960) used the term "iconic memory" to describe the passing trace of a perceptual event. Miller, Galanter, and Pribram (1960) used the term "working memory" to describe the neural mechanism that allows the brain to form, modify, and execute plans. Anderson and Bower (1973) used the term "working memory" to describe an active partition of long-term memory that supports ongoing processing. Baddeley and Hitch (1974) used the term "working memory" to describe processes that maintain task-relevant information during the performance of a task. The common theme across these definitions is that working memory refers to a temporary storage buffer that allows an organism to extend the ongoing representation of a stimulus beyond the termination of that stimulus for some short duration of time and then use that stored representation. More broadly, the stimulus represented in working memory might come from any perceptual channel (e.g., it might be visual or auditory) or from long-term storage, and the representation might code for any ontological category (e.g., what the stimulus is, where the stimulus appeared, when the stimulus occurred).

Current conceptualizations of working memory seem to agree on this general definition. For example, Cowan et al. (2005) define working memory as "the set of mechanisms capable of retaining a small amount of inform-ation in an active state for use in ongoing cognitive tasks" (p. 43). Conway, Kane, Bunting, Hambrick, Wilhelm, and Engle (2005) define working memory as "a multicomponent system responsible for active maintenance of information in the face of ongoing processing and/or distraction" (p. 770). However, when these definitions are recast as measurement tasks, differ-ences in the conceptualization of working memory become apparent. For example, Cowan et al. (2005) view working memory within the context of adjustable attentional focus, and particularly as reflecting the scope of this attentional focus. Specifically, if experience is conceptualized as the transitory activation of representational processes, working memory refers to the limited capacity to extract chunks of information from these active processes, thus allowing the information to be used in some explicit memory-dependent response. Consider this example: You wake up in the darkness, hear a resonant gong, and realize that you have been awakened by the chimes of a grandfather clock. It occurs to you to wonder what time it is, and you do a scan of your memory: "I think I heard bong-bong-bong, so it must be 3:00." From the Cowan et al. perspective, the extraction of "bong-bong-bong" from the transient repository of perceptual experience is an example of working memory. Moreover, successful extraction of a two-bong representation requires less working memory capacity and extraction of a 10-bong representation requires considerably more working memory capacity.

Working memory measurement procedures are consistent with the Cowan et al. approach if they meet various constraints, but the key components seem to be that grouping and rehearsal processes are limited during presentation and maintenance of stimuli. For example, in the *memory for ignored speech task*, participants are engaged in a cognitive task, are simultaneously hearing (and ignoring) a list of digits, and must respond to occasional probes that assess memory for the most recently presented digits (e.g., Cowan, Saults, Nugent, & Elliott, 1999). Similarly, in the *running memory span task*, verbal items are presented at a fast pace in a list that ends unpredictably, and participants are asked to recall the most recently presented items (e.g., Hockey, 1973). Finally, Luck and Vogel (1997) have developed a *visual-array comparison task* in which participants see a large array of items followed by a second array that is either identical to the first or that has one item that has undergone a change, and the participant attempts to determine whether the second array is changed or unchanged.

The definition of working memory proposed by Conway et al. (2005) puts more emphasis on the processes whereby transitory information is retained. In this multi-component system, converging processes actively maintain information in the context of other ongoing processes that can be more or less distracting. As a realistic example, imagine being asked to dial a phone number, which you are holding in memory, when you realize that you need to enter an access code before dialing the number. The processes that you use to retain the original number and not forget it in the context of ongoing activity can be considered working memory. Interestingly, the term "attention" is relevant here as well, but in a different sense. Kane and Engle (2002) define executive attention as the capability to maintain memory representations in an active state in the face of interference. From this perspective, working memory must be assessed in a storage-and-processing context in which information is maintained despite more or less direct interference. For example, in the *reading span task*, participants read sentences and try to remember words from the sentence (e.g., Daneman & Carpenter, 1980) or an unrelated word (Engle, Tuholski, Laughlin, & Conway, 1999). In an *operation span task*, participants evaluate equations while remembering words (e.g., Turner & Engle, 1989). Finally, in a *counting span task*, participants count items in successive arrays and attempt to remember how many items were in each array (Case, Kurland, & Goldberg, 1982). Each of these examples is structured to require participants to use attentional processes to hold information in working memory intentionally in the context of ongoing processing or blatant distraction, either of which prevents or undermines rehearsal.

The definition of working memory in infants and toddlers should be informed by the definition of working memory in adults, although a role-reversal is possible, with developmental aspects of the phenomenon having theoretical relevance for conceptualizations of adult working memory. As noted in the previous paragraphs, conceptualizations of working memory are of limited utility until they are linked to measurement operations. The specific procedures that are used to assess infant and toddler working memory are addressed in a subsequent section. An important first step is to defend the claim that infants and toddlers do indeed possess working memory and to highlight the significance of this fact.

If we agree that working memory refers to a temporary storage buffer that allows an organism to extend the ongoing representation of a stimulus beyond the termination of that stimulus for some short duration of time, then the best evidence for the availability of working memory is the presence of behavioral abilities that would be thus enabled. For example, by late in the first year, infant humans can solve goal-oriented problems (Mosier & Rogoff,

1994; Willatts, 1984, 1999), communicate about intentions and desires using words and gestures (Bates, Beninni, Bretherton, Camaioni, & Volterra, 1979; Bruner, 1975; Harding & Golinkoff, 1979), and engage in shared attention coordinated with a partner regarding some external event (Bakeman & Adamson, 1984; Bates, 1976; Seibert, Hogan, & Mundy, 1982). These sophisticated cognitive abilities require holding a goal in mind, enacting a strategy, or processing an ongoing flow of information and thus would be impossible without working memory.

From a more philosophical perspective, working memory allows an organism to move out of a simple existence in the present and attain a higher level of consciousness that includes a past and a future. That is, working memory provides the operational space and processes that allow an organism to retain information that has already occurred and to use this information to direct behavior toward future goals. For example, consider an infant who has a very limited working memory capacity. When she sees a pacifier, processes of recognition and learning can cause a positive emotional response to the pacifier and support behavior directed toward obtaining the pacifier. However, if a young infant with limited capacity for working memory sees her pacifier disappear, her pacifier no longer exists in a mentalistic sense. Months later, when working memory capacity is much stronger, the same infant might retain a representation of the absent pacifier, and on the basis of this information, use a more or less effective behavioral strategy in order to obtain the goal that she now has in mind (e.g., search in the location where the pacifier now resides, seek help from an adult in obtaining the pacifier). In any circumstance in which intentional action is ascribed to an organism, an underlying assumption is that behavior is being driven by a goal, which is simply another way of saying that a target representation is available in working memory. To quote from James's poetic description of the phenomenon I am calling working memory:

> [T]he practically cognized present is no knife-edge, but a saddle-back, with a certain breadth of its own on which we sit perched, and from which we look in two directions into time. The unit of composition of our perception of time is a duration, with a bow and a stern, as it were— a rearward- and a forward-looking end.
>
> (1890/1981, p. 574)

METHODOLOGICAL ISSUES

Most procedures for assessing working memory in adults depend on some degree of verbal fluency (either to understand instructions or to provide a response), and the stamina and motivation needed to endure a long series of trials. Obviously, infants fail to align on both of these dimensions, and thus a different array of measurement procedures is needed.

Some of the issues that confront researchers who study adult working memory attain a different relevance when applied to infants and toddlers. For example, Cowan et al. (2005) suggest that participants whose working memory is being tapped must be prevented from grouping information into chunks and from rehearsing. There could be perceptual processes that infants use to align, configure, or categorize stimuli (e.g., the phenomenon of categorical perception in which the auditory system ignores discriminable speech contrasts and groups similar sounds into phonetic categories), but these processes seem quite dissimilar to such processes as the chunking of single digits into larger numbers or the semantic categorization that might aid in short-term storage. Furthermore, it seems highly unlikely that infants are capable of engaging in any sort of deliberate rehearsal process because they lack the relevant verbal skills, the broader ability to form and use a strategy, and the motivation to do so. Given that we do not know if intrinsic or implicit rehearsal processes are available to non-verbal organisms, the parsimonious assumption is that rehearsal is not a factor that influences recall in non-verbal organisms. So, from the chunking and rehearsal perspective, there is no reason for concern that working memory is not being tapped.

A second issue that has unique relevance when applied to infants and toddlers is whether ongoing processes are present that can be more or less distracting (Conway et al., 2005). Infants cannot respond to complex instructions that urge them to do two things at once, thus some approaches to this problem are simply not feasible. However, research with infants suggests that cognitive processing in this age group is so fragile and unstable that almost any coterminous activity is distracting, and paradigms can be engineered to insure distraction. For example, infants who are holding information in mind are distracted when they interact with an examiner. Also, when a task includes multiple trials, sampling with replacement across trials introduces the distraction of proactive interference as the infant attempts to discard or update previous memory traces.

If issues related to chunking, rehearsal, and ongoing distraction are held in abeyance, a straightforward assessment of working memory can be reduced to three key steps. The participant is first presented with a specific piece of information (e.g., a location or an identity), which presumably can be represented by the participant's perceptual apparatus. After the information is presented, the presentation ends and a delay is imposed during which the participant must maintain the information using mental processes (i.e., there is no clue present or detectable rule that can be used instead of the original information). Finally, at the conclusion of the delay, the participant must perform some action that indicates that the original information is still available. In this context, working memory capacity can be defined from at least two perspectives. One perspective on capacity is the span of time between presentation and performance during which the participant maintains the representation of the original information. A second perspective on capacity is the amount of information maintained.

Delayed-response task

Hunter (1913) introduced a procedure that fits this description, which he referred to as a delayed-reaction procedure, but the more recent terminology is *delayed-response task*. Hunter's goal was to compare typical mammalian behavior when a so-called "determining stimulus" was absent at the moment of response, and he developed a procedure that was applicable and effective for rats, dogs, raccoons, and children. In a subsequent study, Hunter modified the apparatus to test his daughter when she was 13–16 months old (Hunter, 1917). Thayer watched her father hide a toy inside one of three, small, lidded boxes. Hunter then distracted Thayer by covering her eyes or turning her away from the apparatus or engaging her in an interaction. After a delay of between 3 and 35 seconds, Thayer was allowed to search for the toy, which she did with relative success if the delay was less than 17 seconds. Hunter's study implicitly defined working memory capacity as the number of seconds over which the hiding location was maintained, but alternative approaches would include allowing the participant to choose between various numbers of boxes or to search for various numbers of objects. It would take greater working memory capacity to remember a location for 35 seconds rather than for 3 seconds, to find a hidden object when the choice is between 3 rather than 2 boxes, or when 2 objects are hidden rather than 1 object.

In the 90 years since Hunter's study, the delayed-response task has been used in more or less this exact format in hundreds of studies, and it is gener-ally accepted as the canonical procedure for assessing working memory with non-verbal participants (Goldman-Rakic, 1987). The delayed-response task has been a productive research procedure because it taps into fundamental survival skills (i.e., foraging for food) and is fun (i.e., it mimics games like peek-a-boo or hide-and-seek). Some variations of the delayed-response task would be expected to affect performance but not the theoretical interpret-ation of the phenomenon being assessed. For example, performance could be affected by the salience and distinctiveness of the target. Bell (1970) found that infants are more likely to search for their mother than for a toy, and it is obvious that a hungrier animal is more likely to search for food. Huttenlocher, Newcombe, and Sandberg (1994) allowed children to search for an object in an undifferentiated box of sand, and DeLoache and Brown (1979) had children find a toy hidden in a room. The basic delayed-response syntax is the same in both procedures, although the tasks do introduce some difficulty as a result of spatial orienting.

Another variation is the use of an orienting response rather than a reach-ing response. For example, Gilmore and Johnson (1995) cued infants with a visual stimulus at a particular location in the peripheral visual field. Schwartz and Reznick (1999) showed infants an examiner appearing in a window and communicating with the infant and then noted the infant's ability to gaze toward the location where the examiner had appeared. The orient versus reach parameter is particularly salient because infants tend to perform better in a delayed-response task when they are allowed to gaze toward a correct location rather than reach for that location (Diamond, 1985; Hofstadter & Reznick, 1996). Pelphrey and Reznick (2003) offer various interpretations to explain this phenomenon. In the paradigm developed by Schwartz and Reznick, infant behavior across multiple trials of this "peek-a-boo" game can be interpreted as an effort to find the hidden examiner, but it is important to note that orienting toward a location and reaching toward a location do not necessarily support the same psychological interpretation.

The delayed-response task, as described earlier, is a clear measure of working memory. However, it is important to note that the task is amenable to embellishments that alter the measurement goal. For example, when the pattern of hidings is modified to present several trials at one location and then a trial at a new location, the participant must not only remember a new location but also inhibit a strong, prepotent response to the previously correct location. This so-called *A-not-B procedure* was used by Piaget to assess the infant's emerging object concept (Piaget, 1954), and from recent theoretical perspectives, the procedure can be viewed as tapping the executive function labeled "response inhibition" or the lack thereof, which is labeled "perseveration." In a related version of the task, after an object has been hidden, its hiding location can be modified through a series of displacements. Piaget interpreted the child's ability to process complex displacements as evidence of an increasingly mature object concept. Finally, a spatial transformation can be introduced after the hiding (e.g., the table is rotated or the infant is moved to the other side of the table) and the delayed-response task can be used to study aspects of infant spatial knowledge including place learning or cue learning (e.g., Acredolo, 1978).

A more controversial variation of the delayed-response task is a version in which infants do not actively search for a hidden object. In the *violation-of-expectation procedure*, the infant sees an object hidden at a particular location. After a delay, the contents of the location are revealed. In the control condition, the expected object is present. In the memory challenge condition, either the expected object is not present or an unexpected object is revealed. In either case, greater visual attention to the violation-of-expectation condition is interpreted as evidence that the infant maintained the location and/or identity of the hidden object in working memory. For example, Wilcox, Nadel, and Rosser (1996) report that infants as young as 10 weeks are attentive when a toy is retrieved from an unexpected location after 5 seconds, and Baillargeon and colleagues report that 8-month-olds respond to an unexpected retrieval up to 70 seconds after the toy was hidden (Baillargeon, DeVos, & Graber, 1989; Baillargeon & Graber, 1988). More recently, Luo, Baillargeon, Brueckner, and Munakata (2003) familiarized 5-month-olds with a scenario in which a box was hidden behind a screen in a position that should or should not block a tall cylinder from moving back and forth behind the screen. Infants looked longer at the unexpected scenario after a 3- or 4-minute delay, and given the duration of the test trials, the actual delay was

6 or 7 minutes. Luo et al. suggest that this evidence supports the claim that infants can "remember" the hidden box for several minutes. Other versions of the violation-of-expectation procedure have been used to support claims about working memory for the identity of specific objects (e.g., Kaldy & Leslie, 2005).

Infants in the violation-of-expectation procedure obviously are manifesting memory in some sense, but can we say that this procedure is tapping working memory in the usual sense in which the construct is used? The community of researchers who study infant memory can be seen as divided into those who accept this interpretation and those who do not, and there are considerable implications depending on the side chosen. Specifically, if the violation-of-expectation procedure is tapping working memory, this methodology is much more sensitive than the *delayed-response task*. Moreover, data from the violation-of-expectation procedure suggest that working memory is available to infants early in the first year, and that these infants sustain information in their working memory for minutes, which is longer than the span of working memory generally attributed to adults.

A compelling resolution of the counterintuitive claim that very young infants have adult-like working memory capacity is to suggest that although the violation-of-expectation procedure could tap working memory, in some instantiations it also taps other, more robust aspects of memory. Specifically, implicit memory refers to the phenomenon in which past experience affects current performance even though there is no conscious or intentional recollection of the previous experience (Graf & Masson, 1993). For example, consider the experience of staring at a colleague without knowing why and then eventually realizing that the colleague has new glasses or a new hair style. Staring at the colleague in this scenario is driven by a violation of expectation in some sense, but the expectation is not explicit and certainly is not being retained in working memory. In a typical implicit memory experiment with children (e.g., Mecklenbrauker, Hupbach, & Wippich, 2003), the child sees a series of pictures and is asked to name each picture and describe its color. In a subsequent task, children are given a category name and are asked to produce exemplars of that category. Previously seen items are more likely to emerge as category responses even though children have no explicit memory for having seen the exemplar, and they certainly have not maintained a representation of the exemplars in working memory.

A large body of research suggests that implicit memory ability is strong and stable from 3 years of age to adulthood (Murphy, McKone, & Slee, 2003). We know very little about implicit memory in infants and toddlers because the standard assessment procedures require more or less complicated instructions and tend to use verbal responses. From the present perspective, it seems reasonable to interpret the violation-of-expectation procedure as a measure of implicit memory. That is, an infant could stare at an unexpected event without having any explicit expectation regarding the event, and particularly without holding any relevant representation of the event in working memory.

In other words, the infant is looking at the event because implicit memory indicates that something is amiss, just as the infant stares at a physical event that violates the regularity of previous experience (Baillargeon, 1987, 1995; Spelke, 1988, 1994; Wynn, 1992). This behavior does not imply working memory (or knowledge of physics or mathematics)—just that young infants have a functional implicit memory system that is sensitive to statistical regularities in the environment (Saffran, Aslin, & Newport, 1996; Marcus, Vijayan, Rao, & Vishton, 1999). This not only explains the anomalous claims regarding working memory that emerge from the violation-of-expectation procedure, but also is consistent with current views regarding the stability and relatively early development of implicit memory (Murphy et al., 2003).

A second interpretation of looking behavior in the violation-of-expectation procedure is that the infant is responding to the unexpected event because of information being stored in long-term memory rather than working memory per se. From this perspective, we could say that the infant has learned that an object is hidden at a particular location, and that this specific fact could be stored and retained after a considerable delay. For example, McDonough (1999) reports that infants in a delayed-response task can recall the location of a hidden object for 90 seconds, even after a significant distraction. The important point is that each infant in McDonough's study only participated in a single trial and thus only had to learn that an object had been hidden at a particular location. More dramatically, Moore and Meltzoff (2004) report that 14-month-old infants who saw a bell hidden in a container were highly likely to search for the bell in that container when they were allowed to search for the bell 24 hours later. These findings illustrate that the interpretation of a single successful trial in a memory task can be ambiguous when different memory systems are potentially involved. Given that an infant who searches correctly on a particular trial after a delay of a few seconds might also have searched correctly after a delay of hours or days, how can we be certain that working memory is being tapped? A key to assuring that working memory is being assessed is that performance be contrasted across multiple trials with a random assignment of correct locations. This protocol requires the infant to replace short-term representations with new representations and thus reduces the possibility that performance reflects information being retrieved from long-term representations.

Other procedures

Several procedures that are used to measure working memory in adults have been adapted to explore infant and toddler working memory. In an *observe–perform procedure*, a sequence of actions is presented, a delay is imposed, and the participant attempts to repeat the sequence of actions. For example, in the Corsi blocks test (Corsi, 1972) an examiner taps a sequence of blocks and the participant attempts to repeat the sequence of taps immediately afterward. Memory capacity is challenged with longer tap sequences defined by sampling with replacement among the set of blocks. Infants who observe a multistep action sequence are likely to produce those actions when given the opportunity at a later time (Kagan, 1981; see Bauer, 2002, for a review), thus enabling this approach to be used to measure working memory if the steps in the action sequence are independent and if sequence steps are sampled with replacement across successive trials. For example, Alp (1994) reported an imitation sorting task in which an examiner sorted disparate objects into two containers, then retrieved the objects and gave them to 12- to 36-month-olds. Older children imitated the examiner's sort correctly for an increasingly large set of objects.

In a *familiarize–recognize procedure*, participants see a set of stimuli (e.g., digits). If they are subsequently able to recognize specific probes as members of the familiarized set of stimuli, this suggests that the original stimuli were held in working memory (Sternberg, 1966). This procedure can be used with infants. For example, de Saint Victor, Smith, and Loboschefski (1997) familiarized 10-month-old infants with a set of one, two, or three photographs of objects (e.g., a bike, a ball, a bunny) and then presented test trials pairing a familiar stimulus with a novel stimulus. Fixation to the familiar stimulus increased as a function of familiarization set size, suggesting that infants perform an item-by-item scan of the contents of working memory to determine that the stimulus was familiar. Ross-Sheehy, Oakes, and Luck (2003) have developed an alternative approach to the familiarize–recognize format that holds promise as an assessment of infant memory. Infants see displays on two separate computer monitors. The stimulus on one display remains constant over trials, while the stimulus on the other display changes on each trial (e.g., a square changes color). An infant who forms a representation of the color of the stimulus and keeps that representation active during the inter-trial interval would be attracted to the changing display. There are various reasons why an infant might not prefer the changing display, but a lack of working memory is a salient interpretation.

As described earlier, some caution is warranted in interpreting these results because it is unclear whether implicit memory is involved and whether short-term or long-term memory processes are being engaged. An infant might respond to a particular stimulus on the basis of implicit memory and might respond similarly to that stimulus when it is presented hours, days, or weeks later (e.g., Fantz, 1956), which undermines the claim that an active representation was sustained during the interval and questions the interpretation that working memory is being tapped.

WHAT DO WE KNOW ABOUT WORKING MEMORY IN INFANTS AND TODDLERS?

Our phenomenological experience of the stimulus representation process gives us a strong impression that events do not necessarily extinguish in the mind as abruptly as they may vanish from the ambient environment. For example, the physical pressure wave that we hear as the tolling of a clock dissipates almost immediately, but the experience of having heard a sound and the characteristics of that sound might linger for seconds or minutes. The definition of working memory that has been adopted in this article implies neither a sophisticated representation (i.e., chunking or categorization) nor rehearsal. If working memory is, at minimum, the simple reverberation of an event in the context of competing cognitive processes, a nervous system that can represent physical stimulation and that is likely to have some capacity for maintaining that representation after the physical stimulation is over has some level of working memory. On the other hand, it is important to ask at what point in development working memory can be demonstrated. From a phylogenetic perspective, animals that efficiently forage for food, hunt, or avoid predators are easily described as using working memory to act on transitory information (e.g., systematically avoid a location that no longer has food, monitor and predict the location of unseen prey, or calibrate an escape route that takes into account the path of a pursuer). This category of "creatures with working memory" would include a wide array of sophisticated nervous systems that have working memory.

From an ontogenetic perspective, the structure and functionality of a nervous system change over time and thus each organism must transition from a developmental phase without working memory, and possibly through phases with minimal or limited working memory, before attaining mature working memory capacity. This fact tempts us to ask, "When do human infants have sufficient working memory to be detectable in an experimental procedure?" Any answer to this question must be arbitrary because the answer will be generated on the basis of the working memory assessment techniques that are available at the time. If the delayed-response task is regarded as the "gold standard," the earliest evidence for behavior clearly reflecting working memory is in 5- to 6-month-old infants. Reznick, Morrow, Goldman, and Snyder (2004) had an examiner appear in one of two windows and interact with an infant who was seated on the mother's lap. The examiner then disappeared behind a curtain and used her hand to draw the infant's attention to the center of the apparatus. After a delay of 1–2 seconds, the examiner opened the curtains to reveal empty windows. This action attracted the infant's gaze toward one of the windows, and if the first gaze was toward the window where the examiner had disappeared, this was considered to be a successful search. The location of the correct window was counterbalanced between the left and right windows across 12 trials. Several approaches to data analysis suggested that by the end of their sixth month, most infants had sufficient working memory capacity to allow them to retain the location where the examiner had disappeared and to use this information to guide their subsequent orienting response.

It seems obvious that the subsequent development of working memory would be marked by a more or less linear increase in capacity, and that banal summary is the best that the field can offer at the present time. For example, Fox, Kagan, and Weiskopf (1979) tested infants longitudinally from 6 to 14 months on a delayed-response task with a 1-, 3-, or 7-second delay. No 7-month-old reached to the correct location at the 7-second delay, and most 12-month-olds solved the problem easily. Diamond and Doar (1989) used a 16-trial, two-location delayed-response task with infants tested longitudinally from 6 to 12 months. Ability to span a delay increased linearly at a rate of 2 seconds per month from approximately 2 seconds at 7.5 months to roughly 10 seconds at 12 months. This developmental function was confirmed in a cross-sectional cohort, where infants tolerated delays of 0, 3, and 8 seconds at 8, 10, and 12 months, respectively. These findings both replicated and diverged from other findings in the literature. Their results replicated findings from Harris (1973) and Brody (1981) indicating comparable ability in this age range, and are consistent with research by Pelphrey et al. (2004) exploring working memory for location in infants aged 6–12 months using a cross-sectional design, with assessments defined by orientation and reaching, and with working memory capacity challenged across varying delays and across a varying number of locations. However, Diamond and Doar's results diverge from findings by Allen (1931) and Reznick, Fueser, and Bosquet (1998). Allen's results indicated that 12-month-old infants could tolerate delays far greater than the 10-second delays suggested by Diamond and Doar's data. Reznick et al. (1998) allowed 9-month-old infants to search for a toy hidden in one of three possible locations. Infants searched correctly after delays of 2 and 3 seconds, a finding compatible with Diamond and Doar's estimate of working memory capacity at 9 months. However, when infants who had searched incorrectly were allowed to select from the two remaining locations after delays of 10 to 20 seconds, they were correct on approximately 62% of their responses, significantly more than would be expected by chance. Rose, Feldman, and Jankowski (2001) and Ross-Sheehy et al. (2003) used alternative methodologies and found results that are consistent with these developmental trends.

Working memory capacity should continue to improve in toddlers, and this claim is consistent with the limited evidence that is available. Kagan (1981) administered a memory-for-locations task in cross-sectional and longitudinal designs to children in the United States and abroad and found a steep improvement across the second year. Reznick, Corley, and Robinson (1997) reported comparable results for a large sample of identical and fraternal twins. Barth and Call (2006) reported above-chance performance in 2.6-year-old children who searched for an object hidden in one of three cups after a delay of 30 seconds. Cowan and others (e.g., Cowan, 1997; Cowan, Saults, & Elliott, 2002) have described changes in working memory across childhood, with some articulation of relevant dimensions and processes. This level of detail is possible because older children can be given task instructions, provide verbal responses or well-trained motor responses, and participate in multiple tasks. Unfortunately, the toddler age range is more difficult to work with, and some procedures that are effective with younger and older children are not appropriate.

RELEVANCE OF RESEARCH WITH ADULTS AND NON-HUMANS

Hunter's initial study using the delayed-response task (Hunter, 1913) included children, raccoons, dogs, and rats, thus indicating that the delayed-response approach as well as the construct of working memory obviously have broad applicability. Harlow (1932) compared performance in apes and monkeys, and the following section describes research with animals that has been used for identifying the neural circuitry that supports working memory performance.

Barth and Call (2006) administered a basic delayed-response task (as well as various modifications of the task) to 24 great apes representing a wide range of species, and found almost perfect performance after a 0-second delay and above-chance performance after a 30-second delay. These results are comparable to the performance of 2.6-year-old children tested in the same context, and they suggest that relatively sophisticated organisms who live in a world in which they must find food and shelter, and avoid predators and injury, are endowed with a significant working memory capacity.

RELEVANCE OF COGNITIVE NEUROSCIENCE

There is an impressive body of research that links working memory to the functioning of a distributed network of brain regions, with the prefrontal cortex (PFC) and the hippocampus playing a major role. Although the focus of this research has tended to be on the functionality of specific brain regions, it is obvious that the whole brain and particularly the brain's interconnecting circuits are relevant for performance on any task. More generally, this research is relevant because maturation of the underlying neural structures and interconnecting circuitry is likely to be a limiting factor in, if not a cause of, increases in working memory capacity.

Jacobsen (1936) found that PFC damage produced selective deficits in the ability to respond to situations on the basis of dynamic information (see Goldman-Rakic, 1987, for a detailed review of the early literature on this topic). Fuster and Alexander (1971) and Kubota and Niki (1971) detected cells in the monkey's PFC that have a firing frequency correlated with performance on delayed-response tasks. Subsequent work ruled out alternative interpretations and strengthened the conclusion that neuronal activity in PFC is related to the short-term storage of spatial-location information in non-human primates (Funahashi, Bruce, & Goldman-Rakic, 1989) and in humans (Petrides, Alivisatos, Evans, & Meyer, 1993; McCarthy et al., 1994).

Most research highlights the structural aspect of the link between working memory and PFC, but the functionality of the dopamine system is also relevant. For example, neural activity in PFC that is associated with working memory can be enhanced by local application of dopamine (Sawaguchi, Matsumura, & Kubota, 1988) and a D_2 receptor agonist (Luciana, Depue, Arbisi, & Leon, 1992), and can be decreased by application of a D_1 receptor antagonist (Sawaguchi & Goldman-Rakic, 1991).

The link between working memory and PFC is quite specific, suggesting a direct relation between working memory capacity and PFC activation. For example, Cohen et al. (1997) and Jonides et al. (1997) report neuroimaging data from *n-back tasks*, in which participants see a sequence of letters and report the immediate target or a letter that was 1, 2, or 3 back in the sequence (in the Cohen et al. task) or judge whether the present letter matches a letter that was 1, 2, or 3 back (in the Jonides et al. task). Both studies indicate that PFC activation increases as a function of load. A second aspect of capacity is the need to manage two or more tasks at once. D'Esposito, Detre, Alsop, Shin, Atlas, and Grossman (1995) monitored sites in PFC using fMRI while participants performed a semantic-judgment task, a spatial-rotation task, or both. Neither task activated PFC individually, but when both tasks were performed simultaneously, PFC was involved.

If violation-of-expectation tasks are accepted as evidence for working memory, early developing neural systems are also relevant. For example, Kaldy and Sigala (2004) focus their review of the neurobiology of working memory on temporal cortex, thalamic, and hippocampal structures rather than the frontal lobes. The conception of dorsal and ventral pathways with differential specialization for information about identity versus location has been an influential perspective on neural development (Goodale & Milner, 1992; Milner & Goodale, 1995) and would be highly relevant for infant working memory if one accepts the interpretation on the basis of data from the *violation-of-expectation procedure* that young infants hold information about the identity of a hidden object in their working memory (e.g., Kaldy & Leslie, 2005). However, from the perspective of evidence on the basis of the *delayed-response task*, the neural mechanisms associated with the frontal lobes have hegemony.

Finally, researchers have attempted to link infant working memory with underlying neural maturation. For example, Bell and Fox (1992) found that increases in electrical activity in the frontal lobes measured using electro-encephalogram techniques correlate strongly with increases in the ability to span longer delays during 7- to 12-month-old infants' performance in a version of the delayed-response task. More recently, Bell (2002) found that the 6–9 Hz frequency band discriminated among different stages of cognitive activity and also between correct and incorrect responses in 8-month-olds. Finally, Baird, Kagan, Gaudette, Walz, Hershlag, and Boas (2002) recorded near-infrared spectroscopic images from 5- to 12-month-olds who attempted to retrieve a hidden toy after a 3-second delay. Successful performance on this task, which ranged from 6.0 to 8.3 months and averaged 7.1 months, was associated with an increase in hemoglobin concentration in the frontal cortex.

APPLICATIONS

One important application of working memory is that deterioration of working memory capacity has been noted in a wide range of circumstances. In the context of typical development, working memory deterioration may underlie various aspects of the poorer performance of older adults on cognitive tasks that involve reasoning (Phillips & Forshaw, 1998), updating (Hartman, Bolton, & Fehnel, 2001), overcoming interference (Lustig, May, & Hasher, 2001), storage (Belleville, Rouleau, & Caza, 1998), or cognitive processing (Salthouse, 1996). Working memory has also been implicated to some degree in Down syndrome (Lanfranchi, Cornoldi, & Vianello, 2004), fragile X syndrome (Munir, Cornish, & Wilding, 2000), autism (Mottron, Belleville, & Menard, 1999), Turner's syndrome (Cornoldi, Marconi, & Vecchi, 2001), and traumatic brain injury (Ewing-Cobbs, Prasad, Landry, Kramer, & DeLeon, 2004).

We do not know why working memory is affected in these conditions. One possibility is that working memory deficits are yet another symptom of disease-related deterioration of neural structures and processes. A more intriguing possibility is that in some conditions, working memory deterioration is the focal disease-related event and that the deterioration of this critical cognitive component leads to a broad range of subsequent problems in cognitive or social-emotional domains (e.g., poor language or reasoning, poor social cognition).

TO-DO LIST

From a scientific perspective, working memory is nothing more than the term that we use to describe a family of related processes and functions that support the ability to temporarily extend the representation of a stimulus and then use that stored representation. Infant and toddler working memory is a particularly important topic for various reasons. Working memory is a critical component of the cognitive infrastructure that supports such significant developmental accomplishments as language acquisition, goal-oriented behavior, and joint attention. We know very little about atypical development of working memory, but given the relation between working memory and various problematic outcomes, atypical development of working memory should be a relevant topic. Finally, that working memory either emerges or undergoes dramatic improvement during this age range should warrant considerable attention.

Rather than offer a banal "more research is needed" admonition, I would suggest that the most important step toward a cumulative science of infant

and toddler working memory would be the development of better methodology and a broader knowledge base that includes data from a rich array of
procedures. It is clearly a mistake to bind any scientific construct to a single
measurement operation and to ignore the variance that reflects the operation
of different processes and functions. The delayed-response task has been a
workhorse for the study of infant and toddler working memory and is clearly
the "gold standard," but procedural variations are needed to offset task-
related error of measurement and at a higher level, myopic adherence to an
essence rather than appropriate differentiation of relevant components. At
a minimum, multiple assessments across trials, sessions, or procedural variations can improve measurement of working memory. For example, Pelphrey
et al. (2004) assessed infant working memory in multiple procedures administered in multiple sessions to obtain robust estimates of working memory
capacity for each participant. An additional issue is the choice between a
multi-item test battery in which problems are selected to span a wide range of
difficulty and a stair-step approach in which each participant starts at a minimal level of challenge and moves through increasingly difficult challenges
until attaining a level of challenge that is too difficult. The former method
yields a percentage correct across a common denominator of items. The latter
method yields an absolute level of competence.

An additional step toward better methodology and better science is to
develop new procedures for measuring relevant constructs. The observe–
perform procedure and the familiar–recognize procedure described earlier
both hold promise as measures of infant and toddler working memory.
Another promising approach is to use mismatch negativity in evoked potential as an index of working memory (Cheour, Leppanen, & Kraus, 2000;
Thierry, 2005). For example, Gomes, Sussman, Ritter, Kurtzberg, Cowan,
and Vaughan (1999) presented sequences of auditory stimuli that included
either standard or deviant tones with either a 1-second or 8-second gap
between tones. Children aged 6–12 years displayed mismatch negativity when
the gap between a standard and a deviant tone was 1 second, but only older
children did so when the gap was 8 seconds, suggesting that their working
memory capacity had been exceeded. Inferences about memory derived from
mismatch negativity are correlated with more traditional measures (e.g.,
Ceponiene, Service, Kurjenluoma, Cheour, & Maatanen, 1999). Given the
passive nature of the mismatch negativity task, it might be productively
applied to infants and toddlers.

The development of alternative measurement tasks is a worthy goal, but
this endeavor is only beneficial if tasks are constructed within the bounds of a
common nomological network. Contemporary research on adult working
memory can be viewed as a Tower of Babel in which the term "working
memory" is used without reference to a specific measurement operation and
thus without meaning. Recent interpretations of violation-of-expectation
data and single-trial delayed-response experiments seem to be having the
same effect on discussions of infant and toddler working memory. One

fundamental step will be to combine data from multiple perspectives in the context of a single study to identify shared variance or subdivide the term "working memory" into the unique components and processes that are being tapped.

A second important area of research concerns divergent validity. The pattern of correlations among working memory measures and other measures of cognitive performance should cause concern that working memory could become the "new IQ" in the sense that it correlates with everything. The theoretical utility of working memory requires that it be differentiated from other cognitive abilities and competencies. This differentiation will be a difficult challenge in infants and toddlers because so many abilities are emerging and expanding during this phase of life, but without a more refined articulation, working memory is at risk for becoming merely a proxy for growth.

In addition to differentiating working memory from constructs that it might support, we must also explore the relation between working memory and constructs with which it is intimately related. For example, as described earlier, some theoretical conceptions view working memory as an aspect of attention that allows an individual to moderate the scope and focus of attention in the context of ongoing distraction. If working memory and attention are merely different names for the same thing, we need to adjust our definitions. More likely, we need to differentiate among constructs and measurement procedures related to memory and attention, and thus be able to describe and explain how these two concepts are interrelated.

ACKNOWLEDGMENTS

I thank Jerome Kagan and Barbara Goldman for their helpful comments on drafts of this manuscript.

REFERENCES

Acredolo, L. P. (1978). Development of spatial orientation in infancy. *Developmental Psychology*, *14*, 224–234.

Allen, C. N. (1931). Individual differences in the delayed reaction of infants. *Archives of Psychology*, *19* (Whole No. 127).

Alp, E. (1994). Measuring the size of working memory in very young children: The imitation sorting task. *International Journal of Behavioral Development*, *17*, 125–141.

Anderson, J. R., & Bower, G. H. (1973). *Human associative memory*. Washington, DC: Winston.

Baddeley, A. D., & Hitch, G. J. (1974). Working memory. In G. Bower (Ed.), *The psychology of learning and motivation* (Vol. 8, pp. 47–90). New York: Academic Press.

Baillargeon, R. (1987). Young infants' reasoning about the physical and spatial properties of a hidden object. *Cognitive Development, 2*, 179–200.

Baillargeon, R. (1995). A model of physical reasoning in infancy. In C. Rovee-Collier & L. Lipsitt (Eds.), *Advances in infancy research* (Vol. 9, pp. 305–371). Norwood, NJ: Ablex.

Baillargeon, R., DeVos, J., & Graber, M. (1989). Location memory in 8-month-old infants in a non-search A-not-B task: Further evidence. *Cognitive Development, 4*, 345–367.

Baillargeon, R., & Graber, M. (1988). Evidence of location memory in 8-month-old infants in a non-search A-not-B task. *Developmental Psychology, 24*, 502–511.

Baird, A. A., Kagan, J., Gaudette, T., Walz, K. A., Hershlag, N., & Boas, D. A. (2002). Frontal lobe activation during object permanence: Data from near infrared spectroscopy. *Neuroimage, 16*, 1120–1125.

Bakeman, R., & Adamson, L. (1984). Coordinating attention to people and objects in mother–infant and peer–infant interaction. *Child Development, 55*, 1278–1289.

Barth, J., & Call, J. (2006). Tracking the displacement of objects: A series of tasks with great apes (Pan troglodytes, Pan paniscus, Gorilla gorilla, and Pongo pygmaeus) and young children (Homo sapiens). *Journal of Experimental Psychology: Animal Behavior Processes, 32*, 239–252.

Bates, E. (1976). *Language and context: The acquisition of performatives*. New York: Academic Press.

Bates, E., Beninni, L., Bretherton, I., Camaioni, L., & Volterra, V. (1979). *The emergence of symbols*. New York: Academic Press.

Bauer, P. J. (2002). Long-term recall memory: Behavioral and neuro-developmental changes in the first 2 years of life. *Current Directions in Psychological Science, 11*, 137–141.

Bell, M. A. (2002). Power changes in infant EEG frequency bands during a spatial working memory task. *Psychophysiology, 39*, 450–458.

Bell, M. A., & Fox, N. A. (1992). The relations between frontal brain electrical activity and cognitive development during infancy. *Child Development, 63*, 1142–1163.

Bell, S. M. (1970). The development of the concept of the object as related to infant–mother attachment. *Child Development, 41*, 291–311.

Belleville, S., Rouleau, N., & Caza, N. (1998). Effect of normal aging on the manipulation of information in working memory. *Memory and Cognition, 26*, 572–583.

Brody, L. R. (1981). Visual short-term cued recall memory in infancy. *Child Development, 52*, 242–250.

Bruner, J. S. (1975). The ontogenesis of speech acts. *Journal of Child Language, 2*, 1–19.

Case, R., Kurland, D. M., & Goldberg, J. (1982). Operational efficiency and the growth of short-term memory span. *Journal of Experimental Child Psychology, 33*, 386–404.

Ceponiene, R., Service, E., Kurjenluoma, S., Cheour, M., & Maatanen, R. (1999). Children's performance on pseudoword repetition depends on auditory trace quality: Evidence from event-related potentials. *Developmental Psychology, 35*, 709–720.

Cheour, M., Leppanen, P. H. T., & Kraus, N. (2000). Mismatch negativity (MMN) as a tool for investigating auditory discrimination and sensory memory in infants and children. *Clinical Neurophysiology, 111*, 4–16.

Cohen, J. D., Perlstein, W. M., Braver, T. D., Nystrom, L. E., Noll, D. C., Jonides, J., et al. (1997). Temporal dynamics of brain activation during a working memory task. *Nature, 386*, 604–608.

Conway, A. R. A., Kane, M. J., Bunting, M. F., Hambrick, D. Z., Wilhelm, O., & Engle, R. W. (2005). Working memory span tasks: A methodological review and user's guide. *Psychonomic Bulletin and Review, 12*, 769–786.

Cornoldi, C., Marconi, F., & Vecchi, T. (2001). Visuospatial working memory in Turner's syndrome. *Brain and Cognition, 46*, 90–94.

Corsi, P. M. (1972). *Human memory and the medial temporal region of the brain.* Unpublished doctoral dissertation, McGill University, Montreal.

Cowan, N. (1997). The development of working memory. In N. Cowan & C. Hulme (Eds.), *The development of memory in childhood* (pp. 163–199). Hove, UK: Psychology Press.

Cowan, N., Elliott, E. M., Saults, J. S., Morey, C. C., Mattox, S., Hismjatullina, A., et al. (2005). On the capacity of attention: Its estimation and its role in working memory and cognitive aptitudes. *Cognitive Psychology, 51*, 42–100.

Cowan, N., Saults, J. S., & Elliott, E. M. (2002). The search for what is fundamental in the development of working memory. In R. Kail & H. W. Reese (Eds.), *Advances in child development and behavior* (Vol. 29, pp. 1–49). New York: Academic Press.

Cowan, N., Saults, J. S., Nugent, L. D., & Elliott, E. M. (1999). The microanalysis of memory span and its development in childhood. *International Journal of Psychology, 34*, 353–358.

Daneman, M., & Carpenter, P. A. (1980). Individual differences in working memory and reading. *Journal of Verbal Learning and Verbal Behavior, 19*, 450–466.

de Saint Victor, C., Smith, P. H., & Loboschefski, T. (1997). Ten-month-old infants' retrieval of familiar information from short-term memory. *Infant Behavior and Development, 20*, 111–122.

DeLoache, J. S., & Brown, A. L. (1979). Looking for Big Bird: Studies of memory in very young children. *Quarterly Newsletter of the Laboratory of Comparative Human Cognition, 1*, 53–57.

D'Esposito, M., Detre, J. A., Alsop, D. C., Shin, R. K., Atlas, S., & Grossman, M. (1995). The neural basis of the central executive system of working memory. *Nature, 378*, 279–281.

Diamond, A. (1985). Development of the ability to use recall to guide action, as indicated by infants' performance on A-not-B. *Child Development, 56*, 868–883.

Diamond, A., & Doar, B. (1989). The performance of human infants on a measure of frontal cortex function, the delayed-response task. *Developmental Psychobiology, 22*, 271–294.

Engle, R. W., Tuholski, S. W., Laughlin, J. E., & Conway, A. R. A. (1999). Working memory, short-term memory and general fluid intelligence: A latent variable approach. *Journal of Experimental Psychology: General, 128*, 309–331.

Ewing-Cobbs, L., Prasad, M. R., Landry, S. H., Kramer, L., & DeLeon, R. (2004). Executive functions following traumatic brain injury in young children: A preliminary analysis. *Developmental Neuropsychology, 26*, 487–512.

Fantz, R. L. (1956). A method for studying early visual development. *Perceptual and Motor Skills, 6*, 13–15.

Fox, N., Kagan, J., & Weiskopf, W. (1979). The growth of memory during infancy. *Genetic Psychology Monographs, 99*, 91–130.

Funahashi, S., Bruce, C. J., & Goldman-Rakic, P. S. (1989). Mnemonic coding of visual space in the monkey's dorsolateral prefrontal cortex. *Journal of Neuro-physiology*, *61*(2), 331–349.

Fuster, J. M., & Alexander, G. E. (1971). Neuron activity related to short-term memory. *Science*, *173*, 652–654.

Gilmore, R. O., & Johnson, M. H. (1995). Working memory in infancy: Six-month-olds' performance on two versions of the oculomotor delayed response task. *Journal of Experimental Child Psychology*, *59*, 397–418.

Goldman-Rakic, P. S. (1987). Circuitry of primate prefrontal cortex and regulation of behavior by representational memory. In F. Plum & V. Mountcastle (Eds.), *Handbook of physiology* (Vol. 5, pp. 373–417). Bethesda, MD: American Physiological Society.

Gomes, H., Sussman, E., Ritter, W., Kurtzberg, D., Cowan, N., & Vaughan, H. G., Jr. (1999). Electrophysiological evidence of developmental changes in the duration of auditory sensory memory. *Developmental Psychology*, *35*, 294–302.

Goodale, M. A., & Milner, A. D. (1992). Separate visual pathways for perception and actions. *Trends in Neuroscience*, *15*, 20–25.

Graf, P., & Masson, M. E. J. (1993). *Implicit memory: New directions in cognition, development, and neuropsychology*. Hillsdale, NJ: Lawarence Erlbaum Associates, Inc.

Harding, C. G., & Golinkoff, R. M. (1979). The origins of intentional vocalization in prelinguistic infants. *Child Development*, *50*, 33–40.

Harlow, H. F. (1932). Comparative behavior of primates: III. Complicated delayed reaction tests on primates. *Journal of Comparative Psychology*, *14*, 241–252.

Harris, P. L. (1973). Perseverative errors in search by young infants. *Child Development*, *44*, 29–33.

Hartman, M., Bolton, E., & Fehnel, S. E. (2001). Accounting for age differences on the Wisconsin Card Sorting Test: Decreased working memory, not inflexibility. *Psychology and Aging*, *16*, 385–399.

Hockey, R. (1973). Rate of presentation in running memory and direct manipulation of input-processing strategies. *Quarterly Journal of Experimental Psychology (A)*, *25*, 104–111.

Hofstadter, M., & Reznick, J. S. (1996). Response modality affects human infant delayed-response performance. *Child Development*, *67*, 646–658.

Hunter, W. S. (1913). The delayed reaction in animals and children. *Behavior Monographs*, *2*, 1–86.

Hunter, W. S. (1917). The delayed reaction in a child. *Psychological Review*, *24*, 74–87.

Huttenlocher, J., Newcombe, N., & Sandberg, E. (1994). The coding of spatial location in young children. *Cognitive Psychology*, *27*, 115–147.

Jacobsen, C. F. (1936). Studies of cerebral function in primates. *Comparative Psychology Monographs*, *13*, 1–68.

James, W. J. (1981). *The principles of psychology, Volume 1*. Cambridge, MA: Harvard University Press. (Original work published 1890)

Jonides, J., Schumacher, E. H., Smith, E. E., Lauber, E. J., Awh, E., Minoshima, S., et al. (1997). Verbal working memory load affects regional brain activation as measured by PET. *Journal of Cognitive Neuroscience*, *9*, 462–475.

Kagan, J. (1981). *The second year*. Cambridge, MA: Harvard University Press.

Kaldy, Z., & Leslie, A. M. (2005). A memory span of one? Object identification in 6.5-month-old infants. *Cognition*, *97*, 153–177.

Kaldy, Z., & Sigala, N. (2004). The neural mechanisms of object working memory:

What is where in the infant brain? *Neuroscience and Biobehavioral Reviews, 28,* 1113–1121.

Kane, M. J., & Engle, R. W. (2002). The role of prefrontal cortex in working memory capacity, executive attention, and general fluid intelligence: An individual-differences perspective. *Psychonomic Bulletin and Review, 9,* 637–671.

Kubota, K., & Niki, H. (1971). Prefrontal cortical unit activity and delayed alternation performance in monkeys. *Journal of Neurophysiology, 34,* 337–347.

Lanfranchi, S., Cornoldi, C., & Vianello, R. (2004). Verbal and visuospatial working memory deficits in children with Down syndrome. *American Journal on Mental Retardation, 109,* 456–466.

Luciana, M., Depue, R. A., Arbisi, P., & Leon, A. (1992). Facilitation of working memory in humans by a D_2 dopamine receptor agonist. *Journal of Cognitive Neuroscience, 4,* 58–68.

Luck, S. J., & Vogel, E. K. (1997). The capacity of visual working memory for features and conjunctions. *Nature, 390,* 279–281.

Luo, Y., Baillargeon, R., Brueckner, L., & Munakata, Y. (2003). Reasoning about a hidden object after a delay: Evidence for robust representations in 5-month-old infants. *Cognition, 88,* B23–B32.

Lustig, C., May, C. P., & Hasher, L. (2001). Working memory span and the role of proactive interference. *Journal of Experimental Psychology: General, 130,* 199–207.

Marcus, G. F., Vijayan, S., Rao, S. B., & Vishton, P. M. (1999). Rule learning by seven-month-old infants. *Science, 283,* 77–80.

McCarthy, G., Blamire, A. M., Puce, A., Nobre, A. C., Bloch, G., Hyder, F., et al. (1994). Functional magnetic resonance imaging of human prefrontal cortex activation during a spatial working memory task. *Proceedings of the National Academy of Science, USA, 91,* 8690–8694.

McDonough, L. (1999). Early declarative memory for location. *British Journal of Developmental Psychology, 17,* 381–402.

Mecklenbrauker, S., Hupbach, A., & Wippich, W. (2003). Age-related improvements in a conceptual implicit memory test. *Memory and Cognition, 31,* 1208–1217.

Miller, G. A., Galanter, E., & Pribram, K. H. (1960). *Plans and the structure of behavior.* New York: Holt, Reinhart & Winston.

Milner, A. D., & Goodale, M. A. (1995). *The visual brain in actions.* Oxford: Oxford University Press.

Moore, M. K., & Meltzoff, A. N. (2004). Object permanence after a 24-hr delay and leaving the locale of disappearance: The role of memory, space, and identity. *Developmental Psychology, 40,* 606–620.

Mosier, C. E., & Rogoff, B. (1994). Infants' instrumental use of their mothers to achieve their goals. *Child Development, 65,* 70–79.

Mottron, L., Belleville, S., & Menard, E. (1999). Local bias in autistic subjects as evidenced by graphic tasks: Perceptual hierarchization or working memory deficit? *Journal of Child Psychology and Psychiatry and Allied Disciplines, 40,* 743–755.

Munir, F., Cornish, K. M., & Wilding, J. (2000). Nature of the working memory deficit in Fragile-X syndrome. *Brain and Cognition, 44,* 387–401.

Murphy, K., McKone, E., & Slee, J. (2003). Dissociation between implicit and explicit memory in children: The role of strategic processing and the knowledge base. *Journal of Experimental Child Psychology, 84,* 124–165.

Pelphrey, K. A., & Reznick, J. S. (2003). Working memory in infancy. In R. Kail (Ed.),

Advances in child development and behavior (Vol. 31, pp. 173–227). New York: Academic Press.

Pelphrey, K. A., Reznick, J. S., Goldman, B. D., Sasson, N., Morrow, J., Donahoe, A., et al. (2004). Development of visuospatial short-term memory in the second half of the first year. *Developmental Psychology*, *40*, 836–851.

Petrides, M., Alivisatos, B., Evans, A. C., & Meyer, E. (1993). Dissociation of human mid-dorsolateral from posterior dorsolateral frontal cortex in memory processing. *Proceedings of the National Academy of Science, USA*, *90*, 873–877.

Phillips, L. H., & Forshaw, M. J. (1998). The role of working memory in age differences in reasoning. In R. H. Logie & K. J. Gilhooly (Eds.), *Working memory and thinking* (pp. 23–43). Hove, UK: Psychology Press.

Piaget, J. (1954). *The construction of reality in the child*. New York: Basic. (Original French edition, 1937)

Reznick, J. S., Corley, R., & Robinson, J. (1997). A longitudinal twin study of intelligence in the second year. *Monographs of the Society for Research in Child Development*, *62*(1, Serial No. 249).

Reznick, J. S., Fueser, J. J., & Bosquet, M. (1998). Self-corrected reaching in a three-location delayed-response search task. *Psychological Science*, *9*, 66–70.

Reznick, J. S., Morrow, J. D., Goldman, B. D., & Snyder, J. (2004) The onset of working memory in infants. *Infancy*, *6*, 145–154.

Rose, S. A., Feldman, J. F., & Jankowski, J. J. (2001). Visual short-term memory in the first year of life: Capacity and recency effects. *Developmental Psychology*, *37*, 539–549.

Ross-Sheehy, S., Oakes, L. M., & Luck, S. J. (2003). The development of visual short-term memory capacity in infants. *Child Development*, *74*, 1807–1822.

Saffran, J. R., Aslin, R. N., & Newport, E. L. (1996). Statistical learning by 8-month-old infants. *Science*, *274*, 1926–1928.

Salthouse, T. A. (1996). The processing-speed theory of adult age differences in cognition. *Psychological Review*, *103*, 403–428.

Sawaguchi, T., & Goldman-Rakic, P. S. (1991). D1 dopamine receptors in prefrontal cortex: Involvement in working memory. *Science*, *251*, 947–950.

Sawaguchi, T., Matsumura, M., & Kubota, K. (1988). Dopamine enhances the neuronal activity of a spatial short-term memory task in the primate prefrontal cortex. *Neuroscience Research*, *5*, 465–473.

Schwartz, B. B., & Reznick, J. S. (1999). Measuring infant spatial working memory with a windows and curtains delayed-response procedure. *Memory*, *7*, 1–17.

Seibert, J. M., Hogan, A. E., & Mundy, P. C. (1982). Assessing interactional competencies: The Early Social Communication Scales. *Infant Mental Health Journal*, *3*, 244–245.

Spelke, E. S. (1988). The origins of physical knowledge. In L. Weiskrantz (Ed.), *Thought without language* (pp. 168–184). Oxford: Oxford University Press.

Spelke, E. S. (1994). Initial knowledge: Six suggestions. *Cognition*, *50*, 431–445.

Sperling, G. (1960). The information available in brief visual presentations. *Psychological Monographs: General and Applied*, *74*, 1–30.

Sternberg, S. (1966). High speed scanning in human memory. *Science*, *153*, 652–654.

Thierry, G. (2005). The use of event-related potentials in the study of early cognitive development. *Infant and Child Development*, *14*, 85–94.

Turner, M. L., & Engle, R. W. (1989). Is working memory capacity task dependent? *Journal of Memory and Language*, *28*, 127–154.

Wilcox, T., Nadel, L., & Rosser, R. (1996). Location memory in healthy preterm and full-term infants. *Infant Behavior and Development, 19,* 309–323.

Willatts, P. (1984). Stages in the development of intentional search by young infants. *Developmental Psychology, 20,* 389–396.

Willatts, P. (1999). Development of means–end behavior in young infants: Pulling a support to retrieve a distant object. *Developmental Psychology, 35,* 651–667.

Wynn, K. (1992). Addition and subtraction by human infants. *Nature, 358,* 749–750.

14 Developments in the study of the development of memory

Peter A. Ornstein
University of North Carolina at Chapel Hill, USA

Catherine A. Haden
Loyola University of Chicago, USA

At the 1971 meetings of the Society for Research in Child Development, John Flavell organized a now-celebrated symposium on children's memory. The title of that symposium—"*What is memory development the development of?*"—posed a question that has to a considerable extent defined the nature of research on children's memory for more than three decades. Certainly, the answers to this question have changed dramatically over the years, as a function of changes in research paradigms, theoretical frameworks, and even the ages of the children being studied. Indeed, as theories and research paradigms have evolved, so too has knowledge of the surprising mnemonic competence of young children and of age-related differences in memory performance. Nonetheless, as we look at the field in historical perspective, we see a remarkable consistency in its focus on the characterization of *something* (e.g., strategies, underlying knowledge, basic capacity) that is thought to be changing with age. In contrast, there have been only a few investigations of changes over time in the memory skills of individual children, and thus, as a consequence, little attention has been paid to describing the ways in which early examples of that *something* (e.g., a naming strategy) give way to later and more sophisticated variations (e.g., a more complex rehearsal strategy). Moreover, still less attention has been devoted to the more difficult question of "What are the factors that operate to bring about developmental change?" As is apparent in the chapters of this excellent volume, the net result is that a great deal is now known about the contrasting memory skills of children of different ages. These advances notwithstanding, we suggest that what has not been explored very systematically is the process of development, and in this chapter we outline our vision for the type of research that is still needed.

Our position, essentially, is that cognitive developmentalists interested in memory have focused remarkably well on issues of *memory* development, but not very much on the *development* of memory (Ornstein & Haden, 2001; Ornstein, Haden, & Hedrick, 2004). We discuss this important distinction in the context of what we take to be three critical "tasks of the developmentalist." From our perspective, a developmental analysis of memory (or of any other set of skills, for that matter) requires that we: (1) characterize the skills of children of different ages, or in other words, make cognitive "diagnoses"; (2) map age-related changes (and constancies) by tracing the development of individual children longitudinally; and (3) search for mediators of developmental change. The aim of this chapter is to offer a "score card" on how well memory researchers have done in terms of these tasks in the 10 years since the original edition of this significant volume.

As we make this accounting, it is important to acknowledge the salient place that the study of memory has come to occupy in the many areas of contemporary psychology. Within developmental psychology, for example, an understanding of the developing memory system is of obvious importance for thinking about children's changing abilities to remember, but it is also at the core of analyses of age-related progressions in other cognitive skills. In addition, the development of memory figures prominently in discussions of topics not typically viewed as "cognitive," such as the emergence and refinement of a sense of self and personal identity (see Chapter 8 by Howe, Courage, & Rooksby, and Chapter 11 by Fivush, this volume). Moreover, increasingly in recent years, basic research on children's memory has proved to be highly relevant to some difficult applied issues, as, for example, in the debates concerning the reliability of children's testimony and the accuracy of adult claims of recovered memories (see Chapter 9 by Paz-Alonso et al., and Chapter 10 by Pipe & Salmon, this volume). Indeed, the research on children's memory that has been amassed in the years since Flavell's seminal symposium has had considerable reach, strongly influencing current work in developmental psychology, and making a difference in the real world in the lives of children and families. Given then the centrality of investigations of children's skills for remembering, how well have we done in meeting the tasks of the developmentalist? We begin this assessment with the task of cognitive diagnosis.

CHARACTERIZING CHILDREN'S MEMORY

The corpus of research on age-related changes in children's mnemonic skills has expanded in an impressive fashion. Indeed, researchers have done rather well in terms of providing precise "diagnostic" information about the skills of children at different ages. Two themes describe the voluminous literature. First, under supportive conditions of assessment, infants and young children demonstrate surprising mnemonic competence, as is amply documented in this volume (see, e.g., Chapters 2, 3, 6, and 13 by Rovee-Collier & Cuevas; Hayne & Simcock; Bauer; Reznick, this volume). Second, with the exception of some aspects of implicit (as opposed to explicit) memory (see Chapter 5 by Lloyd & Newcombe, this volume), the literature documents the presence of substantial age differences in most aspects of memory performance (e.g., see Chapters 4, 7, 8, 9, 10, 11, and 12 by Hudson & Mayhew; Bjorklund, Dukes,

& Brown; Howe et al.; Paz-Alonso et al.; Pipe & Salmon; Fivush; Cowan & Alloway). These themes represent a distillation of evidence that is drawn from research paradigms ranging from conditioning and elicited and deferred imitation to those involving the production of narrative accounts of previous experiences and verbal measures of both strategy use and remembering. To illustrate how far the field has come in characterizing children's memory, we offer an overview of our current understanding of young children's skills based on work that is discussed in greater depth in this volume.

Mnemonic competence in infancy and toddlerhood

Innovative research programs that make use of nonverbal measures of memory provide us with examples of the remarkable mnemonic skills of infants and toddlers. For example, Rovee-Collier and Cuevas (Chapter 2, this volume) describe a very creative line of inquiry in which conjugate reinforcement procedures are utilized to provide information on infants' learning and memory. With this technique, a ribbon is tied to an infant's foot and connected to a mobile suspended over a crib, and the baby learns that kicking makes the mobile move. Once the operant response has been acquired, remembering after varying intervals can readily be assessed under conditions of extinction in which the ribbon is disconnected from the mobile. Memory is then inferred if the rate of kicking observed in these test periods is greater than that seen in the baseline period, and under these conditions, two fundamental patterns of age differences in performance in the first 6 months of life have been reported: both speed of learning and length of retention increase with age. Thus, older infants acquire the kicking response more rapidly than younger children, and when trained to the same criterion of performance, retain it longer than their younger peers (e.g., Hill, Borovsky, & Rovee-Collier, 1988).

Programmatic research with this mobile conjugate reinforcement task has also revealed two other important features of early memory. First, under some conditions, memories that would seem to be forgotten can be cued and recovered. Partial reminders of a previous experience (i.e., reinstatement; Campbell & Jaynes, 1966) and procedures in which a component of the original event is presented toward the end of the delay interval (i.e., reactivation; Spear & Parsons, 1976), can extend considerably the retention of the kicking response over days and even weeks (e.g., Sweeney & Rovee-Collier, 2001). Second, the kicking response can be remarkably sensitive to changes in aspects of the mobile and/or the context in which the response was acquired. Even a change in a single element of the mobile or the decoration on the crib liner can lead to substantial disruptions in performance (Hartshorn et al., 1998; Hayne, Greco, Earley, Griesler, & Rovee-Collier, 1986; Rovee-Collier, Schechter, Shyi, & Shields, 1992; see also Rovee-Collier & Cuevas, Chapter 2, this volume, for further discussion).

As described in Chapters 3 and 6 by Hayne and Simcock and Bauer, other researchers (e.g., Barr & Hayne, 2000; Bauer, 2007a; Hayne, Barr, & Herbert,

2003; Meltzoff, 1985, 1995) have been equally creative in utilizing nonverbal indices of remembering that are derived from elicited and deferred imitation paradigms. With these techniques, memory is demonstrated when a young child is able to use props to reproduce an action sequence that had been previously modeled by an examiner. Consider, for example, the acts involved in constructing a gong: putting a crossbar atop two posts, hanging a metal plate on the crossbar, and then hitting the plate with a plastic mallet. After a baseline period in which a young child interacts freely with these materials, an experimenter demonstrates the sequence that will lead to the construction of the gong, while under some conditions providing simple labels for each of the actions. Typically in the elicited but not the deferred imitation procedure, the modeling of these actions is accompanied by a verbal description of the target actions and the goal of the event sequence. Moreover, in the elicited imitation paradigm, an immediate assessment of memory is usually obtained, with the child being invited to imitate the modeled sequence of actions (e.g., "Now you show me how to make a gong"). Memory is often also assessed after a delay, with and without the verbal cue. In contrast, in the deferred paradigm, imitation is assessed but without much verbal prompting, and only following a delay.

   Despite the procedural differences that can lead to differences in memory performance (see Hayne & Simcock, Chapter 3, this volume, for discussion), converging evidence from the elicited and deferred imitation paradigms shows that the age-related changes in performance that begin in infancy—in the extent to which information can be held in memory—continue to be observed during toddlerhood. For example, 6-month-olds are able to produce parts of a three-step action sequence 1 but not 2 days after it is modeled (Barr, Dowden, & Hayne, 1996), although there is no evidence that the children can produce the components of the sequence in order, either immediately or after a 24-hour delay. In contrast, by 9 months of age, infants are able to recall individual components of novel two-step sequence after 5 weeks, and approximately half of the infants studied were able to produce the sequences in the correct temporal order following this delay interval (Carver & Bauer, 2001). The latter part of the first year of life is a period in which skills for remembering change in a dramatic fashion, as illustrated by the fact that by 10 months, children evidence ordered recall of two-step events at delays of both 1 and 3 months (Carver & Bauer, 2001).

   Although this improvement in performance is certainly impressive, it should nonetheless be emphasized that the temporally ordered recall of 9- and 10-month-olds is still rather limited. First, the length of time over which information can be remembered is quiet short, and second, recall at this age is dependent on multiple exposures to each modeled events sequence. Third, the length of the event sequences that are to be remembered is rather small (Bauer, 2006). Each of these limitations is overcome to a considerable extent over the course of the second year of life. Not only do older toddlers remember longer (e.g., Barr & Hayne, 2000), they do not require multiple exposures to an event in order to remember it over a delay of several months (Bauer, Hertsgaard, & Wewerka, 1995). Moreover, in contrast to the two-step events that are remembered by 9- and 10-month-olds, children at 24 months of age can produce sequences of five steps in length (Bauer & Travis, 1993). Finally, the length of time across which ordered recall can be observed increases dramatically during this time period; indeed 100% of children at 20 months of age are able to recall in an ordered fashion after a month, with more than half evidencing memory for portions of the to-be-remembered sequences after delays as long as a year (Bauer, Wenner, Dropik, & Wewerka, 2000).

Verbal recall of personally experienced events

Building on their remarkable nonverbal memory skills, young children produce well-organized accounts of recurring day-to-day events—such as going to a grocery store or to a fast food restaurant—soon after they begin to speak, although descriptions of these types of events become more "script"-like with increases in age and experience. As is outlined in Chapter 4, by Hudson and Mayhew (this volume), research on memory for recurring events has moved well beyond the pioneering demonstrations of change over time in preschoolers' verbal scripts (e.g., Nelson, 1986; Nelson & Gruendel, 1979). In this regard, recent research has generated important questions about the ways in which general event knowledge that is formed over repeated experiences of the same event can facilitate children's memory for a single episode. The evidence suggests that scripts can enhance remembering of the objects and actions that are typically or always a part of the event (i.e., "fixed items," such as the presence of a cake at a birthday party). However, experiencing an event multiple times can also lead to distortions in memory, particularly for so-called "variable features" that occur only sometimes during an event (such as a treasure hunt at a birthday party). Moreover, other research on memory for recurring events has focused on linkages between knowledge for familiar event routines and (1) advances in children's skills for planning for future experiences, and (2) the development of an understanding of future time. For example, despite demonstrations of poor planning for novel activities, 5-year-olds appear to be quite able to form and execute plans for familiar, recurring events, suggesting that they are putting their general event knowledge to use to anticipate what might occur in the future (see Hudson & Mayhew, Chapter 4, this volume, for further discussion).

Over the preschool years, children also make dramatic gains in their abilities to talk about "one-time" experiences. As indicated in Chapters 8 and 11 in this volume by Howe, Courage, and Rooksby and by Fivush, with increases in age and experience, children's reporting of novel events becomes more richly detailed and complex, and less dependent on the scaffolding provided by adult conversational partners (e.g., Fivush, Haden, & Adam, 1995; Haden, Haine, & Fivush, 1997). Moreover, as is documented in Chapters

9 and 10, by Paz-Alonso et al. and by Pipe and Salmon (this volume), in comparison with younger children, older children respond to questions about salient personal experiences with higher levels of overall recall, providing greater amounts of information in response to open-ended questions. As such, as children get older there is less need for interviewers to make extensive use of yes/no probes (e.g., Baker-Ward, Gordon, Ornstein, Larus, & Clubb, 1993; Fivush & Hamond, 1990). Further, older children evidence less forgetting over time (Brainerd, Kingma, & Howe, 1985; Brainerd, Reyna, Howe, & Kingma, 1990), and are less susceptible to suggestive questions (Ceci & Bruck, 1993).

New research on children's memory for salient events has yielded important information about linkages between emotion and memory, especially about the ways in which stress impacts children's memory for painful medical procedures such as a voiding cystourethrogram or VCUG (e.g., Brown, Salmon, Pipe, Rutter, Craw, & Taylor, 1999; Goodman, Quas, Batterman-Faunce, Riddlesberger, & Kuhn, 1994; Merritt, Ornstein, & Spicker, 1994), injuries and resulting emergency room procedures (e.g., Burgwyn-Bailes, Baker-Ward, Gordon, & Ornstein, 2001; Howe, Courage, & Peterson, 1994; Peterson & Whalen, 2001), and natural disasters (e.g., Ackil, Van Abbema, & Bauer, 2003; Bahrick, Parker, Fivush, & Levitt, 1998; Sales, Fivush, Parker, & Bahrick, 2005). These investigations indicate age-related improvements in remembering, just as with memory for more mundane experiences. For example, within a few weeks of experiencing a VCUG, children generally remembered the procedure quite well (Goodman et al., 1994; Merritt et al., 1994), indeed, better than more routine medical events (e.g., Merritt et al., 1994), but older children recalled more than their younger peers, and in some cases provided more accurate information (e.g., Goodman et al., 1994; Salmon, Price, & Pereira, 2002). Further, children who are older than 2 or 3 at the time of a stressful or traumatic experience are significantly more likely than younger children to remember it in the long term. To illustrate, children who experienced an injury and emergency room treatment prior to 18 months of age (Peterson & Rideout, 1998), or a VCUG test prior to the age of 3 (Quas, Goodman, Bidrose, Pipe, Craw, & Ablin, 1999), were unlikely to demonstrate clear memory for the experience, whereas those who were older at the time of these events evidenced at least some memory for them.

Learning to be strategic

As young children develop expertise in talking about their past experiences, they also evidence increasing skill in the deployment of deliberate strategies for remembering information. To a considerable extent, their growing competency in talking about the past reflects age-related improvements in the incidental encoding of information—which in turn stems from children's greater understanding of the situations that they encounter—as well as improvements in retrieving and reporting information from memory. In contrast to the more or less incidental nature of event memory, the use of specific mnemonic techniques for remembering requires that a child behave intentionally in order to prepare for a future assessment of memory (Folds, Footo, Guttentag, & Ornstein, 1990; Wellman, 1988). A consensus view two decades ago was that children were rather "astrategic" before the elementary school years. However, as described by Bjorklund et al. (Chapter 7, this volume) it turns out that preschoolers just do not make use of the rehearsal and organizational types of strategies that are evident after the age of 8, but rather use simpler techniques. For example, 18-month-olds begin to evidence rudimentary strategies such as verbalizing, looking, and pointing when they are faced with the task of remembering the location of attractive objects they had watched a researcher hide (e.g., DeLoache, Cassidy, & Brown, 1985). Similarly, preschoolers' memory goals can be seen in their spontaneous use of study-like behaviors such as naming and visual examination to remember an arbitrary set of materials in an object memory task (Baker-Ward, Ornstein, & Holden, 1984).

With increases in age, not only are children more likely to engage in some form of strategy in response to the challenges of a memory goal, but what they do to meet this goal changes dramatically. When asked to remember verbal materials, children in the early years of elementary school engage in seemingly passive, rote-type memorization procedures, but older children's strategies are more active and involve a deliberate integration of the to-be-remembered information with existing knowledge. Nevertheless, even when the same strategy appears to be used by children of different ages, the procedure routinely has a more facilitative effect on the recall of older, as opposed to younger, children. For example, although Baker-Ward et al. (1984) showed that 4-, 5-, and 6-year-olds prepared for a memory goal in the context of an object-memory task by using quite comparable strategies of naming and visual examination, they also found that these strategies only facilitated the memory performance of the 6-year-olds. These data—and other demonstrations of *utilization deficiencies* (Bjorklund & Coyle, 1995; Miller, 1990)—illustrate that young children may understand the importance of doing "something" in order to respond to a memory demand, but what they chose to do may be quite ineffective.

This brief treatment of early strategies that do not "work" should underscore the fact that *intentionality* represents only one facet of strategic behavior. Two other features of strategy application—*effectiveness* and *consistency*—are central to any account of children's increasing mastery over the elementary school years of a set of strategies for remembering. Concerning effectiveness, research on utilization deficiencies suggests that young children's initial strategic efforts often do not facilitate remembering, and even when their strategies do affect performance, young children routinely benefit less than do older children (Folds et al., 1990; Ornstein, Baker-Ward, & Naus, 1988). Further, novice strategy users are not consistent in their use of mnemonic techniques, and the application of any given procedure is initially restricted to supportive contexts. In contrast, when children become skilled strategy users, they have a command over a broad set of strategies (e.g., rehearsal, organization, elaboration, and later, study skills) and are able to use them skillfully in many settings that call for remembering (see Bjorklund et al., Chapter 7, this volume; Ornstein et al., 1988).

Diagnosing skill

The research briefly reviewed here provides a picture of the quite remarkable mnemonic competencies of young children, as well as clear age-related differences in many aspects of memory performance. Much is thus known about *memory* development, that is, the memory skills of children of different ages. However, we are very conscious of the fact that our conclusions as to the competency of the child are driven by the settings in which we make our observations, and that minor contextual changes may result in quite different impressions of skill (Ornstein et al., 1988; Ornstein & Myers, 1996). In addition, because most investigations focus on remembering in the context of one or another task, relatively little is known about linkages across tasks that vary in their information processing requirements. Yet this is exactly the type of information that is necessary to characterize adequately mnemonic skills at any age level and to determine just what is changing with age and experience. In short, any description of competence is incomplete until we can incorporate these measures.

To illustrate our vision of the type of research that is needed, consider Bauer's (2006) comparison of infants' abilities to imitate enabling versus arbitrary action sequences in the elicited imitation task. With enabling sequences, each action must be performed in a temporally invariant pattern in order to reach the end state (e.g., making a gong), whereas with arbitrarily ordered sequences (e.g., making a party hat), there are no inherent constraints on the placements of any of the actions. For example, in making a hat that is decorated with a pompom and a sticker, it does not matter whether the pompom is put on top before or after the sticker is placed on the front. As we see it, the contrasts within individual children in nonverbal memory performance under these differing conditions of support provide important information about the level of competency of the child. Similarly, the diagnostic usefulness of a multitask assessment strategy is illustrated in Guttentag, Ornstein, and Siemens' (1987) within-participant exploration of children's rehearsal under contrasting levels of support. Consistent with the bulk of the literature, Guttentag et al. observed that third graders rehearsed passively when the list of to-be-remembered items was presented in the typical item-by-item fashion. Although most of these children continued to rehearse passively when given an opportunity to continue to view each item after it had been presented, some of them changed spontaneously to an active multi-item rehearsal strategy. The contrast in the children's performance under these two presentation conditions provided useful diagnostic information about the level of children's skills and in the Guttentag et al. study was related to their performance as fourth graders a year later. Indeed, the use of a multi-item strategy was better predicted by the children's performance as third graders in the supportive (items visible) presentation condition than by what they did in the standard version of the task.

These contextual variations imply that adequate assessment of children's skills requires measurements in contrasting settings and summarization in the form of profiles of performance (Folds et al., 1990). Although this view of cognitive diagnosis jibes nicely with efforts to explore the *zone of proximal development* (e.g., Cox, Ornstein, & Valsiner, 1990) by measuring children's performance under conditions of varying task support, it is not congruent with the bulk of the literature in which between-subjects comparisons are most common. Nonetheless, we suggest that the incorporation of within-subjects assessments involving contrasts in children's performance across conditions that vary in their information processing requirements may pay substantial dividends. However, we also argue that such a step is not enough! Rather, as we see it, this assessment strategy must be coupled with longi-tudinal analysis to meet the second task of a developmentalist—that of describing developmental change—to which we now turn.

LONGITUDINAL ASSESSMENT

As our brief summary indicates, the last 35 years have witnessed a patent increase in our knowledge of both the early mnemonic competencies of young children and age-related differences in memory performance. Moreover, the impressive chapters of this volume catalog the most significant contributions to the field in the years since the publication of the first edition.

These advances in our understanding of *memory* development notwith-standing, we suggest that we still know relatively little about the *development* of memory. To understand the development of skills for remembering it is necessary to establish longitudinal samples and trace linkages between early skill as reflected, say, in elicited or deferred imitation, later ability to talk about the past, and still later competence in situations that call for deliberate memorization.

As is evident in this volume, researchers in the field have favored cross-sectional designs in which the performance of children of different ages is contrasted, and longitudinal designs in which the same children are tracked over time have been used infrequently. Involving as they do parallel samples of children, cross-sectional methods are ideal for characterizing the cognitive skills of children of different ages, but they cannot provide information about the developmental course of remembering within individual children. Indeed, cross-sectional studies do not permit serious statements to be made about the emergence and refinement of skills for remembering as a function of age and experience. In contrast, longitudinal designs in which children are traced over time are essential for describing the ways in which early demonstrations of skill are related to later articulations of cognitive competency.

To illustrate the important insights into development that are derived from longitudinal work, consider two separate longitudinal studies of children's developing memory strategies that have been carried out by Schneider and his colleagues (see Bjorklund et al., Chapter 7, this volume, for more information). In the Munich Longitudinal Study on the Genesis of Individual Competencies (Sodian & Schneider, 1999), children were tracked between 4 and 18 years of age, whereas in the Würzburg Longitudinal Memory Study (Schneider, Kron, Hünnerkopf, & Krajewski, 2004), children were observed multiple times between 6 and 9 years of age. These studies make two important contributions to our understanding of children's memory skills and their development. First, the characterization of the average level of children's performance at various age points maps on well to the findings reported in the cross-sectional literature. However, second, the picture that emerged at the level of the individual child was quite different than the impression of a smooth, gradual developmental function that is implied by the cross-sectional data. Rather, in both investigations improvements in the use of strategies seemed to be rather dramatic "leaps," as opposed to gradual increments in sophistication over time.

Related to longitudinal investigations are microgenetic studies in which frequent and intense observations of children are made over relatively short intervals (see Bjorklund et al., Chapter 7, this volume, for further discussion). The repeated assessment of children—at times during which they are thought to undergo rapid developmental change—has resulted in several important contributions to our understanding of the emergence and consolidation of mnemonic skill. To illustrate, Siegler's (2006) examination of a range of cognitive strategies suggests that age-related changes from passive to active strategies may not reflect adequately the complexities of children's growing strategic competence. Indeed, he reports that children frequently make use of less effective techniques in tandem with more complex and effective strategies that have been recently acquired.

In an insightful discussion of these patterns, Siegler (1996) articulates an "overlapping waves" theory for characterizing elementary school children's mastery of a mix of strategies at any point in time. From this perspective, development is seen as change as a function of age and experience in the composition of this strategy mix. Moreover, consistent with the Munich and Würzburg longitudinal studies, microgenetic work carried out by Schneider and his colleagues confirms the finding that children do not routinely transition from simple to more advanced strategies in a gradual fashion. For example, Schlagmüller and Schneider (2002) studied fourth and fifth graders who had been identified in the Würzburg study as non-users of a categorization strategy and gave these children nine sort-recall tasks over the course of an 11-week period. Importantly, the children who acquired the organizational strategy did so at different times in an all-or-none fashion, with strategy use being preceded by metamnemonic insights and followed by recall improvements.

As these studies illustrate, longitudinal and microgenetic analyses of children's memory can clearly extend the cross-sectional data base in critical ways by providing a truly developmental account of the acquisition of skill. To be sure, cross-sectional studies can generate valuable information about the abilities of children of different ages, thus suggesting age-related trends, but statements about development within individual children can only be made when researchers employ designs in which the changing abilities of the same children are tracked over time. Yet, as difficult as these descriptions of change may be to obtain, we hasten to point out that they too are not enough. Paradoxically, not all longitudinal studies are really developmental in character. To meet the third task of the developmentalist, therefore, we must build into these studies explorations of factors that may account for age-related progressions in skill. As we discuss in the next section, it is of critical importance to speak meaningfully about these potential mediators of developmental change.

MEDIATORS OF CHANGE

When it comes to the exploration of factors that affect developmental change, inspection of this volume reveals that we have a number of candidates, ranging from the biological (see Bauer, Chapter 6, this volume), to the cognitive (see Bjorklund et al., Chapter 7, this volume) to the social (see Chapters 7 and 11, by Bjorklund et al., and by Fivush, this volume). We turn now to a brief treatment of several of these factors that may impact children's abilities to remember the past and prepare for future assessments of memory and serve to mediate observed age-related progressions in these skills (see also Ornstein, Haden, & San Souci, 2008).

Biological factors

A complete account of memory and its development requires an understanding of the neural substrate that supports the core processes involved in remembering: encoding, consolidation and storage, and retrieval. Neuroscientists (see, e.g., Eichenbaum & Cohen, 2001) have made considerable progress in identifying associations between a complex neural network that includes both medial-temporal and cortical structures and these fundamental memory processes. In contrast, as discussed by Bauer (Chapter 6, this volume), research identifying linkages between developmental changes in underlying brain systems and corresponding changes in mnemonic skill has essentially just begun (e.g., Bauer, 2004; Nelson & Webb, 2002). This new line of work (see Bauer, 2007b, and Chapter 6, this volume), however, is very promising, as timing differences in the maturation of various neural systems—contrast the relatively early-maturing medial temporal structures with the later-developing prefrontal cortex and dentate gyrus—may be seen as "rate-limiting" variables that impact the development of memory. Using this perspective as a guide to research with a combination of electrophysiological (e.g., ERP) and behavioral (e.g., elicited imitation) measures, Bauer has argued convincingly that age-related differences in encoding and consolidation contribute to variability in recall in the first 2 years of life. Extending this exciting line of research linking maturational changes in neural structures to (potentially) corresponding changes in children's remembering can certainly advance our understanding of the ways in which biological factors affect development.

Cognitive factors

Developmental changes in a range of cognitive skills certainly underlie corresponding changes in children's ability to remember. In addition to children's developing facility with language and ability to use narrative conventions to report on their experiences, at least three interrelated factors should be mentioned. First, changes in the underlying knowledge base in permanent memory are known to influence dramatically the flow of information within the memory system (Bjorklund, 1985; Ornstein & Naus, 1985). Indeed, the current state of a child's knowledge system can impact autobiographical memory, as well as strategy selection and execution. Moreover, as suggested above, children's strategic efforts may first be evident in supportive settings that involve salient and meaningful materials, with gradual generalization being observed to less supportive settings. Second, age-related reductions in the attentional resources needed to carry out mnemonic strategies may contribute to the observed developmental progression in strategy effectiveness, as was demonstrated in Guttentag's (1984) work on the changing effort requirements of a cumulative rehearsal strategy. In the early stages of strategy acquisition, young children may need to devote more cognitive resources to processing than to storage operations (Case, 1985), with little or no capacity being available for encoding and storing information. However, processing efficiency may increase with age, as a function of corresponding increases in the speed of information processing (Kail, 1991) and the *functional* capacity of the cognitive system that stems from the automatization of skill associated with experience and practice (Case, 1985; Ornstein et al., 1988; Siegler, 1996). Third, changes with age in the capacity of working memory (Cowan, & Alloway, Chapter 7, and Reznick, Chapter 13, this volume) contribute to children's increasing abilities to manipulate information that is held in memory. These changes, reflecting in part increases in processing efficiency, may account for children's increasing abilities to handle complex strategies and to take advantage of social input (e.g., elaborative mother–child conversation), a topic to which we now turn.

Social factors

Children's abilities to remember develop in the context of social interactions with adults, primarily their parents and teachers. When children first begin to report past experiences in conversations with their parents, there are substantial individual differences in the "reminiscing styles" that mothers use to structure these discussions (see Fivush, Haden, & Reese, 2006; Fivush, Chapter 11, this volume, for reviews). In contrast to parents who use a *low elaborative* style, those with a *high elaborative* style pose many questions, follow-in on their children's efforts to contribute to the conversation, and continue to add new information, even when their children are contributing little to the discussion. Importantly, Reese, Haden, and Fivush (1993) have shown that these differences in reminiscing styles in the early years are associated with later differences in children's independent abilities to recall personally experienced events (see Fivush, Chapter 11, this volume; Harley & Reese, 1999; Peterson, Jesso, & McCabe, 1999).

Supplementing this work on the social origins of independent skills in remembering the past, researchers have focused on the classroom setting as a context for the development of children's deliberate memory skills. In this regard, Ornstein, Coffman, McCall, Grammer, and San Souci (in press) reported that it is quite rare to find explicit instruction in mnemonic techniques in the elementary school grades (see also Moely et al., 1992). However, even though strategies are not taught explicitly, Ornstein and his colleagues observed that first grade teachers engage in memory "talk"—including indirect requests for deliberate remembering, strategy suggestion, and metacognitive questioning—in their whole-class instruction. Moreover, children in first grade classes taught by *high mnemonic* teachers who use more of this type of memory talk were better able to take advantage of strategy training than were those children with *low mnemonic* teachers (Coffman, Ornstein, & McCall, 2003; Ornstein, Coffman, et al., in press). As such, this work suggests that just as "parent talk" about the past can impact preschoolers' developing abilities to talk about past events (e.g., Reese et al., 1993), "teacher talk" may also be relevant for the emergence and refinement of mnemonic skills.

LOOKING AHEAD

Given the theoretical and applied significance of children's memory, it is of critical importance that as we take stock of the progress that has been made, we move to address the serious gaps in current understanding. Although much is known about *memory* development, our cognitive diagnoses of the skills of children of different ages are still incomplete. To increase the precision of our diagnostic statements, it is critical to examine children's performance on multiple tasks that vary in their information processing requirements.

Moreover, researchers have yet to shed much light on the *development* of memory. Simply put, we understand relatively little about the critical question of the forces that propel the development of skilled remembering. From our perspective, an understanding of this critical developmental question requires that we design longitudinal studies that illuminate underlying mechanisms that drive development.

As suggested above, there are many factors that may serve as mediators of developmental change in cognitive skill. Moreover, it is almost certain that these factors differ in their impact and in the points in development at which they exert their influence on remembering. We thus should not be searching for *the* principal force that drives development, but rather for the ways in which these different factors combine to facilitate the growth of mnemonic skill. From our perspective, our future progress is going to depend on our abilities to take the best of the information processing tradition—in terms of its abilities to specify the effort and attentional demands of different types of tasks—and to meld it with the best of the cognitive neuroscience and social constructivists traditions as we seek to discover potential mediators of developmental change.

In sum, what we need is a greater commitment to longitudinal research that informs understanding of the development of memory. As we embrace longitudinal research designs, clearly we recognize that it is important not to abandon completely the analytic precision of cross-sectional experiments. Rather, because longitudinal research designs are inherently correlational in nature, longitudinal studies should be married, when possible, with parallel experimental investigations in which hypothesized mediators of change are brought under experimental control. These experimental interventions (e.g., Boland, Haden, & Ornstein, 2003; Carr, Kurtz, Schneider, Turner, & Borkowski, 1989) are necessary if the aim is to make causal statements about factors that serve to bring about developmental change. From this perspective, through this integration of methods, it is possible to study both *memory* development and the *development* of memory.

REFERENCES

Ackil, J. K., Van Abema, D. L., & Bauer, P. J. (2003). After the storm: Enduring differences in mother–child recollections of traumatic and nontraumatic events. *Journal of Experimental Child Psychology, 84*, 286–309.

Bahrick, L. E., Parker, J. F., Fivush, R., & Levitt, M. (1998). The effects of stress on young children's memory for a natural disaster. *Journal of Experimental Psychology: Applied, 4*, 308–331.

Baker-Ward, L., Gordon, B. N., Ornstein, P. A., Larus, D. M., & Clubb, P. (1993). Young children's long-term retention of a pediatric examination. *Child Development, 64*, 1519–1533.

Baker-Ward, L., Ornstein, P. A., & Holden, D. J. (1984). The expression of memorization in early childhood. *Journal of Experimental Child Psychology, 37*, 555–575.

Barr, R., Dowden, A., & Hayne, H. (1996). Developmental changes in deferred imitation by 6- to 24-month-old infants. *Infant Behavior and Development*, *19*, 159–170.

Barr, R., & Hayne, H. (2000). Age-related changes in imitation: Implications for memory development. In C. Rovee-Collier, L. P. Lipsitt, & H. Hayne (Eds.), *Progress in infancy research* (Vol. 1, pp. 21–67). Mahwah, NJ: Lawrence Erlbaum Associates, Inc.

Bauer, P. J. (2004). Getting explicit memory off the ground: Steps toward construction of a neuro-developmental account of changes in the first two years of life. *Developmental Review*, *24*, 347–373.

Bauer, P. J. (2006). Event memory. In D. Kuhn, R. S. Siegler, W. Damon, & R. M. Lerner (Eds.), *Handbook of child psychology: Vol. 2. Cognition, perception, and language* (6th ed., pp. 373–425). Hoboken, NJ: John Wiley & Sons.

Bauer, P. J. (2007a). *Remembering the times of our lives: Memory in infancy and beyond*. Mahwah, NJ: Lawrence Erlbaum Associates, Inc.

Bauer, P. J. (2007b). Recall in infancy: A neurodevelopmental account. *Current Directions in Psychological Science*, *16*, 142–146.

Bauer, P. J., Hertsgaard, L. A., & Wewerka, S. S. (1995). Effects of experience and reminding on long-term recall in infancy: Remembering not to forget. *Journal of Experimental Child Psychology*, *59*, 260–298.

Bauer, P. J., & Travis, L. L. (1993). The fabric of an event: Different sources of temporal invariance differentially affect 24-month-olds' recall. *Cognitive Development*, *8*, 319–341.

Bauer, P. J., Wenner, J. A., Dropik, P. L., & Wewerka, S. S. (2000). Parameters of remembering and forgetting in the transition from infancy to early childhood. *Monographs of the Society for Research in Child Development*, *65* (4, Serial No. 263).

Bjorklund, D. F. (1985). The role of conceptual knowledge in the development of organization in children's memory. In C. J. Brainerd & M. Pressley (Eds.), *Basic processes in memory development* (pp. 103–142). New York: Springer.

Bjorklund, D. F., & Coyle, T. R. (1995). Utilization deficiencies in the development of memory strategies. In F. E. Weinert & W. Schneider (Eds.), *Memory performance and competencies: Issues in growth and development* (pp. 161–180). Hillsdale, NJ: Lawrence Erlbaum Associates, Inc.

Boland, A. M., Haden, C. A., & Ornstein, P. A. (2003). Boosting children's memory by training mothers in the use of an elaborative conversational style as an event unfolds. *Journal of Cognition and Development*, *4*, 39–65.

Brainerd, C. J., Kingma, J., & Howe, M. L. (1985). On the development of forgetting. *Child Development*, *56*, 1103–1119.

Brainerd, C. J., Reyna, V. F., Howe, M. L., & Kingma, J. (1990). The development of forgetting and reminiscence. *Monographs of the Society for Research in Child Development*, *53*(3–4, Serial No. 222).

Brown, D. A., Salmon, K., Pipe, M.-E., Rutter, M., Craw, S., & Taylor, B. (1999). Children's recall of medical experiences: The impact of stress. *Child Abuse and Neglect*, *23*, 209–216.

Burgwyn-Bailes, E., Baker-Ward, L., Gordon, B. N., & Ornstein, P. A. (2001). Children's memory for emergency medical treatment after one year: The impact of individual difference variables on recall and suggestibility. *Applied Cognitive Psychology*, *15*, S25–S48.

Campbell, B. A., & Jaynes, J. (1966). Reinstatement. *Psychological Review, 73*, 478–480.

Carr, M., Kurtz, B. E., Schneider, W., Turner, L. A., & Borkowski, J. G. (1989). Strategy acquisition and transfer among American and German children: Environmental influences on metacognitive development. *Developmental Psychology, 25*, 765–771.

Carver, L. J., & Bauer, P. J. (2001). The dawning of a past: The emergence of long-term explicit memory in infancy. *Journal of Experimental Psychology: General, 130*, 726–745.

Case, R. (1985). *Intellectual development: Birth to adulthood.* New York: Academic Press.

Ceci, S. J., & Bruck, M. (1993). Suggestibility of the child witness: A historical review and synthesis. *Psychological Bulletin, 113*, 403–439.

Coffman, J. L., Ornstein, P. A., & McCall, L. E. (2003, July). *Linking teachers' memory relevant talk to children's memory performance.* Poster presented at the biennial meeting of the Society for Applied Research in Memory and Cognition, Aberdeen, Scotland.

Cox, B. D., Ornstein, P. A., & Valsiner, J. (1990). The role of internalization in the transfer in mnemonic strategies. In L. Oppenheimer & J. Valsiner (Eds.), *The origins of action: International perspectives* (pp. 101–131). New York: Springer-Verlag.

DeLoache, J. S., Cassidy, D. J., & Brown, A. L. (1985). Precursors of mnemonic strategies in very young children's memory. *Child Development, 56*, 125–137.

Eichenbaum, H., & Cohen, N. J. (2001). *From conditioning to conscious recollection: Memory systems of the brain.* New York: Oxford University Press.

Fivush, R., Haden, C., & Adam, S. (1995). Structure and coherence of preschoolers' personal narratives over time: Implication for childhood amnesia. *Journal of Experimental Child Psychology, 60*, 32–56.

Fivush, R., Haden, C. A., & Reese, E. (2006). Elaborating on elaborations: Role of maternal reminiscing style in cognitive and socioemotional development. *Child Development, 77*, 1568–1588.

Fivush, R., & Hamond, N. R. (1990). Autobiographical memory across the preschool years: Toward reconceptualizing childhood amnesia. In R. Fivush & J. A. Hudson (Eds.), *Knowing and remembering in young children* (pp. 223–248). New York: Cambridge University Press.

Folds, T. H., Footo, M. M., Guttentag, R. E., & Ornstein, P. A. (1990). When children mean to remember: Issues of context specificity, strategy effectiveness, and intentionality in the development of memory. In D. F. Bjorklund (Ed.), *Children's strategies: Contemporary views of cognitive development* (pp. 67–91). Hillsdale, NJ: Lawrence Erlbaum Associates, Inc.

Goodman, G. S., Quas, J. A., Batterman-Faunce, J. M., Riddlesberger, M. M., & Kuhn, J. (1994). Predictors of accurate and inaccurate memories of traumatic events experienced in childhood. *Consciousness and Cognition, 3*, 269–294.

Guttentag, R. E. (1984). The mental effort requirement of cumulative rehearsal: A developmental study. *Journal of Experimental Child Psychology, 37*, 92–106.

Guttentag, R. E., Ornstein, P. A., & Siemens, L. (1987). Spontaneous rehearsal: Transitions in strategy acquisition. *Cognitive Development, 2*, 307–326.

Haden, C., Haine, R., & Fivush, R. (1997). Developing narrative structure in parent–child conversations about the past. *Developmental Psychology, 33*, 295–307.

Harley, K., & Reese, E. (1999). Origins of autobiographical memory. *Developmental Psychology*, *35*, 1338–1348.

Hartshorn, K., Rovee-Collier, C., Gerhardstein, P., Bhatt, R. S., Klein, P. J., Wondoloski, T. L., et al. (1998). The ontogeny of long-term memory over the first year-and-a-half of life. *Developmental Psychobiology*, *32*, 69–89.

Hayne, H., Barr, R., & Herbert, J. (2003). The effect of prior practice on memory reactivation and generalization. *Child Development*, *74*, 1615–1627.

Hayne, H., Greco, C., Earley, L., Griesler, P., & Rovee-Collier, C. (1986). Ontogeny of early event memory: II. Encoding and retrieval and 2- and 3-month olds. *Infant Behavior and Development*, *9*, 461–472.

Hill, W. L., Borovsky, D., & Rovee-Collier, C. (1988). Continuities in infant memory development. *Developmental Psychobiology*, *21*, 43–62.

Howe, M. L., Courage, M. L., & Peterson, C. (1994). How can I remember when "I" wasn't there: Long-term retention of traumatic experiences and the emergence of the cognitive self. *Consciousness and Cognition: An International Journal*, *3*, 327–355.

Kail, R. (1991). Developmental changes in speed of processing during childhood and adolescence. *Psychological Bulletin*, *109*, 490–501.

Meltzoff, A. N. (1985). Immediate and deferred imitation in fourteen and twenty-four-month-old infants. *Child Development*, *56*, 62–72.

Meltzoff, A. N. (1995). What infant memory tells us about infantile amnesia: Long-term recall and deferred imitation. *Journal of Experimental Child Psychology*, *59*, 497–515.

Merritt, K. A., Ornstein, P. A., & Spicker, B. (1994). Children's memory for a salient medical procedure: Implications for testimony. *Pediatrics*, *94*, 17–22.

Miller, P. H. (1990). The development of strategies of selective attention. In D. F. Bjorklund (Ed.), *Children's strategies: Contemporary views of cognitive development* (pp. 157–184). Hillsdale, NJ: Lawrence Erlbaum Associates, Inc.

Moely, B. E., Hart, S. S., Leal, L., Santulli, K. A., Rao, N., Johnson, T., et al. (1992). The teacher's role in facilitating memory and study strategy development in the elementary school classroom. *Child Development*, *63*, 653–672.

Nelson, C. A., & Webb, S. J. (2002). A cognitive neuroscience perspective on early memory development. In M. de Haan & M. H. Johnson (Eds.), *The cognitive neuroscience of development* (pp. 99–125). Hove, UK: Psychology Press.

Nelson, K. (1986). *Event knowledge: Structure and function in development.* Hillsdale, NJ: Lawrence Erlbaum Associates, Inc.

Nelson, K., & Gruendel, J. (1979). At morning it's lunchtime: A scriptal view of children's dialogues. *Discourse Processes*, *2*, 73–94.

Ornstein, P. A., Baker-Ward, L., & Naus, M. J. (1988). The development of mnemonic skill. In F. E. Weinert & M. Perlmutter (Eds.), *Memory development: Universal changes and individual differences* (pp. 31–50). Hillsdale, NJ: Lawrence Erlbaum Associates, Inc.

Ornstein, P. A., Coffman, J. L., McCall, L. E., Grammer, J. K., & San Souci, P. (in press). Linking the classroom context and the development of children's memory skills. In J. Meece and J. Eccles (Eds.), *Handbook of research on schools, schooling, and human development.* Mahwah, NJ: Lawrence Erlbaum Associates, Inc.

Ornstein, P. A., & Haden, C. A. (2001). *Memory* development or the *development* of memory? *Current Directions in Psychological Science*, *6*, 202–205.

Ornstein, P. A., Haden, C. A., & Hedrick, A. M. (2004). Learning to remember: Social-communicative exchanges and the development of children's memory skills. *Developmental Review, 24*, 374–395.

Ornstein, P. A., Haden, C. A., & San Souci, P. (2008). Children's memory development. In J. H. Byrne (Ed.-in-Chief) & H. Roediger, III (Vol. Ed.), *Learning and memory: A comprehensive reference: Vol. 4. Cognitive psychology of memory.* Oxford: Elsevier.

Ornstein, P. A., & Myers, J. T. (1996). Contextual influences on children's remembering. In K. Pezdek & W. P. Banks (Eds.), *The recovered memory/false memory debate* (pp. 211–223). San Diego: Academic Press.

Ornstein, P. A., & Naus, M. J. (1985). Effects of the knowledge base on children's memory strategies. In H. W. Reese (Ed.), *Advances in child development and behavior* (Vol. 19, pp. 113–148). New York: Academic Press.

Peterson, C., Jesso, B., & McCabe, A. (1999). Encouraging narratives in preschoolers: An intervention study. *Journal of Child Language, 26*, 49–67.

Peterson, C., & Rideout, R. (1998). Memory for medical emergencies experienced by 1- and 2-year-olds. *Developmental Psychology, 34*, 1059–1072.

Peterson, C., & Whalen, N. (2001). Five years later: Children's memory for medical emergencies. *Applied Cognitive Psychology, 15*, 17–24.

Quas, J. A., Goodman, G. S., Bidrose, S., Pipe, M.-E., Craw, S., & Ablin, D. (1999). Emotion and memory: Children's long-term remembering, forgetting, and suggestibility. *Journal of Experimental Child Psychology, 72*, 235–270.

Reese, E., Haden, C. A., & Fivush, R. (1993). Mother–child conversations about the past: Relationships of style and memory over time. *Cognitive Development, 8*, 403–430.

Rovee-Collier, C., Schechter, A., Shyi, G., & Shields, P. (1992). Perceptual identification of contextual attributes and infant memory retrieval. *Developmental Psychology, 28*, 307–318.

Sales, J. M., Fivush, R., Parker, J., & Bahrick, L. (2005). Stressing memory: Long-term relations among children's stress, recall and psychological outcome following Hurricane Andrew. *Journal of Cognition and Development, 6*, 529–545.

Salmon, K., Price, M., & Pereira, J. K. (2002). Factors associated with young children's long-term recall of an invasive medical procedure: A preliminary investigation. *Journal of Developmental and Behavioral Pediatrics, 23*, 347–352.

Schlagmüller, M., & Schneider, W. (2002). The development of organizational strategies in children: Evidence from a microgenetic longitudinal study. *Journal of Experimental Child Psychology, 81*, 298–319.

Schneider, W., Kron, V., Hünnerkopf, M., & Krajewski, K. (2004). The development of young children's memory strategies: First findings from the Würzburg Longitudinal Memory Study. *Journal of Experimental Child Psychology, 88*, 193–209.

Siegler, R. S. (1996). *Emerging minds: The process of change in children's thinking.* New York: Oxford University Press.

Siegler, R. S. (2006). Microgenetic analyses of learning. In D. Kuhn, R. S. Siegler, W. Damon, & R. M. Lerner (Eds.), *Handbook of child psychology: Vol. 2. Cognition, perception, and language* (6th ed., pp. 464–510). Hoboken, NJ: John Wiley & Sons.

Sodian, B., & Schneider, W. (1999). Memory strategy development: Gradual increase, sudden insight, or roller-coaster? In F. E. Weinert and W. Schneider (Eds.), *Individual development from 3 to 12: Findings from the Munich Longitudinal Study* (pp. 61–77). New York: Cambridge University Press.

Spear, N. E., & Parsons, P. J. (1976). Analysis of a reactivation treatment: Ontogenetic determinants of alleviated forgetting. In D. L. Medin, W. A. Roberts, & R. T. Davis (Eds.), *Processes of animal memory* (pp. 135–165). Hillsdale, NJ: Lawrence Erlbaum Associates, Inc.

Sweeney, B., & Rovee-Collier, C. (2001). The minimum duration of reactivation at 6 months: Latency of retrieval and reforgetting. *Infant Behavior and Development, 24,* 259–280.

Wellman, H. M. (1988). The early development of memory strategies. In F. E. Weinert and M. Perlmutter (Eds.), *Memory development: Universal changes and individual differences* (pp. 3–29). Hillsdale, NJ: Lawrence Erlbaum Associates, Inc.

Author Index

Subject Index

Note: **bold** page numbers denote references to Figures/Tables

Ignored speech task 319, **319**, **320**, 344
Imitation
    peer and sibling interactions 56–57
    picture books 60–62
    television 58, 60, *see also* deferred
        imitation; elicited imitation
Implicit memory 4–5, 28, 93–113,
        350–351, 352, 368
    clinical populations 107–108
    conceptual priming 94, 95, 97–99, 100,
        101, 102–103
    false memory 99–101
    neuroscience 105–107
    perceptual priming 94, 95–97, 98, 102,
        106–107, 108
    priming and explicit memory
        interaction 101–102
    sequence and statistical language
        learning 103–105, *see also*
        procedural memory
Independent locomotion 49–50
Infantile amnesia 3, 11, 34–35, 63, 214
    cognitive structures 181
    frailty of infant memory 178–179
    human nature of 180
    neurobiological constraints 183
Inferior temporal cortical regions 182
Information processing 1, 2, 7, 374, 380
    age-related changes 378
    capacity 162
    emotional appraisals 208
    memory strategies 146
    working memory 309, *see also* cognitive
        processing
Intellectual disability (ID) 260, 261, 264,
    see also learning disabilities
Intelligence
    forensic context 261, 267
    memory strategies 166
    working memory 332
Internal state language 292
Internal working models (IWMs) 223,
    224

Knowledge
    abstract 69–70, 74, 85
    autobiographical memory 183, 185,
        190
    cognitive development 378
    conceptual priming 99, 103
    episodic/semantic memory distinction
        54–55
    implicit 94, 102
    long-term 64
    memory strategies 161–164
    metamemory 164
    neural correlates 72–73
    pre-event 219

script 208
    working memory 308, 324, 325–326,
        see also general event knowledge

Labels 51–52, 60
Language 4, 7, 262
    acquisition of language skills 50–53
    autobiographical memory 6, 187–190,
        284, 285
    forensic context 266–267
    infantile amnesia 11, 34
    internal state 292
    maltreated children 260
    mnemonic utterances **54**
Language disorders 330
Learning
    early memory for nonhuman species
        179
    purpose of memory 64
    sequence 103–105
Learning disabilities 332, *see also*
    intellectual disability
Lesion studies 72–73, 119, 123, 182
Letters 306, 307
Locomotion 49–50
LOGIC, *see* Munich Longitudinal Study
    on the Genesis of Individual
    Competencies
Longitudinal studies 158–159, 220, 290,
    375–377, 380
Long-term memory 3–4, 6, 11, 304
    activation 311, 312, 334
    age-related changes in retention 45–48,
        47
    attention control 324
    conditioning 13–14
    constructivist accounts 73
    embedded-processes model **310**
    retrieval strategies 153
    verbal cues 51
    violation-of-expectation procedure 351

"Magic Shrinking Machine" 34, 52, 53,
    63
Magnetic resonance imaging (MRI) 122,
    123, 133, 216, *see also* functional
    magnetic resonance imaging
Mathematics 331–332
Media 56
Medial-temporal structures 117, 118,
    124–125, 182, 377–378
    amnesia 120, 123
    consolidation and storage 120–121, 136
    functional maturity 128
Mediation deficiency 147
Mediators of developmental change
    377–379, 380
Medical procedures 219, 221, 372